Great Stories
OF AMERICAN
Businessmen

Above, the first New York Stock Exchange building as shown in an engraving from its collection; opposite, the coat of arms of the Virginia Company, one of the earliest corporations, from Stow's Survey of London *(1633)*

Great Stories
OF AMERICAN
Businessmen

from
AMERICAN HERITAGE
The Magazine of History

Introduction by
Oliver Jensen

Published by
American Heritage Publishing Co., Inc., New York

CONTENTS

AMERICAN HERITAGE
PUBLISHING CO., INC.

PRESIDENT AND PUBLISHER
Paul Gottlieb

EDITOR-IN-CHIEF
Joseph J. Thorndike

EDITOR, AMERICAN HERITAGE MAGAZINE
Oliver Jensen

SENIOR EDITOR, BOOK DIVISION
Alvin M. Josephy, Jr.

EDITORIAL ART DIRECTOR
Murray Belsky

GENERAL MANAGER, BOOK DIVISION
Kenneth W. Leish

INTRODUCTION

There are thirty-nine articles in this book, just as there are in the official creed of the Church of England, and if they are published on lesser authority they nevertheless reflect an important creed of their own, the business faith which built the American economic colossus. All of them are taken from our magazine of history, AMERICAN HERITAGE, in its first eighteen years of life, but they cover three centuries. They begin with tiny coastal communities in a time when the miller was our first industrialist and the ship owner (or smuggler, in many cases) our first trader, and they end with the trusts and the giants of our time.

Along the way, we hope those who read this book will enjoy a strange and diverting cast of characters, Yankee peddlers, tinkering inventors, glib-tongued salesmen, genial swindlers, rough oil-drillers, stealthy manipulators, and even gentle philanthropists. Some of them are largely forgotten, like Samuel Slater, an English mechanic with a photographic memory for complex looms and spindles; he transplanted the industrial revolution to America when British law forbade the export of either spinning machines or designs. And there is Elias Hasket Derby, whose trade with the East Indies made him our first millionaire in a day when Salem was a great port; and profligate Isaac Singer, who thought up the little combination of devices that made a practical sewing machine; and John Matthews, who gave us the soda fountain and the first real competition the saloon ever had. But the whiskey distillers are here, too, a very sizable enterprise, against whom it was once necessary to mobilize the President, the Secretaries of War and the Treasury, and an army as large as any that ever took the field in the Revolution. Not to put them out of business, of course; just to get them to pay their taxes.

More modern times bring more familiar names: brisk, bustling, evangelistic Andrew Carnegie; the imperious J. P. Morgan (who could organize the end of a financial panic single-handed in the days before Big Government); that shrewd, suspicious, small-town genius, Henry Ford; grasping Commodore Vanderbilt, collecting railroads; Jay Gould wrecking them; Jim Hill building westward. The greatest of them all, of course, is the richest man in the world, frugal, quiet John D. Rockefeller, the Sunday-school teacher who became the most-hated acquisitor in America. And in the wake of these titans appear, inevitably, the correctives—the labor leaders, the reformers, the regulators.

If there is a theme that runs through it all it is that America, in its brief two independent centuries, has had the most free economy in history, so that our getting and spending has not only been dramatic, both in its good and in its evil, but also that it has been the central activity of our history. We have given it most of our time and our effort and our ingenuity; our most creative men, as Lord Bryce the historian observed over eighty years ago, were not our politicians but our business-men, however much this fact may distress philosophers. It angered the gentlemanly Charles Francis Adams, Jr., scion of an older society, who said, "I am a little puzzled to account for the instances I have seen of business success—money-getting. It comes from a rather low instinct." John D. Rockefeller put it differently: "You know that great prejudice exists against all successful business enterprise—the more successful, the greater the prejudice."

That great speeding machine, the free American economy, turned out in our new century to have certain inconveniences. It was hard to control and it had no brakes, as we discovered in a series of crashes. The greatest of them is described here by John Kenneth Galbraith, and one of the largely futile attempts to install brakes—the Sherman Anti-Trust Act—is discussed at the close of the book by a man who tried to make it work, the late Thurman Arnold. And, of course, in recent years so many people have crowded into the driver's seat of the economy that its motion is necessarily erratic. The old freedom in any event is gone, regretted even by those who killed it, swallowed as much in the purposeless immensity of conglomerates as in the regulatory spider web of government, the stranglehold of labor, and the grasp of enormous financial institutions. Perhaps it was all inevitable, like the growth of a snowball coming down the hillside, especially since no hill has yet been devised without a bottom. But the problem of reconciling bigness, utility, and freedom is the unenviable province of the economist and his "dismal science." The business of the historian, which we believe our distinguished company of contributors have executed here very well, is to describe the trip, the route we followed, and the high excitement on the way.

—Oliver Jensen, Editor of AMERICAN HERITAGE Magazine

Written and illustrated by ERIC SLOANE

The MILLS of EARLY AMERICA

An artist recalls the picturesque

devices that helped a young nation get ready

for the age of machinery

Revolving head

Stationary tower

Tail-pole

1813 Mill at Watermill L.I.

A typical old-time windmill, with tail pole and revolving head by which the miller could adjust it to varying winds.

While the antiquarian still coos over many a useless relic of the past, the American miller and his mill have often been forgotten. Like the farmer and the barn builder, his name is seldom recorded; but his place in the fabric of our history is distinct.

The miller was America's first industrial inventor. He was builder, banker, businessman and host to the countryside. When highways were no wider than today's bridle paths, the first good roads were built to the mills. Where there was a mill site, there was a nucleus for a town. America had so many Millvilles, Milltowns, Milfords and other towns named after original mills, that the Post Office Department sponsored the changing of many such names to stop the confusion.

There are still abandoned millponds, forgotten mill roads and millstreams that wind through the "old sections" of cities. But the structure with its machinery, once the hub of the village, is usually lost in the oblivion of a vanished landscape.

Over a hundred years ago, roads were used for travel, but almost never for commercial transportation. Even to transport a simple wagonload of wood could cost more than the value of the load; to move salt from Long Island to Danbury, Connecticut, by horse, cost eight times its worth. In Philadelphia, coal shipped from Newcastle, England, cost less than coal hauled over the road from nearby Richmond, Virginia. Every small village had to depend upon itself for almost

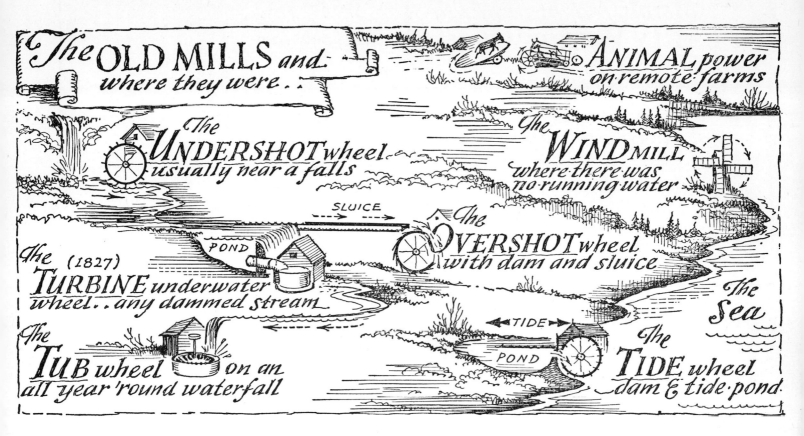

The OLD MILLS and where they were...

The UNDERSHOT wheel usually near a falls

ANIMAL power on remote farms

The WINDMILL where there was no running water

SLUICE

The OVERSHOT wheel with dam and sluice

POND

The (1827) TURBINE underwater wheel...any dammed stream

The Sea

TIDE

POND

The TUB wheel on an all year 'round waterfall

The TIDE wheel dam & tide pond

every necessity, and the mills were the answer. It would have a sawmill and a gristmill; there would also be mills for making cider, salt, flax, plaster, linseed oil, tobacco, barrel staves, axes, bone meal, mustard, and on down to smaller mills that turned out simple necessities of everyday life. In the hamlet of New Preston, Connecticut, there is still a water-powered sawmill. Its saws are actuated by a new turbine which operates underwater and therefore does not ice up the way its original water wheels did. The small stretch of waterway that feeds its turbine is no longer than you can walk in a minute or two, yet there were once about thirty mills on it, almost as many mills as there were residences.

People of today might think of the old-time miller as just another merchant. But if they could step inside an early water-wheeled mill and watch it at work, the miller might be added to their list of American greats. The ponderous wheels and massive gears spring to life with a surge of power that makes the mill house shudder, and which explains why early mills had hand-hewn beams of such tremendous proportions.

"Killed in his mill" was a frequent epitaph of two hundred years ago. The careless miller's life was a short one, and whether he was lifted aloft and thrown from a windmill, whacked in the head by a spar or caught by his hand or clothing in the gigantic gears and ground up, his everyday work had to be as exacting and careful as that of an airplane pilot.

Millstones have a lore and language of their own. The *runner* stone turned above the fixed *nether* stone, and according to the *dress* of the *run* (pair), different consistencies of meal were ground. Because of the resemblance to plowed land, the millstone dresses, or pattern of cut grooves, were called the *furrows*, while the uncut area was called the *land*. The interesting patterns of millstone dresses are becoming lost records, yet many a Pennsylvania barn's hex sign and farm wife's patchwork quilt has been inspired by some favorite millstone design.

The first mills were hand-turned mortar and pestle arrangements. The first water-powered mill had no wheel; it consisted of a pounding mortar that was lifted upward by the weight of water running into a box on one end of a beam. When the box filled, it lowered and tipped itself, actuating the beam up and down ceaselessly and pounding a stone pestle into a hollowed tree mortar. Travelers could tell when they were nearing a village by the steady beat of these "plumping mills."

We think of the windmill as being entirely Dutch, yet travelers from Holland were impressed by the windmills of New York. "As we sailed into the harbor," wrote one Hollander, "the horizon was pierced by scores of windmills, taller than any we have seen elsewhere." Sailing ships set their sails according to the position of windmills and Long Island ferries advertised "daily services except when the windmills on

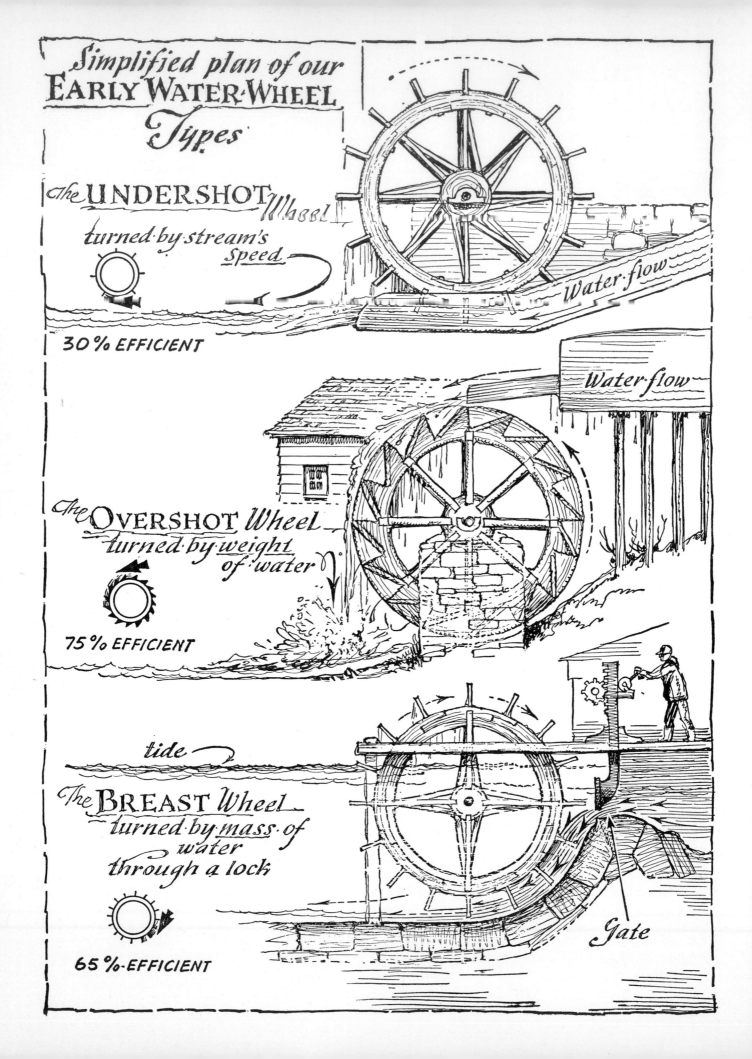

Simplified plan of our
EARLY WATER·WHEEL
Types.

The UNDERSHOT Wheel
turned by stream's speed.

Water·flow

30 % EFFICIENT

Water·flow

The OVERSHOT Wheel
turned by weight of water

75 % EFFICIENT

tide

The BREAST Wheel
turned by mass of water
through a lock

Gate

65 %·EFFICIENT

the opposite shore have taken in their sails."

The Dutch erected windmills in Manhattan in 1640 and the idea spread to Long Island, where the mills pumped sea water into large vats for the manufacture of salt. Although wind-powered mills were designed for riverless areas, they had an advantage over water-wheeled mills in that they did not freeze. During the great cold winters of early New England days, the water wheels were often frozen solid for months.

Except for a few restored or ornamental examples, time has run out on the American windmill. But the water-wheeled mill still turns in many a hidden glen throughout the country, grinding meal and doing other chores, just as if progress had never come through the land. City folks drive long distances to see these mills and to pay fancy prices for stone-ground corn meal, but few realize they are purchasing more than quaintness. The country people know that the best corn bread only comes from a water-powered burrstone mill, where the meal has absorbed the dampness of the mill site and has not been scorched by fast-moving machinery. When the meal is fresh from the slow turning stones, "as warm as from the underside of a settin' hen," it makes bread the country way.

Nearly all the early water wheels were variations of three basic designs: the overshot wheel, the undershot wheel and the breast wheel. The overshot wheel was fed from above, and the weight of falling water gave it the most efficiency. The undershot wheel was moved by the velocity and mass of a moving stream; the breast wheel was fed from the middle section, often by tidewater. There were bucket wheels and tub wheels and countless inventions of the American mind, but these three designs, hewn from native timber, have become Americana despite earlier overseas models. From their pattern has evolved the industrial machinery that electricity now actuates and even in the jet airplane engine you may find early mill theories put to use.

When steam power took over, the mill had reached its Rube Goldberg age, and even the smallest farm owned treadmill machines where oxen and horses and even dogs churned butter, sawed logs and ground out linseed oil for barn paint. Even the spit in the fireplace was turned by a dog or a tame squirrel in a treadmill cage. Wherever animals, wind or water could make chores simpler, the American mind enjoyed the spectacle.

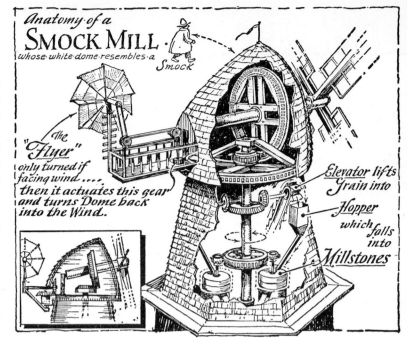

A windmill could be complicated. This cut away diagram shows some of the intricate machinery by which the wind's power was put to work. The sketches below show various stages in the development and use of the earliest mills.

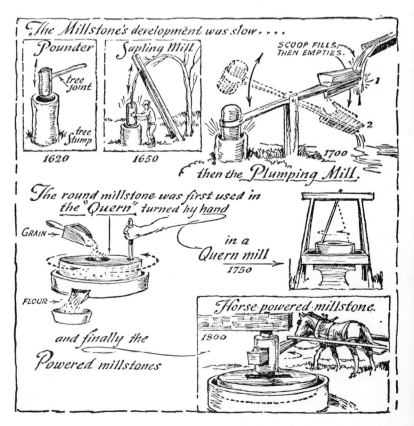

War

Blackbeard, whose real name was Edward Teach, derived his nickname from the "large quantity of hair, which, like a frightful meteor, covered his whole face." Long considered the very archetype of a villain (although later history debunks him somewhat), he seems to have enjoyed playing the role. Blackbeard was a fine showman who sported a scarlet silk sash and three braces of pistols. With a two-foot knife between his teeth and lighted matches under his hat, he was "such a figure that imagination cannot form an idea of a fury from hell to look more frightful." His victims, understandably, rarely put up a fight. Blackbeard operated off the American coast during the early Eighteenth Century, enjoying the blessing of the corrupt governor of North Carolina. When he was finally killed by a naval officer, his head, complete with beard, was hung from the bowsprit of the ship for the triumphal voyage home.

makes thieves, peace hangs them

In an era that condoned smuggling and lawbreaking

the transition from privateer to pirate was easy

By ROGER BURLINGAME

Piracy along the American coast began with legalized plunder. Sea warfare in colonial times was only partly an affair of navies. The rest was free private enterprise. If an individual adventurer could reap a fortune from a war, he had the satisfaction of knowing that his riches were patriotically gained.

In the war which England waged in the late years of the Seventeenth and the early years of the Eighteenth centuries, the American colonies were of considerable assistance. The king authorized colonial governors to distribute "letters of marque and reprisal" liberally among the seafaring men of the New England and middle colonies. Such a letter entitled its holder to capture all the enemy ships he could, bring them into port, and there claim a major portion of ship and cargo. If he could not bring the ship into port, he would relieve her of her cargo and crew and sink her. Enormous sums of money were made in this way, especially from the sale of the rich cargoes of captured Spanish merchantmen.

King William's War between England and France ended in 1697. Queen Anne's War, which was a part of the War of the Spanish Succession, began in 1701, and involved both France and Spain. In both wars there was sea fighting, and colonial "privateers" carried on a lucrative business. In Queen Anne's War which involved most of Europe, both English and colonial ships worked the Spanish Main. There shipmasters became familiar with the hundreds of island hide-outs, the inlets, the coves, and the rivers that gave shelter for escape and surprise attack.

Privateering was a free, adventurous, exciting life. The risks were great but so were the rewards. There was an almost total absence of restraint, of regulation, of discipline. The privateer was entirely on his own. He was only authorized to capture enemy ships, but neutrals sometimes fell into his hands, and it was easy to explain that the neutral ships were carrying contraband of war. He must use his own judgment. There was no one to give him advice. The seas were wide and empty and, once over the horizon, a ship was out of range of communication.

The life was so good, indeed, that when the war was over, the men who had enjoyed it became restless. They had lost their taste for the hard work of legitimate trade. They had grown intimate with the merchants of the seaport cities but these friendships, built through the sale of rich, exotic cargoes, had nothing to sustain them when peace came. In the uneasy peace that followed King William's War at the turn of the century, there was depression throughout the colonies. The bungled Treaty of Ryswick ending that war had given concessions to the French that nearly ruined the New England cod fisheries. In the middle colonies the price of wheat fell because of English competition in the West Indies trade. This general climate of depression was anything but congenial to the ex-privateer who despised slow, laborious ways of earning a living.

Thus the temptation to find his way back to some sort of predatory seafaring was hard to resist. It was easy to move across the vague lines set by a treaty; to plunder what were no longer enemy vessels; to move, in short, from privateering to piracy. In England, this process had been practiced since the days of Francis Drake; it was hardly surprising that it appeared in the American colonies in the intervals between wars.

By no means all the buccaneers who operated along the American coast were colonials. Indeed, some of the most masterful were natives of the British Isles. But America was the natural scene of their operations, whatever their origin. Its intricately indented coastline furnished ideal hiding places for the ships that flew the black flag. Still more useful was the colonial tradition of lawbreaking. Certain kinds of smuggling had been universal among New England traders. After years of winking at this practice officials in the northern seaports had grown corrupt. Finally, dealing in contraband goods had made the seaport merchants rich and powerful and they, in turn, had brought pressure even on the royal governors to ignore the illicit trade.

In the northern colonies, smuggling had become necessary to survival. The Navigation Acts had created this necessity. They prohibited, among other things, trade with those islands of the West Indies that were not British. In the North, where winters were long and there was no such staple crop as tobacco or rice, agriculture alone could not pay for the goods the people had to buy from England. They turned, therefore, to other occupations: mainly fishing, sea trade, and the manufacture of rum. Rum became the staple, so to speak, of New England. It was made of molasses brought from the sugar islands of the Caribbean. The British islands could not supply all the molasses the Yankees needed; also, the French product was cheaper. So the smuggling of molasses became a universal practice. To the proud northern colonials it was a demonstration of their independence of drastic English law. As time went on and the laws became more restrictive, evasion, for some New Englanders, became a sort of patriotic duty just as, some two centuries later in the Prohibition era, many Americans proudly defied the Eighteenth Amendment and encouraged bootlegging in the name of liberty. By that time, however, English-

men who were shocked by such American lawlessness had forgotten that the same sort of evasion had once been forced by their ancestors upon ours.

In those early years there was hardly a customs official in the colonies who enforced the unwelcome statutes. It was, of course, profitable to them to let the contraband through. Payment for protection was an item of the merchant's budget. If there were officials who were above this sort of corruption they were rare characters indeed, and so unpopular that ways would surely have been found to force them out of office. Thus, all along the coast there developed an atmosphere of genial, easygoing disrespect for law that made it an ideal hunting ground for every kind of freebooter. If one contraband article could be smuggled, why not another? If a port inspector could be bribed, why not the man higher up? If the bribe was big enough, where, indeed, was the royal governor who could not be bought?

Almost any American school child, asked to name the most notorious pirate in American history, will automatically reply, "Captain Kidd." William Kidd has become a legend. Boys of many generations living in the vicinity of Long Island Sound have dreamed of finding his buried treasure. As the historians George Francis Dow and John Henry Edmonds tell us in their *Pirates of the New England Coast:* "Captain Kidd as he is recalled today is a composite type. All the pirates who have frequented the New England coast have become blended into one and that one—Captain Kidd." His death did much to nourish the legend. Hanged at Execution Dock on the Thames water front, his body was then bound in chains and left hanging in view of every ship on the lower river as a macabre warning.

Recent researchers have tried to debunk the legend. According to Kidd's latest biographer, Willard Bonner, in his extremely readable *Pirate Laureate*, he was "a reputable trader and navigator of old New York," and Bonner presents evidence that the "unfair" trial given the Captain was part of a political conspiracy. That Kidd had admittedly killed a number of his crew was, however, the first charge against him.

Whatever may have been the whole truth—and it will perhaps never be disclosed—Kidd illustrates the sort of progress from privateering to other predatory operations that is typical. In September, 1696, he sailed out of New York with a royal commission to command a "private Man of War" and orders to capture and bring to justice "Pirates, Free booters, and Sea Rovers," wherever he might find them. Specifically mentioned were the notorious villains, Thomas Tew of Rhode Island and Thomas Wake and William Maze of New York, supposed at the time to be in the neighborhood of the international pirate headquarters on the island of Madagascar. In this enterprise, Kidd was financed by five peers of the realm and one New Yorker. As usual, all these gentlemen were to profit heavily from the patriotic venture.

Kidd disappeared entirely for three years. Apparently he had fallen on evil times. Cruising in the dreadful heat of the Red Sea, he had missed his prizes, and his men, who had expected to share in the booty, had become unruly. Finally, according to Kidd, they had mutinied, made him prisoner, and turned his ship, the *Adventure Galley,* from a man-of-war into a pirate craft. This, at any rate, was Kidd's story as he sailed into the home port with his ship loaded with treasure. Meanwhile, the story had circulated in England that the Captain had turned pirate. He was, therefore, arrested in Boston; not, however, until after he had buried part of the loot on Gardiners Island off Long Island where men and boys have been vainly digging ever since. The hidden treasure is the most probable part of the legend.

Kidd's story of the mutiny was typical. Many an alleged pirate made a similar tale part of his defense. Often enough it was true. It was common practice for a pirate to force the master of a captured vessel to join him in further robberies. It may be doubted, however, that the prisoner was always as reluctant as he maintained to bow to his captor's will. The temptation to turn from the dull life of a merchantman skipper to the fabled adventure of a buccaneer was usually irresistible as soon as he saw the tangible evidence of the rich rewards.

Among the pirates who entered the profession in this way were Howel Davis, Captain England, "Red Legs" Greaves, David Herriott, Benjamin Jefferys, John Phillips, Bartholomew Roberts, John Upton, and Thomas White. It was surprising how many men had started life as respected citizens in their communities—lawyers, doctors, merchants, or well-to-do gentlemen—and had turned at last to piracy. Such, for example, was Stede Bonnet, a former major in the British Army and a wealthy landowner in the Barbados. Once started on his new career, however, he became one of the most brutal pirates of all—the only one, indeed, against whom it was proved that he made his prisoners walk the plank. So outrageous was his behavior and so complete the change from his former way of life that his island neighbors blamed his nagging wife for having driven him mad. According to the contemporary biographer Charles Johnson, Bonnet was "rather pitty'd than condemned, by those that were acquainted with him, believing that this Humour of going a-pyrating proceeded from a Disorder in his Mind . . . which is said to have been occasioned by some Discomforts he found in a married State. . . ."

Yet in the early years of the Eighteenth Century, piracy was not as disreputable—at least in America—as it later became. Like smuggling, it was often thought to be a protest against the injustices of British maritime law. The tough, hard-drinking, picturesquely profane Samuel Bellamy echoed these sentiments in a speech he delivered to an unhappy law-abiding skipper whose sloop he had captured, plundered, and sunk. He apologized for the sinking, which he said had been done by his crew contrary to his wishes, but he added:

"Tho', damn ye, you are a sneaking Puppy, and so are all those who will submit to be governed by Laws which rich Men have made for their own Security, for the cowardly Whelps have not the Courage otherwise to defend what they get by their Knavery; but damn ye altogether: Damn them for a Pack of crafty Rascals, and you, who serve them, for a Parcel of hen-hearted Numskuls. They villify us, the Scoundrels do, when there is only this Difference, they rob the Poor under the Cover of Law, forsooth, and we plunder the Rich under the Protection of our own Courage; had you not better make One of us . . . ?"

As early as 1700, the city of New York had acquired a reputation for greed, sharp trading, and cynical corruption. Established by the Dutch as a trading depot, it had continued under the English with business the main preoccupation. Hither had come people from all parts of Europe, each seeking some kind of fortune. Politically there had been chaos. The stupid, drunken, or prideful Dutch governors had been followed by a succession of weak or corrupt Englishmen. In 1691 the insurgent German-born Jacob Leisler had almost brought the colony to civil war. A few years later, while Benjamin Fletcher occupied this powerful and despotic post, New York became a utopia for pirates.

During Fletcher's administration, the New York merchants attained a position of wealth and arrogance they had never known. One of the great sources of their riches was the vast, wild no man's land of Mada-

gascar off the southeast coast of Africa. As the island belonged to no one but the savage tribes that had always inhabited it, the pirates were safe there; they made it their rendezvous, the depository for their stolen goods, and a market for trade with New Yorkers. Ships out of New York would land at Madagascar laden with goods the pirates wanted—mainly liquor and ammunition. The profits to the New Yorkers were astronomical. Rum that sold for two shillings a gallon in New York would bring £3 a gallon in Madagascar. A pipe of Madeira wine costing £19 in New York could be sold for £300 there. Coming back, the merchantmen brought the loot the pirates had captured all the way to India. Encouraged by the friendliness the New Yorkers showed them in Madagascar, the pirates came themselves to New York and were welcomed.

They had, to be sure, to make it worthwhile for the collector, the customs officers, and the magistrates at New York not to have them arrested. When these gentlemen were taken care of, it was customary to make friends with the Governor. Fletcher seems, from his later testimony, to have been confused as to who was a privateer and who a pirate. It was estimated that before a pirate and his crew could land, the cost of protection was £100 per man. The buccaneer Edward Coates, a frequent visitor to the city, maintained that he had paid some £1,300 directly to Governor Fletcher.

Once the sea robbers had paid the price of the racket, they were free to dine at the houses of the best families—who often found it good business to invite them—or to swagger through the streets, drunk, boastful, and exceedingly generous with silver and gold. They were popular with rich and poor alike. People of all conditions gathered round them to hear their yarns. They sold their loot at bargain prices, underselling legitimate goods. Some they gave away to adorn the houses of important officials.

The genial Governor seems to have justified himself by the fact that war with France was in progress during his administration and that some of the alleged pirates had privateer commissions. This did not, of course, entitle them to capture neutral and even English ships or to carry on the Madagascar trade, and it failed to explain the presents the Governor received.

When, in 1697, the King replaced Fletcher with the Earl of Bellomont and instructed the new governor to

These three venerable stone fortresses, seen (left) as they looked from the front and (right) as they looked from the rear, are typical of those that stood at vantage points along the coasts to protect the ports and the populace from attack. Nevertheless, pirates like Morgan dared to attack them.

end the piratical trade in New York, the situation there was wholly out of hand. Bellomont found not only that the powerful merchant body was solidly behind Fletcher, but also that there were no instruments of law enforcement that he could use. In his report to the home government he stated that he would rather have an honest New York judge than a man-of-war. He found the city literally a nest of pirates. Everywhere they were living in luxury, sheltered by the merchants.

In his first year, however, Bellomont did meet with some success—at least, in 1698, he so reported.

"'Tis almost incredible," he wrote, "what a vast quantity of East India goods would have been brought into this port, had there not been a change in government. Two men in this town had for their share twelve thousand pounds each, which were brought from Madagascar and got there with the barter with pirates. . . ."

We must allow for a certain excess of zeal in the Earl's reports. Anything approaching a total suppression of the piratical trade was beyond the powers of any one man. An illustration of the complexity of the situation is the fact that Bellomont had himself been one of the backers of Captain Kidd. The news that Kidd, in 1698, had turned pirate must have suggested the possibility of arousing distrust of the Governor at home. In New York Bellomont had become universally unpopular; the rich merchants had brought vilifying accusations against him and these had been conveyed to powerful connections in the English aristocracy. It was natural, therefore, for him to exaggerate his effectiveness in his letters home. Actually, documents in the city archives show that New York was still haunted by pirates as late as the summer of 1717.

The thirty-year piratical era came to an end in 1718, not in New York but in Virginia. There, that rare creature, an honest royal governor, had turned up in Alexander Spotswood. Meanwhile, a change in colonial fortunes had made piracy unpopular.

Queen Anne's War had ended in 1713. It was followed by circumstances very different from those consequent upon King William's War. The Peace of Utrecht was the opposite of that of Ryswick. It put an end to French commercial competition. As a result, prosperity instead of depression came to the American colonies. Legitimate trade became more profitable and far less risky than the shadowy negotiations with Madagascar.

At the same time, Queen Anne's War had produced a new breed of privateer-pirates. They were bold and

savage men, drunk with the fortunes they had reaped and, for the most part, utterly ruthless. Also, even before the war was over, they had begun to prey, not only on enemy or neutral vessels, but on colonial shipping as well. When peace came and the newly prosperous American sea traders were carrying their legitimate rich cargoes, these new pirates became an intolerable scourge. Also, they made raids on the seaports, terrorizing the inhabitants, burning, pillaging, and making prisoners of those who resisted. Horrible stories drifted back of prisoners stripped, lashed to a mast, and whipped to death; of others marooned on desert islands to starve.

The most formidable of these postwar pirates was a man whose name was variously reported as Thatch, Thack, and Teach, but who was commonly known as Blackbeard because of his abundant, fancily braided coal-black whiskers. Teach had started life as a crewman on an English privateer in the war. Deserting, he had fallen in with a veteran pirate named Hornigold at New Providence in the Bahamas. Hornigold was exceptional in having a conscience and refusing to capture British ships; wherefore Blackbeard left him and carried on operations on his own at Charleston and along the southern coast, hiding, between exploits, in one of the many coves of North Carolina. There he was protected by one Tobias Knight, secretary of the colony, whom he rewarded abundantly as, in fact, he

Jean and Pierre Laffitte left France to become highly successful pirates off the Louisiana coast around 1810. This rude woodcut purports to show them taking a prize by shooting a cannon point-blank at their huddled victims.

seems to have done the governor, Charles Eden, as well. Wrote Henry Brooke in his *Book of Pirates* (1841):

"As governors are but men, and not unfrequently by no means possessed of the most virtuous principles, the gold of Black Beard rendered him comely in the governor's eyes, and by his influence, he obtained a legal right to the great ship called 'The Queen Anne's Revenge.'"

Brooke adds that the Governor liked Blackbeard enough to attend his wedding when he took as his fourteenth wife a sixteen-year-old girl of Bath, North Carolina.

The Governor of the neighboring province of Virginia, however, was otherwise inclined. Teach had made devastating raids on Virginia shipping. Governor Spotswood was not subject to pirate bribery and Teach kept out of his way, usually escaping to a North Carolina shelter after his attacks. Presumably, a Virginia governor would never trespass upon another province to pursue him. But Blackbeard did not know his hotheaded adversary.

In a twenty-gun sloop, Spotswood sent Lieutenant Robert Maynard, one of his bravest officers, to find Blackbeard and end his career. He found him in Ocracoke Inlet, North Carolina. All night the two ships maneuvered among the treacherous shoals of the inlet. On his ship, Teach is reported to have sat all night below, drinking. In the morning his men attacked Maynard's sloop, killing and wounding 29 Virginians. Maynard sent his remaining men below and appeared on his deck alone. Blackbeard, thinking he had only one man to contend with, boarded Maynard's sloop. At a given signal, the crew came on deck and overwhelmed the pirate. There are various accounts of this fight but all agree that it was a desperate battle and that, in the end, Teach's bearded head was stuck on a pole and carried triumphantly ashore at Hampton, Virginia, followed by the members of his crew, who were duly tried at Williamsburg and hanged. The more credulous people of Hampton believe that the headless ghost of Blackbeard still walks there at night.

In the same year, 1718, Stede Bonnet of the "disordered mind" was taken at Charleston. Thus piracy along the colonial coast came to an end. In the bad years, it had flourished. In the economic upturn, it could not endure.

ROBERT MORRIS
AND THE
"Art Magick"

Skillful money-juggling by America's first financier aided

the new nation but led Morris himself to utter ruin

By JOHN DOS PASSOS

Early in the Yorktown year of 1781 the Continental Congress heard the report of a committee which had been at work estimating the debts of the United States. The committee failed to find enough income even to meet interest charges. The Continental paper had reached a point where it cost more to print a bill than it was worth in the market place. Next day the members of Congress voted unanimously to dump the whole mess in the lap of Robert Morris.

The Financier, as he came to be called, was the center of a web of commercial enterprises which included most of the banking and land speculation and shipping of the middle states. He was openhanded, approachable, a bold trader who exuded that prime commercial quality described as confidence. He was thought to be the richest man in America.

Martha Washington's grandson, George Washington Custis, used to say that of all the Revolutionary leaders it was Robert Morris for whom Washington felt the warmest personal friendship. He was a sanguine, hearty, thick-necked man. He had two town houses and a country house above the Schuylkill, where his table was famous for good food and good drink and cheerful entertaining; he was always ready to crack a friendly pot. He was obliging, particularly to people of influence. He made an opening for one of Washing-

ton's nephews in his country house. He was helpful to the General and to many a member of Congress about discounting notes and cashing bills of exchange. When Jefferson after his wife's death left his eleven-year-old daughter in Philadelphia for her schooling, Mr. and Mrs. Morris couldn't have been more considerate. The great magnate arranged loans for congressmen; he gave advice to his many friends about investments; he was everybody's banker.

Of his appointment as superintendent of finance, Washington wrote: "I have great expectations of the appointment of Mr. Morris, but they are not unreasonable ones; for I do not suppose that by art magick, he can do more than recover us, by degrees, from the labyrinth in which our finance is plunged." Art magick! High finance was regarded with awe and astonishment in those days, almost as a form of sorcery. What Robert Morris did, in that mysterious realm, no other man in America could have done. The Financier played such a crucial role in the affairs of the Confederacy that, by the time Washington rode home to Mount Vernon in December, 1783, he was left the most influential figure in the government.

Yet there was always ground for suspicion. Joseph Reed of Pennsylvania, who had been Washington's aide in the old days of the investment of Boston, was a

A hearty, sanguine man, "The Financier" of the Revolution rose from poverty to become reputedly America's richest man and ended in debtor's prison.

vain and thin-skinned politician but a man of good education and a shrewd observer. After Morris' appointment as superintendent of finance he described him to Nathanael Greene as a "pecuniary dictator. . . . It would not be doing justice not to acknowledge that, humiliating as this power is, it has been exercised with much advantage for the immediate relief of our distresses, and that the public have received a real benefit from Mr. Morris's exertions. At the same time those who know him will also acknowledge that he is too much a man of the world to overlook certain private interests which his command of the paper, and occasional speculations in that currency, will enable him to promote. It seems to have ever been a ruling principle with him to connect the public service with private interest and certainly he has not departed from it at this time of day."

Part of the confusion over Morris' honesty as a public servant arose from the complexity of the commercial dealings of the time. Bookkeeping was rudimentary. Since American merchants had to deal with the fluctuating paper currencies of thirteen separate provinces, transactions were basically by barter. Morris would trade so many hogsheads of tobacco estimated in Maryland paper currency, say, for a shipload of molasses in St. Kitts estimated in pounds sterling. In default of

other currency, bills of lading would have to pass as a medium of exchange, so that half the time he would be using the bill of lading for the shipload of molasses to meet an obligation for a shipment of straw hats held by a merchant in Leghorn.

Bills of exchange circulated that could be met part in cash, part in commodities, part in credit. Due to the slowness in communications, years might go by before any particular transaction was completed and liquidated. Add to that the hazards of wartime captures and confiscations, and the custom, so as not to have all their eggs in one basket, of a number of shippers sharing in a shipload of goods. "The commonest things," Morris wrote to a friend, "become intricate when money has anything to do with them."

Everything depended on the individual merchant's personal standing in the world-wide commercial community—what Robert Morris, in the parlance of the time, spoke of as his "integrity." It was considered ethical for a merchant who had in his hands a shipload of lumber consigned to him, say, in Boston, to exchange it, if he saw the chance for a good deal, with the bill of lading for a shipload of hides in Cadiz, without consulting the original owners who might be merchants in St. Eustatius or in Baltimore or in Savannah. In dealing with public funds Robert Morris behaved in

Morris renamed his estate "Castle Defiance" as he sought to elude his creditors in 1798.

the same way. As Joseph Reed pointed out, he was never too curious to find out whether he was using the negotiable paper of the United States for a speculation to his own advantage, or whether he was using his own funds for the benefit of the United States.

He would hardly have been human if he hadn't encouraged the legend to grow that he was risking his private fortune to finance the Revolution. To a certain extent this may have been true; to a large extent the opposite was true. Of one thing we may be sure: the commercial career of Robert Morris was interlocked with the successes and failures of the American cause.

Morris' appointment as sole superintendent of finance came as the climax of a brilliantly successful business career. It was a career all of his own making.

Born in England in 1734, he was the son of a Liverpool man of a seafaring family who had set himself up as a tobacco factor at Oxford on the Eastern Shore of Maryland. It is doubtful whether his mother and father were legally married. His grandmother brought him up. When the father's business began to flourish he sent for his son to join him in America. Young Robert Morris was then about thirteen.

He arrived in Oxford to find that his father had set up housekeeping with a lady named Sarah Wise, whom he had never taken the trouble to marry. Young Robert was placed with a merchant friend of the elder Morris' in Philadelphia to be educated, and in due time was apprenticed in the countinghouse of the Willing family's notable import and export firm. He served as a supercargo on trading journeys and showed such enterprise and application that he became one of the Willings' indispensable men.

He was only sixteen when his father died. Young Robert inherited about £2,500 in Maryland currency. Sarah Wise's daughter was provided with a hundred pounds and another hundred was left "to the infant with which she was then with child." When this infant turned out to be a boy whom the mother named Thomas, Robert Morris raised him as his own son.

When the Willing firm was reorganized, some time after young Thomas Willing came back from London, Morris, although he was only 21, was taken in as a junior partner. He had made good use of his father's little legacy in private adventures on the Willing ships, and he had already a substantial sum to invest. He and young Willing became firm friends.

Thomas Willing was a cautious, thoughtful individual who in later life was known in Philadelphia as "Old Squaretoes." His conservatism combined with Morris' reckless enterprise made the classical combination for a business partnership. The firm of Willing & Morris was successful indeed.

Morris became one of the great men of fast-growing Philadelphia. His easy, convivial manner made him friends in all directions. He married Mary White, a lady from a respected Maryland family who was reputed a great beauty. He acquired a town house on Front Street and a country house across the Schuylkill. This place, The Hills, was known for its fruit and for the products of the vegetable garden and greenhouse. "You see I continue my old practice of mixing business and pleasure," he wrote one of his friends, "and ever found them useful to each other."

It was natural that he should push to the fore in the Philadelphia Committee of Merchants during the Stamp Act agitation. He sat in the Pennsylvania Assembly. He was appointed to the Continental Congress. Though he opposed the Declaration of Independence as untimely, when the day came to sign the document he put his name to it in a bold scrawl at the head of the Pennsylvania delegation.

With his practical knowledge of shipping he immediately became the most active member of the Committee of Commerce and of the Marine Committee that handled naval affairs. He saw to it that his firm's network of correspondents in the West Indies and in European ports became indispensable in the procurement of war materials. He treated the Continental Congress and the state of Pennsylvania as he would commercial partners. While he procured them the munitions they needed he indulged in profitable speculations on his own.

As early as the fall of 1777 Willing and Morris dissolved their main partnership, though they remained associated in a number of enterprises. It is likely that the cautious Willing was already finding Morris' speculations a little giddy. The failure of young Thomas Morris may have had something to do with Willing's decision to dissolve the partnership. Robert Morris had given his young half brother "the best education that could be obtained in Philadelphia," had brought him up in his own countinghouse and had sent him off to Europe to represent Willing & Morris and the United States in a number of delicate negotiations. Thomas took to drink and gambling, fell into the hands of sharpers, and finally died in France in a desperate fit of dissipation. This was not the way Old Squaretoes believed in doing business. It is possible, too, that Willing was suffering some doubts that winter about the success of the American cause. When Howe occupied Philadelphia he chose to remain in the city as a noncombatant.

Morris, on the other hand, was thoroughly committed to independence. As a merchant, by this time, he was quite able to stand alone. His investments were scattered over the middle and southern states and all of the Atlantic ports. He was involved in nine major partnerships in various American seaports, as well as in numberless smaller enterprises. By the time the fighting ended his fortune was thought to be without equal in America.

No man could rise to such heights without making enemies. All along, Morris had been a vigorous partisan in local Pennsylvania politics. In the enthusiasm of 1776 the Pennsylvanians had ditched their old charter, and installed a constitution which merged most of the powers of government in a single chamber elected by popular vote. Two parties sprang up, a party of western settlers and of the mechanics and artisans in the towns, most of them recent immigrants of Scotch-Irish origin, Presbyterian in religion, who supported the constitution; and a party of merchants, Quakers, and Church of England people who wanted to revise it. The constitutionalists were for printing-press money, price-fixing, legal tender acts, and radical measures against suspected Tories; their opponents, who called themselves Republicans, were for the protection of property, freedom of opinion, and hard money. Robert Morris was a leader of the Republicans.

Since Philadelphia was the seat of the Continental government during these years, Pennsylvania politics had a disproportionate influence on the opinions of members of Congress. The rancor between the two parties in Philadelphia flared into open violence. The constitutionalists threatened to run the Republicans out of town, and Robert Morris and a group of the "hard money" leaders found themselves besieged in James Wilson's house. This riot, in which a few men were killed and wounded, proved the beginning of the decline of the "Furious Whigs." Moderate men began to put their heads together. The Assembly cut off prosecutions by an act of oblivion. It wasn't long before the Republicans would be carrying the executive council. Robert Morris was elected to the Assembly.

When Congress appointed him superintendent of finance, one of the conditions he laid down was that he be allowed to hold his seat in the Assembly long enough to vote against a new issue of paper money which he considered particularly obnoxious.

Robert Morris set up his office in a building next to the large brick mansion where he lived on Front Street. Immediately he became known as the Financier. He was going to conduct the affairs of the United States as he would his own business. Even before his appointment was confirmed his office filled up with men with long bills demanding to be paid. He was beset by Continental officers with pathetic stories of want asking for advances. Sea captains poured out tales of capture and pillage on the high seas. Butchers, bakers, clothiers, drovers, crowded round his desk trying to turn their dog-eared bills into cash.

The Financier was a businessman who believed in giving his subordinates full responsibility. In the case of his half brother he had made a mistake, and an expensive one. In choosing an assistant superintendent of finance he chose wisely indeed.

He called in a young New Yorker who bore the same name but who came from a very different family background. Gouverneur Morris was the son of the second lord of the manor at Morrisania in Westchester County. There was a brilliant self-assurance about his language in debate that threw elder men off. Some of the delegates spoke of him with dismay as "the tall boy."

When the two Morrises took over the finances of the Confederacy, inflation had destroyed the value of the paper currency and was fast destroying that of the loan office certificates which were the government bonds of the period. Foreign loans were every day harder to come by. As the war emergency became less acute after Yorktown, it became harder for Congress to raise money from the states.

Paradoxically, at a time when Congress and most of the state governments were in a condition of bankruptcy, the country as a whole was prosperous. Privateering and wartime procurement had brought new wealth into the seaport towns. The rural districts, except where they had actually been laid waste by ravaging armies, were harvesting fine crops. The war had brought more prosperity than it had ruin to the thirteen states.

The problem that faced the Morrises was how to turn the fundamental financial health of the new nation to account. Their first measure was to establish a national bank.

Alexander Hamilton had been agitating for a bank for some time. He pointed out that the blunders and failures in American affairs had resulted not from the disaffection of the people, but from the mismanagement of the Confederacy. When the members of a federation were more powerful than the head, a stable and unified command was impossible. The cure was to enlarge the powers of Congress. Hamilton agreed with the two Morrises that a national bank would be the cornerstone of a stable central government.

Robert Morris went to work to push a charter through Congress. "I mean to render this a principal pillar of American credit," he wrote Franklin, who was busy in Passy trying to coax a fresh loan out of the foreign office at Versailles, "so as to obtain the money of individuals for the benefit of the Union and thereby bind these individuals more strongly to the general cause by ties of private interest."

Robert Morris as financier dominated the bank's operations from behind the scenes. To back up Congress' credit he had the supreme effrontery to print notes of his own, backed only by the glamour of his name. The Robert Morris notes were generally accepted at a premium over the Continental paper. Never since the days of the Mississippi Bubble had a money man trodden such dangerous heights. To build the edifice of credit he needed on such a very small foundation in actual specie, he had to have recourse more and more to what Washington had called the "art magick."

Financing the government became a race with time to meet daily obligations. "It seems as if every Person connected in the Public Service," Morris wrote in his daybook, "entertains an Opinion that I am full of Money for they are constantly applying even down to the common express Riders and give me infinite interruption so that it is hardly possible to attend to Business of more consequence."

Year after year the two Morrises kept having to put off their "Business of more consequence." They did manage to reduce expenses and to put order into the paper work of their department and to list and to certify the heterogeneous congressional debt. They appointed Continental collectors of taxes for the various states, thereby laying the foundation for an internal revenue system.

All their projects failed when Congress forwarded them to the states for ratification, in spite of the fact that they were backed by most of the younger men of the "continentalist" side. Jefferson lobbied in vain for Morris' impost in Richmond. Even Tom Paine, whom Robert Morris hired at Washington's suggestion at $800 a year to promote the cause of a Continental tax on imports, failed to make any immediate impression on the public mind. In the end Virginia and Rhode Island between them managed to defeat the tax on imports.

To add to his troubles Morris' own enormous investments were endangered by the severe depression that the end of the war had induced in the seaport towns. Merchants found themselves overstocked with goods bought in Europe at inflated wartime prices. The carrying trade to the West Indies, which before the war had been the lifeblood of colonial commerce, was choked off by the British through a series of new interpretations of the Navigation Acts in reprisal for American independence. Shipbuilding was at a standstill. Morris' investments, based on loans against securities borrowed from Peter to pay Paul, had expanded to a dangerous degree.

He held on in the Finance Office even after Gouverneur Morris resigned, in the hope of at least balancing his books before giving up. With the congressional income still insufficient to pay the interest on Congress' multifarious indebtedness, and with Franklin writing from Passy that he had to have cash to keep up interest payments on the foreign loans, Morris was forced more and more to apply the "art magick" to meet current expenditures. His days were spent dreaming up recourses to bolster the value of the Continental paper, and of his own Robert Morris notes. When credit faltered, men who his critics claimed were his own agents were ostentatiously paid in clinking silver at the Bank of North America.

He carried the art of kiting checks and bills of exchange to a high degree of perfection. The fact that sailing ships took so long to cross the Atlantic made it possible to meet an obligation in Philadelphia with a note drawn on some Dutch banker in Amsterdam. That would give the Financier three months to find negotiable paper with which to appease the Dutchman when he should threaten to protest the note. In the end it was the loan John Adams raised in Holland that extinguished the threat of a protest in Amsterdam which would have ruined Congress' credit abroad. Robert Morris could now resign with the books of the Finance Office tolerably balanced. He was not so lucky with his procurement transactions. In the final statement of the affairs of the old Congressional Committee of Commerce it was found that Robert Morris still owed the United States $93,312.63.

Robert Morris' real crime, in the eyes of the men who were trying to keep the states in the ascendant, was his use of public finance to centralize government. As resentment against the impost grew in the state legislatures, Congress filled up with delegates instructed to demand the Financier's resignation. Morris resigned before the movement against him came to a head. Even his friends had found him highhanded. Hamilton, the most ardent of continentalists, wrote Washington, who he knew held the Financier in high personal esteem, that he felt that the way Morris had tried to bludgeon the members of Congress by holding the threat of his resignation over their heads had been unwise. Still, he added, he had to admit that "no man in this country but himself could have kept the money machine a-going during the period he has been in office."

Only the Financier knew how desperately his own investments needed shoring up. He kept up the confident front. Men who had dealings with the retired Financier came away awed and excited by the bustle of vast speculations that filled his life. In New York he was loading a vessel with ginseng, that mysterious root, so cheap to gather in America, for which the Chinese mandarins were willing to pay enormous prices. Rumors trickled out of his scheme to corner the entire American tobacco market in a deal with the French farmers-general. He was putting out enormous sums to keep a controlling interest in western land companies. New York State lands were particularly prized. At one point Morris took title to a million and a quarter acres in Genesee country alone.

Over the Madeira after dinner his table hummed with talk of vast profits to come. There were profits all right. The *Empress of China* sailed safely back into New York in 1784 after inaugurating the great China trade. The grand old *Alliance,* bought from Congress by a syndicate in which Morris took part, was dispatched to the Far East in the opposite direction. Settlers were pouring into the western country. The corner in tobacco lowered the price disastrously for the planters in Maryland and Virginia, but the farmers-general made their advance payments on schedule in His Christian Majesty's good silver coin. Morris' difficulty, like that of the Continental Congress, was that his income never could keep up with the vast inflation of his credit. It was only by an extraordinary use of the "art magick" that he staved off bankruptcy as long as he did.

After Washington's election as President and the formation of a general government on the new plan the Constitution had sketched out, a rumor went around that Robert Morris would be secretary of the treasury, but even Washington, who loved him, felt his affairs were too involved. It would be risking "animadversions" to offer him public office.

L'Enfant's baroque plans for a new town house for the Financier had put him to ruinous expense and made him a laughingstock. "Morris's Folly" people called it. He lost a vast block of Georgia land for nonpayment of taxes. He defaulted on payment on 6,000 lots he had bought inside the ten-mile square of the new capital city where he, with a partner, had contracted to build 120 brick houses. The difficult year of 1797, when the failure of the Bank of England extinguished credit for a while throughout the whole Atlantic trading community, put an end to him. "Who in God's name has all the Money?" he wrote plaintively.

For fifteen years since his resignation as financier, the man whose financial judgment and whose taste in worldly things Washington had always deferred to, had managed somehow to keep in the air, by endless juggling of paper and kiting of promissory notes, an unbelievable structure of interlocking partnerships, land options, loans, mortgages, speculations in everything from ship's timbers to snuffbottles. Now ingenious men figured that Morris and his last partner John Nicholson were between them in default of something like 34 millions of dollars.

By the fall of 1797 the bailiffs closed in. Morris no longer dared venture on the streets for fear of arrest. There was hardly a man in the country he didn't owe money to. He retreated to The Hills and there held the process servers and sheriff's deputies at bay for three months. His spirit never faltered. "Castle Defiance" he called his country house in his desperate notes to Nicholson, who was holding out in similar fashion in what he called "Castle Defense" downtown. "If I ever get square I shall never contract another

Morris' costly Philadelphia town house, widely known as "Morris's Folly," was sold under the auctioneer's hammer.

debt," Morris confided to his accomplice in dishonor.

While Morris was still holding out in the upper story of The Hills, with the front door barred and a fowling piece in his hand, the estate was knocked down under the auctioneer's hammer. L'Enfant's marble folly, Morris' old downtown mansion, the house where President Washington had lived during his second Administration, the choice building lots, everything went. At last on February 15, 1798, Morris gave himself up and was carted off to the debtors' section of the Prune Street Jail. There he remained until the passage of a bankruptcy act late in 1801.

When George Washington, as commander in chief of Hamilton's provisional army during the troubles

with the French Directory, visited Philadelphia for the last time he made a point of dining with his old friend. Instead of at The Hills, where the asparagus and strawberries were always so fine in the spring and the apricots and plums in summer and the pears and hothouse grapes in the fall, and where the claret and Madeira and the roast meats were of the rarest, Washington dined with Morris and his wife in a dim, ill-smelling room with barred windows.

When George Washington, erect and stately in his buff and blue uniform with the shining epaulets, strode with a jingle of spurs into the prison room which Mrs. Morris had worked hard to make a little homelike with a few faint evidences of former grandeur, he found both Morrises pale and shrunken after their ordeal of that summer. As soon as he had heard that a fresh epidemic of yellow fever had begun, Washington, who knew they were in financial difficulties but did not realize to what extent, had written to his old friends to come at once to stay with him at Mt. Vernon.

When Washington's letter reached him the door was already locked on the Financier. His wife, who had taken what Abigail Adams, who called on her there, described as a small neat room nearby, refused to leave him. Together they braved the yellow fever. The streets around were filled with dead. Imprisoned debtors died in the adjoining rooms. They had been spared. They were grateful to God.

Even in this last extremity Morris couldn't keep his sanguine spirits down. He was already revolving vast new schemes by which he could take advantage of some sudden rise in values to pay off his creditors and spend himself into wealth once more. Though he was eventually to regain his freedom and to live obscurely for a few years after, his great days were over. It was all his good friend Gouverneur Morris could do to salvage a small income for Mrs. Morris out of the wreckage of America's greatest fortune.

Even in failure and disgrace Robert Morris' friends thought of him with a certain indulgent affection. Gouverneur Morris and Alexander Hamilton always visited him at Prune Street when they passed through Philadelphia. Thomas Jefferson, no friend of financiers, who had bitterly fought the Morris tobacco monopoly when he was in France as American minister, while he was planning his cabinet with the help of Madison and Gallatin after his election to the presidency, still had enough regard for Morris' ability and patriotism to consider him for secretary of the navy. The chief obstacle was that no one could imagine any way of getting him out of the Prune Street Jail.

A Tax on Whiskey?

To the backwoods distillers of Pennsylvania, that was like taxing the air they breathed. But the government was deadly serious: the Constitution itself was at stake

At Fort Cumberland, Maryland, in mid-October, 1794, President George Washington donned his general's uniform to review troops dispatched to put down the Whiskey Rebellion. The painting was done by Frederick Kemmelmeyer, who witnessed their departure.

Never!

By GERALD CARSON

When one recalls that the President of the United States, the Secretary of War, the Secretary of the Treasury, and the governors of four states once mobilized against the farmers of western Pennsylvania an army almost as large as ever took the field in the Revolutionary War, the event appears at first glance one of the more improbable episodes in the annals of this country. Equipped with mountains of ammunition, forage, baggage, and a bountiful stock of tax-paid whiskey, thirteen thousand grenadiers, dragoons, foot soldiers, pioneers, a train of artillery with six-pounders, mortars, and several "grasshoppers," paraded over the mountains to Pittsburgh against a gaggle of homespun rebels who had already dispersed.

Yet the march had a rationale. President George Washington and his Secretary of the Treasury, Alexander Hamilton, moved to counter civil commotion with overwhelming force because they well understood that the survival of the new U.S. Constitution was involved. Soon after he assumed his post at the Treasury, Hamilton had proposed, to the astonishment of the country, that the United States should meet fully and promptly its financial obligations, including the assumption of the debts contracted by the states in the struggle for independence. Part of the money was to be raised by laying an excise tax upon distilled spirits. The tax became law on March 3, 1791.

In the back country settlements that produced the whiskey and drank the lion's share of it, the news of the passage of the measure was greeted with a roar of indignation. The duty was laid uniformly upon all the states, as the Constitution provided; if the West had to pay more, the Secretary of the Treasury explained, it was only because it used more whiskey. The East could, if it so desired, forego beverage spirits and fall back on cider and beer. The South and the frontier West could not, for they had neither orchards nor breweries. To Virginia and Maryland the excise tax appeared to be as unjust and oppressive as the well-remembered Molasses Act and the tea duties of George III. "The time will come," predicted Georgia's fiery James Jackson in the House of Representatives, "when a shirt shall not be washed without an excise."

Kentucky, then thinly settled, but already producing its characteristic handmade, copper-fired, whole-souled liquor, was of the opinion that the law was unconstitutional. Deputy revenue collectors throughout the Bluegrass region were assaulted, their papers stolen, their horses' ears cropped, and their saddles cut to pieces. On one wild night the people of Lexington dragged a stuffed dummy through the streets and hanged in effigy Colonel Thomas Marshall, the chief collector for the district.

Yet, in no other place did popular fury rise so high, spread so rapidly, involve a whole population so completely, or express so many assorted grievances as in the Pennsylvania frontier counties of Fayette, Allegheny, Westmoreland, and Washington. There, in 1791, a light plume of wood smoke rose from no less than five thousand log stillhouses. The rates went into effect on July 1. The whiskey-maker could choose whether he would pay a yearly levy on his still capacity or a gallonage tax on his actual production.

Before the month was out, "committees of correspondence," in the old Revolutionary phrase, were speeding horsemen over the ridges and through the valleys to arouse the people to arm and assemble. The majority, but not all, of the men who made the whiskey decided to "forbear" from paying the tax. Revenue officers were thoroughly worked over. Robert Johnson, for example, collector for Washington and Allegheny counties, was waylaid near Pigeon Creek by a mob disguised in women's clothing. They cut off his hair, gave him a coat of tar and feathers, and stole his horse.

The Pennsylvania troubles were rooted in the economic importance and impregnable social position of mellow old Monongahela rye whiskey. The frontier people had been reared from childhood on the family jug. They found the taste pleasant, the effect agreeable. Whiskey kept the population cool in summer. In winter, it was the old settlers' equivalent of central heating. Whiskey was usually involved when there was kissing or fighting. It beatified the rituals of birth and death. It provided almost the only diversion, while enjoying at the same time a high reputation as the West's greatest therapeutic agent, effective against fevers, ague, snake bite, or general decline. The doctor kept a bottle in his office for his own use, with the protective label, "Arsenic—Deadly Poison."

Whiskey lubricated the machinery of government. The lawyer produced the bottle when the papers were signed. Whiskey was available at the prothonotary's office when the trial list was made up. Jurors got their dram, and the constable drew his ration for his services on election day. The hospitable barrel and the tin cup were the mark of the successful political candidate. The United States Army issued a gill to a man every day. Ministers of the gospel were paid in rye whiskey, for they were shepherds of a devout flock, Presbyterians mostly, who took their Bible straight, especially where it said:

"Give strong drink unto him that is ready to perish, and wine unto those that be of heavy hearts."

"Let him drink, and forget his poverty, and remember his misery no more."

With grain the most abundant commodity west of the mountains, the farmers could eat it or drink it, but they couldn't sell it in distant markets unless it was reduced in bulk and enhanced in value. Thus a Pennsylvania farmer's "best holt" was whiskey. A pack horse could move only four bushels of grain. But it could carry twenty-four bushels if it was condensed into two large wooden kegs of whiskey slung across its back, while the price of the goods would double when they reached the eastern markets. So whiskey became the frontier remittance for salt, sugar, nails, bar iron, pewter plates, powder and shot. Along the western rivers, where men saw few shilling pieces, a gallon of good, sound rye whiskey was a stable measure of value.

The bitter resistance of the western men to the whiskey tax involved both practical considerations and principles. First, the excise payment was due and must be paid in scarce hard money as soon as the water-white distillate flowed from the condensing coil. The principle concerned the whole repulsive idea of an internal revenue levy. The settlers of western Pennsylvania were a bold, hardy, emigrant race from Scotland and northern Ireland, who had set up their mashing tubs, fermenters, and pot stills before the last Indian war whoop ceased to echo among the hills. They brought with them also bitter memories of oppression in the old country under the excise laws, involving invasion of their homes, confiscation of their property, and a system of paid informers. Revenue collectors were social outcasts in a society which might have warmly seconded Doctor Samuel Johnson's definition of excise: "a hateful tax levied upon commodities, and adjudged not by the common judges of property, but wretches hired by those to whom excise is paid."

The whiskey boys of Pennsylvania, then, saw it as simply a matter of sound Whig principles to resist the exciseman as he made his rounds with a Dicas hydrometer to measure the proof of the whiskey and his marking iron to brand the casks with his findings. Earlier, the state had taxed spirits, except that whiskey produced for purely private use was exempt. William Findley of Westmoreland County, a member of Congress at the time and a sympathetic interpreter of the western point of view, looked into this angle. To his astonishment, he learned that all of the whiskey distilled in the west was for purely personal use. So far as the excise tax was concerned, or any other state tax, the sturdy Celtic peoples of the Monongahela region had cheerfully returned to a state of nature: they just didn't pay. About every sixth man made whiskey. But all were involved in the problem, since the other five took their rye and corn to the stillhouse where the master distiller turned it into liquid form.

But now matters had taken a more serious turn. The new federal government in Philadelphia was dividing the whole country up into "districts" for the purpose of collecting the money, and cutting the districts up into smaller inspection "surveys." The transmontane Pennsylvanians found themselves in the grip of something known as the fourth survey, with General John Neville, hitherto a popular citizen and leader, getting ready to enforce the law. Rewards would be paid to informers and a percentage of the taxes given to the collectors, who appeared to be a rapacious set.

The first meeting of public protest against the United States excise of 1791 was held in July at Redstone Old Fort (now Brownsville, Pennsylvania). The proceedings were moderate on that occasion, and scarcely went beyond the right of petition. Another meeting in August, more characteristic of others which were to follow, was radical in tone, disorderly, threatening. It passed resolves that any person taking office under the revenue law was an enemy of society.

When warrants were issued in the affair of the molested revenue agent, Robert Johnson, the process server was robbed, beaten, tarred and feathered, and left tied to a tree in the forest. As the inspectors' offices were established, they were systematically raided. The familiar Liberty poles of the Revolution reappeared as whiskey poles. The stills of operators who paid the tax were riddled with bullets in attacks sardonically described as "mending" the stills. This led to a popular description of the whiskey boys as "Tom the Tinker's Men," an ironical reference to the familiar, itinerant repairer of pots and kettles. Notices proposing measures for thwarting the law, or aimed at coercing the law-abiding distillers, were posted on trees or published in the Pittsburgh *Gazette* signed, "Tom the Tinker," nom de plume of John Holcroft and other anti-tax propagandists. Congressman Findley, one of the prominent men of the region who tried to build a bridge of understanding between the backwoodsmen and the central government, described the outbreak as not the result of any concerted plan, but rather as a flame, "an infatuation almost incredible."

An additional complaint against the tax grew out of the circumstance that offenders were required to appear in the federal court at Philadelphia, three hundred miles away. The whiskey-makers saw this distant government as being no less oppressive than one in London, and often drew the parallel. Some democrats, oriented sympathetically toward the Jacobin Clubs of Paris, whispered that the whole whiskey issue was a scheme of the Federalists to transfer the powers of government from the people to an aristocratic junto.

A mounting clamor of protest led Congress to modify the severity of the excise tax law in 1792 and again in 1794. A further conciliatory step was taken. To ease the hardships of the judicial process, Congress gave to the state courts jurisdiction in excise offenses so that accused persons might be tried in their own vicinity. But some fifty or sixty writs already issued and returnable at Philadelphia resulted in men being carried away from their fields during harvest time. This convinced the western leaders that the aristocrats in the east were seeking a pretext to discipline the democratic west.

One day in July, 1794, while the processes were being served, William Miller, a delinquent farmer-distiller and political supporter of General Neville, saw the General riding up his lane accompanied by a stranger who turned out to be a United States marshal from Philadelphia. The marshal unlimbered a paper and began to read a summons. It ordered the said Miller to "set aside all manner of business and excuses" and appear in his "proper person" before a judge in Philadelphia. Miller had been planning to sell his property and remove to Kentucky, but the cost of the trip to Philadelphia and the fine for which he was liable would eat up the value of his land and betterments.

"I felt my blood boil, at seeing General Neville along, to pilot the sheriff to my very door," Miller said afterward. "I felt myself mad with passion."

As Neville and the marshal rode away, a party from the county militia which was mustered at Mingo Creek fired upon them, but there were no casualties. When the General reached Bower Hill, his country home above the Chartiers Valley, another party, under the command of John Holcroft, awaited him and demanded his commission and official papers. The demand was refused, and both sides began to shoot. As the rebels closed in on the main house, a flanking fire came from the Negro cabins on the plantation. The whiskey boys were driven off with one killed and four wounded.

The next day, Major James McFarlane, a veteran of the Revolutionary War, led an attack in force upon Neville's painted and papered mansion, furnished with such marvels as carpets, mirrors, pictures and prints, and an eight-day clock. The house was now defended by a dozen soldiers from Fort Fayette at Pittsburgh. A fight followed during which a soldier was shot and McFarlane was killed—by treachery, the rebels said, when a white flag was displayed. The soldiers surrendered and were either released or allowed to escape. Neville was not found, but his cabins, barns, outbuildings, and finally the residence were all burned down. Stocks of grain were destroyed, all fences levelled, as the victors broke up the furniture, liberated the mirrors and clock, and distributed the General's supply of liquor to the thirsty.

The funeral of McFarlane caused great excitement. Among those present were Hugh Henry Brackenridge, author, lawyer, and one of the western moderates, and David Bradford, prosecuting attorney for Washington County. The former wished to find ways to reduce the tension; the latter to increase it. Bradford was a rash, impetuous Marylander, ambitious for power and position. Some thought him a second-rate lawyer. Others disagreed. They said he was third-rate. But he had a gift for rough mob eloquence. Bradford had already robbed the United States mails to find out what information was being sent east against the conspirators. He had already called for the people to make a choice of *"submission or opposition . . .* with *head, heart, hand* and *voice."*

At the McFarlane funeral service Bradford worked powerfully upon the feelings of the mourners as he described "the murder of McFarlane." Brackenridge also spoke, using wit and drollery to relieve the pressure and to make palatable his warning to the rebels that they were flirting with the possibility of being hanged. But the temper of the throng was for Bradford, as clearly revealed in the epitaph set over McFarlane's grave: "He fell . . . by the hands of an unprincipled villain in the support of what he supposed to be the rights of his country."

The high-water mark of the insurrection was the occupation of Pittsburgh. After the fight and the funeral, Bradford called out the militia regiments of the four disaffected counties. They were commanded to rendezvous at Braddock's Field, near Pittsburgh, with arms, full equipment, and four days' rations. At the field there was a great beating of drums, much marching and counter-marching, almost a holiday spirit. Men in hunting shirts practiced shooting at the mark until a dense pall of smoke hung over the plain, as there had been thirty-nine years before at General Braddock's disaster. There were between five and seven thousand men on the field, many meditating in an ugly mood upon their enemies holed up in Pittsburgh, talking of storming Fort Fayette and burning the town as "a second Sodom."

Bradford's dream was the establishment of an independent state with himself cast as a sort of Washington of the west. Elected major general by acclaim, he dashed about the field on a superb horse, in a fancy uniform, his sword flashing, plumes floating out from his hat as he issued orders, harangued the multitude, and received applications for commissions in the service of—what? No one quite knew.

Marching in good order, strung out over two-and-a-half miles of road, the rebels advanced on August 1, 1794, toward Pittsburgh in what was hopefully termed a "visit," though the temper of the citizen-soldiers was perhaps nearer to that of one man who twirled his hat on the muzzle of his rifle and shouted, "I have a bad hat now, but I expect to have a better one soon." While the panic-stricken burghers buried the silver and locked up the girls, the mob marched in on what is now Fourth Avenue to the vicinity of the present Baltimore & Ohio Railroad station. A reception committee extended nervous hospitality in the form of hams, poultry, dried venison, bear meat, water, and whiskey, and agreed to banish certain citizens obnoxious to the insurrectionists. One building on a nearby farm was burned; another attempt at arson failed to come off. The day cost Brackenridge four barrels of good old Monongahela. It was better, he reflected, "to be employed in extinguishing the fire of their thirst than of my house."

Later in the month of August armed bands continued to patrol the roads as a "scrub Congress"—in the phrase of one scoffer—met at Parkinson's Ferry, now Monongahela, to debate, pass resolutions, and move somewhat uncertainly toward separation from the United States. Wild and unfounded rumors won belief. It was said that Congress was extending the excise levy to plows at a dollar each, that every wagon entering Philadelphia would be forced to pay a dollar, that a tax was soon to be established at Pittsburgh of fifteen shillings for the birth of every boy baby, and ten for each girl.

It was evident that the crisis had arrived. The President requisitioned 15,000 militia (of whom about 13,000 actually marched) from Pennsylvania, New Jersey, Virginia, and Maryland. Would the citizens of one state invade another to compel obedience to federal law? Here one gets a glimpse of the larger importance of the affair. Both the national government and the state of Pennsylvania sent commissioners to the west with offers of pardon upon satisfactory assurances that the people would obey the laws. Albert Gallatin, William Findley, Brackenridge, and others made a desperate effort to win the people to submission, though their motives were often questioned by both the rebels and the federal authorities. The response to the offer of amnesty was judged not to be sufficiently positive. Pressed by the Secretary of the Treasury, Alexander Hamilton, to have federal authority show its teeth, Washington announced that the troops would march.

The Army was aroused. In particular, the New Jersey militia were ready to exercise lynch law because they had been derided in a western newspaper as a "Water melon Army" and an uncomplimentary estimate made of their military capabilities. The piece was written as a take-off on the kind of negotiations which preceded an Indian treaty. Possibly the idea was suggested by the fact that the whiskey boys were often called "White Indians." At any rate, in the satire the Indians admonished the great council in Philadelphia: ". . . Brothers, we have that powerful monarch, Capt. Whiskey, to command us. By the power of his influence, and a love to *his person* we are compelled to every great and heroic act . . . We, the Six United Nations of White Indians . . . have all imbibed his principles and passions—that is a love of whiskey . . . Brothers, you must not think to frighten us with . . . infantry, cavalry and artillery, composed of your watermelon armies from the Jersey shores; they would cut a much better figure in warring with the crabs and oysters about the Capes of Delaware."

Captain Whiskey was answered hotly by "A Jersey Blue." He pointed out that "the water-melon army of New Jersey" was going to march westward shortly with "ten-inch howitzers for throwing a species of melon very useful for curing a *gravel occasioned by whiskey!*" The expedition was tagged thereafter as the "Watermelon Army."

The troops moved in two wings under the command of General Henry (Light Horse Harry) Lee, Governor of Virginia. Old Dan Morgan was there and young Meriwether Lewis, five nephews of President Washington, the governors of Pennsylvania and New Jersey, too, and many a veteran blooded in Revolutionary fighting, including Captain John Fries of the Bucks County militia and his dog, which he had named after a drink he occasionally enjoyed—Whiskey.

The left wing marched west during October, 1794, from Virginia and Maryland to Fort Cumberland on the Potomac, then northwest into Pennsylvania, to join forces with the right wing at Bedford. The Pennsylvania and New Jersey corps proceeded via Norristown and Reading to Harrisburg and Carlisle. There, on October 4, President Washington arrived, accom-

In an old etching, a mob of Pennsylvania frontier farmers protesting the whiskey excise have just tarred and feathered a federal revenue agent. Violent acts of this sort led President Washington to call out the Army in 1794.

panied by Colonel Alexander Hamilton. The western representatives told the President at Carlisle that the army was not needed, but Hamilton convinced him that it was. Washington rode down to Fort Cumberland on October 16 to review the troops of the left wing, which had assembled there. He then went on to Bedford, the rendezvous, to survey final plans before returning to Philadelphia for the meeting of Congress. Meanwhile Hamilton ordered a roundup of many of the rebels and personally interrogated the most important ones. Brackenridge, incidentally, came off well in his encounter with Hamilton, who declared that he was satisfied with Brackenridge's conduct.

By the time the expedition had crossed the mountains, the rebellion was already coming apart at the seams. David Bradford, who was excluded from the subsequent amnesty, fled to Spanish Louisiana, where he finished out his life as a planter. About 2,000 of the best riflemen in the west left the country, including many a distiller who loaded his pot stills on a pack horse or a Kentucky boat and sought asylum in Kentucky, where, hopefully, a man could distill "the creature" without giving the public debt a lift.

The punitive expedition moved forward in glorious autumn weather, raiding chicken coops, consuming prodigious quantities of the commodity which lay at the heart of the controversy. Richard Howell, governor of New Jersey and commander of the right wing,

revived the spirits of the Jersey troops by composing a marching song, "Dash to the Mountains, Jersey Blue":

> *To arms once more, our hero cries,*
> *Sedition lives and order dies;*
> *To peace and ease then bid adieu*
> *And dash to the mountains, Jersey Blue.*

Faded diaries, old letters, and orderly books preserve something of the gala atmosphere of the expedition. At Trenton, New Jersey, a Miss Forman and a Miss Milnor were most amiable. Newtown, Pennsylvania, was noted as a poor place for hay. At Potts Grove a captain of a cavalry troop got kicked in the shin by his horse. Among the Virginians, Meriwether Lewis enjoyed the martial excitement and wrote to his mother in high spirits of the "mountains of beef and oceans of Whiskey," sent regards "to all the girls," and announced that he would bring "an Insergiant Girl to se them next fall bearing the title of Mrs. Lewis." If there was such a girl, he soon forgot her.

Yet where there is an army in being, there are unpleasant occurrences. Men were lashed. Quartermasters stole government property. A soldier was ordered to put an insurgent under guard. In execution of the order, he ran the rebel through with his bayonet, of which wound the prisoner died. At Carlisle, a dragoon's pistol went off and hit a countryman in the groin; he

31

too died. On November 13, long remembered in many a cabin and clearing as "the dismal night," the Jersey Horse rounded up suspects whom they described grimly as "the whiskey pole gentry," dragging them out of bed, tying them back to back.

In late November, finding no one to fight, the army turned east again, leaving a volunteer force under General Morgan to conciliate and consolidate the position during the winter. Twenty "Yahoos" were carried back to Philadelphia and were paraded by the Philadelphia Horse through the streets of the city with "Insurrection" labels on their hats. It was an odd Federalist version of a Roman triumph. The troop was composed, as an admirer said, of "young gentlemen of the first property of the city," with beautiful mounts and uniforms of the finest blue broadcloth. They held their swords elevated in the right hand, while the light flashed from the silver stirrups, martingales, and jingling bridles. Stretched over half a mile they came, first two cavalrymen abreast, then a pair of prisoners, walking; then two more mounted men, and so on.

The army, meditating upon their fatigues and hardships, called for a substantial number of hangings. Samuel Hodgson, the commissary-general, wrote to a Pittsburgh confidant: "We all lament that so few of the insurgents fell—such disorders can only be cured by copious bleedings . . . ," while Philip Freneau, friend and literary colleague of Brackenridge, suggested in retrospect—ironically, of course—the benefits which would have accrued to the country "If Washington had drawn and quartered thirty or forty of the whiskey boys . . ." Most of the captives escaped any punishment other than that of being held in jail without a trial for ten or twelve months. One died. Two were finally tried and sentenced to death. Eventually both were let off.

If the rising was a failure, so was the liquor tax. The military adventure alone, without ordinary costs of collection, ran up a bill of $1,500,000, or about one-third of all the money that was realized during the life of the act. Meanwhile the movement of the army to the Pennsylvania hinterland had brought with it a flood of cash which furnished the distillers with currency for paying their taxes. Gradually the bitterness receded. During Jefferson's administration, the tax was quietly repealed. Yet the watermelon armies and the whiskey boys made a not inconsiderable contribution to our constitutional history. Through them, the year 1794 completed what 1787 had begun; for it established the reality of a federal union whose law was not a suggestion but a command.

THE farewell previous to the WESTERN EXPEDITION.

*Above, a young militiaman bids farewell to his sweetheart
as he prepares to join the fight against the whiskey boys.*

PACK-ROAD
TO
YESTERDAY

What the old-time peddler meant

in the development of the American frontier

By PENROSE SCULL

The sea and the deep broad bays and rivers sweeping far into the continent offered the early American colonists their easiest and cheapest highroad for commerce and communications. There were literally tens of thousands of miles of shore line which could be reached handily by boat, yet because of some perverse streak in man's nature it wasn't long before a number of restless people packed their scanty possessions and struck out for the heavily wooded, hilly interior.

As these deflectors from the tidewater areas moved inward, cleared their land and established outposts of colonial civilization, they presented a challenging opportunity to other men whose minds were occupied with trade and commerce. Each farm, each gristmill, each nucleus of some future village had its constant need for a supply of worldly goods and its surplus of produce to offer to the seaboard. It was a market that couldn't be ignored—and it wasn't for very long. Thus it came about that a band of stout-legged men hoisted trunkloads of merchandise on their backs and trudged

off into the pathless forests to trade with the people who had moved inland.

These were the peddlers. For the next two centuries they were to follow doggedly in the shadows of far-wandering Americans as they rafted down the Ohio and the Mississippi, trekked along the Wilderness Road and the Santa Fe Trail, and ultimately moved in on the Spaniards on the far side of the Rockies in California.

Considering the number of easier and more sedate ways there were to earn a living, one wonders why men chose to become peddlers. In almost every respect it was a dog's life, knocking around the raw back country of America. When the peddlers went out on the road, they were quite literally on the road—afoot, sloshing through mud ankle-deep in winter, or scuffing up a cloud of dust in summer. They were snapped at by vicious dogs, shot at by Indians, nipped by frost, and pounced upon by hijackers. Many were stung by rattlesnakes, and all of them were feasted upon by fleas,

John Whetton Ehninger's Yankee Peddler *(1853), looking prosperous and talking fast, appears ready to clinch another sale.*

gnats, mosquitoes, bedbugs, leeches, and other flying and crawling species of tormentors.

But despite all of these occupational hazards, there were many overriding reasons why so many men chose such a precarious profession. Adventure was one of them, and from all accounts they encountered enough of that. A chance to get about and travel was another; early Americans had a consuming curiosity about the make-up of their country, and for a man with a restless foot, peddling gave it plenty of exercise.

But the main reason for "going peddling" was opportunity. Peddling required no experience and very little capital. A peddler could quickly enough learn his trade as he made his rounds, and for as little as twenty or thirty dollars in cash he could buy enough stock to set himself up in business. The market for the peddlers' goods was rapidly expanding; many peddlers accumulated enough money after several years to retire from traveling and settle down at home as merchants and traders.

Thousands of others spotted remote villages which they figured would some day become bustling centers of trade and transportation. To these places with a future the peddlers returned and sank their roots. Some opened stores and became prosperous merchants. Others became jobbers and wholesalers. In hundreds of American cities and towns—Albany, Buffalo, Cincinnati, Fargo, Albuquerque, Sacramento—firms begun long ago by peddlers are still in business.

The first of the Yankee peddlers carried a general line of housewares and notions. Pots and pans, axes, handmade nails, thread, buttons, scissors, and combs were fastest-selling items. Biggest profits were earned on such frivolities as bits of lace and ribbon and fancy cloth, mirrors, toilet waters, spices, tea, coffee, and nostrums.

There were limits, naturally, as to how much of a load of these things a man could carry or how much he could manage to stow upon his horse. Such weight and space limitations led some of the peddlers to become

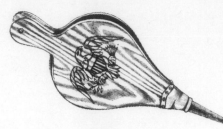

specialists in certain lines. Instead of loading up with a hodgepodge of general merchandise, the specialists handled spices only, or tinware, or herbs and medicines. In later years there were clock peddlers, furniture peddlers, sewing machine peddlers. There were even peddlers of wagons and carriages—men who hitched together a string of three or four vehicles and drove around until they found buyers for the new rigs.

There was no end to the peddlers' ingenuity in finding customers. They tracked down the remotest farmhouse and loneliest cabin, and turned up at every fair or carnival. In the Deep South they paddled up and down the rivers and bayous in canoes and drew their customers from plantation mansions and shanties by blowing on a bugle or a conch shell. But mostly the peddlers walked, pacing off the long lonely miles with their heavy loads on their backs and the dream of riches and the future easing their way.

The peddler's trunk was a long, rather narrow box usually made of tin. A strong peddler starting out on a selling expedition carried two such trunks, one on each shoulder. The stowing of merchandise in these trunks was a major undertaking requiring great skill. Dishes and pans of varying size were nested. Into pots went buttons, pins, nails, and ribbons. Gingham and bright calicoes were wrapped around long-handled forks.

So packed, each trunk weighed up to fifty or sixty pounds. And, paradoxically, the more a peddler sold the heavier became his trunks, for, often as not, the buyers had only grain, honey, furs, and homemade woodenware to exchange for the peddler's wares. These products, which often weighed more than those the peddler had sold, had to be carried back to his home base and sold to the merchants and wholesalers. How successfully the peddlers traded off these country wares determined their ultimate profits.

There were compensations, however. Wherever the peddler called he was a welcome visitor. Housewives stopped their work, men came in from the fields, children gathered around, and the trunks were opened. There was no great hurry. Everybody wanted to see all the fascinating goods and hear every scrap of the latest news. And the peddler was in no hurry either, for he welcomed a chance to rest his road-weary legs. Besides, if it was morning when the peddler arrived, he could usually drag out negotiations long enough

to be asked to stay for the noonday meal, and if he arrived in the afternoon, there was a good chance of an invitation to stay over for supper and the night.

As roads improved some peddlers rode on horseback, carrying their wares strapped to their horses. Others used wagons which were capable of carrying full-sized loads. These improvements in transportation increased the importance of the peddler in our early commerce. He was able to go farther, carry more stock and take a greater volume of goods in trade or barter.

But the peddlers still had their troubles, as is attested to by the following letter written by a peddler of bonnets (paper hats called Navarinos) to his supplier in western Massachusetts:

Tioga June 22nd 1830 NYK
Mr. Thomas Hurlbut. Sir.
From Bainbridge I arrived here today at 12 o'clock by driving 12 miles yesterday in the rain. In consequence of the heavy rains that have fallen in this country the past ten days the roads are *tremendous* bad they are so rutted that I have been obliged to fasten a roap to the top of my box and hold on. I have just met with a Dry Goods Pedler who trades through all parts of Pennsylvania. he says the roads are much worse than they are here however I am not discouraged yet. my horses stand it well except they are galled a little by driveing yesterday and today in the rain & for Bonets I have found no chance for any sales of consequence yet.
The Small Pox is spreading over this country.
don't send out another Pedler with so high a box.
In haste yours
Rodney Hill
I am in good health.

By early March the farm families in New England were on the lookout for the man with the packs on his back. Long before his arrival they had carefully listed the wares they *must* have—a dozen buttons, a paper of pins (very expensive in those days), a new jackknife, two pewter mugs, six needles—and as an appendage to that list of essentials there was a much longer list of the things they would *like* to have.

The meeting between the farm family and the peddler was a lively swapping session, with the peddler in much the stronger position to get the better of every transaction. First of all, the peddler was working in

DECORATIONS BY DUO

what was pretty much of a seller's market. His offering included items which the family could not do without. Then, too, he was selling to people who understandably were eager to add the slightest luxuries to their meager possessions. People possessing so little as did the early colonists found it difficult to resist a jew's-harp for the children, a stick of candy, a bit of gay ribbon or of lace, or a pretty piece of chinaware to set on the bare mantel over the kitchen fireplace. Sales resistance was low—even among the most frugal people—and the country people were uninformed about goods and prices.

If a peddler held out for a 600 per cent markup for pepper, he would blandly explain that the price was high due to an obscure war at sea which had shut off imports from the Spice Islands. So, too, would he justify his exorbitant prices for other articles by fixing the blame somehow on the English king or the avarice of the merchants in Boston, New York, or Philadelphia. His customers were in no position to dispute the peddler's laments about the skyrocketing prices in the market places, and they paid through the nose for the goods they bought.

But when it came their turn to offer goods to the peddler in payment, the farm families invariably found that the market for such things as they had for sale was poor indeed. Honey was a drug on the market, according to the peddler; the merchants in town were

not much interested that year in coonskins and beaver pelts or beautifully hand-carved chairs. If the peddler was to be believed, he could resell such items at very depressed prices, hardly more than it would cost him to transport the stuff back to town.

Very often a peddler who marked up an item by 1,000 per cent knew that this was unrealistic. He started high so that he could magnanimously come down to, say, about 500 per cent profit—a process of repricing which was an exhilarating experience both for the peddler and his customer. One of the most enduring myths in our colonial folklore is that the peddlers were guilty of foisting wooden nutmegs and sanded sugar upon unsuspecting housewives. There has never been any evidence uncovered to back up these tales of deliberate dishonesty, but there is evidence aplenty that the peddlers were masters of the art of deception and overpricing.

Unquestionably, a minority of the peddlers were first-class bums and crooks. Their drunken brawls, bloody fights and shady deals were well publicized, and drew sharp blasts from newspaper editors. Many inns and taverns posted notices bluntly announcing that peddlers were unwelcome.

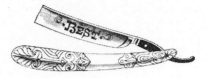

The spellbinders who peddled a nauseous brew of raw alcohol, roots, herbs, and branch water as a cure-all for every ailment from ague to housemaid's knee did their profession a disservice. And there are, in fact, no really new stories about the traveling man and the farmer's daughter, for the same ribald stories told today were in currency soon after the first peddlers passed along the country lanes in staid old New England. In the South the peddlers were referred to as "those damn Yankees from Connecticut," and throughout the land they were scorned by pious folks as ungodly ne'er-do-wells only a cut or two better than gypsies.

But for all the unsavory publicity generated by the few bad eggs among them, the peddlers served a useful purpose. Importers and small manufacturers depended upon them as an outlet for a large portion of their goods. Several million people relied on these wandering merchants to bring them the goods they needed, and to carry away the things they had produced. This army of walkers was a primitive and inefficient way of carrying on trade, but when the peddler's trunks were opened up, and he began his persuasive sales pitch, one historian remarked that "wants dawned on the minds of the household that they had never known before."

The peddler's salesmanship and physical endurance kept alive the first stirrings of our industrial economy. He has gone now, but for two hundred years he was an important man among men engaged in important affairs.

In 1805, when Salem and the Crowninshield family were both riding the flood tide of the East India trade, George Crowninshield, Sr., commissioned George Ropes to paint this scene of Crowninshield Wharf. At the outer end of the wharf lies the *America*, famous pepper trader commanded by Captain Benjamin Crowninshield (see below) and later a privateer in the

In July, 1805, Captain George Crowninshield and his sons waited impatiently for their ship *America*, under comand of a cousin, Benjamin Crowninshield, to arrive from Sumatra. Their impatience was not joyful since the market at that moment was glutted with pepper and the *America*'s cargo would only depress the price even more. They had no one to blame except themselves for the expected cargo since they had given strict orders to Captain Ben to proceed to Sumatra for pepper and to go to no other port to

trade, as the captain was so fond of doing. When the word arrived that the vessel was coming into Salem harbor, old George Crowninshield with his sons went out to meet it, hoping that Captain Ben had disobeyed his orders this time. While being rowed out to the slowly moving ship, they sat tensely and sniffed in hopes they could smell the cargo. Suddenly the men caught the odor of coffee in the air! Young Ben Crowninshield sang out through his speaking trumpet, "What's your cargo?" Captain Ben, with a solemn

War of 1812. Next to her lies the *Fame,* another East Indiaman. In the counting house at the far left a watcher with a spyglass scans the harbor for sail. The warehouses on the wharf are filled with the treasure of the Indies: silks from China, coffee from Mocha, sisal from Manila, iron from Kronstadt, salampores from India, ivory and gold from the Guinea Coast.

face, answered from the quarter deck, "Pepper!" "You lie! I smell coffee," shouted the merchant while Captain Ben stood at the rail grinning.

Pepper had been such a bonanza just a few years before that the house of Crowninshield had been led, in this instance, to depart from the time-tested Salem policy of giving a shipmaster full freedom of action. Captain Ben's experience only proved the wisdom of the usual policy. On the outward voyage he had put into Isle of France (Mauritius), a favorite refreshment

place for ships bound to and from the Orient, and here, on this island in the middle of the Indian Ocean, he discovered that most of the vessels bound for the States had pepper in great quantity but not one of them reported any coffee. Having his owner's interests in mind, he decided to disregard his orders and, instead of proceeding to Sumatra, set sail for the steaming little coffee port of Mocha on the Red Sea. Such independence, coupled with a fine business sense, was the basis of Salem's East India trade.

The bark *Richard* sailed chiefly in the South American trade but was painted off Marseilles in 1831. Later she was a whaler.

The little port of Salem, in these thirty years between the Revolution and "Mr. Madison's War" of 1812, was a powerhouse of world commerce. Seldom a day passed when a vessel did not clear for foreign ports or when some sharp-eyed boy did not come running to "King" Derby to collect a Spanish silver dollar for the news that a returning Salem ship stood off Baker's Island.

It was a full century since the last witch had been hanged on Gallows Hill, a century and a half since Governor Winthrop had advised his hard-pressed farmers to seek their fortunes on blue water. The men of Salem had learned their seamanship in the rigorous school of Grand Banks fishing and long before the Revolution they had developed a thriving trade with the West Indies. Their trim little schooners carried the produce of New England—chiefly codfish and lumber—to the Indies and brought back cargoes of sugar, salt or molasses. Often they ventured to the wine islands or to the Mediterranean ports and rarely to the coast of Africa. But neither before nor after the

Revolution was there any important trade in slaves, for it took a pretty hardened skipper, even if he cared nothing for the law of Massachusetts, to walk into the old East Church with slave-trading money in his pocket and face the accusing Congregational eye of the Reverend Dr. Bentley.

The Revolution offered New England the greatest challenge of its maritime history. Salem's response was

This painting by the French artist Antoine Roux shows how the little brig *Eunice* had her bottom cleaned at St. Paul Island in 1817. Her Salem crew careened her on the beach but, because of the slight

40

The bark *Patriot,* built in 1809, served in both the Baltic and the East India trade. She was painted off Copenhagen.

a fleet of 158 privateers, some of them converted traders and some newly built, which issued from the port to prey on England's commerce and carry naval warfare to the very shores of the British Isles. In 1781, the surrender of Cornwallis left Salem with a double problem. The privateers were built too large for the coastwise or the West Indian trade; and the British West Indian ports which had been open to Salem

Mediterranean tide, could not float her off. Advised by local fishermen, they "casked" her in wooden staves and then, with the help of two small fishing vessels, rolled her back into the water like a barrel.

masters as colonials were closed to them as citizens of the new Republic. Casting about for new opportunities, the merchants fixed their gaze on the Orient, until then the exclusive trading province of the European East India companies.

Elias Hasket Derby, whose business acumen and imagination did much to build Salem's prosperity, sent one of his larger vessels, the *Grand Turk,* to the Cape of Good Hope in 1784, with a cargo of rum, cheese, salt meat, sugar and butter. The cargo was to be exchanged at the Cape for tea and other China goods. But there was one flaw in the plan: the British East India Company vessels were not allowed to break bulk at that place. By luck Captain Jonathan Ingersoll was able to buy tea, silks and nankeens from the East India Company ship *Calcutta,* which had been forced to put into the Cape.

The success of this voyage prompted Derby to make another attempt to trade in the same region. In December, 1785, the *Grand Turk* was sent to Isle of France with the following cargo: pitch, tar, flour, rice, tobacco,

41

House flags of the Salem merchants, along with flags of some individual ships, were painted about 1835 by an unknown artist.

butter, claret wine, bar iron, sugar, oil, chocolate, brandy, beef, rum, bacon, ham, candles, soap, anise seed, fish, beer, porter, and pork. Included in this typical cargo of a maritime Yankee peddler were not only the native products of New England but goods gathered from all around the shores of the North Atlantic.

Captain Ebenezer West put into Cape Town to sell his cargo, but finding the market slow, he moved on to Isle of France. Conditions there were not much better, but he sold his cargo and then he received the offer of a freight to Canton from a French merchant. The *Grand Turk* of Salem was the third American vessel into China, having been preceded by the *Empress of China* and the *Hope*, both of New York. The return cargo was largely tea—315½ chests of Bohea, 2 chests of Hyson, 52 chests of Souchong and 32 chests of Bohea Congo—together with 130 chests of cassia, 10 chests of cassia buds, and 75 boxes of chinaware.

For American seamen the approach to Canton was a trip into fairyland. From shore to shore the Pearl River was alive with ferryboats and canal boats, sampans housing whole families, elegant barges, junks with gaudily painted eyes on their prows, flower boats with tinkling music and all manner of craft for business or pleasure. Leaving their vessels at Whampoa Reach, the Americans picked their way through this strange, uncounted fleet to the warehouses or "Hongs" where, by imperial edict, foreigners must live and trade. The heads of the Hongs were merchants of great wealth who sometimes won, as Houqua did, the respect and lifelong friendship of Yankee captains.

Yet despite oral tradition and despite the fascination that Canton held for the young New England seamen, the China trade never played an important part in Salem's commerce. There were great profits to be made from the teas and silks and chinaware that Canton offered, but it was hard to find anything that the self-sufficient Chinese would take in return. One product in demand was ginseng, a medicinal root which resembles a man in form and, according to the doctrine of signatures in medieval medicine, is good for the whole body. But since ginseng grew mostly in the Middle Atlantic states, New York and Philadelphia got the lion's share of this trade, as Boston did of the trade in sea otter skins from the Pacific Northwest coast.

After 1800 Salem's Canton business picked up when Joseph Peabody's captains discerned a vast Chinese appetite for the *bêche-de-mer,* a sea slug which the mandarins prized for soup. The *bêche-de-mer* lived on the islands of the South Pacific and there the Salem captains hunted them. In doing so many a Salem boy had his horizons widened by meeting up with exotic island girls, with cannibals and headhunters, and with pieces of native art which he carried home to his mother and aunts in Salem. The great Pacific collection of the Peabody Museum, America's greatest ethnological treasure of the South Seas, is largely a by-product of this odd hunt for a marine worm to flavor Chinese soup.

The China trade has always been the most romantic one of Oriental commerce, but, as far as Salem was concerned, the trade with British India was more important. During the period from 1784 to 1800, when twelve voyages were made to Canton, 54 voyages were made to India. The ship *Lighthorse,* Ichabod Nichols master, owned by Elias Hasket Derby, was in Calcutta in 1788 where she loaded cotton to be taken to China. Captain John Gibaut took the *Astrea* to the Orient in 1791, stopping at Cape of Good Hope and Isle of France, then heading for the Coromandel Coast to trade. She put into Colombo and went on to Madras where she found a freight to Rangoon. At that port she was seized by the Sultan of Pegu to transport sup-

Elias Hasket Derby was the leader in Salem's East India trade. With one blue eye and one brown he watched over a global enterprise which made him America's first millionaire.

Nathaniel Silsbee was an East India captain at 19, later a U. S. Senator.

Jacob Crowninshield was the dashing son of a great merchant family.

Joseph Peabody, last of the merchant princes, employed 7,000 men.

plies to his army, then making war in Siam, and her master was held as a hostage. When the *Astrea* was released in 1793 she was in such bad condition that Captain Gibaut was forced to sell her in Calcutta and return home on another vessel. In 1794 Elias Hasket Derby's second *Grand Turk* arrived in Salem with 1,200,000 lbs. of sugar, 60,000 lbs. of pepper, and about $50,000 worth of general merchandise, largely textiles.

A group of life-size clay portrait figures of Hindu and Parsee merchants sits as if in conference in the Peabody Museum today. These portrait figures, dressed in clothes actually worn by the Indian merchants themselves, were sent to Salem merchants, just as we send photographs to distant friends and relatives today.

In the language of the Eighteenth Century the term "India" included not only the Asian subcontinent but all the Southern lands and islands beyond the Cape of Good Hope. In this vast watery empire, extending 5,000 miles from Table Mountain to Java Head, Salem ships opened scores of ports to American trade. The *datu* of Quallah Battoo was not the only native prince who believed, well into the Nineteenth Century, that Salem was a sovereign nation.

Of all the branches of the East India trade the Sumatra pepper trade was the most exciting. The Dutch had maintained nominal control over the island for several centuries but had never extended actual control beyond a little trading post of the Dutch East India Company. The British East India Company also had a trading post, called Fort Marlborough, on the island, and it was to these two settlements that the Malays brought their pepper to sell. Neither of the East India Companies had sought to develop the pepper trade but had been content to accept what they could get at the trading posts and charge a high price for it in Europe.

The discovery by Americans that pepper could be purchased easily on the island of Sumatra was made by two Salem adventurers, Captain Jonathan Carnes and William Vans, who sailed from Salem as master and supercargo respectively of the brig *Cadet*. After a voyage that lasted two years, the pair arrived in the port of New York with a cargo of pepper and various other spices. Jonathan Carnes, realizing he had an opportunity to open a new field of trade, approached his uncle, Jonathan Peele, who supplied him with the schooner *Rajah* and a cargo of brandy, gin, scrap iron, tobacco and fish. The schooner sailed in November, 1795, disappeared from sight for nearly two years and then came into New York with a full cargo of pepper. Salem buzzed with the news and there was speculation in all the counting houses as to where Carnes had found his cargo, but neither Peele nor Carnes would tell. Tradi-

The focal point of the China trade was the waterfront of Canton. Flags of the Western nations (left to right: Denmark, Spain, the United States, Sweden and England) fly over the Hongs or factories where foreigners were required to trade.

PAINTING BY MICHELE FELICE CORNÉ

tion says that a profit of 700% was realized on the investment.

With the return of the *Rajah,* Salem entered upon a trade which built the fortunes of many merchants and made Salem for a time the capital of the world's pepper market. This should have been an idyllic trade. Sumatra is a tropical island with a strip of lowland along the coast and green towering peaks beyond; the sea breaks over the coral reefs and only ripples reach the palm-fringed shore; just beyond the strip of white sand lie the villages, groups of nipa huts peopled with Malays dressed in gay-colored sarongs. In the trading days a vessel arrived, the captain came ashore and dickered with the local *datu* for pepper. When a price was agreed upon the ship's crew brought a beam balance and weights on shore to weigh the pepper, which was carried out to the ship in *praus* (native boats). In this green paradise the serpent was the Malay himself, who reasoned, logically, why bring pepper to sell when we can capture the vessel, kill the crew, take the cargo and money. The master who relaxed his vigilance lost his vessel and often his life. Many times sailors and mates new to the coast dismissed the pirate tales as mere imagination, only to discover the laughing innocent Malay transformed in an instant into a murderous pirate.

Off the pepper coast in 1806 Captain William Story was sitting in the cabin of the Gardners' ship *Marquis de Somereulas* when he heard his first mate, Mr. Bromfield, cry out that he was "creesed." There followed a brief scuffle between the four seamen left on deck and a band of native pirates armed with the wicked Malay short sword called a *kris* or, in Salem spelling, creese. Rallying his men, the captain started up the companionway, only to be beaten back by the Malays, who now controlled the deck. Before making a second attempt, Captain Story stationed a man by the powder magazine with instructions to apply a match and blow up the ship if the Malays won the fight. Thereupon the captain and crew rushed the deck, only to find the natives unaccountably making for shore in the *praus* that brought them.

The net profit on this voyage of the *Marquis de Somereulas* was $99,751.50. Such profits help to explain why, despite all the perils, men still went to Sumatra.

Foreign trade before the advent of modern communication, fast steamships and submarine cables, depended largely on the good judgment of the master, since both the navigation of the vessel and the disposal of the cargo were entrusted to him. At the start of each voyage the owner handed the captain a letter of instructions that gave him not only directions as to the voyage but also an amazing liberty in the conduct

From his first pepper voyage to Sumatra Captain Jonathan Carnes in 1797 brought back an elephant's tooth, a double-stemmed Batta pipe and a goblet carved from rhinoceros horn. These trophies launched the great collection of the East India Marine Society at the Peabody Museum in Salem.

A great friend of American captains was Houqua *(below)*, senior Hong merchant at Canton and one of China's richest men. They found him fair and honorable but one added: "Houqua is rather dear, loves flattery and can be coaxed."

of his business. The following letter to Captain William D. Waters of Salem is quite typical:

June 18th 1824

Capt Wᵐ Waters

Sir! You being Master & part owner of the Brig Otter now . . . ready for sea we advise you to proceed to the port of Manilla in the Island of Luconia & there invest your funds in such produce as you think will pay the most profit in this Market such as Sugar, Hides, & Indigo, Turtle-shell, dye wood & Manilla grass, bearing in mind however that the latter as well as Indigo & Turtle shell may not be so high next year as it is this. You will therefore be governed by the best information you can obtain & your own prudent judgment. If you find in Manilla that you can obtain a cargo that would answer better for Europe this you are at liberty to do or if you can obtain a freight from there to Europe or any other part of the world if you think it for our advantage, you are at liberty to employ your vessel as long as you think you can make it profitable. Should you not succeed at Manilla in procuring a cargo for this country or Europe you may then proceed to any Island or Port in India where you think best for the benefit of the voyage. You will receive for your services 3 p.c. of the Nett proceeds of the cargo at her port of discharge in Europe or the United States. If you should return to the United States you will hoist a white flag for your signal & proceed to Boston.

Should any accident befal you during this voyage to deprive us of your services, your first Officer will take charge of the property so as to obtain a cargo & return to the United States.

Since the *Otter* was a new vessel a common instruction was omitted in the letter, viz., the permission to sell the ship itself. Such is found in the letter of William Gray to Captain Clifford Crowninshield of the ship *Ceres* in 1789:

". . . sell the cargo now on board for the most it will fetch, and if you can, sell the Ceres . . ."

If the master found a good market for his cargo and also found an abundant return cargo, he frequently bought or chartered another vessel and freighted the two of them.,

A ship's captain was not a mere employee, even though he received a monthly wage, but had certain privileges. He received from 1% to 8% of the net profits of the voyage, a great inducement to careful trading, and in addition was allowed to carry up to five tons of goods to trade on his own account. On the early Salem voyages, each seaman was allowed a certain number of cubic feet of hold space for his own private trading stock, which might be a few kegs of tobacco or some large New England cheeses. From such an allotment fortunes were built.

Seldom, indeed, has Opportunity knocked so insistently on a boy's door as it did in Essex County dur-

Indian merchants sent these clay figures of themselves, together with their clothes, as gifts to Salem merchants. They are ranged, as if in conference, at the Peabody Museum.

Salem's worst disaster occurred in 1802 when the ship *Ulysses* and two others were driven onto Cape Cod by a blizzard. Eighty-seven seamen froze to death in the triple disaster.

PAINTING BY MICHELE FELICE CORNÉ

Salem's most distinguished man of intellect was Nathaniel Bowditch, who served as clerk and captain of Salem ships. Finding 8,000 errors in the British maritime tables, he compiled *The American Practical Navigator*, which, after 70 editions, is still the standard work. Osgood painted him under the bust of Laplace, whose *Mécanique Céleste* he translated into English.

ing the early years of the East India trade. Though Salem in 1785 was the sixth largest city in the country (after New York, Philadelphia, Boston, Baltimore and Charleston), it still had only 6,665 people and in the main seafaring age group of sixteen to thirty it numbered but 694 males. From all the surrounding countryside farm lads, catching the smell of adventure and fortune, made their way to the Salem wharves, each laden with a bagful of belongings, a few books or comforts from his anxious mother and such stern advice as this from a Boston uncle: "If you meet the Devil, cut him in two and go between the pieces."

Except for the merchants' sons, who went to Harvard, their schooling was sound but short. Nathaniel Bowditch, the great mathematician and navigator, had no formal schooling after he was ten and went to sea when he was fourteen. But these youths were men of the world when most of their compatriots were stuck behind a plow. Many a Salem boy had seen Calcutta and the Coromandel Coast before he ever set foot in Boston.

The captains themselves, in many cases, were hardly more than boys. When Nathaniel Silsbee took Mr. Derby's *Benjamin* out of Salem in 1792, on a voyage that lasted eighteen months and brought its owner a profit of 100%, he was nineteen years old; his first

mate was twenty and his clerk was nineteen. But Nathaniel Silsbee was a seasoned skipper, having been at sea since he was fourteen and captained a sloop in the West Indies trade. His two brothers both commanded ships before they were twenty and all three of them, having made small fortunes, left the quarterdeck to set up as merchants before they were thirty.

Very few Salem merchants inherited wealth; most of them worked up from common seamen. Elias Hasket Derby, son of the merchant Richard Derby, was the great exception. Young Mr. Derby had never gone to sea, yet he knew the whole world almost as well as he knew the long wharf where he unloaded his ships or the fine mansion which he built across the street from it. Before the Revolution he was the leading merchant of the West Indies trade and when war broke out he took the lead in building and outfitting privateers. Few merchants knew as much about the design and building of a ship and none had his mastery of a worldwide business empire. His neighbors knew that Mr. Derby was a man of great fortune but few suspected its size until he died. He was America's first millionaire.

"King" Derby had a fine talent for picking men. Joseph Peabody, Nathaniel Silsbee, Stephen Phillips, Jacob Crowninshield, George Crowninshield, Benja-

---

A Note About the Peabody Museum

The East India Marine Society, organized in Salem in 1799, was made up of shipmasters and supercargoes (owner's representatives) who "shall have actually navigated the Seas near the Cape of Good Hope and Cape Horn." The Society, which had 403 members before the last India captain died, had three purposes. One was to help the needy families of mariners engaged in a hazardous enterprise. Another was to gather a library of information tending to improve navigation. The third was to form a museum of objects found on distant shores.

To each member bound to sea the Society gave a blank journal, to be filled with the log of the voyage, descriptions of channels, ports, reefs and headlands and, in some cases, with sketches or even water colors of coastlines and foreign craft. Salem mariners made the first navigational charts of the waters in and around the Malay archipelago. Their sea journals now stand, row on row, in the Peabody Museum of Salem, a unique record of an era in maritime history.

The Museum itself had its start when Captain Jonathan Carnes, returning from his second pepper voyage, brought it an elephant's tooth, a Batta pipe and a rhinoceros-horn goblet (see page 45). Over the years it accumulated one of the world's great collections of Oriental objects.

The Society's proudest day came in 1824 when President John Quincy Adams dedicated its present building. After eighteen toasts were drunk Mr. Adams retired—but the hardy mariners stayed on to drink 25 more. Some forty years later, when the decline of Salem's foreign trade threatened the Society with extinction, its collection was saved by a gift from the great Salem-born London merchant, George Peabody, whose name the Museum now bears.

min Hodges and Ichabod Nichols, all of whom were well-known Salem merchants, started their careers on Mr. Derby's vessels.

The firm of George Crowninshield and Sons was made up of George Sr., George Jr., Benjamin W., Jacob, John, and Richard. The sons learned their business on their father's vessels on the West Indies run and then were transferred to the Oriental trade. Before 1805 the five sons had made nearly twenty voyages to the Indies. The firm broke up during the early Nineteenth Century when Jacob became a member of Congress, Benjamin, Secretary of Navy under Madison, and John and Richard turned to manufacturing. George, Jr., kept his interest in the sea and during the War of 1812 he outfitted the ship *America* as a privateer. With the coming of peace he built the brig *Cleopatra's Barge,* the first American ocean-going yacht, and made a cruise of the Mediterranean, entertaining princes and potentates and stirring up rumors that he was going to rescue Napoleon from St. Helena. A replica of the cabin saloon, complete with original furnishings, can be seen at the Peabody Museum.

The flood tide of East India commerce brought Salem not only wealth but a cosmopolitan air and a taste for beautiful things which set her apart from most American cities. "The fruits of the Mediterranean are on every table," wrote Harriet Martineau, an English visitor. "They have a large acquaintance in Cairo . . . wild tales to tell of Mozambique and Madagascar." A merchant, in his progress down Essex Street, might be followed by a Chinese boy in bright silks. A turbaned lascar might serve his dinner. Or he might, like Jacob Crowninshield, bring back from Africa the first elephant seen in the United States. Almost certainly, before he died, he would build one of the square Federal mansions which have made Chestnut Street the finest street, architecturally, in America.

This was the zenith. In the seven years between 1807 and 1814 Federalist Salem endured first Jefferson's hated Embargo and then Madison's unpopular war. Once more Salem privateers made a brilliant record at sea, but the cost was heavy. Of more than 200 sail at the start of the war, only 57 remained under Salem registry at the close. The fleet was soon rebuilt and Salem entered a long Indian summer of trade in which Joseph Peabody, last of the great merchant princes, enjoyed as great a primacy as E. H. Derby had a generation before. But the tide was running against the port. Salem's harbor, inferior to a dozen others on the Atlantic coast, was too shallow for the larger ships of the 1820's and 30's. Salem had no great river or hinterland to feed it commerce. Slowly the business shifted to Boston and with it, many of the merchant houses.

It was not until 1893 that the last Salem ship, owned by the great old house of Silsbee, Stone and Allen, left Derby Wharf to become a coal barge. But by 1846, when Nathaniel Hawthorne wanted a sinecure post in which to write his novels of Salem decadence, he wangled an appointment as Surveyor of the Port of Salem. In the big drafty Customs House, built at the close of Salem's great mercantile era, only a few old shipmasters remained to doze in the sun, record the arrival of a coastwise lumber schooner and swap tales of great days in distant seas.

In 1836, when Salem became a city, it adopted a seal showing an East Indian with a parasol standing under a palm tree with a ship in the distance. Engraved on this unique American city seal is the motto: *Divitis Indiae usque ad ultimum Sinum,* which is rendered: "To the farthest port of the rich East."

Brig   Brigantine   Bark

Young Samuel Slater smuggled a cotton mill out of England—in his head—

and helped start America's Industrial Revolution

FATHER *of our* FACTORY

Samuel Slater

Feats of memory, particularly of the kind of memory derided as "photographic"—for all the cornucopias of wealth they sometimes pour over television contestants—are looked down on in modern times, but they have their role in history. Consider, for example, the story of Samuel Slater. It would be impolite to call him a spy, for he would not have considered himself one. Furthermore, he was a man of peace. Yet in his own time this cotton spinner's apprentice achieved with his prodigious memory an effect as great as or greater than any successful military espionage has brought about in our own. For he successfully transplanted the infant Industrial Revolution, which was in many ways an English monopoly, across an ocean to a new country.

To understand Slater's feat, one must look back to the economic situation of England and America in the days directly after the Colonies had achieved their independence. If Britain no longer ruled her former colonies, she clung tenaciously to her trade with them. Thanks to her flourishing new textile industry, she was able to sell large quantities of cotton goods in the United States at prices so low there was little incentive left for making cloth over here by the old-fashioned hand methods. To maintain this favorable dependency as long as possible, England went to fantastic lengths to guard the secrets that had mechanized her cotton industry, and so effective were these measures that America might well have continued solely as an agricultural nation for years, had it not been for Samuel Slater.

Slater's first mill: In the tall building at the river's edge, once a fuller's mill, he designed from memory intricate machines like a 48-spindle Arkwright spinning frame (right).

SYSTEM

By ARNOLD WELLES

Slater was born near the town of Belper, in Derbyshire, and served his apprenticeship in Jedediah Strutt's cotton mills (foreground).

live and work with Strutt. When William Slater died shortly afterward, in 1783, young Samuel Slater signed his own indenture to learn cotton spinning as an apprentice in Strutt's factory until the age of 21.

During the early days of his term the boy became so engrossed in the business that he would go for six months without seeing his family, despite the fact that they lived only a mile away, and he would frequently spend his only free day, Sunday, experimenting alone on machinery. In those days millowners had

Slater was born in 1768 on his family's property, Holly House, in Derbyshire, England. His father, William Slater, was an educated, independent farmer and timber merchant, the close friend and neighbor of Jedediah Strutt, successively farmer, textile manufacturer, and partner of England's famous inventor, Sir Richard Arkwright, whose spinning frame had revolutionized the manufacture of cotton yarn. Three years after Samuel Slater's birth, Strutt had financed Arkwright's factory at Cromford—the world's earliest authentic cotton mill—where water power replaced humans and animals in moving the machinery, and where the whole operation of spinning yarn could be accomplished for the first time automatically under one roof. Within five years Arkwright's mills were employing over 5,000 workers, and England's factory system was launched.

It was in this atmosphere of industrial revolution that young Slater grew up. He showed signs of his future mechanical bent at a tender age by making himself a polished steel spindle with which to help wind worsted for his mother, and whenever he had the chance, he would walk over to nearby Cromford or Belper on the Derwent River to see the cotton mills which Strutt and Arkwright owned. In 1782 Strutt began to erect a large hosiery factory at Milford, a mile from the Slater property, and he asked William Slater's permission to engage his eldest son as clerk. Slater, who had noticed the ability and inclinations of his younger son, Samuel, recommended him instead, observing that he not only "wrote well and was good at figures" but was also of a decided mechanical bent.

Thus, at the age of fourteen, Samuel Slater went to

to build all their own machinery, and Slater acquired valuable experience in its design, as well as its operation, and in the processes of spinning yarn. Even before completing his term of indenture he was made superintendent of Strutt's new hosiery mill.

But Slater had become concerned about the chances for an independent career in England. Arkwright's patents having expired, factories had sprung up everywhere, and Slater could see that to launch out on his own he would need more and more capital to stay ahead of the technical improvements constantly taking place. His attention had been drawn to the United States by an article in a Philadelphia paper saying that a bounty of £100 had been granted by the Pennsylvania legislature to a man who had designed a textile machine. Young Slater made up his mind that he would go to the United States and introduce the Arkwright methods there. As his first step, even before his term with Strutt expired, Slater obtained his employer's permission to supervise the erection of the new cotton works Arkwright was then starting, and from this experience he gained valuable knowledge for the future.

There were, it was true, grave risks to consider. Britain still strictly forbade the export of textile machinery or the designs for it. With France entering a period of revolution which might unsettle the economy of the Old World, it was even more important that the large American market be safeguarded for British commerce. As a result, the Arkwright machines and techniques were nowhere in use in America at the time, and various attempts—in Pennsylvania, Massachusetts, Connecticut, Maryland, and South Carolina— to produce satisfactory cotton textiles had borne little fruit. Without Arkwright's inventions it was impossible to make cotton yarn strong enough for the warps needed in hand-loom weaving.

Enterprising Yankees undertook all kinds of ingenious attempts to smuggle out modern machines or drawings. Even the American minister to France was involved in some of them: machinery would be quietly purchased in England, dismantled, and sent in pieces to our Paris legation for transshipment to the United States in boxes labeled "glassware" or "farm implements." British agents and the Royal Navy managed to intercept almost all such shipments, however, and skilled workers who attempted to slip away with drawings or models were apprehended on the high seas and brought back. Passengers leaving England for American ports were thoroughly searched by customs agents before boarding ship.

Slater knew of these handicaps and determined to take along nothing in writing save his indenture papers. Even these he was careful to conceal. As the time of his departure drew near he did not reveal his plans even to his family, telling his mother only that he was taking a trip to London. On September 1, 1789, in the warm sunlight of late summer, he cast one last look at the pleasant meadows and orchards of Holly House and set off through the lovely Derbyshire countryside.

In London he decided to spend a few days sightseeing, inasmuch as this was to be his first and last visit to the capital. Then, after posting a letter home revealing his intended journey, he boarded ship for New York, assuming the guise of a farmer to escape detection. The role was not difficult for the son of a Derbyshire yeoman, and except for the hidden indenture there was nothing to link the young man with the cotton textile industry. But he was carrying with him in a very remarkable memory the complete details of a modern cotton mill.

After a passage of 66 days, Slater's ship reached New York. He had originally intended to go to Philadelphia, but when he learned of the existence of the New York Manufacturing Company on Vesey Street in downtown Manhattan, he showed his indenture and got a job there instead. The company had recently been organized to make yarns and cloth, but the yarn was linen and the machinery, hand-operated, was copied from antiquated English models. This was a far cry from the factories Slater had supervised in Derbyshire, and he was unimpressed.

Fortunately, about this time, the newcomer happened to meet the captain of a packet sailing between New York and Providence, Rhode Island, and from him learned of the interest in textile manufacturing shown by a wealthy, retired merchant of Providence, Moses Brown, later to become one of the founders of Brown University. A converted Quaker and a man of large imagination and business acumen, Brown had invested considerable cash in two rough, hand-operated spinning frames and a crude carding machine as well as in a couple of obsolete "jennies." But all his attempts to produce cotton yarns had ended in failure, and he could find little use for his expensive machinery. Such was the situation when he received a letter from Slater:

New York, December 2d, 1789

Sir,—

A few days ago I was informed that you wanted a manager of *cotton spinning*, etc., in which business I flatter myself that I can give the greatest satisfaction, in making machinery, making good yarn, either for *stockings* or *twist*, as any that is made in England; as I have had opportunity, and an oversight of Sir Richard Arkwright's works, and in Mr. Strutt's mill upwards of eight years. If you are not provided for, should be glad to serve you; though I am in the New York manufactory, and have been for three weeks since I arrived from England. But we have but *one card, two machines*, two spinning jennies, which I think are not worth using. My *intention* is to erect a *perpetual card and spinning*. (Meaning the Arkwright patents). If you please to drop a line respecting the amount of encouragement you wish to give, by favor of Captain Brown, you will much oblige, sir, your most obedient humble servant.

Samuel Slater

N.B.—Please to direct to me at No. 37, Golden Hill, New York.

Slater's letter fired the shrewd Quaker's imagination, and he hastened to reply, declaring that he and his associates were "destitute of a person acquainted with water-frame spinning" and offering Slater all the profits from successful operation of their machinery over and above interest on the capital invested and depreciation charges. His invitation concluded: "If the present situation does not come up to what thou wishes, and, from thy knowledge of the business, can be ascertained of the advantages of the mills, so as to induce thee to come and work ours, and have the *credit* as well as the advantage of perfecting the first water-mill in America, we should be glad to engage thy care so long as they can be made profitable to both, and we can agree."

Moses Brown, a Quaker merchant, was Slater's financial backer.

These lithographs are from an unusual series called The Progress of Cotton, *published in the early nineteenth century, which shows all the steps in the processing of cotton from field to finished product. Three of the steps are illustrated here: at left, carded "ends," or*

Tempted and flattered, and assuming that the Providence operation needed only an experienced overseer to make it a success, Slater decided to accept. He took a boat in January, 1790, reached Providence on the eighteenth of the month, and immediately called on Moses Brown.

The two men were in striking contrast. Slater, only 21, was nearly six feet tall and powerfully built, with ruddy complexion and fair hair. Moses Brown, in his soft, broad-brimmed Quaker hat, was well past middle age, of small stature, with a pair of bright, bespectacled eyes set in a benevolent face framed by flowing gray locks. Satisfied from a glance at the Strutt indenture that his young caller was bona fide, Brown took Slater in a sleigh to the little hamlet of Pawtucket, a community consisting of a dozen or so cottages on both sides of the Blackstone River, just outside Providence. They stopped at a small clothier's shop on the river's bank, close by a bridge which linked Rhode Island and Massachusetts. Here was assembled Brown's ill-assorted machinery.

Slater took one look and shook his head, his disappointment obvious. Compared to Strutt's splendid mill this was almost a caricature. He spoke bluntly: "These will not do; they are good for nothing in their present condition, nor can they be made to answer." Brown urged him to reconsider, to give the machines

a try, but the young Englishman was not to be persuaded. At last, in desperation, the old merchant threw Slater a challenge:

"Thee said thee could make machinery. Why not do it?"

Reluctantly, Slater finally agreed to build a new mill, using such parts of the old as would answer, but only on one condition: that Brown provide a trusted mechanic to make the machinery which Slater would design and that the man be put under bond neither to disclose the nature of the work nor to copy it.

"If I don't make as good yarn as they do in England," Slater declared, "I will have nothing for my services, but will throw the whole of what I have attempted over the bridge!" Brown agreed, arranging in addition to pay Slater's living expenses.

Then the old merchant took his visitor to the cottage of Oziel Wilkinson, an ingenious ironmaster, with whom Slater could board. Wilkinson, also a Quaker, operated a small anchor forge using water power from the river, and there he turned out ships' chandlery, shovels, scythes, and other tools. As the young Englishman entered the Wilkinson home, his host's younger daughter shyly scampered out of sight, but Hannah, the elder, lingered in the doorway to look at the stranger. Slater fell in love with her. (Within two years they would be married, and Hannah Slater would later

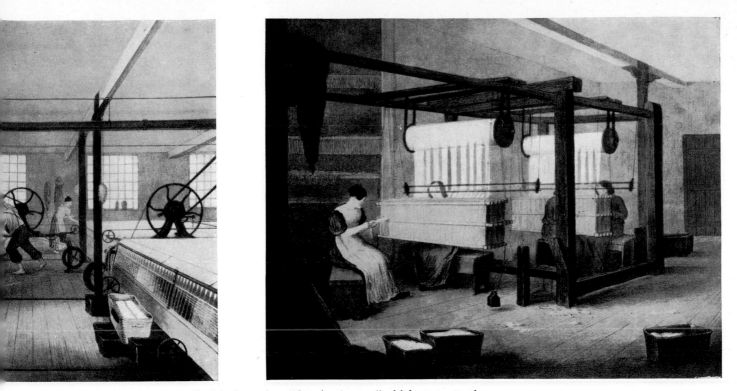

"slivers," of cotton are fed from cylindrical cans into "drawing frames," which attenuate them to produce more even slivers; the "mule" (center) stretches and spins the yarn and winds it on bobbins; in the "warp-winding" process (right) the yarn is attached to frames for weaving.

acquire fame in her own right as the discoverer of cotton sewing thread, which she first produced from the fine yarns her husband manufactured.) In the Wilkinson household young Slater found new parents who helped him overcome his homesickness and encouraged him in the first difficult months.

Part of that winter he spent experimenting with Moses Brown's crude carding machine, and he was able to improve the quality of cotton fleece it turned out. This, when spun by hand on the jennies, produced a better yarn, but one which was still too weak and uneven to be used as warp in the hand-weaving of cloth. Slater was downhearted; he realized that he must build everything from scratch.

The rest of the winter he spent assembling the necessary materials for constructing the Arkwright machines and processes. He lacked even the tools with which to make the complicated equipment, and he was forced to make many of them himself before any building could commence. Furthermore, without models to copy, he had to work out his own computations for all measurements. One of the most ingenious elements of the Arkwright inventions was the variation in speeds of various parts of the machines. Mathematical tables for these were not available anywhere save in England; Slater had to rely on his own extraor-

dinary memory. Nevertheless, by April, 1790, he was ready to sign a firm partnership agreement to build two carding machines, a drawing and roving frame, and two spinning frames, all to be run automatically by water power. He was to receive one dollar a day as wages, half-ownership in the machinery he built, and, in addition, one-half of the mill's net profits after it was in operation. Moses Brown had turned over the supervision of his textile investments to William Almy, his son-in-law, and Smith Brown, his cousin, and these two men became Slater's new partners.

Now, behind shuttered windows in the little clothier's building on the riverbank, young Slater began to design the first successful cotton mill in America. As he drew the plans with chalk on wood, Sylvanus Brown, an experienced local wheelwright, cut out the parts from sturdy oak and fastened them together with wooden dowels. Young David Wilkinson, Slater's future brother-in-law and like his father a skilled ironworker, forged shafts for the spindles, rollers for the frames, and teeth in the cards which Pliny Earle, of Leicester, Massachusetts, prepared for the carding machines. Before iron gearwheels and card rims could be made, Slater and Wilkinson had to go to Mansfield, Massachusetts, to find suitable castings. By autumn, working sixteen hours a day, Slater had more than fulfilled his agreement: he had built not two but three carding machines, as well as the drawing and roving frame and the two spinning frames. At last he was ready for a trial.

Taking up a handful of raw cotton, Slater fed it into the carding machine, cranked by hand for the occasion by an elderly Negro. This engine was one of the most important elements of the Arkwright system, for in it the raw cotton was pulled across leather cards studded with small iron teeth which drew out and straightened the fibers, laid them side by side, and formed them into a long, narrow fleece called an "end," or "sliver." This was then placed on the drawing and roving frame to be further stretched, smoothed, and then twisted before being spun into yarn on the spinning frame. Before the cotton was run through the cards, the fibers lay in every direction, and it was essential that the carding be successful if the "end" was to be suitable for the subsequent steps. But when Slater fed the test cotton into his machine it only piled up on the cards.

Slater was greatly perplexed and dismayed. The machinery had already taken a long time to make, and his partners were becoming impatient. Slater sensed their growing doubts and knew he would forfeit their confidence if this first trial failed. Yet he had nobody who could check on the correctness of his designs. The Wilkinson family later described his anxiety. Standing before their fireplace, he sighed deeply, and they saw tears in his eyes. Mrs. Wilkinson, noting his distress, asked, "Art thou sick, Samuel?" Slater answered sadly, "If I am frustrated in my carding machine, they will think me an impostor."

After a number of sleepless nights, Slater determined that the trouble arose from a faulty translation of his design into reality, for Pliny Earle had never before made cards of that description. Slater decided that the teeth stood too far apart, and that under pressure of the raw cotton they fell back from their proper places instead of standing firm and combing the cotton as it moved past. He pointed out the defect to Earle, and together, using a discarded piece of grindstone, they beat the teeth into the correct shape. Another test was made and the machine worked satisfactorily.

The final stage was now at hand. Almost a year had passed in preparation for this moment. Would the machinery operate automatically by water power? That was the miracle of the Arkwright techniques, which gave them their name, "perpetual spinning." A connection was made to the small water wheel which had been used by the clothier in whose little shop Slater's new machinery now stood. It was deep winter, and the Blackstone River was frozen over, so that Slater was obliged to crawl down and break up the ice around the wheel. When the wheel turned over, his machinery began to hum.

On December 20, 1790, Samuel Slater's mill produced the first cotton yarn ever made automatically in America. It was strong and of good quality, suitable for sheetings and other types of heavy cotton goods; soon Slater was turning out yarn fine enough to be woven into shirtings, checks, ginghams, and stockings, all of which had until then been imported from Europe. Good cotton cloth woven at home from English yarn had cost from forty to fifty cents per yard, but soon Slater brought the cost down as low as nine cents. For the remainder of that first winter, unable to get anyone else to do the job, Slater spent two or three hours each morning before breakfast breaking the river ice to start the water wheel. Daily it left him soaking wet and numb from exposure; his health was affected for the rest of his life.

The little mill started with four employees, but by the end of one month Slater had nine hands at work, most of them children. In this he was following the practice in England, where entire families were employed in the mills. Early English millowners had found children more agile and dexterous than adults, their quick fingers and small hands tending the moving parts more easily. Slater, like other pioneer millowners dealing with small working forces, was able to maintain a paternalistic attitude toward the young persons in his charge; until the coming of the factory system and absentee ownership, child labor was not the evil it later became. Slater introduced a number of social customs he had learned in the Arkwright and Strutt mills. For his workers he built the first Sunday school in New England and there provided instruction in reading, writing, and arithmetic, as well as in religion. Later he promoted common day schools for his mill hands, often paying the teachers' wages out of his own pocket.

Proudly Slater sent a sample of his yarn back to Strutt in Derbyshire, who pronounced it excellent. Yet Americans hesitated to use it, preferring traditional hand-spun linen yarn or machine-made cotton yarn imported from England. Within four months Moses Brown was writing to the owners of a little factory in Beverly, Massachusetts, run by a relative, proposing a joint petition to Congress: Why not raise the duties on imported cotton goods? Some of the proceeds could be given to southern cotton farmers as a bounty for upgrading their raw cotton, and some could be presented to the infant textile industry as a subsidy.

Next, Brown arranged to transmit to Alexander Hamilton, secretary of the treasury and already known as a supporter of industry, a sample of Slater's yarn and of the first cotton check made from it, along with various suggestions for encouraging the new textile manufactures. He reported to Hamilton that within a year machinery and mills could be erected to supply enough yarn for the entire nation. Two months later, when Hamilton presented to Congress his famous *Report on Manufactures,* he mentioned "the manufactory at Providence [which] has the merit of being the first in introducing into the United States the celebrated cotton mill."

By the end of their first ten months of operations, Almy, Brown & Slater had sold almost 8,000 yards of cloth produced by home weavers from their yarns. After twenty months the factory was turning out more yarn than the weavers in its immediate vicinity could use; a surplus of 2,000 pounds had piled up. Desperately, Moses Brown appealed to Slater, "Thee must shut down thy gates or thee will spin all my farms into cotton yarn."

It was at this point that the full force of Slater's revolutionary processes began to become apparent. To dispose of their surplus the partners began to employ agents in Salem, New York, Baltimore, and Philadelphia, and so encouraging were the sales that it became obvious to them that their potential market was enormous. In 1791, therefore, they closed the little mill and built nearby a more efficient factory designed to accommodate all the processes of yarn manufacturing under one roof. It was opened in 1793. (Now the Old Slater Mill Museum, the building still stands today.)

As of December, 1792, the partners' ledgers had shown a credit in Slater's name of £882, representing his share of the proceeds from the sale of yarn spun by

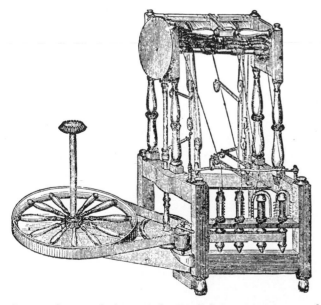

One of the foundations of the English factory system, and a machine with which Slater was familiar, was the Arkwright spinning frame, or throstle frame, invented about 1768.

his mill. From then on both he and the infant industry he had helped to create prospered rapidly. The factory was no longer a neighborhood affair but sought its markets in a wider world. When the War of 1812 had ended, there were 165 mills in Rhode Island, Massachusetts, and Connecticut alone, many of them started by former employees of Slater who had gone into business for themselves. By this time Slater, too, had branched out; he owned at least seven mills, either outright or in partnership. An important mill town in Rhode Island already bore the name of Slatersville. Around three new cotton, woolen, and thread mills which he built in Massachusetts, a new textile center sprang up which became the town of Webster. Later, his far-reaching enterprise carried him to Amoskeag Falls on the Merrimac River; in 1822 he bought an interest in a small mill already established there, and in 1826 erected a new mill which became the famous Amoskeag Manufacturing Company, hub of an even greater textile center—Manchester, New Hampshire.

President James Monroe had come to Pawtucket in 1817 to visit the "Old Mill," which was then the largest cotton mill in the nation, containing 5,170 spindles. It had started with 72. Slater himself conducted his distinguished visitor through the factory and proudly showed him his original spinning frame, still running after 27 years. Some years later another President, Andrew Jackson, visited Pawtucket, and when he was told that Slater was confined to his house by rheumatism brought on from that first winter of breaking the ice on the Blackstone, Old Hickory went to pay his respects to the invalid. Courteously addressing Slater as "the Father of American Manufactures," General Jackson said:

"I understand you taught us how to spin, so as to rival Great Britain in her manufactures; you set all these thousands of spindles to work, which I have been delighted in viewing, and which have made so many happy, by a lucrative employment."

Slater thanked his visitor politely and with the dry wit for which he was well known replied:

"Yes, Sir, I suppose that I gave out the psalm, and they have been singing to the tune ever since."

By the time he died in 1835, Slater had become generally recognized as the country's leading textile industrialist. In addition to his cotton and woolen manufactures, he had founded a bank and a textile-machinery factory and had helped promote several turnpikes, including a road from Providence to Pawtucket and another from Worcester, Massachusetts, to Norwich, Connecticut. At his death Moses Brown, who survived him, estimated Slater's estate at $1,200,000—a remarkable achievement in those early days of the nineteenth century.

The industry Slater had founded 45 years earlier had shown phenomenal growth by the year he died. In 1790 the estimated value of all American manufactured goods barely exceeded $20,000,000, and the domestic cotton crop was about 2,000,000 pounds. By 1835 cotton manufactured goods alone were valued in excess of $47,000,000, and that single industry was consuming almost 80,000,000 pounds of cotton annually. Few men in our history have lived to see such tremendous economic changes wrought in one lifetime by their own efforts.

The social changes which Samuel Slater witnessed and helped to further were even more far-reaching. When he arrived in 1789 America was a nation of small farmers and artisans. By the time he died, and to a considerable extent because of his accomplishments, many artisans had become mill hands.

Three years after Slater's mill began operations, a young Yale graduate named Eli Whitney, visiting a Georgia plantation, devised the cotton gin, and this, in combination with English cotton mills and American ones like Slater's in New England, enormously stimulated the cotton economy (and the slave-labor system) of the South. Simultaneously, and paradoxically, Slater and Whitney helped fasten on the North an industrial economy which would defeat the South when the long-standing economic conflict between the two sections flared out at last in civil war.

Portrait

OF A

Yankee Skipper

From his great-grandfather's papers a poet re-creates that hard-working man of

many parts—sailor, farmer, merchant financier—the New England sea captain

By ARCHIBALD MAC LEISH

The principal difference between history and life is that history is simpler. Things are themselves in history; in life they are generally something else. Take, for obvious example, the New England sea captain of the early 1800's. In history he is a sea captain and nothing more: the master of magnificent brigs and ships on all the oceans, survivor of dreadful storms, proud and often successful adversary of the swiftest patrols the British or the French could send against him.

In life, however, if my great-grandfather, Captain Moses Hillard, was at all typical of his colleagues, he was a great deal more besides: he was a buyer and seller of goods of all kinds, from castor oil and cowitch through rum, coffee, and cotton to garden seeds of curious kinds and the best stockings and shawls to be purchased on the Paris market; he was a dealer in foreign exchange in a number of currencies, including, together with the Russian and the usual European varieties, the complicated coinages of the Spanish Main and those domestic American valuations which were expressed in such terms as "27½ Lawfl money is £13.2.6 or $43.75 cts."

He was a sea lawyer skilled in the filling out of bills of lading in quadruplicate, one to be sworn to before consul or judge affirming United States ownership and three to be sent home, each one in a different vessel; he was a student of long-range and short-range markets in a number of Atlantic ports, a close observer of world affairs (particularly wars), a diplomat of sorts (especially at his own table), a master-rigger, a bit of a doctor, his own laborious secretary, a pleasant companion to his passengers, and a good bit of a man of the world wherever the world might be—in Demerara or New York or Paris.

And in addition to all this he was, or might be, a farmer. My great-grandfather was. How many Yankee sea captains had farms to which they returned between their months-long, often years-long, voyages, I have no means of knowing. The Atlantic coasts of Rhode Island and of eastern Massachusetts and Maine, where the hay mowings run down to salt water and

No picture of any of Hillard's ships is known to survive, except perhaps for this one by Antoine Roux, labeled the Lovely Matilda, *and painted in Marseilles in 1808. Since Hillard had the* Amiable Matilda *that year, and since* aimable *in French means* lovely, *this may indeed have been his ship.*

half the pasture fences are tidal creeks, have a look which suggests that the combination may have been fairly common. Captain Hillard's farm was none of these. It lay out of sound and smell of the sea, some ten miles, perhaps, from the head of navigation, in the little Connecticut town of Preston where the Captain was born in 1780, and where the journey home at the end of a voyage was a long one: by schooner from New York to New London and up the Thames to Norwich, and thence by horseback or cart across the bridge and through the country lanes to 130 acres of ungrateful land and a small unpainted house.

And yet, for some inexplicable reason, that house was closer to the ocean than many built along its shore. Captain Hillard's gravestone in the Long Society Burying Ground stands beside the stones of three of his brothers, no one of whom is buried in that ground. George Hillard's body is somewhere on the island of Madeira, Captain Chester Hillard's lies in a cemetery in Havana, and Benjamin Franklin Hillard was lost at sea off Spain in his nineteenth year.

It would be a mistake, however, to think of the Hillards, or any other sea captain's family with a foot ashore, as farmer-sailors. The farm was all very well in its way—a place to return to and a place to leave one's wife and children—but a man's life was the sea and his profession also. Jefferson's embargo proved that, if any proof was necessary, to hundreds of land-locked sailors up and down the coast and to my great-grandfather neither least nor last. In a letter written in January, 1809, to a seafaring friend in New York, the relative values of land and sea in his universe are made pungently plain, as well as the politics and temper of the man himself:

"Of a Sunday morning and a Stormy Day that Deprives me of my Usual Sundays tour of going to meeting and with a handful of Sore fingers bruised getting wood for this Cold weather and A heart worse bruised by the tyrannical Acts of our Government I sit down to Inform you of my and my family's good health and to Enquire After yours and family's who I hope are Enjoying everything that our present oppressed Situation will allow of your Enjoying. for my share I can assure you there is but little left for people of my profession to Rejoice in. however to keep off the blue Devils my brothers and myself are busying ourselves in Getting wood out of a Dismal Swamp. we have already 100 loads out heaped up so that of freezing we are in no Danger if tom Jefferson and his thundering Administration Starve us out we will go to hell with a fire. . . .

"If I have Raved in my Expressions when you Consider me Compelled to Abandon my own profession and Knock about here in the woods with broken shins and jammed fingers growling like A bear with A Sore head I trust your goodness will Excuse me . . . for I am beating up Against wind and tide and dam hard work to hold my own Every now and then Splitting a Sail. Although Already on Soundings I shant Anchor in hopes that the Current of political influence will soon be changing as I Already See A Damd Strong Eddy Current not far from the Ship which may Set up Strong I hope Ere the Barkee is Ashore. . . ."

Why he loved the sea as he did is a question no sea captain of that difficult time could have answered logically. Captain Hillard was one of the best on the North Atlantic—a man whose passengers wrote him letters of tribute to his "connaissances supérieures en marine" and his agreeable "manière d'agir envers tous les passagers"—but there was little in his career to recommend it to his softer descendants, or, at least, to this one.

His second voyage, when he was nineteen, ended in a French prison on Guadeloupe and he was constantly being searched at sea by arrogant British officers such as the captain of the *Leander* who, as Captain Hillard wrote his owner, Joseph Otis of New York, in 1804, boarded him, "Sandy Whook bearing WNW dist 219 Miles," and treated him "in A most Rascally Manner Who Plundered us of A Number of Small articles and Left Us for a Parcle of Saucy Yankeys Assuring us he had taken A Number of our Countrymen and Were in hopes of taking More."

Furthermore, the wages were not impressive, even when allowance is made for the depreciation of the currency. On his first voyage to Hamburg, Moses Hillard was paid $22 a month; on his second, to the West Indies, the rate was $17; and even when he became captain, as he did in 1803 at the age of 22, $40 or thereabouts was the average pay—though he carried, of course, small "adventures" for himself and seems to have shared, toward the end of his career, in the profits of his voyages. It must be added however—as a commentary on the economy of Preston if not on his own—that the Captain's assessment for the Fifth

School District, Second Society,* in October, 1820, was the highest on the list, in consequence of which he was made chairman of the committee to build and repair the schoolhouse and defray its expenses.

And over and above all this there was, of course, the sea itself—or rather the sea in its relation to such ships as the time afforded: staunch, well-built Yankee vessels but small indeed by any modern standard. Captain Hillard's first command was the brig *Neptune* of 123 tons and his two largest were the ship *Amiable Matilda,* 232 tons, and the ship *Favorite,* 274. Smaller craft by far have crossed the Atlantic, but rarely and

MRS. RALPH BLOMELEY

Direct descendants of Moses Hillard still own this portrait done by a French artist.

with little pleasure in the waters which the Yankee skippers frequented and at the seasons which found them afloat. What happens to a vessel of 160 tons in the North Sea in December and January is recorded with restraint in Captain Hillard's "minet" on a voyage of his brig, the *Havana Packet,* to Toningen with a cargo of logwood at the end of the year 1809.

From the Banks of Newfoundland on, they had "but little else than Constant and Severe Gales of wind generally from the westward till passing the Shetland Islands During Which time we had our head Rails and Quarter boards Washed Away by the Sea and our Crew were very Much Disabled from the fa-

* A kind of parish under the Congregational Church, not disestablished in Connecticut until 1818.

tigue of the passage. After Entering the North Sea which was on the 30th December had tolerable Moderate weather and Constant thick fog for most of the time till 15th January 1810 for the last ten Days of Which time were never more than Seventy or Eighty miles from Heiligoland nor had an Observation & on the 15th Jany Made the Island of Heiligoland at which time the wind was blowing a verry hard Gale and Excessive Cold which Gale Drave us past the Horn Reef to the Northward the vessel Much loaded with Ice and our Crew Mostly frozen and Disabled from the Severity of the Weather found it to be Impossible with Such Weather in our Disabled State to Remain Much longer at Sea. . . ."

This, one gathers, was a more or less routine voyage, worth no more than fifteen lines or so to the owner. The *Havana Packet,* "having no more than two well men on board," made port eventually in Norway, her general destination. Nevertheless one may be permitted to feel, at this remove, that there are better, or at least easier, ways of earning $40 a month.

Not all voyages, moreover, turned out even as well as this. Any sea captain of the time who followed the sea long enough was likely to lose a ship and Captain Hillard was no exception. He lost the *Oneida* in a January storm in 1817 and very nearly lost his wife, Sally Pride, with her, for that adventurous lady was on her first trip to Paris at the time. Only the bare facts of the disaster are recorded in the "Protest" made by Captain Hillard, his chief mate, and a seaman, before Robert Monroe Harrison, consul of the United States for the island of St. Thomas, where half the ship's company was eventually brought ashore, but something more can be guessed from the Captain's letters and other sources. For one thing, the *Oneida* was apparently a famous ship in the North Atlantic, with a great reputation among passengers between Le Havre and New York; for another, if a stubborn but unverified tradition in the Hillard family is true, she was involved in one of the several plots for the escape of Napoleon after Waterloo; and finally she was her master's favorite vessel.

The story of the plot is as vague as it is intriguing. What it comes down to is the Captain's assertion to his son, Elias Brewster Hillard, my grandfather, who was not born until ten years after the battle, that friends of the Emperor had approached the *Oneida*'s master in Paris after Waterloo to attempt to arrange for passage through the blockading British fleet. The Captain, who had no love for British men-of-war either alone or in combination, was willing enough and went so far as to build a false bottom in a water butt, but though he lay on and off at the point agreed for the

better part of a night no Bonaparte appeared. It is a tale one has heard before. I can say only this for its probability: that Captain Hillard had a reputation for truthfulness.

Of the Captain's passion for the *Oneida,* however, there can be no question. She was, in a very particular sense, his ship, for the Talcotts bought her, apparently on his advice, in his own home port of Norwich where she lay under attachment, "her top Masts and yards down and all her Standing Rigging hanging overhead in the weather.' She was a sad sight and in the slowly recovering ship industry, shaken by the Embargo and brought close to ruin by the war, it was difficult work getting her calked and rigged and painted, but the job was eventually done. There are five letters from captain to owners in the month of March, 1815, telling the whole story in a detail which would delight a sailor even now, and before the month was out he had brought her over the Norwich bar "with as light a draft of water as possible"—seven feet nine inches—a northwest gale having lowered the tides in the Thames for some days past.

It was a four-day gale from the same quarter which prepared the destruction of the *Oneida* two years later. Bound for Le Havre, she had passed the east end of Long Island at three in the morning of January 20 when the wind began, driving her without rest or intermission until the night of the twenty-fourth when, as the "Protest" recounts, the wind suddenly "veered around to South East and blew a Perfect Hurricane. when laying too at 11 PM the Ship was struck by a Sea and thrown on her beam ends with the lee Combings of the Hatches in the water which Obliged them to get up their axes in Readiness to cut away the masts when the wind suddenly shifted to N.W. blowing a gale at which time the Ship Righted and it was Discovered that She had opened a Dangerous leak. . . ."

For the next seventeen days passengers and crew, Captain and wife, held precariously to a miserable, frozen hope. First, the crew being exhausted with the intense cold and only two of them "capable of Doing Duty . . . the Passengers were prevailed upon to go to the Pumps." Then, the leak still increasing, they encountered "another Dreadful gale" and the ship's upper works threatening, under the strain, to separate from the bottom, they "commenced heaving overboard the spare spars Cables and everything that could be got at and stove the water casks but Retaind the long boat for the purpose of saving their lives. . . ." By this time "the Passengers were compelled to work at the Pumps without intermission."

By the first of February, after the anchor had been hove and as much of the cargo—ashes, flour, beeswax—as they could get at, and after the small boat had been "stove over the stern," the passengers and crew were "falling at the Pumps in Despair" but the gale still continued and her upper works were now "so loose that it was expected every roll that they would seperate from her bottom." Finally, on the ninth of February, after they had begun to put a raft together, "a sail passed to windward but took no Notice of our Signals of Distress." The next day, however, there was a second sail which bore down and proved to be the schooner *Mars* of Newport, George W. Carr, master, bound from New York to Surinam.

Captain Carr was prevailed upon "to Receive them on board 24 in number with a part of their baggage and a small Quantity of Provisions" and the *Oneida* was abandoned "in Latd 33″ 20 North and Longd 59″ 00 she having then 4 feet water in the hold and the Pumps Stopped. . . ." Two weeks later the over-crowded little *Mars* fell in with the Bremen ship *Dido*, bound for the Virgin Islands, and fourteen of the 24 were transferred, including Captain Hillard and his wife. They reached St. Thomas on the fifth of March, a season when the trade wind is steady in those parts, the sun hot, and the sea unusually blue.

I never fly over that lovely port now on my easy, safe, and comfortable way to the Leewards without seeing it, or trying to, as it must have looked to my great-grandfather in March of 1817. Disasters at sea are the common lot of sailors, but few are called upon to live through as long, persistent, and relentless a trial as the ship's company of the *Oneida*. As one thinks of the frostbitten, helpless crew and the despairing passengers at the pumps, and the Captain's wife in whatever shelter that wracked and leaking wreck afforded, one can imagine how much rest Moses Hillard found in those twenty days.

One can imagine also with what conflicting emotions he saw the harbor of St. Thomas. He had saved his passengers and crew. His wife was alive, though the voyage, as he wrote the Talcotts, had been "almost too much for her"—one can well believe it. But he had lost his cargo and, above all, he had lost his ship.

I suppose a sailor in those troubled years, like a sailor in any generation, balanced the bad off against the good and then refrained from striking a balance. The bad, in Moses Hillard's computations, would have included, along with the wreck of the *Oneida,* the loss of the brig *Caroline,* and the failure of a voyage in the *Amiable Matilda,* but neither disaster would have been chargeable to the sea. The French sank the *Caroline* somewhere north of St. Lucia on his second voyage in 1800, and a British man-of-war, combined with the French Army, cost him the voyage in 1808. This second misadventure is reported in a letter from the Mediterranean to the Captain's owners, William and Samuel Craig of New York. A "British cruizer," he wrote them, had forced him into Gibraltar Roads and endorsed his register forbidding him to enter any port from which the British flag was excluded. This act, combined with the occupation of Barcelona by the French, "Blasts all our hopes of A voyage" and left him with no choice but to "Return Direct to NewYork as the best possible thing that I Can Do for your Interest in this Dreadful Dilemma. I shall sail with the first Ship of force that goes through the Gut for a Convoy and make the best of my way home."

The loss of the brig *Caroline* is recorded in quite another form. From his first voyage ("July 2nd 1799 took my Departure from my father's house in Preston and Sailed from Norwich for NewYork got to New-London and Set off from there in a light westerly wind") Moses Hillard had kept a diary of sorts in a little, homemade journal covered with a rag of sailcloth which is now in the library at Yale. The last pages record the voyage of the *Caroline* which began at New London on May 8, 1800. St. Lucia, in the Windwards, was reached on June 13 and thereafter the journal entries are in lead pencil and now all but illegible:

Monday June 23 sailed from St. Lucia for America with a fair wind.

Tuesday June 24 at 8 A.M. was taken by a French Privateer of 4 guns and fifty men and robbed of most of our clothes and adventures [i.e. goods for sale on adventure] and scuttled the brig after taking us all on board the privateer.

Wednesday June 25 took an American ship and put us all in irons.

Thursday June 26 this day kept close confined and under water most of the time.

Friday June 27 after having had several skirmishes [?] arrived in Basse-Terre not allowed to leave our irons on any emergency.

Saturday June 28 This day was put on shore and turned to prison after being robbed of our money one and all and most of our cloathes thus we are set naked and helpless ashore in a foreign country.

It was a mean business. The prisoners were allowed "two or three ounces of pork poor stuff and bread in proportion" and lived "toughing it out in the usual way half starved." Some, including the Captain of the *Caroline,* were sent off in a cartel within a few days, but it was not until the twenty-eighth of July that Moses Hillard, having spent half his time in prison and the rest "working out" on the fitting of French sloops or prizes "to keep alive," found himself in a cartel headed for St. Kitts.

On the other side of the mariner's balance would stand, in Captain Hillard's case, the voyage of the *Thomas* from Archangel to London to New York in 1812-13, which earned him his footnote in the history of the Republic. N. and D. Talcott of New York, the owners for whom the Captain most frequently sailed, had sent the *Thomas* to Archangel in the previous year, where the Russians had detained her on suspicion, real or pretended, as to her neutrality. Her captain and most of her crew had deserted her, her equipment had been tampered with, bills amounting to three or four thousand rubles were outstanding against her, and the situation generally was one to worry the American consul almost as much as it pained the owners.

Furthermore the War of 1812 was in the offing and the future handling of the ship, even if she could be cleared from Archangel, presented uncommonly difficult problems. In these circumstances—and it was a tribute to the regard in which he was held in the profession—Captain Hillard was asked to get together a skeleton crew of five or six able seamen and make his way to Archangel to take whatever action was possible. A credit for £4,000 was opened in his name, he was given full power of attorney to act for the owners, and the decision whether to sell the ship, freight her, or load her was left entirely to his discretion.

The mission, so far as the *Thomas* was concerned, was successfully completed. The Captain was able to get possession of his ship, man her and equip her and take her out. Financially, however, the owners suffered. Agents, apparently British, so managed the exchange of funds in Archangel as to absorb a considerable part of the sterling credit, and Moses Hillard always felt that, had he understood Russian currency a little better, he might have saved the money loss as well as the ship itself. But it was not the finances of the voyage which gave it its importance but the news the *Thomas* brought home with her.

New York had not heard of Napoleon's defeat in Russia until "the elegant corvette-built ship *Thomas,* Hillard, 48 days from London in ballast to N and D Talcott" came up the bay on the sixth of January, 1813, and even then some New Yorkers, including the editor of the *Post,* refused to believe it. Only after reflection did the *Post* announce to its readers that the "auspicious and glorious" report of the defeat of Murat and the flight of Bonaparte was "entitled to full faith

This is the English section from a multilingual "sea letter" which in 1803 commended Hillard to all the powers of the earth, who are listed in sonorous precedence. It is signed (see portion visible, center) by "Th. Jefferson," a man this long-embargoed Yankee skipper cordially detested.

and credit." "The boasted conqueror of the north has been compelled already to quit Moscow in disgrace. . . ."

The principal significance of the voyage of the *Thomas* to men of our time, however, is the light it throws on the character of the sea captain's profession as it was practiced at the beginning of the last century. Seamanship was undoubtedly the first requirement but only the first. Judgment, commercial and political as well as nautical, was demanded, and coolness (the *Thomas* was boarded on Georges Bank by a British squadron in pursuit of Commodore Rogers) was as necessary as courage. In addition a knowledge of commercial law and international banking was clearly desirable, as well as an ability to deal with bureaucrats and functionaries of many habits and traditions. A letter from Joseph Otis, owner of the brig *Sussex*, which Captain Hillard commanded at the age of 25, gives a succinct idea of what was expected of the master of a vessel in 1805. He was no mere carrier of cargoes bought and sold by others but a merchant—a sort of glorified Yankee peddler—as well:

New York 12 Oct. 1805—

Capt. Moses Hillard
    Sir,

The Brig Sussex under your Command, being now Loaded & ready for Sea, you will proceed with all possible Dispatch for La Guira and there dispose of your Cargo on the best Terms the market will admit and invest the proceeds in such Articles as you may Judge most for Our Interest & return direct for this Place— In Case you are not permitted an Entry at La Guira, You will if You think it advisable try one Other Port on the main, and also St. Thomas if it becomes necessary.

Your Cargo is valuable and the Articles comprising the same are of the first Qualities and will warrant recommending with Safety. We therefore trust you will obtain the highest Prices, be very Careful in Purchasing Your return Cargo, & see that every thing is free of damage, and of Good Qualities—be extremely Cautious in all your Dealings, do nothing that Shall in the Least endanger the Property under your Care. You will write every opportunity & communicate every Particular relative to your Situation, Prospects & Destination.

Your Vessel & Cargo being Insured, you will in Case of any Accident procure the requisite Papers to enable to recover of the Underwriters. We are allowed by the Charter-party, thirty Lay Days in the West-Indies from the Time of Entry at the Custom House, beyond that Time we must pay a heavy Demurage. It therefore becomes necessary that every

Exertion be used to facilitate Your Business. At foot you have the present prices of a few Articles for your Government. Wishing you a Safe & pleasant Voyage—

Your Obt Servant
Joseph Otis

Coffee 27 to 30 Cents
Cocoa 35 to 38 Dols for 112
Hides 11 to 12 cents
Indigo 1¾ to 2¼ Dols

A few years later, when the Captain was a bit older and when his reputation was firmly established, his owner's instructions would have been less peremptory, but the responsibilities they defined would have been the same or greater. The master of a Yankee ship 150 years ago was, in addition to everything else, the executive head of a wholesale house which happened to be afloat.

One other preconception would also correct itself, I think, in the mind of any careful reader of Captain Hillard's papers. Ever since Mencken began his babbitization of American history it has been standard doctrine that the New England Protestants of the great New England period were repressed and blue-nosed characters whose influence on the country has been harmful if not actually disastrous. Captain Hillard, as his letters demonstrate, was a church-going man with at least enough religious fervor to have produced one clergyman among his sons, but there was nothing even remotely puritanical about life on his ships.

A conscientious passenger, an Englishman named Matthew Carter, writes him at Le Havre to apologize because Mr. Carter had left the ship in such haste he had been "unable to arrange for the payment of the little amounts toward the dinner at Justins and the losses at Cards which were to be appropriated to the Cost of the dinner." And numerous exchanges with French friends in Paris make it quite clear that the Captain knew that city as well as he knew Le Havre. Indeed, to perform his duties as buyer and seller as well as sailor, he would have had to walk its streets and sit over long meals in its restaurants much as other Americans have walked and sat in later generations.

I suspect it was something more than the thought of crossing the sea which induced Sally Pride Hillard to sail with her husband on the last voyage of the *Oneida*. I suspect he had told her tales of a Paris which those imaginary Puritans were not supposed to know.

The Second Bank of the United States had its home in this Philadelphia building. On the opposite page, its mortal enemy, Andrew Jackson, seems ready to stamp out this "hydra of corruption."

JACKSON'S FIGHT WITH THE 'MONEY POWER'

Old Hickory's attack on Biddle's bank had some unexpected consequences.

By BRAY HAMMOND

"Relief, sir!" interrupted the President. "Come not to me, sir! Go to the monster. It is folly, sir, to talk to Andrew Jackson. The government will not bow to the monster. . . . Andrew Jackson yet lives to put his foot upon the head of the monster and crush him to the dust."

The monster, "a hydra of corruption," was known also as the Second Bank of the United States, chartered by Congress in 1816 as depository of the federal government, which was its principal stockholder and customer. The words were reported by a committee which called on President Jackson in the spring of 1834 to complain because he and Secretary of the Treasury Roger Taney had removed the federal deposits from the federal depository into what the Jacksonians called "selected banks" and others called "pet banks." The President was disgusted with the committee.

"Andrew Jackson," he exclaimed in the third person

as before, "would never recharter that monster of corruption. Sooner than live in a country where such a power prevailed, he would seek an asylum in the wilds of Arabia."

In effect, he had already put his foot on the monster and crushed him in the dust. He had done so by vetoing a new charter for the Bank and removing the federal accounts from its books. So long as the federal Bank had the federal accounts, it had been regulator of the currency and of credit in general. Its power to regulate had derived from the fact that the federal Treasury was the largest single transactor in the economy and the largest bank depositor. Receiving the checks and notes of local banks deposited with it by government collectors of revenue, it had had constantly to come back on the local banks for settlements of the amounts which the checks and notes called for. It had had to do so because it made those amounts

67

immediately available to the Treasury, wherever desired. Since settlement by the local banks was in specie, i.e. silver and gold coin, the pressure for settlement automatically regulated local bank lending; for the more the local banks lent, the larger the amount of their notes and checks in use and the larger the sums they had to settle in specie. This loss of specie reduced their power to lend.

All this had made the federal Bank the regulator not alone of the currency but of bank lending in general, the restraint it had exerted being fully as effective as that of the twelve Federal Reserve Banks at present, though by a different process. With its life now limited to two more years and the government accounts removed from its books, it was already crushed but still writhing.

As the Bank's president, Nicholas Biddle, aristocratic, a bit naïve—and a good banker —bore the brunt of Jackson's attack. Henry Inman painted this fine miniature.

The Jacksonian attack on the Bank is an affair respecting which posterity seems to have come to an opinion that is half hero worship and half discernment. In the words of Professor William G. Sumner, the affair was a struggle "between the democracy and the money power." Viewed in that light, Jackson's victory was a grand thing. But Sumner also observed— this was three-quarters of a century ago—that since Jackson's victory the currency, which previously had owned no superior in the world, had never again been so good. More recently Professor Lester V. Chandler, granting the Bank's imperfections, has said that its abolition without replacement by something to take over its functions was a "major blunder" which "ushered in a generation of banking anarchy and monetary disorder." So the affair stands, a triumph and a blunder.

During Andrew Jackson's lifetime three things had begun to alter prodigiously the economic life of Americans. These were steam, credit, and natural resources.

Steam had been lifting the lids of pots for thousands of years, and for a century or so it had been lifting water from coal mines. But only in recent years had it been turning spindles, propelling ships, drawing trains of cars, and multiplying incredibly the productive powers of man. For thousands of years money had been lent, but in most people's minds debt had signi-

fied distress—as it still did in Andrew Jackson's. Only now was its productive power, long known to merchants as a means of making one sum of money do the work of several, becoming popularly recognized by enterprising men for projects which required larger sums than could be assembled in coin. For three centuries or more America's resources had been crudely surmised, but only now were their variety, abundance, and accessibility becoming practical realities. And it was the union of these three, steam, credit, and natural resources, that was now turning Anglo-Saxon America from the modest agrarian interests that had preoccupied her for two centuries of European settlement to the dazzling possibilities of industrial exploitation.

In the presence of these possibilities, the democracy was becoming transformed from one that was Jeffersonian and agrarian to one that was financial and industrial. But it was still a democracy: its recruits were still men born and reared on farms, its vocabulary was still Jeffersonian, and its basic conceptions changed insensibly from the libertarianism of agrarians to that of *laissez faire*. When Andrew Jackson became President in 1829, boys born in log cabins were already becoming businessmen but with no notion of surrendering as bankers and manufacturers the freedom they might have enjoyed as farmers.

There followed a century of exploitation from which America emerged with the most wealthy and powerful economy there is, with her people the best fed, the best housed, the best clothed, and the best equipped on earth. But the loss and waste have long been apparent. The battle was only for the strong, and millions who lived in the midst of wealth never got to touch it. The age of the Robber Barons was scarcely a golden age. It was scarcely what Thomas Jefferson desired.

It could scarcely have been what Andrew Jackson desired either, for his ideals were more or less Jeffersonian by common inheritance, and the abuse of credit was one of the things he abominated. Yet no man ever did more to encourage the abuse of credit than he. For the one agency able to exert some restraint on credit was the federal Bank. In destroying it, he let speculation loose. Though a hard-money devotee who hated banks and wanted no money but coin, he fostered the formation of swarms of banks and endowed the country with a filthy and depreciated paper currency which he believed to be unsound and unconstitutional and from which the Civil War delivered it in the Administration of Abraham Lincoln thirty years later.

This, of course, was not Andrew Jackson's fault, unless one believes he would have done what he did had his advisers been different. Though a resolute and decisive person, he also relied on his friends. He had his official cabinet, largely selected for political expediency, and he had his "kitchen cabinet" for informal counsel. Of those advisers most influential with him, all but two were either businessmen or closely associated with the business world. The two exceptions were Major William B. Lewis, a planter and neighbor from Tennessee who came to live with him in the White House; and James K. Polk, also of Tennessee, later President of the United States. These two, with Jackson himself, constituted the agrarian element in the Jacksonian Administration. Several of the others, however, were agrarian in the sense that they had started as poor farm boys.

Martin Van Buren, probably the ablest of Jackson's political associates, was a lawyer whose investments had made him rich. Amos Kendall, the ablest in a business and administrative sense, later made the telegraph one of the greatest of American business enterprises and himself a man of wealth. He provided the Jacksonians their watchword, "The world is governed too much." He said "our countrymen are beginning to demand" that the government be content with "protecting their persons and property, leaving them to direct their labor and capital as they please, within the moral law; getting rich or remaining poor as may result from their own management or fortune." Kendall's views may be sound, but they are not what one expects to hear from the democracy when struggling with the money power.

Roger Taney, later Chief Justice, never got rich, but he liked banks and was a modest investor in bank stock. "There is perhaps no business," he said as Jackson's secretary of the treasury, "which yields a profit so certain and liberal as the business of banking and exchange; and it is proper that it should be open as far as practicable to the most free competition and its advantages shared by all classes of society." His own bank in Baltimore was one of the first of the pets in which he deposited government money.

David Henshaw, Jacksonian boss of Massachusetts,

In the view of cartoonist-lithographer H R. Robinson, the withdrawal of federal funds in 1833 brought the walls tumbling in on the Bank-subsidized editors and politicians.

69

was a banker and industrialist whose advice in practical matters had direct influence in Washington. Henshaw projected a Jacksonian bank to take the place of the existing institution but to be bigger. (A similar project was got up by friends of Van Buren in New York and one of the two was mentioned favorably by Jackson in his veto message as a possible alternative to the existing United States Bank.) Samuel Ingham, Jackson's first secretary of the treasury, was a paper manufacturer in Pennsylvania and later a banker in New Jersey. Churchill C. Cambreleng, congressional leader of the attack on the Bank, was a New York businessman and former agent of John Jacob Astor. These are not all of the Jacksonians who were intent on the federal Bank's destruction, but they are typical.

There was a very cogent reason why these businessmen and their class generally wanted to kill the Bank of the United States. It interfered with easy money; it kept the state banks from lending as freely as they might otherwise and businessmen from borrowing.

New York, for example, was now the financial and commercial center of the country and its largest city, which Philadelphia formerly had been. The customs duties collected at its wharves and paid by its businessmen were far the largest of any American port, and customs duties were then the principal source of federal income. These duties were paid by New York businessmen with checks on New York banks. These checks were deposited by the federal collectors in the New York office of the Bank of the United States, whose headquarters were in Philadelphia and a majority of whose directors were Philadelphia businessmen. This, Amos Kendall observed, was a "wrong done to New York in depriving her of her natural advantages."

It was not merely a matter of prestige. As already noted, the United States Bank, receiving the checks of the New York businessmen, made the funds at once available to the secretary of the treasury. The Bank had therefore to call on the New York banks for the funds the checks represented. This meant that the New York banks, in order to pay the federal Bank, had to draw down their reserves; which meant that they had less money to lend; which meant that the New York businessmen could not borrow as freely and cheaply as they might otherwise. All this because their money had gone to Philadelphia.

Actually the situation was not so bad as my simplified account makes it appear. For one thing, the goods imported at New York were sold elsewhere in the country, and more money came to New York in payment for them than went out of the city in duties paid the government. But I have described it in the bald, one-sided terms that appealed to the local politicians and to the businessmen prone to grumbling because

money was not so easy as they would like. There was truth in what they said, but it amounted to less than they made out.

New York's grievance was special because her customs receipts were so large and went to a vanquished rival. Otherwise the federal Bank's pressure on the local banks—all of which were state banks—was felt in some degree through the country at large. Wherever money was paid to a federal agency—for postage, for fines, for lands, for excise, for import duties—money was drawn from the local banks into the federal Bank. The flow of funds did not drain the local banks empty and leave them nothing to do, though they and the states' rights politicians talked as if that were the case. The federal Bank was simply their principal single creditor.

And though private business brought more money to New York and other commercial centers than it took away, the federal government took more away than it brought. For its largest payments were made elsewhere—to naval stations, army posts, Indian agents, owners of the public debt, largely foreign, and civilians in the government service throughout the country. In the normal flow of money payments from hand to hand in the economy, those to the federal government and consequently to the federal Bank were so large and conspicuous that the state banks involved in making them were disagreeably conscious of their size and frequency.

These banks, of course, were mostly eastern and urban rather than western and rural, because it was in eastern cities that the federal government received most of its income. Accordingly, it was in the eastern business centers, Boston, New York, Baltimore, and Charleston, that resentment against Philadelphia and the federal Bank was strongest. This resentment was intensified by the fact that the federal Bank's branch offices were also competitors for private business in these and other cities, which the present Federal Reserve Banks, very wisely, are not.

General Jackson's accession to the presidency afforded an opportunity to put an end to the federal Bank. Its charter would expire in seven years. The question of renewal was to be settled in that interval. Jackson was popular and politically powerful. His background and principles were agrarian. An attack on the Bank by him would be an attack "by the democracy on the money power." It would have, therefore, every political advantage.

The realities behind these words, however, were not what the words implied. The democracy till very recently had been agrarian because most of the population was agricultural. But the promoters of the assault on the Bank were neither agrarian in their current interests nor representative of what democracy implied.

In the western and rural regions, which were the most democratic in a traditional sense, dislike of the federal Bank persisted, though by 1829 it had less to feed on than formerly. Years before, under incompetent managers, the Bank had lent unwisely in the West, had been forced to harsh measures of self-preservation, and had made itself hated, with the help, as usual, of the state banks and states' rights politicians. But the West needed money, and though the Bank never provided enough it did provide some, and in the absence of new offenses disfavor had palpably subsided by the time Jackson became President.

There were also, in the same regions, vestiges or more of the traditional agrarian conviction that all banks were evil. This principle was still staunchly held by Andrew Jackson. He hated all banks, did so through a long life, and said so time after time. He thought they all violated the Constitution. But he was led by the men around him to focus his aversion on the federal Bank, which being the biggest must be the worst and whose regulatory pressure on the state banks must obviously be the oppression to be expected from a great, soulless corporation.

However, not all agrarian leaders went along with him. For many years the more intelligent had discriminated in favor of the federal Bank, recognizing that its operations reduced the tendency to inflation which, as a hard-money party, the agrarians deplored. Altogether, it was no longer to be expected that the agrarian democracy would initiate a vigorous attack on the federal Bank, though it was certainly to be expected that such an attack would receive very general agrarian support.

Martin Van Buren

It was in the cities and within the business world that both the attack on the Bank and its defense would be principally conducted. For there the Bank had its strongest enemies and its strongest friends. Its friends were the more conservative houses that had dominated the old business world but had only a minor part in the new. It was a distinguished part, however, and influential. This influence, which arose from prestige and substantial wealth, combined with the strength which the federal Bank derived from the federal accounts to constitute what may tritely be called a "money power." But it was a disciplined, conservative money power and just what the economy needed.

But it was no longer *the* money power. It was rivaled, as Philadelphia was by New York, by the newer, more vigorous, more aggressive, and more democratic part of the business world.

The businessmen comprising the latter were a quite different lot from the old. The Industrial Revolution required more men to finance, to man, and manage its railways, factories, and other enterprises than the old business world, comprising a few rich merchants, could possibly provide. The Industrial Revolution was set to absorb the greater part of the population.

Yet when the new recruits, who yesterday were mechanics and farmers, offered themselves not only as laborers but as managers, owners, and entrepreneurs requiring capital, they met a response that was not always respectful. There was still the smell of the barnyard on their boots, and their hands were better adapted to hammer and nails than to quills and ink. The aristocrats were amused. They were also chary of lending to such borrowers; whereupon farmers' and mechanics' banks began to be set up. These banks found themselves hindered by the older banks and by the federal Bank. They and their borrowers were furious. They resisted the federal Bank in suits, encouraged by sympathetic states' rights politicians, and found themselves blocked by the federal courts.

Nor were their grievances merely material. They disliked being snubbed. Even when they became wealthy themselves, they still railed at "the capitalists" and "the aristocrats," as David Henshaw of Massachusetts did, meaning the old families, the Appletons and Lawrences whom he named, the business counterparts of the political figures that the Jacksonian revolution had replaced. Henshaw and his fellow Jacksonian leaders were full of virtue, rancor, and democracy. Their struggle was not merely to make money but to demonstrate what they already asserted, that they were as good as anyone, or more so. In their denunciation of the federal Bank, one finds them calling it again and again "an aristocracy" and its proprietors, other than the federal government, "aristocrats."

The Jacksonians, as distinct from Jackson himself, wanted a world where *laissez faire* prevailed; where, as Amos Kendall said, everyone would be free to get rich; where, as Roger Taney said, the benefits of banks would be open to all classes; where, as the enterprising exploiters of the land unanimously demanded, credit would be easy. To be sure, relatively few would be rich, and a good many already settling into an urban industrial class were beginning to realize it. But that consideration did not count with the Jacksonian leaders. They wanted a new order. But what they achieved was the age of the Robber Barons.

The attack on the old order took the form of an attack on the federal Bank for a number of reasons which may be summed up in political expediency. A factor in the success of the attack was that the president of the Bank, Nicholas Biddle, was the pampered scion of capitalists and aristocrats. He was born to wealth and prominence. He was elegant, literary, intellectual, witty, and conscious of his own merits. When at the age of 37 he became head of the largest moneyed corporation in the world he was wholly without practical experience. In his new duties he had to rely on brains, self-confidence, and hard work.

With these he did extraordinarily well. He had a remarkable grasp of productive and financial interrelations in the economy. The policies he formulated were sound. His management of the Bank, despite his inexperience, was efficient. His great weakness was naïveté, born of his ignorance of strife.

This characterization, I know, is quite contrary to the conventional one, which makes Biddle out a master of intrigue and craft such as only the purity of Andrew Jackson could overcome. But the evidence of his being a Machiavelli is wholly the assertion of his opponents, whose victory over him was enhanced by a magnification of his prowess. One of these, however, the suave Martin Van Buren, who knew him well and was a judge of such matters, ascribed no such qualities to him but instead spoke of the frankness and openness of his nature. It was in Daniel Webster that Van Buren saw wiliness.

Nicholas Biddle's response to the Jacksonian attack was inept. He was slow in recognizing that an attack was being made and ignored the warnings of his more astute friends. He expected the public to be moved by careful and learned explanations of what the Bank did. He broadcast copies of Jackson's veto message, one of the most popular and effective documents in American political history, with the expectation that people in general would agree with him that it was a piece of hollow demagogy. He entered a match for which he had no aptitude, impelled by a quixotic sense of duty and an inability to let his work be derogated. He engaged in a knock-down-drag-out fight with a group of experts as relentless as any American politics has ever known. The picture he presents is that of Little Lord Fauntleroy, lace on his shirt and good in his heart, running into those rough boys down the alley.

In his proper technical responsibilities Nicholas Biddle was a competent central banker performing a highly useful and beneficial task. It is a pity he had to be interrupted, both for him and for the economy. For him it meant demoralization. He lost track of what was going on in the Bank, he made blundering mistakes, he talked big. These things his opponents used tellingly against him. He turned from able direction of the central banking process to the hazardous business of making money, of which he knew nothing and for which his only knack lay in an enthusiastic appraisal of America's great economic future. In the end his Bank of the United States broke, he lost his fortune, he was tried on criminal charges (but released on a technicality), and he died a broken man.

This was personal misfortune, undeserved and severe. The more important victim was the American people. For with destruction of the United States Bank there was removed from an overexcitable economy the influence most effective in moderating its booms and depressions.

Andrew Jackson had vetoed recharter in 1832 and transferred the federal accounts to the pet banks in 1833 and 1834. The Bank's federal charter expired in

Roger B. Taney

1836, though Nicholas Biddle obtained a charter from Pennsylvania and continued the organization as a state bank. The period was one of boom. Then in 1837 there was panic, all the banks in the country suspended, prices fell, and business collapsed. It was all Andrew Jackson's fault, his opponents declared, for killing the federal Bank. This was too generous. Jackson was not to blame for everything. The crisis was world-wide and induced by many forces. It would have happened anyway. Yet certainly Jackson's destruction of the Bank did not help. Instead it worsened the collapse. Had the Bank been allowed to continue the salutary performance of the years immediately preceding the attack upon it, and had it been supported rather than undermined by the Administration, the wild inflation which culminated in the collapse would have been curbed and the disaster diminished. Such a course would have been consistent with Jackson's convictions and professions. Instead he smote the Bank fatally at the moment of its best performance and in the course of trends against which it was needed most. Thereby he gave unhindered play to the speculation and inflation that he was always denouncing.

To a susceptible people the prospect was intoxicating. A continent abounding in varied resources and favorable to the maintenance of an immense population in the utmost comfort spread before the gaze of an energetic, ambitious, and clever race of men, who to exploit its wealth had two new instruments of miraculous potency: steam and credit. They rushed forward into the bright prospect, trampling, suffering, succeeding, failing. There was nothing to restrain them. For about a century the big rush lasted. Now it is over. And in a more critical mood we note that a number of things are missing or have gone wrong. To be sure, we are on top of the world still, but it is not very good bookkeeping to omit one's losses and count only one's gains.

That critical mood was known to others than Jackson. Emerson, Hawthorne, and Thoreau felt it. So did an older and more experienced contemporary of theirs, Albert Gallatin, friend and aide in the past to Thomas Jefferson, and now president of a New York bank but loyal to Jeffersonian ideals.

"The energy of this nation," he wrote to an old friend toward the end of Andrew Jackson's Administration, "is not to be controlled; it is at present exclusively applied to the acquisition of wealth and to improvements of stupendous magnitude. Whatever has that tendency, and of course an immoderate expansion of credit, receives favor. The apparent prosperity and the progress of cultivation, population, commerce, and improvement are beyond expectation. But it seems to me as if general demoralization was the consequence;

I doubt whether general happiness is increased; and I would have preferred a gradual, slower, and more secure progress. I am, however, an old man, and the young generation has a right to govern itself. . . ."

In these last words, Mr. Gallatin was echoing the remark of Thomas Jefferson that "the world belongs to the living." Neither Gallatin nor Jefferson, however, thought it should be stripped by the living. Yet nothing but the inadequacy of their powers seems to have kept those Nineteenth-Century generations from stripping it. And perhaps nothing else could.

But to the extent that credit multiplies man's economic powers, curbs upon credit extension are a means of conservation, and an important means. The Bank of the United States was such a means. Its career was short and it had imperfections. Nevertheless it worked. The evidence is in the protest of the bankers and entrepreneurs, the lenders and the borrowers, against its restraints. Their outcry against the oppressor was heard, and Andrew Jackson hurried to their rescue. Had he not, some other way of stopping its conservative and steadying influence could doubtless have been found. The appetite for credit is avid, as Andrew Jackson knew in his day and might have foretold for ours. But because he never meant to serve it, the credit for what happened goes rather to the clever advisers who led the old hero to the monster's lair and dutifully held his hat while he stamped on its head and crushed it in the dust.

Meanwhile, the new money power had curled up securely in Wall Street, where it has been at home ever since.

Amos Kendall

SHEAVES OF GOLDEN GRAIN

Cyrus McCormick fought hard to win the "harvester war"

—and brought the machine age to America's farms

A wheat field on the McCormick farm in northern Rockbridge county, Virginia, where Cyrus McCormick invented the reaper. This shows the field as it looked in July, 1952.

By MARSHALL FISHWICK

It's the snugness that makes the valley. On both sides blue mountains hem it in, brooding over the farmhouses like a mother hen brooding over her chicks. There is a time, just when the sunlight touches the crest of the Blue Ridge, when there is too much beauty for believing. This is land to come to and not leave. The Indians loved it, and named it Shenandoah —"Daughter of the Stars." They came to hunt in the thick green foliage, to drink the cool water, and to make up poetic stories that expressed their love for the valley.

White men, coming first in the late Seventeenth Century, found grass growing from the limestone soil so high that they could tie it across their saddles. Many kinds of people came to settle. In the northern portion were Palatinate Germans, Mennonites, and Lutherans. Farther south were the Scotch-Irish, a brave and iron-veined people, who had such a fear of God that it left no room in their hearts for fear of any man. They liked this land, this gateway to the West. Fifteen hundred feet above sea level, with a brisk, pleasant climate, it was ideal for stock, grain, orchards, and tobacco. Settlers could stand on the crest of the Blue Ridge, wash their faces in the clouds, and look out over miles of land as bonny as that of Scotland.

This is the story of a Scotch-Irish family that came, and one member of it who changed our agricultural history.

Like many a Shenandoah saga, this begins not in the lonely valley, but in crowded Philadelphia. In the spring of 1735 Thomas McCormick and his wife Elizabeth Carruth disembarked there and set out to make a new home in Cumberland County, Pennsylvania. They eked out a living and brought five sons into the world. The fifth, Robert, fought with Washington's army against the British, returned home to marry Martha Sanderson, and then set off to the Virginia frontier. Halfway up the valley he found the right place, rolling fields into which he wanted his wooden plow to bite.

Though it was only 1779, the land had already had four owners. Benjamin Borden was the first; he obtained a grant of 100,000 acres in 1737 and opened the area for white settlement. Borden sold a portion of the tract to Tobias Smith, who in turn sold it to William Preston on May 12, 1760. On August 5, 1765, Preston deeded it to Daniel McCormick, who was no relation to the newcomer, Robert McCormick. Daniel's heirs were willing to sell 450 acres and the two log structures erected by Tobias Smith, right on the boundary between Rockbridge and Augusta counties.

There exists no exact account of the buildings which Robert McCormick bought, but they doubtless had hewn logs for walls, shingles for the roof, plank floors cut with a whipsaw and trimmed with a broadax. There must have been an open stone fireplace, a pine table with benches, garners for holding grain, beds filled with straw or chaff. To the modern eye, little comfort here; but to the pioneers, home.

The newly established immigrants did the one thing all newcomers had to do. They got to work. That was the only way to put down roots, to belong to the land. Robert McCormick and the family he had brought with him worked hard; at the time of his death he would leave three slaves and eight horses. His only Virginia-born son, also named Robert, was born on June 8, 1780. Young Robert grew up, learned to work the land, and married Mary Ann Hall, who lived two miles down the Great Path. Until they could build a

home of their own, they lived in one of the log cabins on the McCormick homestead.

A year later, on a cold February night in 1809, their first child was born. They named him Cyrus Hall McCormick.

These were hardheaded, hard-working country people. Even if they had had time, they would not have daydreamed much about the little baby's future. Surely they would not have supposed he would become one of the most important persons in the nation—any more than would another log cabin family out in Kentucky, the Lincolns, who had also had a new son just three

THE TESTING OF THE FIRST REAPING MACHINE NEAR STEELE'S TAVERN, VA. A.D. 1831.

An old print showing how an artist believed the first test of the McCormick reaper looked to those who watched. Inset, upper right, McCormick himself; upper left, the twine binder.

days earlier and had named him Abraham.

The world Cyrus grew up in was simple, solid, and sweaty. Like most farm boys of his time, he had little formal education, picking up what book learning he could at the hearth and the old field school. He studied Webster's speller, Murray's grammar, Adams' geography, and (most of all) the Bible. He learned much from nature too; learned of the mystery, the wonder, the symmetry of things. He listened to the sassy, chirpy insects as the rich, green grain blew in the wind. In the fall there was a transformation in the valley, colored now with scarlet, russet, gold, and umber. The sun stayed hot in September and October. The men went out with their hand instruments, mopped their brows, and harvested the grain. If they didn't finish before the rain came, the crop was ruined. Innately mechanical, Cyrus devised a locust-wood cradle which made the job a bit easier. But not easy enough. He thought and wondered about the problem. Inside his mind wheels began to turn.

In 1822 Cyrus' father decided it was time to build a new house. Aided by his sons and his servants, he erected a red brick residence, 50 by 65 feet, with a broad hallway and eight rectangular rooms on two floors. He included wainscoting, broad fireplaces, and a porch on which he could sit and rock in the springtime. McCormick had named his home Walnut Grove.

The porch is still there; with the right kind of chair, it makes for good rocking. The spring behind the house still flows fresh and free; on the right kind of hot afternoon, it makes for good drinking.

Like most Shenandoah Valley homes, Walnut Grove was practically self-sufficient. There were flax and wool for clothing. Sheep, cattle, and hogs furnished plenty of meat. There were hides for shoes and harness, grain for flour and whisky, vegetables and fruit for the table, wood for the fires and sawmill.

Young Cyrus was proud of his father's place and the growing things all about it. He enjoyed riding about on the back of his white-footed sorrel, Peacock. Most of all, he liked to putter about in the smith and to work on the tools that were broken or bent. Cyrus was so reserved as a boy that his neighbors commented on it, and so concerned with his dress that barefoot boys poked fun at his broadcloth coat and black beaver hat, which he liked to wear to church.

Like all young men everywhere, Cyrus had an eye for pretty girls. On October 31, 1831, he wrote to a friend:

"Mr. Hart has two fine daughters, rite pretty, very smart, and as rich probably as you could wish; but alas! I have other business to attend to and can . . . devote but a small proportion of my time to the enjoyment of their society. . . ."

The "other business" was to carry the name of Cyrus McCormick to the four corners of the world.

That business was the developing and perfecting of the reaper. Earlier machines, both here and abroad, had paved the way for McCormick's success, and the involved story of just what had and had not been done before his famous demonstration in the midsummer of 1831 need not be told here. The incontestable point is that here on this Virginia field a machine was tried which included all the basic parts of the modern grain-cutting machines—the straight reciprocating knife, reel, knife-guards, platform, main wheel, the principle of cutting to one side of the line of draft, and the divider at the outer end of the cutting bar.

Cyrus McCormick paid $30 to the United States Treasury for a patent extending "the full and exclusive right and liberty of making, constructing, using, and vending to others to be used, the said improvement." The next season saw exhibitions on half a dozen Rockbridge County farms and brought a commendation from the editor of the Lexington *Union*. Encouraged by this and a glowing account in Edmund Ruffin's *Farmers' Register,* he took out a second patent on a self-sharpening horizontal plow. The "other business" was about to get under way.

Oddly enough, the Panic of 1837 speeded up the process. The year before father and son had gone into the iron business with a furnace they called Cotopaxi. When this failed in the panic, leaving Cyrus and his father deep in debt, the two of them decided to concentrate everything on the reaper.

To appreciate just what a revolution the reaper brought about for agriculture, one has to realize that up to 1830 the Industrial Revolution had been concentrated in the factories, not the fields. Centuries-old methods still held in the country, and the sickle held unchallenged sway over the harvest fields of the world. Since grain was a staple crop throughout the temperate zone, an invention which allowed the farmer to reap as much as he could sow quite literally affected the whole culture. "This machine," Dr. William Hutchinson points out, "was necessary if the increasing millions of city dwellers were to have low-priced bread. City and country life must be complementary for industrial society to exist. Cyrus McCormick conspicuously aided in maintaining this equilibrium."

Few things could have benefited the young Republic as much as the device perfected by the Virginia farm boy. Transportation facilities, especially in the West, were so poor that it was actually a waste of land and labor to harvest more than could be used in the home. Farm laborers were scarce, and were frequently lured to the cities. The problems of transportation, labor, markets, and inventions were interwoven. In addition to its importance in the fields themselves, the new reaper stimulated the extension of railroads, increased European migration and city growth, and improved methods of cultivation and productivity.

Plainly this invention touched one of mankind's basic needs—food. From now on there would be fewer backaches and tired fingers throughout the world. McCormick ushered in a new era in agriculture, replacing muscles with mechanical power on a job that had to be done. That he also gave to the North one of the devices that unquestionably helped win the Civil War is one of the ironies of American history.

But Cyrus McCormick's battles were not over when his reaper cut the grain, they were only beginning. He had invented a reaper; if it were to get onto thousands of American farms, he would have to invent a business.

No easy task, this. After a decade of planning and promoting, he was worse off than he had been when he began. His iron business collapsed, his partner evaded all financial responsibilities, his farm was gone, and creditors hounded him day and night. A teamster named John Brains even sent the constable out with a summons when Cyrus defaulted on a $19.01 debt. McCormick pleaded for, and got, a little more time. Fortune smiled; he sold a reaper, and Brains' debt was paid. But it wasn't a very good year so far as placing reapers on America's farms was concerned. The McCormicks sold seven.

But Cyrus had assets other than his reapers. Inside him was a little machine that drove him on. He knew what he wanted to do. At night, when he lay in the darkness thinking, he saw something "so enormous that it seemed like a dream—like dwelling in the clouds—so remote, so unattainable, so exalted."

Next year an order for a reaper came in from Illinois. Cyrus was elated—until someone asked how he would get it to the buyer. He would have to send it on a wagon to Scottsville, on the canal to Richmond, on a barge to Norfolk, on a packet boat around Florida to New Orleans, on a Mississippi River boat up to Illinois. Then he'd have to have it loaded on another wagon and try to get it out to the farm.

This would never do. Out west the land was flat, the grain was thick, and the labor was scarce. In some places they turned hogs and cattle into wheat fields because there were no hands to harvest the grain. Maybe Virginia wouldn't accept his reaper, but the West would have to.

So Cyrus McCormick left Walnut Grove, his total fortune of $300 tucked in his belt and his visions still sharp in his mind. For ten days he traveled towards the setting sun which he had seen all his life through the twigs and leafage of trees. Then finally he stepped out into the open, standing at last with the forests behind him, gazing with dazzled eyes at the American prairies.

This was the land for the reaper.

He was not hasty in choosing the place for his factory. He traveled thousands of miles before he decided. He talked and looked and pondered. When he made public his decision, people found it hard to take him seriously. The town he favored, one of the youngest and ugliest in the West, was the residuum of a broken land boom. In its ten years of existence it had struggled with dust, debt, panic, and cholera. The only paved street was one block long, made of wood. The unpainted frame shanties where people lived didn't even have numbers. There was no railroad, no gas, no sewer, no telegraph, no stockyards. The harbor, into which six small schooners sailed in 1847, was blocked by a sand bar. The entire region was a dismal swamp, better for beavers than businessmen. Even the name was discouraging. Who could be expected to remember a name like "Chicago"?

McCormick's choice was the master stroke of his business career. Buffalo, Cleveland, Milwaukee, St. Louis, and Cincinnati were more prosperous. But as other men were to see, after Cyrus McCormick had first seen, it was Chicago which would link the Great Lakes and the Great West.

Having neither money nor credit, McCormick went into partnership with Chicago's first mayor, William Ogden. With Ogden's money McCormick built the largest factory in the city.

In the half century that followed, one of America's major business empires was established. It was the story of hard-slugging laissez-faire capitalism. To the Nineteenth Century, it was a glorious and inspiring spectacle. To the early Twentieth Century, committed to greater social and economic justice, the story of the carnivorous Robber Barons was a black page in our national history. In the last decade the historical pendulum, gradually having swung from the thesis to the antithesis, has moved back towards the synthesis. The early economic leaders may not have been demigods, but they were not soulless scoundrels. They were human beings, acting out their roles in an entirely human manner. Few people ever do more.

An important question for the historian, so far as McCormick is concerned, is this one: How did this tinkering farm boy emerge as one of our major industrialists? Even Norbert Lyons, who has written a whole volume which debunks Cyrus and his part in the invention of the reaper, admits he was "one of America's ablest *industrial* pioneers and leaders." Stewart Holbrook, whose much better balanced account, *The Age of the Moguls,* is perhaps the best book we have on the self-made men who got to the top echelon, pays McCormick an even greater compliment: "Cyrus McCormick was perhaps unique among wealthy industrialists of his era in that he was a genuine inventor, a creator who also had business ability such as almost no other inventor, until Thomas Edison, displayed."

McCormick's chief business asset was his system. In an age when business was conducted on the principle of buyer beware, he gave with every purchase a written guarantee which warranted the performance of the reaper in every respect. At a time when the seller got the highest price he could, McCormick sold at a fixed price, and no haggling. A farmer could have a reaper for $30 down, with six months to pay the rest. If crops were bad or times hard, he got an extension of time without interest. Knowing that a farmer who needed a reaper needed one in a hurry, McCormick set up nineteen assembling plants at strategic points in the Mississippi River Valley, and he made that valley the chief food-producing region of the world.

Cyrus might have been generous with farmers, but he was hell on politicians, inventors, lawyers, and judges who crossed his path. Certainly it is significant

"WESTWARD THE COURSE OF EMPIRE TAKES ITS WAY" WITH McCORMICK REAPERS IN THE VAN.

Late in the Nineteenth Century the McCormick Harvester Company distributed this litho-graph as a way to emphasize the westward movement brought about by the reaper.

many as forty machines in a single day. Mowers were even chained back to back and then forcibly torn apart to test relative strength.

International fame caught up with McCormick in 1851, when the Virginia inventor went to the London International Exposition. To the London *Times* his machine seemed to be "a cross between an Astley chariot, a wheelbarrow, and a flying machine." But the English grins disappeared when the Yankee put his contraption to work in a grain field. So did they vanish in the other countries where the reaper went.

Back home in Chicago, the business boom continued. Cyrus mowed down competitors as his machine mowed down wheat. Then, in 1871, came the great Chicago fire. All the McCormick property and machinery went up in smoke. It was typical of Cyrus that he was in the midst of the fire-fighting and had the coat burned off his back.

After the fire, McCormick promptly got to work. His was the first factory in the city rebuilt and put into operation. When his family admonished him for working too hard, he replied, "I know of no better place for a man to die than in the harness."

McCormick died in 1884. He had been born in a land that had a few small loaves; before he died, he made it possible to feed the multitudes. He gave his nation a hunger-insurance policy.

that not one of his patents was at any time removed, and that in order to insure his $40,000 royalties up to 1858, he spent $90,000 in litigation! No man of his time was more obdurate. He dominated his lawyers, alienated members of his own clan, and lashed out at competitors with an Old Testament fervor.

After the Civil War, when grain binders, hayrakes, and corn binders were perfected, a full-scale "harvester war" developed. Cyrus stayed on the front line for the duration. The enemy's strategy was to stage field trials, in which the advantages of their products could be demonstrated. One rival, William Whitely, hitched himself in the horse's place and pulled his new mower. Cyrus competed against as

When his body lay in state in Chicago, many people came to pay him a last homage, and to place a floral wreath at the foot of his coffin. The design was that of a reaper, with the main wheel broken. At the very end, one of Cyrus McCormick's oldest associates leaned over and dropped something on his breast. It was a sheaf of golden yellow wheat, from American land on which he had long worked, and which he left so much more workable.

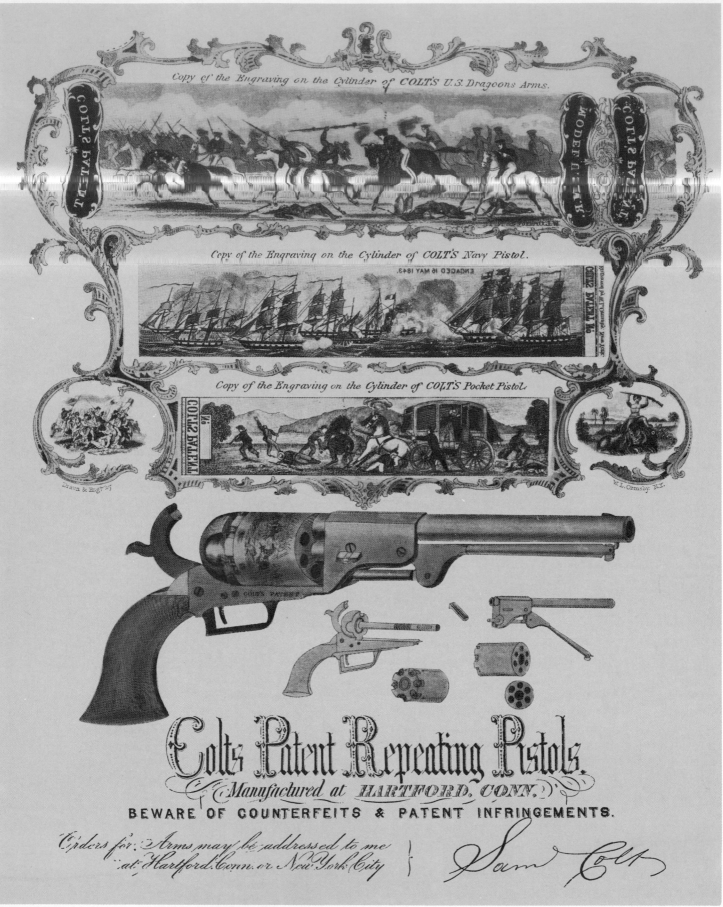

This advertising broadside of the 1850's shows engravings that identified as well as decorated particular Colt pistols.

Samuel Colt's life was brief but eventful.
He was an imaginative inventor and
an ambitious pitchman whose legacy included scandal
and success—and firearms that were
revolutionary in more ways than one

Gunmaker to the World

By ELLSWORTH S. GRANT

The funeral of Samuel Colt, America's first great munitions maker, was spectacular—certainly the most spectacular ever seen in Hartford, Connecticut. It was like the last act of a grand opera, with threnodial music played by Colt's own band of immigrant German craftsmen, supported by a silent chorus of bereaved townsfolk. Crepe bands on their left arms, Colt's 1,500 workmen filed in pairs past the metallic casket in the parlor of Armsmear, his ducal mansion; then followed his guard—Company A, 12th Regiment, Connecticut Volunteers—and the Putnam Phalanx in their brilliant Continental uniforms.

A half mile away the largest private armory in the world stood quiet—its hundreds of machines idle, the revolvers and rifles on its test range silent. Atop the long dike protecting Colt's South Meadows development drooped the gray willows that furnished the raw material for his furniture factory. Beneath the dike a few skaters skimmed over the frozen Connecticut River. To the south, the complex of company houses was empty for the moment, as was the village specially built for his Potsdam willow workers.

On Armsmear's spacious grounds snow covered the deer park, the artificial lake, the statuary, the orchard, the cornfields and meadows, the fabulous greenhouses. At the stable, Mike Tracy, the Irish coachman, stood by Shamrock, the master's aged, favorite horse, and scanned the long line of sleighs and the thousands of bareheaded onlookers jamming Wethersfield Avenue. After the simple Episcopal service the workers formed two lines, through which the Phalanx solemnly marched—drums muffled, colors draped, and arms reversed. Behind them, eight pallbearers bore the coffin to the private graveyard near the lake.

Thus, on January 14, 1862, Colonel Samuel Colt was laid to rest, at the age of only forty-seven. At the time, he was America's best-known and wealthiest inventor, a man who had dreamed an ambitious dream and had made it come true. Sam Colt had raced through a life rich in controversy and calamity and had left behind a public monument and a private mystery. The monument, locally, was the Colt armory; in the world beyond, it was the Colt gun that was to pacify the western and southern frontiers and contribute much to their folklores. The mystery concerned his family, whose entanglements included lawsuits, murder, suicide, and possibly bigamy and bastardy. His had indeed been a full life.

On that January afternoon a kaleidoscope of colorful memories must have crowded the minds of the family and intimates who were present. The foremost mourner was the deceased's calm and composed young widow, Elizabeth, holding by the hand their three-year-old son Caldwell, the only one of five children to survive infancy. Elizabeth was to become Hartford's *grande dame,* and her elaborate memorials would ennoble Colt's deeds at the same time that they would help conceal the shadows of his past. Her mother, her sister Hetty, and her brothers Richard and John Jarvis, both Colt officials, sat behind her. Richard, then the dependable head of Colt's willow-furniture factory, would in a few years become the armory's third president. Only the year before, the Colonel had sent John to England to buy surplus guns and equipment. Colt had been extremely fond of both these men, in contrast to his tempestuous relationships with his own three brothers. Near the Jarvises sat Lydia Sigourney, Hartford's aging, prolific "sweet poetess," who had

Right: Samuel Colt looked every inch the industrial tycoon to Charles Loring Elliott, who also painted the widowed Elizabeth Hart Colt and son Caldwell (left) in 1865. The 1863 photograph above is of Samuel Caldwell Colt, the Colonel's nephew— or, perhaps, his illegitimate son.

been Colt's friend from his youth and who looked upon Mrs. Colt as "one of the noblest characters, having borne, like true gold, the test of both prosperity and adversity."

Four of the pallbearers had played major roles in Colt's fortunes. They were Thomas H. Seymour, a former governor of Connecticut; Henry C. Deming, mayor of Hartford; Elisha K. Root, mechanical genius and head superintendent of the armory; and Horace Lord, whom Colt had lured away from the gun factory of Eli Whitney, Jr., to become Root's right-hand man.

And in the background, obscured by the Jarvises and the Colt cousins, was a handsome young man named Samuel Caldwell Colt. In the eyes of the world he was the Colonel's favorite nephew and the son of the convicted murderer John Colt, but according to local gossip he was really the bastard son of the Colonel himself by a German mistress.

Hartford was stunned by Colt's early death. True, he had suffered for some time from gout and rheumatic fever; he had indulged fully in the pleasures of life; he had labored from dawn to dusk to the point of exhaustion; then, at Christmas, he had caught a cold and become delirious. Perhaps pneumonia had set in. Whatever the cause of the Colonel's death, the general reaction was, as one lady put it, that "the main spring is broken, and the works must run down."

Sam Colt had made his mark in Hartford—and in the world—in less than fourteen years, beginning with his return to his native city to achieve his life's ambition of having his own gun factory. In the two decades before that he had been a failure at school and in business, but not as an inventor, pitchman, and promoter of himself and his wares.

To many, his brash nature and new-fangled ideas made him seem an outsider—a wild frontiersman

rather than a sensible Yankee. Yet Sam's maternal grandfather, John Caldwell, had founded the first bank in Hartford, and his own father was a merchant speculator who had made and lost a fortune in the West Indies trade. Widowed when Sam was only seven—the year the boy took apart his first pistol—Christopher Colt had had to place his children in foster homes. At ten, Sam went to work in his father's silk mill at Ware, Massachusetts, and later spent less than two years at a private school at Amherst. Sam became in-

terested in chemistry and electricity, and fashioned a crude underwater mine filled with gunpowder and detonated from shore by an electric current carried through a wire covered with tarred rope. On July 4, 1829, he distributed a handbill proclaiming that "Sam'l Colt will blow a raft sky-high on Ware Pond." The youngster's experiment worked too well: the explosion was so great that water doused the villagers' holiday best. Angrily they ran after the boy, who was shielded by a young machinist whose name was Elisha Root.

This peaceful view of the Connecticut River and Colonel Samuel Colt's gun factory, with its distinctive blue cupola, was done about 1857 by an unknown American artist. The oval is one of a pair; the companion piece, painted from the southeast, is a view of Hartford with the large Colt armory shown at the left.

Yearning for high adventure, Colt in 1830 persuaded his father to let him go to sea. It was arranged for him to work his passage on the brig *Corvo,* bound for London and Calcutta. "The last time I saw Sam," a friend wrote to Sam's father, "he was in tarpaulin [hat], checked shirt, checked trousers, on the fore topsail yard, loosing the topsail. . . . He is a manly fellow."

During this, his sixteenth year, Sam conceived, by observing the action of the ship's wheel, or possibly the windlass, a practical way for making a multishot pistol.

Probably from a discarded tackle block, he whittled the first model of a rotating cylinder designed to hold six balls and their charges. The idea was to enable the pawl attached to the hammer of a percussion gun to move as the gun was cocked, thus turning the cylinder mechanically. Colt thus became the inventor of what would be the definitive part of the first successful revolver. Although he later claimed he had not been aware of the existence of ancient examples of repeating firearms until his second visit to London in 1835,

85

it is likely that he had inspected them in the Tower of London in 1831, when the *Corvo* docked in the Thames. Moreover, he may have seen the repeating flintlock with a rotating chambered breech invented by Elisha Collier of Boston in 1813 and patented in England in 1818. But since Collier's gun was cumbersome and the cylinder had to be rotated by hand, Colt cannot be said to have copied its design.

Colt returned to Boston in 1831 with a model of his projected revolver. With money from his father he had two prototypes fabricated, but the first failed to fire and the second exploded. Out of funds, Sam had to scrimp to make his living and to continue the development of his revolver, which he was certain would make him a fortune. At Ware, his exposure to chemistry had introduced him to nitrous oxide, or laughing gas. Sam now set himself up as the "celebrated Dr. Coult of New York, London and Calcutta" and for three years toured Canada and the United States as "a practical chemist," giving demonstrations for which he charged fifty cents admission. Those who inhaled the "exhilirating" gas became intoxicated for a few minutes; they would perform ludicrous feats, to the delight of the audience.

In the meantime, Colt had hired John Pearson of Baltimore to make improved models of his revolver, but he was at his wit's end trying to keep himself and the constantly grumbling Pearson going. Borrowing a thousand dollars from his father, Colt went to Europe and obtained patents in England and France. In 1836, aided by the U.S. commissioner of patents (a Hartford native named Henry Ellsworth), Colt received U.S. Patent No. 138, on the strength of which he persuaded a conservative cousin, Dudley Selden, and several other New Yorkers to invest some $200,000 to incorporate the Patent Arms Manufacturing Company of Paterson, New Jersey. Sam got an option to buy a third of the shares (though he was never able to pay for one of them), a yearly salary of $1,000, and a sizable expense account, of which he took full advantage to promote a five-shot revolver in Washington military and congressional circles. (The five-shooter was more practical to produce than a six-shot model based on Colt's original design.) At the time, the Army Ordnance Department, facing boldly backward, was satisfied with its single-shot breech-loading musket and flintlock pistol. A West Point competition rejected Colt's percussion-type arm as too complicated. Mean-

Part of the Colt munitions complex was destroyed by fire in February of 1864; the Aetna Insurance Company promptly incorporated the disaster into its advertising (left). Above is Armsmear, Colt's mansion; employee-inventor Charles Billings poses (right) in an armory band uniform.

while, Cousin Dudley was growing impatient with Sam's lavish dinner parties, lack of sales, and mounting debts. At one point he chastised Colt for his liquor bill: "I have no belief in undertaking to raise the character of your gun by old Madeira."

The clouds began to break in December of 1837, when Colonel William S. Harney, struggling to subdue the Seminole Indians in the Florida Everglades, ordered one hundred guns, stating, "I am . . . *confident that they are the only things that will finish the infernal war.*" Still, Colt failed to win over the stubborn head of Ordnance, Colonel George Bomford, until the summer of 1840, when another trial proved his gun's superiority and forced Bomford to give in slightly; Colt got an order for one hundred carbines at forty dollars apiece. It was a Pyrrhic victory, though, because sales were otherwise too meager to sustain the little company, and in September of 1842 its doors closed for good.

Colt wound up in debt and in controversy with his employers, whom he suspected of fiscal skulduggery. Disgusted with bureaucrats, he determined to be his own boss thereafter. To a member of the family he confided in his half-educated but colorful way:

To be a clerk or an office holder under the pay and patronage of Government, is to stagnate ambition & I hope by hevins I would rather be captain of a canal bote than have the biggest office in the gift of the Government . . . however inferior in wealth I may be to the many who surround me I would not exchange for there treasures the satisfaction I have in knowing I have done what has never before been accomplished by man. . . . Life is a thing to be enjoyed . . . it is the only certainty.

During this period Sam Colt was also involved in a trying and frustrating family tragedy. His erratic but usually mild older brother, John, who was struggling to earn a living by writing a textbook on bookkeeping, had rented a small office in New York City. Then, in September of 1841, he killed his irascible printer, Samuel Adams, after the two had fought over the accuracy of the printer's bill—their versions differed by less than twenty dollars. John (in self-defense, he claimed) struck Adams with a hatchet, then stuffed the body into a packing case and had it delivered to a

TEXT CONTINUED ON PAGE 94

A PORTFOLIO OF ILLUSTRATIONS BEGINS OVERLEAF

Catlin & Colt

Sam Colt was an aggressive merchandiser, and during the 1850's he arranged for George Catlin, the prominent and peripatetic painter of American Indians, to do a series of canvases to illustrate the use of Colt firearms in a variety of exotic settings. Six of the paintings were lithographed and widely distributed—and a powerful advertising campaign was launched. Four of the scenes in the following portfolio were actually part of the sextet; the others (the ostrich, flamingo, and jaguar hunts) were done in much the same general spirit and format—Catlin the hunter using Colt weaponry—but were not used to push the armory's line. The last illustration (pages **92** and **93**) is a reproduction of one of the actual advertising lithographs, which today are quite rare. Apart from the zest of the paintings proper, Catlin's enthusiasm for his task is repeatedly borne out in passages from his *Life Among the Indians* and *Last Rambles Amongst the Indians of the Rocky Mountains and of the Andes,* both published in the 1860's. Catlin's was a breezy, freewheeling prose style; one of his favorite devices was to attribute personality to "Sam." "Sam! who's Sam?" he would challenge the reader in his chatty, rhetorical way. "Why *Sam Colt,* a six-shot little rifle, always lying *before* me during the day and *in my arms* during the night, by which a tiger's or alligator's eye, at a hundred yards, was sure to drop a red tear. . . ." During his South American travels Catlin disdained to use blowguns and poisoned arrows: "I don't wish to poison anybody! and game enough 'Sam' and I can always kill without it—powder and ball from Sam are *rank poison.*" So confident was Catlin of his armament ("made expressly for me by my old friend Colonel Colt," he proudly wrote) that, before an ostrich hunt in Argentina, he said he was reckoned a literal one-man band: "I . . . with 'Sam' in hand and a six-shot revolver in my belt, was considered equal to a war party." Faced with such vigorous testimonials—to say nothing of the exciting lithographs in the ads—what man of action could resist buying a Colt?

Catlin's Colt revolver fells a buffalo in Texas.

Catlin and "Sam" hunt ostriches in Argentina.

Catlin remains alert during a pause on Brazil's Rio Trombetas.

The artist tries to rescue a companion treed by peccaries.

Catlin portrayed himself as a mighty hunter of Texas flamingos.

Catlin nears his kill—a Brazilian jaguar.

The artist-hunter awes a group of Carib Indians with his repeating rifle.

packet bound for New Orleans. A heat wave was his undoing; discovery of the decomposing corpse led to his arrest. Sam went to John's defense, engaging Cousin Dudley and Robert Emmet as attorneys and scrounging about for funds.

The trial was the newspaper sensation of the year, for it had all the elements of melodrama: a crime of passion, a voluble defendant with friends of influence and means, an aroused populace, a lovely black-eyed blonde, and a bizarre climax.

The girl in the story was Caroline Henshaw, an unschooled young woman who gave birth to a son just before the trial opened in January of 1842. She told the court that she had met John Colt in Philadelphia in 1840, but did not live with him until she came to New York the following January. He taught her to read and write, but eschewed marriage, he said, because of his poverty. Another version had it that Caroline was of German birth, and that it was Sam, not John, who met her first. On his trip to Europe in 1835, the story went, Sam met Caroline in Scotland and brought her back to America as his wife. According to this account, Sam was so preoccupied with his inventions and was away so much that John had, out of pity, made Caroline his common-law wife. Furthermore, because of their social differences, Sam was only too glad to be rid of a partner who might impede his career, which he always placed above personal ties.

In any event, John Colt was convicted of murdering Sam Adams and was sentenced to be hanged on November 18, 1842.

As dawn broke that day, Sam Colt was the first to see John. At about eleven o'clock, Dr. Henry Anthon, rector of St. Mark's Church, visited the prisoner, who had decided, after conferring with his brother, to make Caroline his lawful wife. John handed the minister five hundred dollars to be used for Caroline's welfare; he had received the money from Sam—a sizable gift from a man whose factory had failed the month before. A little before noon, Caroline, worn and nervous but smartly dressed in a claret-colored coat and carrying a muff, arrived with Sam. She and John were married by Dr. Anthon. For nearly an hour she remained alone with John in his cell. Then she departed with Sam, and John was left undisturbed.

At five minutes to four the sheriff and Dr. Anthon entered the cell to escort John to the scaffold. But the prisoner lay dead on his bed, a knife with a broken handle buried in his heart. The New York *Herald* speculated that Colt's relatives knew of his intention to commit suicide and that they might have smuggled the knife into his cell. The allegation was never proved—or disproved.

Colt secretly arranged for Caroline and her young son to go to Germany. He told his brother James that she "speaks and understands German and can best be cared for in the German countries. . . . [I have] made all the necessary arrangements and will somehow provide the needful." At his insistence she changed her name to Miss Julia Leicester, but the boy grew up as Samuel Caldwell Colt.

Caroline and her son remained abroad, supported by Sam. Eventually she became attracted to a young Prussian officer, Baron Friedrich Von Oppen, whose father questioned her background and suspected that money, not love, was Caroline's motive. But Colt used all his influence to insure a quiet marriage and afterward did everything possible to make the couple and fifteen-year-old Samuel happy.

Apparently the boy did not like book learning any better than Sam himself, so Colt brought him back to America and placed him in a private school. He loaned Caroline $1,000 to enable her husband, who had been disinherited, to enter business. The money was soon dissipated, and Caroline feared debtor's prison. Sam came to the rescue again, making the Baron his agent in Belgium. But Von Oppen and Caroline drifted apart, and she was lonely without her child. She appealed to Sam to bring her back to America—and there the curtain drops: the beautiful, tormented Caroline Henshaw Colt Von Oppen vanished from Samuel Colt's life just as he reached the pinnacle of success. She never appeared again, except in a portrait that hung beside one of John Colt at Armsmear, and in the persistent stories (Hartford residents have never let them die) about her true relationship to Samuel Colt.

Even before the demise of the Paterson company in 1842, Colt had been working on two other inventions. In the late thirties he began developing a waterproof cartridge out of tin foil, and he also returned to his experiments with underwater batteries. About the latter he wrote to President John Tyler in 1841:

Discoveries since Fulton's time combined with an invention original with myself, enable me to effect instant destruction of either Ships or Steamers . . . on their entering a harbour.

The Navy granted him $6,000 for a test. Using copper wire insulated with layers of waxed and tarred twine, he made four successful demonstrations, one of which blew up a sixty-ton schooner on the Potomac before a host of congressmen. But neither the military nor Congress took to the idea, which John Quincy Adams branded an "unChristian contraption," and Colt's Submarine Battery Company never surfaced.

The waterproof cartridges had a better reception, including an endorsement by Winfield Scott, General in Chief of the Army. In 1845 Congress spent one quarter of its $200,000 state militia appropriation on Colt's ammunition.

Meanwhile, Colt had become acquainted with Professor Samuel F. B. Morse and his electro-magnetic telegraph. The two inventors hit it off from the start. If Colt's cable could carry an electrical impulse under water to trigger an explosive charge, then it probably could carry telegraphic messages across lakes and rivers. Colt supplied Morse with batteries and wire and won a contract for laying forty miles of wire from Washington to Baltimore. In May of 1846, the same month in which war was declared on Mexico, the New York and Offing Magnetic Telegraph Association was incorporated by Colt and a new set of investors, with the rights to construct a telegraph line from New York City to Long Island and New Jersey. But again the operation was mismanaged, partly because of Colt's negligence, and at thirty-two he once more found himself as "poor as a churchmouse." Desperate, he sought—in vain—a captaincy in a new rifle regiment.

Although Colt was not destined to fight in the Mexican War, his guns were. For the five-shot Paterson pistol, having won acceptance against the Seminoles in Florida, had gained further renown in the hands of the Texas Rangers in the early forties. (The six-shot Colt .45, or "Peacemaker," the gun that supposedly won the West, did not appear until the early 1870's.) In the summer of 1844, for instance, Captain John C. Hays and fifteen rangers engaged some eighty Comanches in open combat along the Pedernales River and with Colt guns killed or wounded half of them. Altogether, 2,700 Paterson guns, mostly .34 and .36 caliber, were made for the frontiersmen in pocket, belt, and holster sizes. At the close of 1846, without money or machines but still possessed of his patent rights, Colt approached Ranger Captain Samuel H. Walker about buying "improved" arms for his men, who had been mustered into the United States Army. A veteran Indian fighter, Walker needed little encouragement. He wrote Colt:

Without your pistols we would not have had the confidence to have undertaken such daring adventures. . . . With improvements I think they can be rendered the most perfect weapon in the World for light mounted troops. . . . The people throughout Texas are anxious to procure your pistols.

That was certainly the case with General Zachary Taylor, commanding troops in Texas in the autumn of 1846. Taylor wanted one thousand Colts within three months, but Colt lacked even a model with which to start manufacturing again. That did not overly distress Colt, because Captain Walker wanted a simpler yet heavier gun—.44 caliber—that would fire six shots. So Colt designed the so-called Walker gun.

Armed with a $25,000 government order, Sam persuaded Eli Whitney, Jr., the Connecticut contractor for Army muskets, to make the thousand revolvers. They were ready six months later. A pair of guns for Walker, who had hounded Colt for delivery, arrived in Mexico only four days before he was killed in action. To General Sam Houston, who had praised the guns' superiority, Colt wrote:

I am truly pleased to lern . . . that your influance unasked for by a poor devil of an inventor has from your own sense of right been employed to du away the prejudice heretofore existing among men who have the power to promote or crush at pleasure all improvements in Fire arms for military purposes.

In the early 1830's the would-be arms maker, struggling to make ends meet, was billing himself as the "celebrated Dr. Coult"—purveyor of laughing gas at fifty cents a whiff.

His appetite whetted, Colt obtained an order for another thousand Walker guns. He borrowed about $5,000 from his banker cousin Elisha Colt and other Hartford businessmen, leased a factory on Pearl Street, and hired scores of hands. Thus, in the summer of 1847, Colt started his own factory, promising to turn out five thousand guns a year. To a friend in Illinois he wrote a letter that reveals much of the basic Colt:

I am working on my own hook and have sole control and management of my business and intend to keep it as long as I live without being subject to the whims of a pack of dam fools and knaves styling themselves a board of directors . . . my arms sustain a high reputation among men of brains in Mexico and . . . now is the time to make money out of them.

Alert to the new methods being used in New England's machine-tool industry, Colt quickly adapted the system of interchangeable parts to the mass production of guns. Though two other Connecticut gunmakers, Simeon North and Whitney, had been the first to standardize parts, Colt perfected the technique to the point where eighty per cent of his gunmaking was done by machine alone.

Vital to his success was his able staff, especially Elisha Root, whom he had first met at Ware and whom he had now lured away from the Collins Axe Company by offering him the unheard-of salary of $5,000 a year. As Colt's head superintendent, Root designed and constructed the incomparable Colt armory and installed its equipment. During his tenure, Root invented many ingenious belt-driven machines (some of which are still operative) for turning gun stocks, boring and rifling barrels, and making cartridges.

Root's quiet, firm, perfectionist leadership made Colt's factory a training center for a succession of gifted mechanics, some of whom went on to apply his modern methods in their own companies. Charles E. Billings and Christopher M. Spencer started a company (now defunct) for making a variety of hand tools; Spencer invented the Spencer rifle, used in the Civil War, as well as the first screw-making machine. Other armory graduates included Francis A. Pratt and Amos Whitney, who together founded a machine-tool company that today is part of Colt Industries.

While Root managed the factory, Colt functioned as president and salesman extraordinary. Far more than his competitors, he appreciated the necessity of creating demand through aggressive promotion. He paid military officers and others to act as his agents in the West and the South and as his lobbyists in Congress, while Colt himself solicited patronage from state governors. Until the approach of the Civil War, however, government sales were scanty compared to the thousands of revolvers shipped to California during the Gold Rush, or to foreign heads of state. From 1849 on, Colt travelled abroad extensively, wangling introductions to government officials and making them gifts of beautifully engraved weapons.

In May of 1851 Colt exhibited five hundred of his machine-made guns and served free brandy at London's Crystal Palace Exposition. He even read a paper, "Rotating Chambered-Breech Firearms," to the Institute of Civil Engineers. Two years later he became the first American manufacturer to open a branch abroad, choosing a location on the Thames for supplying the English government with what he termed "the best peesmakers" in the world. So backward did he find England's mechanical competence, however, that he was forced to send over both journeymen and machines. Colt was ultimately unable to convince the English of the superiority of machine labor, and the London factory was sold in 1857, but not before it and the main plant in Hartford had between them supplied two hundred thousand pistols for use in the Crimean War.

Colt had been successful in obtaining a seven-year extension of his basic American patent and in crushing attempts at infringement. He had become a millionaire in less than a decade. As a loyal Democrat he had finally won his long-sought commission, becoming a colonel and aide-de-camp to his good friend Governor Thomas Seymour.

As demand and production continued to soar, Colt had to seek larger quarters. By the early fifties his dream was to build the largest private armory anywhere. He turned his attention to two hundred acres of lowlands along the Connecticut River below Hartford, which he planned to reclaim by building a dike nearly two miles long against spring flooding. His dike, with French osiers planted on top to prevent erosion, was finished in two years at a cost of $125,000.

Behind the dike soon rose the brownstone armory, with a blue onion-shaped dome topped by a gold ball and a stallion holding a broken spear in its mouth. A giant 250-horsepower steam engine, its flywheel thirty feet in diameter, drove four hundred various machines by a labyrinth of shafts and belts. By 1857 Colt was turning out 250 finished guns a day.

The buildings were steam heated and gas lighted. Around them he constructed fifty multiple dwellings, in rows, for his workmen and their families; he had streets laid out and a reservoir built. Colt paid good wages but insisted on maximum effort in return. Said one factory notice, evidently written by Colt himself:

EVERY MAN EMPLOYED IN OR ABOUT MY ARMOURY WHETHER BY PIECEWIRK OR BY DAYS WIRK IS EXPECTED TO WIRK TEN HOURS DURING THE RUNING OF THE ENGINE, & NO ONE WHO

By "inside contracting" Colt kept his own employment rolls to less than a fourth of the total number who earned their living from the armory. His thirty-one contractors assumed responsibility for their particular operations or departments, hiring their own men and receiving materials and tools from Colt.

The willow trees grew so well on top of the dike that Colt set up a small factory to manufacture willow furniture, which became especially popular in Cuba and South America because of its lightness of weight and its coolness. For his German willow workers he erected a row of two-family brick houses modelled after their homes in Potsdam, and gave them a beer-and-coffee garden as well. For his own pleasure and theirs, he formed them into a brightly uniformed armory band. His final, most forward-looking contribution to his employees' welfare was Charter Oak Hall, named after the Charter Oak tree that fell in 1856, the year the hall was dedicated.* Seating a thousand people, the hall was a meeting place for workers; there they could read, hear lectures or concerts, and hold fairs or dances.

Through it all, Sam Colt had remained a rather bibulous bachelor, a well-fleshed six-footer whose light hazel eyes were beginning to gather more than a few wrinkles about them. But Colonel Colt was now at the peak of his career, and he needed a wife and home; these he acquired with his usual dispatch and pomp. Four years earlier he had met the two daughters of the Reverend William Jarvis of Middletown, downriver from Hartford. He chose as his bride the gracious and gentle Elizabeth, who at thirty was twelve years younger than he. The extravagance of their wedding, on June 5, 1856, rocked Hartford's staid society. The steamboat *Washington Irving*, which Colt chartered for the occasion, carried him and his friends to the wedding in Middletown. They boarded in front of the flag-bedecked armory; there was an immense crowd of spectators, and Colt mechanics fired a rifle salute from the cupola. Two days later the Colonel and his bride sailed on the *Baltic* for a six-month trip to Europe. On their return, Sam began to build his palatial Armsmear on the western edge of his property.

When Armsmear was finished, Colt's investment in the South Meadows was close to two million dollars—truly a gigantic redevelopment project for that era (and one that he accomplished without borrowing from the bankers he so roundly detested). Yet its importance was largely lost upon the city fathers, and Colt's father-in-law complained, "Though he pays nearly one tenth of the whole city tax, yet there has been a determination on the part of the Republicans to do nothing for him, or the many hundreds who reside on his property in the South Meadows."

Although the city finally gave him some tax relief for his improvements, its only physical contribution was three street lamps. And when Sam started a private ferry from the armory across the Connecticut to East Hartford to convey mechanics who could not be accommodated in company housing, the hostile Hartford *Courant* accused him of trying to "dodge the rights of the Hartford Bridge Company." So exasperated did the Colonel become over such treatment—which was undoubtedly aggravated by his own brashness—that he made a major change in his will, depriving Connecticut of what would surely have been a great educational institution. He had originally planned to leave a quarter of his estate for "founding a school for the education of practical mechanics and engineers."

By the end of 1858 the Colonel, his lady, and young Caldwell were comfortably ensconced in Armsmear. The family saw little of Colt, however; as the North and South raced toward cataclysm, Colt was busy making enormous profits by filling the demands of both sides for what he sardonically called "my latest work on 'Moral Reform.'" He seriously considered building a branch armory in either Virginia or Georgia. The Armory's earnings averaged $237,000 annually until the outbreak of the Civil War, when they soared to over a million. His last shipment of five hundred guns to the South left for Richmond three days after Fort Sumter, packed in boxes marked "hardware."

Colt regarded slavery not as a moral wrong but as an inefficient economic system. He abhorred abolitionists, denounced John Brown as a traitor, and opposed the election of Lincoln for fear the Union would be destroyed—and a lucrative market thereby lost. Like many other Connecticut manufacturers, he believed that an upset of the status quo would be ruinous to the free trade on which the state's prosperity depended. Thus, he took a conservative stand on slavery and supported the Democrats because they stressed Union and the Constitution. But at the same time, he shrewdly prepared the armory for a five-year conflict and for the arming of a million men; the prevailing sentiment in Hartford was that a civil war, if it broke out, could not last two months. During a vacation in Cuba in early 1861, Colt wrote Root and Lord, exhorting them to "run the Armory night & day with a double set of hands. . . . Make hay while the sun shines."

---

* The Charter Oak long had been a symbol of Connecticut's passion for independence. In 1687 the British royal governor was frustrated in his attempt to take away the colony's charter when a local resident stashed the document in the ancient tree.

During the 1860 state elections Colt's political convictions and their manifestations caused a stir in the press, the *Courant* leading the attack and the Hartford *Times* waging a vigorous defense. Colt was known to have used dubious methods in previous campaigns, including having ballot boxes watched to make sure his workers supported Democratic candidates. This time the hostile press accused him of discharging, outright, "66 men, of whom 56 are Republicans. Many of these were contractors and among his oldest and ablest workmen." Asserting that their dismissals amounted to "proscription for political opinion," the discharged Republican workers resolved that "the oppression of free labor by capital, and the attempt to coerce and control the votes of free men, is an outrage upon the rights of the laboring classes." Colt quickly issued a flat denial:

In no case have I ever hired an operative or discharged one for his political or religious opinions. I hire them for ten hours labor . . . and for that I pay them punctually every month. . . .

Yet a few months earlier he had suggested to a politician friend that he pen a resolution urging "us [manufacturers] all to discharge from our imploymen every Black Republican . . . until the question of slavery is for ever set to rest & the rights of the South secured permanently to them."

Now Colt's immense business responsibilities were beginning to wear down his seemingly inexhaustible energies. Bothered by frequent attacks of inflammatory rheumatism and distressed by the death of an infant daughter, he drove himself as if he knew his days were numbered. Smoking Cuban cigars, Colt ruled his domain from a roll-top desk at the armory, often writing his own letters in his left-handed scrawl.

Shortly before he died, he handed the family reins to his brother-in-law, Richard Jarvis, with the admonition that "you and your family must do for me now as I have no one else to call upon. You are the pendulum that must keep the works in motion." Two of his own brothers were dead, and the other, James, a hot-tempered ne'er-do-well and petty politician, had proved a miserable failure as Colt's manager in the short-lived London plant and later as an official of the armory. The entire estate, which Mrs. Colt and their son Caldwell controlled, was valued at $15,000,000—an enormous sum in those days—giving Elizabeth an income of $200,000 a year for life. Caldwell grew up to be a good sportsman, an international yachtsman, and a lover of beautiful women; although a vice president, he took little interest in the company, and died a mysterious death in Florida at the age of thirty-six.

Other than Elizabeth and Caldwell, Colt's major beneficiary was Master Samuel Caldwell Colt, "son of my late brother John Caldwell Colt," whom even Mrs. Colt regarded favorably. When Sam and his southern bride were married in a large and fashionable wedding at Armsmear in 1863, Elizabeth presented the couple with a house across the street; at her death she left them many of her personal effects. For a short time this handsome, retiring man worked at the armory; he became a director but eventually moved to Farmington and took up gentleman farming. He was always loyal to the memory of Colonel Colt, who his descendants believe was his true father.

Colonel Samuel Colt had adopted as his motto *Vincit qui patitur*, "He conquers who suffers." But a better-fitting key to his character is found in a remark he once wrote to his half-brother William: " 'It is better to be at the head of a louse than at the tail of a lyon!' . . . If I cant be first I wont be second in anything."

Colt's ambition was to be first and best, and his means were money and power, both of which he had in full measure. His patriotism, while stronger than that of the average munitions maker, was ever subordinate to his desire to see maintained a commercially favorable status quo between North and South. Colt was not above using bribery and was unashamed of profiteering; he seldom reflected on the moral implications of dealing in weapons of death and destruction.

In fairness, Colt was not alone in his evident amorality: the turbulence of the age had thrown out of focus more than a few of the old values for more than a few of his countrymen. Especially to Connecticut Yankees, who had made their state an arsenal for the nation since colonial days, gunmaking could be no sin. What did bother the diluted Puritan conscience of Colt's time was that a Hartford aristocrat flouted the tenets of the Congregational Church to which he was born— by a bizarre career, a love of high living, and an overbearing pride and flamboyance.

It can scarcely be denied that Sam Colt was one of America's first tycoons, a Yankee peddler who became a dazzling entrepreneur. The success of his many mechanical inventions and refinements was due less to their intrinsic merits—which were considerable—than to his showmanship in telling the world about them. He achieved his goals despite continual adversity for nearly three fourths of his short life. Proud, stubborn, and farsighted, he was a man apart; he was impatient with the old ways, preferring, as he said, to be "paddling his own canoe."

CITIES

OF THE

MIDDLE BORDER

Some became great, others stayed as they were—

and their story tells of the rise of the Midwest

By PAUL M. ANGLE

One hundred and fifty years ago the story of America was a story of the open country—of rural people, living for the most part in villages or on farms. A great part of the country had not even been explored, and huge sections of it did not belong to the United States. By 1830, although the number of Americans living west of the Alleghenies was fast approaching the number east of them, many intelligent men seriously believed that it would take anywhere from 500 to 2,000 years to settle and develop the country.

Today, in contrast, the story of America has become very largely a story of the city. Of all the changes that have come to America, one of the most striking has been the country's amazing urbanization. A few generations ago the average American was a farmer; today he is a city dweller.

At the beginning of the Nineteenth Century, Boston, New York, Philadelphia, and Baltimore were the only cities in the United States with white populations of more than 10,000. When the 1950 census was taken, 484 cities had passed the 25,000 mark, and within their limits lived 41 per cent of the entire population.

Nowhere has the change been more dramatic than along what used to be called the Middle Border—the great Middle West, an open land of frontier communities and small towns only a century ago, today a thickly settled, highly industrialized area of thriving cities that have burgeoned far beyond anything imaginable in 1856.

The enormous difference can be seen, visually, in such exhibits as the set of contrasting lithographs and photographs recently arranged by the Chicago Historical Society. But while the visual disparity is evident, what is not so clear is the reason behind the cities' changing faces.

What happened, out on the Middle Border, to make some of these cities double, treble, or quadruple their populations in so short a time? Why should one city grow so much faster than another? Why should St. Paul, Minnesota, have a population of 300,000 today while Davenport, Iowa, has 75,000—when both were approximately the same size a hundred years ago?

We start with Galena, Illinois, not because the town is typical, but because it is not. Almost alone among middle western cities, Galena has lost population over the last hundred years. In 1856 it had 10,000 inhabitants; today it has fewer than 5,000.

GALENA, ILLINOIS

This center of lead mining in 1856 was all bright promise, but growth stagnated and the town today is smaller than it was.

DAVENPORT, IOWA

This is the thriving young river town in 1856. It prospered, yet St. Paul, tiny at that time, has long since outstripped it.

As anyone who knows Latin could guess, lead made Galena. As early as 1816, when the first rank of advancing settlers was still hundreds of miles to the south and east, miners were taking lead from the hills in which Galena nestles. Production increased steadily until 1845, when the region accounted for 54,500,000 pounds of the 65,000,000 pounds of lead mined in the entire country. Steamboats regularly poked their way through the narrow Fever River to the town's busy wharves, and the inhabitants built solid, comfortable homes, churches, and public buildings on the sides and crests of the hills. It is significant that the first railroad to be built out of Chicago was named the Galena and Chicago Union (though it never managed to get to Galena), while the Galena Branch of the Illinois Central, as originally conceived, was considered of no less importance than the Chicago connection. A *Harper's Magazine* reporter, visiting Galena in 1857, was awed, not only by the rush of trains and steamers, and by the churches and schools, but also by the "thousands of tons" of zinc and copper ore, dug up in the course of lead mining but simply abandoned for want of coal to smelt them. "Galena will not go backward," reported *Harper's*.

But lead unmade Galena. By 1845, the miners had just about exhausted the easily accessible, high-yield deposits. Costs rose, production dropped. For a decade the distribution of lumber and merchandise more than made up for the loss of revenue from mining, but the railroad, which everyone expected to be a boon, took away more business than it brought. Miners drifted away to California and Nevada. The Panic of 1857 hit hard. In the depression that followed, Galena slipped from her place as the metropolis of northwestern Illinois to the undistinguished status of a county seat. Her citizens have made repeated efforts to resuscitate the little city, but today its principal asset is the aura of the past that makes it a delight to artists, antiquarians, and tourists.

In some ways the story of Dubuque parallels that of Galena. Iowa too had its lead deposits, and Dubuque stood at their center. And when mining shrank in importance, wholesale merchandising made up the losses as it did in Galena. But here the similarity ends. Dubuque—or rather the eastern shore of the Mississippi opposite the town—was the terminus of the Illinois Central; Galena was only a station near the end of the line. Settlers were swarming into Iowa's fertile prairies; Dubuque was their natural place of supply. Nathaniel H. Parker, the author of a contemporary gazetteer, *Iowa As It Is in 1856*, asserted that Dubuque, "the present terminus of two important railroads, has recently become a place of great commercial importance." In that year 85,045 people registered in Dubuque hotels.

The decline of river traffic, which hurt Galena badly, affected Dubuque not at all. Railroads, fanning out beyond the Mississippi, needed ties and telegraph poles. Huge rafts of logs floated down from Wisconsin and Minnesota, and Dubuque's sawmills did the rest. Thus the Iowa city found new industries to sustain its growth while Galena wilted for the lack of anything to replace its lead mines.

But Dubuque differed from Galena only in degree. As other cities grew along the Mississippi and in the interior of Iowa—Davenport, Burlington, Waterloo, Des Moines—Dubuque's importance as a trading center declined. And finally the lumber trade played out. A residue of furniture factories and a still sizeable commercial area kept the city from losing population. It has, in fact, grown, but far less rapidly than the United States as a whole, and less rapidly, even, than other cities along the great river.

Davenport is an example. As late as 1855 Daven-

THE BUSTLING WEST OF 1857

"The hurry of life in the Western part of this country, the rapidity, energy, and enterprise with which civilization is there being carried forward, baffles all description, and, I think, can hardly be believed by those who have seen it. Cities of magnificent streets and houses, with wharves, and quays, and warehouses, and storehouses, and shops full of Paris luxuries, and railroads from and to them in every direction, and land worth its weight in gold by the foot, and populations of fifty and hundreds of thousands, where, within the memory of men, no trace of civilization existed, but the forest grew and the savage wandered.

"I was at a place called Milwaukee, on Lake Michigan, a flourishing town where they invited me to go and read Shakespeare to them, which I mention as an indication of advanced civilization, and one of the residents, a man not fifty years old, told me that he remembered the spot on which stood the hotel where I was lodging, a tangled wilderness through which ran an Indian trail. Does not all that sound wonderful?"

from a letter by Fanny Kemble
April 7, 1857

ST. LOUIS, MISSOURI

This view in the 1850's looks down from the bluffs at Lucas Place. Across the Mississippi is Illinoistown (now East St. Louis). In the white-domed building at right, Dred Scott lost his first legal battle for freedom; here an unsuccessful ex-army captain named U. S. Grant was selling real estate. Busy, attractive St. Louis lived up to its early promise.

port was no more than a village. Kennedy's *Progress of the Republic*, a comprehensive geography published in 1853, does not mention it. Fisher's *Gazetteer of the United States*, published in the same year, accords Davenport a population of 3,400 and states that it was destined to be a place of importance—but that was a prediction with which the author flattered almost every crossroads in the country.

Isabella Bird, an English traveler who visited the town in 1855, would probably have smiled at Fisher's prediction. Crossing the river from Rock Island, her party landed at what she called "a clearing containing the small settlement of Davenport." There, "in a long wooden shed with blackened rafters and an earthen floor," she breakfasted on "johnny-cake, squirrels, buffalo-hump, dampers, and buckwheat, tea and corn spirit [bourbon whiskey?], with a crowd of emigrants, hunters, and adventurers." Evidently Davenport held no other attraction, for the party immediately re-embarked for Rock Island.

But there was more to the settlement in the clearing than Mrs. Bird saw. She appears to have overlooked the piers of a bridge rising in the Mississippi, the first to span the mighty river in its entire length. The bridge would be finished in the spring of 1856, and after that the cars of the Rock Island Railroad would run on to Davenport. Already the town was exporting large quantities of grain and thousands of hogs and cattle; with the completion of the bridge its commercial importance would double and treble. Like Dubuque, Davenport enjoyed a thriving lumber business, sawing the logs that came down the river and sending ties and planks into the rapidly settling interior.

Did culture languish in these new settlements? Writers of the time apostrophize their libraries and "historical" institutions, and this anecdote was printed in New York exactly a hundred years ago: A New Yorker meets a young man from Davenport, who says he has come to the East to buy goods for his store back home:

"What goods?"

"Music and musical instruments."

"What! For Davenport, where the stumps are hardly dug out?"

"Yes, sir. I sell music and musical instruments."

"Only?"

"Yes, to the amount of five thousand dollars a year."

For forty years—from 1860 to 1900—Davenport and Dubuque kept pace in population. Then Davenport pulled ahead. In 1950 it counted 75,000 inhabitants with 5,000 more in contiguous Bettendorf; Dubuque had 50,000. The reason for the disparity lies in the fact that when the lumber trade died away Dubuque had nothing to replace it, while Davenport had found other industries. In the 1880's nearby limestone quarries were opened and the manufacture of cement was begun. Plants for fabricating iron and steel were founded about the same time. Davenport became, and remains today, a city of diversified industry, at least keeping pace with the country as a whole in growth.

Industry, transportation, and a location that brings trade—these seem to be the factors that make cities. Certainly these are the factors that made St. Louis. When Pierre Laclède Liguest picked its site in December, 1763, he announced that he was establishing a settlement "which might hereafter become one of the finest cities in America." Each passing decade has proved that the prediction was not idle talk. Before the Revolutionary War St. Louis had become the center of the western fur trade. The acquisition of Louisiana Territory made it the crossroads of western expansion. Year after year caravans of settlers bound for the West crossed the Mississippi at St. Louis and bought their outfits for the long trip across the plains.

But it was the traffic on the river that made a city. By 1840, after 77 years, St. Louis had a population of 16,400. In 1850 the census takers counted 78,000; in 1860, 160,000. These were the years when the stacks and masts of the river steamers tied up at St. Louis looked like the denuded trunks in a burned-over forest. The rivermen sinned boisterously in the dives along the wharves and brawled in the streets, but in spite of their picturesque ways, the city impressed visitors by its substance and maturity. Richard Cobden, the English reformer, visiting there in 1859, spoke for many when he recorded in his diary:

"The city of St. Louis is, in the solidity of its buildings, the extent of its commerce, and the reputed wealth of its capitalists the third in importance in the States.—I have seen no place in the interior which gives the same impression of solid wealth and extensive commerce."

Chicagoans, a boastful breed, like to recall that in forty years their own upstart city passed long-established St. Louis, and subsequently left it far behind. The implication is that when the railroads supplanted the river steamers, St. Louis withered and Chicago bloomed. But St. Louis didn't wither. Railroads could be built to and from the city on the Mississippi as well as anywhere, and they quickly replaced the commerce that the river had carried. Industry, moreover, was firmly established as early as 1850.

Optimistic St. Louisans predicted in 1850 that by 1900 the city would have a population of a million. The actual 1900 figure turned out to be 575,000, but that represented a steady, decade-by-decade gain which has continued in the Twentieth Century. In 1950,

ST. PAUL, MINNESOTA
The city in 1856 had an advantageous position, but much of its growth was due to one man—the railroad builder Jim Hill.

CINCINNATI, OHIO
This is the "Queen City of the West" as it looked in 1853. It still thrives, but other midwestern cities overcame its lead.

Kansas City, Missouri, as it looked in 1855.

with 850,000 inhabitants, St. Louis ranked eighth among the cities of the country.

St. Louis, in fact, outran a rival that had taken what appeared to be, in the first thirty or forty years of the Nineteenth Century, a lead that would hold up forever. During most of these years Cincinnati deserved to be called the Queen City. Even the acidulous Frances Trollope, who lived there from 1828 to 1831, admitted that in spite of all shortcomings it was "a city of extraordinary size and importance." Later English visitors were less restrained. In 1859 Cobden recorded in his diary:

"The City has a substantial and prosperous appearance.—Like Philadelphia it depends very much on its manufactures, besides being the centre of a very rich agricultural region, its pork market being the most famous in America.—Lying along the right bank of the Ohio river, with its wooded banks on both sides and its graceful reaches as it winds its course below the City, it is one of the most beautiful sites for a town I have ever seen.—The population is about 200,000 [actually it was 160,000] of which nearly one half are Germans & Irish. . . . At dinner at the hotel heard a discussion as to the number of people in Cincinnati who are worth $500,000, when it seemed to be the opinion that there were 20 to 25 persons owning that amount of property.—It was thought there were hundreds possessing $100,000."

Mrs. Trollope confessed that upon her arrival she thought "the many tree-covered hills around, very beautiful," but went on to say that she tired of the view so quickly that long before she left she would have welcomed the sight of Salisbury Plain. But to Isabella Bird, in 1855, the view from any of the hills which ringed the city was magnificent. "I saw it first bathed in the mellow light of a declining sun," she wrote, ". . . hill beyond hill, clothed with the rich verdure of an almost tropical clime, slopes of vineyards just ready for the wine-press, magnolias with their fragrant blossoms, and that queen of trees the beautiful ilanthus, the 'tree of heaven' as it is called; and everywhere foliage so luxuriant that it looked as if autumn and decay could never come."

But Cincinnati had more to be proud of than pleasing vistas. In mid-century, no other city in the interior United States could offer more convincing evidence of industry and prosperity. Mrs. Bird catalogued the signs of well-being: "heavily laden drays rumbling along the streets—quays at which steamboats of fairy architecture are ever lying—massive warehouses and rich stores—the side walks a perfect throng of foot-passengers—the roadways crowded with light carriages, horsemen with palmetto hats and high-peaked saddles, galloping about on the magnificent horses of Kentucky—an air of life, wealth, bustle, and progress." The city's factories turned out furniture, boots and shoes, locks, guns, tools, and carriages, and enough salted and pickled pork to earn for it the name, "Porkopolis."

Yet Cincinnati had reached its zenith, at least comparatively. The city had profited from the westward movement of the American people; but the flood tide had passed. After 1850 Cincinnati would grow so slowly that at the end of a century seventeen cities would rank ahead of it. Even in Ohio, it would slip to second place, outstripped by what was a mere village when Cincinnati was the queen of the old Northwest.

In 1850 Cleveland had a population of 17,034. But Cleveland also had a fine harbor, canal connections, and ten miles of railroad. By 1860 the population had jumped to 43,417, and the ten miles of railroad had become hundreds, connecting the city with the eastern seaboard and with Chicago, Cincinnati, and St. Louis. And by 1860 Cleveland was an iron ore port with a red avalanche spilling on its docks to be distributed for smelting to the coal-rich neighboring area. To this day, the flow continues.

Oil soon paired with ore to push Cleveland ahead. For ten years after Edwin L. Drake brought in the nation's first great oil field in northwestern Pennsylvania, Pittsburgh, the nearest large city to the wells, held first place as a refining center. Then Cleveland's superior transportation facilities—a water route and two competing railroad connections with the East against Pittsburgh's one—made the city on the lake the oil capital of the country.

The two great industries attracted manufacturers of other products. New railroads were built to transport raw materials and finished products. Thousands of foreigners flocked in to fill the ever-increasing number of jobs. Cleveland grew—to 160,000 in 1880, to 380,000 in 1900. In the Twentieth Century Cleveland spurted to fifth place among American cities, but by 1950 a newcomer, Los Angeles, and an old stalwart in the East, Baltimore, had forced it back to seventh place. Yet with almost a million inhabitants, fine transportation facilities that will become even better with the completion of the St. Lawrence Seaway, and a solid base of diversified industry, Cleveland should hold its high relative position indefinitely.

Cleveland had natural advantages, but it also had, to a remarkable degree, another asset often ignored when attempts are made to appraise the forces that raise one city above another. Cleveland had bold, imaginative, and highly successful enterprisers. Samuel L. Mather and Stephen V. Harkness in iron and steel; Daniel P. Rhodes and his son-in-law, Mark Hanna, in coal, ore, and lake shipping; John D. Rockefeller and Henry M. Flagler in oil—to these men, one could contend, Cleveland owes as much as it owes to all the other factors in its expansion.

The same case can be made for the last of our seven cities, St. Paul. When St. Paul became the capital of the newly created Minnesota Territory in 1849, it was a frontier village with fewer than a thousand inhabitants, many of whom were French Canadians and half-breeds. After ten years St. Paul counted 10,000 inhabitants, most of them brought up the Mississippi by wood-burning side-wheelers which returned downriver loaded with furs and buffalo robes from the Indian country to the north and west.

By this time, the city had given up its early name,

Pig's Eye—the change is understandable—and was beginning to ship its grain to the East.

Among the immigrants, Swedes and Germans and Irishmen, who poured in to make St. Paul large and powerful, one would not have particularly noticed James Jerome Hill. All that marked this little fellow of eighteen was a blind eye, put out by an arrow in his native Ontario, and a yen to continue west, to the Pacific, with the next brigade of trappers. Because no brigade left soon after his arrival, Jim Hill had to wait. He got a job, labeling the flour bags aforesaid, and St. Paul gained a maker of cities, who transformed the little settlement into a great trading center. Here was a railroad builder not ashamed to doff his fine coat and spell the workmen digging his own railroad, a man of choler who would, according to his whim, put a town on the railroad or not, in the manner of the Lord giving or taking away. Acquiring control of the St. Paul and Pacific Railroad in the 1870's, Hill expanded it into the Great Northern, extended its lines, and induced many thousands of ambitious men from Europe and the older states of the East to settle in the territory it served. The Northwest prospered, the Great Northern prospered, St. Paul prospered. By 1900 the village of 1850 had became a city of 163,000; fifty years later it had almost doubled in size. To credit this result to James J. Hill alone would be the grossest kind of oversimplification, yet one can easily imagine slower growth, and a smaller city today, had chance led the well-named Empire Builder to some other place of residence.

One certain deduction can be made from this cursory survey of what has happened to seven cities of the interior United States in the last hundred years. Of all the factors which contribute to growth, the greatest is industry. But industry has brought blight as well as wealth. Look at the attractive, almost bucolic aspect of the cities shown in the old lithographs. Discount the pictures, if you please, on the score that they were made to sell, and that the buyers wanted realism no more than the subject of a portrait photograph desires it. The old prints still represent pleasanter surroundings than we live in today. But not, perhaps, pleasanter surroundings than we might enjoy if we only wanted them badly enough to zone our cities properly and keep them as clean and attractive as they once dreamt of being, in the fresh youth of the Middle Border.

COLLECTION OF MRS. STEPHEN C. CLARK; KODACHROME BY FRANCIS G. MAYER

IDYL'S BEGINNING: *Winslow Homer's* The Morning Bell *caught the spirit of the early New England mill girl: coming from a rural background—and free to return to it whenever she wished —she stepped across a footbridge into a new world, and brought to it her own sturdy virtues.*

Dusk fell over the city of Lawrence, Massachusetts, a few minutes before five o'clock on January 10, 1860. In the five-story brick textile factory owned by the Pemberton Manufacturing Company, lamps began to flicker in the ritual of "lighting-up time." The big building—nearly three hundred feet long and eighty-five wide—rumbled unceasingly with the noise of its hundreds of machines for turning cotton into cloth: its scutchers and spreaders, carders, drawing frames and speeders; its warpers and dressers; and its power looms for weaving the finished fabric. Inside, the noise was higher-pitched, a relentless squeak, clatter, and whirr from the belt-and-shaft system that transmitted water power to the machinery. Some six or seven hundred "hands," mostly women, were at work that afternoon. Those near the windows could look through the twilight at the factory yard, with its two lower buildings running out at right angles from the ends of the main plant. Next to the yard lay the canal which carried the waters of the Mer-

rimack River to the giant water wheels, and beyond that was a row of frame boardinghouses for the employees. Sometime after seven o'clock, bells would jangle and the workers would stream across footbridges over the canal, home to dinner.

But not that night. Suddenly there was a sharp rattle, and then a prolonged, deafening crash. A section of the building's brick wall seemed to bulge out and explode, and then, literally in seconds, the Pemberton Mill collapsed. Tons of machinery crashed down through crumpling floors, dragging trapped, screaming victims along in their downward path. At a few minutes after five, the factory was a heap of twisted iron, splintered beams, pulverized bricks, and agonized, imprisoned human flesh.

Bonfires, lit to aid rescue workers, made pockets of brightness in the gathering night. But the darkness was merciful, hiding sights of unforgettable horror. Girls and men were carried out on stretchers, with arms and legs torn from their bodies, faces crushed

THE
WORKING
LADIES
OF
LOWELL

By BERNARD A. WEISBERGER

Harper's Weekly, JANUARY 21, 1860

IDYL'S END: *The collapse of the shoddily built Pemberton Mill at nearby Lawrence, Massachusetts, symbolized the end of utopias like Lowell; the dream had been shattered.*

beyond recognition, open wounds in which the bones showed through a paste of dried blood, brick dust, and shredded clothing. The worst was yet to come, however. At about 9:30 P.M., the moans of pain, delirium, and cold coming from those still pinned in the wreckage changed to screams of panic. Someone scrambling through the ruins had upset an oil lantern. Flames raced through the oil-soaked wood and cotton waste, drove back doctors, rescue crews, and spectators (many of them relatives of the mill workers), and snuffed out the final shrieks. Next morning saw only a black and smoking mass of "brick, mortar and human bones . . . promiscuously mingled" at the scene of the tragedy.

There were ninety dead—fourteen of them unidentifiable or never found—and a long list of crippled and hospitalized. The casualty list read like a cross section of New England's labor force. There were Yankee girls like Mary York, of Brighton, Maine, and men like Ira Locke, of Derry, New Hampshire. But there were also Nancy Connelly and Bridget Doyle and Kate Harridy,

and many others whose names were of Ireland's "ould sod." There were men like the Swiss George Kradolfer, the German Henry Bakeman, and the Scotch-Irish Robert Hayer, who had come a long way to suffer at the edge of a New England canal. And there was not a church in Lawrence—Catholic, Methodist, Baptist, Presbyterian, Congregational, Unitarian, Universalist, Episcopalian—that did not have parishioners to mourn or to console on the Sunday after the accident.

What had gone wrong? A lengthy coroner's inquest did a certain amount of hedging, but certain unpleasant facts emerged. During the factory's construction, in 1853, cast-iron pillars supporting the floor beams had been shown to be cheap and brittle. They went in nevertheless. Extra machinery had been crowded into the upper floors, ignoring already questionable load limits. Brick walls had not been sufficiently reinforced against the outward thrust of those overburdened floors. After the disaster, the ministers of Lawrence spoke sermons on God's inscrutable wrath, but it was

clear that human oversight and corner-cutting on expenses bore much of the blame.

This seemed to point the finger at the owners, David Nevins and George Howe, who had bought the factory from its first owners in 1857, during a financial panic. Yet neither man was callous or dishonest. Both undoubtedly shared the shocked dismay of their fellow businessmen in the New England Society for the Promotion of Manufactures and the Mechanic Arts, who, ironically, had scheduled a dinner in Boston for that dreadful January 10. Nevins and Howe had acted in response to pressures which they themselves did not fully understand, and such guilt as they bore was partly the guilt of the generation of men who had brought industry to New England's hills forty years before. Those men had nursed lordly dreams of progress and profit through the machine, and some of their visions of growth and gain and uplift had been realized. But industrialism, as America was to learn, brought pain and perplexity with it as well. The horror at the Pemberton Mills was a symbol of another collapse: that of an experiment in creating a strifeless industrial society showering blessings alike on workers and capitalists. Like most such experiments, it expected too much of human nature and counted too little on the unforeseen. For a time, however, it gave a thrill of promise. Its beginnings went back beyond Lawrence, to the early days of the Republic.

In the years just after 1789, the "establishment of manufactures" was a focus of debate. Men like Alexander Hamilton and Tench Coxe looked upon the few domestic workshops of the infant nation and found them good. They urged that the national government should protect and nurture these producers of "American" clothing, gunpowder, rope, paper, rum, iron, leather, and a miscellany of other articles. From other quarters, however, came warnings that liberty and industry made poor partners. Thomas Jefferson was only one among many to point to England's experience and predict that factory workers would inexorably sink into pauperism. They would be forced by the workings of human nature and economic law to "the maximum of labor which the construction of the human body can endure, & to the minimum of food . . . which will preserve it in life." Malthus, Marx, and Ricardo together could not have put it more grimly. Jefferson's implication needed no spelling out—plainly, an impoverished (and therefore vice-ridden and ignorant) laboring class would be indigestible in a democratic republic.

By and large, the Jeffersonians had the better of the argument for some twenty-five years. Capital, markets, and skilled labor—all necessary to a manufacturing economy—were scarce in an undeveloped America, which still found adequate rewards for its work in the soil, the ocean, and the forest. There were a few significant experiments in industry. In Rhode Island, by way of example, two farsighted Quaker merchants, Moses Brown and William Almy, set up in 1790 a "factory" for spinning cotton yarn and thread. They used many of the new machines developed in England during the preceding fifty years to mechanize the spinning process. (The British jealously guarded against the export of those machines or plans for them, but Almy and Brown found a young immigrant from England named Samuel Slater. Slater had stored away the details of the new devices in an incredible memory and come to the United States precisely in the hope of finding sponsors like Almy and Brown. He built their first plant "by heart" and made his fortune and theirs as planned.

Almy and Brown had their new machinery tended by the children of families whom they induced to settle in the factory neighborhood, and they paid their workers, sometimes, in store orders for Almy and Brown merchandise. Thus high-mindedly did they plant the seeds of the company town and child labor in New England soil. With the coming of the cotton gin in 1793, and with years of wartime high prices, they prospered, and even had a few imitators. Yet for all these, "industry" in any real economic sense remained all but nonexistent in the United States. The

real breakthrough came in 1812, and one of the many forces behind it was, as so often, a hunch in a gifted man's mind.

The man was Francis Cabot Lowell, member of a family which was to crowd the American hall of fame with merchants, ministers, legislators, judges, poets, soldiers, and educators. In 1812, this particular Lowell was visiting England for his health, and, like so many Yankees apparently "resting," was deep in meditation. His mind ranged over a number of diverse facts. One was that the impending war would severely shake the Lowell family importing business. Another was that "yarn factories" were not a bad substitute investment. A third was that fresh inventions in the field of power looms had opened up still newer profit opportunities in clothmaking. In Great Britain, weaving factories were at last keeping pace with the healthy output of spinning factories. Francis Lowell, thirty-six years old in 1812, synthesized these facts into a dazzling American vision. Why not put spinning and weaving machines under one roof? Why not have southern cotton delivered at one end of a factory, while from the other end bales of finished yard goods emerged to find a ready market, swept clean of British competitors by war? Power would come from New England streamlets; capital from Boston's countinghouse aristocracy. Machinery? That was a little harder, but not impossible. Lowell, an amateur mathematician and scientist, visited the factories of unsuspecting British business contacts, and gave himself a quick course in the intricate process of machine weaving, which saw cotton fibers fluffed, combed, rolled, twisted, stretched, toughened, and cross-laced, moving from winding to winding and machine to machine in a complex and brilliantly-timed ballet of rollers, spindles, and flyers. Returning home to Boston, he took Paul Moody, a talented Massachusetts mechanic, into his confidence. The two of them perspired over drawings, imported a few devices, copied, redesigned, invented where they had to—and had their factory set up in Waltham, near Boston, by 1815. Meanwhile, Lowell's brother-in-law, Patrick Tracy Jackson, had helped to round up the

By 1835, only a dozen years after the Merrimack Company put up the first factory there (second from left), the five other mills shown on these pages were also humming away at Lowell, turning a hamlet of 200 into a sprawling and still-growing city of 17,000. These engravings decorated the borders of a map of Lowell and its environs published in 1850.

initial capital, and its donors had been incorporated in 1813 as the Boston Manufacturing Company.

Power, capital, machinery—all were ready. But what of labor? The more complex weaving machinery could not be run by children, and yet the cotton factory did not demand the skill and strength of grown men for most of its jobs. Obviously women workers were the answer. New England indeed had what was then called a "fund" of "female labor" in the daughters of its rural folk. But what of that supposed indissoluble bond of union between "manufactures" on the one hand, and "vice and poverty" on the other? Would Yankee farmers send their daughters into the factories to become part of a permanent force of degraded wage workers? Clearly not! Then how would the Boston Manufacturing Company recruit its labor? The answer was an invention as intriguing as any new mechanical gadget for mass-producing cloth. One of Patrick Jackson's biographers explained it, years later.

By the erection of boarding-houses at the expense and under the control of the factory; putting at the head of them matrons of tried character, and allowing no boarders to be received except the female operatives of the mill; by stringent regulations for the government of these houses; by all these precautions, they gained the confidence of the rural population who were now no longer afraid to trust their daughters in a manufacturing town. A supply was thus obtained of respectable girls; and these, from pride of character as well as principle, have taken especial care to exclude all others.

It was soon found that an apprenticeship in a factory entailed no degradation of character, and was no impediment to a reputable connection in marriage. A factory-girl was no longer condemned to pursue that vocation for her life; she would retire, in her turn, to assume the higher and more appropriate responsibilities of her sex; and it soon came to

111

be considered that a few years in a mill was an honorable mode of securing a dower. The business could thus be conducted without any permanent manufacturing population. The operatives no longer form a separate caste, pursuing a sedentary employment, from parent to child, in the heated rooms of a factory; but are recruited, in a circulating current, from the healthy and virtuous population of the country.

"In a circulating current." There was the trick. The fathers of Waltham had not invented the notion of an employer's personal responsibility for the physical and moral welfare of the worker. That was a legacy from indentured labor, apprenticeship—even slavery. But the new factory owners had built a new structure on that foundation. If they brought young girls to the factory for a brief period between maturing and marrying, and if they boarded them under safeguards approved by church, family, and all the gods of respectability, then a *rotating* labor force would escape the ills of industrial decay. It was simple country logic. Standing water stank; a running stream or a spring-fed pond stayed pure and clear.

So the experiment was tried at Waltham. Not much is known about early working conditions, but from a business viewpoint, success was enormous. The owners played a shrewd game from the start. They concentrated on plain and simple fabrics, marketed through a single firm, and they successfully lobbied, in 1816, for a certain measure of tariff protection. Francis Lowell died prematurely in 1817. He did not live to see another twenty years of dividends rarely falling below ten per cent, even while the price to the consumer dropped from twenty-one to six cents a yard. He did not need to; even by 1817, his kind of textile factory, mass-producing cheap, utilitarian goods, had won a clear decision over the dying system of decentralized craft production. By 1821, the leaders of the Boston Manufacturing Company were looking for new worlds to conquer, hunting for a site for a new factory, to turn out printed calicoes.

They found their spot in December of 1821, in a peaceable little farm community called East Chelmsford, some twenty-five miles from Boston. It was at the junction of the Concord and Merrimack rivers, a quiet place, where men could still fish tranquilly for salmon and alewives in their season. A no-longer-used canal around a fall in the Merrimack was quickly bought by the promoters of the new factory. It gave them water power and an iron grip on any future mill-building in the area. A new corporation, the Merrimack Manufacturing Company, was created—but its owners were predominantly the Waltham founders. For years they remained a well-knit group, holding tightly to patents and controlling blocks of stock, and admitting outsiders only when they could pass inspection—and pay!

But if the ownership elite did not grow swiftly, the enterprise did. The Merrimack factory was up in December of 1823. Within three years more, little East Chelmsford, with its scattered farmhouses, gristmills, store, and tavern, was ready for incorporation as a village. Its leading businessmen, landowners, and citizens—the mill owners, naturally—renamed it Lowell. And Lowell mushroomed, geysered, exploded. Two new mills went up in 1828, another in 1830, three more in 1831, still another in 1835. The population of 200 in 1820 jumped to 6,477 in 1830, and 17,633 in 1836. A bank appeared, then another, then a hotel, a library, two schoolhouses, and Episcopalian, Baptist, Congregational, Universalist, and Unitarian churches. In 1835 the Boston and Lowell Railroad—one of the country's

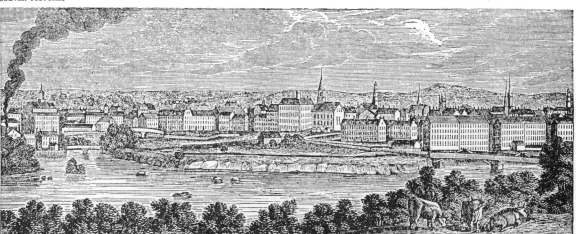

The mills of Lowell crowded the banks of the Merrimack in 1839.

earliest—was opened in a flourish of band music and spread-eagle oratory. By 1845 Lowell, population over 30,000, had become a modern factory town in less time than it took small boys who once had fished undisturbed in the Concord to reach the ripe age of thirty.

Lowell was more than a success. It was a showpiece. Its population consisted mostly of factory girls living in the company boardinghouses. From 1823 to about 1845, it seemed to show that the fond hopes of those who planned a rotating and virtuous labor force might be realized. Foreign tourists—Michel Chevalier of France, Harriet Martineau and Charles Dickens of England—and famous Americans like Andrew Jackson, Henry Clay, and David Crockett visited it to wonder and admire. The focus of attention was the band of New England country girls who had turned themselves into mill hands. They had done so for a number of reasons, among them to show, as one of their number put it, that "it is the laborer's privilege to ennoble his work by the aim with which he undertakes it, and by the enthusiasm and faithfulness he puts into it."

What kind of girls were they? Precisely as planned, they were farm girls, and not only did they come off the farms as expected, they went back to them according to prediction. In 1845 the author of a small book on Lowell inquired of several mill owners to learn whence came their "hands," and how long they stayed. In one factory employing 173 workers, 21 were from Massachusetts, 45 from Maine, 55 from New Hampshire, 52 from Vermont. Only five had worked more than ten years, and 114 of them—nearly two-thirds of the total force—had been there for less than four. Even allowing for some shifting from mill to mill, the turnover in Lowell's population was brisk.

The New England farmer's daughter was anything but a peasant. She might be classed technically as an "unskilled" laborer, but that was only so far as factory production was concerned. She could grow fruits and vegetables, and put them into pies and preserves of breathtaking quality. She could cook for one man or for twenty at harvest time. She could knit, sew, embroider, and sometimes spin and weave. She could keep a two-story frame house spotless, raise small animals and baby brothers and sisters, and nurse sick aunts and grannies as occasion demanded. She could make such varied household products as cheese, brooms, candles, and soap. Independence came as naturally to her as to her brothers, who at seventeen and eighteen were working their own fields or commanding fishing smacks, trading schooners, and whalers. She had the equivalent of a grade-school education, often kept her father's books if he was a small businessman on the side, and took as naturally as she breathed to reading

or to attending two-hour lectures and sermons.

One of these girls, Lucy Larcom, who later became a well-known poet and editor of a children's magazine, recalled her childhood in the port town of Newburyport. She remembered leisure hours spent in devouring Aesop, Bunyan, *Gulliver's Travels*, *The Vicar of Wakefield*, and *Arabian Nights*. The stories in them were no more wonderful than those that she got from retired seamen, who brought home gorgeously colored tropical parrots to squawk from perches in New England parlors, and who spoke to friends (addressed as "shipmate") about voyages to Calcutta and Hong Kong as casually as they might refer to a pony ride to the next village. Lucy knew the local farmers, too, who tramped into her father's store in thick boots and coarse trousers, smelling of hay, dung, and honest sweat. When her widowed mother moved to Lowell to run one of the boardinghouses, Lucy, aged eleven, was prepared for hard work and for leisure rigorously spent in self-improvement.

In the mills there was work in plenty. From April to October, operations began about 5 A.M. and ran until close to 7:30 in the evening, with half-hour interruptions for breakfast at 7 A.M. and dinner at 12:30 in the afternoon. In the shorter months, breakfast was served before daylight, and the working day was finished under lamps. Six days of eleven to thirteen hours' actual work made a long week, but not necessarily a prohibitive one to girls used to being up with the rooster and rarely idle until the sewing basket was set aside for nine o'clock bedtime. (The American factory schedule, in fact, copied farmer's hours—up at dawn to feed stock before breakfast, home for dinner in hottest daytime, late supper after barnyard chores.)

Nor was the factory work unremittingly taxing. Lucy's first job was as a bobbin girl, watching a spinning frame and replacing filled spools with empty ones. It was almost fun to watch a bobbin wax fat, and lift it off at the right moment. Those at spooling, warping, and dressing machines had harder work. The "buzzing and hissing and whizzing of pulleys and rollers and spindles and flyers . . . often grew tiresome." But a lucky girl, near a window, could tend flowers in a window box or read (when such things were permitted, as they were at first) or simply daydream. Daydreaming was discouraged, of course, for one real purpose of having attendants at the machinery was to watch for broken threads, overfilled bobbins, twisted belts, spindles that slipped off their shafts—any one of which could in seconds create an ungodly jam of twisted fibers and stalled machinery.

At the looms, the girls had more to watch—warp threads rising and falling regularly to the tug of the heddles, shuttles jerking back and forth between the warp threads at an even 120 picks to the minute, warp-beam and cloth-beam rolling, and reed beating the cross-threads tight together in even thumps. A wary eye was needed here for breaks and snarls, and for shuttle boxes that needed to be changed; but if a girl had only one or two looms to tend, it was not overly burdensome. Then there were other jobs of varying skill and distastefulness—from minding the whippers and pickers which fluffed the newly arrived cotton, to folding, measuring, and packing finished goods in the cloth room. When Lucy Larcom grew up, she chose to work there. It paid less than machine-tending, but left more quiet hours for reading; an overseer once found his intellectual little mill girl deeply absorbed in Cotton Mather's pedantic *Magnalia Christi Americana* while she was folding cloth.

For the girl who grew a little weary of it all, it was always possible to go home for a month or two. With Lowell booming and growing, there would always be a job when she returned to the factory. What was more, farm girls did not need to accept assignments that they regarded as unfair. A young woman who knew that she was only a day's trip from home, where there were chickens in the henyard, milk in the springhouse, and squash in the garden, took no "sass" from an overseer. Early mill records duly chronicled the dismissal of some girls for "insolence," which undoubtedly meant telling overseers what they thought of them. Wherever industry had not completely displaced a rural way of life, workers had an extra bit of protection. The English-woman, Harriet Martineau, noted that the boot and shoe makers of Lynn, Massachusetts, as late as 1835, knocked off in summers to earn money by fishing. In Pennsylvania in the 1820's, the overseer at an iron foundry carefully recorded that a batch of molten iron had been ruined because, when it was ready to pour, nobody was on hand. "The men," he sorrowfully noted, "was out hunting with their guns."

And if, somehow, the hours did seem to stretch a bit toward the close of the day, there were the tangible rewards in cash to consider. It is not easy to generalize about Lowell wages from 1830 to 1845, particularly since much of the pay was by the piece. In 1840 a careful Scot, James Montgomery, made a study of the comparative costs of cotton manufacture in Great Britain and the United States. He estimated that American owners had to figure on paying girls at various spinning machines $2.50 to $3.50 a week. Weavers could earn twenty-five cents per "piece," which meant that a girl who was willing to work an extra loom might earn as much as $4.50 or even $5.50. (The gap in pay between the rank and file and the "non-coms" in the industrial army was not very great. Bookkeepers rated

$9.50 weekly, overseers $12, and superintendents $25. It seems safe to say that the mill girls, in this period, averaged $3.50 a week in wages. In Lowell in 1840, five cents bought a half-dozen eggs, fifteen cents an entire chicken, and two dollars a carcass of mutton. The companies charged the girls $1.25 for their board and lodging, which left $2.25—nearly $5 every fortnight, or $9 every month, according to how paydays fell—for spending or for saving.

In rural New England a century and a quarter ago, that was no inconsiderable sum of cash. The girls saved what must have been a considerable amount of it. In 1845, according to the Reverend Henry Miles in his *Lowell As It Was And As It Is,* half of the two thousand depositors in the Lowell Savings Bank were factory girls, and their bankbooks showed a total of more than $100,000 laid away. Between 1829 and 1845, the bank had taken in $2,103,-500 and paid out $1,423,500, much of it in the girls' earnings. The girls used this money for their own dowries; they lifted mortgages from fathers' farms; they supported fatherless nephews, nieces, and cousins; and, apparently not infrequently, they put brothers through college.

Francis Cabot Lowell

But what counted was not whether the girls spent their pay on ribbons and shawls or saved it for the future. What counted was that as women, they had money of their own. This was an age when a woman's property was still in the absolute control of her husband, and when the single or widowed woman who did not choose to become a seamstress or a housemaid lived on family charity. Another of those literate mill girls, Harriet Hanson Robinson, summed up the advantages of having one's own income:

The law took no cognizance of woman as a money-spender. She was a ward, an appendage, a relict. Thus it happened, that if a woman did not choose to marry, or, when left a widow, to re-marry, she had no choice but to enter one of the few employments open to her, or to become a burden on the charity of some relative. . . . The cotton-factory was a great opening to these lonely and dependent women. . . . At last they had found a place in the universe; they were no longer obliged to finish out their faded lives mere burdens to male relatives. . . . For the first time in this country woman's labor had a money value. . . . And thus a long upward step in our material civilization was taken; woman had begun to earn and hold her own money, and through its aid had learned to think and to act for herself.

Harriet remembered what a blessing the factory was to those unhappy and lonely older women who sat in New England chimney corners, meekly enduring the teasing of the children, the gruffness of the men, and the sharpness of female in-laws who had kitchens and hearthsides of their own. Some went into the factories, and

. . . after the first pay-day came, and they felt the jingle of silver in their pockets, and had begun to feel its mercurial influence, their bowed heads were lifted, their necks seemed braced with steel, they looked you in the face, sang blithely among their looms or frames, and walked with elastic step to and from work.

To talk of wage slavery to such women was futile; to them the factory gates had opened the way to independence.

When work was done, the girls returned to the boardinghouses. They were usually two or three story frame buildings, standing in neat rows separated from the factory by squares of greenery. They were run by older women, often widows like Mrs. Larcom, or like the mothers of Nathaniel Banks and Benjamin F. Butler, both of whom were to become Massachusetts political leaders and Civil War generals. The houses had kitchens attached in the back, dining rooms and parlors on the ground floor, and bedrooms in which two or four girls roomed together.

They did not seem to regard that a hardship. Companionship, as a matter of fact, took the sting out of initial homesickness. Harriet Robinson remembered how the wagons which had gone into the back country to recruit would pull up before a boardinghouse and discharge a cluster of farm girls, followed by a pile of neat, small trunks, often bound in home-tanned, spotted calfskin on which the hair still showed. The new arrivals would gaze wide-eyed and white-faced at the huge buildings, the crowds, and the rushing canal. As an old woman, Harriet still recalled one girl with a large tear in each eye, pathetically clutching a bandbox on which the name "Plumy Clay" was carefully lettered.

Yet after a few weeks in which Plumy and Samantha and Keziah and Elgardy and Leafy and Ruhamah had come to be friends, it all seemed rather adventuresome. The girls chatted in their rooms in the evening, or sometimes read to each other from books that might have been found on the shelves of any middle-class home of the period. There were such "holy" works as Baxter's *Saints' Rest,* and *Pilgrim's Progress,* of course, but in addition, such popular (and less uplifting) novels as *Charlotte Temple, The Castle of Otranto,* and *The Mysteries of Udolpho.* On the table in the parlor were the newspapers to which the girls jointly sub-scribed—religious sheets like the *Christian Register, Christian Herald,* and *Signs of the Times,* abolitionist journals such as *The Liberator* and *Herald of Freedom,* and ordinary dailies like the *Boston Daily Times.* The mill girls read and discussed the contents of these organs of opinion, and debated among themselves the fads and fancies of the yeasty 1830's and 1840's—phrenology, mesmerism, Grahamism, Fourierism. One boardinghouse even contained a Mormon Bible!

Undoubtedly it was only a small number of the girls who were grimly intellectual, but they gave a tone to the entire enterprise. They were the ones who went to lectures at the lyceum in Lowell, and solemnly took note of the pearls of wisdom that fell from the lips of John Quincy Adams, Edward Everett, Ralph Waldo Emerson, John Greenleaf Whittier, and the other gods of New England. They were the girls who took books into the factories, and later, when this was tabooed, pasted pages of newspaper poetry to their looms and frames and memorized as they worked. Some girls felt that the Bible ought to be exempt from the rule, and brought their pocket Testaments to work, creating a nice problem for pious overseers. Under the rules, they had to confiscate all literature discovered, but it went hard for some to wrest the Scriptures from a girl. "I did think," said one of them ruefully to a victim of such a seizure, "you had more conscience than to bring that book in here." One group of these "factory ladies," relentlessly bent upon improving each shining hour, flabbergasted Charles Dickens (who visited Lowell in 1841) by clubbing together to buy a piano for their boardinghouse parlor. The novelist was not merely confounded by such a genteel instrument in what was, after all, a home for "working-class" women, but he shared the amazement which a modern reader must feel that girls who worked a fourteen-hour day could be interested in anything more taxing in the evening than climbing wearily into bed.

Perhaps the most astonishing fact of all was that some of the girls, after a dawn-to-dusk session in the mill, not only found time to read literature, but to make it. Some of the ministers whose congregations included a sprinkling of highly literate mill girls had taken the lead in forming "improvement circles" as early as 1838. At the meetings of these groups—as in the literary clubs of the colleges of that day—members read their own compositions to each other for mutual criticism. The Reverend Abel Thomas, of Lowell's First Universalist Church, gradually accumulated a drawerful of essays, short stories, and poems by the members of his "circle." Enthused by what he read, he raised enough money to issue a collection of the pieces in a pamphlet entitled *The Lowell Offering.* Some of the money came from the company, which sensed the publicity value of the scheme, in the form of a large order for copies.

Having still more material on hand, Thomas undertook to edit the *Offering* as a regular periodical. Four numbers appeared in 1840 and 1841. Meanwhile an "improvement circle" in the First Congregationalist Church had independently launched an *Operatives' Magazine*. In 1842 the Reverend Mr. Thomas turned the editorship of the *Offering* over completely to two of the millworkers, Harriot F. Curtis and Harriet Farley. Presumably, he wanted to prove once and for all that the "operatives" could write, edit, and publish a magazine entirely under their own power. The two women merged the *Lowell Offering* and *Operatives' Magazine*, and managed to run it for five volumes. It finally died, as conditions began to change in Lowell, and a few efforts to revive it under other titles failed.

The *Lowell Offering* was by no means the cream of American periodical literature of the mid-nineteenth century. Yet it was an incredible production to emerge from a factory working force. It contained, Harriet Robinson recalled, "allegories, poems, conversations on physiology, astronomy, and other scientific subjects, dissertations on poetry, and on the beauties of nature, didactic pieces on highly moral and religious subjects, translations from French and Latin, stories of factory and other life, sketches of local New England history, and sometimes chapters of a novel." The poetry was in the mold of popular female bards of the period like Lydia Sigourney; the prose had overtones of Addison, Goldsmith, and the briskly selling lady novelist, Lydia Maria Child. The fifty-seven girls who contributed to it chose pen names as far from "Harriet," "Lucy," "Abby," and "Sarah" as they could get—"Ella," "Adelaide," "Aramantha," "Oriana," "Dolly Dindle," and "Grace Gayfeather." Two or three of the contributors continued as writers in later life; others became missionaries, schoolteachers, and suffragettes, and at least one—Margaret Foley—was a successful sculptor.

All of this was a long way from the factory slums of Birmingham and Manchester, which, in those very 1840's, were furnishing ammunition for the assaults on capitalism of Engels and Marx. The girls were aware of their uniqueness, and in the brief moments between sleep and work they undertook their mental cultivation proudly and self-consciously. They were, in their own eyes, pioneers, demonstrating that "woman" could be independent, that "manual labor" could be combined with character and intellect, and that the "impossible" concept of a highly educated working class was realizable in the United States. *They* knew that in their dignity and pride they were the equals of the capitalists who employed them, whatever their in-

comes. Their writing and poetizing and piano playing were meant to prove, as Lucy Larcom said, that "honest work has no need to assert itself or to humble itself in a nation like ours, but simply to take its place as one of the foundation-stones of the republic." At Brook Farm, not too far from Lowell, a number of better-educated men and women were conducting an experiment that was not too different. Pitching hay in the afternoons and reading Greek in the evenings in West Roxbury were ways of vindicating the dignity of labor, too.

And so, willingly, the girls accepted the discipline of the boardinghouses. They went to church regularly, were in by 10 P.M., avoided improper conduct and language, and shunned idle companions—all of which came to them easily enough. They were trying to make of their factory community "a rather select industrial school for young people," Lucy Larcom wrote in 1889. And then she added, proudly: "The girls were just such girls as are knocking at the doors of young women's colleges today."

So there was Lowell in 1845 at its high noon, and whether the credit belonged to the tariff or American democracy or creative capital or the frontier or Jehovah who smiled upon America was hard to say. It was not really typical of the growing factory system. But all observers agreed that it was a sight to admire. President Jackson visited Lowell in June of 1833, and rode under triumphal arches amid a procession of drums, militiamen, citizens, schoolchildren, and 2,500 of the factory girls, carrying parasols and wearing stockings of silk. Reputedly Jackson swore that "by the Eternal," they were pretty women. Congressman Crockett of Tennessee came the next year, and if we can believe the statement in the largely fraudulent *Autobiography* ghostwritten for him, found the girls "well-dressed, lively, and genteel," looking as if "they were coming from a quilting frolic." Henry Clay came to beam at the success, in 1834, of the domestic manufactures whose protection he had so long and eloquently advocated.

Charles Dickens, as late as 1841, found that the whole city still had a fresh, new appearance (except for the mud). Its shiny buildings looked like those of a cardboard toy town, fresh out of the wrappings. He inspected the factories, he watched the girls at work, and he carried off four hundred pages of the *Offering* to read. Dickens disliked industrialism, and at that time he disliked the United States. He would have been glad, undoubtedly, to pour a little humanitarian spite on an exploitative American industrialism. But after looking long and hard, he declared: "I cannot recall or separate one young face that gave me a painful impression; not one young girl whom, assuming it to be a matter of necessity that she should gain her daily bread by the labour of her hands, I would have removed from those works if I had had the power."

In another twenty years Dickens' thoughts might have been different. For shortly after that first visit of his, Lowell began to decline. The cotton factories moved away from the golden day, toward the era of Lawrence, the Pemberton Mill disasters, and bitterness.

The change came gradually, but even in the heyday a sharp eye might have seen the warning signals going up. There was, to begin with, an iron streak in the companies' paternalism. Their control of the force was as rigid as that of any army. Girls who quit "properly," giving their employer two weeks' notice, received an "honorable discharge" (the very words entered on company records) signed by their superintendent. Not a single mill would hire an experienced worker without such a discharge, which meant that a girl who was

Cotton-weaving looms had been improved by 1857, when this engraving appeared in The Family Christian Almanac, *but the lives of the mill girls had become harder. Few had time —or permission—to tend flower pots on the window sills.*

fired, or left for any reason not approved by her employers, was barred from factory work for good. It also meant that there was no competitive bidding among bosses, and no way of improving conditions, therefore, except as the bosses chose. And since the companies did not hesitate to discharge girls who received bad conduct reports from the boardinghouse matrons, their "stewardship" sometimes became a kind of punitive spying into the employees' personal lives.

As the bloom wore off the noble experiment, there were murmurs of discontent. Fourteen hours of daily indoor work, broken only for two hastily gulped meals, took some of the spring out of the millworkers. Those whose health broke down could enter a company-built hospital, but had to pay three dollars a week for the privilege, and often emerged with a heavy debt to be worked off. The hardy few who had energy left to enjoy the "advantages" of the boardinghouses began to leave. Labor reformer Seth Luther sardonically compared those who remained to the horse of a hardfisted farmer, who explained that his animal had "a bushel and a half of oats, *only he ain't got no time to eat 'em.*" Luther, and others like him, resented the corporation owners' growing sense of superiority, however patriarchal it might be. A small but articulate labor press denounced the "mushroom aristocracy of New England, who so arrogantly aspire to lord it over God's heritage."

The real sin of the mushroom aristocrats, however, was nothing so impalpable as an attitude. The truth was that as early as 1836, in the face of growing competition, they began to cut costs at the expense of the workers. In that year the wages of the Lowell mill girls were reduced by a dollar each week. Some 1,500 girls staged a "turn out" in protest. It was a decorous enough affair: they walked through the streets waving their handkerchiefs and singing a parody of a popular tune:

Oh! isn't it a pity, such a pretty girl as I—
Should be sent to the factory to pine away and die?
Oh! I cannot be a slave,
I will not be a slave,
For I'm so fond of liberty
That I cannot be a slave.

It was charming, intelligent, and utterly futile. The companies did not restore the cuts—then or later. In addition, they began to increase the number of frames and looms each girl had to watch, and then to overcrowd the boardinghouses, assigning as many as eight to a room. The operatives began, after all, to look like the washed-out and exhausted creatures of Jefferson's most dire predictions.

For the girls who had come on the scene early, of course, there was the option of going home. That appealed to them even more than striking, which had an unladylike and un-Christian character about it, hardly becoming to the virtuous daughters of independent yeomen. They would return to the farm until the owners, short of hands, saw reason. In time, the girls believed, they must see it, for in America there was no "irrepressible conflict" between capital and labor.

So the more aggressive and independent girls drifted

away from Lowell. But the owners were not concerned with the problem of replacements. For in the 1840's a mighty tide of immigration was setting in, much of it Irish. A few of Erin's sons had been in Lowell in Lucy Larcom's day—some six hundred in 1835—living with their large families in shanties on the town's fringe. Sometimes on their way to work Lucy and her friends would toss a slice of boardinghouse bread to an elderly Irishwoman in order to elicit a musical flood of grateful brogue.

There was nothing quaint about the effect of the Irish on the labor market, however. By 1860 they constituted nearly half the population of Lowell. There were no friendly farms to which *they* could retreat when conditions worsened. The roofs that they could call their own were in Lowell only, and they were not the decent roofs of the boardinghouses, but overcrowded, jerry-built, or decaying homes. The companies were spared the expense of boardinghouses in this way, a point not lost upon them. And the millowners did not worry especially about the "moral character" of their Hibernian operatives, being quite willing to leave that to the priests and the police.

While the labor force thus changed, so did the nature of the owning group. The new ownership was well represented by a man like Amos Lawrence, ancestor of many pious churchmen, whose name was bestowed on a new mill town on the Merrimack, built up in the 1840's. Lawrence was a nonsmoker and nondrinker who demanded the same abstinence of his male employees. Plagued with stomach trouble, he dined briefly and frugally on watery gruel, and he was not a man to listen sympathetically to complaints that a worker's salary did not buy an adequate diet. Reproached by some critics with his great wealth, he is said to have snarled: "There is one thing you may as well understand; I know how to make money, and *you* cannot prevent it." There was something hard here that made the older, paternalistic, nationalistic outlook of the founders of Waltham seem archaic. The difference between Lawrence and Lowell, the towns, was something like the difference between Lawrence and Lowell, the men.

In addition, as stockholding in the corporations finally became a little more widespread, the personal link between owner and worker was snapped. The original Boston promoters had been drawn from the same Yankee stock as the mill hands. But the difference between a Boston attorney with a few shares of Suffolk Manufacturing Company in his safe, and Bridget Doyle at her spinning frame, was more than one of money. It was a gap between ways of life and understanding. Moreover, as some stock passed into the hands of guardians and estate administrators, company treasurers were at last able to invoke piously the interests of widows and orphans, as they maintained dividends while slashing wages and stretching out tasks.

Through the 1850's the labor scene darkened as industry spread through the nation. Prices rose in response to gold strikes and industrial booms, but wages remained at ancient levels. Factory workers struck more frequently—and were more frequently replaced by immigrant strikebreakers. Some leaders, despairing of direct action by labor, turned to state legislatures and petitioned for laws restricting the hours of labor and the employment of women and children. Some small gains were made in legislative cutting of the work burden of children under twelve, but most "ten-hour" legislation proposed in New England in the fifties died in the state capitals. The slogans of progress which had justified the beginnings of Waltham and Lowell now rang out to justify a *status quo* maintained at the price of increasing bitterness.

So it was that in 1860 something more than a single defectively built factory lay in ruins in Lawrence. In all New England there was evidence that the United States was going to have to find another way toward justice for labor—was going to have to walk the long road through decades of violence, organization, degradation, cruelty, bitterness, and protest, before the light would dawn again. The short cut to Utopia had run into a dead end, and Lowell was not, as it turned out, the harbinger of a perfect, harmonious, and just industrial society, in which a "circulating current" of laborers gained bread, education, and stature at the machines. It was not the only utopian experiment of the Jacksonian era to fail. Like the others, it remains in American history as a memory, the surviving token of a lost innocence that believed in the impossible, and for a few short hours in a simpler time, seemed to make it work.

The First Great Cheerful Giver

George Peabody made fourteen million dollars and gave
nine million away — with no tax deductions to urge him on

By GEOFFREY T. HELLMAN

In a day when it is no secret that the very rich can, and do, practice philanthropy at bargain rates— about nine cents on the dollar, or, by a judicious transfer of stocks, paintings, or incunabula, bought cheap and appraised dear, at no cents on the dollar; or, indeed, with even better luck, at a profit—it requires a historical perspective to understand the mood in which the Western world reacted to the death in London of George Peabody on November 4, 1869. As a man who began to combine large-scale acquisition with large-scale distribution in the 1850's, Peabody was the first great American philanthropist. At a time when the Astors, far richer than he, were giving little away, he was disposing of millions. Peter Cooper, to be sure, built and endowed The Cooper Union "for the advancement of science and art" during this decade, but his total bill was $900,000—a fraction of Peabody's benefactions. Peabody munificently founded free libraries, museums, lecture halls, and musical conservatories, and he established the country's first true foundation—the Peabody Education Fund, which helped put southern education on its feet after the Civil War. In the view of the late Dr. Abraham Flexner, an expert on funds and foundations, it was "the pioneer [fund] in the United States in combining private and unofficial with public and official endeavor. . . . To a considerable extent [it] determined the course that future educational benefactions would take." It was after a conversation with Peabody on the pleasures of giving money away that Johns Hopkins made out a will leaving seven million dollars for a university and hospital. The trail that Peabody blazed was later followed, more lavishly but relatively no more generously, by Mrs. Russell Sage, Andrew Carnegie, Julius Rosenwald, the Fords, the Guggenheims, and the Rockefellers.

George Peabody was born in 1795 in South Danvers, Massachusetts, nineteen miles north of Boston, toward the end of an astrological period—on February 18— that all fellow Aquarians (socially minded, eager to improve the lot of the human race) will recognize as appropriate. During his lifetime, out of a fortune of approximately fourteen million dollars, he gave away some nine million for public purposes—without, of course, a penny of tax deduction for his largesse. He had made a great deal of his money in England, where

Few hometown-boys-made-good ever came back to such a fever of adulation as Danvers, Massachusetts, worked up in 1856 when favorite son George Peabody returned to visit after spending twenty years and earning several million dollars elsewhere. The lithographs on the preceding page, framing a photograph of the philanthropist, suggest the occasion's plethora of parades, wreaths, arches, dinners, and speeches.

he lived for the last three decades of his life, and he gave a great deal of it away in England; but he also gave much away in America, which he continued to think of as his home, never relinquishing his American citizenship.

The Peabody benefactions were not only generous; they were thoughtfully planned and thoughtfully set up. Stemming from principle rather than impulse, they were calculated to help people help themselves and to prevent poverty rather than cure it. And they were executed by able men, chosen by the founder. In England, for example, the early trustees of the £500,-000 Peabody Donation Fund—established to build homes for the poor in London—included Charles Francis Adams, the American minister to Great Britain; Lord Stanley, the Postmaster General; and Junius Spencer Morgan, a Peabody partner in London who was the father of the first John Pierpont Morgan. In America, where the Peabody Education Fund had to work in a war-torn area sensitive to northerners, the Fund's original trustees were drawn from North and South alike and included General Grant, Admiral Farragut, and the governors of New York, Massachusetts, Virginia, and South Carolina. Among successor trustees were Presidents Hayes, Cleveland, McKinley, and Theodore Roosevelt; J. P. Morgan, Anthony J. Drexel, Joseph H. Choate, and Bishop William Lawrence of Massachusetts. The Fund's first general agent, or administrator, was Dr. Barnas Sears, who relinquished the presidency of Brown University to assume this post, and of whom the *Dictionary of American Biography* reports:

His inauguration of the work for which the Fund was devised was perhaps the most important achievement of his career. The specific recommendations regarding the ends to be sought and the methods to be employed contained in his first report became the stereotyped policy of the trustees. In carrying it out Sears met a difficult and delicate situation with a patience, tact, and wisdom that won confidence and support in the South and ensured success.

The emphasis on housing and education of Peabody's two major single philanthropies may well have reflected the fact that their author, in his youth, was poorly housed and modestly educated. He was born in a two-story, four-room, yellow frame house on the outskirts of South Danvers, the third son and fourth child (in a family of five boys and five girls) of Thomas and Judith Dodge Peabody. Although the family name was well known in New England, little is recorded of his father beyond the fact that he had fought in the Revolution. The boy who was to give $2,000,000 to southern education, $150,000 to Yale, $150,000 to

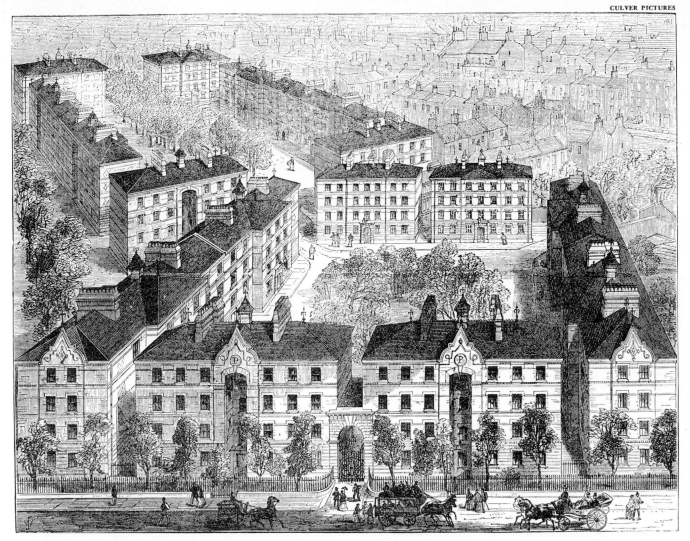

The Peabody Square model dwellings, generously built for "the laboring poor of London," were a private prototype for the public low-rent housing projects that in modern times have become familiar urban features both abroad and in America.

Harvard, $60,000 to Washington College (now Washington and Lee), $25,000 to Phillips Academy (Andover), and $25,000 to Kenyon College, attended district school between the ages of seven and eleven, where he did badly in arithmetic and well in penmanship. He was then apprenticed by his father to the neighboring general store of a Captain Sylvester Proctor, where four years of handling groceries and dry goods and bartering them for farm produce netted him thirty dollars and a suit of clothes. His next three business connections were still far from Rothschildian. At fifteen he worked for a year on the Vermont farm of Jeremiah Dodge, his maternal grandfather, performing such chores as clearing hillsides of sumac trees; the following year, 1811, he joined his brother David, twice his age, in a newly opened dry-goods store in Newburyport, Massachusetts. Shortly thereafter their father died, leaving their mother and several small

children to support; the store was destroyed that same year in a great Newburyport fire; and George, at seventeen, moved on to Georgetown, in the District of Columbia, to clerk in another family dry-goods store, that of an uncle, John Peabody. Uncle John had already gone bankrupt once in the business; creditors were after him, and he installed his nephew, partly as a cover, as titular head of the business. In this reverse nepotism, George flourished. Within two years he was running the store, but his uncle's situation made him apprehensive. In 1814, when Elisha Riggs, a successful competitor in the District, suggested a merger, George accepted. He had saved a little over a thousand dollars, which he invested in Riggs & Peabody, but if the capital was largely Elisha's, the business genius was largely George's. The firm began to export southern cotton to England and import finished goods to the United States. In 1815 it moved to Baltimore to acquire ship-

121

ping facilities, and in 1822 it established branches in Philadelphia and New York. It was by this time a supplier of credit to facilitate the movement of cargoes by others. Peabody made his first trip to London in 1827. Two years later Riggs retired, leaving his partner in sole charge and well on his way toward a typical nineteenth-century American business metamorphosis—that of dry-goods merchant into banker.

This metamorphosis subsequently exemplified in the careers of Henry Clews, Levi P. Morton, Junius Spencer Morgan, and the founding partners of J. & W. Seligman and Company and Kuhn, Loeb and Company—was dramatically highlighted in 1835. The state of Maryland, in severe financial trouble, appointed Peabody as one of three commissioners to negotiate loans. The merchant went to London and sold $8,000,000 worth of state bonds there, thus maintaining Maryland's credit and upping his own. He refused a $60,000 commission and received a vote of thanks from the state legislature.

In 1837, the now-prosperous Peabody took the step that was to qualify him, geographically, for an impressive collection of British honors. He moved to London, where under the sign of George Peabody & Company he began to specialize in foreign exchange and American securities. The Panic of 1837 found him a heavy buyer of depreciated bonds of the American states at what turned out to be bargain rates. During the next few years, his firm became the leader in trading American securities in Europe and the house on which American letters of credit were most generally drawn. Meanwhile, Peabody himself became a kind of unofficial American ambassador. In 1851, when a World's Fair was scheduled at the Crystal Palace in London, Congress made no appropriation for the American exhibitors. Peabody personally advanced the $15,000 needed to fit up galleries and arcades for the display of Colt's revolver, McCormick's reaper, Hoe's printing press, Hobbs' unpickable lock, Bond's spring governor, and Hiram Powers' famous statue of *The Greek Slave*. A mortified Congress later paid him back.

On each Fourth of July, Peabody gave a British-American banquet graced by such consequential guests as the octogenarian Duke of Wellington. His offices, well-furnished with American newspapers and magazines, became headquarters for travellers from the United States. One of them, described anonymously as "an American writer in London," had this to say about Peabody's habits of entertainment:

During 1851 Mr. Peabody commenced inviting to dinner every person who brought a letter of credit on his house. The thing had been unknown heretofore. He showed to the stranger particular attentions. A day or two after his arrival there was a polite note of invitation to dinner at the 'Star and Garter' or to a Sunday's fete at Hampton Court, or to a sail on the Thames, or, at least, to an 'At Home' at Club Chambers . . .

At the head of the dinner-table, as the host of the numerous fetes given at Richmond Hill, Blackwall, and Hampton Court, in his spacious suite of apartments at Club Chambers, or among guests at his extemporized pleasure-parties, Mr. Peabody was one of the most genial of men. . . . Where the Duke [of Wellington] went all could go. It [the July 4, 1851 dinner] was without exaggeration the affair of the season. Mr. Peabody spared no expense. Lablache, Alboni and Grisi, lent the concert the aid of their voices; duchesses waltzed with Governors of States, and members of Parliament flirted with Massachusetts belles, long past the small hours of the night; newspapers chronicled the wonderful success of the rich American's banquet; and on the morning of July 5, 1851, George Peabody's name was in the mouths of half the kingdom.

It was during this period of increasing fame, as his capital was rising into the millions, that Peabody became aware of an occupational problem: what to do with his money. He never married; a story, possibly apocryphal, has it that he carried a lifelong torch for a Providence girl, who, travelling in Europe with friends, met him and became engaged to him, only to jilt him for a former fiancé. His habits, other than those connected with business entertainment, were frugal. He carried his lunch to his office in two small tin boxes, and when not with clients he dined, by preference, in cheap chophouses. He liked to fish, to play whist and backgammon, to sing Scottish songs, and to talk. He employed a valet only during the last year of his life, when he was ill and feeble. During most of the 1860's, when his income was more than $300,000 a year, he drew only one per cent, $3,000, for

Harper's Weekly, NOVEMBER 3, 1866

A gold snuff box was presented to Peabody by the Mayor and Citizens of London— perhaps with the thought that it might bring frequent blessings upon its owner.

personal expenses. He helped support an army of poor relatives, but the surplus remained alarming. He hit upon philanthropy as the answer to the problem.

For Peabody, charity began at home. In the summer of 1852, when he was invited to the centennial celebration of the severance of the town of Danvers from Salem, he was too busy to show up; but he sent the centennial committee $20,000, to which he later added $230,000 more, to establish a Peabody Institute. This opened in 1854 with a museum, lecture hall, and library, and Peabody visited it two years later, on his first trip to America in nineteen years. A lavish welcome awaited him. Contemporary lithographs depict grand processions of silk-hatted citizens, an Institute inscribed "Dedicated to Knowledge and Morality," and other local buildings and triumphal arches bearing banners inscribed with such devices as "Danvers Welcomes Her Favorite Son," "Danvers Welcomes a Nation's Guest," "Honor to Him, Who Loves to Honor His Country," "A Friend at Home and Abroad," and "George Peabody Respected and Honoured on Both Sides of the Atlantic." A reception was held, followed by a dinner for fifteen hundred, at which, if we can believe the erratically spelled bill of fare, more than fifty dishes were served, namely:

Boiled: Mutton, Caper Sauce. Turkey, Oyster Sauce. Chickens, Celery Sauce. Saltpetred Beef. Ham. Tongue.
Roast: Turkeys. Geese. Chickens. Ducks. Lamb. Beef. Pigs.
Entrees: Potted Pigeons. Beef á la mode. Chicken Salad. Stewed Oysters. Brazed Tongue. Escalloped Oysters. Lobster Salad. Chicken Mayornase.
Game: Black Ducks. Widgeons. Teal. Red Head Ducks.
Pastry: Charlotte Russe. Tipsey Cake. Chess Cake. Cream Cake. Glacee Pudin. Custard Pudding. Washington Pies. Pies of various kinds. Cake of all kinds.
Ice Cream: Vanilla. Pine Apple. Lemon. Strawberry. Sherbet. Punch.
Fruit: Oranges. Raisins. Apples. Peaches. Pears. Grapes. Melons. English Walnuts. Almonds. Pecan Nuts.
Table Ornaments: Tea. Coffee.

These were downed to the accompaniment of thirteen speeches (including one by Peabody); one song of welcome, rendered by a relative of the guest of honor—Mrs. Joel R. Peabody, who started out, *Welcome! illustrious friend and guest! / Aye, more than welcome here, / And be the day forever blessed / That brings back one so dear;* two odes, sung by other ladies; and a score of toasts, commencing with one to Rufus Choate ("An adopted son of old Danvers") and moving with great sweep to King Alfred, Bacon, Shakespeare, and Milton ("They are ours by inheritance. Our share in their glory is that of brotherhood with the elder branch of the family").

The Favorite Son bore up admirably. "Mr. Peabody appeared in our streets the next morning, apparently as fresh and vigorous as usual," a published account of the proceedings states. "He made personal inquiry and observation of all matters relating to the Institute, examining the Treasurer's books."

Thus awakened to the pleasures of philanthropy, the banker went on to revisit Baltimore and to present *it* with a Peabody Institute. His initial gift was $300,000, which he eventually increased to $1,500,000. His founding letter to the trustees called for an extensive library; a lyceum for lectures on science, art, and literature; a "Gallery of Art in the department of Painting and Statuary"; an Academy of Music with "a capacious and suitably furnished saloon" (today the Peabody Conservatory of Music); and "ample and convenient accommodation for the use of the Maryland Historical Society." Peabody was a practical man of his time, and his letter reveals a double standard of rewards as applied to the sexes. It provided for an annual grant of $1,200, of which $500 was to be awarded in cash prizes of from $50 to $100 each to "graduates of public Male High Schools adjudged most worthy, from their fidelity to their studies, their attainments, their moral deportment, their personal habits of cleanliness and propriety of manners"; $200 was set aside for ten $10 gold medals and twenty $5 gold medals to reward female high-school graduates for similar virtues. The remaining $500 was to be given to meritorious School of Design graduates of the Mechanics Institute of Baltimore. The Institute itself, Peabody's third biggest single benefaction, was completed in 1861 but the Civil War postponed its opening until 1866. Its treasurer was Enoch Pratt, a wholesale-iron millionaire who, like Johns Hopkins, became a philanthropic disciple of Peabody's. In the 1880's, he presented the city of Baltimore with a $1,000,000 Pratt Free Library.

During the Civil War, Peabody invested some $9,000,000 in Union bonds. Although his influence in Great Britain was on the side of neutrality, his early days in the South had left him without animus. "Never during the War or since," he said when it was over, "have I permitted the contest or any passions engendered by it to interfere with the social relations and warm friendships which I have formed for a very large number of the people of the South." His establishment of the Peabody Education Fund in 1867 was influenced by this regional interest. He had retired from business in 1864, when he turned George Peabody & Company over to its younger partner, Junius Spencer Morgan, who changed its name to J. S. Morgan & Company. Morgan's son John Pierpont had worked in the Peabody firm for a year in 1856; and *his* subsequent banking houses in New York presently acted as the American representatives of J. S. Morgan.

Thus the man who gave J. P. Morgan his first job and whose bank was the progenitor of the House of Morgan was close to seventy when, for the first time in his life, he was free to act as a full-time humanitarian. Actuated by the postwar impoverishment of the southern states, the concomitant collapse of education there, and the pressing needs of the emancipated slaves, and particularly their children. Peabody set up the Education Fund "for the promotion and encouragement of intellectual, moral, or industrial education among the young of the more destitute portions of the Southern and Southwestern States of our Union." It was endowed on the books with $3,500,000, but $1,500,000 of this was invested in Mississippi and Florida state bonds that never paid their coupons and were eventually repudiated. It divided its income between the promotion of free public schools and the professional training of teachers. It awarded scholarships in all the southern states (those in Mississippi and Florida were withheld until 1892), and in 1875 it created the State Normal College in Nashville, Tennessee, which in 1889 became the Peabody Normal College and in 1905 the George Peabody College for Teachers. The founder had stipulated that the Fund might be terminated after thirty years; actually, it continued for forty-seven, until 1914. Its residue was divided, unequally, between the George Peabody College and the John F. Slater Fund, set up in 1882 for industrial education for Negroes—the Slater Fund got $350,000 and Peabody College got $1,500,000, to which the Rockefeller-founded General Education Board afterward added many millions. "Of all [Peabody's] gifts," President Calvin Coolidge wrote in 1926, "the most remarkable was the Peabody Education Fund. . . . George Peabody, who has been called 'the father of modern educational philanthropy' . . . was a pioneer. He blazed the trail. He pointed out the path."

Queen Victoria might have challenged the first part of this statement. Was the Education Fund any more remarkable than the £500,000 Donation Fund, established in 1862 for the purpose of slum clearance and "the building of lodging-houses for the laboring poor of London"? Several blocks of buildings were erected and the laboring poor invited in at an average room rental of two shillings sixpence a week. "The London press with one accord proclaimed the gift as unparalleled in the history of the world," the Reverend O. S. Butler observed in 1895, at a centennial celebration of Peabody's birth. "The whole nation joined in a chorus of praise and thanksgiving, from the throne to the poorest hamlet in the realm. The children of poverty clapped their bony fingers and shook their emaciated forms with wild delight, to realize that one man was found that remembered the poor. In our own country the news was received with unmingled satisfaction."

In England, after one hundred years, Peabody's charitable project still flourishes. Today London's Donation Fund, with a capitalization of nearly £3,000,000 and a board of governors headed by Sir Charles J. Hambro of Hambros Bank, runs five thousand flats inhabited by some eighteen thousand tenants, ranging, according to a recent annual report, from bagmakers, brewers' men, and costermongers to lamplighters and needlewomen.

There were other Peabody benefactions which, while relatively minor, grew to be exceedingly fruitful. A fine example was the $150,000 that he gave to Yale. This founded the Peabody Museum of Natural History, the leading institution of its kind in New England. During its first quarter-century it was run by Professor Othniel Charles Marsh, a nephew of Peabody's who had persuaded his uncle to put up the money for it. Marsh, whom Peabody generously supported far beyond Yale's judicious stipends, was a pioneer in vertebrate paleontology. Thanks to his discoveries and vast collections in this field, gathered chiefly in the western states, "The Peabody's" accumulations of fossil vertebrates are extraordinary to this day. If the uncle had no other memorial, the nephew's

The Peabody Institute in Baltimore, opened in 1866, offered the public a library, a lecture hall, an art gallery, and an academy of music, plus the funds to keep them going.

museum would suffice. As early as 1868, when it had been paid for but not yet built, George T. Dole, a Yale man of the 1830's, delivered before the Phi Beta Kappa Society of Yale College an original poem, "Yale Revisited," in which he anticipated *A grand Museum, where, in bright array,/The Cabinets their rich stores shall display* and went on to immortalize its founder.

> *But who the rich Maecenas that supplies*
> *Funds, this idea to fitly realize?*
> *One whom no College ever graduated,*
> *Nor classic institution cultivated:*
> *From a New England common school sent forth,*
> *He stands, at length, with magnates of the earth,*
> *A prince of merchant princes; aye, a prince*
> *Of the high order of beneficence.*
>
> * * * * * *
>
> *Let all the rich, who mean, when they shall die,*
> *To do great things by way of legacy,*
> *How to make sure a worthy end, and see,*
> *And taste the pleasure, learn of PEABODY.*

It was only a year later that the "prince of merchant princes" was himself dead, having by that time seen and tasted the pleasure of a great many of his good works. He had also been suitably rewarded with much esteem and praise in high places, perhaps even more notably in England than in the United States. Congress had ordered a medal struck in his honor in 1868; but Queen Victoria had offered him a baronetcy (which he refused), and had presented him with a miniature enamel portrait of Her Majesty wearing the Koh-i-noor Diamond, the Order of the Garter, and a jewelled cross given her by Prince Albert. It was inscribed, "Presented by the Queen to Geo. Peabody, Esq., the Benefactor of the Poor of London," and it is said to have cost its donor $70,000. There was also a statue of Peabody, unveiled by the Prince of Wales in 1869 on Threadneedle Street, in the heart of the London financial district.

Peabody was given three impressive funerals, and—elaborately embalmed—spent over three months between deathbed and grave. During the first of these obsequies, held in Westminster Abbey, London shopkeepers lowered their blinds and closed up shop. The mourners included Prime Minister William Gladstone, and an obituary sermon was delivered by the Bishop of London. After thirty days of lying in state in the Abbey, the body was transported to the United States, on the Queen's order, by Great Britain's newest and biggest warship, H.M.S. *Monarch*. There was some grumbling in America about the propriety of this. On the whole, however, it was taken as a gesture of Anglo-American friendship to relieve the tension caused by American reparation claims for the depredations of the British-built *Alabama* against Union ships during the Civil War. President Grant dispatched the U.S.S. *Plymouth* to accompany the *Monarch* as an escort, and on January 25, 1870, the two ships steamed into the harbor at Portland, Maine—chosen over Boston because its deeper channel could accommodate the big *Monarch*.

After several days of lying in sentinelled state at Portland's city hall, where services included a choral rendition from Handel's *Messiah* by 300 voices, Peabody's remains went by special train to Peabody, Massachusetts. (It was his old home town of South Danvers, which in 1868 had gratefully changed its name in honor of its famous son.) There was a flurry of excitement and controversy when it was rumored that Robert E. Lee (who had known Peabody briefly but fondly) might attend the final funeral there; but Lee was ill and sent his regrets—to the satisfaction of those who felt that a man like Lee had no ceremonial business north of the Mason-Dixon Line. But the young Prince Arthur, Queen Victoria's third son, who had recently come from a tour of Canada, appeared with his retinue for the ceremony, which took place in the South Congregational Church on February 8, after another week of lying in state—this time at the Peabody Institute Library. Numerous American dignitaries were also present: the governors of Massachusetts and Maine, mayors of half a dozen cities, the trustees of the Peabody benefactions from at least as many different other places. The first great American philanthropist had been an unconscionable time a-burying, but at length he was put to rest in a granite sarcophagus he himself had ordered six months before.

Among the elegies from well-known persons in various parts of the world there was one from Victor Hugo. "Yes," wrote the famous French author, "America has reason to be proud of this great citizen of the world and great brother of all men—George Peabody. . . . Like Jesus Christ, he had a wound in the side: this wound was the misery of others. It was not blood that flowed from this wound: it was gold which now came from a heart. . . . It is on the face of [such] men that we can see the smile of God." It was a tribute no doubt somewhat too Gallic in its expression for American taste, but the sentiment, nonetheless, seemed appropriate.

HOW THE FRONTIER SHAPED THE AMERICAN CHARACTER

By RAY ALLEN BILLINGTON

Since the dawn days of historical writing in the United States, historians have labored mightily, and usually in vain, to answer the famous question posed by Hector St. John de Crèvecœur in the eighteenth century: "What then is the American, this new man?" Was that composite figure actually a "new man" with unique traits that distinguished him from his Old World ancestors? Or was he merely a transplanted European? The most widely accepted—and bitterly disputed—answer was advanced by a young Wisconsin historian named Frederick Jackson Turner in 1893. The American was a new man, he held, who owed his distinctive characteristics and institutions to the unusual New World environment—characterized by the availability of free land and an ever-receding frontier —in which his civilization had grown to maturity. This environmental theory, accepted for a generation after its enunciation, has been vigorously attacked and vehemently defended during the past two decades. How has it fared in this battle of words? Is it still a valid key to the meaning of American history?

Turner's own background provides a clue to the answer. Born in Portage, Wisconsin, in 1861 of pioneer

TEXT CONTINUED ON PAGE 129

Although John Gast painted this canvas in 1872, twenty years before Turner's essay on the significance of the frontier, its theme might have sprung straight from the pages themselves. Here is Turner's procession of civilization—"the buffalo following the trail to the salt springs, the Indian, the fur-trader and hunter, the cattle raiser, the pioneer farmer."

Turner states his frontier theory: 1893

Excerpt from "The Significance of the Frontier in American History"

In a recent bulletin of the Superintendent of the Census for 1890 appear these significant words: "Up to and including 1880 the country had a frontier of settlement, but at present the unsettled area has been so broken into by isolated bodies of settlement that there can hardly be said to be a frontier line. In the discussion of its extent, its westward movement, etc., it can not, therefore, any longer have a place in the census reports." This brief official statement marks the closing of a great historic movement. Up to our own day American history has been in a large degree the history of the colonization of the Great West. The existence of an area of free land, its continuous recession, and the advance of American settlement westward, explain American development. . . .

[This] development has exhibited not merely advance along a single line, but a return to primitive conditions on a continually advancing frontier line, and a new development for that area. American social development has been continually beginning over again on the frontier. This perennial rebirth, this fluidity of American life, this expansion westward with its new opportunities, its continuous touch with the simplicity of primitive society, furnish the forces dominating American character. . . .

The frontier is the line of most rapid and effective Americanization. The wilderness masters the colonist. It finds him a European in dress, industries, tools, modes of travel, and thought. It takes him from the railroad car and puts him in a birch canoe. It strips off the garments of civilization and arrays him in the hunting shirt and the moccasin. It puts him in the log cabin of the Cherokee and Iroquois and runs an Indian palisade around him. Before long he has gone to planting Indian corn and plowing with a sharp stick; he shouts the war cry and takes the scalp in orthodox Indian fashion. In short, at the frontier the environment is at first too strong for the man. He must accept the conditions which it furnishes, or perish. . . . Little by little he transforms the wilderness, but the outcome is not the old Europe, not simply the development of Germanic germs. . . . The fact is, that here is a new product that is American. . . .

BROWN BROTHERS

Frederick Jackson Turner

The Atlantic frontier was compounded of fisherman, fur-trader, miner, cattle-raiser, and farmer. Excepting the fisherman, each type of industry was on the march toward the West, impelled by an irresistible attraction. Each passed in successive waves across the continent. Stand at the Cumberland Gap and watch the procession of civilization, marching single file—the buffalo following the trail to the salt springs, the Indian, the fur-trader and hunter, the cattle-raiser, the pioneer farmer—and the frontier has passed by. Stand at South Pass in the Rockies a century later and see the same procession with wider intervals between. . . .

The most important effect of the frontier has been in the promotion of democracy here and in Europe. . . . The frontier is productive of individualism. Complex society is precipitated by the wilderness into a kind of primitive organization based on the family. The tendency is anti-social. It produces antipathy to control, and particularly to any direct control. The tax-gatherer is viewed as a representative of oppression. . . . To the frontier the American intellect owes its striking characteristics. That coarseness and strength combined with acuteness and inquisitiveness; that practical, inventive turn of mind, quick to find expedients; that masterful grasp of material things, lacking in the artistic but powerful to effect great ends; that restless, nervous energy; that dominant individualism, working for good and for evil, and withal that buoyancy and exuberance which comes with freedom—these are traits of the frontier, or traits called out elsewhere because of the existence of the frontier. Since the days when the fleet of Columbus sailed into the waters of the New World, America has been another name for opportunity. . . . What the Mediterranean Sea was to the Greeks, breaking the bond of custom, offering new experiences, calling out new institutions and activities, that, and more, the ever retreating frontier has been to the United States directly, and to the nations of Europe more remotely. And now, four centuries from the discovery of America, at the end of a hundred years of life under the Constitution, the frontier has gone, and with its going has closed the first period of American history.

parents from upper New York state, he was reared in a land fringed by the interminable forest and still stamped with the mark of youth. There he mingled with pioneers who had trapped beaver or hunted Indians or cleared the virgin wilderness; from them he learned something of the free and easy democratic values prevailing among those who judged men by their own accomplishments rather than those of their ancestors. At the University of Wisconsin Turner's faith in cultural democracy was deepened, while his intellectual vistas were widened through contact with teachers who led him into that wonderland of adventure where scientific techniques were being applied to social problems, where Darwin's evolutionary hypothesis was awakening scholars to the continuity of progress, and where searchers after truth were beginning to realize the multiplicity of forces responsible for human behavior. The young student showed how well he had learned these lessons in his master's essay on "The Character and Influence of the Fur Trade in Wisconsin"; he emphasized the evolution of institutions from simple to complex forms.

From Wisconsin Turner journeyed to Johns Hopkins University, as did many eager young scholars of that day, only to meet stubborn opposition for the historical theories already taking shape in his mind. His principal professor, Herbert Baxter Adams, viewed mankind's development in evolutionary terms, but held that environment had no place in the equation; American institutions could be understood only as outgrowths of European "germs" that had originated among Teutonic tribes in the forests of medieval Germany. To Turner this explanation was unsatisfactory. The "germ theory" explained the similarities between Europe and America, but what of the many differences? This problem was still much in his mind when he returned to the University of Wisconsin as an instructor in 1889. In two remarkable papers prepared during the next few years he set forth his answer. The first, "The Significance of History," reiterated his belief in what historians call "multiple causation"; to understand man's complex nature, he insisted, one needed not only a knowledge of past politics, but a familiarity with social, economic, and cultural forces as well. The second, "Problems in American History," attempted to isolate those forces most influential in explaining the unique features of American development. Among these Turner believed that the most important was the need for institutions to "adapt themselves to the changes of a remarkably developing, expanding people."

This was the theory that was expanded into a fullblown historical hypothesis in the famous essay on "The Significance of the Frontier in American History," read at a conference of historians held in connection with the World Fair in Chicago in 1893. The differences between European and American civilization, Turner stated in that monumental work, were in part the product of the distinctive environment of the New World. The most unusual features of that environment were "the existence of an area of free land, its continuous recession, and the advance of American settlement westward." This free land served as a magnet to draw men westward, attracted by the hope of economic gain or adventure. They came as Europeans or easterners, but they soon realized that the wilderness environment was ill-adapted to the habits, institutions, and cultural baggage of the stratified societies they had left behind. Complex political institutions were unnecessary in a tiny frontier outpost; traditional economic practices were useless in an isolated community geared to an economy of self-sufficiency; rigid social customs were outmoded in a land where prestige depended on skill with the axe or rifle rather than on hereditary glories; cultural pursuits were unessential in a land where so many material tasks awaited doing. Hence in each pioneer settlement there occurred a rapid reversion to the primitive. What little government was necessary was provided by simple associations of settlers; each man looked after his family without reliance on his fellows; social hierarchies disintegrated, and cultural progress came to a halt. As the newcomers moved backward along the scale of civilization, the habits and customs of their traditional cultures were forgotten.

Gradually, however, newcomers drifted in, and as the man-land ratio increased, the community began a slow climb back toward civilization. Governmental controls were tightened and extended, economic specialization began, social stratification set in, and cultural activities quickened. But the new society that eventually emerged differed from the old from which it had sprung. The abandonment of cultural baggage during the migrations, the borrowings from the many cultures represented in each pioneer settlement, the deviations natural in separate evolutions, and the impact of the environment all played their parts in creating a unique social organism similar to but differing from those in the East. An "Americanization" of men and their institutions had taken place.

Turner believed that many of the characteristics associated with the American people were traceable to their experience, during the three centuries required to settle the continent, of constantly "beginning over again." Their mobility, their optimism, their inventiveness and willingness to accept innovation, their materialism, their exploitive wastefulness—these were frontier traits; for the pioneer, accustomed to repeated moves as he drifted westward, viewed the world through rose-colored glasses as he dreamed of a better future, experimented constantly as he adapted artifacts and customs to his peculiar environment, scorned culture as a deterrent to the practical tasks that bulked so large in his life, and squandered seemingly inexhaustible natural resources with abandon. Turner also ascribed America's distinctive brand of individualism, with its dislike of governmental interference in economic functions, to the experience of pioneers who wanted no hindrance from society as they exploited nature's riches. Similarly, he traced the exaggerated nationalism of the United States to its roots among frontiersmen who looked to the national government for land, transportation outlets, and protection against the Indians. And he believed that America's faith in democracy had stemmed from a pioneering experience in which the leveling influence of poverty and the uniqueness of local problems encouraged majority self-rule. He pointed out that these characteristics, prominent among frontiersmen, had persisted long after the frontier itself was no more.

This was Turner's famous "frontier hypothesis." For a generation after its enunciation its persuasive logic won uncritical acceptance among historians, but beginning in the late 1920's, and increasingly after Turner's death in 1932, an avalanche of criticism steadily mounted. His theories, critics said, were contradictory, his generalizations unsupported, his assumptions inadequately based; what empirical proof could he advance, they asked, to prove that the frontier experience was responsible for American individualism, mobility, or wastefulness? He was damned as a romanticist for his claim that democracy sprang from the forest environment of the United States and as an isolationist for failing to recognize the continuing impact of Europe on America. As the "bait-Turner" vogue gained popularity among younger scholars of the 1930's with their international, semi-Marxian views of history, the criticisms of the frontier theory became as irrational as the earlier support rendered it by overenthusiastic advocates.

During the past decade, however, a healthy reaction has slowly and unspectacularly gained momentum. Today's scholars, gradually realizing that Turner was advancing a hypothesis rather than proving a theory, have shown a healthy tendency to abandon fruitless haggling over the meaning of his phrases and to concentrate instead on testing his assumptions. They have directed their efforts primarily toward re-examining his hypothesis in the light of criticisms directed against it and applying it to frontier areas beyond the borders of the United States. Their findings have modified

These two photographs of the same pioneer couple, the Ephraim Swain Finches, show how rapidly change came to the frontier. Above, the Finches stand before

many of the views expressed by Turner but have gone far toward proving that the frontier hypothesis remains one essential tool—albeit not the only one—for interpreting American history.

That Turner was guilty of oversimplifying both the nature and the causes of the migration process was certainly true. He pictured settlers as moving westward in an orderly procession—fur trappers, cattlemen, miners, pioneer farmers, and equipped farmers—with each group playing its part in the transmutation of a wilderness into a civilization. Free land was the magnet that lured them onward, he believed, and this operated most effectively in periods of depression, when the displaced workers of the East sought a refuge from economic storms amidst nature's abundance in

130

the West. "The wilderness ever opened the gate of escape to the poor, the discontented and oppressed," Turner wrote at one time. "If social conditions tended to crystallize in the east, beyond the Alleghenies there was freedom."

No one of these assumptions can be substantiated in the simplified form in which Turner stated it. His vision of an "orderly procession of civilization, marching single file westward" failed to account for deviations that were almost as important as the norm; as essential to the conquest of the forest as trappers or farmers were soldiers, mill-operators, distillers, artisans, storekeepers, merchants, lawyers, editors, specu-

the mayor reduced to a mere figurehead.

The pioneers who marched westward in this disorganized procession were not attracted by the magnet of "free land," for Turner's assumption that before 1862 the public domain was open to all who could pay $1.25 an acre, or that acreage was free after the Homestead Act was passed in that year, has been completely disproved. Turner failed to recognize the presence in the procession to the frontier of that omnipresent profit-seeker, the speculator. Jobbers were always ahead of farmers in the advance westward, buying up likely town sites or appropriating the best farm lands, where the soil was good and transportation outlets available. When the settler arrived his choice was between paying the speculator's price or accepting an inferior site. Even the Homestead Act failed to lessen speculative activity. Capitalizing on generous government grants to railroads and state educational institutions (which did not want to be bothered with sales to individuals), or buying bonus script from soldiers, or securing Indian lands as the reservations were contracted, or seizing on faulty features of congressional acts for the disposal of swampland and timberland, jobbers managed to engross most of the Far West's arable acreage. As a result, for every newcomer who obtained a homestead from the government, six or seven purchased farms from speculators.

their log-and-mud hut in Nebraska in the 1880's; twenty years later, prospering, they built a sturdy frame house, complete with scroll-saw decorations.

lators, and town dwellers. All played their role, and all contributed to a complex frontier social order that bore little resemblance to the primitive societies Turner pictured. This was especially the case with the early town builders. The hamlets that sprang up adjacent to each pioneer settlement were products of the environment as truly as were the cattlemen or Indian fighters; each evolved economic functions geared to the needs of the primitive area surrounding it, and, in the tight public controls maintained over such essential functions as grist-milling or retail selling, each mirrored the frontiersmen's community-oriented views. In these villages, too, the equalitarian influence of the West was reflected in thoroughly democratic governments, with popularly elected councils supreme and

Those who made these purchases were not, as Turner believed, displaced eastern workers fleeing periodic industrial depressions. Few city-dwelling artisans had the skills or inclination, and almost none the capital, to escape to the frontier. Land prices of $1.25 an acre may seem low today, but they were prohibitive for laborers earning only a dollar a day. Moreover, needed farm machinery, animals, and housing added about $1,000 to the cost of starting a farm in the 1850's, while the cheapest travel rate from New York to St. Louis was about $13 a person. Because these sums were always beyond the reach of factory workers (in bad times they deterred migration even from the rural East), the frontier never served as a "safety valve" for laborers in the sense that Turner employed the term. Instead, the American frontiers were pushed westward largely by younger sons from adjacent farm areas who migrated in periods of prosperity. While these generalizations apply to the pre-Civil War era that was Turner's principal interest, they are even more applicable to the late nineteenth century. During that period the major population shifts were from country to city rather than vice versa; for every worker who left the factory to move to the farm, twenty persons moved from farm to factory. If a safety valve did exist at that time, it was a rural safety valve, drawing off surplus farm labor and thus lessening agrarian discontent during the Granger and Populist eras.

Admitting that the procession to the frontier was more complex than Turner realized, that good lands were seldom free, and that a safety valve never operated to drain the dispossessed and the malcontented from industrial centers, does this mean that his conclusions concerning the migration process have been completely discredited? The opposite is emphatically true. A more divergent group than Turner realized felt the frontier's impact, but that does not minimize the extent of the impact. Too, while lands in the West were almost never free, they were relatively cheaper than those in Europe or the East, and this differential did serve as an attracting force. Nor can pages of statistics disprove the fact that, at least until the Civil War, the frontier served as an indirect safety valve by attracting displaced eastern farmers who would otherwise have moved into industrial cities; thousands who left New England or New York for the Old Northwest in the 1830's and 1840's, when the "rural decay" of the Northeast was beginning, would have sought factory jobs had no western outlet existed.

The effect of their exodus is made clear by comparing the political philosophies of the United States with those of another frontier country, Australia. There, lands lying beyond the coastal mountains were closed to pioneers by the aridity of the soil and by great sheep ranchers who were first on the scene. Australia, as a result, developed an urban civilization and an industrialized population relatively sooner than did the United States; and it had labor unions, labor-dominated governments, and political philosophies that would be viewed as radical in America. Without the safety valve of its own West, feeble though it may have been, such a course might have been followed in the United States.

Frederick Jackson Turner's conclusions concerning the influence of the frontier on Americans have also been questioned, debated, and modified since he advanced his hypothesis, but they have not been seriously altered. This is true even of one of his statements that has been more vigorously disputed than any other: "American democracy was born of no theorist's dream; it was not carried in the *Susan Constant* to Virginia, nor in the *Mayflower* to Plymouth. It came out of the American forest, and it gained a new strength each time it touched a new frontier." When he penned those oft-quoted words, Turner wrote as a propagandist against the "germ theory" school of history; in a less emotional and more thoughtful moment, he ascribed America's democratic institutions not to "imitation, or simple borrowing," but to "the evolution and adaptation of organs in response to changed environment." Even this moderate theory has aroused critical venom. Democracy, according to anti-Turnerians, was well advanced in Europe and *was* transported to America on the *Susan Constant* and the *Mayflower;* within this country democratic practices have multiplied most rapidly as a result of eastern lower-class pressures and have only been imitated in the West. If, critics ask, some mystical forest influence was responsible for such practices as manhood suffrage, increased authority for legislatures at the expense of executives, equitable legislative representation, and women's political rights, why did they not evolve in frontier areas outside the United States—in Russia, Latin America, and Canada, for example—exactly as they did here?

The answer, of course, is that democratic theory and institutions were imported from England, but that the frontier environment tended to make them, in practice, even more democratic. Two conditions common in pioneer communities made this inevitable. One was the wide diffusion of land ownership; this created an independent outlook and led to a demand for political participation on the part of those who had a stake in society. The other was the common social and economic level and the absence, characteristic of all primitive communities, of any prior leadership structure. The lack of any national or external controls made self-rule a hard necessity, and the frontiersmen, with their experience in community co-operation at cabin-raisings, logrollings, corn-huskings, and road or school building, accepted simple democratic practices as natural and inevitable. These practices, originating on the grass roots level, were expanded and extended in the recurring process of government-building that marked the westward movement of civilization. Each new territory that was organized—there were 31 in all—required a frame of government; this was drafted by relatively poor recent arrivals or by a minority of upper-class leaders, all of whom were committed to democratic ideals through their frontier community experiences. The result was a constant democratization of institutions and practices as constitution-makers adopted the most liberal features of older frames of government with which they were familiar.

This was true even in frontier lands outside the United States, for wherever there were frontiers, existing practices were modified in the direction of greater equality and a wider popular participation in governmental affairs. The results were never identical, of course, for both the environment and the nature of the imported institutions varied too greatly from country to country. In Russia, for instance, even though it promised no democracy comparable to that of the United States, the eastward-moving Siberian frontier, the haven of some seven million peasants during the nineteenth and early twentieth centuries, was notable for its lack of guilds, authoritarian churches, and all-powerful nobility. An autocratic official visiting there in 1910 was alarmed by the "enormous, rudely democratic country" evolving under the influence of the small homesteads that were the normal living units; he feared that czarism and European Russia would soon be "throttled" by the egalitarian currents developing on the frontier.

That the frontier accentuated the spirit of nationalism and individualism in the United States, as Turner maintained, was also true. Every page of the country's history, from the War of 1812 through the era of Manifest Destiny to today's bitter conflicts with Russia, demonstrates that the American attitude toward the world has been far more nationalistic than that of non-frontier countries and that this attitude has been strongest in the newest regions. Similarly, the pioneering experience converted settlers into individualists, although through a somewhat different process than Turner envisaged. His emphasis on a desire for freedom as a primary force luring men westward and his belief that pioneers developed an attitude of self-sufficiency in their lone battle against nature have been questioned, and with justice. Hoped for gain was the magnet that attracted most migrants to the cheaper lands of the West, while once there they lived in units where co-operative enterprise—for protection against the Indians, for cabin-raising, law enforcement, and the like—was more essential than in the better established towns of the East. Yet the fact remains that the abundant resources and the greater social mobility of frontier areas did instill into frontiersmen a uniquely American form of individualism. Even though they may be sheeplike in following the decrees of social arbiters or fashion dictators, Americans today, like their pioneer ancestors, dislike governmental interference in their affairs. "Rugged individualism" did not originate on the frontier any more than democracy or nationalism did, but each concept was deepened and sharpened by frontier conditions.

His opponents have also cast doubt on Turner's assertion that American inventiveness and willingness to adopt innovations are traits inherited from pioneer ancestors who constantly devised new techniques and artifacts to cope with an unfamiliar environment. The critics insist that each mechanical improvement needed for the conquest of the frontier, from plows to barbed-

wire fencing, originated in the East; when frontiersmen faced such an incomprehensible task as conquering the Great Plains they proved so tradition-bound that their advance halted until eastern inventors provided them with the tools needed to subdue grasslands. Unassailable as this argument may be, it ignores the fact that the recurring demand for implements and methods needed in the frontier advance did put a premium on inventiveness by Americans, whether they lived in the East or West. That even today they are less bound by tradition than other peoples is due in part to their pioneer heritage.

The anti-intellectualism and materialism which are national traits can also be traced to the frontier experience. There was little in pioneer life to attract the timid, the cultivated, or the aesthetically sensitive. In the boisterous western borderlands, book learning and intellectual speculation were suspect among those dedicated to the material tasks necessary to subdue a continent. Americans today reflect their background in placing the "intellectual" well below the "practical businessman" in their scale of heroes. Yet the frontiersman, as Turner recognized, was an idealist as well as a materialist. He admired material objects not only as symbols of advancing civilization but as the substance of his hopes for a better future. Given economic success he would be able to afford the aesthetic and intellectual pursuits that he felt were his due, even though he was not quite able to appreciate them. This spirit inspired the cultural activities—literary societies, debating clubs, "thespian groups," libraries, schools, camp meetings—that thrived in the most primitive western communities. It also helped nurture in the pioneers an infinite faith in the future. The belief in progress, both material and intellectual, that is part of modern America's creed was strengthened by the frontier experience.

Frederick Jackson Turner, then, was not far wrong when he maintained that frontiersmen did develop unique traits and that these perpetuated form the principal distinguishing characteristics of the American people today. To a degree unknown among Europeans, Americans do display a restless energy, a versatility, a practical ingenuity, an earthy practicality. They do squander their natural resources with an abandon unknown elsewhere; they have developed a mobility both social and physical that marks them as a people apart. In few other lands is the democratic ideal worshiped so intensely, or nationalism carried to such extremes of isolationism or international arrogance. Rarely do other peoples display such indifference toward intellectualism or aesthetic values; seldom in comparable cultural areas do they cling so tenaciously to the shibboleth of rugged individualism. Nor do residents of non-frontier lands experience to the same degree the heady optimism, the rosy faith in the future, the belief in the inevitability of progress that form part of the American creed. These are pioneer traits, and they have become a part of the national heritage.

Yet if the frontier wrought such a transformation within the United States, why did it not have a similar effect on other countries with frontiers? If the pioneering experience was responsible for our democracy and nationalism and individualism, why have the peoples of Africa, Latin America, Canada, and Russia failed to develop identical characteristics? The answer is obvious: in few nations of the world has the sort of frontier that Turner described existed. For he saw the frontier not as a borderland between unsettled and settled lands, but as an accessible area in which a low man-land ratio and abundant natural resources provided an unusual opportunity for the individual to better himself. Where autocratic governments controlled population movements, where resources were lacking, or where conditions prohibited ordinary individuals from exploiting nature's virgin riches, a frontier in the Turnerian sense could not be said to exist.

The areas of the world that have been occupied since the beginning of the age of discovery contain remarkably few frontiers of the American kind. In Africa the few Europeans were so outnumbered by relatively uncivilized native inhabitants that the need for protection transcended any impulses toward democracy or individualism. In Latin America the rugged

terrain and steaming jungles restricted areas exploitable by individuals to the Brazilian plains and the Argentine pampas; these did attract frontiersmen, although in Argentina the prior occupation of most good lands by government-favored cattle growers kept small farmers out until railroads penetrated the region. In Canada the path westward was blocked by the Laurentian Shield, a tangled mass of hills and sterile, brush-choked soil covering the country north and west of the St. Lawrence Valley. When railroads finally penetrated this barrier in the late nineteenth century, they carried pioneers directly from the East to the prairie provinces of the West; the newcomers, with no prior pioneering experience, simply adapted to their new situation the eastern institutions with which they were familiar. Among the frontier nations of the world only Russia provided a physical environment comparable to that of the United States, and there the pioneers were too accustomed to rigid feudal and monarchic controls to respond as Americans did.

Further proof that the westward expansion of the United States has been a powerful formative force has been provided by the problems facing the nation in the present century. During the past fifty years the American people have been adjusting their lives and institutions to existence in a frontierless land, for while the superintendent of the census was decidedly premature when he announced in 1890 that the country's "unsettled area has been so broken into by isolated bodies of settlement that there can hardly be said to be a frontier line" remaining, the era of cheap land was rapidly drawing to a close. In attempting to adjust the country to its new, expansionless future, statesmen have frequently called upon the frontier hypothesis to justify everything from rugged individualism to the welfare state, and from isolationism to world domination.

Political opinion has divided sharply on the necessity of altering the nation's governmental philosophy and techniques in response to the changed environment. Some statesmen and scholars have rebelled against what they call Turner's "Space Concept of History," with all that it implies concerning the lack of opportunity for the individual in an expansionless land. They insist that modern technology has created a whole host of new "frontiers"—of intensive farming, electronics, mechanics, manufacturing, nuclear fission, and the like—which offer such diverse outlets to individual talents that governmental interference in the nation's economic activities is unjustified. On the other hand, equally competent spokesmen argue that these newer "frontiers" offer little opportunity to the individual—as distinguished from the corporation or the capitalist—and hence cannot duplicate the function of the frontier of free land. The government, they insist, must provide the people with the security and opportunity that vanished when escape to the West became impossible. This school's most eloquent spokesman, Franklin D. Roosevelt, declared: "Our last frontier has long since been reached. . . . Equality of opportunity as we have known it no longer exists. . . . Our task now is not the discovery or exploitation of natural resources or necessarily producing more goods. It is the sober, less dramatic business of administering resources and plants already in hand, of seeking to reestablish foreign markets for our surplus production, of meeting the problem of under-consumption, of adjusting production to consumption, of distributing wealth and products more equitably, of adapting existing economic organizations to the service of the people. The day of enlight-

ened administration has come." To Roosevelt, and to thousands like him, the passing of the frontier created a new era in history which demanded a new philosophy of government.

Diplomats have also found in the frontier hypothesis justification for many of their moves, from imperialist expansion to the restriction of immigration. Harking back to Turner's statement that the perennial rebirth of society was necessary to keep alive the democratic spirit, expansionists have argued through the twentieth century for an extension of American power and territories. During the Spanish-American War imperialists preached such a doctrine, adding the argument that Spain's lands were needed to provide a population outlet for a people who could no longer escape to their own frontier. Idealists such as Woodrow Wilson could agree with materialists like J. P. Morgan that the extension of American authority abroad, either through territorial acquisitions or economic penetration, would be good for both business and democracy. In a later generation Franklin D. Roosevelt favored a similar expansion of the American democratic ideal as a necessary prelude to the better world that he hoped would emerge from World War II. His successor, Harry Truman, envisaged his "Truman Doctrine" as a device to extend and defend the frontiers of democracy throughout the globe. While popular belief in the superiority of America's political institutions was far older than Turner, that belief rested partly on the frontier experience of the United States.

These practical applications of the frontier hypothesis, as well as its demonstrated influence on the nation's development, suggest that its critics have been unable to destroy the theory's effectiveness as a key to understanding American history. The recurring rebirth of society in the United States over a period of three hundred years did endow the people with characteristics and institutions that distinguish them from the inhabitants of other nations. It is obviously untrue that the frontier experience alone accounts for the unique features of American civilization; that civilization can be understood only as the product of the interplay of the Old World heritage and New World conditions. But among those conditions none has bulked larger than the operation of the frontier process.

As the ever-observant Gibbon noted long ago, mankind is much more liberal with applause for its destroyers than for its benefactors. What other explanation can there be for the fact that nowhere, despite thousands of parks and squares bristling with military statuary, has his adopted country erected a statue to John Matthews? A benefactor of the first rank, Matthews gave us the soda fountain and popularized carbonated drinks, yet his only personal memorial is his grave in Greenwood Cemetery, Brooklyn. It is, to be sure, no mean monument, for above a recumbent marble likeness of Matthews rises a granite Gothic canopy and spire to a height of thirty-six feet, richly carved all over with gargoyles, evangelists, expiring Matthews relatives, flora, fauna, and elaborate bas-reliefs representing great moments in the life of the deceased. De-

signed and partially executed in his own workshop, this imposing potpourri looks very much like one of Matthews' own "cottage" soda fountains at the height of that eclectic art form. But the benefactor's true monument is to be found in nearly every drugstore, luncheonette, and department store in America; his handiwork lives on every Main Street.

Natural carbonated waters have, of course, been bubbling up out of springs and spas since the dawn of history. Paracelsus, Lavoisier, and Dr. Joseph Priestley observed and experimented with them. A Swedish chemist named Bergman produced artificial carbonated or mineral water in 1770, and Professor Benjamin Silliman of Yale began manufacturing and bottling small quantities in New Haven in 1806. An early fountain was dispensing various homemade Vichy, Kissingen, and Apollinaris "seltzers" in New

THE SODA Fountain

Of bubbling waters, sacred marble, and old John Matthews, father of an industry and a flamboyant art form

By JOSEPH L. MORRISON

York by 1810; they were supposed to cure obesity. But it was the arrival of John Matthews in New York about 1832 that made soda-water drinking an industry and, incidentally, offered the grogshop and the saloon the first real competition they had ever encountered.

As students of the Matthews mausoleum can learn by twisting their necks to observe the canopy's carved ceiling, the benefactor-to-be began as an apprentice in the London shop of Joseph Bramah, inventor, among other things, of the permutation bank lock, a hydraulic press, and a new kind of seamless lead tubing. There, in eternal stone, is young John, learning how to construct machinery to make carbonic acid gas. In an adjoining panel, he appears again, aged twenty-one, taking ship to seek his fortune in New York, doubtless convinced that there was no future for a seltzer man in a nation of confirmed tea-drinkers.

Matthews hung out his shingle at 55 Gold Street and was soon manufacturing carbonating machinery and selling charged water to retail stores. The equipment was simple enough—a cast-iron box, lined with lead, where carbonic acid gas was formed by the action of sulphuric acid (then often called oil of vitriol) on marble dust. The gas was then purified by passing it through water, and conducted into a tank partially filled with cool water. An employee rocked the tank for a quarter to a half hour, until the water was impregnated and bubbly. To imitate popular mineral waters, one added their salts to the mixture.

The introduction of marble chips was an American development, for Bramah had used whiting and chalk. But marble was easier and cheaper to come by in New York: the enterprising Matthews firm at one point acquired all the scrap from the building of St. Patrick's Cathedral in New York. Although a few of the devout thought this use unseemly, these chips alone supplied some twenty-five million gallons before the supply gave out. Pressure, of course, is always a hazard in gas manufacture, and there were a number of noisy explosions among Matthews' competitors in the early days, but his firm had a special, if rather unusual, method of keeping the pressure from rising above the optimum level of 150 pounds.

The safety valve was an ex-slave named Ben Austen, one of the earliest employees, a man of intelligence and, above all, strength. When the force of a new batch of soda water needed measuring, the job fell to Ben, who simply placed his powerful thumb over the pressure cock. When it blew his thumb away, the Matthews people estimated they had reached 150 pounds and that the water was fully charged. "Ben's Thumb" was long a term in the jargon of the trade. During the Civil War draft riots, when angry Irish mobs roamed the New York streets seeking to hang any Negro they could find, Matthews was obliged to ship Ben out to safety in a packing case, as though he were a tank of the product.

As time went on, several strong competitors entered the field—John Lippincott of Philadelphia, A. D. Puffer of Boston, and James W. Tufts of Somerville, Massachusetts (he did so well eventually that he founded Pinehurst, North Carolina)—but the next great breakthrough, and the one which brought them all prosperity, was made in 1838 or 1839 by Eugene Roussel, a Frenchman who was selling plain soda water at his perfume shop in Philadelphia. With the ingenuity that characterizes all Frenchmen when dealing with the opposite sex, he decided to add flavors to his customers' drinks. As simple as that, but no one had thought of it. Soon the crude soda fountains of Matthews and his competitors were all keeping syrups on hand, in orange, cherry, lemon, teaberry, ginger, peach, and many other flavors. Root beer and birch beer and sarsaparilla appeared, bottled or made at the fountain. Attempts were made to imitate, without alcohol, the flavors of various wines and champagnes, but apparently less successfully.

For a very modest investment, Matthews could put any chemist or other entrepreneur in business. Here is one offering:

1 upright generator	$115.00
1 four-gallon fountain frame	25.00
1 draught apparatus for counter	40.00
6 patent soda tumblers	1.25
1 case extracts for syrups	6.00
1 barrel Matthews' ground marble (Ah, there, St. Patrick!)	2.00
165 lbs. sulphuric acid with carboy	6.53
	195.78

Only six tumblers were provided, but they could be washed in a jiffy. They were simply rinsed in cold water, for germs concerned nobody, and their existence was not suspected. Ice cooling had been introduced and business was booming, so that Art, which had been waiting in the wings, could now step forward and embrace Commerce. The Leonardo of the soda fountain was one G. D. Dows, of Lowell, Massachusetts, who decided to try his hand at improving the looks of the crude soda fountain in his brother's store, and wound up with a combination fountain and ice shaver housed in a white Italian marble box. It became so popular that Dows opened his own place in Boston.

The "cottage" fountain, as this kind of design was later called, now took over the field. Basically boxes resting on a counter, they ran riot through the art of decoration—Gothic, Roman, Byzantine, Egyptian, Japanese, Brooklyn Hittite, anything in any combination—

and bore names like The Frost King, The Icefloe, The Egyptian, The Avalanche, and The Cathedral. Fanciful spigots led out of tombs and temples and chalets decorated with sphinxes, lions, nymphs, knights; allegory ran wild. Names of flavors and famous mineral waters would appear on the larger models. There is a tale of an old lady who walked around a giant fountain displayed at a fete in the Seventh Regiment Armory in New York, reading off to herself the distinguished names graven next to each spigot: Saratoga, Deep Rock, Kissingen, Washington. Then she turned to the attendant. "I didn't know," she said, "that the gallant Seventh had fought in all these battles."

In 1870, John Matthews was gathered to his fathers and entombed in the elegant manner we have described. Meanwhile the "cottage" became too small a device, what with the hundreds of flavors now offered, and great wall-models now appeared, erected like altars behind the counter, gleaming in marble and onyx and with even more fanciful architecture. One boasted 300 flavors. Another cost $40,000, a fortune in those days.

Now another great benefactor appeared, who united the ice cream parlor and the soda fountain. Although he has rival claimants, the historians of the industry press the accolade for inventing the ice cream soda upon Robert M. Green, the soft-drink concessionaire at the Franklin Institute Exposition held in Philadelphia in 1874. Among the drinks he had been selling was one concocted of fresh sweet cream, syrup, and carbonated water, but one busy day he ran out of cream. In desperation he bought some vanilla ice cream, intending to melt it, but the customers were so pressing that he used it in its congealed form. Apparently the drinkers uttered glad cries of joy, for Green thereafter made ice cream sodas *on purpose,* and the recipe spread over the country.

By the end of the century, the soda fountain was big business. The four original firms had combined, as was then stylish, into a trust. It was no longer necessary for soda-fountain proprietors to make their own gas, behind the counter or in the cellar, because it could now be purchased in portable steel cylinders. The wall temples began to disappear in favor of the modern counter, with the apparatus hidden inside it, and the great empty space where the old fountain had stood was covered with an ornate looking-glass and clever displays of tumblers—washed nowadays in hot water. Food too was now offered for sale, and in the twenties came mechanical refrigeration. It was a long way from Lavoisier, from the dissenting parson Priestley shaking up the first glass of artificial mineral water with gas acquired at a nearby brewery, from Ben's thumb, and from that great silent soda fountain in Greenwood Cemetery. But a great thirst had at last been quenched.

Our mementos of John Matthews include an old billhead (above) showing one of his early factories and, at far right, one of the earliest of his surviving soda fountains, made of silver-plated copper. Ice was kept inside to cool a coil through which the beverage passed. It is topped by a thirsty Cupid and flanked with elephant heads; the soda flowed through their trunks, and to draw it you turned the elephant's ears. Today this old urn decorates the Chapel Hill, North Carolina, estate of George Matthews, Jr., great-grandson of "the Father of American Soda Water." (He himself hated the term, because there is no soda in it, and preferred "aerated water.") Below, shown in both front and side views, is a great Matthews marble wall-model, The Angelo. Is the art reference clear?

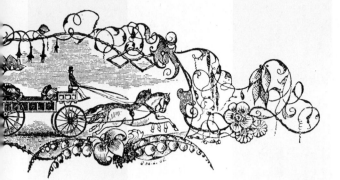

JOHN MATTHEWS:
He started it

BEN AUSTEN:
Human pressure gauge

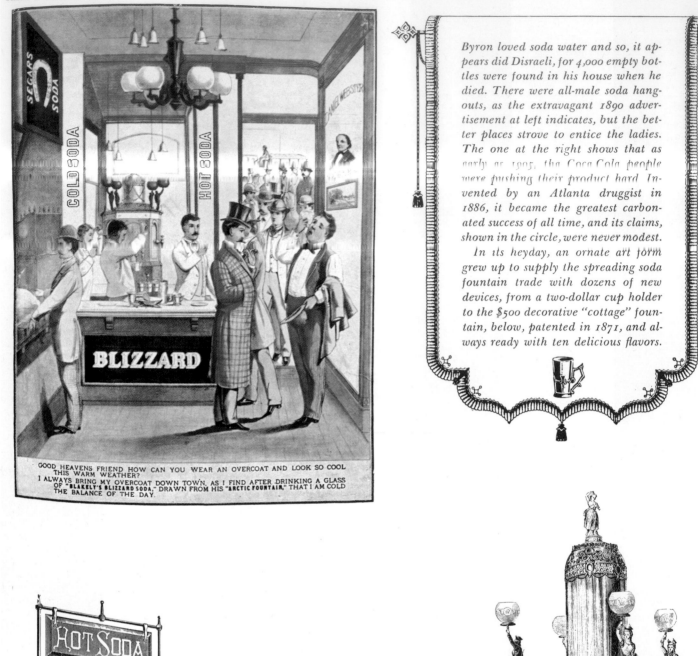

GOOD HEAVENS FRIEND HOW CAN YOU WEAR AN OVERCOAT AND LOOK SO COOL
THIS WARM WEATHER?
I ALWAYS BRING MY OVERCOAT DOWN TOWN, AS I FIND AFTER DRINKING A GLASS
OF "BLAKELY'S BLIZZARD SODA," DRAWN FROM HIS "ARCTIC FOUNTAIN," THAT I AM COLD
THE BALANCE OF THE DAY.

Byron loved soda water and so, it appears did Disraeli, for 4,000 empty bottles were found in his house when he died. There were all-male soda hangouts, as the extravagant 1890 advertisement at left indicates, but the better places strove to entice the ladies. The one at the right shows that as early as 1905, the Coca-Cola people were pushing their product hard. Invented by an Atlanta druggist in 1886, it became the greatest carbonated success of all time, and its claims, shown in the circle, were never modest.

In its heyday, an ornate art form grew up to supply the spreading soda fountain trade with dozens of new devices, from a two-dollar cup holder to the $500 decorative "cottage" fountain, below, patented in 1871, and always ready with ten delicious flavors.

In fact, hot water

Matthews' Change Holder

The Monitor, by the Tufts Company

Spoon Holder

Tumbler Washer

Tumbler Holder

Ice Plane and Mitten

When it came to colored lithographs, it was hard to beat A. D. Puffer & Sons, of Boston; this flight of fancy clearly links the product to all that arctic ice, to a good many races, to those happy monkeys, and even to the wise old owl. Could that be the young John Glenn beside him? The date: approximately 1875.

SODA
PUFFER'S
MAGIC FOUNTAIN

WARSHAW COLLECTION OF BUSINESS AMERICANA

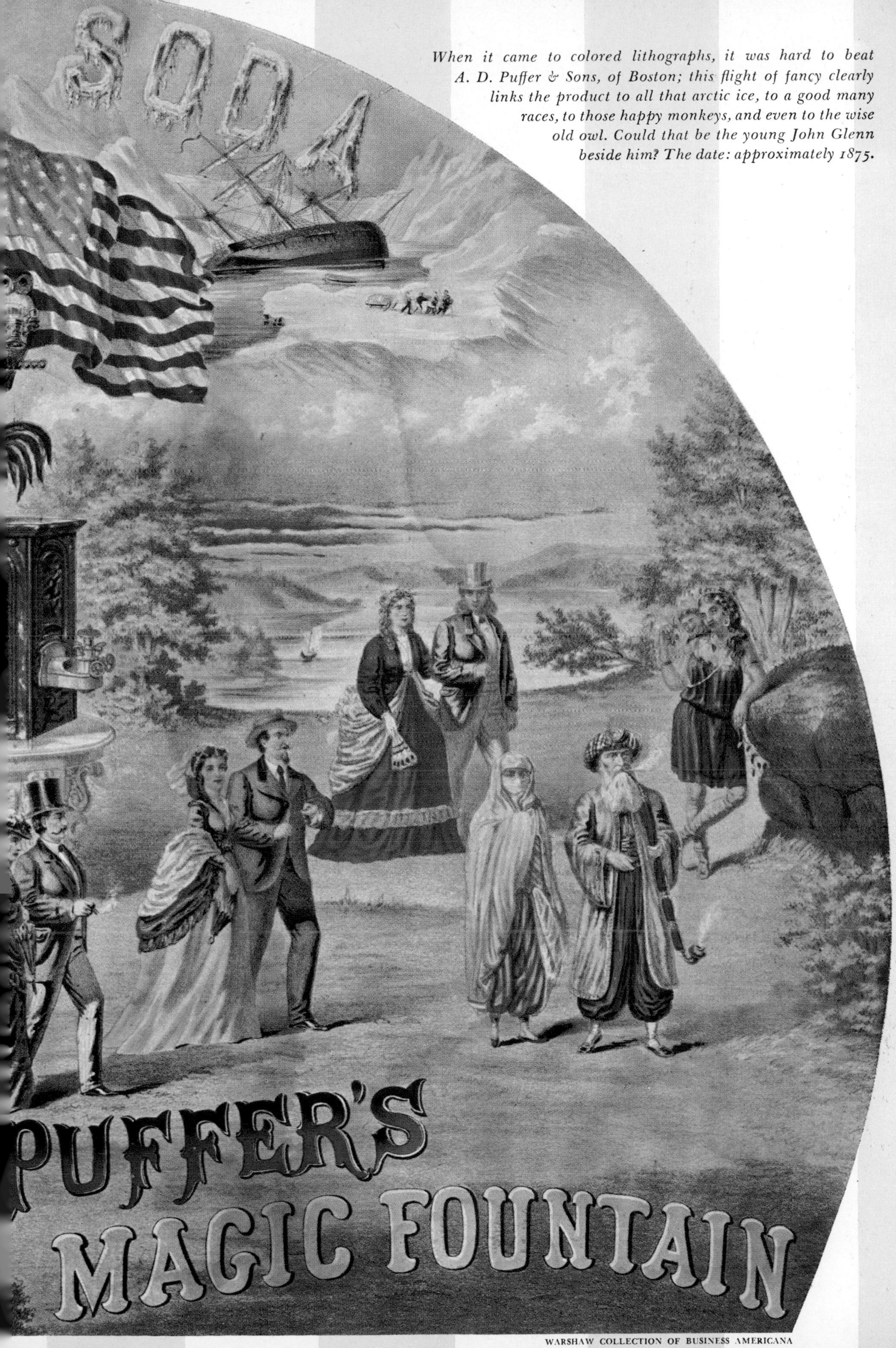

AMERICAN HERITAGE *is grateful to George Matthews, Jr., and John Poulos for making their collections of old catalogues and pictures available; and to Miss Janice Devine and Leslie Dorsey for picture and caption research.*

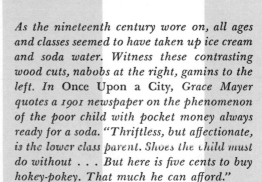

As the nineteenth century wore on, all ages and classes seemed to have taken up ice cream and soda water. Witness these contrasting wood cuts, nabobs at the right, gamins to the left. In Once Upon a City, Grace Mayer quotes a 1901 newspaper on the phenomenon of the poor child with pocket money always ready for a soda. "Thriftless, but affectionate, is the lower class parent. Shoes the child must do without . . . But here is five cents to buy hokey-pokey. That much he can afford."

John Matthews, who started it all, believed in catching soda-water drinkers early, made a street dispensing cart, and waxed lyrical about his product: "Youth, as it sips its first glass, experiences sensations which, like the first sensations of love, cannot be forgotten but are cherished to the last." Who will argue with the old gentleman?

Finis

ISAAC SINGER SEWING

An erratic genius and his sober-sided partner

built fortunes which their numerous progeny

By PETER

Edward Clark, a respectable forty-year-old lawyer, found himself, in the summer of 1851, in a disconcerting position. He was (or so it seemed to Clark) newly yoked in partnership with a man of spectacular depravity, a man so lost to shame as to seem that he had never had any to lose. Everything Clark had discovered about his new partner dismayed him; everything in Clark's character and background demanded that he dissolve the partnership. Yet if he did, a glittering fortune would, he feared, go glimmering. For Clark's wife, the choice was simple. "Sell out," she urged him, "and leave the nasty brute." But still Clark hesitated. He might, he argued, somehow conceal from the world the excesses of his abandoned partner; indeed, with good management and a generous admixture of luck he might pluck good from evil and even succeed in presenting the scoundrel in the unlikely guise of mankind's benefactor. And so Clark decided to stick.

Some odd results can be traced back to that decision. Had he chosen otherwise, baseball's Hall of Fame might not stand at Cooperstown; Marcel Proust would have had to shape somewhat differently the character he called the Marquise de Sainte-Euverte; Time Inc. would have had harder sledding in its early days; Palm Beach would not stand as the lush resort it is today; an excellent gallery of French impressionist paintings would not be offered to the public, improbably, on the Mohawk Trail in Williamstown, Massachusetts; and the incumbent president of the National Association of Manufacturers would be some other. But at the time, Clark's decision was only that he should collaborate with Isaac Merritt Singer in the manufacture and sale of the sewing machine that Singer had invented.

In condemning his new partner Clark made no more shocked a judgment than would all of New York society a few years later. Subsequent chroniclers have likewise looked down their noses at Singer; they have either pilloried him with some disgust as a lecher or with labored hilarity have cited his career as a single-handed effort to disprove the Malthusian hypothesis. A more dispassionate verdict is simply that Singer was born in the wrong time and place. He would have fitted nicely into the Rome of the later Caesars; Renaissance Italy would have made him welcome; it is easy

In 1901 the Singer Company sought to boost its sales of 1,000,000 machines a year with this folder, probably designed to publicize its

to imagine him roistering through Europe with the Chevalier de Seingalt, Giacomo Casanova; but that he was too rich for the blood of Pecksniffian New York in the pre-Civil War era there can be no doubt.

What uniformly offended Singer's critics was that in the 36 years from 1834 to 1870 he sired 24 children. From a biological point of view there is nothing exceptional about such an achievement, but socially it was unusual in that, of the five different women who bore his two dozen children, Singer was married to only two; moreover, he managed to involve him-

and his WONDERFUL MACHINE

made their product a household necessity and have spent in ways both beneficent and bizarre

LYON

awards at the Pan-American Exposition. As early as 1861 Singer was doing more than half its business through far-flung foreign agents.

self with the three others simultaneously. These informal liaisons were all in hand by 1851; hence Clark's dismay and disgust.

Clark had other objections to Singer. He was, in the first place, obviously no gentleman. The eighth of a brood of children born to a poverty-stricken German immigrant millwright, he was hot-tempered, arrogant, and habitually profane. In the second place, he was practically illiterate; indeed, Clark suspected he had never had any formal schooling whatever. As if this were not enough, Singer had spent most of his adult years as an actor, and he had all the actor's egotism. Sinking even lower, if possible, in the social scale, he had been an advance man for a traveling theatrical troupe. How was it conceivable that such a man could have stumbled upon an important mechanical invention?

There was in fact nothing accidental about Singer's accomplishment. He had from boyhood been adept with machinery; his first efforts to earn his own living, shortly after he had run away from home at the age of twelve, had been as apprentice to a machinist in Rochester, New York. But no matter his talent for it, the trade bored him. Moreover, he was hopelessly stage-struck. Illiterate or no, he committed to memory huge chunks of Shakespeare as well as of various fustian scripts advocating temperance. Here was the life: rollicking about the country with complaisant young actresses, bedazzling small-town girls, swaggering about a stage with a mouthful of iambics—while flowers bloom in the garden, why work?

Only when he found himself irremediably at liberty would young Singer reluctantly consider working at his trade. So resolutely did he fight shy of a regular wage that in twenty years he held only three jobs outside the theater. The first was in New York City with Robert Hoe, the well-known manufacturer of printing presses; by that time he was 24 and already married and a father. The second job was four years later, in 1839; he went to work with an older brother, helping to dig the Illinois waterway at Lockport. He found the drudgery so intolerable that he was inspired to develop his first invention, a machine for drilling rock. Fecklessly, he disposed of his patent rights for $2,000, which he promptly squandered by forming his own theatrical company, the Merritt Players. With a repertory that included *Richard III* and *The Stumbling Block, or, Why a Deacon Gave Up His Wine*, he barnstormed throughout the Midwest, at length fetching up, flat broke, in Fredericksburg, Ohio. This was so tiny a settlement that the only job Singer could find was in a sawmill; here he was obliged to toil for two years before he could hit upon another invention —a machine for carving wood-block type. He patented it, and, in easy stages, came to New York.

He had by now compelling reasons to lay hands on some money. Besides his wife, the former Catharine

Isaac Singer spent his happiest years with Isabella Boyer, his second wife and the last of the many women in his life. This faded snapshot, taken about 1870, shows them with little Winnaretta, the second of their six children.

Maria Haley, whom he had long since left with two children to feed, he had taken up with a comely young woman named Mary Ann Sponsler, who, in the course of tagging around the country with him, had borne him six more children, all out of wedlock. He was approaching his fortieth year, and his time for playing *jeunes premiers* was running out. There was the bank account to consider.

Into Singer's life at this juncture, like a plump hen advancing confidently into a den of foxes, came a would-be capitalist of a commonplace sort. This innocent, a man called George Zieber, paid Singer some $3,000 for the Massachusetts rights to the type-carving device and rented space in a Boston machine shop at 19 Harvard Place, not far from the Old South Meeting House. Singer went along to demonstrate the machine to prospective buyers, but, these proving conspicuous by their scarcity, he found time to take notice of his surroundings.

The chief business of the machine shop, owned by Orson Phelps, was supposed to be the manufacture of sewing machines. Owing to some defect in their design, however, more time was spent in repairing the old than in making the new. This was a monotonously familiar complaint against all the early sewing machines, no matter by whom designed or manufactured.

Actually, by 1850 there was nothing new about the idea of a sewing machine. Patents had been granted in England (1790), Austria (1814), the United States

(1826), and France (1830) on mechanical devices for sewing. The French machine was reasonably efficient, but its manufacture was summarily halted by the passion of a mob of Parisian tailors who feared the loss of their livelihood. Something of the same sentiment blocked development of a machine constructed by a remarkable American inventor, Walter Hunt, in 1833. Hunt was the sort of man who could contrive anything if he were given a bit of wire and a half hour; to his credit, among dozens of commodities, are the paper collar and the safety pin. But he was a Quaker with an active conscience about the economic morality of his contraptions, and so, after devising an adequate sewing machine, he referred to his daughter the decision as to whether he should go further with it. She entered a veto—on the ground, as she later testified, that "the introduction of such a machine . . . would be injurious to the interests of hand-sewers. I found that the machine would at that time be very unpopular and . . . refused to use it." In consequence, Hunt decided not to seek a patent.

Such compunctions did not trouble other American inventors, of whom the most important was Elias Howe, Jr., who, on September 10, 1846, was granted a patent on a lock-stitch machine with an eye-pointed needle and shuttle. There was only one difficulty attending on Howe's machine, as well as on others patented about the same time: they didn't work efficiently. Ten letters patent were extended to inventors of mechanical sewing devices in 1849-50; the fourth of them was granted to Lerow & Blodgett late in 1849; and theirs was the machine that Singer inspected with mild interest, a little less than a year later, in Orson Phelps's shop.

Singer thought the machine could be made to work. Phelps was skeptical. "If," he retorted, "you can make a really practical sewing machine, you will make more money in a year than you can in fifty with that carving affair."

Singer reflected. Theretofore he had considered that the manufacture of sewing machines was a paltry business; but maybe Phelps knew what he was talking about. If there was money in it, Singer was interested. Inventors are popularly credited with being under only one goad: What, they are imagined to ask themselves, can I invent that will lighten the load of my fellow man? Nothing could have been further from Isaac Singer's lively mind. He himself put his motive with admirable succinctness. "I don't," he said, "care a damn for the invention. The dimes are what I am after."

And so he bethought him of his wide-eyed financier, Zieber, who had already sunk more than $3,000 into Singer's unsalable type-carving device. Would Zieber submit to a further plucking? Singer had nothing to lose by trying.

In fact, Zieber proved woefully reluctant—in his own words he was "loth to advance any thing out of the small amount yet remaining in my possession, to make experiments." He added: "I became very much disheartened."

Not so Singer, all of whose enormous vitality was already responding to what seemed to him a golden challenge. He directed the full force of his considerable charm on Zieber, and, on September 18, 1850, the three men concluded an agreement, drawn up by Zieber. The capitalist was to "furnish the sum of Forty Dollars"; Singer was to "contribute his inventive genius"; Phelps was to provide "his best mechanical skill." The contract was, Zieber later maintained plaintively, "sufficient to secure to each the interest to which he was entitled, had all the other parties been honorably disposed."

And now attend, for Isaac Singer is approaching the moment of his life that will ensure him lasting fame, and the first of the world's important household appliances is about to be born.

The circumstances of the invention itself are obscured by clouds of contention. Zieber later deprecated Singer's role, but his was clearly a prejudiced statement. The canonical account of Singer's triumph, published a quarter century later, bore the inventor's name as author, but also the unmistakable, ghostly trace of a company publicity man. It is like all such accounts: the humble man of talent works feverishly (eighteen and twenty hours a day), single-mindedly (only one meal a day), for a ridiculously brief time (only eleven days—for, after all, how long would forty dollars last?); at length the parts are assembled on the eleventh night; the assembled machine repeatedly refuses to function, whilst one by one the workmen take their leave, as though from the proverbial sinking ship; the inventor despairs; a chance remark from a bystander leads to the flash of realization of what has been wrong; the tiny adjustment is made, and— eureka!

Whether all this is blarney or not, one stubborn fact stands out: Isaac Singer had developed the first sewing machine that would work.

Nor is it possible to ascribe the invention to the luck of a rascal. Singer's was a brilliant, perceptive, and original design. Andrew B. Jack of the Massachusetts Institute of Technology, whose studies of early sewing-machine history were aided by examination of all the Singer Company's early letter books, has stated that, to be practical, the device must include ten features: (1) lock stitch; (2) eye-pointed needle; (3) shuttle for second thread, vibratory or double-pointed; (4) continuous thread from spools; (5) horizontal table; (6) overhanging arm; (7) contin-

Singer's partner, steady, sensible Edward Clark, managed the merchandising end of the enterprise.

uous feed, synchronous with needle motion; (8) thread or tension controls, giving slack thread as needed; (9) presser foot; and (10) ability to sew in a straight or curving line. Of all these features, only the ninth and tenth were invented by Singer. Elias Howe had originated the first, second, and fourth; other mechanics, notably J. Bachelder and A. B. Wilson, were responsible for the others; but theirs, like all the early machines, were crude and flawed. Only Singer's embraced all ten features.

Singer's design, which has survived substantially intact, was a radical departure from those of all his contemporaries, but it worked; it was, moreover, adaptable to a variety of jobs, whether in the home or the factory. In contrast, Howe's machine could sew only eighteen stitches before the operator was obliged to remove the cloth for a fresh start; and his tension device was imperfect, so that the thread broke repeatedly. "Credit for the invention of the sewing-machine," Jack declares, "must go to Isaac Merritt Singer." It is difficult to overestimate the importance of his accomplishments.

On the heels of his achievement, Singer visibly expanded. His voice, always resonant, now took on a note of authority quite galling to his two associates. When Phelps suggested that, according to their agreement, his name should be linked with Singer's on the patent application, Singer peremptorily shouted him down. When Zieber attempted to mediate and pacify, Singer hectored both men impartially while privately he urged Zieber to buy up Phelps's interest. When Zieber refused, Singer did the job himself, paying Phelps off from money belonging to all three. In short, he behaved like a ruthless man of business whilst his partners behaved like gentle chuckleheads.

Elias Howe now appeared. Howe was uncomfortably aware that his own machine was less practical than Singer's; he was, moreover, in desperate need of money. On the other hand, he had the basic patent, while Singer as yet had none. Manifestly, there was here the basis for a deal if all hands were reasonable. Howe offered Singer and Zieber the American rights to his patent for $2,000. The niceties of patent law were not calculated to appeal to Singer. He reacted in honest and forthright fashion: he would, he declared, boot Howe downstairs if he didn't clear off the premises under his own steam. In part this gesture must have been motivated by the fact that Singer was finding himself, pleasurably and unexpectedly, with money on his hands. His machine, almost from the start, sold well, and the unit profit was generous. The world was becoming his oyster. He and Zieber decided to move their headquarters from Boston to New York.

The move involved, for the romantic inventor, a measure of intrepidity. Somewhere in New York was his wife, whom he had long since deserted (he called her Maria); there, too, was his consort, Mary Ann Sponsler (he called her Mary); and, under two different roofs, there were his children, who now numbered nine. But he had an imperative motive for settling once again in New York. The fact was, love had come again to Singer, in the shape of Mary Eastwood Walters (he called her Mary), 28 years old and presently the mother of his tenth child. He had not been in New York very long before love came to him again—for he was nothing if not receptive to the little naked god—in the shape of Mary McGonigal (how convenient; he could call her Mary, too), 22 years old and presently the mother of his eleventh child.

All this love cost the inventor money. Indeed, by early in 1851, his expenses were so considerable that the partnership of Singer and Zieber was obliged to open its arms to a third man, Barzillan Ransom, an elderly gentleman from Brooklyn who manufactured cloth bags for salt and was sufficiently impressed by Singer's machine to tender promissory notes worth up to $10,000 in return for a one-third share in the business. But Ransom did not last long. To Singer he was merely another pigeon. Ransom, on the other hand, found Singer an extraordinary specimen, of a kind he had never before had an opportunity to inspect at close range. In March he termed Singer "singular"; by April he had concluded Singer was a "dictator . . . insufferable and unless he alters his hand promptly we must separate." By May he had withdrawn—without having paid his notes.

Here was a blow, but there was worse to come. Elias Howe, angered by the success of various sewing-machine manufacturers and thoroughly embittered by a personal tragedy that he blamed on his earlier poverty, had turned vengefully litigious. He brandished suits, one after another, for patent infringement. From Singer he demanded $25,000. Payment of such a sum was of course out of the question, even presuming Singer for a moment believed he had infringed. He was certain he had not; but he needed a lawyer to prove his case, and he had no money even for a lawyer. He appealed to Ambrose Jordan, the attorney who had accompanied him to Washington when he applied for a patent. Would Jordan, Singer inquired, handle the case—and any subsequent litigation—for a share in the business? Jordan refused, for he found Singer personally distasteful. Instead, he referred him to his junior partner and son-in-law, Edward Clark. A former Sunday school teacher, a graduate of Williams at a time when that college's undergraduate body consisted almost wholly of pros-

NEVER TOO LATE TO MEND.

WHAT I HAVE SEWED TOGETHER LET NO ONE RIP ASUNDER.

THIS COAT WAS SEWED ON A SINGER MACHINE

AND THE DEVIL CAME AND SEWED TABLE

MAKING ENDS MEET.

Comic trade cards (above) were handed out in the 1890's to buyers, would-be buyers, and agents for Singer's newfangled machine. The travel cards (below) were widely distributed at country fairs and testify to the ubiquity of the founder's sales force, which canvassed from the frozen tundra of Archangel to the coral reefs of the Caroline Islands.

ARCHANGEL

ALGERIA.

ALBANIA.

WALES

CAROLINE ISLANDS.

CHINA.

PHILIPPINE ISLANDS 'MANILA'

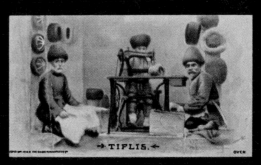

TIFLIS.

pective clergymen and missionaries, Clark nevertheless, as we have seen, accepted.

There were now once again three partners—Singer, Zieber, and Clark—and all three, so unlike in other ways, were united in one respect: each thought there was one partner too many. Zieber, the would-be capitalist, considered Clark a usurper. Neither Clark nor Singer could see that Zieber was of any earthly use. An open rupture, however, was averted when Zieber fell sick of undulant fever; in the fear that he might die and leave a widow harassed by debts, he consented to sell his interest in the company to Singer and Clark for $6,000—an adequate return on the $40 he had originally invested, but microscopic in terms of what the interest was soon to be worth.*

Clark, once he had decided to stay with the firm despite Singer's gaudy peccadilloes, turned out to be precisely the man for the job. By that time he had discovered (or thought he had) how far the warmth of Singer's nature could lead him; but he had discovered as well that Singer's machine was so far superior to any other on the market that, if all went well, he would soon be a very wealthy man indeed. Despite his wife's advice, then, and to protect his stake, Clark plunged enthusiastically into the welter of lawsuits that had been let loose by Elias Howe's charges of infringement.

By 1852 there were a dozen or more manufacturers elbowing their way into the sewing-machine business, each seeking any means, fair or foul, to wring an advantage from the rest. Of these, the largest were I. M. Singer & Co., Wheeler & Wilson Co., and Grover & Baker Co. In addition, Howe, although at first he manufactured no machines, bulked big because of his patent. From 1852 until late in 1856 each of these parties zestfully sued every other in what the press hailed as "the sewing machine war."

It all began quietly enough with a suit brought by Howe against an unimportant company, but by 1854, having won a series of minor victories, Howe was able to force I. M. Singer & Co. to pay $28,000 in settlement of past claims and, furthermore, to pay a license

fee of $10 on every machine sold in the future. By that time Clark had cunningly purchased the rights to a number of early patents, in consequence of which he was ready to bring suit, on behalf of I. M. Singer & Co., against all his rivals. In October, 1854, Clark wondered whether, like himself, those rivals might not be wearying of the struggle. "There are many cogent reasons," he wrote to Howe, "why, in the future, we should act cordially together in respect to the maintenance and enforcement of our various pat

NEW-YORK HISTORICAL SOCIETY

This was Singer's original sewing machine, patented in 1851.

ents." But this reasoning failed; he was obliged to club his mulish competitors over the ears with lawsuits for two more years.

At length, in answer to an action brought by Clark in a United States circuit court at Albany, New York, there assembled the officers and counsel of all the principal sewing-machine manufacturers. Howe was there too, called as a witness. All the interested parties were stopping at the same hotel, Congress Hall, and presently all hands were plunged into negotiations. All night they chaffered and bickered, but a few minutes before the scheduled time for court to sit on the first of the suits, the disputants smiled, shook hands, and initialed a memorable agreement. Under its terms there was established what was called (the phrase had, at the time, no connotations of restraint of trade or competition) the Sewing Machine Combination. It was the archetypal patent pool, the model for similar arrangements later agreed upon in the automotive, aircraft, movie, and radio industries.

The pool was a triumph for Clark. Not only did it put an end to all the expensive litigation; not only did the four principals—I. M. Singer & Co., Grover & Baker, Wheeler & Wilson, and Elias Howe—agree to cross-license all their patents; additionally, all other sewing-machine manufacturers were obliged to pay a license fee of $15, of which $5 went to Howe, $5 to

* In an account of this incident which he wrote some time later —for he survived the fever—Zieber was well-nigh incoherent with rage. He had, he contended, been "robbed," "victimized" by scoundrels. He claimed that he would never have agreed to sell out for a paltry $6,000 had not Singer told him: "The Doctor thinks you won't get over [your sickness]. Don't you want to give up your interest in the business altogether?" Not until later, Zieber claimed, did he discover that Singer had never met the physician and that the physician had never said any such thing. In his account of the affair, however, Zieber reveals himself to be a well-meaning but naïve man, pathetically fated to lose out under the economic code of the nineteenth century—survival of the fittest. "During the month of June, 1860," he wrote, "I disposed of the stock on hand, and went afterwards to Montevideo."

I. M. Singer & Co., and $2.50 to each of the other companies. Howe's royalty was thus cut in half,* and the primacy of I. M. Singer & Co. as manufacturers was acknowledged. It remained only for Clark, as a merchant, to maintain that position.

To attempt to sell a home appliance a century ago was to brave an uncharted wilderness. How to gain consumer acceptance for a brand-new gadget? How to demonstrate that the owner's life would be enriched by its possession? How high to price this innovation? How to merchandise and distribute profitably, on a nationwide basis? How to evaluate the importance of advertising? What share of profits to plow back for expansion and for research and development? In short, how best and most profitably to sell and keep on selling? These are all questions that intensely interest manufacturers, distributors, salesmen, and their advertising agents today; and it is safe to say that today's entrepreneurs are all following the trail that Clark boldly and resourcefully hacked into the forest. Consider just a handful of the problems Clark faced, and his pioneering solutions.

Item: How to overcome the prevailing prejudice that women were too stupid to be trusted with a machine? As early as 1852 there was a girl in the company's Broadway shopwindow, demonstrating how simple the machine was to operate; the crowds that gathered to watch were as big as any that flocked to Phineas T. Barnum's museum, a few steps away. Moreover, Clark established, all over the country, a fully developed system of franchised agencies, each of which was staffed by an agent who was also the salesman, a young woman to demonstrate the machine, and a competent mechanic to service and repair the machines sold. Such a system was unique in its time. "The business we do is peculiar," Clark wrote in 1853, "and we have adopted our own method of transacting it."

Item: How to persuade the customer who already owned a sewing machine that he should buy an improved model, incorporating new features? By February, 1856, Clark announced that any "inferior or wholly worthless" machine—by which he intended the public to understand any machine that was not a new Singer—could be traded in against a new Singer for a cash value of fifty dollars. This was another first for

the sewing-machine industry.

Item: How to influence the market leaders? Clark offered clergymen his machines at half price; newspaper publishers were made the same offer if they would give advertising space to compensate for the other half.

Item: How to sell an appliance costing more than $100 at a time when the American family's average annual income was in the neighborhood of $500? In September, 1856, Clark, taking his cue from New York furniture manufacturers and New England clockmakers, introduced the concept of installment buying, and this was a first for any merchant distributing on a national scale. It was also a startling innovation in commercial relationships. It so bemused a writer for the *Scientific American* that he lost his grip on his syntax: "A psychological fact, possibly new, which has come to light in this sewing machine business," he wrote, "is that a woman would rather pay $100 for a machine in monthly installments of five dollars than $50 outright, although able to do so."

All this commercial pioneering brought a gratifying flood of the dimes that, Isaac Singer had declared, were all he was after. How could it be otherwise when, for a machine priced at $110, the manufacturing costs ran as low as $23? Singer, with only an occasional show of bravura in the commercial sphere, had sedulously devoted himself to improving the product. He left Clark to attend to the business end: the legal questions, the patent problems, the merchandising and the primitive advertising. Singer was even content to have Clark make his machine fancy; "Mr. Singer," Clark wrote to an agent, "is now fully aroused as to the importance of having highly ornamented machines." Singer himself, meanwhile, poured his energies into product research and development and into production. By 1857 he held a dozen patents on various developments. He had spent long hours in the machine shop; one of the mechanics later recalled him as "companionable . . . a good story teller . . . his genius for acting came into good play. The world was made brighter by his presence."

But Singer considered it was time for him to brighten more of the world than just his machine shop. By 1859 his loves and his comforts, like those Desdemona prayed for, began to increase even as his days did grow. Together with his principal consort, Mary Ann Sponsler, he moved to a fashionable address, 14 Fifth Avenue. The count of his progeny was now eighteen: two by his wife, Maria; ten by Mary Ann Sponsler (but of these two had died); one by Mary Eastwood Walters "Merritt"; and five by Mary McGonigal "Mathews." His confidence, always high, had waxed to the point where he could recognize

* But in return, the others agreed that they would license at least 24 manufacturers. Howe's patent expired in 1860; at that time the license fee was cut to $7, and Howe's share to $1. Considering that his invention had never been practical, he did well from it: his royalties are reported to have totaled $1,185,000. Thanks to his victories in the cases for infringement, moreover, to him has been accorded the accolade of history (at least in the United States) as the inventor of one of the most useful of all home appliances, a device described by Louis Antoine Godey, the publisher of *Godey's Lady's Book*, as "next to the plough . . . perhaps humanity's most blessed instrument."

love even when it came to him under some name other than Mary. He engaged to accept the devotion of a pair of Ellens—Ellen Brazee and Ellen Livingston—young ladies whose unions with Singer were, however, never blessed. Heretofore he had been content to wait for love to come to him, but now he grew apprehensive; he seemed to dread that perhaps love was not aware of his change of address. In any event, according to the subsequent testimony of his coachman, he took to waiting for romance to find him on street corners.

Singer kept his coachman busy. He had ten horses, which had cost him $10,000; he maintained three carriages, at a cost of another $3,000. But all this was not enough. He conceived a jumbo equipage on which he actually took out a patent (Number 25,920). It was, said the New York *Herald*, "a regular steamboat on wheels . . . a monster, having all the conveniences of a modern brownstone front, with the exception of a cooking department." This mammoth, weighing nearly two tons and painted, lest anyone fail to notice it, a vivid canary yellow, could seat 31 passengers, inside and out; it was outfitted with a nursery at the back end, "with beds to put the dear ones to sleep"; a small orchestra could be accommodated in seats on the outside, "with guards enough to keep off all outside barbarians"; it was drawn by nine horses: three cream-colored ones in front, then a light-colored cream between two sorrels, and finally a bay between two large gray wheel horses. "Whether," the *Herald*'s reporter commented with pardonable asperity, "this eccentric turnout is intended for speed, comfort or advertisement, the reader must judge."

For a man of Singer's rumbustious tastes and temperament, New York in the years before the Civil War was a congenial playground. A massive man, exploding with vitality, on easy terms with the theatrical and sporting world, Singer ignored the pretensions of Knickerbocker society and by night delighted instead in the more raffish night spots to which he squired actresses of the day. He cut an im-

pressive swath through an unimpressive society, until at length he came a cropper. As might have been predicted, this came about as a result of his ostentation. It could never have happened to a man with only one horse and carriage.

On August 7, 1860, Singer went for a drive up Fifth Avenue with Mary McGonigal. The sun was benign, his curly beard was combed, and all was right with the world until, to his horror, another of his carriages drew up alongside. In it was sitting Mary Ann Sponsler. She looked his way. Hastily he bade his coachman turn down the next street, but too late; Mary Ann's carriage was at his wheels, and Mary Ann's mouth was angrily open.

This incident was the catalyst. Mary Ann had long been privately grieving over the fact that she, the mother of eight Singer children, was not virtuous in the eyes of society. She insisted that she would never have followed him through the Midwest, never have borne his children, had he not promised to divorce Maria Haley and marry her. What irked Mary Ann was that, by August of 1860, Singer was perfectly free to marry again. Six months before, he had at long last divorced his wife, but though he was living with Mary Ann, he had nonetheless refused to make an honest woman of her. And so, on this particular day, her public berating continued through the streets until at last his carriage pulled away from hers and, mercifully, out of range.

Thereafter, just as today, events crowded upon each other according to fixed ritual. She hurried home, but he was there first; there were words, then blows, then appeals to the police, then the cold, white light of public notoriety. Discreetly, Singer decamped to Europe, accompanied, so declared his furious consort, by Kate McGonigal, younger sister of Mary.

In the offices of I. M. Singer & Co., Edward Clark was understandably scandalized. For months he had been seeking general acceptance of the sewing machine by offering it to community leaders—parsons and teachers—at half price. And this was his reward. He sent off one stinging letter of rebuke after an-

On March 6, 1865, Singer employees marched in New York's Grand Procession honoring Lincoln's second inauguration.

other to his chastened partner. When the Civil War broke out, Clark seemed almost to blame that cataclysm, too, on Singer. "Business is pretty much at a standstill," he wrote. "I am suffering for all the large public show of wealth which you made in 1859 and '60. It was industriously spread abroad that the firm was rich. Now all who are rich are expected to be patriotic and to give liberally. . . . I am called on many times a day to subscribe and am obliged to refuse."

Soon after his return to America in 1861, Singer was served with papers by counsel for Mary Ann Sponsler; this time she was suing him for divorce. It was a curious case: a woman who had lived with him intermittently for a quarter century, who had borne him ten children, yet to whom he had never been married, suing for divorce. Her grounds were that Singer had lived with her as his common-law wife for seven months after his divorce from Maria Haley, and in her complaint she made it clear that she had been brooding powerfully for some time over Singer's iniquities. He was, she declared, "a most notorious profligate"; she had concluded, moreover, that "a more dissolute man never lived in a civilized country." This was drawing a very long bow, but apparently the judge agreed with her, for he awarded her $8,000 a year as temporary alimony—a record for the time—pending a permanent settlement. In a commendable effort to save himself still greater notoriety should the suit be prosecuted further, Singer settled out of court: he bought and furnished her a house in 28th Street, paid her lawyers' fees, and gave her $500 in a lump sum and $50 a week for life or for so long as she should not marry. Then he wrote a crestfallen and characteristically illiterate letter to his partner:

Mr. Clark, dear sir, My private afairs (though justly merited) hangs heavy upon me and my soul sicends [sickens] at the prospects befor me and for the well fare of all conserned try to make my load of grief as light as posabl. . . .

This done, Singer retired again to Europe.

In France, he found, matters were managed differently and, he considered, rather better. He stopped at a *pension* in Paris owned by the English-born widow of a Frenchman. This lady, Mme Pamela Boyer, had a daughter—intelligent, attractive, tactful, and gay. Her name was Isabella, and neither she nor her mother knew of a reason why she should not become the rich American's mistress. And so not only love but also a measure of peace came to the distracted Singer. For Isabella Boyer seems, altogether, to have been a remarkably able woman. When they came to America in 1863 (Singer had learned that Mary Ann Sponsler had secretly married, which obliged him to come to a new settlement with her), Isabella promptly endeared herself to all of Isaac's children, whether of the left hand or the right; moreover, though Isaac had been divorced, she somehow managed to inveigle an Episcopal rector into solemnizing her union with him.

But this belated access of respectability did not suffice to appease Edward Clark. Too long had the partners rasped on each other; in July, 1863, they rancorously agreed to dissolve the partnership. I. M. Singer & Co. became The Singer Manufacturing Company, but, at Isaac's stipulation, neither was permitted to be president of the new corporation so long as the other should live. There were, however, compensations. Of an original capitalization of 5,000 shares priced nominally at $100 apiece, Clark and Singer each held 2,075; the balance they sold (at $200 apiece) to seventeen officers and employees of the company. The first dividend was declared in October, and within five years those who had paid $200 a share for their stock had gotten $225 in dividends. The golden flood was still only a trickle; the company has never skipped a dividend. One share in 1863 had become by 1958, through splits and stock dividends, 900 shares, worth about $36,000 at the current market price of about $40 a share, during which long time it had paid cash dividends of $131,340.

By the end of the Civil War the corporation began to expand in earnest. By 1867 the first foreign factory had been built, near Glasgow; and already the Singer salesman, America's first world-wide commercial ambassador, was pressing his obstinate finger on the doorbells of the world. Everywhere he carried the Singer name; everywhere he enhanced his own reputation for pertinacity. He was incredibly competitive: once, when a Singer representative shot and killed a Wheeler & Wilson rival in a frontier saloon near Tacoma, Washington, he found he had gone too far, for he was lynched. Jokes (many of them, to our sophisticated ears, unbearably corny) grew up around the Singer salesman and his product as, two generations later, they would grow up around the Tin Lizzie. Thus:

"Why is a Singer Sewing Machine like a kiss?"

"Because it seams so good."

On its centennial, not long ago, The Singer Manufacturing Company was able to hand out instruction booklets in 54 different languages, boast of more than 100,000,000 machines sold, point to fifteen factories —seven in the United States and the others scattered over Europe and South America—and glory in 5,000 Singer sewing centers all over the world.

But even as early as 1863 his holdings afforded Isaac Singer a very comfortable living. It was in February of that year that Ebenezer Butterick, a Yankee tailor, conceived the notion (he was not the first to do so) of making and selling dress patterns; and the success of his venture gave a boost to the entire sewing-machine industry. Singers were being sold, as well, to the Union Army; in 1865, when Singer employees marched in a vast New York parade celebrating Lincoln's second inauguration, their principal sign proclaimed, "We Clothe the Union Armies—While Grant Is Dressing the Rebels."

On the tide of this prosperity, Isaac Singer coasted into a cozy retirement. If Clark had feared that his partner would go on as before, he erred, for though Singer was still in the prime of life, he suddenly became a model of docile domesticity, a doting father and grandfather. He even submitted to baptism at the hands of an Episcopal minister, his sponsors being his Catholic-born wife and an illegitimate son. He essayed first the life of a Hudson River Valley patroon; but by 1867 it was evident that his wife was languishing, away from France, so he moved his family back to Paris, to a sumptuous mansion in the Rue Malesherbes. In honor of their return, they named Isabella's fourth (and Isaac's twenty-second) child Paris Eugene. The last two Singer children were born there as well; but then, concerned for his wife's health as much as by the Franco-Prussian War, Singer removed first to London and finally, in 1872, to Oldway, a great estate in Paignton, near Torquay, a seaside resort on the Channel coast of Devon.

Now, hedged about as he was with all the perquisites of the landed gentry, Singer might have produced a fascinating memoir if only he had been literate. He had to express himself otherwise.

There was a large house on his grounds, but it was not grand enough for Singer. He chose to spread himself. Working closely with architect and builders, he caused to be reared a palace which he dubbed The Wigwam: it was a Greco-Romano-Renaissance effusion, colonnaded inside and out. In design, it leaned chiefly on the Petit Trianon at Versailles. In addition to the usual 115 rooms there was a completely equipped theater, a circular coach house big enough for half-a-hundred carriages, and a vast marble hall with a grand marble and bronze staircase flanked by an enormous painting by David portraying the coronation of another man celebrated for the gratification of his instincts, Napoleon I. For all this, the onetime star of *Reclaimed, or, the Danger of Moderate Drinking* shelled out $500,000 in old-fashioned money.

Here, at last, was the life. Singer, now past 60, puttered through his marble halls. He amused himself with sketches toward the invention of a steel truss. He delighted in entertaining his various children, no matter who their mother. The Sunday supplements had yet to be circulated in Paignton; in consequence, Singer was regarded by his humble neighbors as odd, but friendly and generous. Even excessively so: periodically he launched monstrous entertainments to which all in the countryside were invited. When he died in July, 1875, he was tendered an impressive funeral, with a mile-long procession of 75 carriages and two thousand mourners; flags in Paignton and Torquay stood at half-mast.

In New York City, Edward Clark joined in "sincerely deploring the loss of this distinguished inventor," and at once got himself elected president of the company.

The distinguished inventor was dead, but his genes went marching on. So, in more decorous fashion, did those of Edward Clark, who by 1882 had followed Singer to the grave. In death as in life, Clark's effects were tidily and prudently disposed among his near and dear, who were neither numerous nor clamorous. Singer's legacy, on the other hand, no matter how carefully he had contrived to order it before he died, caused a scandal as great as any in which he had been involved in life.

Clark's heirs, who have held a dominant share of The Singer Manufacturing Company stock, have used their wealth unexceptionably. The beauty of Cooperstown, New York, testifies to their wisdom, as does the first-rate collection of modern French paintings presently gracing the Sterling and Francine Clark Art Institute in Williamstown, Massachusetts. Their generous support of such institutions as the New-York Historical Society and the Metropolitan Museum of Art is well-known. The family, like its founder, has been uniformly well-bred and well-behaved.

In contrast, Singer's will was bitterly contested from every direction. William and Lillian, his oldest legitimate children, had been given $500 and $10,000 respectively. As far back as 1851 William had disgusted his father by his lack of gumption; "The last two days he spent in the office, Barzillan Ransom said of William, "he was engaged in writing a play for one of the Theatres." Perhaps matters might have gone easier with William had he been an acceptable playwright; but no, he was not even that. Isaac's first wife, Catharine Maria, was likewise morose, for she had been left nothing. The three of them, however, settled for an additional $150,000 paid by the more fortunate heirs. (All the other children were awarded handsome bundles of Singer stock.)

The chief recalcitrant was Mary Ann Sponsler Foster. She had embittered Singer's life and blackened his name. Her own children—save one, John Albert Singer—had turned against her. She had struck a deal with Isaac but concealed from him her violation of it. Now she insisted on $1,000,000, rejected any smaller settlement, and required that her suit be brought in the surrogate's court of Westchester County. In a courtroom crowded with fashionably dressed, scandal-minded onlookers, Mary Ann was her own worst witness. Her attorneys were hard put to find witnesses who would support her, even from among her own children. Only Orson Phelps stepped forward, a figure out of the past, to prate of how, a quarter century before, Singer had spent more time reciting Shakespeare than working on his own invention. At length Mary Ann accepted $75,000, in return renouncing all claims.

The subsequent careers of many of Singer's children recalled the gaudy ways of their progenitor. Of the 22 who survived him, all but six had issue, and they contracted among them 35 marriages. One daughter married Prince Edmond de Polignac and was a friend of Marcel Proust; her musicales were celebrated events in Paris, and when she died she left behind a fund, administered by the *Fondation Singer-Polignac*, to give grants-in-aid to talented artists, musicians, and scientists. Another daughter married the downstart son of an impoverished southern banker, passed her middle years storming the aristocratic citadels of Newport, and retired to the Riviera, where, her husband having died, she engaged a succession of handsome chauffeurs and eventually dwindled away into a Noel Coward joke.

The true throwback among the Singer children was Paris, who died in 1932 but was immortalized in Isadora Duncan's memoirs as her lover (she called him Lohengrin). Paris inherited his father's splendid stature (6'4"), his father's vitality and animal magnetism, a generous slice of his father's fortune (worth, at Paris' majority, perhaps $15,000,000), and his father's faculty for invention (an electric organ and an internal-combustion engine). He was also capable of the grand gesture. Thus, he paid out $200,000 for an option on the old Madison Square Garden as a gift to Isadora Duncan; but when she was not properly appreciative, he allowed the option to lapse and let the $200,000 gurgle down the drain. When they parted in an emotional thunderstorm, Paris consoled himself by staking

Addison Mizner as architect of Palm Beach and by himself becoming that resort's *arbiter elegantiae*; the dissolution of his Florida dreams reduced him to sailing up and down the Nile on chartered dahabeahs.

Thanks to their elders, Singer's grandchildren (there were at least 54) had far less money to spend, and they spent or invested it far more primly—albeit not colorlessly. One shot wild animals in the African veld; one built an unimportant railroad; one made a hobby of attending National Amateur Golf Championships ("It brings out the best in me," asserted Mortimer Singer, Jr.); one married a showgirl who, according to Ziegfeld, had the most beautiful legs in the world; one married a broker, and *her* child, grown to man's estate, in 1922 plunked down a substantial sum of money to back *Time,* then still a struggling infant of a news magazine; one, dying in London, left her will so well hidden that a spiritualist who undertook to locate it by means of its emanations swooned from the strain as he left her premises; one retired as a nun into a French convent.

It is difficult, in surveying this assorted brood, to find a clue to a final judgment of their sire. What was Isaac Singer? Was he merely a Casanova? Was he a Don Juan in the Mozartian sense—a rebel, unscrupulously at war with every convention? Or was he simply an amoral and energetic hooligan blessed with a useful mechanical aptitude?

That there were many women in his life there can be no doubt. That most of them were genuinely fond of him is manifest, and it is the rawest of ironies that, in attempting to assess Singer, we must depend almost entirely on the evidence of the one woman who came to hate him. For the only detailed account of his private life is to be found in the divorce proceedings brought against him by Mary Ann Sponsler. She may be said to have been amply avenged for any hurts he gave her; thanks to her, posterity's picture of Singer is that of a blackguard. Yet surely her account was not disinterested.

A less prejudiced witness might have concluded that Singer, while he was not the most punctilious of men, must have been, more often than not, a charming, likeable vulgarian, bubbling over with animal spirits, with a voracious appetite for life and a ready, if rough, talent for savoring all its delights. And quite apart from what he bequeathed to his children, he gave the world a most useful appliance indeed, the more appropriate since it was the gift of a man who, to put it moderately, must have been aware of the toil necessary to raise and clothe a large family.

"My God, it talks!" said the Emperor of
Brazil. So the new invention did—but not until
Alexander Graham Bell and his assistant
had solved some brain-racking problems

The *Voice Heard Round the World*

By LINCOLN BARNETT

On the afternoon of June 2, 1875, two young men bent over work benches in the hot and stifling garret of a five-story brick building occupied by the electrical workshops of Charles Williams, at 109 Court Street, Boston. They did not speak to one another, for they were in separate rooms some sixty feet apart, at opposite ends of the floor. Between the rooms ran a length of wire.

The younger of the two men was Thomas A. Watson, twenty-one years old, a native of Salem who had left school at the age of thirteen but had become, during several years of employment at the workshop, an able and imaginative technician. His skill had been tested in the construction of virtually all the devices required by Williams' clients—call bells, telegraph keys, galvanometers, annunciators, relays, sounders. He had, moreover, read nearly all of the few books on electricity then available, in the morning of the electrical age. His fingers were deft, his intelligence keen.

The man at the other end of the wire was a tall, rather pale, dark-haired, brown-bearded amateur inventor named Alexander Graham Bell. He was twenty-eight years and three months old. Unlike his collaborator, he had no connection with the Williams workshop. He was, in fact, a teacher of the deaf and a specialist in training teachers of the deaf. He held the title of professor of vocal physiology at Boston University. But for more than a year he had been working with Watson on an invention that he called a "harmonic telegraph." And he had been thinking about it for more than a decade.

The purpose of Bell's harmonic telegraph was to make possible the transmission of several messages over a single telegraph wire at the same time without interference. Thirty-one years had elapsed since Samuel F. B. Morse sent his famous message, "What hath God wrought," over the world's first telegraph circuit, between Washington and Baltimore. During that interval wires had spread like spider webs across the face of the land, and in 1866 the first successful submarine cable spanned the Atlantic Ocean. But as the demand for telegraph service soared, the capacity of each wire remained precisely the same: one message per wire per unit of time. Bell was well aware of the need for multiple telegraphy, and he had formed a notion as to how it could be achieved.

The germ of his idea had first incubated in his mind when, at the age of nineteen, he was teaching elocution and music at Weston House, a boys' school near his native Edinburgh, Scotland. As the son and grandson of teachers of elocution, Bell had already acquired a great deal of knowledge about acoustics and the anatomy of the human vocal apparatus. One day when he was alone it occurred to him to attempt some informal experiments to determine how vowel sounds are produced. Shaping his mouth and tongue into position to pronounce a given vowel, he tapped his teeth or cheeks with his fingernail or a pencil. His trained ear easily

Opposite: In 1892, only seventeen years after the first sentence was transmitted by telephone, Alexander Graham Bell helped dramatize the opening of the World's Columbian Exposition with the first words ever spoken in New York and heard in Chicago. A.T.&T. officials watched with satisfaction.

distinguished the varying resonance pitches of his mouth cavities as they changed form in the production of different vowel sounds. He concluded that every vowel sound is the product of resonances from the changing cavities of the mouth.

Believing that his findings were original, he set them down in an enthusiastic forty-page letter to his father, Alexander Melville Bell, who was then teaching elocution in London. Bell senior passed them on to a friend and professional colleague, Alexander James Ellis, a leader in British philological circles. Regretfully Ellis informed young Bell that his work had been anticipated three years earlier by the great German physicist and physiologist Hermann von Helmholtz, who had reached similar conclusions and described them in a work that has since become a classic, *On the Sensations of Tone*. Helmholtz's experiments had been vastly more elaborate than Bell's, for he had produced vowel sounds not with the human mouth but through combinations of electrically operated tuning forks and resonators. Owing to his limited knowledge of German, Bell could not follow the intricacies of Helmholtz's exposition. But from his study of the accompanying pictures and diagrams of apparatus he concluded that the German scientist had succeeded in transmitting vowel sounds from one point to another over a wire. His assumption was completely wrong; and Ellis, who was then at work translating Helmholtz's treatise into English, corrected him, explaining that the German had simply used electromagnets to keep his tuning forks in continuous vibration.

This episode left several important residuals in Bell's mind. First was his discovery that tuning forks could be made to vibrate continuously by the intermittent attraction of electromagnets. Second was the concept that had grown out of his misreading of the Helmholtz text. For even though he had leapt to an inaccurate conclusion and knew he had done so, his original error began leading a life of its own in his private meditations. If one imagined that vowel sounds *could* somehow be transmitted over a wire, why not the entire spectrum of the human voice? And finally, he had come to realize that he lacked the knowledge of electricity required to undertake the experiments that now began to clamor in his mind for execution. He resolved to repair this deficiency, and in the following year, 1867, while engaged in teaching elocution in the city of Bath, he started experimenting in his leisure moments with telegraph apparatus, electromagnets, and tuning forks. He continued his investigations in London, where, from 1868 until the spring of 1870, he assisted his father with elocution classes and completed his own education at University College.

Then tragedy struck the Bell family. Three years earlier, Graham's younger brother, Edward Charles, had died of tuberculosis. Now, in May of 1870, his older brother, Melville, who had been carrying on the original Bell elocution classes in Edinburgh since his father's move to London, died of the same disease. And Graham himself disclosed symptoms that led doctors to warn that he too was gravely threatened. His father did not delay. Determining to get his surviving son

FAMILY: *Four generations of Bells gathered at Beinn Bhreagh, their summer place in Nova Scotia, in 1903. Left to right: Bell's father; his mother; Bell, with grandson Melville Grosvenor (now National Geographic Society president); Bell's daughter, Elsie Grosvenor.*

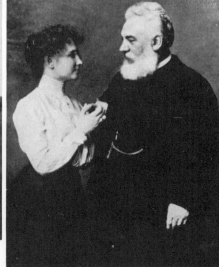

DEAFNESS: *A lifetime concern with the problems of the deaf led Bell to a long and intimate friendship with Helen Keller, here shown at twenty-one in 1901.*

FRESH WATER: *Bell's wideranging mind conceived the idea of condensing fog to obtain fresh water for sailors lost at sea. Here he observes results at Beinn Bhreagh.*

out of London into cleaner, drier air, he abandoned his career at its most prosperous peak, sold his house, and with his wife and Graham sailed for Canada in July. A few weeks later they moved into their new home, a modest, painted brick house perched on a height of land above the Grand River at Brantford, Ontario.*

Here young Bell quickly regained his health, and spent long days continuing to ponder the mysteries of electricity and sound. He also studied the language of the Mohawk Indians, which he mastered so fluently that the Mohawks, pleased, initiated him into their tribe with full ceremonial rites. Sometimes he reclined thoughtfully in a hammock strung between two birch trees on the bluff above the winding river. Sometimes he worked indoors with his tuning forks and electrical circuits, or experimented with the piano. Although he was an accomplished pianist, during this period he was less likely to play music than to strike single notes and listen intently as their harmonics rippled away in the quiet country air.

Gradually it dawned on him, ever more compellingly, that if a tuning fork could be made to vibrate by the intermittent attraction of an electromagnet, the process could be reversed—i.e., a tuning fork vibrating at a certain frequency could, when connected to a circuit with make-and-break points like those of an electric bell, impose its frequency on an electric current. Then if the intermittent current so created were transmitted along a wire to a second tuning fork, the second fork would vibrate in resonance with the transmitting fork. And thus—in accordance with the physical principle of sympathetic vibration—a given note or tone could be sent from one point to another over a telegraph wire.

Extrapolating further, Bell reasoned that if the transmitting fork were also connected to a telegrapher's key that could open and close the circuit, the fork would then become in effect a telegraphic sender, capable of transmitting a series of Morse code signals —dots and dashes—at its own particular frequency. Now suppose further that instead of just one sending fork, you had perhaps six, each with a different pitch, or frequency, and each one paired with a receiving fork of exactly the same frequency at the other end of the line. Then if all six forks began transmitting Morse signals along the same wire at the same time, a complex electrical current carrying six different frequencies would flow through the wire to the receiving end. There each of the six receiving forks, each with its electromagnet and each tuned exclusively to the pitch of its sending partner, would vibrate in resonance with its partner—and only with its partner. The complex signal would thus be unscrambled and each of the six messages sent simultaneously over the same wire would be clearly received. This train of thought led Bell to his conception of the harmonic telegraph.

It was this conception that Bell carried with him from Brantford to Boston in the spring of 1871 when,

* Since Bell evolved many of his fundamental concepts there, the house at Brantford is today maintained as a national monument by the government of Canada.

FLYING: *Intensely interested in aviation, Bell spent many hours in the early 1900's designing and flying special kites to probe the secrets of aerodynamics. Above, he is seen at far right; in the photo at right, he and grandson Melville haul on a big man-lifting kite.*

HYDROFOILS: *In the last years before his death in 1922, Bell anticipated modern developments in hydrofoil boats. This one went seventy m.p.h.*

fully recovered from his illness, he resumed his career as a teacher. He had been offered a fee of five hundred dollars by the Boston school board for a series of lectures on "Visible Speech," a code of written symbols indicating the position and action of the vocal organs in the production of various sounds, which had been devised by his father as a valuable aid in teaching the deaf to speak. Apart from the money involved, the prospect appealed to Bell enormously for several reasons. He was anxious to return to active professional life, he enjoyed teaching, and he had always been profoundly interested in the problems of the deaf. His mother was deaf.

During the ensuing months Bell made up his mind to remain permanently in the United States, and in October, 1872, he opened a school of vocal physiology and the mechanics of speech in Boston, where he demonstrated his father's methods before teachers of the deaf. A year later he received an appointment as professor of vocal physiology at Boston University, and transferred his students there. Through his work with the deaf, Bell met two men who would prove tremendously important to him in the years that lay just ahead. One was Gardiner Greene Hubbard, a Boston lawyer and president of Clarke Institute for Deaf-Mutes in Northampton, Massachusetts; Hubbard's daughter Mabel had lost her hearing through an attack of scarlet fever when she was barely four years old. The other was Thomas Sanders, a prosperous leather merchant of Salem, whose five-year-old son George, born deaf, became one of Bell's private students. Grateful to Bell for his interest in their children, both men became his close friends and within a year of their first meeting, upon learning of his electrical experiments, offered to cover his expenses in return for a share in future patent rights.

Despite his crowded daily teaching schedule, Bell continued his experiments, working far into the night in an effort to perfect the harmonic telegraph. Sometime during the winter of 1873–74 he conceived the idea of improving his device by substituting flexible strips of metal—like organ reeds or flattened clock springs—for the tuning forks. As he envisaged the new apparatus, one end of each reed would be clamped firmly to one pole of an electromagnet; the other end, extended horizontally, would be free to vibrate over the other pole. Each reed would be provided with a tuning mechanism.

Lacking the time and mechanical skill to construct the necessary parts, Bell sought help at Williams' workshop in Court Street. At that time the electrical industry was still in its infancy, and the Williams establishment with its thirty-odd employees ranked as one of the best-equipped shops in the country. Among its employees was Thomas A. Watson, and it was he who came to assist Bell in the modification of his harmonic telegraph. From their initial encounter grew a long and rewarding professional association.

In a memoir written years afterward, Watson recalled: "I made half a dozen pairs of the harmonic instruments for Bell. He was surprised, when he tried them, to find that they didn't work as well as he expected." The failures, however, were blessings in disguise. For, as Watson pointed out, "Had his harmonic telegraph been a well-behaved apparatus that always did what its parent wanted it to do, the speaking telephone might never have emerged from a certain marvellous conception that had even then been surging back of Bell's high forehead for two or three years."

That marvellous conception had slowly flowered through a synthesis of ideas and observations made in the course of his work on the harmonic telegraph. After he had given up on the tuning forks and had started to think in terms of organ reeds, he began to contemplate larger numbers of transmitting units. He knew from his musical experience that if he put his head inside a piano and sang or spoke, a number of strings would respond. Hence if he constructed a "harp transmitter" with enough strings or reeds to pick up every frequency of the human voice, their combined vibrations could be converted into a complex electric current that would vary in intensity with the varying sounds of the voice. And a receiver harp at the other end of the circuit would reproduce those sounds. Although Bell suspected that his theoretical harp transmitter was too big, too complicated, and probably too expensive to be practical, he nevertheless felt that the underlying principles were sound, and the conception persisted in his mind.

Meanwhile, his work with the deaf had taken him one day to the physics laboratory at the Massachusetts Institute of Technology to inspect a remarkable new instrument called the phonautograph. This contrivance was a kind of speaking trumpet, closed at the far end by a stretched membrane. Attached to the membrane was a stylus. When words were spoken into the mouthpiece the membrane vibrated, causing the stylus to trace an oscillating wave pattern on a piece of smoked glass. Bell thought that the instrument might be useful in teaching articulation to the deaf by revealing to them visually the relationship between the sounds they articulated, or tried to articulate, and the patterns traced by the stylus on the smoked glass.

Unfortunately the phonautograph did not work satisfactorily for Bell's purposes. He was struck, however, by a similarity between its mechanism and that of the human ear, and it occurred to him that the phonautograph might be improved were it modelled more closely upon the structure of the ear. Seeking more accurate anatomical information, he consulted a famous Boston ear specialist, Dr. Clarence J. Blake. Somewhat to Bell's surprise, Blake suggested that instead of constructing a phonautograph around a model of the ear, he should use an actual human ear, excised from some donor in the morgue. What was more, the Doctor would provide one. And he did, properly preserved and prepared for scientific study. The experiment proved highly successful. Bell constructed a new phonautograph, using the ear as a component, and found that its tracings of sound patterns on the smoked glass were vastly more accurate than those of the instrument at M.I.T. But what stirred Bell more deeply than this hope of a new device for teaching the deaf was the opening of a new avenue of thought provided by his glimpse into the secret corridors of the inner ear.

Bell carried his apparatus home with him to Brantford in July, 1874, and continued his experiments with it during his summer vacation. He continued to marvel over the mechanisms of the ear, and especially the ability of the tiny diaphragm—the ear drum—to move the relatively heavy bones of the ear. Then suddenly, on July 26, 1874, one of those amazing cross-circuits of thought that happen without premeditation produced a blinding scintillation in his mind. For several hours he had been brooding over the problems inherent in his harp transmitter, wondering if he could not find a less cumbersome device than one involving a whole choir of strings or reeds—and some simpler way to pick up the sounds of the human voice and generate a current that would vary in intensity as the air varied in density during the production of those sounds.

Years later Bell described the exact moment at which he suddenly perceived the solution he had sought: "I do not think that the membrane of the ear could have been half an inch in diameter and it appeared to be as thin as tissue paper. . . . It occurred to me that if such a thin and delicate membrane could move bones that were, relatively to it, very massive indeed, why should not a larger and stouter membrane be able to move a piece of steel in the manner I desired?"

Bell knew now he could discard all the capricious and multitudinous reeds in his harp transmitter. A single diaphragm could take their place. And a single

magnetized reed, attached to the center of the diaphragm and vibrating with the sound of the human voice, could generate a current that would vary in intensity precisely as the air varied in density during the production of that sound.

"At once the conception of a membrane speaking telephone became complete in my mind," Bell related, "for I saw that a similar instrument to that used as a transmitter could also be employed as a receiver."

The vision was there, clear and correct. But many problems of many kinds remained. A technical question that still loomed large concerned the matter of electrical induction. Both Michael Faraday in England and Joseph Henry in America had shown almost concurrently, a few decades earlier, that when a magnetized object is moved toward an electromagnet, a current is induced (generated) in the electromagnet's coil; and when it is moved away from the electromagnet a current of the opposite kind is induced. It was this principle that Bell had invoked. But he wondered now if the current induced by his magnetized reed, vibrating over an electromagnet's pole, would be strong enough to activate the receiver.

A problem of quite another variety now appeared. His financial backers in Boston, Hubbard and Sanders, were sponsoring his experiments in multiple telegraphy, and not his visionary notion of transmitting human speech by wire. Both men were convinced that success for all of them hinged on Bell's ability to perfect and patent the harmonic telegraph with all possible speed. Western Union was stringing lines across the entire continent; it was overwhelmed with more messages than it could transmit; and, most alarming of all, other inventors were aware of the principle of

Life, DEC. 16, 1915

the harmonic telegraph and were competing to win the race. Yet when Bell returned to Boston at summer's end his thoughts were still dominated by the revelations of July. Moreover, he and Watson appeared to be making little progress toward their objective of evolving a workable harmonic telegraph. It continued to balk their best efforts. Night after night they labored vainly to persuade transmitters and receivers to vibrate in monogamistic resonance with their respective mates —and with no others. It seemed that however carefully they adjusted the tuning mechanisms, the pulses that cascaded along the wire overlapped each other in turbulent disarray.

One evening, as they sat down on a bench for a brief recess, Bell decided to take Watson into his confidence and inform him of his summer speculations. As Watson recalled the conversation in later years,

Bell said to me, "Watson, I want to tell you of another idea I have which I think will surprise you!" I listened, I suspect, somewhat languidly, for I must have been working that day about sixteen hours, with only a short nutritive interval . . . but when he went on to say that he had an idea by which he believed it would be possible to talk by telegraph, my nervous system got such a shock that the tired feeling vanished. I have never forgotten his exact words; they have run in my mind ever since like a mathematical formula. "If," he said, "I could make a current of electricity vary in intensity, precisely as the air varies in density during the production of a sound, I should be able to transmit speech telegraphically."

Bell then took a piece of paper and made a sketch of his telephone transmitter as he envisaged it. They discussed it for a while and then went back to their labors on the harmonic telegraph. As Watson remembered later, they agreed that "the chances of its working were too uncertain to impress his financial backers . . . who were insisting that the wisest thing for Bell to do was to perfect the harmonic telegraph; then he would have money and leisure enough to build air castles like the telephone."

Nevertheless Bell did muster up his courage a few days later. He approached Hubbard and Sanders and asked if they would care to sponsor his new conception. The answer was no. They saw no immediate need for such an instrument, while on the other hand there was a great demand for the harmonic telegraph and every urgent reason for bringing it to practical completion. Indeed, they exhorted Bell to hurry to Washington and register his specifications with the Patent Office.

Bell's trip to Washington in February, 1875, proved a fateful one, for while he was in the capital he called upon Joseph Henry, dean of American physicists, inventor of the electric motor, and secretary of the Smithsonian Institution. In later years Bell spoke of this in-

terview as a turning point in his career. For although the great physicist, then nearly eighty years old, listened with courteous interest while Bell described his harmonic telegraph, his interest turned to excitement when the young inventor went on to discuss his hopes of transmitting human speech over a wire. He told Bell that he had "the germ of a great invention" and urged him to forge ahead with his experiments. When Bell expressed fear that he lacked the electrical knowledge necessary to overcome the difficulties, Henry said laconically, "Get it!"

Four months elapsed between Bell's conversation with Henry and the moment of enlightenment that forever afterward Bell and Watson would remember as the crucial episode of their collaboration. Those final months were not easy ones. Watson wrote later:

But this spring of 1875 was the dark hour just before the dawn. . . . The date when the conception of the undulatory or speech-transmitting current took its perfect form in Bell's mind [was] the greatest day in the history of the telephone, but certainly June 2, 1875, must always rank next; for on that day the mocking fiend inhabiting that demonic telegraph apparatus . . . opened the curtain that hides from man great Nature's secrets and gave us a glimpse into that treasury of things not yet discovered. . . .*

In the course of their experiments on the harmonic telegraph, Bell had found the source of their difficulties. The trouble lay in their inability to tune transmitters and receivers into precise and perfect congruence. Since Bell had a musical ear (and Watson did not), it was he who undertook the finicky and seemingly endless job of adjusting the tuning screws. His method was to hold the vibrating spring, or reed, of a receiver close to his ear while the corresponding transmitter in the other room was sending its intermittent current through the electromagnet. He would then manipulate the tuning screw until the vibratory whine emitted by the spring of the receiver appeared to coincide with the whine coming—through the air—from the transmitter.

On the afternoon of June 2, 1875 [Watson continued], we were hard at work on the same old job, testing some modification of the instruments. Things were badly out of tune that afternoon in that hot garret, not only the instruments,

* Watson's literary style is hardly what one would expect from a man who left school at the age of thirteen. However, when he was forty, he entered M.I.T. and took courses in literature, geology, and biology—subjects which dominated his interest in later years. He left the American Bell Telephone Company in 1881 and spent a year in Europe. On his return he went into shipbuilding and founded the Fore River Ship and Engine Company in East Braintree, Massachusetts, which had a large share in building the U.S. fleet that fought the Spanish-American War. In 1904, aged fifty, he retired from business and spent the remaining years of his life in travel. He died in 1934.

The newly invented telephone was soon put to use by the U.S. Army—sometimes in unexpected ways. About 1878 officers at Fort Keogh, Montana Territory, let some members of a Sioux peace delegation talk to others by phone over a considerable distance. Their astonishment was great and left them in a fine mood for negotiation.

but, I fancy, my enthusiasm and my temper, though Bell was as energetic as ever. I had charge of the transmitters as usual, setting them squealing one after the other, while Bell was retuning the receiver springs one by one, pressing them against his ear as I have described.

One of the transmitter springs I was attending to stopped vibrating and I plucked it to start it again. It didn't start and I kept on plucking it, when suddenly I heard a shout from Bell in the next room, and then out he came with a rush, demanding, "What did you do then? Don't change anything. Let me see!"

Bell, at the other end of the line, had heard in his receiver a startling, unbelievable sound, a sound quite different from the familiar whine of the vibrating transmitter. Instead he had heard the distinctive metallic *twang-g!* of a plucked spring, a sound with tones and overtones, a sound that made his heart stand still.

Watson showed him what had happened. The contact screw had been set down so far that it had made permanent contact with the spring. Hence when Watson plucked the spring the circuit remained unbroken. And instead of producing an intermittent current, the spring had acted as a diaphragm and sent an induced, undulating current over the line. In Watson's words,

That strip of magnetized steel by its vibration over the pole of its magnet was generating that marvellous conception of Bell's—a current of electricity that varied in intensity precisely as the air was varying in density within hearing distance of that spring. That undulatory current had passed through the connecting wire to the distant receiver which,

fortunately, was a mechanism that could transform that current back into an extremely faint echo of the sound of the vibrating spring that had generated it.

What was still more fortunate, the right man had that mechanism at his ear during that fleeting moment, and instantly recognized the transcendent importance of that faint sound thus electrically transmitted. The shout I heard and his excited rush into my room were the result of that recognition.

The speaking telephone was born at that moment. Bell knew perfectly well that the mechanism that could transmit all the complex vibrations of one sound could do the same for any sound, even that of speech. . . . All the experimenting that followed that discovery, up to the time the telephone was put into practical use, was largely a matter of working out the details.

For several hours after the unforgettable *twang*, Bell and Watson repeated the experiment, changing places, changing the circuits, testing each pair of transmitters and receivers, and cross-checking each other's observations. On through the afternoon and into the night, "there was little done but plucking reeds and observing the effect"—this time the words are Bell's. But faintly as the signals came through, they were there and they were true. And Bell now knew that his invention could be made to work, for his major and most persistent fear had been resolved. As he expressed it some thirty years afterward, "These experiments at once removed the doubt that had been in my mind since the summer of 1874, that magneto-electric currents generated by the vibration of an armature in front of an electromagnet would be too feeble to produce audible effects that could be practically utilized."

Before they parted company for the night, Bell gave Watson instructions for making the first speaking telephone. The specifications were simply those of the membrane telephone which he had envisaged at his home in Brantford the summer before. Watson promised to have it ready the next day. Bell walked the streets for some time and when he returned to his lodgings found he could not sleep. Though elated, he felt guilty at having invented the telephone when his sponsors expected him to be hard at work on the harmonic telegraph. Before he went to bed he wrote a letter to Hubbard.

"Dear Mr. Hubbard," he began. "I have accidentally made a discovery of the very greatest importance. . . ."

On the next day, June 3, 1875, Watson constructed the first Bell telephone. As a mouthpiece, he arranged a small hollow cylinder, closed at one end by a tautly stretched parchment membrane. To the center of the membrane he attached the free end of a transmitter spring. It was a beautifully simple mechanism. When a person spoke into the mouthpiece, sound waves from his voice caused the membrane to vibrate. The membrane then caused the attached transmitter spring to vibrate. And the transmitter spring, vibrating over one pole of its electromagnet, induced an undulatory current that varied in intensity as the air varied in density during the production of vocal sounds.

That evening Bell and Watson met at the shop, after the workmen had gone home, for the initial tests. Surmising that the signal would be faint at best, and that both he and Bell would doubtless be shouting at the top of their lungs, Watson had taken the precaution of running the wire—the world's first telephone line—from their fifth-floor garret down to the third floor, to lessen the chance of hearing each other directly through the air. On the first test the new telephone was placed on Watson's workbench, while Bell stationed himself at a receiver in the garret. Watson shouted; but Bell, straining his ears, could hear nothing. They then exchanged places, with Bell at the transmitter below and Watson upstairs. This time the results were more encouraging.

"I could unmistakably hear the tones of his voice," Watson recalled later, "and almost catch a word now and then. I rushed downstairs and told him what I had heard. . . . It was enough to show him that he was on the right track, and before he left that night he gave me directions for several improvements in the telephones I was to have ready for the next trial."

Watson attributed the one-way transmission that night not to any defect in the system but to Bell's life-long training in elocution: "The reason why I heard Bell in that first trial of the telephone and he did not hear me, was the vast superiority of his strong vibratory tones over any sound my undeveloped voice was then able to utter." He then added dryly, "My sense of hearing, however, has always been unusually acute, and that might have helped to determine this result."

In any event, the business of what Watson had called "working out the details" continued to be a somewhat sticky one. The experiments went on all summer as Bell and Watson juggled components in an attempt to improve reception. They could hear each other's voices, but only rarely could they distinguish fragments of sentences, isolated phrases, or scattered words. Day after fruitless day they found themselves at a loss as to what to try next. Bell's problems, moreover, were aggravated by other factors. He was deeply involved in drafting specifications and claims for patent rights, foreign and domestic, on both the harmonic telegraph and the telephone *; hence much of his time was con-

* Bell's basic U.S. Patent No. 174,465 covering the telephone—"The method of, and apparatus for, transmitting vocal or other sounds telegraphically, as herein described, by causing electrical undulations, similar in form to the vibrations of the air accompanying the said vocal or other sounds, substantially as set forth"—was granted on March 7, 1876.

sumed in paper work. Then too, his health took a turn for the worse during the hot summer months. And finally, he was beset by financial difficulties. In his zeal to perfect the telephone he had abandoned all his teaching engagements, and now his funds were running low. While his sponsors had agreed to cover his laboratory expenses, no provision had been made for personal expenses. Bell was reluctant to request further assistance, for although both men now saw the potential of the telephone, Sanders had already invested large sums in Bell's work without return, and Bell's relationship with Hubbard was even more sensitive. For he hoped, when he became more solvent, to marry Hubbard's daughter, Mabel.

Seeing no other solution to his predicament, Bell returned briefly to his work with the deaf, lecturing to student teachers and building up a new clientele of private pupils. Toward the end of 1875 his circumstances improved. He was able to move his apparatus from the Williams shop, where it had been eyed by increasing numbers of inquisitive strangers, to private quarters of his own in 5 Exeter Place, Boston. There, through the winter and early spring, Bell continued his experiments and evolved a new and modified transmitter, abetted by a variable battery current. On the night of March 10, 1876, just nine months after Bell's harmonic telegraph receiver gave out its promising *twang,* his telephone pronounced its first complete and intelligible sentence. Watson, who had continued to assist Bell faithfully, constructing his apparatus and working with him night after night no less assiduously than at the workshop in Court Street, was on the receiving end this time, and he recorded the event:

It made such an impression upon me that I wrote that first sentence in a book I have always preserved. The occasion had not been arranged and rehearsed as I suspect the sending of the first message over the Morse telegraph had been years before, for instead of that noble first telegraphic message—"What hath God wrought?"—the first message of the telephone was: "Mr. Watson, come here, I want you." Perhaps if Mr. Bell had realized that he was about to make a bit of history, he would have been prepared with a more sounding and interesting sentence.

Thereafter events moved swiftly. In June, 1876, Bell exhibited his apparatus at the Centennial Exposition in Philadelphia, where he won prizes for both the telephone and his harmonic telegraph. Among the judges were Joseph Henry; the Emperor Dom Pedro of Brazil, who exclaimed, "My God, it talks"; and Sir William Thomson (Baron Kelvin), who later called the telephone "the most wonderful thing [he had seen] in America." There followed a series of demonstrations in both the United States and Canada, with lectures by Bell and gradually lengthening lines of communication. The demonstration circuits began with two miles of wire between Bell's home in Brantford and the neighboring town of Mount Pleasant; by the spring of 1877 a line had been set up from New Brunswick, New Jersey, to New York City, a distance of more than thirty miles. (The wires were leased, for these occasions, from Western Union.) The reactions of audiences ranged from incredulity, through enthusiasm, to skepticism. Some saw in the telephone only an ingenious novelty. Shortly after the Philadelphia Centennial Exposition, the New York *Tribune* commented editorially in this vein:

Of what use is such an invention? Well, there may be occasions of state when it is necessary for officials who are far apart to talk with each other, without the interferences of an operator. Or some lover may wish to pop the question directly into the ear of a lady and hear for himself her reply, though miles away; it is not for us to guess how courtships will be conducted in the twentieth century. It is said that the human voice has been conveyed by this contrivance over a circuit of sixty miles. Music can be readily transmitted. Think of serenading by telegraph!

During this period, when Bell was beginning to win great acclaim but still languished in financial distress, Gardiner Hubbard decided to execute a coup. He approached the Western Union Company and offered to sell them all the Bell patents for a lump sum of $100,-000. He added that Bell would be willing to put on a private demonstration for officers of the company. The president of Western Union spurned the offer of a demonstration and refused the patents, explaining that they "could not make use of an electrical toy." Commenting wryly on this rude rejection, Watson, who was now devoting his full time to the telephone in return for an interest in the Bell patents, observed: "It was an especially hard blow to me, for . . . I had had visions of a sumptuous office in the Western Union Building in New York, which I was expecting to occupy as Superintendent of the Telephone Department of the great telegraph company. However, we recovered even from that. . . . Two years later the Western Union would gladly have bought those patents for $25,000,-000."

Undismayed, Bell and Watson continued with their experiments. They made telephones with every modification and combination of components that they could imagine. They tested all kinds of materials, all kinds of diaphragms, and all kinds of magnets. In the end, after hundreds of experiments, they dispensed with the membrane diaphragm in favor of a thin iron one. They found too that telephones with permanent magnets working without any battery gave better results at a distance than telephones containing electromagnets operated by a battery current. Thus two outstanding characteristics of the later telephone—permanent magnets and metallic diaphragms—had already been added in that early day.

In July, 1877, Bell married Mabel Hubbard and shortly thereafter sailed with his bride to England to introduce the telephone there. He delivered many lectures and gave many demonstrations, most notably one for Queen Victoria at Osborne on the Isle of Wight. But Bell's trip was most memorable for an amazingly prophetic document which he composed on the night of March 15, 1878, at his rented house in Kensington. It was in the form of a prospectus designed to awaken the interest of English investors in the Electric Telephone Company. In view of the fact that the telephone was still in its infancy, the vision embodied in these paragraphs discloses a depth and scope of imagination that matched Bell's inventive genius.

At the present time we have a perfect network of gas-pipes and water-pipes throughout our larger cities. We have main pipes laid under the streets communicating by side pipes with the various dwellings, enabling the members to draw their supplies of gas and water from a common source.

In a similar manner, it is conceivable that cables of Telephone wires could be laid underground or suspended overhead communicating by branch wires with private dwellings, counting houses, ships, manufactories, etc., etc., uniting them through the main cable with a central office where the wires could be connected as desired, establishing direct communication between any two places in the city. Such a plan as this, though impracticable at the present moment, will, I firmly believe, be the outcome of the introduction of the Telephone to the public. Not only so, but I believe that in the future wires will unite the head offices of the Telephone Company in different cities and a man in one part of the country may communicate by word of mouth with another in a distant place.

Thus in the spring of 1878 Bell foresaw clearly how his invention would alter the whole tapestry of human existence. He knew exactly what he had brought into being, and he entertained not the slightest doubt that before very long every home and place of business would possess a telephone, and that through its sorcery the human voice, transcending all barriers of time and distance, would be heard around the world. It is noteworthy too that Bell's prospectus of 1878 introduced some terminology that has remained a basic and permanent part of the lexicon of the telephone. From his concept of a "central office" came the salutation "Hello, Central," which, until the advent of the dial system, was uttered by more people every hour of every day than any other phrase in the English tongue.

By the time Bell and his wife returned to the United States at the end of 1878 the telephone was well on its way to becoming a big business. Never before had a revolutionary invention entered into commercial use so swiftly. The first central switchboard had been established in Boston (with boys as operators, until some inspired but forgotten genius discovered that girls were more polite). The first private line had been strung between Williams' electrical workshop in Court Street and his home in Somerville, Massachusetts. Thereafter, with amazing rapidity wires wove steel traceries across the New England landscape and telephone poles sprouted like autumn weeds. Businessmen, lawyers, doctors, quickly discovered that, quite apart from efficiency and convenience, there was an element of status in owning a telephone. The first directory appeared in New Haven, with a list of fifty subscribers—among them the police department and the post office. And in Boston, Bell's canny business managers, Hubbard and Sanders, supervised the manufacture and rental of telephone instruments, and girded up their loins for the first of an interminable series of legal battles in which the Bell associates would have to defend their basic patents against an army of predators. For it was becoming clear to electrical and telegraph companies that Bell Patent No. 174,465 was a valuable one. As events subsequently showed, it turned out to be *the* most valuable patent ever issued in the history of the U.S. Patent Office. By December of 1879, stock in the New England Telephone Company was selling at $995 a share.

Meanwhile Watson—chief technician in Bell's absence—found himself confronted with the problem of devising a method of summoning people to the telephone. For some reason Bell had not thought of a bell.

It began to dawn on us [Watson recalled] that people engaged in getting their living in the ordinary walks of life couldn't be expected to keep the telephone at their ear all the time waiting for a call, especially as it weighed ten pounds then and was as big as a small packing case, so it devolved on me to get up some sort of a call signal. Williams, on his line, used to call by thumping the diaphragm through the mouthpiece with the butt of a lead pencil. If there was someone close to the telephone at the other end, and it was very still, this worked pretty well, but it seriously damaged the vitals of the machine and therefore I decided it wasn't really practical for the general public; besides, we might have to supply a pencil with every telephone . . .

Then I rigged a little hammer inside the box with a button on the outside. When the button was thumped the hammer would hit the side of the diaphragm where it could not be damaged, the usual electrical transformation took place, and a much more modest but still unmistakable thump would issue from the telephone at the other end. . . .

But the exacting public wanted something better, and I devised the Watson "Buzzer"—the only practical use we ever made of the harmonic telegraph relics. Many of these were sent out. It was a vast improvement on the Watson

A Thomas Nast cartoon of 1886 made it clear that Bell's claims to the invention of the telephone, while they eventually triumphed, did not shake off contestants for many years.

"Thumper," but it still didn't take the popular fancy. It made a sound quite like the horseradish-grater automobile signal . . . and aroused just the same feeling of resentment. It brought me only a fleeting fame for I soon superseded it by a magneto-electric call bell that solved the problem, and was destined to make a long-suffering public turn cranks for the next fifteen years or so, as it never had before or ever will hereafter.

Watson solved another problem at this time which proved important in the future development of the telephone system. In his first version of the magneto call bell he had incorporated a manual switch that had to be thrown one way by hand when the telephone was being used, and then thrown back by hand when the call was terminated in order to put the bell back in circuit again.

But, Watson soon discovered, "the average man or woman wouldn't do this more than half the time, and I was obliged to try a series of devices, which culminated in that remarkable achievement of the human brain—the automatic switch—that only demanded of the public that it should hang up the telephone after it got through talking. This the public learned to do quite well after a few years of practice."

For the next three years after Bell's return from England, both he and Watson were compelled to spend most of their time either testifying in court or preparing to testify. Again and again Watson found himself building reproductions of the original telephone instrument in order to prove to judges and juries that it actually had worked right from the start. The litigation went on for decades, and in time virtually every big electrical and telegraph company in the United States mobilized its technical and legal resources in all-out battles to break the bulwarks of Patent No. 174,465. When Western Union tardily recognized the potential of Bell's invention, just two years after they had haughtily spurned Hubbard's offer to sell it to them for $100,000, they engaged Thomas Edison and Elisha Gray to evolve instruments that would work as well as the Bell telephone and yet evade the restrictions of the basic patent. Edison did, indeed, evolve a carbon-button transmitter that proved superior to Bell's magneto transmitter, as Watson rather ruefully admitted afterward.

"Our transmitter was doing much to develop the American voice and lungs," he observed, "making them powerful but not melodious. This was the telephone epoch when, they used to say, all the farmers waiting in a country grocery would rush out and hold their horses when they saw anyone preparing to use the telephone."

The basic principles involved in Patent No. 174,465 were, however, unique, inimitable, and not subject to disguise or variation. The patent withstood all assaults, and one by one the various adversaries were struck down by the courts—and on several occasions by the U.S. Supreme Court.

Both Bell and Watson separated themselves from the telephone company in the same year, 1881, and turned their restless minds to other interests. By now both young men were financially secure for life; they were, indeed, rich, and they were bored by such matters as law suits and corporate expansion. "Bell was a pure scientist," Watson explained. "Making money out of his idea never seemed to concern him particularly." When the Bell Telephone Company of Canada was incorporated, Bell gave three quarters of his interest to his father and generously dispensed smaller fractions to many others who had helped him. To his wife he gave his entire holdings in the American company as a wedding gift, along with complete control of his financial affairs. Once, while at home in Brantford on vacation, he was asked to return to the States to testify in another patent suit. Throwing up his

hands in exasperation, he declared that he would rather surrender all interest in the telephone and devote the rest of his life to teaching the deaf than participate in one more piece of litigation.

As for Watson, he resigned his position as General Inspector of the New England Telephone Company, partly because the incessant pressures of the embattled and swiftly expanding firm had given him chronic insomnia, and partly because "the telephone business had become, I thought, merely a matter of routine, with nothing more to do except pay dividends and fight infringers." In this latter assumption, events were to prove him incorrect. For the telephone system, from the day it was born, was a living organism that immediately began a process of expansion and technical development that has accelerated with each passing year. The process involved vastly more than the bare necessities of festooning additional miles of wires or manufacturing thousands of new phones. Other original minds, other gifted technicians, took up where Bell and Watson left off. By 1900, less than a quarter century after Bell filed his original patent, more than three thousand patents had been filed in Washington by the second generation of Bell inventors.

Bell's creation of the telephone overshadowed later achievements that by themselves would have insured a degree of immortality to a lesser man. He made important advances toward the development of the photoelectric cell, the phonograph, the iron lung, and the desalination of ocean water. Working with the aviation pioneer S. P. Langley, he contributed valuably to aeronautical theory, in which he was intensely interested; on a practical level, he was the co-inventor of the aileron as a device to control the lateral balance of an airplane.

Yet through all his years of international fame and glory, until his death in 1922, Bell never lost his interest in the problems of the deaf. With $300,000 of his own money he founded the American Association to Promote the Teaching of Speech to the Deaf, and he developed a lifetime friendship with Helen Keller, whom he first knew in 1886 as a six-year-old still almost completely mute. He was always tenderly considerate of his deaf wife, and repeatedly, from the time of his first triumphs in Boston, he declared that he would rather be remembered by posterity as one who had helped the deaf than as the inventor of the telephone.

The Grand Acquisitor

When it was raining
porridge, Lucy Rockefeller
said, John D.'s dish
was always right side up

By ROBERT L. HEILBRONER

The incredibly shrunken face of an animate
mummy, grotesque behind enormous black-
rimmed glasses; the old boy tottering around
the golf course, benign and imperturbable, distributing
his famous dimes; the huge foundation with its medical triumphs; the lingering memory of the great trust
and the awed contemplation of the even greater company; and over all, the smell of oil, endlessly pumping
out of the earth, each drop adding its bit to the largest
exaction ever levied on any society by a private individual—with such associations it is no wonder that the
name has sunk into the American mind to an extraordinary degree. From his earliest days the spendthrift
schoolboy is brought to his senses with: "Who do you
think you are, John D. Rockefeller?"

Yet for all the vivid associations, the man himself remains a shadowy presence. Carnegie, Morgan, or Ford
may not have entered so decisively into the American
parlance, but they are full-blooded figures in our memory: Carnegie, brash, bustling, proselytizing; Morgan,
imperious, choleric, aloof; Ford, shrewd, small-town,
thing-minded. But what is John D. Rockefeller, aside
from the paper silhouettes of very old age and the aura
of immense wealth?

Even his contemporaries did not seem to have a very
clear impression of Rockefeller as a human being. For
forty years of his active career, he was commonly regarded as an arch economic malefactor—La Follette
called him the greatest criminal of the age—and for
twenty years, as a great benefactor—John Singer Sar-
gent, painting his portrait, declared himself in the
presence of a medieval saint—but neither judgment
tells us much about the man. Nor do Ida Tarbell or
Henry Demarest Lloyd, both so skillful in portraying
the company, succeed in bringing to life its central figure; he lurks in the background, the Captain Nemo of
Standard Oil. Similarly, in the reminiscences of his associates we catch only the glimmer of a person—a polite, reserved man, mild in manner, a bit of a stickler
for exactitude, totally unremarkable for anything he
says or for any particular style of saying it. Surely
there must be more to John D. than this! What sort of
man was this greatest of all acquisitors? What was the
secret of his incredible success?

His mother came of a prosperous Scottish farming
family, devout, strait-laced, uncompromising. She
springs out at us from her photographs: a tired, plain
face, deep-set eyes, and a straight, severe mouth announce Eliza Davison Rockefeller's tired, straight, severe personality. Rockefeller later recalled an instance
when he was being whipped by her and finally managed to convince her that he was innocent of a supposed misdemeanor. "Never mind," she said, "we have
started in on this whipping and it will do for the next

time." Her approach to life made an indelible impression—even in his old age Rockefeller could hear her voice enjoining: "Willful waste makes woeful want."

His father, William Avery Rockefeller, was cut from a different bolt of cloth. Big, robust, and roistering, he treated his sons with a curious mixture of affection and contempt. "I trade with the boys," he boasted to a neighbor, "and skin 'em and I just beat 'em every time I can. I want to make 'em sharp." Sharp himself, he was in and out of a dozen businesses in John's youth and, we have reason to suspect, as many beds. Later, when his son was already a prominent businessman, we can still follow his father's erratic career, now as "Doctor" William A. Rockefeller, "the Celebrated Cancer Specialist," peddling his cures on the circuit. Still later, when John D. had become a great eminence in New York, the father drops into obscurity—only to materialize from time to time in the city, where he is shown around by an embarrassed Standard Oil underling. At the very end he simply disappears. Joseph Pulitzer at one time offered a prize of $8,000 for news of his whereabouts, and the rumor spread that for thirty-five years old William had led a double life, with a second wife in Illinois. No one knows.

It was an unpleasantly polarized family situation, and it helps us understand the quiet, sober-sided boy who emerged. His schoolmates called John "Old pleased-because-I'm-sad," from the title of a school declamation that fitted him to perfection; typically, when the boys played baseball, he kept score. Yet, if it was subdued, it was not an unhappy boyhood. At home he milked the cow and drove the horse and did the household chores that were expected of a boy in upstate New York, but after hours he indulged with his brothers, William and Frank, in the usual boyhood escapades and adventures. A favorite pastime, especially savored since it was forbidden, was to go skating at night on the Susquehanna. On one occasion William and John saved a neighbor's boy from drowning, whereupon their evening's sally had to be admitted. Eliza Rockefeller praised their courage—and whipped them soundly for their disobedience.

Always in the Rockefeller home there was the stress on gainful work. Their father may have worked to make them sharp, but their mother worked to make them industrious. John was encouraged to raise turkeys, and he kept the money from their sale in a little box on the mantel until he had accumulated the sum

RETIRED TYCOON: Enemies longing to see Rockefeller get his comeuppance in this world were disappointed. In 1911, a year after this picture was taken, the government dissolved his Standard Oil Trust. But by then he had taken his winnings and severed all connections with the company.

171

of $50. A neighboring farmer asked to borrow the amount at seven per cent for a year, and his mother approved. During that summer John dug potatoes at thirty-seven and a half cents a day. When the farmer repaid the loan with $3.50 in interest, the lesson was not lost on John: the earning power of capital was much to be preferred to that of labor.

He was then only in his teens—he was born in 1899—but already, frugal ways, a deliberate manner, and a strong sense of planning and purposefulness were in evidence. As his sister Lucy said: "When it's raining porridge, you'll find John's dish right side up." But now the time for summer jobs was coming to an end. The family had moved from Moravia and Owego, where John had grown up, to Cleveland, where he went to the local high school in his fifteenth and sixteenth years. For a few months he attended Folsom's Commercial College, where he learned the elements of bookkeeping—and then began the all-important search for the first real job.

That search was performed with a methodical thoroughness that became a hallmark of the Rockefeller style. A list of promising establishments was drawn up —nothing second-rate would do—and each firm was hopefully visited. Rebuffed on the first go-round, John went the rounds again undaunted, and then a third time. Eventually his perseverance was rewarded. He became a clerk in the office of Hewitt & Tuttle, commission merchants and produce shippers. Typically, he took the job without inquiring about salary, hung his coat on a peg, climbed onto the high bookkeeper's stool, and set to work. It was a red-letter day in his life; later, when he was a millionaire many times over, the flag was regularly hoisted before his house to commemorate September 26, 1855.

Work came naturally, even pleasurably to John Rockefeller. He was precise, punctual, diligent. "I had trained myself," he wrote in his memoirs, ". . . that my check on a bill was the executive act which released my employer's money from the till and was attended with more responsibility than the spending of my own funds."

With such model attitudes, Rockefeller quickly advanced. By 1858 his salary (which turned out to be $3.50 a week) had more than tripled, but when Hewitt & Tuttle were unable to meet a request for a further raise, he began to look elsewhere. A young English acquaintance named Maurice Clark, also a clerk, was similarly unhappy with his prospects, and the two decided to form a produce-shipping firm of their own. Clark had saved up $2,000, and John Rockefeller had saved $900; the question was, where to get the last necessary $1,000. John knew that at age twenty-one he was entitled to a patrimony of this amount under his father's will, and he turned to William Rockefeller for an advance. His father listened with mingled approval and suspicion, and finally consented to lend his son the money if John would pay interest until he was twenty-one. "And John," he added, "the rate is ten."

Rockefeller accepted the proposition, and Clark & Rockefeller opened its doors in 1859. The Cleveland *Leader* recommended the principals to its readers as "experienced, responsible, and prompt," and the venture succeeded from the start. In its first year the firm made a profit of $4,400; in the second year, $17,000; and when the Civil War began, profits soared. Rockefeller became known as an up-and-coming young businessman, a man to be watched. Even his father agreed. From time to time he would come around and ask for his loan back, just to be sure the money was really there, but then, unable to resist ten per cent interest, he would lend it back again.

Meanwhile an adult personality begins to emerge. A picture taken just before he married Laura Spelman in 1864 shows a handsome man of twenty-five with a long, slightly mournful visage, a fine straight nose, a rather humorless mouth. Everyone who knew him testified to his virtues. He was industrious, even-tempered, generous, kind; and if it was not a sparkling personality, it was not a dour one. Yet there is something not quite attractive about the picture as a whole. Charitable from his earliest days, he itemized each contribution—even the tiniest—in his famous Ledger A, with the result that his generosity, of which there was never any doubt, is stained with self-observance and an over-nice persnicketiness. Extremely self-critical, he was given to intimate "pillow talks" at night in which he took himself to task for various faults, but the words he recalled and later repeated—"Now a little success, soon you will fall down, soon you will be overthrown . . ." smack not so much of honest self-search as of the exorcising of admonitory parental voices. He was above all orderly and forethoughted, but there is a compulsive, and sometimes a faintly repellent quality about his self-control. He recounts that when he was travelling as a commission merchant, he would never grab a bite in the station and wolf it down, like the others on the train, but "if I could not finish eating properly, I filled my mouth with as much as it would hold, then went leisurely to the train and chewed it slowly before swallowing it."

Yet the faults, far from constituting major traits in themselves, were minor flaws in an essentially excellent character. Rockefeller forged ahead by his merits, not by meanness—and among his merits was a well-developed capacity to size up a business situation coolly and rationally. Living in Cleveland, he could scarcely fail to think about one such situation virtually under his nose. Less than a day's journey by train were the Oil Regions of Pennsylvania, one of the most fantastic locales in America. A shambles of mud, dying horses (their skins denuded by petroleum), derricks, walking beams, chugging donkey engines, and jerry-built towns, the Regions oozed oil, money, and dreams. Bits of land the size of a blanket sold on occasion for three and four hundred dollars, pastures jumped overnight into fortunes (one pasture rose from $25,000 to $1,600,-000 in three months), whole villages bloomed into existence in a matter of months. Pithole, Pennsylvania, an aptly named pinprick on the map, became the third largest center for mail in Pennsylvania and boasted a $65,000 luxury hotel. Within a few years it was again a pinprick, and the hotel was sold for $50.

It is uncertain whether Rockefeller himself visited the Oil Regions in the halcyon early 1860's. What is certain is that he sniffed oil in Cleveland itself, where the crude product was transported by barge and barrel for distillation and refining. In any event, the hurly-burly, the disorganization, and above all the extreme riskiness of the Oil Regions would never have appealed to Rockefeller's temperament. Let someone else make a million or lose it by blindly drilling for an invisible reservoir—a surer and far steadier route to wealth was available to the refiner who bought crude oil at thirty-one or thirty-two cents a gallon and then sold the refined product at eighty to eighty-five cents.

The chance to enter the refining business came to Clark and Rockefeller in the person of an enterprising and ingenious young engineer named Sam Andrews. Andrews, recently come from England (by coincidence, he was born in the same town as Clark), was restive in his job in a lard refinery and eager to try his hand at oil refining. He talked with his fellow townsman and through Clark met Rockefeller. The three agreed to take a fling at the business. Andrews, together with Clark's brothers, took on the production side, and Maurice Clark and Rockefeller the financial side. Thus in 1863 Andrews, Clark & Company was born. Rockefeller, content behind the anonymity of the "Company," had contributed, together with his partner, half the total capital, but he retained his interest in the produce business. The investment in oil was meant to be no more than a side venture.

But the side venture prospered beyond all expectation. The demand for refined oil increased by leaps

COUNTRY SQUIRE: In 1893 Rockefeller started buying land near Tarrytown, New York, and spent the next twenty years moving hills, a college, and a railroad around to improve the estate. In 1913, when his new residence, Kykuit, was completed, his philanthropies amounted to $45,000,000.

and bounds. As Allan Nevins has written: "A commodity that had been a curiosity when Lincoln was nominated, had become a necessity of civilization, the staple of a vast commerce, before he was murdered." And the supply of oil, despite a thousand warnings, auguries, and dire prophecies that the mysterious underground springs would dry up, always matched and overmatched demand.

As the business boomed, so did the number of refineries. One could go into the refinery business for no more capital than it took to open a well-equipped hardware store, and Cleveland's location with its favoring rivers and fortunately placed rail lines made it a natural center for the shipment of crude oil. Hence by 1866, only two years after Andrews, Clark & Company had opened its doors, there were over thirty refineries along the Cleveland Flats, and twenty more would be added before the year was out.

The Rockefeller refinery was among the largest of these. In Sam Andrews had been found the perfect plant superintendent; in Clark and Rockefeller, the perfect business management. From half-past six in the morning, when Andrews and Clark would burst in on their partner at breakfast, until they parted company just before supper, the three talked oil, oil, oil. Slowly, however, Andrews and Rockefeller found themselves at odds with Clark. They had become convinced that oil was to be a tremendous and permanent business enterprise; Clark was more cautious and less willing to borrow to expand facilities. Finally, in 1865, it was decided to put the firm up for auction among themselves, the seller to retain the produce business. "It was the day that determined my career," Rockefeller recalled long afterward. "I felt the bigness of it, but I was as calm as I am talking to you now." When at last Maurice Clark bid $72,000, Rockefeller topped him by $500. Clark threw up his hands. "The business is yours," he declared.

A MAN OF MANY FACES: Over the years John D. Rockefeller's face seemed to go through many changes, especially after an illness cost him all his hair in the 1890's and he started wearing wigs most of the time. This casual collection suggests, to us at least, Rockefeller in these roles:

From the beginning Rockefeller & Andrews, as the new firm was called, was a model of efficiency. Even before acquiring the firm, Rockefeller had become interested in the economies of plant operation. When he found that plumbers were expensive by the hour, he and Sam Andrews hired one by the month, bought their own pipes and joints, and cut plumbing costs in half. When cooperage grew into a formidable item, they built their own shop where barrels cost them only forty per cent of the market price, and soon costs were cut further by the acquisition of a stand of white oak, a kiln, and their own teams and wagons to haul the wood from kiln to plant. The emphasis on costs never ceased; when Rockefeller & Andrews had long since metamorphosed into the Standard Oil Company and profits had grown into the millions, cost figures were still carried to three decimal places. One day Rockefeller was watching the production line in one of his plants, where cans of finished oil were being soldered shut. "How many drops of solder do you use on each can?" he inquired. The answer was forty. "Have you ever tried thirty-eight? No? Would you mind having some sealed with thirty-eight and let me know?" A few cans leaked with thirty-eight, but with thirty-nine all were perfect. A couple of thousand dollars a year were saved.

The zeal for perfection of detail was from the beginning a factor in the growth of Rockefeller's firm. More important was his meeting in 1866 with Henry M. Flagler, the first of a half-dozen associates who would bring to the enterprise the vital impetus of talent, enthusiasm, and a hard determination to succeed. Flagler, a quick, ebullient, bold businessman who had fought his way up from the poverty of a small-town parsonage, was a commission merchant of considerable prominence when Rockefeller met him. The two quickly took a liking to one another, and Rockefeller soon induced Flagler to join the fast-expanding business. Flagler brought along his own funds and those of his father-in-law, Stephen Harkness, and this fresh influx of capital made possible even further expansion. Rockefeller, Andrews & Flagler—soon incorporated as the Standard Oil Company—rapidly became the biggest single refinery in Cleveland.

as Clifton Webb

Bernard Baruch

Eric von Stroheim

the Duke of Windsor

George Arliss

Rameses II, at golf

Flagler brought to the enterprise an immense energy and a playfulness that Rockefeller so egregiously lacked. The two main partners now had a code word in their telegrams—AMELIA—which meant "Everything is lovely and the goose hangs high." And everything *was* lovely. One of Flagler's first jobs was to turn his considerable bargaining skills to a crucial link in the chain of oil-processing costs. All the major refineries bought in the same market—the Oil Regions—and all sold in the same markets—the great cities—so that their costs of purchase and their prices at the point of sale were much alike. In between purchase and sale, however, lay two steps: the costs of refining and the costs of transportation. In the end it was the latter that was to prove decisive in the dog-eat-dog struggle among the refineries.

For the railroads needed a steady flow of shipments to make money, and they were willing to grant rebates to the refiners if they would level out their orders. Since there were a number of routes by which to ship oil, each refiner was in a position to play one road against another, and the Standard, as the biggest and strongest refiner in Cleveland, was naturally able to gain the biggest and most lucrative discounts on its freight. This was a game that Flagler played with consummate skill. Advantageous rebates soon became an important means by which the Standard pushed ahead of its competitors—and in later years, when there were no more competitors, an important source of revenue in themselves. By 1879, when the Rockefeller concern had become a giant, a government investigatory agency estimated that in a period of five months the firm had shipped some eighteen million barrels of oil, on which rebates ran from eleven per cent on the B&O to *forty-seven* per cent on the Pennsylvania Railroad. For the five months, rebates totalled over ten million dollars.

This is looking too far ahead, however. By 1869, a scant three years after Flagler had joined it, the company was worth about a million dollars, but it was very far from being an industrial giant or a monopoly. Indeed, the problem which constantly plagued Rockefeller and his associates was the extreme competition in the oil business. As soon as business took a downturn—as it did in 1871—the worst kind of cutthroat competition broke out: prices dropped until the Titusville *Herald* estimated that the average refiner lost seventy-five cents on each barrel he sold.

AMERICAN INSTITUTION: The passage of time, his great benefactions, and a shower of dimes eventually washed away the muckrakers' charges. For many years Rockefeller had lived very quietly, emerging from his home only for golf, church, or a drive in his automobile. When he died in 1937 at ninety-seven, many people were somehow sorry to see him go.

As the biggest refiner, Rockefeller naturally had the greatest stake in establishing some kind of stability in the industry. Hence he set about to devise a scheme—the so-called South Improvement Company—which would break the feast and famine pattern that threatened to overwhelm the industry. In its essence the South Improvement Company was a kind of cartel aimed at holding up oil prices—by arranging "reasonable" freight rates for its own members while levying far higher ones on "outsiders." Since the scheme was open to all, presumably there would soon be no outsiders, and once all were within the fold, the refiners could operate as a single, powerful economic unit.

The plan might have worked but for the inability of such headstrong and individualistic groups as the railroads and the producers to co-operate for more than a passing moment. When the producers in the Oil Regions rose in wrath against a plan which they (quite rightly) saw as a powerful buying combination against them, the scheme simply collapsed.

The idea of eliminating competition did not, however, collapse with it. Instead, Rockefeller turned to a plan at once much simpler and much more audacious. If he could not eliminate competition, then perhaps he could eliminate his competitors by buying them up one by one—and this he set out to do. The plan was set in motion by a meeting with Colonel Oliver Payne, the chief stockholder in Rockefeller's biggest competitor. Briefly Rockefeller outlined the ruinous situation which impended if competition were permitted to continue unbridled; equally briefly, he proposed a solution. The Standard would increase its capitalization, the Payne plant would be appraised by impartial judges, and its owners would be given stock in proportion to their equity. As for Payne himself, Rockefeller suggested he should take an active part in the management of the new, bigger Standard Oil.

Payne quickly assented; so did Jabez Bostwick, the biggest refiner in New York, and one after another the remaining refiners sold out. According to Rockefeller, they were only too glad to rid themselves of their burdensome businesses at fair prices; according to many of the refiners, it was a question of taking Rockefeller's offer or facing sure ruin. We need not debate the point here; what is certain is that by the end of 1872 the Standard was the colossus of Cleveland. There remained only the United States to conquer.

Rockefeller himself was in his mid-thirties. The slightly melancholy visage of the young man had altered; a thick mustache trimmed straight across the bottom hid his lips and gave to his face a commanding, even stern, aspect. In a family portrait we see him standing rather stiffly, carefully dressed as befits a man in his station. For he was already rich—even his non-oil investments, as he wrote to his wife, were enough to give him independence, and his style of life had changed as his fortune had grown. He and his wife now lived in Forest Hill, a large, gaunt house on eighty acres just east of Cleveland. He had begun to indulge himself with snappy trotters, and on a small scale commenced what was to become in time a Brobdingnagian pastime—moving landscape around.

In town, in his business pursuits, he was already the reserved, colorless, almost inscrutable personality who baffled his business contemporaries; at home, he came as close as he could to a goal he sought assiduously—relaxation. His children were his great delight: he taught them to swim and invented strange and wonderful contraptions to keep them afloat; he bicycled with them; he played daring games of blindman's buff—so daring in fact that he once had to have stitches taken in his head after running full tilt into a doorpost.

It was, in a word, the very model of a Victorian home, affectionate, dutiful, and, of course, rich. An air of rectitude hung over the establishment, not so much as to smother it, but enough to give it a distinctive flavor. Concerts (aside from the performances of their children), literature, art, or theatre were not Rockefeller amusements; in entertaining, their tastes ran to Baptist ministers and business associates. An unpretentious and earnest atmosphere hid—or at least disguised—the wealth; until they were nearly grown up the children had no idea of "who they were."

And of course the beneficences continued and grew: $23,000 for various charities in 1878, nearly $33,000 in 1880, over $100,000 in 1884. But the nice preciseness of giving was maintained; a pledge card signed in 1883 for the Euclid Avenue Baptist Church reads:

Mrs. Rockefeller	$10.00 each week
Self.........................	30.00 each week
Each of our four children......	00.20 each week

How rich was Rockefeller by 1873, a mere ten years after Andrews, Clark & Company had opened its doors? We cannot make an accurate estimate, but it is certain that he was a millionaire several times over. In another ten years his Standard Oil holdings alone would be worth a phenomenal twenty million dollars—enough, with his other investments, to make him one of the half-dozen richest men in the country.

But now a legal problem began to obtrude. The Standard Oil Company was legally chartered in Ohio, and it had no right to own plants in other states. Not until 1889 would New Jersey amend its incorporation laws to allow a corporation chartered within the state to hold the stock of corporations chartered elsewhere. Hence the question: how was the Standard legally to control its expanding acquisitions in other states?

The problem was solved by one of Rockefeller's most astute lieutenants—Samuel Dodd, a round little butterball of a man with an extraordinarily clear-sighted legal mind and an unusually high and strict sense of personal integrity. Because he believed that he could render the best advice to the Standard if he was above any suspicion of personal aggrandizement, he repeatedly refused Rockefeller's offers to make him a director or to buy for him stock which would have made him a multimillionaire.

The sword which Dodd applied to the Gordian knot of interstate control was the device of the trust. In brief, he proposed a single group of nine trustees, with headquarters in New York, who would hold "in trust" the certificates of all Standard's operating companies, including the major company in Ohio itself. In 1882 the Standard Oil Trust was formally established, with John and his brother William Rockefeller, Flagler, Payne, Bostwick, John D. Archbold, Charles Pratt, William G. Warden, and Benjamin Brewster as trustees. (Sam Andrews had sold the last of his stock to Rockefeller four years before, saying the business had grown too big.) In fact, though not in law, one enormous interstate corporation had been created.

Few people even at this time appreciated quite how great the company was. By the 1880's the Standard was the largest and richest of all American manufacturing organizations. It had eighty-five per cent of a business which took the output of 20,000 wells and which employed 100,000 people. And all this before the advent of the automobile. The colossus of the Standard was built not on the internal combustion engine but on the kerosene lamp.

With the creation of the Trust the center of gravity of the concern moved to New York. Rockefeller himself bought a $600,000 brownstone on West Fifty-fourth Street, where the round of teas and dinners for temperance workers, church people, and Standard executives soon went on. The Trust itself occupied No. 26 Broadway, an eleven-story "skyscraper" with gay striped awnings shading its large windows. It was soon known as the most famous business address in the world. There Rockefeller appeared daily, usually in high silk hat, long coat, and gloves—the accepted costume for the big business executive of the time.

At 26 Broadway Rockefeller was the commanding figure. But his exercise of command, like his personality, was notable for its lack of color, dash, and verve. Inquiring now of this one, now of that, what he thought of such and such a situation, putting his questions methodically and politely in carefully chosen words, never arguing, never raising his voice, Rockefeller seemed to govern his empire like a disembodied intelligence. He could be, as always, a stickler for detail; an accountant recalls him suddenly materializing one day, and with a polite "Permit me," turning over the ledger sheets, all the while murmuring, "Very well kept, very indeed," until he stopped at one page: "A little error here; will you correct it?" But he could also be decisive and absolutely determined. "He saw strategic points like a Napoleon, and he swooped down on them with the suddenness of a Napoleon," wrote Ida Tarbell. Yet even that gives too much of the impression of dash and daring. She was closer to the mark when she wrote: "If one attempts to analyse what may be called the legitimate greatness of Mr. Rockefeller's creation in distinction to its illegitimate greatness, he will find at the foundation the fact that it is as perfectly centralized as the Catholic Church or the Napoleonic government." It was true. By 1886 the Standard had evolved a system of committees, acting in advisory roles to the active management, which permitted an incalculably complex system to function with extraordinary ease. It is virtually the same system that is used today. Rockefeller had created the great Trust on which the eyes of the whole world were fastened, but behind the Trust, sustaining it, operating it, maintaining it, he had created an even greater Organization.

"It's many a day since I troubled you with a letter," wrote William Warden, a onetime independent Cleveland refiner who had been bought out and was now a trustee and major official in the Standard, "and I would not do so now could I justify myself in being silent. . . . We have met with a success unparalleled in commercial history, our name is known all over the world, and our public character is not one to be envied. We are quoted as representative of all that is evil, hard hearted, oppressive, cruel (we think unjustly), but men look askance at us, we are pointed at with contempt, and while some good men flatter us, it's only for our money . . . This is not pleasant to write, for I had longed for an honored position in commercial life. None of us would choose such a reputation; we all desire a place in the honor & affection of honorable men."

It was a cry of anguish, but it was amply justified. By the 1880's the Standard was not only widely known —it was notorious. In part its increasingly bad business reputation originated in the business community itself. Stories began to circulate of the unfair advantage taken by the colossus when it bid for smaller properties: the case of the Widow Backus, whose deceased husband's refinery was supposedly bought for a pittance, was much talked about. Many of these tales—the Backus case in particular—were simply untrue. But as the Standard grew in size and visibility, other business practices came to light which *were* true, and which were hardly calculated to gain friends for the company.

Foremost among these practices was an evil device called the drawback. Not content with enjoying a large competitive advantage through its special rebates, Standard also forced the railroads to pay it a portion of the freight charges paid by non-Standard refiners! Thus Daniel O'Day, a particularly ruthless Standard official, used his local economic leverage to get a small railroad to carry Standard's oil at ten cents a barrel, to charge all independents thirty-five cents, *and to turn over the twenty-five-cent differential to a Standard subsidiary.* Another Standard agent, finding that a competitor's car had slipped through without paying the Standard exaction, wrote the road to collect the amount owing, adding: "Please turn another screw."

Such incidents and practices—always denied by the company and never admitted by Rockefeller—plagued the Standard for years. And the impression of highhandedness was not much improved by the behavior of the Standard's officials when they went on public view. John D. Archbold, a key executive called to testify before New York State's Hepburn Committee in 1879, was a typical bland witness. When pressed hard, he finally admitted he was a stockholder of the Standard. What was his function there? "I am a clamorer for dividends. That is the only function I have in connection with the Standard Oil Company." Chairman Alonzo Hepburn asked how large dividends were. "I have no trouble transporting my share," answered Archbold. On matters of rebates he declined to answer. Finally Hepburn asked him to return for further questioning the next day. "I have given today to the matter," replied Archbold politely. "It will be impossible for me to be with you again."

Not least, there was the rising tide of public protest against the monopoly itself. In 1881 Henry Demarest Lloyd, a journalist of passionate reformist sentiments, wrote for the *Atlantic Monthly* an article called "The Story of a Great Monopoly." Editor William Dean Howells gave it the lead in the magazine, and overnight it was a sensation (that issue of the *Atlantic* went through seven printings). "The family that uses a gallon of kerosene a day pays a yearly tribute to the Standard of $32 . . . ," wrote Lloyd. "America has the proud satisfaction of having furnished the world with the greatest, wisest, and meanest monopoly known to history."

Standard's profits were nothing so great as described by Lloyd, but that hardly mattered. If the article was imprecise or even downright wrong in detail, it was right in its general thrust. What counted was Lloyd's incontrovertible demonstration that an industrial concern had grown to a position of virtual impregnability, a position which made it in fact no longer subordinate to the states from which it drew its legal privilege of existence, but their very peer or better in financial strength and even political power. Before Lloyd wrote his article, the Standard was the source of rage or loss to scattered groups of producers, businessmen, or consumers. When he was through with his indictment, it was a national scandal.

That it should be a scandal was totally incomprehensible to John D. The mounting wave of protest and obloquy perplexed him more than it irritated him. Ida Tarbell's famous—and generally accurate—*History of the Standard Oil Company* he dismissed as "without foundation." The arrogance of an Archbold he merely chuckled at, recounting the Hepburn testimony in his *Random Reminiscences of Men and Events* with the comment that Archbold had a "well-developed sense of humor." With his own passion for order, he understood not a whit the passions of those whose demise was required that order might prevail. On one occasion when he was testifying in court, he spied in the courtroom George Rice, an old adversary (against whom, as a matter of fact, the famous screw had been turned, and whom Rockefeller had once offered to buy out). As he left the witness stand, Rockefeller walked over to Rice and, putting out his hand, said: "How do you do, Mr. Rice? You and I are getting to be old men, are we not?"

Rice ignored the hand. "Don't you think, Mr. Rice," pursued Rockefeller, "it might have been better if you had taken my advice years ago?"

"Perhaps it would," said Rice angrily. "You said you would ruin my business and you have done so."

"Pshaw! Pshaw!" rejoined Rockefeller.

"Don't you pooh-pooh me," said Rice in a fury. "I say that by the power of your great wealth you have ruined me."

"Not a word of truth in it," Rockefeller answered, turning and making his way through the crowd. "Not a word of truth in it."

He could not in fact bring himself to believe that there was a word of truth in any of it. There was nothing to argue about concerning the need for giant enterprise, or "industrial combinations" as they were called. They were simply a necessity, a potentially dangerous necessity admittedly, but a necessity nonetheless.

DESIGN FOR A TABLET IN ANTIQUE BRASS
TO BE PLACED IN THE CHICAGO UNIVERSITY

Literary Digest, MAY 6, 1905

"THE AMERICAN BEAUTY ROSE CAN BE PRODUCED IN ALL ITS SPLENDOR ONLY BY SACRIFICING THE EARLY BUDS THAT GROW UP AROUND IT."— John D. Rockefeller, Jr.

Though the direction of Standard Oil was in other, more aggressive hands by 1897, John D. continued to be blamed for its tactics. The lampoon below was published in 1903. His son's defense of business consolidation, from which the caption above was quoted, was delivered in 1905, the same year in which the Collier's cover at left appeared. And that spring came one of the most famous denunciations (lower left): the noted Congregationalist divine Dr. Washington Gladden called a $100,000 gift to his sect's foreign missions "tainted money." Gladden was considerably miffed to find that the donation had in fact been solicited.

COLUMBUS, O., *Dispatch*

DR. GLADDEN—"You can't mix them, John, you can't mix them."

UTICA *Saturday Globe*, MAY 23, 1903

All the rest was ignorance or willful misunderstanding. "You know," he wrote to a university president who offered to prepare a scholarly defense of Standard's policies, "that great prejudice exists against all successful business enterprise—the more successful, the greater the prejudice."

It was common, during the early 1900's, to read thunderous accusations against the Standard Oil Company and its sinister captain, but the fact was that John D. Rockefeller had severed all connection with the business as early as 1897. When news came to him, ten years later, that the great Trust had been heavily fined by the government, he read the telegram and without comment went on with his game of golf. At the actual dissolution of the Trust in 1911, he was equally unconcerned. For already his interests were turning away from business management toward another absorbing role—the disposition of the wealth which was now beginning to accumulate in truly awesome amounts.

Here enters the last of those indispensable subordinates through whom Rockefeller operated so effectively. Frederick Taylor Gates, onetime clergyman, now secretary of the Baptist Education Society, met Rockefeller when Gates played a crucial role in the studies that established the need for a great new university in Chicago. Shortly thereafter Gates became the catalytic figure in instituting the university, having received a generous donation of $600,000 from Rockefeller. (Before he was finished, Rockefeller would give the project eighty million dollars.) Then one morning in 1889, when the two were chatting, Rockefeller suddenly said: "I am in trouble, Mr. Gates." He told him of the flood of appeals which now came by the sackful, and of his inability to give away money with any satisfaction until he had made the most thorough investigation into the cause. Rockefeller continued: "I want you to come to New York and open an office here. You can aid me in my benefactions by taking interviews and inquiries and reporting the results for action. What do you say?"

Gates said yes, and it was under his guidance, together with that of Rockefeller's son, John D., Jr., that the great philanthropies took root: the General Education Board, which pioneered in the educational, social, and medical development of our own South; the Rockefeller Institute for Medical Research, quickly famous for its campaign against yellow fever; the Rockefeller Foundation with its far-ranging interests in the promotion of research. Not that the giving was done hastily. Gates had a meticulousness of approach which suited his employer perfectly. It was not

until 1900 that more than 2 million dollars was given away, not until 1905 that the total of annual giving exceeded 10 million dollars, not until 1913 that the great climactic disbursements began to be made: 45 million dollars that year and 65 million the next, to establish the Rockefeller Foundation; finally 138 million dollars in 1919 to support the philanthropies already endowed.

Gates took his philanthropic duties with ministerial zeal and profound seriousness. Raymond Fosdick, president of the Rockefeller Foundation, recalls Gates' last meeting as a trustee. Shaking his fist at the startled board, he boomed: "When you die and come to approach the judgment of Almighty God, what do you think He will demand of you? Do you for an instant presume to believe He will inquire into your petty failures or your trivial virtues? No! He will ask just one question: *What did you do as a Trustee of the Rockefeller Foundation?*"

Gates was more than just a philanthropic guide. Rapidly he became a prime business agent for Rockefeller in the large business deals which inevitably continued to arise. When Rockefeller came into immense iron properties along the Mesabi Range, it was Gates who superintended their development and the creation of a giant fleet of ore carriers, and it was Gates who carried through their eventual sale to Morgan and Frick at the huge price of 88.5 million dollars. It was the only time in Gates' long association with John D. that he indicated the slightest desire to make money for himself. When the immense iron deal was complete and Gates had made his final report, Rockefeller, as usual, had no words of praise, but listened attentively and without objection and then said, with more emphasis than usual, "Thank you, Mr. Gates!" Gates looked at him with an unaccustomed glint in his eye. "Thank you is not enough, Mr. Rockefeller," he replied. Rockefeller understood and promptly saw to it that Gates was remunerated handsomely.

John D. was becoming an old man now. His face, sharper with age, took on a crinkled, masklike appearance, in the midst of which his small eyes twinkled. Golf had become a great passion and was performed in the deliberate Rockefeller manner. A boy was hired to chant: "Keep your head down," useless steps were saved by bicycling between shots, and even when he was playing alone, every stroke was remorselessly counted. (John D. was once asked to what he owed the secret of the success of Standard Oil; he answered: "To the fact that we never deceived ourselves.")

To the outside world the old man more and more presented a quaint and benevolent image. By the 1920's the antitrust passions of the 1890's and early 1900's had been transmuted into sycophancy of big business; there were no more cries of "tainted money," but only a hopeful queuing up at the portals of the great foundations. The man who had once been denounced by Theodore Roosevelt and Tolstoy and William Jennings Bryan was now voted, in a popular poll, one of the Greatest Americans. Cartoonists and feature writers made the most of his pith helmet and his paper vest, his monkishly plain food, his beaming, almost childlike expression. To the outside world he seemed to live in a serene and admirable simplicity, which indeed he did, in a purely personal sense. But the reporters who told of his afternoon drives did not report that the seventy miles of road over his estate at Pocantico Hills were built by himself, that the views he liked so well were arranged by moving hills around as an interior decorator moves chairs. The perfection of Pocantico became an obsession: some railway tracks that were in the way were relocated at the cost of $700,-000, a small college that spoiled a view was induced to move for $1,500,000, a distant smokestack was camouflaged. It was, to repeat George Kaufman's famous line, an example of what God could have done if He'd only had the money.

In the midst of it all was the never-failingly polite, always slightly disengaged old man, somehow disappointing in close view, somehow smaller than we expect. There are mannerisms and eccentricities, of course, which, when viewed under the magnification of 900 million dollars, take on a certain prominence, but they are peccadilloes rather than great flaws. There is the enormous industrial generalship, to be sure, but it is a generalship of logic and plan, not of dash and daring. There is the generosity on a monumental scale, but then again, not on such a scale as to cut the Rockefeller fortune by ninety per cent, as was the case with Carnegie. Rockefeller gave away over half a billion, but probably he kept at least that much for his family.

In short, the more we look into the life of John D. Rockefeller, the more we look into the life of an incredibly successful—and withal, very unremarkable—man. It is a curious verdict to pass on the greatest acquisitor of all time, and yet it is difficult to avoid the conclusion that John Flynn has perfectly phrased: "Rockefeller in his soul was a bookkeeper." We can see the bookkeeperishness in unexpected but telling places, such as in his *Random Reminiscences,* where he dilates on the importance of friendship, but cites as a dubious friend the man who protests, "I can't indorse your note, because I have an agreement with my partners not to . . ."; or again, when he expands on the nonmaterial pleasures of life, such as gardening, but adds as a clincher: "We make a small fortune out of ourselves, selling to our New Jersey place at $1.50 and $2.00 each, trees which originally cost us only five or ten cents at Pocantico." Whether he turns to friendship or to nature, money is the measure.

These are surely not the sentiments of greatness—but then John D. was not a great man. Neither was he, needless to say, a bad man. In most ways he was the very paragon of the business virtues of his day, and at the same time the perfect exemplar of the unvirtues as well. It is likely that he would have made his mark in any field, but unlikely that any commodity other than oil would have offered such staggering possibilities for industrial growth and personal aggrandizement. He personified in ideas the typical business thought of his day—very Christian, very conventional, very comfortable.

Yet as the image of John D. recedes, we realize the pointlessness of such personal appraisals. We study Rockefeller not so much as a person but as an agent—an agent for better and worse in the immense industrial transformation of America. Viewed against this stupendous process of change, even the largest lives take on a subordinate quality, and personal praise and blame seem almost irrelevant. And Rockefeller was not one of the largest lives only one of the luckiest.

In the end there was only the frail ghost of a man, stubbornly resisting the inevitable. His son, John D., Jr., whom he had fondly called "my greatest fortune," had long since taken over the reins of the great foundations and had begun to refashion the Rockefeller image in his own way: Rockefeller Center, The Cloisters, the restoration of Williamsburg. His grandsons, among them one who would one day aspire to the Presidency of the United States, were already young men, carefully imbued with the family style: determination, modesty on the grand scale, a prudent balance between self-interest and altruism. And the Standard itself, now split and resplit into a handful of carefully noncollusive (and equally carefully noncompetitive) companies, was bigger and more powerful than ever. All in all, it was an extraordinary achievement, and the old man must have enjoyed it to the hilt. For it had indeed rained porridge, and his dish had surely been kept right side up.

TRADE CARDS

Compiled by WILLIAM G. McLOUGHLIN

American manufacturers had a problem in the 1870's. They were beginning to produce and distribute consumer goods on a nationwide scale—but there was no advertising medium of truly national circulation. Their need, together with the perfecting of inexpensive methods of color lithography, gave birth to a fascinating phenomenon, at once folk art and effective business device: the trade card. Inserted in packages at the factory, handed out by retailers with every sale, or mailed to prospective customers, these small cards touted the virtues of almost every imaginable product. The complete sales pitch was usually printed on the back, but an attractive colored picture on the other side of the card was invariably the attention-getter—one that soon proved its tremendous appeal. Thousands of Americans avidly saved these cards, later to exchange them with friends, paste them in albums, or just keep them in a drawer in the parlor, where members of the family could beguile a long winter evening by poring over the collection. The fad flourished until well after the turn of the century; and just as the ads in last week's magazines will one day be of high interest to cultural historians looking for insights into American life of the 1960's, so a sampling of the trade cards of the Gilded Age offers a unique view of how Americans lived then: what they believed in, what they desired, what they were proud of, and what their hidden assumptions were. Such a sampling, together with brief commentaries, follows on the next fifteen pages.

THE GREAT EAST RIVER SUSPENSION BRIDGE.
CONNECTING THE CITIES OF NEW YORK & BROOKLYN.
The Bridge crosses the river by a single span of 1595 ft suspended by four cables 15½ inches in diameter. The approach on the New York side is 2492 ft the approach on the Brooklyn side is 1901 ft. Total length 5898 ft. From high water to roadway 120 ft. From roadway to top 157 ft. From high water to centre of span 135 ft. Width of bridge 85 ft. Total height of Towers 277 ft.

National Emblems

Americans were dazzled, in the 1870's and 80's, by technological feats of such scope and grace that they seemed to be emblems of a strong young nation striding forward to lead all the world in progress. Trade cards made the most of this, and two of the favorite symbols were the Brooklyn Bridge (opened in 1883) and the Statue of Liberty (erected in 1886). The ad men were unabashedly imaginative in adapting both to the promotion of such marvels as Lydia E. Pinkham's Vegetable Compound (opposite) or Eagle Pencils (right, in a trade card with a movable tab to "unveil" the Goddess and reveal her astonishing devotion to the product).

THE EAGLE RISES TO UNVEIL THE STATUE OF LIBERTY.

USE THE BEST EAGLE ROUND AND HEXAGON PENCILS IN SEVEN DEGREES OF HARDNESS No 1-1½ 2-2½ 3-4 5

Compliments of the EAGLE PENCIL COMPANY, N.Y.

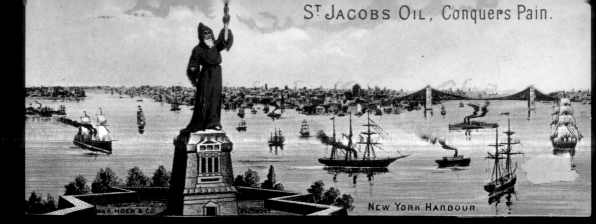

St. Jacobs Oil, Conquers Pain.

New York Harbour.

The happy conviction was dawning upon the country in the last decades of the nineteenth century that everything American was simply the best in the world—especially the things we made. Enormous liberties were taken with Miss Liberty to make this clear, and (opposite page) Uncle Sam was enlisted to suggest complacently how less fortunate peoples might profit by our ingenuity.

BEST IN THE WORLD

The Bartholdi Statue of Liberty
The Largest in the World

The Brainerd & Armstrong Spool Silk
The best in the World

A SUPERIOR SILK IS MANUF BY THE BRAINERD and ARMSTRONG Co.

Liberty. FEEDING THE WORLD

Holmes & Coutts FAMOUS SEA FOAM WAFERS NEW YORK

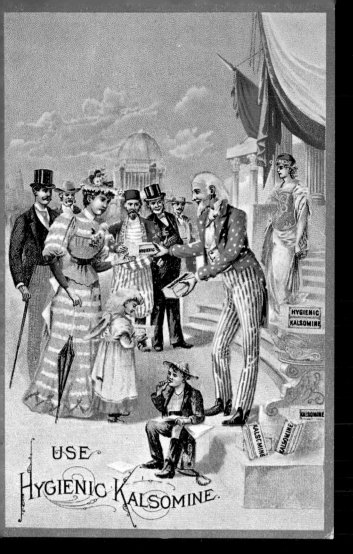

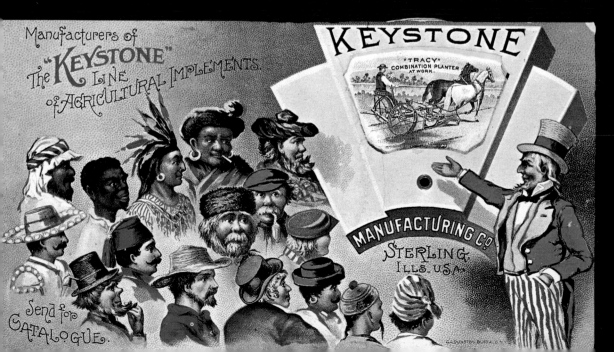

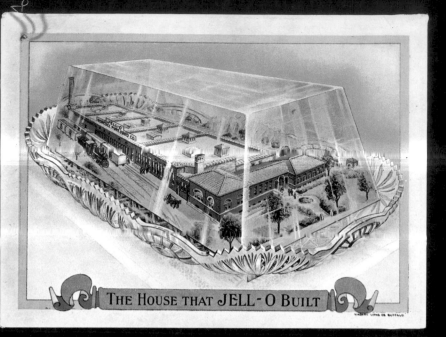

The House that JELL-O Built

The idea, so common in this day of smog control and urban renewal, that a big factory with belching smokestacks is something to be apologetic about would have been incomprehensible to most of our industrial grandfathers. To them their factories were things of beauty, the proudest symbols of the new America; and one of the most popular trade-card subjects was a full-blown rendering of "the works." Jell-O, pulling a neat metonymic switch, exhibited the factory in aspic; Bradley Fertilizer made no excuses for smelling up North Weymouth, Mass., and to Broadhead Mills their gorgeous plant seemed the perfect backdrop for a lightly tripping pretty girl.

"Our Factory"—Proud Symbol of an Era

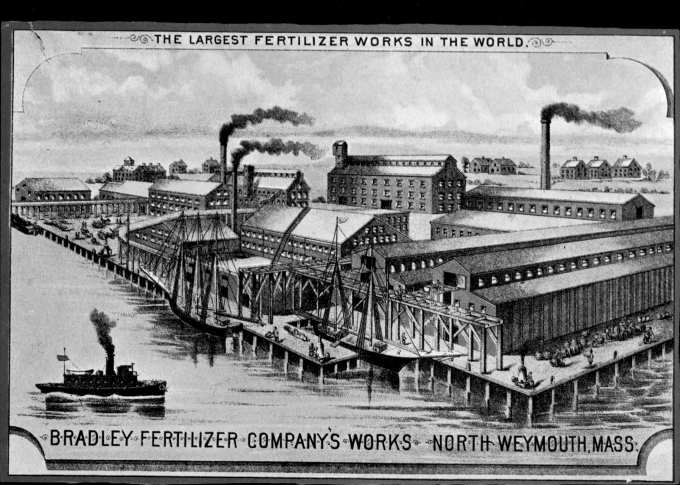

THE LARGEST FERTILIZER WORKS IN THE WORLD.

BRADLEY FERTILIZER COMPANY'S WORKS · NORTH WEYMOUTH, MASS.

HILL'S
CASCARA QUININE
BROMIDE
DANGER
1904
IN DANGER
So are you when you neglect a COLD.~YOU can be CURED by taking
HILL'S CASCARA BROMIDE QUININE TABLETS.
CURES
COLDS, COUGHS
IN
24 HOURS.
CURES
LA GRIPPE
IN
3 DAYS
OR MONEY REFUNDED.

Trade cards, naturally, had to compete for attention just as the things they advertised had to compete for the market. Manufacturers strove for pictorial drama. Innocent Babes and Faithful Fidos were as popular then as now, and so were pretty girls. It would be a good bet that the artist who produced the stirring scene at left for Hill's Cascara Bromide Quinine had done many a similar lithograph to advertise the supercharged melodramas of the period. For Warner's Safe Yeast, a buxom lass was created whose bosom more than hinted at ebullient expansion.

A Splash of Drama—and a Touch of S–x

When a trade card's appeal was broad enough, it could be left blank and later imprinted with the name of any entrepreneur. To make the young lady in the bathtub stand up, turn the page.

Quick to Board the Band Wagon

Innovations in transportation that caught the public imagination
were quickly exploited by the trade-card virtuosos. When the country
began to hear about San Francisco's cable cars (first installed
in 1873), a bright spark at Belding Brothers saw that a
"sectional view" of this intriguing means of locomotion could
be used to imply that Belding's Spool Silk thread was more or less
as strong as a steel cable. The daring introduction of steel
warships in the eighties and nineties stirred someone working for Perry
Davis & Son to substitute still another kind of hull: a bottle of
Davis' Vegetable Pain Killer. (If the principal ingredient of
this medication was that of most such nostrums, the mental association
with the Navy may have sprung from the fact that grog, in one form
or another, was issued to American sailors fairly often in those days.)

Below: the titillating card on the preceding page unfolded
to this rather disappointing scene. But one could always have a beer.

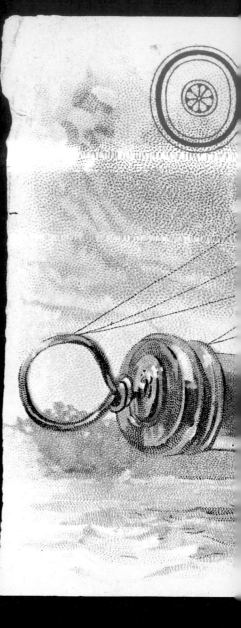

UR NEW NAVY

DAVIS

PERRY DAVIS'
VEGETABLE
PAIN KILLER.
PREPARED BY
PERRY DAVIS & SON
PROVIDENCE, R.I.

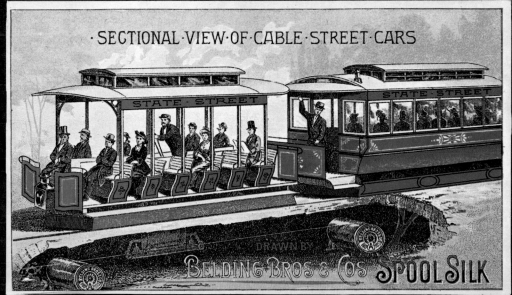

SECTIONAL·VIEW·OF·CABLE·STREET·CARS

STATE·STREET

STATE·STREET

DRAWN BY
BELDING BROS & CO'S SPOOL SILK

Although the colossal day of plastics and electronics was still
far in the future when trade cards flourished, the application of
empirical knowledge to practical matters was in full swing
to answer the growing demand for creature comforts. The Marks
Adjustable Chair suggested that some of the best hours in
one's library might be spent in horizontal reflection on the works
of contemporary masters; it was obvious that operating
the Fort Wayne Improved Western Washer was child's play;
courtship hung in the balance over the purchase of a "Domestic"
sewing machine "with new wood work and attachments";
and the virtues of Rising Sun Stove Polish were brilliantly clear
to the mistress if not to the maid and the delivery boy.
As for Buckeye Force Pumps, they might not quite put out the fire,
but they gave you the satisfaction of knowing that if your
house burned down it was not for want of the latest
equipment, while the Andrews' Gem Folding Bed converted into a
fake armoire so airtight that if anyone happened to get
closed up inside, your guests would never know the difference.

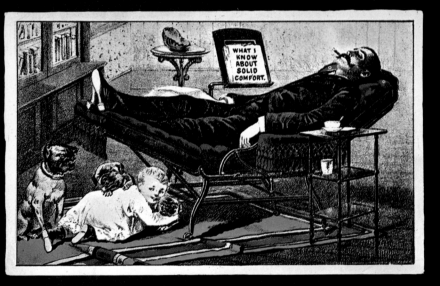

BUCKEYE FORCE PUMPS.

MAST, FOOS & CO.   SPRINGFIELD O.-U.S.A.

MANUFACTURERS OF
BUCKEYE LAWN MOWERS,
IRON TURBINE &
BUCKEYE WIND ENGINE

"AND WHAT CAME OF IT"
ILLUSTRATING THAT

"THE COURSE OF
TRUE LOVE NEVER DID RUN SMOOTH"

BED OPEN

THE ANDREWS' GEM FOLDING BED

Even political satire got into trade cards, or something like them: in 1901 a New York company
put out a folder (below) intended to disparage the Populist movement by showing that
everything might be up to date in Kansas City, but the visiting farmers didn't know what to make of it.

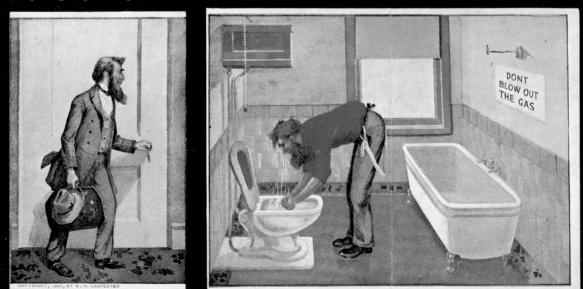

Still Down on the Farm

In spite of the industrial revolution, most Americans still lived in rural surroundings at the end of the nineteenth century, and any randomly chosen stack of trade cards proved it. But even farm life was changing, notably through the steady improvement of agricultural machinery. It isn't quite clear whether the parrot or the girl is speaking, in the card shown below; but nobody was going to deny that the Jackson farm wagon was a very pretty thing. You had no tank to put a tiger in, but if you were well up on the rake's progress you got yourself a J. W. Stoddard Tiger-brand dump rake that turned haying into pure sport — just as a Syracuse chilled steel plow would sail through furrows like a gaff-rigged sloop. The Walter A. Wood Company, catering to a more sobersided set, stressed the safety lever that could instantly raise the cutting bar of their mower and lower the infant mortality rate on the farm.

DAWGY! DAWGY! VERE ISH DAT TAMNED DAWG!

CELLULOID WATERPROOF COLLARS, CUFFS & SHIRT BOSOMS.

THE LAST INVENTION

ECONOMICAL, DURABLE, HANDSOME.

COPYRIGHTED 1892 by POND'S EXTRACT CO.

BOUND FOR DONNYBROOK FAIR
[FULLY EQUIPPED]

Assumptions of a Simpler-minded Time

The public that the typical trade card aimed at was middle class, with middle-class dollars in its pocket and middle-class prejudices in its mind. Its emotions appear — from this evidence — elementary, its sensitivities minimal, its humor often appalling. Observe these stereotypes. Folk heroes, like the fireman, were impossibly courageous and cool. "Foreigners," on the other hand, were thought of as legitimate targets for ridicule, not necessarily bad-tempered but often unkind just the same. The German was fat and stupid, and would never learn to talk without an absurd accent; the Chinese were all laundrymen who had barely missed Mongolian idiocy; the Irish were ever ready for a shillelagh free-for-all. As for the Negro, he was a home-grown alien who was amusingly inferior but always good-natured — though the look on the face of the colored child in Fairy Soap's callous joke suggests that a minor race riot is about to begin. Today, despite echoes that still reverberate, it all seems curiously remote, an embarrassing expression of our national adolescence.

"WHY DOESN'T YOUR MAMMA WASH YOU WITH FAIRY SOAP?"

Made only by THE N. K. FAIRBANK COMPANY.

CHICAGO, ST. LOUIS, NEW YORK, BOSTON, PHILADELPHIA, PITTSBURGH, BALTIMORE.

COPYRIGHT, 1893, THE N.K.FAIRBANK COMPANY, CHICAGO.   (OVER)

THE COMMODORE LEFT TWO SONS

William Henry Vanderbilt   *Cornelius J. Vanderbilt*

—and America's greatest fortune up to that time, some

$100,000,000. The legal battle that followed, full

of tarts and torts and turnabouts, might have been plotted by Dickens

When Commodore Cornelius Vanderbilt expired in New York City on January 4, 1877, with members of his family gathered about his bed singing "Come Ye Sinners, Poor and Needy," he was by far the richest man who had ever died in the United States of America. He had gone to bed for the last time early in May of the previous year. After nearly eighty-three years of strenuous living, his staunch body was finally exhausted by a multitude of ailments, any one of which might have killed an ordinary person. The doughty old Commodore has had his less fervent admirers both before and since his demise, but no one has ever accused him of having been an ordinary person. He fought on through the summer and fall, stubborn and irascible and profanely contemptuous of those whose great expectations were being so maddeningly prolonged by his reluctance to become a decedent.

His residence at 10 Washington Place, then a quiet backwater between the gilded flow of fashion northward from Washington Square and the swirl of commerce up Broadway, was shabby by comparison with the great mansions soon to be built by his favored heirs, and it swarmed with relatives and friends speaking in appropriately hushed voices all through the months of his illness. It must have resembled one of those scenes so relished by writers of popular Victorian novels, with only the favorites permitted to hover solicitously about the deathbed. The aging daughters, who had disapproved of the young wife of their father's declining years

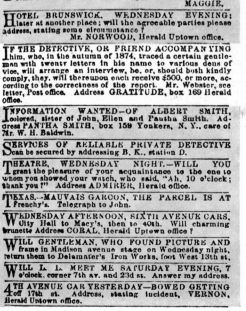

Left: Cornelius Vanderbilt, 1794–1877, called "Commodore" because of his ferries and steamboats, put together the huge New York Central system when past middle age. This portrait of the sturdy old magnate is by Eastman Johnson. Above right: The Personal Column from the Herald *of November 9, 1877—a glimpse at a side of life that rarely gets into history books—contains an ad, signed "Gratitude," which clearly refers to Cornelius J. Vanderbilt (20 letters). One of several mentioned ominously by his lawyers during the trial, it typifies the skullduggery which surrounded the case. No one can say today who "Gratitude" was.*

By FRANK CLARK

and whose mere presence now provoked him into violent rages, were relegated to the hallway outside his chamber, from which they could peek in at him reproachfully whenever the door was opened. At an even farther remove from parental favor, downstairs on the parlor floor, a truly classic example of the wastrel and debt-ridden younger son paced fitfully to and fro, still hopeful of winning a last-minute reprieve.

Down on Wall Street the Commodore's old playmates in the game of swallowing railroads waited ravenously. Their mouths already watered in anticipation of the luscious pickings which would be theirs when the old man's controlling interest in the New York Central was divided among a dozen mutually antagonistic heirs. For some of them the strain was too much; premature announcements of his death were frequently circulated in an effort to drive down the price of Central stock, but the great railroad empire that the Commodore had wrested from the wolves of the Street was impervious to such petty chicanery.

Beyond these financially expectant inner circles was the general public, motivated by nothing more tangible than curiosity as to how the richest man in America, having died, would leave his fortune. This curiosity was considerably whetted by the newspapers, which used relays of reporters to maintain a twenty-four-hour vigil about the house and which printed daily bulletins spiced with assorted rumors and conjectures. Even allowing for this journalistic incitement, the extent of general interest in the imminent demise of a private citizen from natural causes seems hardly credible today. But wealth on such a vast scale as Cornelius Vanderbilt's seemed less credible then. William B. Astor, the son of John Jacob Astor, had died two years earlier leaving forty million dollars, but the Astor fortune had been the product of two lives spanning nearly a century, and it was not nearly so impressive as Vanderbilt's one hundred-odd millions, which he alone had accumulated—and mostly in the last fifteen years of his life. Most of the rich men of the time were worth only a few hundred thousand dollars, but in the extremely solid dollars current in those days, one hundred thousand was a tidy fortune. For a man born poor to amass such a fortune as the Commodore's was a phenomenon so baffling to the imagination that even the rumors grossly underestimated its extent.

The funeral took place on Sunday, January 7. It was described as unostentatious but impressively solemn. After a brief service at the Church of the Strangers around the corner on Mercer Street, the cortege proceeded down Broadway to the Battery, crossed by ferry to Staten Island, and there in the old Moravian burying ground at New Dorp, among generations of

The Commodore got the plain funeral he wanted. Here are the

humble ancestors, Cornelius Vanderbilt was laid to rest.

The next day, promptly at noon, the bereaved family gathered in the home of William K. Thorn, a son-in-law of sufficient independent wealth to be on reasonably good terms with all factions, to hear Judge Charles A. Rapallo read decedent's last will and testament. In the macabre gloom customary in the parlors of that era, with the austere and venerable Judge Rapallo presiding, it must indeed have been a grimly momentous occasion in the lives of the two sons and eight daughters who had grown old awaiting it. Phoebe Jane, the eldest, who was sixty-two, barely survived it.

"I Cornelius Vanderbilt, of the City of New York, do make and publish my last will and testament as follows . . ." Thus commenced the document which would dispose of all the vast accumulation of worldly goods of which decedent had died possessed. First, he gave to his beloved wife, Frank A. Vanderbilt, the sum of $500,000 in five per cent bonds of the United States of America, with the stipulation that this bequest was in fulfillment of an antenuptial contract in which Mrs. Vanderbilt had agreed to waive her dower rights. He also gave to said wife the house and lot at 10 Washington Place, complete with stables and all

carriages outside his house in Washington Place January 7, 1877.

appurtenances thereto, two carriages, and one pair of carriage horses.

The second clause, consisting of one brief paragraph, rapidly disposed of five of his eight daughters by giving to each of them outright $250,000 in bonds of the Lake Shore and Michigan Southern Railroad Company. These were nice bonds to own, even without the picture of the Commodore which adorned them, but there may have been outbursts of filial indignation from the recipients, two of whom were already widows, when they and those husbands who were still living realized that this was all they were going to get.

The third clause took care of the three remaining daughters, and though they fared somewhat better than their sisters, they could well have been even more indignant. Their bequests of $300,000, $400,000, and $500,000, respectively, in five per cent government bonds, were securely tied up in trusts from which they were to receive only the income during their lives. Should they die without surviving issue, the principal would revert to the estate and thence to the residuary legatee "hereinafter named." Not a penny would remain to console a surviving husband in his old age.

With the expectations of the daughters and their husbands written off so neatly, the Commodore, without even deigning to start a new clause, proceeded to the seemingly more delicate and complex problem of deflating the hopes nourished for a lifetime by his younger son. Cornelius Jeremiah Vanderbilt, then in his late forties, had long been in disfavor with his father. The primary reason was not, perhaps, that he was a frequenter of the plush gambling houses and elegant brothels which flourished in that era of extreme feminine prudery, but probably because he had not inherited his parent's zeal for making and holding money. Ever since young Cornelius could remember, he had been afflicted by a sense of the futility of financial enterprise. The insignificant positions he could obtain and the paltry sums he could earn by his own merits should, he felt, have been as embarrassing to his father as to himself. During the Commodore's lifetime he had avoided such embarrassment by struggling manfully along on an allowance from home so miserably inadequate that he was frequently forced to borrow money from friends, acquaintances, and even strangers. But now, after his life had been irrevocably blighted by his father's money, it seemed only fair that he share abundantly in the source of his misfortunes.

Alas, if the old Commodore had had any sympathy for this viewpoint, it was made apparent in his will only to the extent of preventing his son's life from being further blighted by too much money. After setting up a comparatively modest trust fund of $200,000 in five per cent government bonds, he sternly cautioned his trustees that the income thereof was not to be paid over freely but was to be "applied" by them solely "to the maintenance and support of my son, Cornelius Jeremiah Vanderbilt, during his natural life." Even this miserable pittance was hedged with restrictions. It was only to be doled out if Cornelius' behavior was exemplary. Furthermore, any attempt on the son's part to anticipate, assign, or otherwise encumber this income would result in its being withdrawn from his use entirely. It would "thenceforth, during the residue of his natural life, belong to my residuary legatee." But the crowning indignity was yet to come. "Upon the decease of my said son, Cornelius J.," the will continued, "I give and bequeath the last mentioned $200,000 of bonds to my residuary legatee."

The residuary legatee, as everyone could guess by now, was none other than Cornelius' elder brother, William Henry. This industrious plodder, who scrupulously avoided the haunts of gentlemen, had impressed his father with his reverence for money and his real talent for holding on to it. Cornelius detested him. But he was to be one of the trustees to whom Cornelius

201

would be accountable for his behavior, and this was utterly intolerable.

Next were several clauses devoted to minor bequests to twenty-two assorted relatives and friends of sums ranging from $4,000 to $50,000, and totalling less than $300,000. Then came the grand climax in the eighth clause, which in its entirety reads as follows:

All the rest, residue, and remainder of the property and estate, real and personal, of every description, and wheresoever situated, of which I may be seized or possessed, and to which I may be entitled at the time of my decease, I give, devise, and bequeath unto my son, William H. Vanderbilt, his heirs, executors, administrators and assigns, to his and their own use forever.

Perhaps the full majesty of these redundant legal phrases cannot be properly appreciated without the knowledge that the "residue and remainder" to which they refer was still a little more than one hundred million dollars. The will was dated January 9, 1875, and it was signed, with an awesome abbreviation of testator's Christian name, "C. Van Derbilt," a variation of the old Dutch spelling that he favored.

In a codicil made six months after the original will was written, the Commodore took some $11,000,000 worth of New York Central stock away from his residuary legatee, but that step brought no comfort to his eight daughters and his wayward son. If anything, it was the touch needed to complete their humiliation, for this quite significant little bundle of stock was divided among four of the testator's sixteen grandsons. Five million went to his namesake and favorite, Cornelius Vanderbilt II, and two million to each of the other three. All were sons of the residuary legatee, William Henry Vanderbilt.

We do not know what went on in Mr. Thorn's parlor when Judge Rapallo finished reading the will, but it is not unreasonable to suppose that there were bitter outbursts from the "girls" and that Cornelius must have stalked ominously from the premises leaving a trail of threats about seeing his lawyer. All we know for certain is that William, in his capacity as one of the executors, gathered the precious document to his bosom and departed at once for the surrogate's office on Chambers Street to set in motion probate proceedings that would make him the richest man in America. In any event, rumors that the will would be contested spread quickly.

Disputes over the distribution of a decedent's worldly goods have never been uncommon. They were particularly evident in the United States during the late nineteenth century, when there was a bumper crop of parvenu testators, and the records of surrogates' courts of the period are filled with will contests of sensational bitterness. Like other successful men of

CONTINUED ON PAGE 208

202

The William Henry Vanderbilt family was still one of relatively moderate means while the Commodore lived and when this portrait was painted in 1873 by Seymour Joseph Guy, an English emigrant of limited talent. The pictures on the wall are of no consequence, the fixtures merely serviceable, and two servants are included in the background, perhaps out of affection, perhaps (since they are blurred) for ostentation. The family of any mill owner or banker or local nabob in any small eastern city might have looked the same in those years. From the left they are: father William H.; son Frederick; Mrs. William H.; son George; daughter Florence (later Mrs. Twombly); son William K.; daughters Eliza (later Mrs. Webb) and Margaret; Margaret's husband, Elliott Fitch Shepard; daughter Emily (Mrs. Sloane); Cornelius II's wife, Alice Gwynne; Emily's husband, William Sloane; son Cornelius II. An interesting age: Mr. Shepard was a strict sabbatarian who bought the Fifth Avenue horse-drawn bus line in order to stop its profane Sunday service.

THE INHERITORS
A glimpse at the House of Vanderbilt

THIRD GENERATION

Here are all eight of William Henry's children — grandchildren of the Commodore — plus two of their more notable spouses. These were the château builders, horsy, showy, viewed askance by the old aristocracy until the Mrs. Astor finally left her card at their front door.

Cornelius II, the eldest son, managed the family railroad empire, built The Breakers.

Margaret L. Shepard, a quiet type, built a Y.W.C.A. home and financed Spence School.

William K. and his determined wife Alva (later Mrs. O.H.P. Belmont and a militant suffragette) got the family into Society in 1883 by giving New York a dazzling fancy dress ball, built Marble House at Newport, bought their daughter a duke.

FOURTH GENERATION

Here in battle dress is a group of William Henry's grandchildren, plus two granddaughters-in-law. Of those shown here, the survivor is Harold, who fought Robert Young for the family railroad.

Cornelius III designed a practical new locomotive tender, made brigadier general in World War I. His wife, whom he married over family opposition, was Grace Wilson, who became the great party-giving Mrs. Vanderbilt of her era. He rarely appeared.

Gertrude (Mrs. Harry Payne Whitney), a sculptress of talent, founded the Whitney Museum.

Alfred Gwynne owned a polo field, four yachts, loved coaching, died bravely on the *Lusitania*.

Reginald, a sporty type always at horse shows, married Gloria Morgan, sired the well-known Gloria shown below.

FIFTH GENERATION

It is impossible to find any common denominator but Vanderbilt blood in our sample of the current generation, now mostly middle-aged. Not horses. Not even money. Rebels have appeared, belatedly. There are some public-spirited men, and some genuinely talented ones — but no one rivals the founder.

Cornelius IV, the family iconoclast, was once asked by J. P. Morgan what he would like to become. "A journalist," said the boy. "That's awful," replied Morgan. "Neil" did. It was.

Gloria, in and out of the tabloids for her marriages (notably to Leopold Stokowski), also dabbles in the arts.

Second Alfred G. is an outstanding horseman, like a true Vanderbilt. He owns Native Dancer.

George, once a PT boat skipper like his brother Alfred, has sponsored auto races, hunted big game.

William A. M. Burden, a grandson of Mrs. Twombly, has held many government posts, including that of ambassador to Belgium, is a financier and art patron.

Dave Hennen Morris, Jr., served in two world wars, is a banker. His father, like Burden, was ambassador to Belgium.

Grace, daughter of Cornelius III, married one Henry Gassaway Davis III. After divorce, Davis married her second cousin, Consuelo, at right.

Consuelo, this one the daughter of William K., Jr., was first married to broker Earl E. T. Smith, envoy to Cuba in 1957-1959, a Kennedy crony.

Flora Whitney (Mrs. G. Macculloch Miller) is president of the museum her mother founded.

The Vanderbilts, the ones who have made the headlines now for nearly a century, are all descendants of the redoubtable Commodore's eldest son, the able William Henry. He inherited most of the money, built up the railroad system even further, and launched the family on its highly individualistic course. (See him at left, driving his fine trotters, soberly garbed, the Piccadilly whiskers flying.) Of his numerous posterity, we illustrate a sampling below. Unlike later arrivals in the big money, they are not known for enormous tax-exempt foundations or pious monuments; they did some things of that kind, but mainly they lived interesting, sometimes spectacular lives, as any good aristocracy should.

Emily, widow of a member of the W. & J. Sloane family, later married diplomat Henry White.

Fred, first Vanderbilt college graduate (Yale, '78S) ran a paltry ten million legacy up to over seventy. Education pays.

Florence, as Mrs. Hamilton McK. Twombly, became a lavish, legendary dowager who sent private train for guests.

Eliza married a physician, William Seward Webb, who gave up practice for finance, became head of the Wagner Palace Car Co. He was a famous horse breeder, with a great hackney stable at Shelburne, Vt., owned a vast game preserve in the Adirondacks.

George Washington put up the family's first great baronial palace, the huge Biltmore estate.

Gladys, a retiring sort, married Count László Széchenyi, who became Hungarian minister to the U.S. and Britain.

Consuelo tearfully gave in to Mama and married the Duke of Marlborough, later told her story in *The Glitter and the Gold*.

William K., Jr., encouraged auto racing in early days, then turned to ocean yachting, and set up a marine museum.

Harold, a very active Vanderbilt, invented contract bridge, as a yachtsman has thrice defended America's Cup.

J. Watson Webb, one of Eliza's three sons, won wide fame as a polo player, married Electra Havemeyer, a dynamic collector of American art and artifacts. They personally organized the notable museum at Shelburne, Vt.

Alice, one of Gladys Széchenyi's five daughters, married a count. Three others also wed noblemen, breaking Vanderbilt records.

William Jay Schieffelin, Jr., grandson of Margaret, is 6th generation to have run Schieffelin & Co. (drugs, wines, spirits), a firm founded in 1781, antedating even the in-laws' railroads.

Cornelius Vanderbilt ("Sonny") Whitney has been active in aviation, Democratic politics, racing, mining, matrimony, movie-making. Not to be confused with his cousin, "Jock" Whitney, who is not a Vanderbilt.

John Spencer-Churchill, tenth Duke of Marlborough, Consuelo's son, Sir Winston's cousin, has Blenheim Palace, more titles and hereditary positions than a centipede has feet.

Frederick Vanderbilt Field, Harvard '27, rebelled against his background to join and aid Communist fronts, was once jailed for the Cause.

John Henry Hammond, descended via Emily, is an NAACP official, jazz expert, recording executive credited with "discovering" Benny Goodman.

Alice Hammond, John's sister, liked Goodman too and married the "King of Swing" in 1942.

William Douglas Burden, of another Burden family than William A. M., is a practicing explorer, author, and naturalist.

William B. Osgood Field, Frederick's brother, is a glaciologist and geographer with the American Geographical Society.

Derick V. Webb, son of late Vanderbilt Webb, was recently elected to Vermont state senate as a Republican in a heavily Democratic district.

The present William H., active in cancer research, Florida real estate, and Planned Parenthood, served in the Navy in two wars and was governor of Rhode Island.

Commodore Vanderbilt lived in a plain house and saw no odds in drinking champagne when "sody water" would bubble just as satisfactorily. His show place was Grand Central Depot (an older one), and one of his few extravagances was the triumphal frieze of trains and steamboats at left, which once stood atop old St. John's Park freight station. (The statue of him alone survives, in front of the present Grand Central.) But how his lucky heirs could spend! America had never seen such pleasure domes, such costly fancies. We offer a glimpse of them here.

FRUITS OF THE LEGACY

Unlike the Fifth Avenue châteaux, most of the Vanderbilt country mansions still stand. This was Margaret Louisa Shepard's place, now the Sleepy Hollow Country Club at Scarborough, N. Y.

Fred built Rough Point (above) in Newport; Mrs. Twombly roughed it (below) in Madison, N.J.

For George Washington Vanderbilt II's stunning Biltmore, at Asheville, N.C., Richard Hunt took ideas from Chambord and Blois in France; F. L. Olmsted did landscaping, Gifford Pinchot the forests.

One also built for the public

Old Vanderbilt Clinic, Sloane Maternity Hospital, College of Physicians and Surgeons were early family benefactions, now moved uptown.

St. Bartholomew's doors, a gift, designed by Stanford White.

Former Vanderbilt Hotel, on Park Ave., will be apartments.

The Commodore founded Vanderbilt University with one million. Descendants have given another 25. Harold heads its board.

Unable to get boxes at earlier hall, Vanderbilts backed a new Metropolitan Opera.

And indulged many mighty whims

Old William H. laid in $1,500,000 of clean, safe art; every picture told a story. He also paid to bring this obelisk, Egypt's gift, to New York.

The Coronet Sweepstakes, once a main event for the Four Hundred, found the Vanderbilts steady scorers; one duke, four counts, one earl, one plain "hon."

One can, given a fortune big enough, collect anything. For instance, the large tortoise (right) was picked up in the South Seas by William K. Jr., who showed such marine exhibits at his Centerport, L. I., house (row above). Nicholas Murray Butler, on the other hand, was "collected" by George Washington Vanderbilt II when in 1887 he gave "brain money" and later land to a struggling young educational association. The money hired Butler (later president of Columbia, a Nobel Prize winner in 1931), and the result was Teachers College, a force in U.S. education.

One's house was definitely one's castle

Vanderbilt town houses dominated Fifth Avenue from No. 640 (above, left) at 51st Street all the way up to 58th. William H. built himself 640. His daughters Margaret and Emily occupied the adjoining twin mansion, partly visible. The last of these houses to come down, 640 paid taxes of $184 a night by 1941.

Richard Morris Hunt was the architect of W. K. Vanderbilt's Renaissance château at 660. Just showing at right is the manse of his son W. K., Jr., at No. 666.

684 was Florence Vanderbilt Twombly's; at left once stood sister Eliza Webb's.

Cornelius II carried on his almost excessively blameless life in this block-long castle at 57th Street. He once moved his bedroom to avoid shock of a rear view of a naked stone nymph in a city fountain.

Should Cornelius II weary of his city castle he could go to his Newport "cottage," The Breakers.

Not far from The Breakers, Cornelius II's brother William K. built (as a birthday favor for his wife Alva) Marble House, a kind of seaside White House in white Italian marble, looming enormously on what Henry James called a "miniature spot of earth." It cost two million to build, nine more to decorate.

Thrifty Fred sold off Rough Point but kept a place at Bar Harbor, put up a mansion in Hyde Park for mere $660,000.

Palm Beach is full of Vanderbilts; Harold's house appears above. Finally most Vanderbilts go to the vault (right) on Staten Island

G. W. II gave city a library.

Electra Webb moved old lighthouse, plus a steamboat, to her dry-land museum at Shelburne.

Vanderbilt Hall, one of several gifts the family gave Yale, was memorial by Cornelius II to his son William H., who died in college. It cost $575,000. Room 31 was reserved for any Vanderbilts matriculating at Yale.

Long Island mansion of W. K. Vanderbilt, Jr., now museum of fish, shells, art, antiques.

Architect Marcel Breuer's model shows soon-to-be-completed Whitney Museum of American Art, third building to house collection begun by sculptress Gertrude Whitney.

With his J boat *Ranger* (left) Harold won 1937 America's Cup. Yachting has been a Vanderbilt specialty ever since the Commodore steamed *en famille* to Europe with his *North Star* in 1853. The ship above is W. K. Jr.'s *Alva*, 264 feet long, which carried a seaplane and cost in all $2,500,000. She was delivered in 1931, when Central stock sank to 25 from the 1929 high of 256½. Trouble? No, the family by then owned relatively little of the railroad.

A Vanderbilt auto racing cup

Blood will tell, especially a railroad man's. According to Wayne Andrews in *The Vanderbilt Legend*, after Gladys wed Count Széchenyi and went to live in Budapest, she soon controlled the local trams. She was decorated for her war relief work there.

Vanderbilts have always loved horses—for trotting, polo, coaching, racing. Alfred's Native Dancer won $513,425 in his best year (1953). Sonny Whitney's stable (above) was huge; Dr. Webb's in Shelburne seemed even bigger. The Commodore loved fast trotters, and son William broke the mile record with his famous trotting horse Maud S. In Paris, senior W. K. thrice won the Prix du Jockey Club.

the time, Cornelius Vanderbilt was proud of his fortune, and he wanted it preserved intact as long as possible. He figured that the most likely way to insure the continuity of both his name and railroad was to leave as much of his money as possible to his ablest son, who had himself produced male offspring, and the devil take the rest. Undoubtedly his lawyers must have advised him that such an inequitable distribution would incur the risk of a will contest and would create a good deal of unhappiness as well. But this was probably the sort of reasonable business risk which would have appealed to the Commodore, and there is no evidence to show that he ever gave a rap about making everybody happy.

During the following weeks, William denied publicly and solemnly that there was any ill feeling among the heirs. No one could have been very much surprised, however, when late in February, nearly two months after the testator's death, Cornelius and two of his dissatisfied sisters—Mrs. Ethelinda Allen, beneficiary of a $400,000 trust fund, and Mrs. Marie Alicia La Bau, recipient of $250,000 of Lake Shore bonds—informed Surrogate Delano Calvin that they most certainly did intend to contest the validity of their father's will. The Surrogate put the case on his calendar for March 13. In the meantime, formal objections were filed with the court. The contestants charged that the will was obtained by fraud, circumvention, and undue influence pressed against and upon the decedent by William H. Vanderbilt and other persons as yet unnamed.

On the appointed day, Surrogate Calvin's courtroom in the county courthouse in Chambers Street buzzed with rumors: Jay Gould, the sinister financier, was backing the contestants' suit in the hope of winning a ghoulish post-mortem victory over his old adversary and eventually gaining control of the New York Central; gamblers, equally sinister, to whom young Cornelius was hopelessly indebted, were threatening his life if he did not go through with the suit; most sinister of all, unknown parties were threatening his life if he *did* go through with it. There were even a few kill-joys who spread the word that William had finally settled everything by giving each contestant half a million dollars. Surely, it was argued, William would not allow the family skeletons to be rattled in public for the sake of a few paltry millions.

The crowded courtroom, tense with anticipation of the degrading arts that would be revealed, was stunned into glum silence when ex-Congressman Scott Lord, chief of counsel for the contestants, rose to his feet and abruptly announced that he had been instructed by his clients to withdraw their objections to the probate of the will. Although apparently quite as bewildered as the spectators, Surrogate Calvin recovered sufficiently to admit the will to probate. Mr. Lord told reporters later that he knew nothing of any settlement. All he knew was that late on the previous day he had received a note from his clients ordering him to withdraw the objections. It had come as a complete surprise to him, he said, and, judging from his manner, as a considerable shock. After all, as one indignant but anonymous member of the bar exclaimed to reporters, "It's highway robbery. It robs the profession of a million dollars!"

The contestants themselves were not in court when Mr. Lord made his devastating announcement. William, already launched on the career of bad relations with the

Puck, NOV. 21, 1877

VANDERBILTIANA.

1. In early life he determined to make his mark.

2. His father treated him harshly.

3. But he never talked back. No, he only whined like a little dog.

4. He acquiesced in the idea of putting his Ma in a lunatic asylum.

5. And tried to get a "governess" to suit the "old man."

6. So he crawled after the "old man"—

7. Till the "old man" died, when he skipped off with $95,000,000.

8. And now Cornelius John is trying to draw one of his eye-teeth!!

9. Cornelius John trying to pull down the young American Centaur.

$ 95,000,000

KEPPLER

press that was to culminate some years later in his famous misinterpreted remark, "the public be damned," hastily retreated to his private office in Grand Central Depot and refused to issue any statement whatsoever. There were, of course, the usual "friends of the family and other reliable sources" who scoffed at the idea of any compromise settlement but were confident that William would treat his brother and sisters munificently once the will was probated and the fortune was legally clenched in his fist. The real reason for the last-minute withdrawal, they insisted, was simply and obviously Cornelius' reluctance to expose the lurid details of his private life to public scrutiny. Cornelius himself, when finally tracked down, was not in the mood to see reporters either. A friend quoted him as insisting that he had absolutely nothing to say regarding a settlement.

Two months went by in which rumors of a compromise settlement mounted. Finally, on May 14, the rumors seemed substantiated when Cornelius went into state supreme court and filed a complaint against his brother for failure to keep an agreement allegedly made on March 12, the day before the anticlimax previously enacted in Surrogate Calvin's courtroom. Cornelius claimed that he had been promised one million dollars if he withdrew his objections to the will. Spokesmen for William refused to comment, pointing out how improper it would be to do so now that the matter was in litigation. William himself was not available. He was on the high seas bound for England when Cornelius filed his complaint. According to some of the usual informed sources, the purpose of the trip was to pacify two of his sisters living abroad, who were now claiming that they had not been properly represented at the probate proceedings. Whatever the reason for the trip, before William could return, Mrs. La Bau was back in surrogate's court, demanding (as was her right within a year) that probate be reopened and the will proved anew. Mrs. Allen, the other of the three original contestants, had dropped out, apparently feeling that she could rely on her brother's munificence. Cornelius Jeremiah could not be a legal party to Mrs. La Bau's action because of his pending suit in supreme court, although he undoubtedly gave her all the moral support he could muster. Surrogate Calvin put the case on his calendar for July 12, and the expectations of press and public again ran high.

Interest in the case as a public spectacle became even greater when the rosters of opposing counsel were made known. In those days, when the county courthouse still provided the nation with one of its staple brands of popular entertainment, legal luminaries enjoyed a public renown somewhat comparable to that accorded today to ballplayers, prizefighters, and television performers. Their strategy in conducting a case, their skill in cross-examination, and their forensic ability were all highly and learnedly appreciated by large numbers of courtroom buffs. Among connoisseurs of legal form, counsel for the proponents of the will (Wil-

liam, two of his sons, and a nephew) were generally rated the pretrial favorites. Henry L. Clinton, their field captain, had distinguished himself for many years in the criminal courts of New York State by an uncanny ability to obtain acquittals for unfortunately situated defendants. A client seen with blood on his hands in the immediate vicinity of the corpus delicti did not daunt Mr. Clinton, and his talent for confusing prosecution witnesses and discrediting their testimony was expected to be useful to William H. Vanderbilt in this case.

The master strategist of William's defense of the will was George F. Comstock, a former chief justice of New York State's highest tribunal, the court of appeals, whose opinions are still quoted. Less spectacular than Mr. Clinton, Judge Comstock was a lawyer's lawyer, ranked by many of his contemporaries as the greatest legal mind of his day. What was more, he looked the part. He was tall and spare, with an impressive mane of silvery hair; his mere presence in a courtroom was said to give weight to his client's case.

Joseph Hodges Choate was the reserve force of proponent's legal team. He was somewhat younger and less experienced than his two illustrious colleagues but was already renowned for the role he had played a few years earlier in liberating New York from the grip of Boss Tweed.

Although the odds were against them, counsel for the contestant were not without their backers. Scott Lord, fresh from a term in Congress, had been the law partner of Senator Roscoe Conkling and was an experienced infighter. Uninhibited by legal niceties, he was a particularly good man in a will contest. His colleague, Ethan Allen, had served for a number of years earlier in his career as a United States district attorney.

As a pinch hitter of formidable endowment when legal eloquence was in order, the contestant had retained the services of Jeremiah S. Black, a former chief justice of the supreme court of Pennsylvania and a Cabinet member under both Buchanan and Lincoln. Judge Black had the reputation of being the most magnificent orator at the American bar. His snow-white, shaggy eyebrows belied the bright auburn wig he customarily wore. Twirling a silver tobacco box on the end of an enormous chain and followed by a Negro valet, Judge Black was a familiar figure in courtrooms throughout the nation. The power of his argument was said to rise with the number of spittoons he filled.

There are three grounds on which to break a will, assuming it has been properly drawn and attested, and when the case finally got under way in earnest on November 12, 1877, before Surrogate Calvin, Mr. Lord made it clear in his opening that he was not going to overlook any of them. The contestant would offer evidence to show, first, that the testator had been of unsound mind at the time he made his will; second, that he had been subjected to undue influence; and, third, that the will was the product of a fraudulent conspiracy. "Undue influence" and "fraud-ulent conspiracy" are, in practice, virtually synonymous. The usual tactic is to demonstrate that the unsound con-dition of the testator's mind, weakened by physical dis-ability and insane delusions, made him readily susceptible to a fraudulent conspiracy designed to influence him un-duly. In addition to the lurid charges that Mr. Lord alleged would prove the will invalid on strictly legal grounds, he embellished his opening remarks with lofty rhetorical ef-fects of a moral nature. The division of the estate under the terms of the will was, he declaimed, contrary not only to the spirit of the law but to the morals of a democracy. This may have impressed the public but hardly Surrogate Calvin, who was undoubtedly aware that, in the words of one of his contemporaries, "a will may be mean, unjust and inequitable . . . [and] public sentiment and the moral sense of the community may condemn the instrument and its author to no avail."

Mr. Lord himself, of course, was fully aware of the formidable task confronting him. Not only did he have to battle great wealth and impressive legal talent, but he also had to demonstrate that the testator's mind was of ques-tionable soundness, if he hoped to win his case. That would be tremendously difficult. The mere ability to perform an ordinary business transaction was, and still is, considered sufficient proof of testamentary capacity, regardless of aber-rations and debilities of the most startling sort. Surrogate Calvin himself was fond of citing the case of a testator who believed that in order to go to Heaven he had to eat Boston crackers every morning; nevertheless, his will was duly probated. Judged by this criterion, Cornelius Vander-bilt, who was still juggling railroads successfully in the closing years of his life, was perhaps the sanest of men. Thus, Mr. Lord served notice that contestant's case would reveal the diabolical conspiracies William H. Vanderbilt had been carrying out for years to influence his aging fa-ther. Mr. Lord admitted that many of the charges which would be proved were of a scandalous nature, but he laid the blame for making them public squarely on William himself. The press, of course, was in a dither, devoting col-umns of space to Mr. Lord's "startling performance," and his "amazing allegations."

It was also apparent from this opening that Cornelius Jeremiah, though technically not a contestant in Mrs. La Bau's suit, was to be the central figure in the case and was undoubtedly the moving spirit behind it. For it was pri-marily against him that the alleged undue influence had been exercised. As a direct consequence, Mr. Lord said, his voice quivering with righteous indignation, "his father subjects [young Cornelius] to a degradation unparalleled in the history of wills . . . in this will he puts the son bearing his Christian name under a vassalage so odious that every instinct of his manhood revolted against it."

According to the press, popular sympathy was with Cor-nelius and his sisters, not so much, perhaps, because they got too little as because William and his family got too much. Nevertheless, the will had its supporters—solid, pillar-of-society types who remained unmoved by the piteous spec-tacle of young Cornelius in his $10,000-a-year vassalage.

Mr. Lord then opened his assault. He called to the stand an impressive array of medical experts who had either at-tended Commodore Vanderbilt during his last illness or participated in the autopsy. Their testimony was intended to establish that the physical condition of the deceased had been such that he could not possibly have been of sound mind. What it did establish beyond question was that the old gentleman had suffered from a remarkable variety of afflictions and had had a truly remarkable constitution. The autopsy itself revealed in grisly detail that, except for the heart (which was found to be unusually small), there was hardly an organ in his vast cadaver which was not diseased. Yet it had been peritonitis of only several days' duration which finally killed him. Mr. Clinton objected strenuously to most of this on the ground that it proved nothing about decedent's mental condition when he made his will two years before his death and was, therefore, ir-relevant.

In sum, the testimony of the medical experts, although it had shown the testator to be a man abundantly afflicted with the physical infirmities of old age, had failed to de-velop the picture of a doddering old fool. On the contrary, the more ailments the experts revealed, the more the Com-modore stood forth as an exceptionally strong-willed old curmudgeon rising triumphantly above his bodily ills.

Contestant's real hope of establishing that the Commo-dore was of unsound mind lay in demonstrating that he was subject to various insane delusions. Mr. Lord proposed to do this by proving, first, that the decedent had believed in clairvoyance and spiritualism, and, second, that the Com-modore had had a mania, amounting to insanity, for wealth and personal fame.

The key witness to the influence of the spirits on the testator was Mrs. Jennie W. Danforth. She was a sprightly little woman, who said she was a "magnetician" or "mag-netic healer." Magnetic healing, a heady mixture of spiritu-alism, hypnotism, and electricity, generously spiked with pure hokum, was one of the numerous branches of the non-medical healing arts which flourished in that era of be-mused wonder at the apparently limitless marvels of sci-ence. Some of its practitioners may have been sincere in the sense that they were merely as naïve and gullible as their patients; many, however, were unmitigated frauds. The notorious Claflin sisters, Tennessee and Victoria, for example, made their debut in New York as versatile prac-titioners of the occult arts. They then went on to greater things, including blackmail, free love, and a friendship with Commodore Vanderbilt that was, according to contemporary gossip, not entirely devoted to communion with the spirits (it was known that Vanderbilt's generosity brought the sisters gains on the stock market). During the contest over the will, the Claflin sisters were frequently mentioned as star witnesses for the contestant, and, when they departed suddenly for England, it was widely rumored that they had been bribed by William's faction to put themselves beyond the jurisdiction of the court. In any event, in lieu of Tennie and Victoria on the witness stand, Mr. Lord had to manage with Mrs. Danforth and her far less alluring magnetic arts.

According to her testimony, the Commodore had frequently sent for her in the spring and summer of 1876, during the early stages of his last illness. These were evidently memorable occasions in her career, and she would drop everything to bring the great financier the solace of her miraculous healing powers. She was equally co-operative on the witness stand with Mr. Lord. She recalled with enthusiastic alacrity that the Commodore had absolutely assured her that he believed in clairvoyance and communication with the dead. In fact, on one occasion he had asked her to communicate with his first wife, Sophia, who had died in 1868. Mrs. Danforth had promptly done so. Unfortunately, however, it had been her sad duty to report that Sophia's spirit was in a very distressed state indeed. To this the Commodore said he knew why and that he would certainly have to make another will to set things right with his wife's spirit. At this, Mr. Clinton finally erupted with violent objections to admitting Mrs. Danforth's testimony, in whole or in part. It was, he said, entirely irrelevant. Some courtroom observers felt it was entirely too relevant to be credible. Surrogate Calvin, for his part, said he would like to listen to arguments from both sides before making his decision.

There was very little legal precedent by which to judge the effects of a belief in spiritualism on testamentary capacity. Isaac Redfield, one of the few legal authorities who had commented on the subject, had written in his treatise "The Law of Wills," published in 1876, ". . . [Spiritualism] may be a species of religious belief . . . but [we] can scarcely dignify [it] by the name of science . . . We believe the courts fully entitled to assume, as matter of law, that what is contrary to the acknowledged laws of nature cannot have any standing in a court of law . . . and that a will which is the off-spring of such assumptions cannot be maintained."

Mrs. Danforth's testimony, of course, did not show that the will was the offspring of the spirits, and Mr. Lord did not intend it to do so. Its purpose was to show that the testator had been a true believer in the spirits and in the possibility of communicating with them. This in itself, Mr. Lord contended, was evidence of a state of mental weakness which would render him susceptible to a fraudulent conspiracy designed to influence him unduly.

Arguing for the proponents, Mr. Clinton stated vehemently that Mrs. Danforth's testimony was irrelevant simply because her visits to the Commodore did not take place until more than a year after he had drawn his will. Furthermore, if belief in clairvoyance was to be admitted as proof of insanity, then the witness herself was insane and her testimony was void. Judge Comstock, Mr. Clinton's learned associate, did not much care whether the witness' testimony was relevant or not; it was worthless in any case. The idea that belief in clairvoyance and spiritualism was in itself any proof of mental weakness was, he said, ridiculous. Thousands of intelligent people believed in it. He also pointed out, with remorseless logic, that there were supernatural elements in all religions.

At this crucial point, when it appeared that the evidence of testator's senility was either irrelevant or untenable, or both, Mr. Lord hastily called for reinforcements. Judge Black, rumbling into position beside a convenient spittoon, commenced his argument by brushing aside the question of the relevance of Mrs. Danforth's testimony as of minor importance. Instead, he launched a vigorous attack on the character of the deceased.

"Commodore Vanderbilt was the weakest of living men," Judge Black declaimed. "He was one who more completely misunderstood all the duties he owed to his own family and himself, and was more utterly ignorant of those principles of natural justice which he ought to have thought of and understood and applied to this transaction, than any other man that ever lived or ever died. And the evidence shows that he was so."

Surrogate Calvin, obviously annoyed and, also, a bit bewildered by this highly nonlegal approach to the question at issue, interrupted sharply to ask what there was in the evidence to show the decedent to have been of weak mind.

"His whole life shows it," Judge Black thundered. "All he has ever done or said about the disposal of his property. He had one faculty that was preternaturally enlarged, and that was for accumulating property. It was so enlarged that it dwarfed every other moral sentiment and every intellectual power. Sanity depends upon the balance that has been preserved between the different intellectual faculties and moral sentiments so that all of them bear their proper proportions to one another. Suppose a man's liver to be enlarged beyond what it ought to be, is that man a healthy man? Cornelius Vanderbilt's bump of acquisitiveness, as a phrenologist would call it, was in a chronic state of inflammation all the time. [Phrenology was another of the new "sciences" popular at this period.] It grew wonderfully. And he cultivated it, and under his cultivation all the intellectual faculties that ministered to the gratification of that passion at the expense of everything else. Morally and intellectually his mind was a howling wilderness. He did not content himself by worshipping Mammon alone, though certainly he was a very zealous devotee of that meanest and least erect of the spirits that fell, whose worship is most sure to demoralize the mind and to corrupt while it weakens the understanding. When this is carried to a very great extent, unquestionably its victim cannot be considered a sane man. His love of money amounted to a mania, which would render any act of his void if it could be shown to be the offspring of the delusion under which he labored."

Judge Black's phrenological approach might have beguiled a nonlegal mind, but it failed to impress Surrogate Calvin. He simply ignored it. In order for Mrs. Danforth's testimony to be acceptable as indirect evidence of insanity, the Surrogate ruled that the contestant must first get in evidence something to show that Commodore Vanderbilt was actually insane at the time his will was drawn. This had not been done. Therefore, the witness' testimony was irrelevant and Mr. Clinton's objection was sustained.

"What it amounts to," Mr. Clinton had said in winding up his own argument, after commenting on the fact that Mrs. La Bau had also been a patient of Mrs. Danforth, "is that counsel seeks on behalf of a crazy client and through a crazy witness to influence this court to let in all kinds of crazy testimony."

Deprived of help from the spirits, Mr. Lord put on the stand a number of witnesses whose testimony was supposed to prove the testator's mania for wealth and personal fame. E. D. Worcester, an official of the New York Central and hardly a friendly witness, told of an employee who had stolen twenty dollars from the railroad. It had troubled his conscience so much that he had given the money to his priest to return to the Commodore. His mission accomplished, the priest took the opportunity to mention the poverty and need of his church, but the Commodore was not moved. He turned the money over to Mr. Worcester for credit to the proper account, saying, "There is considerable good in religion after all."

Oakey Hall, the debonair ex-mayor who turned his varied talents to playwrighting after his political career had been brought to an untimely end by the disclosure that he was a member in good standing of the Tweed Ring, came to the stand to tell the inside story of how the heroic statue of the Commodore, which then decorated the façade of the St. John's Park freight terminal and which now graces the southern approaches to Grand Central Terminal, had been paid for. It had cost $100,000 which ostensibly had been raised by public subscription; actually, according to Mr. Hall, the decedent had had to foot the entire bill himself. These two incidents, Mr. Lord contended, were proof of the old man's mania for fame.

In mid-December, with the trial more than a month old and with public interest commencing to languish, Mr. Lord, like a good showman, suddenly shifted his attack from the public to the private life of the deceased and his family. He sought permission to add the names of Mrs. Frank Vanderbilt, the bereaved widow, and her mother, Mrs. Crawford,

to that of William Henry Vanderbilt as parties to the alleged conspiracy to influence the testator. In support of his motion, Mr. Lord revealed that the two ladies had actually been named in the original allegation when it was first prepared but that their names had been stricken out by Mrs. La Bau from motives of delicacy. Since then, however, such strong evidence of their complicity had been obtained that his client was forced to suppress any such sentiments in the interests of justice. Public interest was revived, and Mr. Clinton was more infuriated than ever. He denounced the motion as "an effort to build up a case by defamation of the living and the dead." It was another attempt, Mr. Clinton said, "to prove impossible facts by incredible witnesses." But it was to no avail. Surrogate Calvin said he would have to grant the motion as he must assume it to be in good faith. The idea of assuming anything good on the part of opposing counsel was more than Mr. Clinton could bear. He was so incensed that he defied the Surrogate's admonishments to temper his remarks. He openly accused Mr. Lord of trying his case in the newspapers by scurrilous allegations because his witnesses were either nonexistent or so worthless that he did not dare to call them.

This was not a nice thing to say of a fellow member of the bar, and Mr. Lord was, to all appearances, genuinely indignant. Nevertheless, it was hard to deny that very little evidence had thus far been produced that would invalidate the will. The contestant's lawyers seemed simply to be piling one scandalous allegation upon another until William Henry should capitulate in order to save the family name. For a legalized blackmailing operation of this sort, the offers of counsel to prove an allegation were just as effective as the sworn testimony of reputable witnesses. The press could be relied upon to publish the sordid details in its news columns as it salved its conscience with pious editorials defending "the sanctities of private life" and castigating those who violated them. William Henry himself was accused of unnatural greed in permitting the family name to be dragged through the mire. But, in spite of it all, William showed no sign of loosening his grasp on all his "rest, residue and remainder."

In the light of later events it would seem that Mr. Lord had really been conducting a delaying action until his star witnesses either could be found or, having been found, could be prevailed upon to appear. But now, apparently goaded beyond endurance by Mr. Clinton's unkind accusations, he unlimbered his heavy artillery. The opening barrage was the testimony of Cornelius J. Vanderbilt, the chief victim of the alleged conspiracy engineered by his brother William. When his name was called by Mr. Lord, there was a ripple of excitement in the crowded courtroom. Now, surely, the skeletons supposedly rattling in the family closet would dance merrily into public view.

"Young Corneel," as he was familiarly known, was, alas,

one of the skeletons himself. From contemporary accounts, he must have looked the part. He was tall and gaunt and badly stooped, and a dank goatee added a satanic touch to his cadaverous features. Even the languid manner which he affected, and which was then *de rigueur* for men about town and scions of wealth, was impaired by a disjointed twitchiness of movement. For him to take the stand was either an act of considerable moral courage or irrefutable evidence that he was every bit the fool his father had thought him to be.

Piloted by Mr. Lord's gentle questioning, Cornelius skimmed blithely over and around the shoals of his misspent life. He'd always been told that he'd been born in 1831, so that would make him about forty-six years old. He had lived at home, more or less, until he was eighteen, when he had gone out on his own, more or less. There was no special reason for his leaving home, although his father was rather rough in his treatment and it was not very agreeable to be at home. He simply preferred it outside, and he supposed his father preferred it too. His father gave him an allowance of about $100 a month, and he had boarded around in New York. This arrangement had continued for six or seven years until in 1856, at the age of twenty-five, he had married Ellen Williams of Hartford, Connecticut, a girl of modest circumstances, and the allowance was increased to $150. They had lived near Hartford on a farm his father had given him. He didn't care much for farming. After about a year, on the plea of his wife and her family, the allowance was increased to $200, and there it remained until her death in 1872. Since then young Corneel had been boarding around in New York again, or travelling, or staying with friends, and the allowance had been increased to $250, for no apparent reason that he could think of except that his father was much richer in 1872 than he had been in 1856 and he supposed it cost more for a single man in his position to live in the city.

With the vital statistics filled in, more or less, Mr. Lord got down to the real business at hand. Did Mr. Vanderbilt remember being arrested and taken to a lunatic asylum in January of 1854? He should say he did remember it. In fact, he would never forget it. It was early of a Sunday evening, just as he was dressing to keep a supper engagement, when, without the slightest warning or explanation, he had been rudely arrested and hauled off to the Bloomingdale Asylum away up on 117th Street and Morningside Heights. It had been rather an upsetting experience at the time, of course, and he had not been very amiable about it. His lack of co-operation had induced Dr. D. Tilden Brown, the director of the institution, to admit that the commitment papers were insufficient to hold him against his will, and early the next morning he and Dr. Brown had driven into the city and gone before Judge Ingram to swear out a writ of habeas corpus. William H. Vanderbilt and Judge Charles A. Rapallo, who had signed the commitment papers, had appeared in court to oppose the writ. William, in a most unbrotherly fashion, had told Cornelius that he had better withdraw his writ and return quietly to the asylum. Otherwise, he would be arrested on a forgery charge brought by a downtown merchant, and his father, who lay desperately ill at the time, would surely disinherit him. Cornelius had indignantly refused. He was innocent of any forgery, and, in any event, he would rather be considered a damned rascal than a damned lunatic. There was great laughter at this, and to restore order Surrogate Calvin had to threaten to clear the courtroom.

Judge Ingram had granted Cornelius' writ and released him, and he had gone directly to see the merchant. The merchant had denied any intention of charging him with forgery for what was, after all, merely another unpaid bill. So far as Corneel was concerned, that would have been the end of the matter. But sometime later that year, while he was paying one of his infrequent visits to his parents on Washington Place, the subject of the Bloomingdale episode had come up again. One word had led to another, as it usually did, and his father had commenced one of his tirades of abuse. Corneel had been about to leave when suddenly, much to the astonishment of both his father and himself, his mother had turned on his father and told him to stop being such a fool. Then, of course, she had burst into tears at her audacity, but finally managed to calm down enough to tell his father that it was William who had planned the whole thing. It was not the first time, either. She hated to say it because she loved all her children, but William had always been scheming and telling lies to cause trouble between the witness and his father. Even more surprising than his mother's outburst, however, had been his father's reaction to it. He had hung his head sheepishly and maintained a glum silence, as though saddened by the realization that no man as rich as he was could ever really trust anyone, not even his first-born son. The witness himself, more than twenty years later, was still saddened by his memory of that unhappy scene. He took out a handkerchief and blew his nose. William, for his part, appeared unaffected by his brother's testimony, or by the suffering visible on the faces of his lawyers.

Mr. Lord, with appropriate hems and haws, now broached a rather delicate subject. Had the witness ever been afflicted in any way? With head bowed and voice trembling, Cornelius replied that he had been afflicted with epilepsy in its severest form from childhood until he was about thirty-eight. Since then the attacks had become less frequent and less severe, but it was still necessary for him to be accompanied by a friend at all times. This led into Mr. Lord's next question. Did he recall where he was during October and November, 1874? Yes, he certainly did. He was with Mr. George Terry, his friend and constant companion, travelling about from one place to another. His memory was so good on this point because he had consulted a diary which he had kept then and which he kept now.

"During those months, or at any other time," Mr. Lord asked, "were you in the habit of frequenting the Fifth Avenue Hotel every morning?"

No, he certainly was not. Of course, he may have been there once or twice during the summer and three or four times during the winter. After all, it would have been quite impossible to avoid it entirely.

In those days, in the seventies and on into the early eighties, the original Fifth Avenue Hotel played a role in New York City that no single hotel was ever to enjoy again. Standing at the intersection of Broadway and Fifth Avenue at Twenty-third Street, in the days when the city's life was centered at the crossing of those avenues, it was the Plaza and the Ritz of the fashionable, the Astor and the Knickerbocker of the theatrical and sporting set, the Algonquin of the literary, and the old Waldorf of the *nouveaux riche*.

With a weather eye on Mr. Clinton, who was commencing to fret and fume in his seat, Mr. Lord launched his next question. During those two apparently unique months of October and November, 1874, did the witness visit any gambling house, or gambling hell, as it is called? Before Cornelius could reply, Mr. Clinton was on his feet with a strenuous objection. The witness was not a party to the contest of the will and his habits or whereabouts, good, bad, or indifferent, were entirely irrelevant and immaterial. Surrogate Calvin seemed inclined to agree and requested Mr. Lord to reveal where his line of questioning would lead. Counsel for contestant was delighted to explain. Such testimony, he said, was directly related to the foul conspiracy which William H. Vanderbilt, desperate because of his brother's long abstention from gambling, whoring, and drinking, had cunningly devised in October and November, 1874, in order to hoodwink his aging father. It did not matter that the victim of this vicious plot was the much-maligned Cornelius rather than Mrs. La Bau, the actual contestant. If any part of the will was fraudulently produced, then the whole was a fraud. Surrogate Calvin, after some deliberation, ruled in Lord's favor. It was the first important victory for Mrs. La Bau's side, and a murmur of gratification welled up from the section of the courtroom where the contestant's partisans were gathered. Cornelius returned at once to the stand to answer Mr. Lord's question triumphantly. No, he had not been in the habit of frequenting gambling houses, or hells, in October and November of the year 1874.

"Or houses of ill-fame?"

"No!"

"Or of drinking to excess?"

"No!"

For his last question Mr. Lord lowered his voice to the hushed tone reserved for speaking of the dead to their bereaved ones. How many times had he seen his father during his last illness? He had called at the house two or three times every day during the last three or four months, he replied sorrowfully, but his stepmother had permitted him to see his father only once in all that time.

And now came one of the most eagerly awaited moments of the trial—the ordeal by cross-examination of young Corneel. Mr. Clinton, making no effort to conceal his impatience with filial grief, went to work immediately. There were, as he put it, a few things he was confused about and would like to have cleared up. For instance, had Mr. Vanderbilt ever been in Bloomingdale before his visit there in 1854? Well, yes, he had been there once before—in 1850, when he was about nineteen. Could he tell them a little more about it? Well, he had been down in Washington and he had drawn some money on his father, but his father hadn't paid it. So the authorities, or whoever it was, communicated with his father and he came on and settled it. Cornelius went back to New York with his father and went into Bloomingdale of his own volition. He did not think he was insane, nor did anyone else. How long had he stayed there? About six months, more or less. Well, he must have liked it then, more or less. What did he do next? After some difficulty the witness recalled that he had gone to work in the law office of Horace Clark, his brother-in-law. In what capacity? "I could not tell," Cornelius replied languidly, and Mr. Clinton suggested that possibly he had not been there long enough for it to be determined. And then what did he do? He went into the leather business with William F. Miller & Co. at the head of Gold Street. How long had he lasted there? About three months. Why had he left? He did not care to stay. No, he was not requested to leave. He had left voluntarily. He simply did not relish the business very much. And then what? Well, after his marriage, he had run the farm his father had given him. But that was five or six years later, wasn't it? He supposed it was, more or less.

Mr. Clinton seemed quite perplexed about the witness' name. Hadn't he been christened Cornelius Jeremiah Vanderbilt and not Cornelius Vanderbilt, Jr.? Inasmuch as he was only a few weeks old at the time, the witness said he really couldn't recollect whether he had or not. It got quite a laugh from the spectators, but Mr. Clinton, who was not amused, persisted. What was his real name? Well, his mother said it was Cornelius, Jr., and his father said it was Cornelius Jeremiah. To save any trouble about the matter he used both of the names.

Mr. Clinton now undertook to set the record straight as to the number of times the witness had been arrested. Mr. Vanderbilt thought three times sounded about right. That is, three times in civil suits charged with fraud. Mr. Clinton was not satisfied and the following exchange took place:

Q: Haven't you been arrested four times by Deputy Sheriff McCulligan?

A: I don't know the man.

Q: Would you know him if you saw him?

A: I don't think I should. They are a class of people I don't particularly fancy.

Q: Isn't it true that you have been arrested thirty times? The witness thought not, but he was rather vague about it, and when Mr. Clinton confronted him with the names of some thirty-five creditors to whom he had allegedly given checks on banks where he had no accounts, he was hazier than ever. He could not recollect, he did not remember, he had forgotten, or he would not swear either way. His arrangements with banks, it developed, were somewhat unusual. He had never in his life bothered to keep a regular account in any bank. As the occasion arose he simply drew checks on whichever bank was most convenient and then deposited sufficient funds to cover them. For instance, he had a standing arrangement with the teller of the Hartford County Bank to pay such checks as might come in and then to notify him of the amount needed to cover them. Of course, this method might be a bit disconcerting to banks that were unfamiliar with it, and sometimes, too, he forgot to deposit the money or found it inconvenient to do so for one reason or another.

Mr. Clinton seemed fascinated by Mr. Vanderbilt's extraordinary talent for borrowing money and not paying it back. Under prolonged questioning the witness admitted borrowing and not paying in Utica, Rochester, Cincinnati, San Francisco, and Philadelphia, but he could not recollect as to Buffalo, Toledo, Chicago, St. Louis, or Baltimore. Finally Mr. Clinton thought it would be simpler if the witness could name one city in which he had not borrowed money. He claimed he could mention several, but he would need time to think; Mr. Clinton decided to spare him the effort. All in all the witness thought he owed about $90,000.

Mr. Clinton professed to be highly mystified by all this, particularly as to how the witness had managed to incur such a large indebtedness, living as he did on a small farm in the country. Mr. Vanderbilt explained that he needed four or five servants, as he frequently entertained prominent men in his home; that he had to have an attendant at all times; and that his expenses were very large generally, inasmuch as he was expected to sustain the family name and his father's honor. Mr. Clinton found it most difficult to understand how he had sustained the honor of his father's name by borrowing money from his guests, which he had done. Mr. Vanderbilt did his best to explain that although he may have borrowed money from men in Hartford who had been guests in his house, he had never done so while they were guests. It was a fine distinction that only a highly cultivated person could appreciate, and he seemed quite proud of it. He did admit making one exception to this rule, but he felt that the circumstances warranted it. A man was invited for a few days and stayed several months. He was quite a bore, really, so the host

borrowed a little money from him to get rid of him. Of course he had never paid it back. Had he ever paid back any of the money he had borrowed from those who were *not* bores? He thought he had, but he couldn't recollect their names or the amounts offhand.

He firmly denied that the greater part of his indebtedness had been caused by gambling—his total losses for his whole life did not exceed $10,000. In fact, he seemed to feel quite keenly that it was a shameful reflection both on his father's honor and his own manhood to confess that he had never lost even as much as $500 at a sitting. Possibly he had borrowed money from gamblers, but not for gambling. And, no, he didn't think he had ever assigned his monthly allowance to anyone except John Daly, a very good friend of his who merely happened to be a professional gambler. He didn't even know Alex Howe, who ran a place on Twenty-ninth Street; he knew of George Thompson only by hearsay, although he would not swear he had never met him. A man in his position meets so many people. Of course he had often been in Matthew Danser's place at 8 Barclay Street. Danser ran a downtown day game patronized by the Wall Street crowd. And it went without saying that he had been in George Beers' elegant establishment at University Place and Thirteenth Street. The late Mr. Beers had been a gentleman and scholar who had catered to the town's young bloods.

Mr. Clinton was particularly interested in the witness' relations with one Zachariah Simmons. Mr. Simmons in his day was widely famed as a lottery man (lotteries were a

C. Vanderbilt

The Commodore's signature, in the old-fashioned Dutch way

forerunner of what we know as the "numbers racket" and were equally lucrative for their operators). Did Mr. Vanderbilt owe Mr. Simmons any money? Well, he supposed he did, but he could not be certain of the amount. Possibly $10,000 or so, more or less. When had he last seen Mr. Simmons? The witness said he couldn't recall exactly, offhand. He saw so many people, you understand. Mr. Clinton did not understand, and said he wanted an answer to his question. Well, it was fairly recently. How recently? Yesterday? No, he was sure it wasn't yesterday. What about the day before yesterday? He wasn't so sure about that. Before the witness could make up his mind, Mr. Lord bounced up with a vigorous objection to this line of questioning as being entirely irrelevant. Surrogate Calvin directed Mr. Clinton to explain where it was leading. The latter said he could not reveal his purpose at this time. He would say, however, that at the proper time, and in direct relation to his question, there would be disclosed one of the rankest conspiracies ever encountered in the history of jurisprudence. The

Henry L. Clinton, chief counsel of the proponents

Surrogate said he might continue and directed the witness to answer the question. Mr. Vanderbilt now admitted that he had indeed last seen Mr. Simmons on Monday. If this was Wednesday, that would make it the day before yesterday. After further cross-examination Mr. Clinton finally got the witness to concede that he had probably borrowed money from Simmons within the last six months but he could not tell the amount without referring to his books. He did not think he had borrowed money from Simmons to finance the trial, but he did concede that he might have used some of the loan for one thing or another connected with the trial. It was another of those fine distinctions that Mr. Clinton was incapable of appreciating.

"The harrowing ordeal of young Corneel," as one over-wrought journalist called it, lasted nearly four days, but he still had some fight left in him when Mr. Clinton gave him back to Mr. Lord for re-direct examination. Where did he expect to get the money to pay his debts? Why, from the same source that his brother William expected to get his, naturally. It got quite a laugh from the spectators and it seemed to restore Corneel's own morale, too. As to his gambling habits, Cornelius claimed, after consulting his diary, that he had gambled only sixteen times in all of 1876, in spite of the strain imposed on him by his father's last illness. The fact that he had gambled at all was due entirely to the disheartening indifference with which his father had received his exemplary behavior of 1874. At this point Mr. Lord attempted to put in evidence two letters which Cornelius had written to his father in the fall of 1874 and which his father had not deigned to answer.

Mr. Clinton himself, during cross-examination, had already demonstrated that Cornelius was a prolific letter writer with an addiction to high-flown phrases. He had put in evidence a series of letters Cornelius had written to Wil-

liam in 1867 during another period of remorse and good resolutions—and incidentally, of acute financial embarrassment. "If you think proper," he had written from an institution in Northampton, Massachusetts, in his rich epistolary style, "to reciprocate the warm and liberal views which I have fully determined shall hereafter form the nucleus of my future relations towards yourself, I shall be most happy to receive such an assurance, and I doubt not that the line of policy which I have likewise laid down as regards the regulation of my general behavior will in a short time cause the many stigmas that now hover around my name to vanish like the morning dew, and that the insane, disgraceful tendencies of the past will soon be forgotten, and in lieu thereof the honorable workings of a subdued spirit and an expanded brain be promptly acknowledged and handsomely proclaimed." William, alas, had not thought proper to reciprocate even to the trifling extent of $150, the amount Corneel was requesting.

Mr. Lord now tried to put in evidence letters from Cornelius to his father, composed in the period of allegedly unblemished behavior in the fall of 1874. In these Cornelius alluded to similar promises of reformation and demanded to know if such promises had not now been fulfilled. Should his father fail to reply, he warned in language of suitable grandeur, his silence would be taken for assent. Counsel for the proponents objected strenuously, both to the admission of these letters as evidence, and to the assumption that the witness, lacking an answer from his father, had thereby been judged a reformed character. Judge Comstock summed up their argument with merciless logic. "Here," he said, "was a son worthless and dissipated. He writes to his father and tells him that he has been good, and says to him, now answer and tell me if you are satisfied with me, or else I will hold you to strict accountability for your silence. Why, the father had no means of knowing whether he had been good or not, and so he did not answer the letter." Mr. Lord took violent exception to the phrase "worthless and dissipated" and called Judge Comstock a liar. Judge Comstock replied in kind and the courtroom was in an uproar. Surrogate Calvin banged his gavel for order, and excluded the letters as evidence.

While young Corneel may not have been an ideal witness, he had borne up fairly well under the embarrassment of having his personal peccadilloes so harshly exposed to the public eye. His testimony, while far from conclusive, did lay the groundwork for evidence as to the great conspiracy allegedly hatched by William Henry to discredit Corneel's reformation of late 1874. Furthermore, the Surrogate had in effect ruled that proof of such a conspiracy would invalidate the entire will. Thus, if William's accomplices could be produced in court, as Mr. Lord seemed confident they could, and if their testimony stood up, it would not matter that the contestant had been unable to show that the testator was of unsound mind. In a day when the courts abounded with professional witnesses who would swear to anything for a reasonable fee, it must have been a harrowing time for William, too, even if he were entirely innocent of any wrongdoing.

In fact, it was a bad time for both sides. A month's adjournment was called to enable Surrogate Calvin to get caught up with other business, but even after this lull, the star witnesses to the Great Conspiracy were still reluctant to make their entrance. Mr. Lord did his best to fill time by bringing a motley assortment of characters to the stand, most of whom were seeking personal publicity or had old grudges against the Commodore and his family. Surrogate Calvin refused to admit the testimony of most of them, but, of course, their stories got into the papers. John J. Ogden, for instance, a hitherto obscure stockbroker who had desk space in the offices of Woodhull, Claflin & Co., was anxious to tell how he had escorted the seductive Tennie Claflin, the spiritualist, to the Commodore's office on numerous occasions and had once overheard the Commodore tell her that he would have kept his promise to marry her but for the interference of his family. (The best he had been able to do, according to contemporary gossip, was to set Wall Street on its ear by putting up the money for Tennie and her astonishing sister, Victoria Woodhull, to establish the only female brokerage firm in the world.) Mr. Ogden claimed that on another occasion he had heard the Commodore boast that many young ladies bought New York Central stock because of his picture on it. All of this showed, according to Mr. Lord, that the Commodore had had loose notions about marriage and a diseased mind generally. Whatever it showed, Surrogate Calvin ruled it irrelevant.

Daniel Drew, once a market manipulator rivalling Vanderbilt himself but now a tottering old bankrupt, Buckman ("Buck") Claflin, the Micawberish father of Tennie and Victoria, along with magneticians and electrical healers, paraded through the courtroom without noticeably advancing the contestant's case.

After several weeks in which the accomplices still did not appear, Mr. Clinton complained about the delay with bitter sarcasm. "Where is that cloud of devastating witnesses counsel promised to bring down upon us?" he demanded. As it turned out, that was exactly what Mr. Lord himself had been trying to learn. Finally, on March 19, at the insistence of the court, he reluctantly admitted that his key witnesses had been mysteriously detained in Chicago, where, of course, it was well known that anything might happen. He told a tale of threats, pursuit, bribery, and other "sinister influences at work to discourage" their appearance in court. In several formal affidavits requesting extensions of time, Mr. Lord revealed for the first time the identity of the witnesses—three private detectives—and details of the plot to discredit Cornelius in which they had allegedly been involved. Then, there had been a rash of ominous

"Notices to Whom It May Concern" in the Personal Column of the *Herald*, a favorite medium, in those days before the telephone, for arranging assignations and other devious activities. The notices, Mr. Lord said, were unmistakably part of the plot.

The effect of these revelations on Surrogate Calvin was such that he decided, much to the disgust of counsel for the proponents, to adjourn the case until June 11 to give Mr. Lord ample time to assemble his elusive detectives.

According to his own sworn statements, Mr. Lord had first learned of what came to be known as The Great Conspiracy in June, 1877, nearly a month after his client's contest of the will had formally commenced. Young Cornelius had turned over to him a letter he had received from one Franklin A. Redburn, relating how a certain "head detective" (Redburn himself) had been approached in the fall of 1874 by a "genteel-appearing stranger." "A singular change," the stranger was quoted as saying, "for which no one could account had come over Commodore Vanderbilt. The old gentleman had become affected with the delusion that his prodigal son had returned to the paths of virtue and honor and would yet shed glory on the family name, whereas in truth 'young Corneel' had never in his life been guilty of greater excesses and prodigality than he was now practising daily." Even William shared his father's delusion.

As a result the stranger, whom Redburn later revealed to be none other than Chauncey M. Depew, felt duty-bound, as a devoted family friend and a responsible official of the New York Central Railroad, to undertake whatever action might be required so that the Commodore and William would be convinced of their error. In short, he wanted Head Detective Redburn to have Cornelius followed until the evidence needed to set matters straight could be obtained. Redburn readily agreed to undertake the job. They arranged to meet the next day at the Fifth Avenue Hotel, Redburn to bring with him one of his most reliable operatives, who would do the actual work of trailing young Vanderbilt. As it turned out, and as Redburn said he realized later, there was something extremely "providential" about this meeting. Neither he nor his subordinate knew the intended quarry by sight, and they so informed Mr. Depew. While the three of them were still conferring at the hotel, however, who should saunter through the lobby on his way to the bar but a man whom Mr. Depew promptly pointed out as young Corneel himself. At once Redburn's reliable operative, George A. Mason, went into action.

Detective Mason's technique, as revealed in a sworn statement he gave Mr. Lord in August of 1877, was simple but effective. Mornings he would loiter about the Fifth Avenue Hotel, a pastime so pleasant that many young blades engaged in it by choice, until his man appeared. It was not difficult to keep track of him after that. According to Mason's deposition, Corneel's day would go like this:

Arriving at the hotel between 10 and 11 A.M., he would proceed directly to the bar, where he would indulge in a few drinks with various friends and acquaintances. Then, with the morning gone and well aglow with spirits, said Cornelius together with several of his boon companions would leave the hotel and journey down to Ann Street aboard a Broadway stage. There, in the shadow of St. Paul's Church, they had their choice of several of those insidious institutions known as "day games." These "day games," which then abounded in the blocks off Broadway between Fulton and Chambers streets, were faro games operated primarily for the benefit of businessmen who worked in the area. They were also patronized by gentlemen of leisure like young Cornelius and his cronies, who found it irksome to wait until midafternoon for the uptown establishments to open their doors. These downtown excursions usually lasted two or three hours. Afterwards, they would return to the Fifth Avenue Hotel for more refreshments and for discussion of what to do next. Would they saunter across Twenty-fourth Street to John Morrissey's luxurious parlors, where they could enjoy a sumptuous free meal before settling down to an afternoon of serious gambling? Or would they pay their respects to the charming ladies to be found in certain elegant, if notorious, establishments along West Twenty-fifth Street? It was not always an easy decision to make. On occasion it took so long to make it that they were in no condition to carry it out.

Once or twice a week said Cornelius would desert his cronies after the return from Ann Street and proceed purposefully down Fifth Avenue to Fourteenth Street, where, as if by chance, he would meet a lady. She would accompany him for a seemingly casual stroll down University Place to Eleventh Street. There they would suddenly vanish into Solari's, a restaurant discreetly and cozily equipped with private rooms, and there would remain until evening. Upon emerging, said Cornelius would be so much the worse for wear that it would be all he could do to crawl into a cab and be driven home.

So it went day after day until Detective Mason commenced to have difficulty keeping up with his man, who was by now growing suspicious. Mason decided, therefore, that what he needed was an assistant to enable him, as he put it, to follow said Cornelius into dens of vice into which Mason could not always obtain admission alone or into which he did not deem it advisable to venture unaccompanied. For this purpose he selected one William H. Clark, an old and experienced colleague who had entree even into the exclusive establishments on Twenty-fifth Street to which Cornelius was so devoted. The intimate and revealing nature of the report produced by this double coverage was such that Mr. Depew, already bubbling with enthusiasm over Mason's solo efforts, could now no longer contain himself. He hustled the two detectives over to William's office in Grand Central Depot for a repeat performance. William, according to Mason's somewhat pedestrian account, professed much sorrow on learning of his brother's behavior but made only a feeble objection when Mr. Depew suggested that the report be given to the Commodore.

Detective Clark's account of this occasion, in the affidavit he gave Mr. Lord, reveals him as a much more acute observer than the matter-of-fact Mason, quite capable of penetrating beneath the deceptive surfaces of human behavior. Here is his version: ". . . That said William H. Vanderbilt, as he listened to Mason's report, professed to be disappointed and distressed at the intelligence of his brother's delinquencies, but that deponent [Clark] insists on saying herein that there was something in the manner and looks of said William H. Vanderbilt and in the glances he exchanged with his 'soi-disant' friend that constrained deponent to believe, and a little later in the day to remark to said Mason, that notwithstanding William H. Vanderbilt's ostensible grief, deponent was confident that he was delighted with the reports of his brother's infamy, and that said Mason replied that he did not like to think, much less to say so, but that, nevertheless, he had received the same impression as deponent. That deponent afterward accompanied the said 'soi-disant' friend and said Mason to the office of Commodore Vanderbilt. That the moment the Commodore understood the nature of their visit he exclaimed, addressing himself to said self-styled friend, 'I suppose you have now come to kill me and make an end of it.' Whereupon the person addressed declared that the business was not half so serious as that, and when the Commodore replied that he could see through it all, and that he wished to God he had never been born, that said self-styled friend remarked, 'If you would stop, Commodore, to reflect what the country would have been out without you, you would never have made such an unpatriotic wish,' and that the Commodore then said, 'No, I don't wish that, but I wish that this son of mine had never been born; that's what I do wish.'"

His patriotism restored, the Commodore braced himself for the ordeal of listening to Mason's report. He could not, however, conceal his true feelings from Detective Clark, who wrote in his affidavit "that the Commodore appeared to be half-suffocated with the intelligence of his son's depravity; that it seemed to deponent that grief and indignation, love and hatred, and all the conflicting passions, had engaged in a battle royal in which his bosom was receiving the hardest blows. That a few expressions of anger seemed to relieve the Commodore when, after asking deponent a few questions, he cried, 'Go away, go away, and never let me see you again.'"

A few days later Mason and Clark were informed by Redburn that their mission had been accomplished to the complete satisfaction of the "soi-disant" friend of the family, Mr. Depew. Young Corneel stood revealed for what he was. The case, so far as they were concerned, would have been closed forever but for an embarrassing incident which befell Detective Mason only a little more than two years later, or, as chance would have it, not long after the first rumblings of discontent over the Commodore's will were heard. Late in the spring of 1877, according to the affidavit he gave Mr. Lord, Mason was taking a stroll along Broadway one day with an acquaintance. This acquaintance pointed out a person whom he claimed was none other than Cornelius J. Vanderbilt himself. Mason, who prided himself on an infallible memory for faces, promptly said that that was impossible; it was definitely not the person he had followed every day for nearly a month. But his friend insisted that the man they had seen was young Corneel. The upshot was a wager which, to his chagrin, deponent lost.

Bewildered but indignant, Mason communicated his discovery to Clark, and together they confronted Head Detective Redburn with the facts. Redburn, according to Mason, "seemed surprised and suggested that steps be taken to ascertain the truth." Realizing that they had been the unwitting instruments of a nefarious plot, they quickly concluded that simple justice demanded they do all in their power to repair the damage they had wrought. Redburn therefore composed the letter dated June 22, 1877, to the wronged Cornelius which the latter had passed on to Mr. Lord. Mr. Lord must have grasped it eagerly. Here, if ever there was one, was a fraudulent conspiracy designed to influence a testator unduly. He could hardly have been blamed if he had commenced spending the fat fee which would be his for breaking the will of the richest man in America.

During the adjournment granted by Surrogate Calvin Mr. Lord finally succeeded in coaxing Redburn, Mason, and Clark to return to New York. They promised faithfully to appear in court when the case was resumed on June 11. Finally, all that remained to be done was a last-minute rehearsal of their testimony with Mr. Lord and Judge Black which was scheduled for June 10.

That was how matters stood on the afternoon of June 9, a Sunday, when Mr. Lord opened an envelope which had been slipped under his door at his hotel. It was a letter from Redburn stating that Clark and Mason had gone off together, ostensibly to check on dates and places, but that he would go after them immediately and bring them back. Alas, it had a familiar ring. Apparently those sinister influences of which Mr. Lord had previously complained were again at work. He still had faith in the doughty Redburn, but the testimony of the craven Mason and Clark was essential to his case. Moreover, the next day the most crushing blow of all fell on Mr. Lord. It came in the form of a letter dated June 9, written jointly by Mason and Clark. In it they said that they had discovered that everything to which they had previously sworn was the result of a plot concocted by Cornelius J. Vanderbilt himself, aided and abetted by his friend "Simpson," a big wheel in the lottery racket with powerful political and underworld connections. It was only a few hours before writing the letter that they had finally become convinced of the truth. "We agree perfectly in everything," they wrote, "except as to whether Redburn was one of the original conspirators. One believes he was, while one willingly gives him the benefit of the doubt . . . Finally, Judge Lord, we wish to say that when we made our statements to you, we fully believed them . . . and that you could never have had any reason to doubt them until now, when we give you this disclosure. With great respect, [signed] William H. Clark and George A. Mason."

With two of his key witnesses reneging and all of them vanished, Mr. Lord might well have wished to vanish himself. He was left with a set of affidavits which were worthless as evidence, even if true, and which, in any event, were now apparently discredited. However, he went into court on June 11, bristling with indignation, and presented yet another affidavit of his own in support of a motion to continue the case. Annexed thereto were not only the original affidavits of Redburn, Mason, and Clark, but also (and this was perhaps his master stroke which at once demonstrated his own integrity and confounded his opponents) the joint letter of Mason and Clark in which they denied the truth of their own sworn statements. In his own affidavit, after relating the events of the past months during which he had labored to overcome the detectives' fears, and to obtain sworn affidavits from them, Mr. Lord went on to say that he still believed the statements in those affidavits to be true; if the testimony of Mason and Clark could be taken, he said, the affidavits would be sustained. He did not believe that they could be bribed, or otherwise persuaded, to appear upon the stand and perjure themselves, but he did believe that they could have been induced to write their letter of June 9 and then to put themselves beyond the jurisdiction of the court. The close of Mr. Lord's new affidavit summarized the confusion. "Deponent further says," Lord wrote, "that the communication received by him from said Mason and Clark leads him to believe that they have been in communication with some person or persons in the interest of the proponents, and have been induced by them to put themselves beyond the jurisdiction of this court to avoid testifying, and that this also leads him to believe that had they not refused to testify under oath to the statement of their letter, they would have been allowed to appear in court and testify; and that counsel for the contestant, under all these circumstances, deem it their duty to ask the court for a continuance, so that in a matter of such vital importance the truth may be ascertained."

Mr. Clinton objected strenuously to the reading in court of the Redburn-Mason-Clark affidavits, on the grounds that they were entirely extra-judicial. Every word might be false and yet the authors could not be held for perjury. "It comes to this," he declaimed heatedly, "whether this court is to be used only for the purpose of scandal . . . [and] for getting into the newspapers statements which they have already refused to print." Surrogate Calvin said he did not think reputable counsel would resort to such tactics and permitted the reading to continue, although he made it clear that the affidavits themselves could have no bearing on the outcome of the case.

There was a tense silence in the courtroom as the reading proceeded, broken only by occasional gasps of astonishment from the spellbound audience and by snorts of disgust from counsel for the proponents. William H. Vanderbilt sat with his eyes fixed rigidly upon the ceiling, thus avoiding the fierce glare of his sister, Mrs. La Bau, and the sight of the angry fist which, from time to time, she shook at him. Contestant's counsel also read a statement by Cornelius J. Vanderbilt flatly denying the charge made against him by Mason and Clark in their joint letter of confession, and another by "Zach" Simmons stating that if he was the "Simpson" referred to therein, which he was, he denied all charges.

Counsel for proponents came into court the next day armed with their own affidavits. In sworn statements read by Mr. Clinton, Chauncey M. Depew and William H. Vanderbilt categorically denied everything of which they had been accused by Mr. Lord and his reluctant witnesses. Mr. Clinton then went to work in earnest on the affidavits offered by Mr. Lord. He dealt very harshly with young Cornelius, quoting with caustic relish some of the riper passages which contained the preposterous notion that Cornelius could ever amount to anything, and, most preposterous of all, that the canny old Commodore would ever have been foolish enough to think that he would. Almost equally absurd, Mr. Clinton said, was the story of Chauncey Depew concocting a conspiracy in the lobby of the Fifth Avenue Hotel. Depew may have had his less fervent admirers, but no one ever set him down for a natural-born fool.

"The falsity of these papers is apparent on their face," Mr. Clinton stormed. "They were all written by the same person, and that person is a lawyer."

Counsel for contestant were on their feet screaming in outrage, and Mr. Clinton conceded that he was not referring to any known member of contestant's counsel. This did not exactly mollify Mr. Lord and his associates, but Mr. Clinton refused to retract the suggestion that they were being used as cat's-paws by some sinister legal mind in the employ of young Corneel and his underworld crony, Simmons. Surrogate Calvin himself objected to so grave an accusation. He asked Mr. Clinton if he could suggest an explanation for the motives behind such affidavits.

"Certainly," came the reply. "For the purposes of blackmail. Anyone who knows anything of private detectives understands how ready they are to seize upon anything that promises money. . . . These detectives are too keen to swear to anything for which they can be held responsible . . . They have disappeared just at the time for them to appear in court because they never intended to appear. They thought us weak-kneed, and that we would yield to their demands."

Although it may seem now that Mr. Clinton was being rather harsh in his treatment of private detectives, actually his remarks were quite mild. The profession had a most unsavory reputation at this period. In a time when moral hypocrisy was common, when suspicion flourished, its services were in great demand. Nevertheless, it had become an overcrowded field, and its practitioners, in order to survive, had to promote new business aggressively. As a matter of policy, the customer was always right, and their reports were tailored to fit his needs. Blackmail was an obvious and lucrative sideline, and private detectives had been known to prey upon the guilty and the innocent alike.

Mr. Clinton wound up his argument with a few words for opposing counsel. "Why were not these witnesses subpoenaed?" he demanded. "The affidavits are of no value except to excuse counsel for being humbugged for six months. The whole story is a fabrication."

Surrogate Calvin closed the hearing with some remarks that left the whole affair more confused than ever. "What seems extraordinary to the court," he said, somewhat wistfully, "is that if these detectives were honest men and found they had been deceived by Cornelius J. Vanderbilt, they did not make known their discoveries to the other side. The fact that they have departed in this way is full of suspicion."

In spite of his bewilderment, the Surrogate was not quite willing to give up hope of seeing with his own eyes whether such fantastic witnesses actually existed. He granted Mr. Lord an adjournment of two weeks, urging him to spare no effort to produce at least Redburn, who seemed fairly available, or, at any rate, less mythical than Mason and Clark. Mr. Lord, unabashed by the sneers of opposing counsel, resolutely promised to do his utmost. Two weeks later, alas, he came back into court with the air of a man to whom the fates had been malignantly unkind. Redburn was seriously ill and confined to his home. (He lived in New Jersey, so he was not within the jurisdiction of the court.) Mason and Clark had not returned from wherever it was they had gone, and no one knew where that was. Their existence was becoming very mythical indeed. Mr. Lord endeavored to offset this impression with another of his garrulous lady witnesses whose testimony was discredited by Mr. Clinton on cross-examination.

On July 2, 1878, court adjourned early to allow the participants to attend the funeral of Phoebe Jane Cross, the Commodore's eldest daughter, who had grudgingly accepted her $250,000 worth of Lake Shore bonds; Mr. Clinton wryly remarked that it was "the first time he would not oppose a motion to adjourn." But the next day he was back in action again when Mr. Lord suggested that it might be a good time to adjourn for the summer. It would be very unpleasant in the little courtroom during July and August, and Redburn, suffering from what was described as "intermittent fever," would certainly be unable to appear under such unfavorable conditions. Mr. Clinton, by now running a very high temperature himself, objected violently not only to a summer's adjournment but to allowing the contestant any more time whatsoever; if the case were permitted to drag on indefinitely, Surrogate Calvin's term in office might expire, and then it could be claimed his successor did not have jurisdiction and so it would go—forever.

Surrogate Calvin, striving for a compromise, decided to grant the adjournment, but to allow contestant only eight more days when the case was resumed in the fall. He pointedly warned Mr. Lord that there would be no more adjournments due to the nonappearance of witnesses. The lawyer, his confidence restored by the prospect of over two months' grace, took the warning in stride; as the session closed, he was blandly promising to produce not only Redburn, Mason, and Clark but also a fourth man whom he said he would not name at that time for fear that proponents would, as he put it, "educate him as a witness." Mr. Clinton was left frothing with rage and indignation.

When the case was resumed in the fall, it was at once apparent that something new and ominous for proponents was brewing in the camp of the contestant which had nothing to do with the missing witnesses (who were just as missing as ever). Mr. Lord and his cohorts, swelled to bursting with mystery and importance, ignored any reference to Redburn, Mason, and Clark as a matter too trifling to concern them. Counsel for proponents, now more wary and suspicious than ever, were reinforced by Joseph H. Choate, making his first appearance in court.

Judge Jeremiah Black, one of contestant's counsel

The testimony of contestant's first important witness failed to fulfill the rumors of sensational disclosures with which the corridors of the courthouse had been buzzing. It did, however, reveal a rather subtle shift in Mr. Lord's strategy which would, if successful, enable him to take advantage of decedent's apparent belief in spiritualism. The witness, a Mrs. Mary L. Stone, appeared at first to be yet another of the seemingly endless procession of ladies in straitened circumstances who had visited the Commodore in search of financial aid. Mrs. Stone, a serious-minded lady of some refinement, was in her middle thirties; her deceased father, Henry Chapin, had been a friend and business associate of the Commodore. She testified that she had first approached the Commodore in his office on Fourth Street in October of 1874, a period on which Mr. Lord laid great stress since it was during this time that the last will was being drafted. She wanted help in starting a school. Mrs. Stone got no money, but she did get some advice. The Commodore solemnly told her, she said, that before going further with her enterprise she must seek communion with the spirits of her dear departed. He himself, he assured her, did nothing without advice from the spirits. For example, as a result of communications he had had with the spirit of his dead wife, he was going to leave most of his worldly goods to his son William. Mrs. Stone, alas, was so overwhelmed by the daily problems of her mundane existence that, as counsel for the proponents were to suggest later, the only spirits she was able to commune with successfully were those in a bottle. Nevertheless, she was back in the Commodore's office again several months later, or, as it happened, not long after the final will had been executed, to see if she could get her brother a job as a conductor on one of the Vanderbilt railroads. William, who was hovering about in an officious sort of way, told her bluntly that his father could do nothing for her. With that the Commodore flared up. "You can't have it all your own way," Mrs. Stone quoted him as saying. "You are walking in my shoes now. I have made a will in your favor, and that ought to be enough."

"The Spirits made the will in my favor, Father," William said solemnly. "You said so yourself."

"What if I did," the old man grumbled. "It ought to be enough for you."

Apparently it wasn't enough for William, and Mrs. Stone's brother did not get the job. Mr. Clinton objected to her testimony with all of his customary vigor. What it amounted to, he argued, was that Mr. Lord was trying to commence the case all over again even though he had had no case in the first place. The Surrogate, as even his worthy opponent should be able to recall, had already ruled that testator's belief in spiritualism was of itself no indication of an unsound mind, and that evidence as to such belief was therefore irrelevant and immaterial. Mr. Lord, far from reacting with his usual violence to the gibes of opposing counsel, argued quite calmly—some thought even smugly—that, while he was by no means unaware of the Surrogate's earlier ruling or even of the seeming validity of counsel's objections, nevertheless, new evidence, which his conscience would not permit him to suppress, had dictated reopening this line of inquiry. Mrs. Stone's testimony, he added, would lay the groundwork for showing that the will was the product of a foul conspiracy designed by William H. Vanderbilt to take advantage of his father's belief in communication with the dead. Earlier Mr. Lord had contended that such belief would demonstrate that the Commodore was of unsound mind. Now, if as he claimed he could prove a fraudulent conspiracy, that indispensable ingredient of most successful will contests, the soundness of the testator's mind, would not necessarily be at issue.

This shift in strategy was a little too subtle for Surrogate Calvin to grasp all at once. He decided to stick to his earlier ruling that testimony as to the influence of the spirits should be excluded, at least until the alleged conspiracy itself had been established. Getting a bit spritely himself, he proposed that communication be had with the testator in order to settle the whole question.

Mr. Lord was not in the least amused by what he considered misplaced judicial facetiousness, but he remained undaunted. If he himself could not communicate directly with the Commodore, he was now ready to unveil a witness whose testimony about the influence of the spirits upon the old man would be no joke for the proponents.

The witness was a Mrs. Lilian Stoddard, and as soon as she had swished herself into the witness stand it was evident that the big moment had now arrived. For Mrs. Stoddard, to any discerning masculine eye, was obviously no ordinary woman. In her early thirties, with neither youth nor beauty to commend her, she still retained that sort of saucy girlish bounce which, piquantly mellowed by years of dissipation, inevitably inspires in men's minds visions of all manner of delightfully accessible and deliciously depraved sexual activity. Her testimony, as well as her person, was to have an electrifying effect upon the courtroom. Even Mr. Clinton and his august colleagues, though prepared in advance for the worst, seemed dumbfounded and aghast at the story she had to tell—under, be it remembered, solemn oath.

Mr. Lord conducted his direct examination with a dignified reserve that did not permit unseemly prying into irrelevant and purely personal biographical details. Mrs. Stoddard was, she said, the widow of Dr. Charles Anderson Stoddard, a medical clairvoyant who had died in the spring of 1875; Commodore Vanderbilt had been among his patients. In the summer of 1874, Mrs. Stoddard testified, her late husband was using his supernatural powers to alleviate the aches and pains with which the Commodore's aging body was afflicted. Mr. Lord, in his questioning, was careful to bring out that Mrs. Stoddard herself was invariably present at these treatments. While this may have been a trifle irregular, the manner of her testimony on this point rather suggested that the proximity of her person had such an exhilarating effect upon the patient that he regarded it as an essential part of the therapy.

The treatments had continued in this cozy fashion, two or three times a week over a period of several months, until one fine morning early in September, following a professional visit to the Commodore in his office, the witness and her husband were sitting in Washington Square Park resting from the ardors of their joint therapy when they were approached by a gentleman who introduced himself as William H. Vanderbilt. Accustomed as they were to being abused and persecuted by cynical relatives of their patients, they were quite overwhelmed by Mr. Vanderbilt's cordiality. He told them how impressed he had been by the great faith which his father had in Dr. Stoddard's remarkable powers, and, far from wishing them to cease their ministrations, his only thought was to suggest that a more intense application of those powers might prove beneficial to all concerned. Mr. Vanderbilt's exact words were, according to the witness, "I want you to influence the old man and make him think more of me so that I can control him."

In reply Dr. Stoddard had said that he would be glad to do what he could in his humble way if the circumstances were properly conducive. Thereupon Mr. Vanderbilt nodded his head understandingly and handed Dr. Stoddard a roll of bills which the latter calmly counted and put in his pocket. The witness admitted that she never did learn the exact amount of the fee, but she figured that the roll added up to at least $1,000. In any event, she could tell that her husband was pleased. "This is all right," she quoted him as saying as he pocketed the bills. "I am now ready for business." With the conducive circumstances thus established, Mr. Vanderbilt proceeded to dictate in a brisk, businesslike manner the exact words of the message which he wished to be transmitted from his mother in the world of the spirits to his father here on earth. Dr. Stoddard repeated the message word for word. Mr. Vanderbilt signified his approval, tipped his hat, and went on his way.

Thus inspired and with a prospect of more inspiration to come, Dr. Stoddard on their next visit to the Commodore was able to commune with the spirit of the deceased Mrs. Vanderbilt as soon as he went into his trance. "I seem to have a message for you from your dead wife in the world beyond the grave," Dr. Stoddard whispered. "Are you ready to receive the message?" The Commodore, according to the witness, was a bit shaken, but he replied stoutly enough that he was always ready to hear from his dear Sophie. With that, the spirit of Mrs. Vanderbilt, speaking in the quavery tones of a voice from the sepulchre through the medium of Dr. Stoddard, could be heard to say, "I have a much clearer insight into the affairs of your world than I had before my departure **from it,** and I implore you, in memory of me, to make our son William your successor in all earthly things. Do this and you will make no mistake. The other children hate you. Only William loves you . . . only William . . ." And as the voice of the spirit faded away, the Commodore said solemnly, "I will do as you wish, Sophie. Billy shall have it all."

Variations of this message from the other world were repeated at appropriate intervals over a period of several months, or, to put it crassly, for as long as the fiscal inspiration from William H. Vanderbilt to Dr. Stoddard was maintained. Mrs. Stoddard could not recall exactly how many times her husband had transmitted Sophie's message, but she was quite positive that the last visit had occurred early in January, 1875. She remembered it so well, she said, for two reasons: first, simply because it was, alas, the last visit, and, second, because the Commodore had been so cheerful. Instead of his usual solemn reply to the voice from beyond the grave, his answer had been, "Don't fret about it any more, Sophie. It's all been fixed so Billy will get it all."

Mr. Lord laid particular stress upon the witness' testimony about this final visit because, although of course the Stoddards presumably couldn't have known it at the time, the date coincided remarkably well with the date of the formal signing and execution of the Commodore's last will and testament. Thus, Mrs. Stoddard's testimony, fantastic though it may have sounded, was a matter of grave concern to the proponents, and their lawyers were obviously most unhappy about it. There was no question of its being relevant: the best Mr. Clinton could do on that score was a niggling argument to the effect that actually the testator had disobeyed the spirits, for Billy did not get it all. Furthermore, it opened the door for the seemingly abundant evidence, which the Surrogate had previously refused to admit, that the Commodore had, in fact, been a true believer in spiritualism, even, or perhaps especially, as practiced by charlatans such as Dr. Stoddard and the Claflin sisters. It was, if true, the only material evidence thus far produced to show that in making his will the testator might have been unduly influenced by a fraudulent conspiracy. Even though the will itself might not have differed by so much as a single stray "hereinbefore" without the advice of the spirits, it raised a reasonable doubt; when one hundred million dollars is at stake even a most unreasonable doubt could loom very ominously indeed. Mrs. Stoddard's testimony was of such a nature that it could not be conclusively refuted. Mere denials would not suffice. Before the proponents could again breathe easily, Mrs. Stoddard herself would have to be completely demolished.

Mr. Clinton commenced his cross-examination by asking the witness to tell the court just how her connection with the case had come about. Mrs. Stoddard said that about three weeks before she testified she had received a letter signed "A friend" asking her to call at Mr. Lord's office in a matter of great importance. This "friend" turned out to be a man whom she had seen around, as she put it, but whom she did not know by name and had not seen again. She said that when she had been interviewed by Mr. Lord, she had told him she had nothing to tell but the truth. Mr. Clinton said he was very glad to hear that, and, if she would continue the same policy with him, things should work out splendidly. There were a few minor details in her direct testimony he wanted to clear up. For instance, she had said that she and her husband were living at 64 Charles Street when they had last seen Commodore Vanderbilt. A little later in her testimony, however, she had said they had left 64 Charles Street about six months prior to the death of her husband in May, 1875, which would indicate either that they had last seen the Commodore in November of 1874 instead of the following January, or that she was mistaken as to the date of her husband's death. But of course she could hardly be mistaken about a thing such as that, could she?

Under this steady barrage of seemingly trivial questions about dates and places, Mrs. Stoddard snarled herself in a tangle of contradictions, and gradually it came out that she did not know to the day or even the week when her husband had died. Bit by bit, Mr. Clinton drew from her the admission that her husband had been dead and buried a month or more before she even knew about it. Asked to explain how such a thing could be, the harried witness said it was because her husband had died in Poughkeepsie. Mr. Clinton, now assuming that air of happy bewilderment which can be so exasperating to witnesses who have been driven into a corner, conceded that while Poughkeepsie might not be the best place in the world in which to have one's husband die, surely it was not so bad as to deprive him of her presence. The witness, by now as irritated as she was confused, angrily denied that there was anything particularly strange about this. It just so happened that Dr. Stoddard lived in Poughkeepsie part of the time because he had an office there. A great light seemed to dawn on Mr. Clinton. "I see," he said. "But you didn't live in Poughkeepsie . . . not even part time?" And with the inference established that there was something peculiarly irregular in the relationship between the witness and the late Dr. Stoddard, Mr. Clinton suggested that it was time to call it a day. He had the scent he needed for his private bloodhounds—Poughkeepsie, only seventy miles away on the main line of the Vanderbilt railroad—and he had four days for them to track it down before the next session of court.

News of Mrs. Stoddard's testimony created a sensation in Poughkeepsie. Even after an absence of some fifteen years, she was well remembered there, particularly by righteously indignant friends and relatives of the late Dr. Stoddard. Mr. Clinton's research into the early phases of her career thus proved to be both simple and fruitful. When he resumed his cross-examination, he knew exactly what questions would unfold the saga of a country girl, originally known as "Nell," who had not waited until she got to the big city to go astray.

While still in her early teens Nell had been adopted by a widower named Coe who lived across the river in Ulster County. After a year or so in this ambivalent situation Nell had come back across the river to "keep house," as she called it—although that wasn't what the neighbors called it—for a man named DeGroot near Poughkeepsie. It was during her DeGroot period that she first met Dr. Stoddard and took to calling herself Lilian. The Doctor had been deeply smitten by her charms, even then well-developed, and they were married at Kingston after a three-week courtship spent driving about the countryside in a horse and buggy making frequent stops in country hotels. Lilian might well have become a bit disenchanted at this point when she learned that Dr. Stoddard already had a wife and family living in Poughkeepsie, but, being both good-natured and realistic, she tried to make the best of a difficult situation by moving into the Stoddard home in the role of general houseworker. This arrangement had lasted only a week.

From the formidable appearance of a lady whom Mr. Clinton asked to rise and be identified by the witness as the original, and only genuine, Mrs. Stoddard, it could not have been a very pleasant week for Lilian. The *Times* carried a special dispatch from its Poughkeepsie correspondent which quoted the genuine Mrs. Stoddard as saying, "There was something about her when she came to my house that I did not like, and that was the reason I discharged her." One thing Mrs. Stoddard had not liked was that Lilian called Dr. Stoddard "Charley," although his name was really "Amasa." There were other things, too, but Mrs. Stoddard did not wish to specify what they were. Dr. Stoddard, however, must have liked being called "Charley," and liked the other unspecified things as well, for he now set Lilian up in rooms on Bridge Street in Poughkeepsie, not too far away from his official residence, where she could keep house to her heart's content. This cozy arrangement went on for five or six years. Then, apparently, it had finally dawned on Lilian that Poughkeepsie afforded too limited a field for the full development of her talent for housekeeping, and, in the interests of her career, she had gone to New York. From that time on Dr. Stoddard divided both his professional and his domestic lives between New York and Poughkeepsie. He also had an office in Newburgh, but nothing was known of his domestic arrangements there. Lilian herself quickly developed a considerable talent for dividing her life into multiple compartments, and during the doctor's absences she became widely acquainted in elite circles of the underworld as the consort of forgers, counterfeiters, and confidence men. At one time and another she had been known as Mrs. Benning, Mrs. Draper, and Mrs. Hall—all names of gentlemen renowned in their professions. Mr. Hall, perhaps, represented the pinnacle of her achievement to date, for he was Edward Hall, the celebrated forger. Having achieved such a position, it was little wonder that Lilian became quite incensed when Mr. Clinton asked her if she had ever been arrested for anything so crude as stealing a watch and chain.

"No, sir," she replied haughtily, "I was never arrested, and I would like to see the one to say I was."

Her "marriages" were usually dissolved by the departure of her current "husband" for prison and were not customarily renewed. This made her relationship with Mr. Benning rather unique, as it had been resumed, at least on a part-time basis, after he had been away for two years in New Jersey State Prison. Mr. Clinton was especially interested in the enduring nature of Lilian's attachment to Mr. Benning, for Mr. Benning was a specialist in a highly specialized field. In the jargon of his profession he was what was known as a "straw-bail man." In plain English, he was an expert in the manufacture and distribution of fake testimony for counterfeiters. Mr. Clinton's line of questioning strongly suggested that Mr. Benning's basic technique was readily adaptable to other types of enterprise.

On the whole, Lilian bore up remarkably well under Mr. Clinton's barrage of embarrassing questions. She maintained right to the bitter end that the number of men she had lived with had nothing to do with the truth of her testimony. Nor could Mr. Clinton ever get her to admit that she had known what Benning and his associates were really up to. There were frequent sharp exchanges between the witness and the lawyer, and her saucy and defiant replies were vastly entertaining to the spectators who now filled the courtroom to capacity. When Mr. Clinton tried to get her to admit that she had visited Benning in prison, she rapped her fan emphatically on the railing of the witness stand and said, "I won't answer any more about that State Prison, so there!"

Mr. Lord tried hard in his re-direct examination to refurbish her respectability. "Abraham," he said, "found favor before the Lord although he had more than one wife." He then tried to show that Lilian had received a wedding ring from Dr. Stoddard when they were "married" at Kingston and that she had entered into the ceremony in good faith. If she had acted in good faith, Mr. Lord argued, she had been more sinned against than sinning, and the facts of her later life, however unseemly, did not affect the credibility of her testimony. Surrogate Calvin was not at all impressed with this line of reasoning and promptly excluded the testimony offered to establish her good faith.

Mr. Choate, who had long been straining at the leash, now entered the fray for the first time with a scathing attack upon the witness, calling her "a woman of the town of the most infamous kind." He demanded that she be taken into custody on a charge of willfully committing perjury. But that was not the worst of it. Steeped in crime though she was, such a woman was obviously incapable of constructing a story which "fit into the crevices of the case so cunningly." Only some sinister legal mind lurking in the camp of the contestant could possibly have done that. There was the real criminal who should be brought to book.

This was indeed a serious accusation to make against the opposing lawyers. Counsel for contestant were on their feet seething with indignation. Judge Black was particularly incensed, loudly demanding that Mr. Choate either back up his accusation by naming the person who had concocted Lilian's story so that he personally could withdraw from such an unholy fellowship, or else retract it entirely. Mr. Choate, for his part, refused to do either, although he did grant that Judge Black himself should be excluded from his aspersions at opposing counsel. Furthermore, he persisted in demanding that the witness be arrested at once for perjury, as he supposed there was no one so credulous as to believe a word of "that woman's" testimony. Mr. Lord, of course, was not silent. He hotly denied that there was any evidence either of perjury or of wrongdoing on his part. Of course, he did not wonder that counsel for proponent were a trifle disturbed by such damaging testimony. Let them prove it false, if they could, before making such contemptible accusations.

Surrogate Calvin, trying to maintain a judicial calm, finally brought the wrangling to an end by ruling that it would be improper to allow the motion for perjury to be brought in his court. In spite of his skepticism, he patiently pointed out the great importance of Lilian's testimony: It was, if true, the only conclusive evidence of undue influence thus far presented, and it opened the way for Mr. Lord to present his abundant evidence, originally excluded as irrelevant, of the Commodore's belief in spiritualism.

Mr. Clinton was quite beside himself with frustrated rage as Mr. Lord now happily proceeded to put back on the stand Mrs. Mary Stone, to tell how her efforts to communicate nonspiritually with the Commodore to raise money for her school and to get her brother a job on the railroad had been so cruelly thwarted by William.

With Mrs. Stone's testimony safely on record, Mr. Lord was obviously flushed with success. He then attempted to bring on a witness who would link Mrs. Frankie Vanderbilt, the bereaved widow, to her stepson William in a highly improper manner. Earlier, Surrogate Calvin had sternly excluded such testimony unless it had first been clearly shown that Mrs. Vanderbilt had actually conspired to influence her husband unduly. Mr. Lord's attempt aroused a storm of protest among counsel for proponents; Surrogate Calvin, highly indignant himself, threatened to hold Mr. Lord in contempt if the offer were repeated. Mr. Lord accepted his reprimand with a sardonic bow. No one could do anything, however, to suppress the jeering remarks with which Mrs. La Bau greeted Mr. Choate's references to the unblemished character of her stepmother.

The trial had now been in progress for nearly a year, and opposing counsel urged the Surrogate to instruct Mrs. La Bau's counsel to bring their case to a close. Mr. Lord, of course, protested vociferously, repeating his stock arguments as to the magnitude of the case and the continued absence of vital witnesses. Surrogate Calvin suggested that he name his missing witnesses and the nature of their testimony in an affidavit to support a motion to continue. This Mr. Lord indignantly refused to do. Those whose names had been revealed heretofore, he argued, had been threatened and bribed, and he could not again permit himself to jeopardize his client's interests by his own naïve innocence of the depths of infamy to which opposing counsel would stoop. Apparently touched by Mr. Lord's impassioned plea, Surrogate Calvin ruled that contestant could continue if the names of future witnesses were submitted to him privately. Such an arrangement was not at all to the liking of counsel for the proponents, and they reacted to it with howls of genuine legal anguish. Not only would this arrangement deprive them of the opportunity to do their customary research into the lives of prospective witnesses. It could also mean the indefinite prolongation of the case.

Despite the comforting assurance that the identity of his cast of characters would be kept from opposing counsel, Mr. Lord's long-threatened cloud of devastating witnesses still failed to materialize. And yet a curious air of complacency now seemed to prevail in the camp of the contestant, as of a cat who has finally devised a way to lure the canary from its cage whenever he chooses to do so. Lord's smugness was all the more evident because it was in such marked contrast to the exasperated anxiety of counsel for proponents. Time seemed no longer of any moment to Mr. Lord as he leisurely proceeded, serenely indifferent to Mr. Clinton's caustic comments, to bring forth more of his apparently endless array of medical experts whose testimony proved nothing except what had already been proved: that the testator was an old man more or less subject to the infirmities of his age. Even Mr. Lord himself seemed bored by them. Then, during the early part of November, 1878, Mr. Lord fired what proved to be his last shot.

It started out like another of his medical-expert duds. The expert was Dr. Salmon Skinner, a dentist who had obtained some notoriety by suing Henry Ward Beecher to recover the value of a set of false teeth he had made for Dr. Beecher's father (and who possibly had discovered that being in the legal limelight increased the demand for his product). Dr. Skinner had come forward voluntarily and was prepared to testify that he had treated the Commodore in 1873 and found his mind in a state of such imbecility that he had thought him to be drunk. More careful examination, however, had disclosed that the imbecility arose simply from the natural decay of his faculties. Surrogate Calvin, scanning the private list of prospective witnesses Lord had given him, was shocked to find that it did not even contain the name of Dr. Skinner. The Surrogate refused to permit him to testify.

"Under those circumstances," Mr. Lord announced, very quietly and deliberately, "the contestant closes her case."

Mrs. La Bau clapped her hands and jumped with glee as the courtroom buzzed with excitement. But an astonishing pall of gloom seemed to descend upon William H. Vanderbilt and his counsel as they sat dumbfounded by the inexplicable suddenness with which the event they had been awaiting so impatiently had finally occurred.

"That is all wrong, Mr. Vanderbilt," Sam F. Barger, a friend and himself a lawyer, was heard to say. "I'm afraid that will give them a new trial."

Disinterested attorneys present in the courtroom expressed the opinion that Surrogate Calvin's decision to refuse to allow Dr. Skinner to testify would not be upheld in the Appellate Court. Mr. Lord himself denied any intention of setting a legal snare for the Surrogate, but his manner rather indicated that he was not entirely displeased with himself. New and important evidence, he told reporters, was constantly being discovered, and it might be just as well to let the matter rest for a while. His client, motivated more by a desire for justice than by greed, had nothing to gain by undue haste. It was obvious, of course, that Mr. Lord was quite aware of the infuriating effect that the prospect of indefinite delay in distributing the estate would have upon those who were content with the will as it stood. Until the defense of the will was presented, and the case decided, they were being deprived of the use and enjoyment of the money they felt was rightfully theirs.

On November 19, 1878, nearly two long and galling years after the testator's death, the favored heirs were at last permitted to commence their defense of the will. Mr. Clinton's presentation of their case was simple, direct, and vigorous. Disdaining to make any sort of opening address whatever (much to the consternation of Surrogate Calvin, who felt that such an omission was highly irregular), Mr. Clinton at once set about calling to the stand a procession of gentlemen prominent in government, finance, and the professions, who testified briskly and unanimously to the Commodore's business acumen, his staunch character, and his remarkable clear-headedness until the very end of his life. Ex-Governors E. D. Morgan and John T. Hoffman of New York, as well as Edwards Pierrepont and William E. Dodge, all gentlemen of distinction locally and even nationally, provided an impressive contrast to the magneticians and shady ladies who had testified for the contestant. Mr. Lord rarely bothered to cross-examine them. The only notable exception occurred when Bishop Holland N. McTyeire of the Southern Methodist Church was on the stand. He had been called as a witness primarily to establish the irreproachable character of the Commodore's widow, whom he had known all of her life and through whom he had been able to cajole the great man into giving away $1,000,000 for the purpose of founding Vanderbilt University. Mr. Lord rudely asked the Bishop to tell the court what he knew about an earlier husband of Frankie's who was still living. Before the Bishop could reply, Mr. Clinton, Mr. Choate, and Judge Comstock were all on their feet vigorously protesting that the question was irrelevant, immaterial, and ungentlemanly. The spectators were in a dither. Mrs. La Bau hurried eagerly down the aisle to her lawyers' table so that she could watch Judge Black more closely as he replenished his chewing tobacco and strode before the bench to present their argument. Even William H. Vanderbilt, usually as stolid as a stone, appeared affected for the first time since the trial had started.

"This is not a trifling matter," Judge Black rumbled, speaking slowly and with apparent embarrassment. "Here is a man eighty years old marrying a woman fifty years his junior, who came here a stranger, after separating from a husband who is still living. That there should have been bitterness felt toward this woman by the Commodore's daughters, some of whom were already grandmothers, and that this feeling should have turned the heart of the father against them, are natural results. But there was one exception in the family. William H. Vanderbilt encouraged the marriage, and continued to show as much regard for the woman as though she had not done the injury of marrying the Commodore in his dotage. But the aggravation is immense if, in addition to showing the distress and hatred that this marriage caused, we show that it was unlawful, and that, therefore, whatever influence Mrs. Vanderbilt exerted was not only undue, it was unholy. There are words struggling for utterance here that I am compelled to restrain, and I suppose I have made a bungle of it, but your Honor must understand what I mean."

His Honor, however, apparently as stunned as everyone else in the courtroom, appeared to be beyond understanding. And so, in a voice choking with emotion, Judge Black went on to spell out exactly what he meant. "That a stranger should sell herself to this old man for his money, taking advantage of that weakness of his nature, is not a reason why a will made under such circumstances should be allowed to stand."

When he had finished, Judge Black sat down and buried his flushed face in his hands. His apparently real embarrassment at what the necessities of the occasion had required him to say about a member of the fair sex was quite as moving as his argument. There was hardly a sound in the courtroom. Even counsel for proponents, though dark with rage, remained strangely silent. But it was all in vain. Surrogate Calvin, once he had regained his judicial poise, hastily sustained proponents' objection to Mr. Lord's question, and Bishop McTyeire was permitted to step down.

But the damage had been done, and there was no joy among counsel for proponents at the Surrogate's decision in their favor. The witness they had called to establish the sterling quality of Mrs. Frankie Vanderbilt's character—probably at her own insistence and against their better judgment—had provided opposing counsel with an irresistible opportunity to tarnish it. Judge Black's eloquent plea, illogical and irrelevant though it may have been, probed through the one weak link in proponents' case to an excruciatingly sensitive spot. However great William's reluctance to compromise with his brother and sister, whether from greed or, as seems more likely, from pure cussedness, he had also to consider the feelings of his stepmother. Her good will and co-operation were essential to him, and he did not dare to risk further aspersions upon the propriety of her marriage to his father. As a lady with social ambitions of her own for the future, this was a subject on which she was understandably touchy.

In retrospect it seems clear (as it must have been clear then to any reasonably astute observer of courtroom dramas) that, by the time Judge Black came to the end of his little discourse on the theme of young women who marry very rich and very old men, the contest was really over and that a compromise agreeable to the contestant would be arranged. Even Mrs. La Bau's vindictive hatred of her stepmother seemed finally to have been appeased. Out of respect for judicial form, the last act had still to be played out, but no one seemed to mind when Surrogate Calvin adjourned the trial for two months in order to catch up with a backlog of other matters urgently demanding his attention. There was, for instance, a lady who had developed a penchant for beating her brother on the head with an umbrella in the corridor outside the Surrogate's chambers in connection with the probate of their father's will. In fact, it has been said that the calendar of the Surrogate's Court in New York has never completely recovered from the effects of the Vanderbilt case.

Thus, it was not until March 4, 1879, that the essential legal buttress of proponents' case was hammered solidly into place by Charles A. Rapallo, a jurist distinguished by his long service on the state of New York's court of appeals, the Commodore's confidential legal adviser for many years, and the man who had been drawing wills for the decedent since 1856. All the wills were substantially the same. William had always been named residuary legatee and Cornelius had always been left with a comparatively small annuity.

The next and final witness for the proponents was William H. Vanderbilt himself. Mr. Vanderbilt was calm and dignified as Mr. Choate conducted his examination in the impressively courteous manner for which he was noted. In reply to Mr. Choate's respectfully couched questions the witness denied, briefly but emphatically, all the utterances attributed to him by contestant's witnesses in regard to his influence over his father; he also disclaimed any design to prejudice the Commodore against Corneel or to turn to his own advantage his father's alleged spiritualist beliefs.

Mr. Lord was scarcely less courteous in his cross-examination. After a few questions put with a most gingerly circumspection as to Mr. Vanderbilt's relations with his stepmother (he seemed relieved when assured that they had always been entirely proper), Mr. Lord said quietly that that would be all.

There was a flurry of excitement as the significance of his words became apparent. After it subsided, Mr. Lord told the court that counsel for contestant would submit their case without summing up. Then, in a voice which betrayed repressed emotion, he asked to have stricken from the record everything reflecting upon the character of Mrs. Vanderbilt that had appeared there by their motion, offer, or allegation. To the bewilderment of the spectators, there was a general shaking of hands among opposing counsel, and Mr. Choate made a great point of thanking Mr. Lord for his words on behalf of Mrs. Vanderbilt.

Under the heading "POSITIVE DETAILS OF THE COMPROMISE," the *Tribune* promptly gave its readers an inside version of why the trial had ended so abruptly. It claimed its facts came from a gentleman described as "one who has been intimately connected with the contestants, but who refuses to have his name mentioned." This anonymous gentleman was quoted as saying that "the compromise was the result of a conversation between Judge Rapallo and the person who has all along been backing Cornelius Vanderbilt, Jr., in his suit. I don't mean his sister, who has stood by him nobly when she might have pocketed her half million and avoided any trouble. This friend of young Vanderbilt told very plainly what it was proposed to show by numerous witnesses not yet examined, and the consequence was that it was agreed that Cornelius was to be paid $1,000,000 and costs of his suit in the Supreme Court, and Mrs. La Bau $1,000,000 plus her expenditures in the contest of the will; and that all testimony of a character derogatory to any member of the Vanderbilt family, past or present, was to be suppressed."

As later events would show, the *Tribune*'s version, though somewhat overly generous, was not too far removed from the truth. The proponents, for instance, acknowledged that William H. Vanderbilt stood ready to fulfill the promises he had made before the contest started, but this, of course, would not be a compromise. It would be simply a matter of "free gifts"—the same kind of gifts William had given to his other sisters on their refusal to contest the will. Even Mr. Lord, speaking for the contestant, maintained tartly that "I know nothing of any compromise."

Surrogate Calvin gave his decision on March 19, 1879, two weeks after the end of the trial. While all element of doubt as to the outcome had pretty well vanished, it was, nevertheless, an interesting document. In it the Surrogate took considerable pains to castigate the contestant and her counsel severely for what he described as their "persistent effort to uncover to the public gaze the secrets of a parent's domestic and private life; to belittle his intelligence and his virtues; to distort his providence into meanness; to magnify his eccentricities into dementia, his social foibles into immorality, his business differences into dishonesty and treachery; and to ascribe his diseases to obscene practices."

In fact, the Surrogate said, the testimony showed the testator to have been a man of "very vigorous mind and strong nature, but lacking the amenities of education and culture and a delicate respect for the opinions of his fellow-men." He also dismissed without exception, and with somewhat less rhetorical flourish, every phase of the contestant's case. The only evidence of a fraudulent conspiracy to influence the testator unduly was the extraordinary testimony of the lady from Poughkeepsie, with her background of unusual domestic arrangements, and of the alcoholically inclined Mrs. Stone. In these cases, due to "the discreditable and fraudulent enterprises in which these two witnesses claimed to have been engaged, and their manner of testifying, their discreditable antecedents and associations, together with the intrinsic improbability of their story," Surrogate Calvin reached the conclusion that their testimony was unworthy of credit and refused to accept it as a basis for judicial action. Furthermore, he urged those directly interested to pursue and bring the offenders to merited punishment, together with their guilty suborners, for, as he put it, "it is not to be believed that a mere fondness for an odious notoriety was sufficient to call these witnesses from their obscene associations unsolicited." (Alas for justice and public expectations, the ladies were permitted to resume their accustomed ways unmolested. Any such stern pursuit would only have stirred up more of the unsavory publicity which the Vanderbilts were now so anxious to avoid, and would, in any event, have violated the terms of the treaty of peace.)

An editorial in the *Times* summed up the whole affair quite succinctly: "The most remarkable feature [of the contest] is the obtuse moral perceptions of the children who have uncovered the nakedness of their parent . . . The worst feature has been its vulgarity."

Obtuse moral perceptions or not, these were happy days for Vanderbilts, even poor ones. Cornelius and his sister may have lost a legal battle, but, from their point of view, they had won the war. Although the fruits of their victory were not quite so abundant as was rumored in the press (the version favored by the *Times* gave $1,000,000 to each,

PICTURE CREDITS FOR PAGES 204-205: BROWN BROTHERS; UPI; CULVER PICTURES; EUROPEAN; WIDE WORLD; FABIAN BACHRACH; COLUMBIA RECORDS; ATLANTIC-LITTLE, BROWN, BY TONI FRISSELL; BLACKSTONE-SHELBURNE NEW YORK. PAGES 206-207: BROWN BROTHERS; UPI; PALM BEACH HISTORICAL SOCIETY; COLUMBIANA COLLECTION; COLUMBIA UNIVERSITY; NEW YORK PUBLIC LIBRARY; VANDERBILT MUSEUM, CENTERPORT, N.Y.; WHITNEY MUSEUM OF AMERICAN ART; NINA LEEN, *Life* MAGAZINE; CULVER PICTURES; WIDE WORLD.

plus $250,000 for counsel and expenses), they were still substantial. All we know definitely is that, in addition to the Commodore's original bequests, young Corneel received a $400,000 trust fund and some $200,000 in cash. Mrs. La Bau undoubtedly received a comparable amount; and there must also have been considerable sums for legal fees and expenses, but the exact figures of the total settlement disappeared immediately behind the veil of secrecy with which the Vanderbilts now endeavored to conduct their affairs. Considering the general preposterousness of contestant's case, these sums were munificent indeed. Even Cornelius conceded, in a letter to the *Times* indignantly protesting against the use of the word "compromise" to describe the settlement, that his brother "acted in a just and magnanimous manner . . . and displayed a liberality far beyond my expectations." The rich Vanderbilts, William and his brood, were happily absorbed with the delightful problem of learning how to spend money as ostentatiously as only *the* Vanderbilts could now afford to spend it.

Happiest of all, perhaps, were the lawyers for both sides. Their combined fees exceeded by a vast margin all then-existing world's records for fat legal pickings. Mr. Clinton's fee was reliably reported to have been at least $300,000; rumor put it as high as $500,000. Whatever it was, he was able to retire and devote the remaining twenty years of his life to writing books about the criminal cases which had been his first and true love. The exact amount of Mr. Lord's fee has never been made public, but he did well enough to free himself from financial worries for the remainder of his life. Judge Black was said to have received $28,000, fair pay certainly for the few occasions on which he was called upon to display his eloquence. In the long run, however, perhaps it was young Corneel's *bête noire*, Chauncey M. Depew, who, although not officially of counsel, topped them all. He entrenched himself so solidly with the Vanderbilt family that he went on to become president of the New York Central and, as a sort of fringe benefit frequently bestowed on prominent industrialists in the days before senators were chosen by popular vote, served two terms in the United States Senate.

The only people concerned with the settlement who seem to have been unhappy were Cornelius' creditors in Hartford. Weeks went by and they were still anxiously waiting. According to a dispatch from Hartford there were 217 claimants to whom Corneel allegedly owed an aggregate of $75,000. Most of them were paid eventually; luckily for them, payment of all outstanding debts was a condition of the settlement insisted upon by William.

By December of 1879 Cornelius himself was becoming unhappily restive in the humdrum security of his new existence. Besides, the mere fact of the inaccessibility of the principal of his new trust fund must have had a most disturbing effect upon anyone so sensitive in such matters. Predictably enough, Cornelius' natural reaction to such frustration was to dash off a typical epistolary effusion, asking that half of the fund be released to him immediately. Alas, William replied that "it would not be a sound exercise of judgment to grant your request, however pleasing it might be to gratify your desire." Unable or unwilling to grasp the idea that one of the chief purposes of trust funds is to protect beneficiaries against the use of their own judgment, Cornelius now petitioned the Supreme Court of New York to remove William as a trustee on some vague grounds of fiduciary incapacity. The court promptly denied the motion. When Cornelius insisted on appealing, against the advice of his counsel, the decision was affirmed with a severe rebuke for bringing an application having neither law nor facts to justify it. The brief era of good feeling between William and Cornelius had ended and was never to be revived.

For a thwarted ne'er-do-well, life without great expectations was a dismal, downhill affair. Soon Corneel was reappearing once more in his old haunts, where by the curious logic of finance his credit was not as good as it had been when he was scrounging along on an allowance from home, and he was again being harassed by creditors, particularly by Simmons, whose methods of collection could be rather unpleasant. He spent his last night on earth in a gambling house at 12 Ann Street, returning to his rooms in the Glenham Hotel at 6 A.M. of the morning after, worn and bedraggled. Early that afternoon, April 2, 1882, while Sunday crowds promenaded outside on Fifth Avenue, "young Corneel" shot himself to death. It seems now to have been an unnecessarily grim ending to a life which, from any rational point of view, should have continued happily along on a blithe and debonair course.

In his own will Cornelius treated his sisters just as badly as had his father. He left them each $1,000 to buy something in remembrance of him. The bulk of his estate consisted of the disputed $400,000 trust fund, the principal of which he was never able to touch during his life, but which he could dispose of as he wished in his will. Most of it went to his old friend and companion, in good times and bad, George N. Terry. Mrs. La Bau, his staunch comrade-at-arms during the long will contest, was so incensed by this unbrotherly treatment that she now rushed into court with objections to the probate of *his* will. Later, however, she withdrew them after what was described as "an understanding agreeable to all the parties."

Early in the Great Will Contest, when Mr. Lord was developing some of his particularly scurrilous irrelevancies about the Commodore's alleged weakness for assorted females, the *Tribune,* in an outburst of editorial righteousness, had predicted that "rivers of gold will not wash out the stain . . . The name Vanderbilt will disappear in shame and ignominy." Alas for the prescience of editorial writers, the name Vanderbilt, far from disappearing, was transmuted with almost magical celerity into a national symbol of wealth and social status of such potency that later and far richer parvenu families, strive as they might, have never been able to displace it. Even now, when such things no longer really matter, its spell still lingers.

William more than doubled his inheritance, leaving, upon his death in 1885, an estate worth nearly $200,000,000. With twice as much to distribute, he had something for everyone, and there was nothing resembling a wayward son with great expectations to be prudently blighted. In dividing the kitty, William followed the general pattern set by his father. Each of his four daughters received $5,000,000 outright and $5,000,000 in trust, as did his two younger sons, Frederick and George. The two elder sons, Cornelius II and William K., divvied up the remainder, some $130,000,000.

Although this division did not exactly show equal regard for his offspring, there was not even a rumor of a dispute over the will. None of the eight appeared to feel disinherited, as most of the Commodore's children had in their day. Indeed, it would have been difficult to feel disinherited with a legacy of $10,000,000 in a day when there was no income tax and when a dollar was really a dollar.

One fine November day in 1848 a railroad locomotive christened the *Pioneer* chugged westward out of Chicago a distance of eight miles. It pulled only a single coach, a baggage car temporarily outfitted to carry a handful of prominent Chicagoans being treated to one of the first runs of the Galena & Chicago Union Railroad. Spotting a farmer driving an ox wagon filled with wheat and hides toward Chicago, two of the passengers purchased the goods and transferred them to the baggage car. The train then returned to its home city. This simple event foreshadowed the future course of Chicago's development: within twenty years the modest railroad comprising ten miles of track became the giant Chicago & North Western, one of the roads that made Illinois the nation's leader in railroad mileage; while the city itself grew tenfold to a population of 300,000. The inflow of wheat, which had begun when a group of men on a one-car train hauled a few bushels, amounted to tens of millions of bushels annually.

"Let the golden grain come, we can take care of it all," cried a Chicago newspaper of the 1850's. And come it did. Illinois was a major grain producer, and Chicago—"the New York of the West"—enjoyed a strategic location that made it the key transfer point for transcontinental trade. Systems like the Chicago & North Western and the Illinois Central funnelled in wheat, corn, and barley from the immense cereal carpet that lay to the city's west and northwest. During the sixties it became one of the world's primary grain markets; through the wonder of the telegraph, price fluctuations in the Chicago market were quickly communicated to the world and affected prices in New York and faraway Liverpool. At the center of these transactions stood the Chicago Board of Trade, the focal point for the buying and selling of grains, flour, and other foodstuffs. A contemporary called the Board "the Altar of Ceres," and the label was apt. Grain, and the money it might bring, was indeed a goddess to be worshipped by the restless merchants of the Board of Trade.

To accommodate the huge quantities which flowed in and out of Chicago there developed a most lucrative business, that of storing the grain in warehouses until it was sold and shipped east. (Railroad connections were such that direct shipments to eastern centers were difficult or impossible.) Known as grain elevators, the warehouses were skyscrapers able to hold 500,000 to 1,000,000 bushels in elongated, perpendicular bins that were mechanically loaded by the lifting up of dump buckets fastened to conveyor belts. Once the grain was deposited there, the warehousemen facilitated sales to merchants and speculators by issuing them receipts to represent the amount in storage. These receipts were regarded as

Grain elevators had false bottoms; freight rates had no ceilings. The farmers raised the roof, and government regulation crossed industry's threshold

MUNN v. ILLINOIS

A Foot in the

CHICAGO HISTORICAL SOCIETY

230

Ira Y. Munn

Door

By C. PETER MAGRATH

stable tokens of value comparable to bank bills; and presumably a warehouseman, like a banker, held a position of public trust demanding a high level of integrity. The presumption, however, proved to be quite unjustified.

The history of the great Chicago grain elevators is reflected in the rise and fall of Munn & Scott, a firm founded in Spring Bay, Illinois, in 1844. The two partners, Ira Y. Munn and George L. Scott, ran a small (about 8,000 bushels capacity) warehouse that served the north central part of the state. Munn, who was the firm's driving spirit, soon expanded his operations. Taking advantage of the opportunities presented by the growing commercial ascendancy of Chicago, he established a 200,000-bushel grain elevator there in 1856 under the name of Munn, Gill & Co. Two years later it became Munn & Scott, one of Chicago's thirteen elevator firms, which had a combined storage capacity of over four million bushels.

The next decade—one that belonged to America's capitalists—was enormously prosperous for Munn & Scott. They expanded to four elevators with a total capacity of 2,700,000 bushels; they could receive as many as 300,000 bushels daily and ship out twice that number. With success came power and prestige. Ira Munn emerged as a leading Chicago businessman; he was prominent in the affairs of the Board of Trade, serving as its president in 1860 and as president of the city's Chamber of Commerce in 1868. During the Civil War he participated conspicuously in activities supporting the Union cause. At the same time, good capitalist that he was, Ira Munn diversified his enterprises by engaging in wholesale grain speculation and by investing in newspapers and banks.

On the surface all seemed well for Munn & Scott, but they had their problems. These, in large measure, were of their own making; the age of enterprise was also an age of corruption, and the Chicago warehousemen were not at war with the spirit of their age. By 1868 Munn & Scott and four other firms dominated the field. They were interlocked in a business pool, each owning part interest in each of the others. They could thus fix prices and force farmers, who had to store their grain prior to sale, to pay high storage fees. There were cruder forms of chicanery. The warehousemen commonly made deals with the railway men whereby they were assured of receiving the grain carried by a particular line, regardless of the shipper's consignment. Munn & Scott, for instance, received most of their grain from the Chicago &

Some of the great Chicago grain elevators whose misuse brought on the struggle for government regulation of trade dominate this 1866 lithograph. One of Munn & Scott's elevators is seen at the right.

North Western. Another practice was to issue bogus receipts not backed by actual grain. Yet another favorite trick, performed with allied speculators, was to spread false rumors that the grain was spoiling; unsuspecting merchants would hasten to unload their grain receipts at depressed prices, thus setting up a juicy profit for the warehousemen.

While this sophisticated graft pleased the profiteers, it aroused its victims. As early as 1857, Chicago's grain merchants, acting through the Board of Trade, sought to impose a system of self-regulation upon the grain-elevator owners. Their aim was to get impartial inspectors into the warehouses to report on the condition and quantity of the grain in storage. A related objective was to make the Board a central registration agency which would record incoming shipments of grain and validate their sale, so as to eliminate the practice of issuing bogus receipts. The warehousemen naturally resisted, claiming that as private owners they had an inherent right to exclude outside parties from their property. Since the elevator proprietors also had representation on the Board of Trade, they were usually able to turn the regulatory proposals into meaningless compromises. The upshot was the semblance but not the substance of regulation: grain weighers who were in the employ of the warehousemen; Board inspectors whose admission into the elevators depended upon the owners' good will and who were vulnerable to bribes; and unverifiable reports, filed by the warehousemen, which were as worthless as many of their grain receipts.

The Munn & Scott firm was both a prime cause of complaints and a leader in the fight against effective control by the Board. In 1861, after warehouse "wheat doctors" had camouflaged a huge quantity of spoiled grain and mixed it with good grades, open charges of fraud were voiced. The Board appointed an investigating committee, but by tacit agreement its report was suppressed. When Joseph Medill's crusading Chicago *Tribune* suggested that the report had been shelved because it incriminated many elevator men, Munn & Scott succeeded in getting *Tribune* reporters expelled from Board meetings. Similar newspaper charges hinting at Munn & Scott frauds appeared in 1865; another public furor followed, but the lax inspection procedures remained unchanged.

Four years later almost all of Chicago's receivers, shippers, and dealers united in demanding a system of real inspection. The immediate cause was a raise in storage rates and the imposition of an extra charge for grain that spoiled while in storage. New Board regulations designed to eliminate fraudulent issues of grain receipts were adopted early in 1870; once again the warehousemen, including Munn & Scott, asserted their right to control matters within their own elevators. The

An Unforeseen Collaboration

Left to right: Justices Bradley, Field, Miller, Clifford; Chie

Public feeling against the railroads' exorbitant freight rates was sharply prodded by the Patrons of Husbandry, or Grangers. Organized in 1867 as an agrarian social society, it grew rapidly into a powerful political force against the economic malpractices of railroads and middlemen. By 1873, when economic depression had intensified their woes, the Grangers had founded scores of papers and journals to promote their complaints. The cartoon at left, captioned The Grange Awakening the Sleepers, *puns on a familiar synonym for railroad crossties. Some big-city papers, notably the Chicago* Tribune, *edited by Joseph Medill (right), helped by campaigning vigorously for state regulation of grain elevators. Eventually the Supreme Court of 1877 (below) sided with the Grangers, thus belying its conservative looks.*

Justice Waite; Justices Swayne, Davis, Strong, and Hunt.

fight intensified. Elections for Board of Trade offices in the spring of 1870 split the membership into two factions—one supported the warehousemen; the other, which won most of the positions, insisted that their power be broken.

Businessmen are not customarily champions of governmental regulation, but the warehouse situation had become intolerable. The conduct of complex business relationships, after all, depends in significant part on mutual trust. Unable to control the warehousemen, the Board of Trade turned to the state, asking that Illinois subject them to public regulation. It was necessary, declared the retiring Board president in 1870, to destroy "a monopoly highly detrimental to every interest of the city." Joseph Medill, whose newspaper made warehouse regulation its cause, put it more colorfully when he described the warehousemen as "rapacious, blood sucking insects." These complaints went before the state's constitutional convention of 1869–1870, then in session. The result was one of those strange yet almost typical alliances of American politics: a temporary pact between two normally opposed interests, the grain merchants and the grain producers.

The farmer-merchant alliance was an unusually strange one for 1870 because that year found the midwestern farmer in the grip of depression. Beyond a doubt, the economic balance of the post-Civil War period was heavily weighted against the American farmer. Between 1861 and 1865 he had rapidly expanded production to meet burgeoning needs, but the postwar market absorbed only part of his fantastic output of wheat, corn, and other grains. The farmer, moreover, sold in an unprotected world market at a time of falling prices; wheat, which sold at $1.45 a bushel in 1866, dropped to 76 cents within three years. As prices dropped, the value of money appreciated, and the farmers, who had borrowed in the wartime flush of inflationary optimism, had to meet debts with a scarce and hard-earned currency. Manufacturers, by contrast, were protected by a high tariff which pushed up the cost of the farmers' tools and domestic necessities.

The farmers of the West and Midwest had yet another grievance which became a focus of all their discontents —the great railroad systems whose shiny rails crisscrossed the farm country. No one had welcomed the coming of the railroad more than the western farmer, since it opened up new markets for his products and made farming feasible in otherwise remote areas. Many had mortgaged their property to buy railroad shares; others had cheerfully accepted high local taxes to finance the bonds that lured the iron horse into their territory.

Unfortunately, the harvest was a bitter one. Once established, the railroads treated their clientele with disdain. Company officials were overbearing, charged exorbitant rates, and discriminated in favor of large shippers, who received special discounts. Precisely because the railroads were essential, they could act arrogantly; in any given area a single line usually enjoyed a monopoly and thus could charge as much as the traffic would bear. The railroads, of course, defended their rates as moderate, sufficient only to make good on the immense speculative risks they had undertaken. The farmers were unimpressed. To them the dominant fact was that freight costs ate up a frightful percentage of their income. Sometimes they were even reduced to burning their corn as fuel rather than shipping it to market at a loss.

Their profound discontent soon led them to organize. Oddly, what became the major vehicle for agrarian protest had its start as a fraternal order intended to end the farmers' isolation from social and educational opportunities. In 1867 an idealistic government clerk in Washington, Oliver Hudson Kelley, singlehandedly founded the National Grange of the Patrons of Husbandry. At first his organization existed more on paper than in reality, but Kelley was an indefatigable worker —and also a shrewd observer. He broadened the Grange's appeal by making its primary objectives cooperative purchasing and the control of monopolies. These tactics paid off, and the Grange spread like prairie wildfire. It soon blanketed the entire nation, reaching its peak in 1874 when representatives of some 800,000 farmers convened in St. Louis to proclaim "the art of agriculture" as "the parent and precursor of all arts, and its products the foundation of all wealth."

Although "the Grange" became a synonym for all the agrarian movements of the seventies, there were other highly vocal farmers' associations which antedated the Patrons of Husbandry, and which intervened in politics throughout the Midwest. All shared the same goals: elimination of the middleman's profits, lowered interest charges, and, most insistently, railroad rate regulation. "We were all grangers," a farmer later recalled. "I never belonged to the order but I was a granger just the same."

In Illinois the farmers scored one of their first successes when they joined with Chicago's merchants in getting the state's constitutional convention to authorize railroad and warehouse regulation. Like the Board of Trade, Illinois farmers had just cause for wanting to see the elevators controlled. Typically, a farmer might ship 1,000 bushels of wheat to Chicago, but receive a warehouse receipt for only 950. After paying costly storage charges, he might be told that his grain was "heating" and that, to avoid a complete disaster, he should sell his receipt to the warehouseman at a loss of 10 cents per bushel. Later, the hapless farmer would learn that his grain, perfectly sound, had been sold at a nice profit. But beyond their joint desires to clean up a dirty business, both farmers and merchants were interested in comprehensive regulation. The Board of Trade wanted to make normal business relationships possible; the farmers wanted a stringent limitation on the rates charged by railroads and warehouses.

Acting in response to these pressures, the 1871 legislature passed laws forbidding railroad discriminations and prescribing maximum freight and passenger rates. The warehousemen's fraudulent practices were outlawed, storage rates were limited, and a Board of Railroad and Warehouse Commissioners was created to enforce the regulations.

Enforcement, however, was not easy. The warehousemen proclaimed the law unconstitutional and ignored it. Munn & Scott refused to take out the required license and kept the state-appointed registrar of grain out of their elevators. The state then sued the firm; but the trial proceedings were delayed because of the mass destruction of records by Chicago's Great Fire of 1871. In July, 1872, the state won a judgment of $100; Munn & Scott promptly appealed to the Illinois Supreme Court.

Meanwhile, however, through a series of related events, the downfall of Munn & Scott was beginning. Despite the state regulation (which at first had no practical impact), the Board of Trade continued to seek inspection of the warehouses during 1871 and 1872. Some elevators co-operated with Board inspectors in measuring their grain, but Munn & Scott remained defiant. Finally, in 1872, the firm consented to admit inspectors. It requested, however, that its elevators be inspected last in order to give it time to consolidate its grains and to avoid any implication of particular mistrust of Munn & Scott. The Board agreed, and the firm put the time to good use—flooring over the tops of several bins in one large elevator and covering the false bottoms with grain so as to give the illusion of full bins. The inspectors were fooled until an employee divulged the secret, and it was learned that Munn & Scott grain receipts totaling 300,000 bushels were not backed by grain.

Deplorable as the corruption was, its disclosure merely confirmed what had long been suspected. More immediately damaging were Munn & Scott's financial misadventures in the summer of 1872. Along with three other speculators, the firm attempted to corner all the wheat pouring into Chicago, hoping to dictate its ultimate price in world markets. For a while the corner worked, as Munn & Scott made huge purchases. The heavy buying, however, pushed the price of wheat so high that the farmers, who normally held some grain in reserve in the hope that its value would rise, shipped their surplus to market. This was the crucial stage, for to secure their corner the speculators would have to buy up all the grain. They turned to Chicago's banks for a million-dollar loan, but were unsuccessful: their credit was already severely stretched. They had to stop buying, and wheat prices plummeted forty-seven cents in a twenty-four-hour period. Munn & Scott was ruined, its grain receipts thoroughly discredited. To avoid a complete panic, the powerful George Armour & Co. bought the Munn interests and quietly set about purchasing grain to make its receipts good. Munn and Scott themselves went into bankruptcy; the ensuing court proceedings, as summarized in newspaper headlines, told the story of the Chicago elevator business: IRA Y. MUNN ON STAND LAYS BARE ELEVATOR COMBINATION—PROFITS DIVIDED—AGREEMENT IN 1866—A GENERAL POOL—HISTORY OF CONTRACTS WITH NORTHWESTERN RAILWAY BEGINNING IN 1862 AND RENEWED IN 1866.

The sequel came on December 3, 1872, when Munn and Scott were expelled from the Board of Trade.

The rapidly swelling power of the Grangers was signalled by the crowds that turned out to regional meetings to voice their grievances and demand reform legislation. Above, several thousand gather at Edwardsville, Illinois, in September, 1873.

Although Ira Munn and George Scott passed into oblivion, the regulatory impulse that they and their fellow warehousemen had helped trigger continued unabated. The year 1873 was one of economic panic; grain prices dropped further, and a severe shortage of credit forced numerous mortgage foreclosures. The Granger movement reached floodtide, and its political power was felt in all the midwestern states. Granger votes elected legislators and governors who helped pass laws lowering railroad rates; as the Minnesota governor inelegantly put it, "It is time to take robber corporations by the scruff of the neck and shake them over hell!"

The Granger laws, cursed as communistic in eastern business and financial circles, were a tribute to the political power of organized farmers. But, having failed to prevent the new legislation, the railroads retaliated with a variety of weapons. Their agents fought to repeal or weaken the laws and to persuade the public of their undesirability. They insisted that regulation would discourage further rail construction—an effective point, for even the bitterest foes of "the octopus" wanted increased railroad service at a fair price.

Resistance took other forms as well. In some cases the roads aimed to make the laws backfire: because of technical loopholes they were able to equalize their rates (thus formally ending discriminations) by *raising* them as much as fifty per cent in areas where they had been low. In other cases, they reduced service and forecast its complete abandonment. Wisconsin customers, for example, were subjected to dilapidated cars and erratic service that the railroads suavely blamed on the unusually harsh regulations of the Potter law—"Potter cars, Potter rails, and Potter time."

Mostly, however, the corporations put their faith in the judiciary—not the elective state courts where decisions were likely to mirror popular desires, but the United States Supreme Court. The railroads were supremely confident that rate regulation, no matter how moderate, violated the Constitution for at least three reasons. The first was that the laws contravened the federal contract clause by impairing their right to set rates, a right granted by the states' charters of incorporation. Here the railroads cited the Supreme Court's decision in the Dartmouth College Case of 1819, which stated that a charter was in effect inviolable. (They conveniently overlooked the Supreme Court's later ruling in the Charles River Bridge Case, which modified the doctrine on the ground that the public also had rights and that these could be bargained away only by an *explicit* grant. Furthermore, the railroads' charters had been issued under state constitutions which contained clauses reserving the legislatures'

authority to amend them.) Second, the corporations urged that rate regulation tampered with interstate transportation, thereby impinging on Congress' plenary power over interstate commerce. Lastly, they argued that public rate-setting was a radical innovation unknown in the American experience. It was, they contended, a confiscation which violated the Fourteenth Amendment's prohibition against depriving persons of their property without due process of law.

Corporation resistance quickly led to specific cases in the state and lower federal courts. The Chicago warehousemen who had by now succeeded to the Munn & Scott properties continued to defy the Warehouse Act and carried their case to the state supreme court—unsuccessfully. The state, declared the Illinois judges, might regulate all subjects "connected with the public welfare" in order "to promote the greatest good of the greatest number."

Despite this and other reverses in the lower courts, the business interests were confident of ultimate victory. The assurances of their high-priced legal talent were soothing, and the corporations appealed their cases. In 1873 and 1874 *Munn v. Illinois* and seven railroad cases, which became known as the Granger Railroad Cases, all made their way to the United States Supreme Court, and, so the railroad leaders felt, toward a decision favorable to business.

Their confidence, however, was grossly misplaced. The Court of the 1870's did not regard itself as the judicial handmaiden to entrepreneurial capitalism. Its Chief Justice, Morrison Remick Waite, was a moderate whose deep faith in representative democracy made him tolerant of legislative experimentation. His attitude had been shaped in frontier Ohio, where he had settled in 1838. His politics were solidly Republican, and his experiences in a close-knit community where personal honesty and character mattered as much as business acumen made Waite a typical member of the ante-bellum class of professional and mercantile men to whom wealth was not an end in itself.

Ironically, this man of complete integrity was appointed to the Chief Justiceship through the tawdry maneuverings of the Grant era. When a vacancy occurred in the office in 1873, President Grant tried to please his malodorous entourage with three dubious candidates, but was forced by public outcry to withdraw each in turn. The muddled President then looked for an honest man and found Waite, whose obscure respectability assured his confirmation. An unassuming middle-aged lawyer of medium height, his face clothed in one of those ample beards that were the style of his day, Waite proved himself a first-rate judge and an excellent Chief Justice. While his intelligence was keen, his most valuable assets were an amiable personality and a knack for leading men. "Policy" and "diplomacy" were his self-proclaimed guidelines.

These qualities served him well. Waite's associates were men of uncommon ability, but their vanities and ambitions could easily have mired the Court in a morass of personal conflicts. Unquestionably the best mind and the most learned jurist among them was Joseph P. Bradley. A self-made man, Bradley enjoyed a successful career representing some of New Jersey's leading railroads until appointed to the Court in 1870 by President Grant. Once on the bench, he showed marked independence toward the corporate interests he had formerly defended, frequently upholding economic regulation. Another Court giant was Samuel Freeman Miller. Beginning as a poor Kentucky farm boy, Miller had had two careers, one as a rural doctor and, after studying law on his own, another as a country lawyer. Appointed by Lincoln in 1862, Miller habitually stressed the importance of personal liberties and reflected a hostility to corporate and financial wealth. Blunt, self-confident, and prone to vanity, he was a dominant figure on the Court after the Civil War.

Ward Hunt, Noah H. Swayne, Nathan Clifford, and David Davis, four of the tribunal's lesser lights, generally followed Waite's lead in economic regulation cases. Like Waite, all of them had grown to maturity in Jacksonian America, and they retained a democratic faith that made them favorably disposed to laws passed by the people's representatives.

The remaining two associate justices were exceptions. William Strong was a conservative, sympathetic to corporation views. Stephen J. Field, whose brother Cyrus laid the Atlantic cable, was a transplanted New Englander who prided himself on being a rugged Californian. Through a judicial service of nearly thirty-five years Field outspokenly defended the claims of American business.

Judicial processes are rarely speedy, and the Court of the seventies moved with majestic slowness. Overburdened with a lengthy docket, it required an average of three years to announce decisions. The first Granger case to reach the Court, a challenge to Minnesota's rate law, arrived in October, 1873, and the Illinois, Iowa, and Wisconsin cases were docketed the next year. Oral arguments occupied two sessions during the 1875 term; the Granger Railroad Cases were heard in October, 1875, and *Munn v. Illinois,* the elevator case, was argued early in 1876.

For the oral arguments the business interests marshalled the elite of the nation's bar. William M. Evarts, Orville H. Browning, David Dudley Field (another brother of Justice Field's), and Frederick T. Frelinghuysen were among the assembled legal talent. They strongly argued the three contentions advanced by their side in the lower courts: confiscation of property, impairment of contract obligations, and interference with interstate commerce. To these constitutional arguments they added that rate regulation was almost unheard of in America, and that the Granger laws were "the beginning of the operations of the [Paris] commune in the legislation of this country." In reply, the attorneys for the state governments involved defended the laws as reasonable measures to protect the general welfare against the exactions of private, uncurbed monopolies whose business had in effect become public.

Despite the brilliance of the railroad attorneys and the eloquence of their arguments, seven of the Supreme Court justices cast their votes for the Granger laws. Only Field and Strong dissented on November 18, 1876, when all eight cases were decided together. Chief Justice Waite assigned himself the opinions, well aware of their importance; this was the Court's first major statement on the constitutionality of regulating the new industrial capitalism. He chose the elevator case, *Munn v. Illinois,* for his main opinion. Unlike the companies involved in the Granger Railroad Cases, Munn and Scott were unincorporated partners and their business was not directly involved in interstate transportation. Their case therefore presented the crucial issue, the permissibility of rate regulation, in pure form, uncomplicated by the contract and commerce questions raised in the other disputes.

The Chief Justice devoted the winter to preparing the opinions, later remarking that "they kept my mind and hands at work all the time." Waite did his opinion-writing at home, sitting at a long and cluttered library table in his private study, where he worked in the morning's early hours and often into the night. Admittedly old-fashioned, he spurned secretaries and the newfangled typewriter, making his drafts in longhand. A glimpse of his labors on the *Munn* opinion is preserved on a lined sheet of paper on which he jotted down earlier illustrations of American business regulation. These references to historical practice, some of which appeared in the final opinion, were pertinent. The parties challenging the Granger laws had strongly contended that regulation was alien to America; to demolish their claim Waite naturally referred to the state he knew best, citing precedents from Ohio history.

As Waite prepared the *Munn* opinion, he turned for assistance to Justice Bradley, his closest collaborator on the Court. Bradley in fact deserves recognition as the opinion's co-author: he prepared a lengthy "Outline of my views on the subject of the Granger Cases," from which the Chief Justice freely borrowed. In refuting the business arguments, Bradley, a confirmed legal antiquarian, dug up an obscure seventeenth-century English legal treatise, *De Portibus Maris.* Written by Lord

Chief Justice Hale, it justified regulation of the fees charged in public ports with the following language: "For now the wharf and crane and other conveniences are affected with a publick interest, and they cease to be *juris privati* only." Waite quoted this statement and so introduced the public-interest doctrine to a long life in American constitutional law. Late in February he circulated the draft opinions among the brethren for their final approval. Bradley, the former railroad attorney, responded enthusiastically—"terse, correct, & safe." Miller found the opinions "equal to the occasion which is a very great one."

With these endorsements, the Court released its opinions on March 1, 1877, ruling that the Constitution sanctioned economic regulation in the public interest. Waite's opinion in *Munn v. Illinois* began by stressing the power of the Chicago grain elevators, which, standing at the gateway of commerce to the East, "take toll from all who pass." Their business, he argued, citing Lord Hale, "tends to a common charge, and is become a thing of public interest and use" subject to state control. Noting earlier instances of American price regulation, Waite summarily dismissed the contention that such laws unconstitutionally confiscated private property. Underlying these conclusions was the root assumption of *Munn v. Illinois*—that the popularly accountable legislatures should be the judges of the wisdom of regulatory laws. "For protection against abuses by legislatures the people must resort to the polls, not to the courts," Waite wrote, a remark that symbolizes the opinion's status as one of the Supreme Court's major declarations in favor of judicial self-restraint in economic-regulation cases.

With the Warehouse Act sustained, the Granger Railroad Cases fell easily into place. In brief opinions Waite disposed of them by relying on the public-interest doctrine. He rejected the commerce-clause argument, finding that none of the regulations extended to commerce beyond state lines. He found the claim that the rate laws impaired contract rights to be equally without merit; the states' constitutions had reserved the power to amend charters.

Justice Field, as expected, wrote a fiery dissent labelling the *Munn* decision "subversive of the rights of private property" and predicted that its reasoning implied an almost unlimited scope for the regulatory power: "If the power can be exercised as to one article, it may as to all articles, and the prices of everything, from a calico gown to a city mansion, may be the subject of legislative direction." Field's gloomy prediction was essentially correct in calling attention to the broad implications of the *Munn* decision. In modern-day America the scope of governmental regulation is immense; no one doubts that "the prices of everything"— even calico gowns and city mansions—may be regulated. And this intervention by government in economic affairs finds much of its constitutional sanction in *Munn v. Illinois* and in the line of cases which are its progeny.

During the seventies and eighties, the years when Waite and his majority sat on the Court, the public-interest doctrine, and the underlying assumption that legislative acts are valid unless completely arbitrary, led to further expansions of regulatory power. State railroad regulations were repeatedly upheld, as were laws limiting the rates charged by water companies, prohibiting lotteries, and scaling down the interest and principal owed to the holders of state bonds. Congress' power to regulate federally chartered corporations was similarly upheld by a decision, in the Sinking Fund Cases of 1879, which infuriated corporation and financial leaders.

In later judicial periods, roughly between 1895 and 1937, judges far more committed to free enterprise than Waite, Bradley, and Miller often found reasons for invalidating economic regulations in the due-process clauses of the Fifth and Fourteenth amendments. *Munn v. Illinois* was never overruled, but its public-interest doctrine was radically reinterpreted in the 1920's. The conservative Taft Court struck down a number of state regulatory laws as unconstitutional, declaring that only a narrow category of businesses—enterprises traditionally regulated and large monopolies—were affected with a public interest.

All this came to an end in the next decade. In the 1934 case of *Nebbia v. New York*, sustaining a comprehensive scheme of state milk-price regulation, the Supreme Court returned to a sweeping view of the public-interest doctrine. "A state," it announced in words that Waite would have approved, "is free to adopt whatever economic policy may reasonably be deemed to promote public welfare, and to enforce that policy by legislation adapted to its purpose." Three years later in the case of *NLRB v. Jones and Laughlin Steel Corporation*, when the justices began the process of upholding the economic regulation of the New Deal, the permissive spirit of Waite's *Munn* opinion again triumphed.

Munn v. Illinois, of course, also had a more contemporary impact. The proprietors of the city's grain elevators, the Chicago *Tribune* reported a few days after the Supreme Court's decision, "are thoroughly reconstructed. They bow to the inevitable." They lowered their rates and began co-operating fully with the state's Railroad and Warehouse Commission. Two decades of arrogance by the warehousemen had come to an end; not only were their opponents politically dominant, but the elevator men found their monopolistic power weakened. They faced strong competition from new grain centers at Milwaukee and Minneapolis, and in addition, improved rail connections now permitted farmers to ship grain through Chicago to the East without temporarily storing it.

The railroads also bowed, although many of the midwestern states, responding to powerful railroad lobbies, later repealed or drastically loosened their regulatory laws. Illinois, however, remained a leader in strong railroad regulation; the farmers' influence prevented the repeal of the laws, which were sustained by both state and federal courts.

By 1877 the Patrons of Husbandry, who had provided much of the political support behind the regulatory laws, were but a shadow of their onetime strength. Internal dissensions and the financial collapse of its co-operative enterprises sharply reduced the organization's membership and destroyed its political influence.

In fact, the Grange gradually reverted to its original social purposes and is today a thriving fraternal order. As for the unsavory firm of Munn & Scott, it too was no longer a factor by 1877, for it had passed out of existence.

But ultimately more significant than the immediate results and the conflicting motives of the many participants was the constitutional residue left by the struggles of the seventies: the clear announcement that legislatures might regulate business on behalf of the public interest, a principle that received additional vitality from Chief Justice Waite's assertion that the Court should be reluctant to upset regulatory laws passed by elected representatives. This was the meaning of *Munn v. Illinois,* and it provided a leading precedent for the day when American big business would find itself under continuing government regulation.

"A set of mere money-getters"?

Were the great business tycoons of the nineteenth

By ALLAN NEVINS

For many years critical essayists upon the American businessman, and especially the more implacable assailants of the robber barons, have purred over a verdict once delivered by Charles Francis Adams, Jr., as predatory wildcats might purr over the discovery of a bed of catnip. "As I approach the end," this elder brother of Henry Adams declared, "I am more than a little puzzled to account for the instances I have seen of business success—money-getting. It comes from a rather low instinct. Certainly, as far as my observation goes, it is rarely met in combination with the finer or more interesting traits of character. I have known, and known tolerably well, a good many 'successful' men—'big' financially—men famous during the last half-century; and a less interesting crowd I do not care to encounter. Not one that I have ever known would I care to meet again, either in this world or in the next; nor is one of them associated in my mind with the idea of humor, thought, or refinement. A set of mere money-getters and traders, they were essentially unattractive and uninteresting." They showed a special aptitude and great concentration, Adams added; nothing more.

From frequent use, this quotation is now worn smooth as a pebble in a stream bed. Every time a lecturer or essayist wishes to descant on the meanness of business tycoons, he lugs out Adams' biting statement. It has a special appeal for two reasons. First, nobody can question the fact that its author was an authority upon taste, refinement, and intellectual elevation. All the Adamses were, and particularly the fourth-generation Adamses: Henry, Brooks, and Charles Francis, Jr. When they spoke, no dogs barked. In the second place, Charles Francis had been a businessman himself and really knew the breed. After giving up law, he was for six years head of the Union Pacific Railroad—before being ousted by another businessman. He thus had the honor, as he later ostensibly considered it, of having failed in business. He could speak of "mere money-getters and traders," of their "low instincts," their lack of "humor, thought, or refinement," and their "essentially unattractive and uninteresting" personalities as a man who *knew:* he had been in the midst of this repellent herd.

It is true that some people might suggest that Charles Francis Adams, Jr., would really have been less mordant about the vulgarity, illiteracy, and dullness of businessmen if he had himself succeeded in their field. He was ejected from the presidency of the Union Pacific by Jay Gould, certainly not a high type of business leader. This must have been rather humiliating, especially as Jay Gould accompanied the ejection with some caustic remarks about Adams' lack of talent and vision. But any such suggestion would be unfair. Adams had great ability—even high intellectual distinction; his books, ranging from his *Three Episodes of Massachusetts History* to his biography of Richard Henry Dana, amply prove that. He was, in fact, one of the abler men of his day—the years between 1875 and 1915—in America.

240

century only that? A distinguished historian says no—most emphatically

A more cogent criticism of Adams' rough and cynical verdict upon businessmen might be ventured: that after the family's cross-grained wont, he was rough and cynical about everything and everybody, a veritable Thersites. "I never was sympathetic or popular," he said of his position as a citizen of Quincy, Massachusetts, and we have abundant evidence to support the statement. Again, he once wrote his English friend Cecil Spring-Rice: "My dear fellow, I'm a crank; very few human beings can endure to have me near them. . . ."

But we would be unwise to base any discount of Adams' statement upon the innate moroseness of the Adams tribe. Even a morose man may often hit the nail squarely on the head, and be as right in some diatribes as the cantankerous Thomas Carlyle, or the bumptious H. L. Mencken. Moreover, the critical essayists who quote Adams on businessmen, and who will keep on quoting him, so that his judgment becomes a grand national stereotype about business crassness, will not stop to recall that he made similar remarks about politicians, generals, college professors, writers, lawyers, Negroes, and Abraham Lincoln (about whom he was peculiarly nasty); they will quote him simply as an experienced authority and keen observer, bearing a much-honored name. The attack must either be met directly, or accepted as valid. We must agree that the typical American business leader, the "big" man, was a mere money-getter, a creature of low instincts, without humor, thought, or refinement, and of essentially unattractive and uninteresting personality, or we must prove the opposite.

Proof in any such matter is difficult to furnish, for reasons which we can best illustrate by imagining a conversation between Mr. Adams and one of the great business chieftains of his day. Any reasonable conversation, founded on a thorough knowledge of the two men, will do, for it will show what a complex problem in human communication is involved. Knowing Mr. Adams' mind and experience well, and being thoroughly conversant with the mind and experience of Mr. John D. Rockefeller, I may venture to present the sort of dialogue in which the two might well have joined early in the year 1890. Let us say that, waiting for trains in Philadelphia—Adams going east to Boston, Rockefeller going west to Cleveland—they met by chance in the parlor of an exclusive hotel. They would bow to each other.

CHARLES FRANCIS ADAMS [*short but military-looking*]: I have heard much of you, Mr. Rockefeller, from my friend James Ford Rhodes, who thinks you a man of remarkable discernment and power. Did you know that Mr. Rhodes is working on a large history of the Civil War?

JOHN D. ROCKEFELLER [*quiet and reserved, but briskly incisive*]: I knew Mr. Rhodes well when he was in the iron ore and lake shipping business in Cleveland, and admired his abilities. Since he went east I have not kept in touch with his activities. Is he really wise in taking up history?

MR. ADAMS [*seeing he must try a new tack*]: The year just past, 1889, was one of unusual interest. Everyone will agree that its most important event was the replacement of President

241

Cleveland by President-elect Harrison. For myself, I regard that as unfortunate; I had hoped to see Grover Cleveland carry on his reforms and reduce the tariff.

MR. ROCKEFELLER: I know that you are a mugwump, Mr. Adams. Time will show whether the change is unfortunate. But I do not agree that this was the most important event of the year. For myself, I think that the sudden reappearance of Russia as a tremendous exporter of petroleum, and a rival threatening our American oil industry in half the markets of the world, was the most important event of the year. When I think of her vast extent, her resources, and her concentrated power, I dread Russia.

MR. ADAMS: Russia seems far away to me, and whatever her inroads in the oil market, I think we can leave her to her European neighbors. What I fear is a period of reaction here at home. When I was young, my father was a political reformer, and I knew such men as Charles Sumner and William H. Seward well. Do you take an interest in politics, Mr. Rockefeller?

MR. ROCKEFELLER [*showing irritation*]: The politician I know best is Mark Hanna. He and I were in Cleveland High School together, and we became fast friends. Once, when a bigger boy tried to bully me, Mark was on him like a tiger, and gave him the thrashing of his life. Mark is a practical man, and knows business interests well. But I dare say you would not call him a reformer, Mr. Adams?

MR. ADAMS [*curtly*]: Far from it. A very practical man indeed. [*Sees a new tack is needed again.*] You must have been in the Cleveland high school about the time I was in a Boston secondary school. I went on to Harvard—a family tradition. And you?

MR. ROCKEFELLER [*crisply*]: Went into business. I wished to go to college, but there was no time and no money—much less family tradition. However, I have given a great deal of attention this last year to establishing a new university.

MR. ADAMS: A new university? Well, the East needs some new universities, well officered, nondenominational, with money behind them.

MR. ROCKEFELLER [*himself curt*]: This will be in the West—Chicago. And it will be Baptist—the Baptist Educational Board is advising me.

MR. ADAMS [*horrified*]: Chicago? And a Baptist backing?

MR. ROCKEFELLER [*decisively*]: Yes, Chicago, out by the stockyards. And Baptist, with a Baptist minister, William Rainey Harper, for president; a truly great educator.

MR. ADAMS [*wearily trying a third tack*]: Do you happen to have read William Dean Howells' latest novel? I enjoyed his *Rise of Silas Lapham*. A wonderful picture of one of our business vulgarians [*checks himself*] business leaders, with a special ethical problem.

MR. ROCKEFELLER [*defensively*]: I have scant time for novels, Mr. Adams. In fact, the last novel I read was Lew Wallace's *Ben Hur*. A wonderful book; I couldn't put it down. Is Howells' as gripping as that?

PORTER [*entering center*]: Your trains are almost due, gentlemen.

ADAMS [*exit right*]: The dullest, most ignorant person I ever met!

ROCKEFELLER [*exit left*]: The slowest, stupidest fellow I've seen in years!

As this conversation, or any like it, will reveal, two remarkable men can so totally misunderstand each other that neither sees his companion's remarkable traits. Who is to say that a man is cultivated, literate, or interesting, until we agree on definitions of cultivation, literacy, and interest? The Nobel prize winner in science at Berkeley may think the Harvard classicist abysmally dull and uneducated; a sports editor of the *New York Times* may be bored stiff by the prospect of meeting a Chicago sociologist at dinner. What Charles Lamb called "imperfect sympathies" inevitably play a part in assessments of cultivation, or manners.

One main rebuttal to be brought against Charles Francis Adams' indictment is that it revealed in him an unbecoming and even untenable narrowness. Had he been more tolerant, versatile, and curious, he might have found any businessman fascinating. We do not possess much reliable evidence on the question of whether Carnegie, J. P. Morgan, Sr., E. H. Harriman, John D. Rockefeller, or Henry Ford were "sparkling" conversationalists; what evidence we have suggests a quieter adjective. But they certainly had much to say; and if we heard that Mr. John Doe had sat down with one of them for an hour and had a dull time, we could well suspect that the fault lay with John Doe.

Nevertheless, even allowing for Adams' imperfect sympathies, and for a certain condescension justifiable in a man whose ancestors included two Presidents, whose father had come near nomination for the post, who himself had led a regiment in the Civil War, and who had known almost everybody worth knowing in America and Britain —even allowing for this—the central question remains: Were the great business captains really men of "low instincts," "mere money-getters and traders," without "humor, thought, or refinement," and "essentially unattractive and uninteresting"? We know that Adams thought them unattractive. So, doubtless, did many other people. But on the question of low instincts, submergence in mere money-accumulation, and lack of thought and refinement, more objective tests are available. We need not confine ourselves to subjective judgments.

We open Andrew Carnegie's *Autobiography*, a book which the distinguished art historian John C. Van Dyke felt honored to help him polish for publication, and we read his account of the day when his native town of Dunfermline in Scotland conferred its Freedom upon him. It was "the greatest honor I ever received," he says. And he adds: "I was overwhelmed. Only two signatures upon the roll came between mine and Sir Walter Scott's, who had been made a Burgess." Was there no refinement in the man whose eyes filled with tears as he saw his signature stand beside Sir Walter

Scott's? We read further Carnegie's record of the sequel of his sale of his steel company, and his assumption of the task of disposing of his surplus. He writes:

One day my eyes happened to see a line in that most valuable paper, the *Scottish-American,* in which I had found many gems. This was the line: "The gods send thread for a web begun."

It seemed almost as if it had been sent directly to me. This sank into my heart, and I resolved to begin at once my first web. True enough, the gods sent thread in the proper form. Dr. J. S. Billings, of the New York Public Libraries, came as their agent, and of dollars, five and a quarter millions went at one stroke for sixty-eight branch libraries, promised for New York City. Twenty more libraries for Brooklyn followed.

My father . . . had been one of the five pioneers in Dunfermline who combined and gave access to their few books to their less fortunate neighbors. I had followed in his footsteps by giving my native town a library—its foundation stone laid by my mother—so that this public library was really my first gift. It was followed by giving a public library and hall to Allegheny City, our first home in America. President Harrison kindly accompanied me from Washington and opened these buildings. Soon after this, Pittsburgh asked for a library, which was given. This developed, in due course, into a group of buildings embracing a museum, a picture gallery, technical schools, and the Margaret Morrison School for Young Women.

This is noteworthy not for its record of money-giving, which nowadays seems commonplace enough, but for a certain note of refinement in Carnegie's mention of his debt to the *Scottish-American,* in his filial devotion to his father's memory and to his mother, Margaret Morrison, and in his evident pride in association with the great librarian, surgeon, and educator, John Shaw Billings, and with President Harrison. Elsewhere he betrays the same pride in his friendship with the British author and statesman John Morley, for whom he bought Lord Acton's library; with Matthew Arnold; with "my dear, dear friend, Richard Watson Gilder," the cultivated editor who wrote a poem that led Carnegie to establish his Hero Fund; and with John Burroughs and Mark Twain. He was proud that when he made up the list of trustees for the Carnegie Institution, headed by John Hay, Elihu Root, and "my old friend," the reformer-industrialist Abram S. Hewitt, and showed it to Theodore Roosevelt, the President commented: "You could not duplicate it." Not even Charles Francis Adams would have dared suggest that the men on that list valued Carnegie for his wealth. They valued him for higher reasons, and they found him attractive, interesting, and elevated, as Lord Morley declared years after Carnegie's death:

His extraordinary freshness of spirit easily carried Arnold, Herbert Spencer, myself, and afterwards many others, high

over an occasional crudity or haste in judgment such as befalls the best of us in ardent hours. People with a genius for picking up pins made as much as they liked of this: it was wiser to do justice to his spacious feel for the great objects of the world—for knowledge and its spread, invention, light, improvement of social relations, equal chances to the talents, the passion for peace. These are glorious things; a touch of exaggeration in expression is easy to set right.

Rockefeller had no such genius for friendship as Carnegie; and whereas Carnegie became intimate with authors and statesmen, he was content with the company of ministers, missionaries, educators, and experts in medicine and welfare work. But his parlors on West 54th Street in New York City were filled with them. Rockefeller was far less versatile than Carnegie, but far more gifted in foresight and organizing power; he was much less social and genial, but had a keener sense of humor; he was less an extrovert and individualist, but more efficient in devising co-operative undertakings. He was never for a moment dull or uninteresting to those who approached him cordially, and colorful tributes to his personal gifts were frequent. Not refinement, but something rather better, shines in this passage from his *Reminiscences,* as he describes the exhilarations of—what? Not of money-getting, but of begging for a cause:

When I was but seventeen or eighteen I was elected as a trustee in the church. It was a mission branch, and occasionally I had to hear members who belonged to the main body speak of the mission as though it were not quite as good as the big mother church. This strengthened our resolve to show them that we could paddle our own canoe.

Our first church was not a very grand affair, and there was a mortgage of $2,000 on it which had been a dispiriting influence for years. The holder of the mortgage had long demanded that he should be paid, but somehow even the interest was barely kept up. . . . The matter came to a head one Sunday morning, when the minister announced from the pulpit that the $2,000 would have to be raised, or we should lose our church building. I therefore found myself at the door of the church as the congregation came and went.

As each member came by, I buttonholed him, and got him to promise to give something toward extinguishing that debt. I pleaded and urged, and almost threatened. As each one promised, I put his name and the amount down in my little book, and continued to solicit from every possible subscriber. The campaign for raising the money which started that morning after church, lasted for several months. It was a great undertaking to raise such a sum of money in small amounts ranging from a few cents to the more magnificent promise of gifts to be paid at the rate of twenty-five or fifty cents a week. The plan absorbed me. I contributed what *I* could, and my first ambition to earn more money was aroused by this and similar undertakings in which I was constantly engaged.

But at last the $2,000 was all in hand.

Of J. Pierpont Morgan a great deal could be and has been said in criticism; but nobody ever had the hardihood to suggest that he was uninteresting. Nor could anyone who talked with him of his student days at Göttingen, or who watched him preside over the trustees of the Metropolitan Museum of Art, or who bid against him for a first edition of Milton's *Lycidas* or Shelley's *Epipsychidion,* have dared term him uncultivated or unrefined. He could talk as intelligently of French tapestries as of Wall Street. J. P. Morgan, Jr., who augmented his father's library and dedicated it to research, was an almost equally striking and impressive servant of learning.

Perhaps a greater genius burned in E. H. Harriman; if he exhibited less organizing ability than Rockefeller and less acumen than Carnegie, he had a Napoleonic fire which they lacked. Everyone who has studied the tremendous work he so swiftly accomplished in reorganizing the Illinois Central, the Union Pacific, and other railroads agrees that he brought to his problem an intellectual flash that was unique. He saw all the ramifications of a complex situation in a glance. Californians will not forget how he saved the Imperial Valley when the Colorado River, changing its course and pouring into the Salton basin, threatened its destruction; nor the fact that after the San Francisco earthquake and fire he hauled 224,000 refugees out of the city and brought in 1,600 carloads of supplies without charging a penny.

A man of low instincts, uninteresting and unattractive? The great dream of his later years was an around-the-world transportation system, and to that end he tried to achieve partial control of the South Manchuria Railway, and adumbrated a scheme for a 1,200-mile railroad crossing the Gobi Desert by the old caravan route. C. Hart Merriam, then Chief of the United States Biological Survey, tells us that nobody was a more enlightening conversationalist, for his talk "covered an amazing range of subjects, while his active mind showed a philosophic grasp of many of the problems that disturb our political and industrial worlds." But it is fitting that the warmest praise of Harriman's constructive energies should have come from a citizen of the state he benefited most, California—from old "John of the Mountains," the naturalist John Muir. In a little booklet published after Harriman's death, John Muir, an idealist if one ever lived, wrote that he was a *builder.*

He fairly reveled in heavy dynamical work and went about it naturally and unweariedly like glaciers making landscapes—cutting canyons through ridges, carrying off hills, laying rails and bridges over lakes and rivers, mountains and plains, making the nation's ways straight and smooth and safe. He seemed to regard the whole continent as his farm and all the people as partners, stirring millions of workers into useful action, plowing, sowing, irrigating, mining, building cities and factories, farms and homes. . . .

Ah, yes! defenders of Charles Francis Adams' much-quoted passage will say; this is all very true of Carnegie and Rockefeller, Morgan and Harriman. They were leaders of consummate talents and strength, moving in the largest sphere of action, stimulated by the most dynamic forces of national life. Naturally they took on bigness. But Adams was thinking of businessmen of secondary and tertiary rank, the Jay Goulds who wrecked railroads, the Collis P. Huntingtons who manipulated legislatures, the William A. Clarks who bought their way into the Senate, the Henry Clay Fricks who ground the face of labor into the dust. Surely all would agree that *they* were vulgar money-grubbers, uncultivated, uninteresting, and uninspiring. And in part we must agree. But for every business leader whose career supports Charles Francis Adams' indictment, it is easy to identify ten of his time who do not.

It is plain that in his own special group of transportation executives, Charles Francis Adams did not know, or at least know well, Daniel Willard of the Baltimore & Ohio. Adams was head of the Union Pacific for six years; Willard was head of his road nearly thirty-two years. He began his career as a laborer on the Vermont Central, and worked his way up. In the First World War he was chairman of the War Industries Board. Near the close of the war, Pershing chose him to reorganize the French railway system. His influence with Congress, unapproached by that of any other railroad president, was largely responsible for the passage of the Transportation Act of 1920. In Baltimore he became chairman of the board of trustees of Johns Hopkins University, and a member of the board of the Municipal Art Society. He was one of the Board of Visitors of the Naval Academy. He relaxed with books and music; and, writes President R. W. Brown of the Reading Company, "he always looked more like a college professor than a railroad man. All of us remember the neatness and perfection of his dress—the well-known derby hat and umbrella, and always: *books.*"

One railroad builder and industrialist of his own era that Adams must have known well was Henry Villard. While he does not mention the man in his memoirs, it was impossible for him not to know Villard. It is not enough to say that Villard completed the Northern Pacific Railroad, anticipated James J. Hill in a massive campaign to stimulate immigration to the Northwest—he established 831 local immigration agents in Great Britain, and 124 on the Continent—and that he later helped organize the Edison General Electric Company. This son-in-law of William Lloyd Garrison became owner of the New York *Evening Post* and the *Nation,* giving the editors complete freedom; he paid the debts of the struggling University of Oregon when it was about to go under in 1883, and supported it for two ensuing years of legislative default. He wrote one of the best books of Civil War memoirs; he made important gifts to Harvard and Columbia. Villard, too, was assailed for certain transactions; but it would be preposterous to call this fine champion of many causes in political and social progress narrow, low, unrefined, or uninteresting.

If Adams had been looking for a truly typical businessman of secondary rank in his own transportation field, he might well have lighted upon that fellow Yankee Asa Packer. Leaving a Connecticut farm, Packer arrived at seventeen in Susquehanna County, Pennsylvania, and set to work as a carpenter and joiner. For ten years he lived in a cabin of his own construction so that he could save money to buy a canal boat and begin transporting coal from Mauch Chunk to Philadelphia. He became chief builder of the Lehigh Valley Railroad. Having made a fortune as president of that line, and having broadened his outlook by sitting in Congress, Judge Packer, as one of the original directors of the Bethlehem Iron Company, was struck by the fact that science was revolutionizing industry. Problems of metallurgy, chemistry, and engineering as well as economics challenged young men to master new complexities of science. To help meet the challenge he established Lehigh University, saw it well launched, and at his death left it nearly all of those accumulations that he did not give to the Episcopal Church.

Among his Massachusetts contemporaries, Adams must have heard all about the Chickerings. The first Chickering, son of a blacksmith, was a shy, retiring man who perfected the iron frame for pianos, made many of the best instruments in the country, and became president of the Handel and Haydn Society in Boston. His two sons, carrying on the business, were diligent promoters of musical taste in America.

It would be interesting to know just what comment would have been made upon Adams' assertions by still another son of Massachusetts, who left Amherst College to go to New York: Henry C. Folger. Beginning as a clerk, he rose to be head of Standard Oil of New York. But in college he had been deeply influenced by Emerson, and particularly by Emerson's "Remarks at the Celebration of the 300th Anniversary of the Birth of William Shakespeare." He became an enthusiastic

This cartoon, by the Chicago Tribune's Carey Orr, comments on John D. Rockefeller's vast philanthropies. When he died at the age of 97, he had given away some $550,000,000.

student of Shakespeare and an expert on the vast Shakespeare bibliography. Aided by his wife, a Vassar graduate, he began quietly gathering books until he had an almost unrivalled collection of rarities. For obvious reasons, the British knew more about it than the Americans, and placed tremendous pressure on him to give it to Stratford on Avon. No, he declared, he wished to "help make the United States a center for literary study and progress." In 1928 he quietly announced that he would erect a library for Shakespearean studies in Washington. He then had more than eighty of the 200-odd existing copies of the First Folio, and some 70,000 volumes besides. This has been called the "most munificent gift ever made for the study of literature," a statement that can be challenged only by admirers of another public-spirited businessman, the public transit magnate who founded the much more distinguished Henry E. Huntington Library on the Pacific Coast.

It may be objected that even the great business leaders who founded universities and scattered libraries over the land were not themselves deeply interested in literature, art, or science. Such criticism, however, is not merely shallow, but ignorant. The titans of industry were tremendously busy men, but they used their pitiful leisure time about as well as Presidents and governors did. We may call Collis Huntington's habit of keeping a five-volume set of George Crabbe's

245

poems on his desk and reading in it by snatches an eccentricity, but it was the right kind of eccentricity.

Was there any lack of versatility in the zeal with which Leland Stanford established the great university that bears his name? Or maintained and improved extensive vineyards; bred, trained, and ran fine racing horses, meanwhile raising the equine standard for all California; and made himself a pioneer in the use of instantaneous photography to study the movements of his steeds and other animals? As for Andrew Mellon, a harsh critic might dismiss his magnificent art collection, the heart of our National Gallery, as mere ostentation. But not even the neo-muckraker could shrug off his finely creative passion for the beautification of the national capital, his zeal in giving substance to the Burnham-McKim-Olmsted-Saint-Gaudens plan of 1901, and his role in making Washington one of the most beautiful cities in the world.

Let history take Charles Francis Adams' statement about the tycoons, their "low instincts," lack of "humor, thought, or refinement," and "essentially unattractive and uninteresting" personalities, fold it in an expired bond of the Union Pacific with a sprig of withered rosemary on top, and bury it—where? Under Asa Packer's Lehigh University, or John D. Rockefeller's University of Chicago, or Henry Folger's Shakespeare Library; anywhere, just so history buries it! The question is not why Adams made these assertions, for he liked in his atrabilious way to flutter the dovecotes. The real puzzle is why so many people, including economists, political scientists, and historians, have accepted and repeated the assertions, converting them into a stereotype. Yet it is perhaps not a puzzle after all. Part of the acceptance has been grounded upon ignorance of the real nature of industrialism in this country, its demands upon ability and character, and its achievements. Altogether too little sound industrial history has been written in readable terms. Then, too, many people are consciously or subconsciously envious of the rich man, and prone to discharge that envy in an attitude of intellectual superiority. They say, quite correctly, that American society is too materialistic, and are hence ready, quite incorrectly, to believe most rich men crassly ignoble.

Finally, of course, stereotypes are restful; they save everybody the pain of thinking.

One final observation may have special pertinence. The major industrialists and financiers of the country have sometimes, especially in recent years, played a special role in the shaping of opinion. Far from being mere money-grubbers, they have more and more often been men of large outlook, who profited from their familiarity with the complex forces controlling production, transportation, and investment.

Not only has immersion in large domestic affairs made their judgments and influence valuable, but they have often possessed an international experience that men of lower range have lacked. Walter Lippmann recently remarked, "For a long time, for most of this century, there has been a large divergence inside the business world and inside the Republican party on questions of provincialism and parochialism as against nationalism and internationalism"; and he added that internationalism is championed by "the bigger industrialists and bankers in the big cities, the businessmen who have had a wider experience at home and abroad." To some extent this was true of the greater industrialists and financiers of the nineteenth century as well. The issues did not present themselves in the shape they later assumed, but these men tended to bring a world vision into the restricted American sphere. Andrew Carnegie, who endowed the Hague World Court and a foundation for international peace, was an internationalist; so was John D. Rockefeller, whose business was world-wide, who built the New Bodleian Library and restored Rheims Cathedral, and one of whose foundations stamped out yellow fever around the globe; so was J. P. Morgan, who took risks as the Anglo-French financier in the First World War that he would not have taken had he not felt the deepest affection for England and France; and so was Henry Ford, who established manufacturing plants of huge magnitude in Windsor, Ontario, and Dagenham, England, and lesser factories in France and Germany. This aspect of the minds of our "big" industrialists ought not to be overlooked. Many of them saw further in advance of their time than Charles Francis Adams, Jr., did, or than their other critics ever peered.

THE MEMOIRS OF
FREDERICK T. GATES

My intimate, confidential relationships with Mr. John D. Rockefeller in New York City began in September, 1891.

Up to 1902, when we sold out Mr. Rockefeller's great iron mining and transportation companies, my time and energy had been so engrossed with Mr. Rockefeller's business interests and current benevolence as to leave me little time for the working out of any plans of world benefaction.

I did, indeed, use my leisure in reading and study, and perhaps I could not have hastened matters much even if I had been more free. I was studying civilization, its origin and history, trying to analyze it, separate it into its elements, and find out as best I might in what human progress really consists and in what ways progress is to be promoted.

For the study of world philanthropies, Mr. Rockefeller's office was an excellent laboratory. For we received appeals daily from every sort of agency of human progress and well-being, not only in the United States but in all civilized foreign lands. Not only so, but we were favored with the views and often the elaborate plans of distinguished social reformers and dreamers the world over. These letters and appeals passed through my hands and it was my duty to study them, to inquire about them, to reflect on them, and to encourage such of them as I thought worthy by favorable report to Mr. Rockefeller.

Along with these studies and reflections I was confronted with Mr. Rockefeller's fortune. He continued, as do all men, in the habits and feelings of earlier life. He did not seem to realize, as I sometimes thought, the immensity of his fortune. He was a born money-maker, and a born money-saver. But even had it not been so, even if he had become alarmed at his colossal and every year more colossal accumulation, it was no longer in his power, from the time I first knew him, to prevent or hinder the incoming flood.

And what oppressed me was not merely that Mr. Rockefeller was being inundated with money. I trembled as I witnessed the unreasoning popular resentment at Mr. Rockefeller's riches, to the mass of the people a national menace.

It was not, however, the unreasoning public prejudice against Mr. Rockefeller but what was to be the destiny of his vast fortune that chiefly troubled me.

Was it to be handed on to posterity as other great fortunes have been handed down by their possessors, with scandalous results to their descendants and powerful tendencies to social demoralization? I saw no other course but for Mr. Rockefeller and his son to form a series of great corporate philanthropies for forwarding civilization in all its elements in this land and in all lands; philanthropies, if possible, limitless in time and amount, broad in scope, and self-perpetuating.

I knew very well that Mr. Rockefeller's mind would not work on mere abstract theories. He required concrete practical suggestions and I set about framing them.

It was not until 1905 that I ventured with many misgivings to approach Mr. Rockefeller with the question of the use and disposition to be made of his fortune. It might be urged that I was trespassing on a domain in which I had no proper business. But to myself it was very intimately my business, for I had come clearly to see that unless Mr. Rockefeller were to make some such disposition of his fortune, or a great part of it, my life was doing more harm than good.

So at last I broke my silence. The Rockefeller philanthropies have become world-wide and world-famous for their efficiency. If I were asked to make an estimate of the aggregate benefactions to date of the two Rockefellers—father and son—I could not venture a guess of less than a thousand million dollars, and under the present direction of Mr. John D. Rockefeller, Jr., and his great and varied staff, the outflow of annual benefaction is ever broadening and enlarging.

A study of the Rockefeller benefactions will show that they form a comprehensive and carefully studied plan, comprising quite precisely the elements of civilization as analyzed by distinguished authors. Professor William C. Morey, for illustration, in his summary of the elements of civilization reduced them to six. These consisted of progress in (1) the Means of Subsistence; (2) Government and Law; (3) Language and Literature; (4) Philosophy and Science; (5) Art and Refinement; (6) Morality and Religion. To these I venture to add two more. They are (7) Health and Hygiene; and (8) Reproduction and Eugenics. The Rockefeller philanthropies at home and abroad will be found to fall quite consciously and precisely into these eight categories of civilization.

EPITAPH
for the STEEL MASTER

Who dies rich, dies disgraced, said Andrew Carnegie.

An economist re-examines his brash

career in the light of that noble philosophy

By ROBERT L. HEILBRONER

Toward the end of his days, at the close of World War I, Andrew Carnegie was already a kind of national legend. His meteoric rise, the scandals and successes of his industrial generalship—all this was blurred into nostalgic memory. What was left was a small, rather feeble man with a white beard and pale, penetrating eyes, who could occasionally be seen puttering around his mansion on upper Fifth Avenue, a benevolent old gentleman who still rated an annual birthday interview but was even then a venerable relic of a fast-disappearing era. Carnegie himself looked back on his career with a certain savored incredulity. "How much did you say I had given away, Poynton?" he would inquire of his private secretary; "$324,657,399" was the answer. "Good Heaven!" Carnegie would exclaim. "Where did I ever get all that money?"

Where he *had* got all that money was indeed a legendary story, for even in an age known for its acquisitive triumphs, Carnegie's touch had been an extraordinary one. He had begun, in true Horatio Alger fashion, at the bottom; he had ended, in a manner that put the wildest of Alger's novels to shame, at the very pinnacle of success. At the close of his great deal with J. P. Morgan in 1901, when the Carnegie steel empire was sold to form the core of the new United States Steel Company, the banker had extended his hand and delivered the ultimate encomium of the times:

"Mr. Carnegie," he said, "I want to congratulate you on being the richest man in the world."

It was certainly as "the richest man in the world" that Carnegie attracted the attention of his contemporaries. Yet this is hardly why we look back on him with interest today. As an enormous money-maker Carnegie was a flashy, but hardly a profound, hero of the times; and the attitudes of Earnestness and Self-Assurance, so engaging in the young immigrant, become irritating when they are congealed in the millionaire. But what lifts Carnegie's life above the rut of a one-dimensional success story is an aspect of which his contemporaries were relatively unaware.

Going through his papers after his death, Carnegie's executors came across a memorandum that he had written to himself fifty years before, carefully preserved in a little yellow box of keepsakes and mementos. It brings us back to December, 1868, when Carnegie, a young man flushed with the first taste of great success, retired to his suite in the opulent Hotel St. Nicholas in New York, to tot up his profits for the year. It had been a tremendous year and the calculation must have been extremely pleasurable. Yet this is what he wrote as he reflected on the figures:

Thirty-three and an income of $50,000 per annum! By this time two years I can so arrange all my business as to secure at least $50,000 per annum. Beyond this never earn—make no effort to increase fortune, but spend the surplus each year for benevolent purposes. Cast aside business forever, except for others.

Settle in Oxford and get a thorough education, making the acquaintance of literary men—this will take three years of active work—pay especial attention to speaking in public. Settle then in London and purchase a controlling interest in some newspaper or live review and give the general management of it attention, taking part in public matters, especially those connected with education and improvement of the poorer classes.

Man must have an idol—the amassing of wealth is one of the worst species of idolatry—no idol more debasing than the worship of money. Whatever I engage in I must push inordinately; therefore should I be careful to choose that life which will be the most elevating in its character. To continue much longer overwhelmed by business cares and with most of my thoughts wholly upon the way to make more money in the shortest time, must degrade me beyond hope of permanent recovery. I will resign business at thirty-five, but during the ensuing two years I wish to spend the afternoons in receiving instruction and in reading systematically.

It is a document which in more ways than one is Carnegie to the very life: brash, incredibly self-confident, chockablock with self-conscious virtue—and more than a little hypocritical. For the program so nobly outlined went largely unrealized. Instead of retiring in two years, Carnegie went on for thirty-three more; even then it was with considerable difficulty that he

was persuaded to quit. Far from shunning further money-making, he proceeded to roll up his fortune with an uninhibited drive that led one unfriendly biographer to characterize him as "the greediest little gentleman ever created." Certainly he was one of the most aggressive profit seekers of his time. Typically, when an associate jubilantly cabled: "No. 8 furnace broke all records today," Carnegie coldly replied, "What were the other furnaces doing?"

It is this contrast between his hopes and his performance that makes Carnegie interesting. For when we review his life, what we see is more than the career of another nineteenth-century acquisitor. We see the unequal struggle between a man who loved money—loved making it, having it, spending it—and a man who, at bottom, was ashamed of himself for his acquisitive desires. All during his lifetime, the money-maker seemed to win. But what lifts Carnegie's story out of the ordinary is that the other Carnegie ultimately triumphed. At his death public speculation placed the size of his estate at about five hundred million dollars. In fact it came to $22,881,575. Carnegie *had* become the richest man in the world—but something had also driven him to give away ninety per cent of his wealth.

Actually, his contemporaries knew of Carnegie's inquietude about money. In 1889, before he was world-famous, he had written an article for the *North American Review* entitled "The Gospel of Wealth"—an article that contained the startling phrase: "The man who dies thus rich dies disgraced." It was hardly surprising, however, if the world took these sentiments at a liberal discount: homiletic millionaires who preached the virtues of austerity were no novelty; Carnegie himself, returning in 1879 from a trip to the miseries of India, had been able to write with perfect sincerity, "How very little the millionaire has beyond the peasant, and how very often his additions tend not to happiness but to misery."

What the world may well have underestimated, however, was a concern more deeply rooted than these pieties revealed. For, unlike so many of his self-made peers, who also rose from poverty, Carnegie was the product of a *radical* environment. The village of Dunfermline, Scotland, when he was born there in 1835, was renowned as a center of revolutionary ferment, and Carnegie's family was itself caught up in the radical movement of the times. His father was a regular speaker at the Chartist rallies, which were an almost daily occurrence in Dunfermline in the 1840's, and his uncle was an impassioned orator for the rights of the working class to vote and strike. All this made an indelible impression on Carnegie's childhood.

Steel—and the creation of a steelmaking empire—made Andrew Carnegie the richest man in the world, bridging the gap between the weaver's cottage in Dunfermline, Scotland, where he was born (below, left), and the castle of Skibo, with its battlements and heated swimming pool, which he built for his family on Dornoch Firth (below, right).

The commercial manufacture of steel was made possible in the 1860's by the Bessemer process, in which air forced through molten iron emerges in tall flames and showering sparks. The drama of it appealed to Carnegie, as it did to Aaron Bohrod, who painted The Big Blow *(above) at Weirton, West Virginia, for the National Steel Corporation.*

"I remember as if it were yesterday," he wrote seventy years later, "being awakened during the night by a tap at the back window by men who had come to inform my parents that my uncle, Bailie Morrison, had been thrown in jail because he dared to hold a meeting which had been forbidden . . . It is not to be wondered at that, nursed amid such surroundings, I developed into a violent young Republican whose motto was 'death to privilege.'"

From another uncle, George Lauder, Carnegie absorbed a second passion that was also to reveal itself in his later career. This was his love of poetry, first that of the poet Burns, with its overtones of romantic egalitarianism, and then later, of Shakespeare. Immense quantities of both were not only committed to memory, but made into an integral—indeed, sometimes an embarrassingly evident—part of his life: on first visiting the Doge's palace in Venice he thrust a companion in the ducal throne and held him pinioned there while he orated the appropriate speeches from *Othello*. Once, seeing Vanderbilt walking on Fifth Avenue, Carnegie smugly remarked, "I would not exchange his millions for my knowledge of Shakespeare."

But it was more than just a love of poetry that remained with Carnegie. Virtually alone among his fellow acquisitors, he was driven by a genuine respect for the power of thought to seek answers for questions that never even occurred to them. Later, when he "discovered" Herbert Spencer, the English sociologist, Carnegie wrote to him, addressing him as "Master," and it was as "Master" that Spencer remained, even after Carnegie's lavishness had left Spencer very much in his debt.

But Carnegie's early life was shaped by currents more material than intellectual. The grinding process of industrial change had begun slowly but ineluctably to undermine the cottage weaving that was the traditional means of employment in Dunfermline. The Industrial Revolution, in the shape of new steam mills, was forcing out the hand weavers, and one by one the looms which constituted the entire capital of the Carnegie family had to be sold. Carnegie never forgot the shock of his father returning home to tell him, in despair, "Andra, I can get nae mair work."

A family council of war was held, and it was decided that there was only one possible course—they must try their luck in America, to which two sisters of Carnegie's mother, Margaret, had already emigrated. With the aid of a few friends the money for the crossing was scraped together, and at thirteen Andrew found himself transported to the only country in which his career would have been possible.

It hardly got off to an auspicious start, however. The family made their way to Allegheny, Pennsyl-

251

vania, a raw and bustling town where Carnegie's father again sought work as an independent weaver. But it was as hopeless to compete against the great mills in America as in Scotland, and soon father and son were forced to seek work in the local cotton mills. There Andrew worked from six in the morning until six at night, making $1.20 as a bobbin boy.

After a while his father quit—factory work was impossible for the traditional small enterpriser—and Andrew got a "better" job with a new firm, tending an engine deep in a dungeon cellar and dipping newly made cotton spools in a vat of oil. Even the raise to $3 a week—and desperately conjured visions of Wallace and the Bruce—could not overcome the horrors of that lonely and foul-smelling basement. It was perhaps the only time in Carnegie's life when his self-assurance deserted him: to the end of his days the merest whiff of oil could make him deathly sick.

Yet he was certain, as he wrote home at sixteen, that "anyone could get along in this Country," and the rags-to-riches saga shortly began. The telegraph had just come to Pittsburgh, and one evening over a game of checkers, the manager of the local office informed Andrew's uncle that he was looking for a messenger. Andy got the job and, in true Alger fashion, set out to excel in it. Within a few weeks he had carefully memorized the names and the locations, not only of the main streets in Pittsburgh, but of the main firms, so that he was the quickest of all the messenger boys.

He came early and stayed late, watched the telegraphers at work, and at home at night learned the Morse code. As a result he was soon the head of the growing messenger service, and a skilled telegrapher himself. One day he dazzled the office by taking a message "by ear" instead of by the commonly used tape printer, and since he was then only the third operator in the country able to turn the trick, citizens used to drop into the office to watch Andy take down the words "hot from the wire."

One such citizen who was especially impressed with young Carnegie's determination was Thomas A. Scott, in time to become one of the colorful railway magnates of the West, but then the local superintendent of the Pennsylvania Railroad. Soon thereafter Carnegie became "Scott's Andy"—telegrapher, secretary, and general factotum—at thirty-five dollars a month. In his *Autobiography* Carnegie recalls an instance which enabled him to begin the next stage of his career.

One morning I reached the office and found that a serious accident on the Eastern Division had delayed the express passenger train westward, and that the passenger train eastward was proceeding with a flagman in advance at every curve. The freight trains in both directions were standing

A British Punch *cartoonist called this sketch of Carnegie "The Macmillion," in praise of a grant "Exemplifying his Gospel of Wealth."*

on the sidings. Mr. Scott was not to be found. Finally I could not resist the temptation to plunge in, take the responsibility, give "train orders" and set matters going. "Death or Westminster Abbey" flashed across my mind. I knew it was dismissal, disgrace, perhaps criminal punishment for me if I erred. On the other hand, I could bring in the wearied freight train men who had lain out all night. I knew I could. I knew just what to do, and so I began.

Signing Scott's name to the orders, Carnegie flashed out the necessary instructions to bring order out of the tangle. The trains moved; there were no mishaps. When Scott reached the office Carnegie told him what he had done. Scott said not a word but looked carefully over all that had taken place. After a little he moved away from Carnegie's desk to his own, and that was the end of it. "But I noticed," Carnegie concluded good-humoredly, "that he came in very regularly and in good time for some mornings after that."

It is hardly to be wondered at that Carnegie became Scott's favorite, his "white-haired Scotch devil." Impetuous but not rash, full of enthusiasm and good-natured charm, the small lad with his blunt, open features and his slight Scottish burr was every executive's dream of an assistant. Soon Scott repaid Andy for his services by introducing him to a new and very different kind of opportunity. He gave Carnegie the chance to subscribe to five hundred dollars' worth of Adams Express stock, a company which Scott assured Andy would prosper mightily.

Carnegie had not fifty dollars saved, much less five

But later there were skeptical comments, like this one by W. A. Rogers on Carnegie's statement that the trusts could be trusted, with the bitter title: "A Trustworthy Beast."

hundred, but it was a chance he could ill afford to miss. He reported the offer to his mother, and that pillar of the family unhesitatingly mortgaged their home to raise the necessary money. When the first dividend check came in, with its ornate Spencerian flourishes, Carnegie had something like a revelation. "I shall remember that check as long as I live," he subsequently wrote. "It gave me the first penny of revenue from capital—something that I had not worked for with the sweat of my brow. 'Eureka!' I cried, 'Here's the goose that lays the golden eggs.'" He was right; within a few years his investment in the Adams Express Company was paying annual dividends of $1,400.

It was not long thereafter that an even more propitious chance presented itself. Carnegie was riding on the Pennsylvania line one day when he was approached by a "farmer-looking" man carrying a small green bag in his hand. The other introduced himself as T. T. Woodruff and quite frankly said that he wanted a chance to talk with someone connected with the railroad. Whereupon he opened his bag and took out a small model of the first sleeping car.

Carnegie was immediately impressed with its possibilities, and he quickly arranged for Woodruff to meet Scott. When the latter agreed to give the cars a trial, Woodruff in appreciation offered Carnegie a chance to subscribe to a one-eighth interest in the new company. A local banker agreed to lend Andy the few hundred dollars needed for the initial payment—the rest being financed from dividends. Once again Andy had made a shrewd investment: within two years the

Woodruff Palace Car Company was paying him a return of more than $5,000 a year.

Investments now began to play an increasingly important role in Carnegie's career. Through his railroad contacts he came to recognize the possibilities in manufacturing the heavy equipment needed by the rapidly expanding lines, and soon he was instrumental in organizing companies to meet these needs. One of them, the Keystone Bridge Company, was the first successful manufacturer of iron railway bridges. Another, the Pittsburgh Locomotive Works, made engines. And most important of all, an interest in a local iron works run by an irascible German named Andrew Kloman brought Carnegie into actual contact with the manufacture of iron itself.

None of these new ventures required any substantial outlay of cash. His interest in the Keystone Bridge Company, for instance, which was to earn him $15,000 in 1868, came to him "in return for services rendered in its promotion"—services which Carnegie, as a young railroad executive, was then in a highly strategic position to deliver. Similarly the interest in the Kloman works reflected no contribution on Carnegie's part except that of being the human catalyst and buffer between some highly excitable participants.

By 1865 his "side" activities had become so important that he decided to leave the Pennsylvania Railroad. He was by then superintendent, Scott having moved up to a vice presidency, but his salary of $2,400 was already vastly overshadowed by his income from various ventures. One purchase alone—the Storey farm in Pennsylvania oil country, which Carnegie and a few associates picked up for $40,000—was eventually to pay the group a million dollars in dividends in *one* year. About this time a friend dropped in on Carnegie and asked him how he was doing. "Oh, I'm rich, I'm rich!" he exclaimed.

He was indeed embarked on the road to riches, and determined, as he later wrote in his *Autobiography,* that "nothing could be allowed to interfere for a moment with my business career." Hence it comes as a surprise to note that it was at this very point that Carnegie retired to his suite to write his curiously introspective and troubled thoughts about the pursuit of wealth. But the momentum of events was to prove far too strong for these moralistic doubts. Moving his headquarters to New York to promote his various interests, he soon found himself swept along by a succession of irresistible opportunities for money-making.

One of these took place quite by chance. Carnegie was trying to sell the Woodruff sleeping car at the same time that a formidable rival named George Pullman was also seeking to land contracts for his sleeping

car, and the railroads were naturally taking advantage of the competitive situation. One summer evening in 1869 Carnegie found himself mounting the resplendent marble stairway of the St. Nicholas Hotel side by side with his competitor.

"Good evening, Mr. Pullman," said Carnegie in his ebullient manner. Pullman was barely cordial.

"How strange we should meet here," Carnegie went on, to which the other replied nothing at all.

"Mr. Pullman," said Carnegie, after an embarrassing pause, "don't you think we are making nice fools of ourselves?" At this Pullman evinced a glimmer of interest: "What do you mean?" he inquired. Carnegie quickly pointed out that competition between the two companies was helping no one but the railroads. "Well," said Pullman, "what do you suggest we do?"

"Unite!" said Carnegie. "Let's make a joint proposition to the Union Pacific, your company and mine. Why not organize a new company to do it?" "What would you call it?" asked Pullman suspiciously. "The Pullman Palace Car Company," said Carnegie and with this shrewd psychological stroke won his point. A new company was formed, and in time Carnegie became its largest stockholder.

Meanwhile, events pushed Carnegie into yet another lucrative field. To finance the proliferating railway systems of America, British capital was badly needed, and with his Scottish ancestry, his verve, and his excellent railroad connections Carnegie was the natural choice for a go-between. His brief case stuffed with bonds and prospectuses, Carnegie became a transatlantic commuter, soon developing intimate relations both with great bankers like Junius Morgan (the father of J. P. Morgan), and with the heads of most of the great American roads. These trips earned him not only large commissions—exceeding on occasion $100,000 for a single turn—but even more important, established connections that were later to be of immense value. He himself later testified candidly on their benefits before a group of respectfully awed senators:

For instance, I want a great contract for rails. Sidney Dillon of the Union Pacific was a personal friend of mine. Huntington was a friend. Dear Butler Duncan, that called on me the other day, was a friend. Those and other men were presidents of railroads . . . Take Huntington; you know C. P. Huntington. He was hard up very often. He was a great man, but he had a great deal of paper out. I knew his things were good. When he wanted credit I gave it to him. If you help a man that way, what chance has any paid agent going to these men? It was absurd.

But his trips to England brought Carnegie something still more valuable. They gave him steel. It is fair to say that as late as 1872 Carnegie did not see the future that awaited him as the Steel King of the world. The still modest conglomeration of foundries and mills he was gradually assembling in the Allegheny and Monongahela valleys was but one of many business interests, and not one for which he envisioned any extraordinary future. Indeed, to repeated pleas that he lead the way in developing a steel industry for America by substituting steel for iron rails, his reply was succinct: "Pioneering don't pay."

What made him change his mind? The story goes that he was awe-struck by the volcanic, spectacular eruption of a Bessemer converter, which he saw for the first time during a visit to a British mill. It was precisely the sort of display that would have appealed to Carnegie's mind—a wild, demonic, physical process miraculously contained and controlled by the dwarfed figures of the steel men themselves. At any rate, overnight Carnegie became the perfervid prophet of steel. Jumping on the first available steamer, he rushed home with the cry, "The day of iron has passed!" To the consternation of his colleagues, the hitherto reluctant pioneer became an advocate of the most daring technological and business expansion; he joined them enthusiastically in forming Carnegie, McCandless & Company, which was the nucleus of the empire that the next thirty years would bring forth.

The actual process of growth involved every aspect of successful business enterprise of the times: acquisition and merger, pools and commercial piracy, and even, on one occasion, an outright fraud in selling the United States government overpriced and underdone steel armor plate. But it would be as foolish to maintain that the Carnegie empire grew by trickery as to deny that sharp practice had its place. Essentially what lay behind the spectacular expansion were three facts.

The first of these was the sheer economic expansion of the industry in the first days of burgeoning steel use. Everywhere steel replaced iron or found new uses —and not only in railroads but in ships, buildings, bridges, machinery of all sorts. As Henry Frick himself once remarked, if the Carnegie group had not filled the need for steel another would have. But it must be admitted that Carnegie's company did its job superlatively well. In 1885 Great Britain led the world in the production of steel. Fourteen years later her total output was 695,000 tons less than the output of the Carnegie Steel Company alone.

Charles Graham's 1886 drawing of the Bessemer process in action
Harper's Weekly, APRIL 10, 1886

Second was the brilliant assemblage of personal talent with which Carnegie surrounded himself. Among them, three in particular stood out. One was Captain William Jones, a Homeric figure who lumbered through the glowing fires and clanging machinery of the works like a kind of Paul Bunyan of steel, skilled at handling men, inventive in handling equipment, and enough of a natural artist to produce papers for the British Iron and Steel Institute that earned him a literary as well as a technical reputation. Then there was Henry Frick, himself a self-made millionaire, whose coke empire naturally complemented Carnegie's steelworks. When the two were amalgamated, Frick took over the active management of the whole, and under his forceful hand the annual output of the Carnegie works rose tenfold. Yet another was Charles Schwab, who came out of the tiny monastic town of Loretto, Pennsylvania, to take a job as a stake driver.

Six months later he had been promoted by Jones into the assistant managership of the Braddock plant.

These men, and a score like them, constituted the vital energy of the Carnegie works. As Carnegie himself said, "Take away all our money, our great works, ore mines and coke ovens, but leave our organization, and in four years I shall have re-established myself."

But the third factor in the growth of the empire was Carnegie himself. A master salesman and a skilled diplomat of business at its highest levels, Carnegie was also a ruthless driver of his men. He pitted his associates and subordinates in competition with one another until a feverish atmosphere pervaded the whole organization. "You cannot imagine the abounding sense of freedom and relief I experience as soon as I get on board a steamer and sail past Sandy Hook," he once said to Captain Jones. "My God!" replied Jones. "Think of the relief to us!"

"THE WORKS ARE NOT WORTH ONE DROP OF HUMAN BLOOD"

In his own time there raged about Andrew Carnegie, as about any man who pushes his head above the crowd, many a controversy. From the standpoint of his place in history, none is more important than the great strike that erupted at the Homestead, Pennsylvania, works of the Carnegie Steel Company in the summer of 1892.

Carnegie himself owned a controlling interest in the company, but when the strike broke in July he was, in accordance with his annual custom, on an extended vacation in Scotland. In charge at Homestead was Henry Clay Frick, the company's hard-driving, forty-one-year-old chairman. Frick's attitude toward labor unions was quite blunt: he was against them, and he was out to break the Amalgamated Association of Iron and Steel Workers, which represented the plant's skilled laborers.

Carnegie's labor views, like his attitude toward wealth, were not quite so simple. In two magazine articles in 1886 he had expressed pro-labor sentiments remarkable in a capitalist of his times; where strikebreaking was concerned (and it was to become a key issue in the Homestead strike) he had been particularly forthright: to the traditional Ten Commandments he had suggested adding an eleventh—"Thou shalt not take thy neighbor's job." Nevertheless, before leaving for Scotland in the spring of 1892 he sent Frick a notice to be posted at the works informing the men that after the expiration on July 1 of the existing agreement with the Amalgamated, the Carnegie Steel Company would be operated as a non-union shop.

The union had enrolled only about one-fifth of the workers at Homestead, and when contract negotiations broke down late in June, Frick adopted a tactic calculated to divide the unskilled majority from the organized elite: he declared he would close the mill on July 1 and reopen it on July 6 with non-union men. He surrounded the plant with a high board fence; he topped it with barbed wire, pierced it with portholes—for observation, he later claimed—and erected at strategic intervals platforms equipped with searchlights. To make sure he could fulfill his promise to reopen the works, he arranged secretly for three hundred armed Pinkerton guards to be brought up the Monongahela River from Pittsburgh in the early morning hours of July 6. Clearly, Frick was ready for a fight. But the workers stole a march on him. The unskilled majority, mostly illiterate immigrants, closed ranks with the union men against the company, seized the plant, and assumed control of the town as well.

The night of July 5–6 was foggy, and the Pinkertons headed upriver silently in two covered barges. Union sentries on the bank were not deceived, however, and when the barges tied up at the company wharf at 4 A.M., the strikers were ready for them. At once, gunfire broke out. Early in the fray the tug that had towed the barges steamed away, leaving the Pinkertons stranded at the dock. All day—with dynamite bombs, a small brass cannon, and even oil thrown on the water and set afire—the strikers sought to overwhelm the invaders (right). Finally the Pinkertons surrendered and were permitted to leave Homestead on a train, after being forced to run a gantlet of screaming, rock-throwing, club-wielding workers and their wives. Three Pinkertons and ten strikers had been killed, some thirty Pinkertons and an unknown number of strikers wounded. On July 12 the Pennsylvania National Guard arrived to restore order, and by the fifteenth Frick was able to reopen the mill. Strikebreakers were brought in (eventually about

But Carnegie could win loyalties as well. All his promising young men were given gratis ownership participations—minuscule fractions of one per cent, which were enough, however, to make them millionaires in their own right. Deeply grateful to Jones, Carnegie once offered him a similar participation. Jones hemmed and hawed and finally refused; he would be unable to work effectively with the men, he said, once he was a partner. Carnegie insisted that his contribution be recognized and asked Jones what he wanted. "Well," said the latter, "you might pay me a hell of a big salary." "We'll do it!" said Carnegie. "From this time forth you shall receive the same salary as the President of the United States." "Ah, Andy, that's the kind of talk," said Captain Bill.

Within three decades, on the flood tide of economic expansion, propelled by brilliant executive work and relentless pressure from Carnegie, the company made immense strides. "Such a magnificent aggregation of industrial power has never before been under the domination of a single man," reported a biographer in 1902, describing the Gargantuan structure of steel and coke and ore and transport. Had the writer known of the profits earned by this aggregation he might have been even more impressed: three and a half million dollars in 1889, seven million in 1897, twenty-one million in 1899, and an immense forty million in 1900. "Where is there such a business!" Carnegie had exulted, and no wonder—the majority share of all these earnings, without hindrance of income tax, went directly into his pockets.

Nevertheless, with enormous success came problems. One of these was the restiveness of certain partners, under the "Iron-Clad" agreement, which prevented any of them from selling their shares to anyone but the company itself—an arrangement which meant,

three-fifths of the old workers lost their jobs), and by November the union had surrendered. Sympathy strikes at other Carnegie mills were also defeated by strikebreakers, and it was clear that unionization of the steel industry was a lost cause. As late as 1932 Carnegie's authorized biographer was able to say with some pride: "Not a union man has since entered the Carnegie works."

What had been Carnegie's attitude during the strike? As soon as he heard about it he cabled Frick that he would take the next boat home. Frick and his associates insisted he stay where he was. Even after July 23, when Frick was shot and stabbed (by a Russian-born anarchist who had no connection with the strikers), he insisted in a cable to Carnegie: "There is no necessity for you to come home. I am still in shape to fight the battle out." To the newspapers Frick announced that he was going to fight "if it takes all summer and all winter, and all next summer and all next winter.

Yes, even my life itself. I will fight this thing to the bitter end. I will never recognize the union, never, never!" Carnegie, knowing that if he came home Frick would resign, made his fateful decision: he would back his lieutenant. The day after the Homestead battle he cabled Frick: "All anxiety gone since you stand firm. Never employ one of these rioters. Let grass grow over works. . . ."

This was his public reaction. To friends he showed quite a different face. Stung by criticism of his actions both here and abroad, he wrote to Britain's Prime Minister William E. Gladstone in September: "This is the trial of my life." Frick's hiring of strikebreakers was "a foolish step," he went on, and added: "It is expecting too much of poor men to stand by and see their work taken by others. . . . The pain I suffer increases daily. The Works are not worth one drop of human blood. I wish they had sunk."

The truth was that had Carnegie been on the ground when the strike broke, trouble might never have started, for the men worshipped him. During the dispute he received a cable from the union's officers which said: "Kind master, tell us what you wish us to do and we shall do it for you."

It was that simple: Andrew Carnegie represented a style in industrial relations that was passing, an era of the master who knew his men, who looked out for them in good times and bad, and who could expect in return an unbending loyalty. Frick was the impersonal wave of the future, the inflexible representative of absentee owners.

When Carnegie returned to Homestead that fall, he went through the mills, shaking hands with the old employees he recognized and trying to reconcile them to Frick's management. One of the rollers said to him: "Oh, Mr. Carnegie, it wasn't a question of dollars. The boys would have let you kick 'em, but they wouldn't let that other man stroke their hair."

—*Robert L. Reynolds*

of course, that the far higher valuation of an outside purchaser could not be realized. Particularly chagrined was Frick, when, as the culmination of other disagreements between them, Carnegie sought to buy him out "at the value appearing on the books." Another problem was a looming competitive struggle in the steel industry itself that presaged a period of bitter industrial warfare ahead. And last was Carnegie's own growing desire to "get out."

Already he was spending half of each year abroad, first traveling, and then, after his late marriage, in residence in the great Skibo Castle he built for his wife on Dornoch Firth, Scotland. There he ran his business enterprises with one hand while he courted the literary and creative world with the other, entertaining Kipling and Matthew Arnold, Paderewski and Lloyd George, Woodrow Wilson and Theodore Roosevelt, Gladstone, and of course, Herbert Spencer, the Master. But even his career as "Laird" of Skibo could not remove him from the worries—and triumphs—of his business: a steady flow of cables and correspondence intruded on the "serious" side of life.

It was Schwab who cut the knot. Having risen to the very summit of the Carnegie concern he was invited in December, 1900, to give a speech on the future of the steel industry at the University Club in New York. There, before eighty of the nation's top business leaders he painted a glowing picture of what could be done if a super-company of steel were formed, integrated from top to bottom, self-sufficient with regard to its raw materials, balanced in its array of final products. One of the guests was the imperious J. P. Morgan, and as the speech progressed it was noticed that his concentration grew more and more intense. After dinner Morgan rose and took the young steel man by the elbow and engaged him in private conversation for half an hour while he plied him with rapid and penetrating questions; then a few weeks later he invited him to a private meeting in the great library of his home. They talked from nine o'clock in the evening until dawn. As the sun began to stream in through the library windows, the banker finally rose. "Well," he said to Schwab, "if Andy wants to sell, I'll buy. Go and find his price."

Carnegie at first did not wish to sell. Faced with the actual prospect of a withdrawal from the business he had built into the mightiest single industrial empire in the world, he was frightened and dismayed. He sat silent before Schwab's report, brooding, loath to inquire into details. But soon his enthusiasm returned. No such opportunity was likely to present itself again. In short order a figure of $492,000,000 was agreed on for the entire enterprise, of which Carnegie himself was to receive $300,000,000 in five per cent gold bonds and preferred stock. Carnegie jotted down the terms of the transaction on a slip of paper and told Schwab to bring it to Morgan. The banker glanced only briefly at the paper. "I accept," he said.

After the formalities were in due course completed, Carnegie was in a euphoric mood. "Now, Pierpont, I am the happiest man in the world," he said. Morgan was by no means unhappy himself; his own banking company had made a direct profit of $12,500,000 in the underwriting transaction, and this was but a prelude to a stream of lucrative financings under Morgan's aegis, by which the total capitalization was rapidly raised to $1,400,000,000. A few years later, Morgan and Carnegie found themselves aboard the same steamer en route to Europe. They fell into talk and Carnegie confessed, "I made one mistake, Pierpont, when I sold out to you."

"What was that?" asked the banker.

"I should have asked you for $100,000,000 more than I did."

Morgan grinned. "Well," he said, "you would have got it if you had."

Thus was written *finis* to one stage of Carnegie's career. Now it would be seen to what extent his "radical pronouncements" were serious. For in the *Gospel of Wealth*—the famous article combined with others in book form—Carnegie had proclaimed the duty of the millionaire to administer and distribute his wealth *during his lifetime*. Though he might have "proved" his worth by his fortune, his heirs had shown no such evidence of their fitness. Carnegie bluntly concluded: "By taxing estates heavily at his death, the State marks its condemnation of the selfish millionaire's unworthy life."

Coming from the leading millionaire of the day, these had been startling sentiments. So also were his views on the "labor question" which, if patronizing, were nonetheless humane and advanced for their day. The trouble was, of course, that the sentiments were somewhat difficult to credit. As one commentator of the day remarked, "His vision of what might be done with wealth had beauty and breadth and thus serenely overlooked the means by which wealth had been acquired."

For example, the novelist Hamlin Garland visited the steel towns from which the Carnegie millions came and bore away a description of work that was ugly, brutal, and exhausting: he contrasted the lavish care expended on the plants with the callous disregard of the pigsty homes: "the streets were horrible; the buildings poor; the sidewalks sunken and full of holes . . . Everywhere the yellow mud of the streets lay kneaded into sticky masses through which groups of pale, lean men slouched in faded garments . . ." When the famous Homestead strike erupted in 1892, with its private army of Pinkerton detectives virtually at war with the workers, the Carnegie benevolence seemed revealed as shabby fakery. At Skibo Carnegie stood firmly behind the company's iron determination to break the strike. As a result, public sentiment swung sharply and suddenly against him; the St. Louis *Post-Dispatch* wrote: "Three months ago Andrew Carnegie was a man to be envied. Today he is an object of mingled pity and contempt. In the estimation of nine-tenths of the thinking people on both sides of the ocean he has . . . confessed himself a moral coward."

In an important sense the newspaper was right. For though Carnegie continued to fight against "privilege," he saw privilege only in its fading aristocratic vestments and not in the new hierarchies of wealth and power to which he himself belonged. In Skibo Castle he now played the role of the benign autocrat, awakening to the skirling of his private bagpiper and proceeding to breakfast to the sonorous accompaniment of the castle organ.

Meanwhile there had also come fame and honors in which Carnegie wallowed unashamedly. He counted the "freedoms" bestowed on him by grateful or hopeful cities and crowed, "I have fifty-two and Gladstone has only seventeen." He entertained the King of England and told him that democracy was better than monarchy, and met the German Kaiser: "Oh, yes, yes," said the latter worthy on being introduced. "I have read your books. You do not like kings." But Mark Twain, on hearing of this, was not fooled. "He says he is a scorner of kings and emperors and dukes," he wrote, "whereas he is like the rest of the human race: a slight attention from one of these can make him drunk for a week . . ."

And yet it is not enough to conclude that Carnegie was in fact a smaller man than he conceived himself. For this judgment overlooks one immense and irrefutable fact. He did, in the end, abide by his self-imposed duty. He did give nearly all of his gigantic fortune away.

As one would suspect, the quality of the philanthropy reflected the man himself. There was, for example, a huge and sentimentally administered private pension fund to which access was to be had on the most trivial as well as the most worthy grounds: if it included a number of writers, statesmen, scientists,

it also made room for two maiden ladies with whom Carnegie had once danced as a young man, a boyhood acquaintance who had once held Carnegie's books while he ran a race, a merchant to whom he had once delivered a telegram and who had subsequently fallen on hard times. And then, as one would expect, there was a benevolent autocracy in the administration of the larger philanthropies as well. "Now everybody vote Aye," was the way Carnegie typically determined the policies of the philanthropic "foundations" he established.

Yet if these flaws bore the stamp of one side of Carnegie's personality, there was also the other side—the side that, however crudely, asked important questions and however piously, concerned itself with great ideals. Of this the range and purpose of the main philanthropies gave unimpeachable testimony. There were the famous libraries—three thousand of them costing nearly sixty million dollars; there were the Carnegie institutes in Pittsburgh and Washington, Carnegie Hall in New York, the Hague Peace Palace, the Carnegie Endowment for International Peace, and the precedent-making Carnegie Corporation of New York, with its original enormous endowment of $125,000,000. In his instructions to the trustees of this first great modern foundation, couched in the simplified spelling of which he was an ardent advocate, we see Carnegie at his very best:

Conditions on erth [sic] inevitably change; hence, no wise man will bind Trustees forever to certain paths, causes, or institutions. I disclaim any intention of doing so . . . My chief happiness, as I write these lines lies in the thot [sic] that, even after I pass away, the welth [sic] that came to me to administer as a sacred trust for the good of my fellow men is to continue to benefit humanity . . .

If these sentiments move us—if Carnegie himself in retrospect moves us at last to grudging respect—it is not because his was the triumph of a saint or a philosopher. It is because it was the much more difficult triumph of a very human and fallible man struggling to retain his convictions in an age, and in the face of a career, which subjected them to impossible temptations. Carnegie is something of America writ large; his is the story of the Horatio Alger hero *after* he has made his million dollars. In the failures of Andrew Carnegie we see many of the failures of America itself. In his curious triumph, we see what we hope is our own steadfast core of integrity.

259

"GET THE PROSPECT SEATED . . . AND KEEP TALKING"

By GERALD CARSON

In the autumn of 1885, around harvest time, when a granger was likely to have sold his wheat, a man in a slouch hat, wearing the Grand Army badge, appeared on the piazza of almost every American home. There was nothing in his hands to suggest his errand. Touching his hat respectfully, he would say: "I called to give you an opportunity to see General Grant's book, of which so much has been said in the papers."

The demobilized veteran was a member of a new army. Concealed inside his coat was a prospectus, known in the profession as a "pros," for the *Personal Memoirs of U. S. Grant,* in two volumes at $3.50 each, cash on delivery, or more, according to the binding selected. The agent knew human nature and he knew his book. He was superbly armed with sales arguments, skilled in the art of awakening interest, fanatically devoted to a basic concept of Grant's publisher: "More orders are lost because the agent does not hang on long enough than from any other one cause." In

peace, as in war, discipline, training, the fighting spirit, won through to victory. Grant's *Memoirs* made a never-to-be-forgotten splash in the world of the subscription book.

From earliest times, peddlers and chapmen—flying stationers, in the English phrase—have combed the rural areas of America to bring books, both good and bad, to the people: broadsides and almanacs, catechisms and Indian captivities, songbooks and encyclopedias.

The golden age of the book agent came with the vogue for the bustle and the cast-iron dog on the lawn, i.e., during the thirty years after the Civil War, a time of new wealth, new land, industrial expansion, endless inventions and novelties—including books. In the absence of the modern forms of mass selling, there was no other mechanism for marketing such specialties outside the large cities except the peddler footing it from one door to the next. That is how American

Publishers' come-ons gave the drummer a wide choice of heroics to hawk. A delicate age buried the title of "Prof. Fowler's Great Work" in fine print. It was Sexual Science.

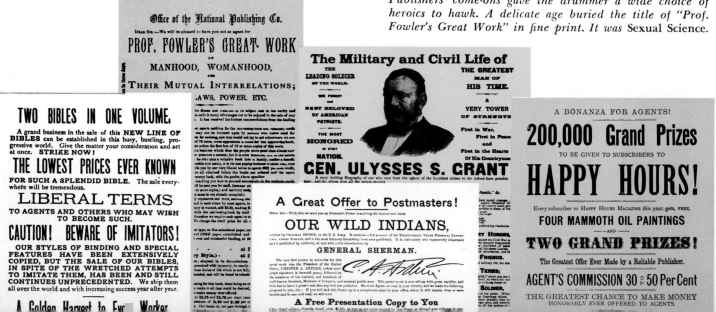

With his smooth spiel and city ways the book agent could sell you the lives of famous men, and if you wanted fame yourself he could arrange that too—for 2½¢ a word

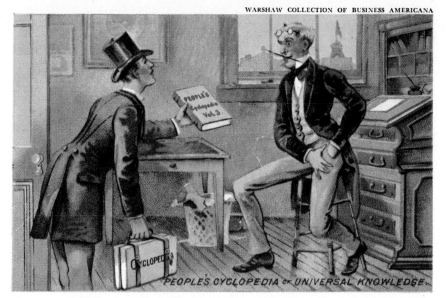

PEOPLE'S CYCLOPEDIA OF UNIVERSAL KNOWLEDGE.

One encyclopedia house furnished its agents with this trade card in the 1890's.

industry introduced a new pie crimper or apple peeler, a darning machine, broom holder, shawl strap, or patented farm gate. And from promoting salve or a new window catch, a man, or his "female agent" counterpart, could easily turn to canvassing for a book.

The greatest reservoir of manpower for canvassing was the soldiers of the late war. No sooner, it seemed, had the armies of Grant and Sherman passed in review along Pennsylvania Avenue on May 23 and 24, 1865, than the ex-soldier without a job would be skirmishing through every four corners and hamlet in the land with Joseph T. Headley's *The Great Rebellion* (sales: 150,000), or Greeley's *American Conflict* (250,000).

But the sales campaign that was put on for Grant's book was the promotional masterpiece of them all. A special interest attaches to this spectacular feat because Grant's publisher was Mark Twain.

General Grant's work was just made for the center table of the eighties, remembered for its marble top and heavy mahogany legs that writhed and curved and dripped carved grapes. Grant's account of the war was made, too, for the holy light which filtered through the lace curtains and fell upon the Bible, centered upon the parlor table and greatly in need of a worthy companion.

All the subscription books of the day were bulky, often over 500 pages in length, printed in large type, emblazoned with gold, lavishly illustrated with woodcuts, steel engravings, and curlicue tailpieces. George Ade recalled that they "did not involve the publishers in any royalty entanglement." "Nobody really wanted these books," continued the Indiana sage. "They were purchased because the agents knew how to sell them,

and they seemed large for the price, and, besides, every well-furnished home had to keep something on the center table."

Into this context came U. S. Grant's two green and gold volumes. It should be said at once, as qualification of Ade's testimony, that the people did want to read Grant, whose military biography frequently has been compared to Caesar's *Commentaries,* and that a very generous author's royalty played a conspicuous part in the publishing arrangements. The first check that Mrs. Grant received after her husband's death was for $200,000; she was ultimately paid between $420,000 and $450,000 by Twain's firm.

The whole country became excited about General Grant's memoirs. Regional or general subscription agents were set up to hire and direct the humbler gleaners. These supervisors were called into New York, and Charles L. Webster, who ran Twain's company, fired them up with a sense of their sacred mission. The promotional effort was tremendous. But it paid off handsomely. Former President Grant thought the sales might reach 25,000. Actually, more than 350,000 sets were moved.

Ten thousand canvassers fanned out over the countryside, all carefully drilled in the principles set forth in a power-packed little manual, *How to Introduce the Personal Memoirs of U. S. Grant,* containing a groundwork of arguments to help the agent deliver a smooth and effective spiel. Go, it said, to the front door; you are selling a parlor book. Introduce yourself by name. Shake hands, if you can. Keep the "pros" concealed from view in a special pocket on the inside of your coat. The confidential instructions told the agent in rich detail exactly what to do, what to say,

261

and how to say it. What chance had a clerk, farmer, or blacksmith, himself a former member of a regiment of volunteer infantry, when the comrade opened up?

"Each volume," he would say, "will contain a facsimile of the Gold Medal presented by Congress to General Grant in 1863 in honor of his successes . . . the first and only medal ever presented to any man by the American Congress . . . this (produce 'pros' and explain) will be the surface size of the volumes, this (showing backs), the thickness. Each volume will contain 600 large octavo pages. Here is a fine steel portrait of the General, from a daguerreotype, taken when he was twenty-one years of age, and Second-Lieutenant in the United States Infantry. The General informs us that he cut twenty cords of wood to pay for the daguerreotype from which this portrait was taken.

"The work, you see, is copyrighted (pointing to copyright) by Ulysses S. Grant, and it is being published for his benefit. . . . The Table of Contents shows the plan and scope of the work. Volume I opens with a brief sketch of his ancestry. . . . This is a sample of the fifteen or twenty maps to be contained in the book. Here is the letter he wrote from Galena at the outbreak of the Civil War, offering his services to his country.

"A fine steel etching . . . shows his birthplace. . . . The frontispiece of the second volume is a steel portrait of Grant as Lieutenant-General . . . a perfect likeness of the General as he looked at the close of the war."

The agent then mentioned all the battles of the war fought under Grant and finally arrived at McLean's house at Appomattox. "It was in the parlor of this house . . ." and so on. "There will be a facsimile of the original document . . . even to the yellow paper on which it was written. . . ." The canvasser now turned to a strip mounted on the inside of the binding that showed the cloth style, saying: "Bound in this style of binding, the work will be furnished at three fifty (Do not say dollars). Bound in full Library leather it will be furnished at four fifty per volume. . . . You see, General Grant owns this book himself, and the publishers simply issue it under his direction." The half morocco was $5.50, but the full morocco was not mentioned until the name was down on the dotted line. Then the agent shot for the really expensive editions, all the way up to the tree calf at $12.50.

Leafing casually through the pages of the canvassing sample, the agent now said, "I presume it is simply a question with you as to your choice of bindings, as no American will want to have it said that he has not read General Grant's book, a work that will descend to your children and will increase in value with every

The subject of this sketch was born in Westerlo, Albany Co., N.Y., Nov. 9, 1797. He was the eldest son, in a family of seven sons and seven daughters. . . .

Until Eliakim was twelve years of age he remained at home on the farm, receiving very limited opportunities for obtaining any education from books, but at that age went to live with his uncle, Abijah Reed, a merchant. . . . Here he remained as a clerk until he was some twenty-four years of age. During these years he received a careful business education, expanded his natural ability and tact, and developed a business talent and shrewdness not common among young men of that day. In the spring of 1822, leaving his uncle, he started business for himself in what is now Oneonta . . . and became one of the pioneer merchants of that part of Otsego County. His capital in cash was small . . . yet, what was of much more importance, he possessed a capital stock of good, sound common sense and practical business habits, together with his energy and will to do, [placed him] among the best business men of his day.

July 21, 1823, he married Miss Harriet, daughter of Ira Emmons and Jane Hotaling . . . both among the early settlers of the town of Davenport.

From the first his success was well assured. Ford's store became widely known, and its affable and gentlemanly proprietor as widely esteemed. He never forgot his responsibilities as a citizen. Every project for the promotion of the general good met in him a generous and hearty response, and no better proof of this can be adduced than his interest in the construction of the Albany and Susquehanna railroad. . . . He was one of its strongest advocates. He saw what many failed to see,—the great advantages

Town and county histories of the nineteenth century reflect a kind of never-never land of wealth and gentility that never, alas, quite existed. The editors had but one style, the adulatory, for the paying subjects, which transformed every struggling farmer into a "prominent agriculturist" and every village law-giver into a Pericles. The biography of Eliakim and Harriet Ford (above) comes from The History of Otsego

Harriet E. Ford

that must result. . . . He showed his own faith by his liberal contributions. . . . Others faltered, but his own faith never wavered. The time of success was sure to come; and it did come. It was a proud day for him . . . that saw the completion of the grand project. . . . He stood vindicated before the world, the correctness of his judgment proved, and the purity of his motives shown. Though it was for him a day of triumph, he showed no spirit of exultation . . . only consciousness of having aided in the accomplishment of a good work.

Mr. Ford was a man of strong and earnest character. He had a sound judgment; his views were broad, comprehensive, and practical, and he possessed a deep insight into the character and motives of others. In his business relations he was methodical and exact in his surroundings; in the appointments of his home everything seemed to wear the appearance of solidity and endurance. The defects in his early education had in a great measure been overcome by his own efforts. . . . Few men were better informed on the current topics of the day.

Mr. Ford was for many years a prominent member of the Baptist church of the village. . . . He will long live in the memory . . . and hearts of the needy poor whom he delighted to assist.

Mrs. Ford possesses those rare qualities of sociability and character which make home attractive, and however the world might frown, or friends grow cold, he was always sure of [her] sympathy.

Mrs. Ford is now in her seventy-third year, familiar with the various changes of the county's growth, from its rude log cabins, replaced by palatial residences of wealth and grandeur, from a wilderness to a settled county of schools, churches, and manufactories, and agricultural interests unsurpassed in the State.

County, New York (*1878*) *and the view of the "beautiful residence and farm" of George German* (below) *from* The History of Oakland County, Michigan (*1877*). *Mr. German, the* History *observed, was "hospitable, sociable and universally . . . honored." So, apparently, was everyone else in the county, but one wonders whether the farmer actually spent much time playing croquet in a frock coat and a tall silk hat.*

generation." (Return to subject of bindings.) "You see the styles your neighbors are taking. Which style do *you* prefer? . . . (Do not wait for a reply to your question, but keep advancing argument after argument . . . Do everything quickly . . . above all have faith to believe you *will* get the order.)"

Among the Aids and Arguments contained in the Key were the answers to "Can't afford it" and to questions about Grant's politics ("Grant should be dear to *all* Americans"). A big card was the delayed payment (next December, next March). The book was sold as an investment (better than real estate), and on the need of the Grant family (pitiful). The manual said, "People . . . expect to hear you talk, and you must not disappoint them . . . keep pouring *hot shot* at them. . . ." The peripatetic bookman had every reason of self-interest to do so, for he did not get his full commission unless he met a quota of one hundred orders per thousand population. "Anyone outside the poor house," the kit said, "can acquire the book if he wants to."

When he sensed the moment to move in for the kill, the agent broke off and said, "Just put your name on that line . . . on *that* line, please." (But if the prospect is not ready, keep talking.) To teachers, read educator testimonials. To young men, quote Ben Franklin and warn all against competitors—"so-called 'Lives of Grant.'" Get the prospect seated, in a fence corner, behind a stump, on the plow beam. Put the book right in his lap, but *you* turn the leaves . . . and keep talking. Remember Grant's perseverance. Keep the pressure up. Avoid "the Bull Run voice, Bull Run appearance, Bull Run walk, and BULL RUN LUCK." Notice the children, smell the flowers, and watch for that *but* . . . The agent aimed to make ten to twenty exhibitions daily in towns, eight to fifteen in the country. He was admonished to avoid controversy, keep away from saloons, learn to read men. "You can often satisfy people as to your honesty by admiring it in others." Make your voice "similar to David's harp," and if you lose, retreat in good order, with colors flying: "Let your last glance be full of sunshine."

The atmosphere changed at collection time. When the agent came back to deliver the books and pick up the money, he was told to be brisk and use the word *contract* freely. As the lady paid up, he departed with the exit line, "A thing of beauty is a joy forever."

The New York *Tribune* asserted in the 1870's that "there is not a cross-road in any part of the country that is not at some time visited by the book agent." In addition to Grand Army men, the ranks were recruited from aging clergymen and spinsters, and seasonally from schoolteachers and youths attending fresh-water colleges who wished to rub up against the world. Many obviously were in the trade only temporarily and passed on to other careers. Grant himself is said to have sold one of Washington Irving's books after resigning from the army before the war. Another future President, Rutherford B. Hayes, canvassed in Ohio. Blaine, an almost-President, went on the road with a life of Henry Clay. Bret Harte, Jay Gould, P. T. Barnum, and Dr. S. B. Hartman, the Bible salesman who later blessed the world with Peruna, each sold books before achieving fame of his own choosing. But there always remained a cadre, a hard core of professionals, who appraised each new announcement of a subscription book and sent for the outfit, or didn't, according to their judgment of what literature would go in the market they knew.

In addition to the memoirs and biographies of great men, the agents lugged to farm and frontier heavy compilations of territorial and state statutes, surveys of natural resources in the new western country, emigrants' guides, family advisers on medicine and commercial law, books of etiquette, of escape and travel, adventure, and inspiration for an agricultural population on the way up in the social scale. There were, too, works of religious piety, Bible commentaries, dictionaries, and such ephemera from the literary underworld as joke books. Finally, there were expensive art books and native poets, and, in a last effulgent sunburst before the close of the nineteenth century, standard English and Continental authors—in pretentious sets, or issued serially in numbered, paper-bound parts at a modest price per installment. But the charges were stiff enough when the time came to bind them up!

About the time that the professional buffalo hunters were ranging over the Great Plains, the book agents made a killing of equally epic proportions out of local history. Regional, town, and county histories had begun to appear before the Civil War, usually the work of some dedicated local antiquarian. After the war, the Mississippi River basin in particular became a kind of Garden of Eden for commercialized localism.

A mood of retrospect and recovery was stimulated by the national observance of the Centennial of American Independence. Congress passed a resolution, dated March 13, 1876, that recommended "to the people . . . that they assemble in their several counties or towns . . . and that they cause to have delivered . . . an historical sketch of said county or town from its formation, and that a copy of said sketch may be filed, in print or manuscript, in the Clerk's office of said county, and an additional copy . . . in the office of the Librarian of Congress."

The orations, pamphlets, Fourth of July addresses, and the burgeoning subscription book industry all expressed a real grass roots impulse. "Local history deals with people, with folk, in a good Elizabethan and Ohioan idiom," Stanley Pargellis, Librarian of the Newberry Library in Chicago, has pointed out. It is, he adds, "the largest and most vital part of our history as a folk and as a nation." The Middle West was just old enough, just prosperous enough, to support a large-scale effort in this field.

The county history school of historiography got its start in New England, where the town is the significant community unit, with town plat books or wall maps made by surveyors and draftsmen. They showed boundaries, streams, farms and houses, the physical geography of the area. Distances were obtained by the odometer, a kind of clock mounted on a wheelbarrow, the prototype of the automobile speedometer. It was wheeled over the town roads and by the revolution of the wheel registered distances on a dial. The odometer itself proved to be a great advertisement. The curious Yankee would examine it, and before he knew it he had ordered a map or atlas.

By the time the scheme got to the Middle West, the map was a county project, mounted on cloth with a roller, bound with tape on the edges. Each township had its own color, and the whole was surrounded with two rows of beautiful, large lithographic views.

"Every house and farm will be shown," the polite, well-dressed stranger had said, "with the pictures of your finest buildings surrounding the map. It will be about six feet square, with rings to hang it by, and the whole thing for only six dollars. You don't have to pay a cent for it until it is hung in your home. As I said before, Mr. Jones. . . ."

In fact, the only catch to the whole beautiful idea, the salesman implied, was whether the project would actually be carried through. It seemed that the expenses of the business were enormous and that it was quite unprofitable. And while this part of the county, populated by prosperous, intelligent "white men" like present company, represented the finest flower of our farming population, there were so many Irish and Bohemians in the other sections, who of course wouldn't patronize the work, that it might never be completed.

"Mr. Brown has ordered six," the man continued. "Many order extras to send east to be hung in public places so as to induce good men to locate in this section. The maps will return large profits," he continued earnestly, "in this way of securing a heavy immigration to Jackson county." He read the list of subscribers, remarked again that "this is the best township in the county in point of intelligence," and slipped his subscription book with pencil under the farmer's nose. "Sign right there . . . thank you, Sir. . . ."

The possibilities of the scenes arranged around the edge of the map were tapped by the next caller. He was the "viewer" who persuaded the subscriber to have an artist visit the farm and "make drawings from nature," with such changes or embellishments, of course, as the owner might like. For instance, he could take away that woodpile, the rubbish in the back yard, put a picket fence in front instead of showing the rails that were actually there, "as you would be doing that soon anyway."

"Put a pump in the well. We might make the barn larger, give the house a coat of paint and we can put a grass lawn in front. A few evergreen trees would look well—and there is the kind of yard you will probably have anyway in three or four years."

The salesman, who might be typed as a "cosmopolitan Yankee," displayed samples of other similar jobs. Then he produced a dummy of the proposed map, with most of the spaces marked "sold." But fortunately the farmer was able to select a choice spot near a rich neighbor for only $36. He was also to receive absolutely free 25 copies of his own farm scene. Just the thing for framing and hanging in the parlor or sending to relatives back east so that they could properly appreciate the fatness of farm life in Illinois or Iowa.

Only a few days later the "sketcher" appeared at the gate. He worked for two hours with the subscriber breathing down his neck, then put away his sketch block, explaining that he would fill in the details down at the hotel. To the customer's surprise, he requested payment and presented the contract. Sure enough, there it was, in good strong black and white: "payment to be made on completion of design, draught or sketch."

From the wall map the atlas was evolved. It was, in essence, a map cut up into book or folio size, with one township to a page, more views of buildings, and new features—more history and an entirely new wrinkle, tabular matter giving the names of subscribers, their business or occupation, where they came from and when, plus something of their early lives and hard times. This biographical material cost the subscriber two and a half cents per word, "just to pay for typesetting."

Thus, the atlas and farmers' directory for Peoria County, Illinois, memorialized not only the president of the Peoria Steam Marble Works, not only the proprietor of the City Livery Stables and the local agent for Blatz Beer and the director of Spencer's Military Band, but also devoted a full page to the Peoria Agricultural & Trotting Society, whose officials, the atlas said, were all public-spirited men anxious to make it possible for the people of Peoria County to have, and I quote, "a place where they can witness trials of speed and contests for supremacy. . . ."

As the biography angle was enlarged, the portrait artist had a soft snap. Portraits rose to $100, but the demand continued strong not only for a likeness of Jedediah himself, but of his wife, too, and of Susan Jane, John Thomas, Hannah, Edward, Lucy, Frank, and little Allie. As a logical extension of the idea, the Hambletonian horse went in, the Shorthorn cattle, the Poland China hogs, and the fine merino sheep. With such rich sources of inspiration, the final stroke was to get the customer to enlarge the tiny view space he had originally authorized to the panoramic scale necessary for preserving for posterity the life and good times of the Johnsons.

The economics of the game went something like this: An atlas for Peoria County, Illinois, sold 2,140 copies. The total receipts were $33,218; the costs, $15,663. Knock off 5 per cent for uncompleted contracts, and the history men were in the clear for about $15,000. Illinois showed up somewhat better than Iowa: more money, equal vanity. These works, it should be said, were not humbugs or swindles. If many of the subscribers did not need them, these maps, atlases, and county histories nevertheless often preserved information obtainable in no other place.

Incidents occurred that are not without their amusing side. One grain and stock dealer of Maquoketa, Iowa, a Mr. Blandings at heart, owned an empty city lot. He had a view of his dream house engraved for the county map, but lost his money before he could build the palace depicted by the engraver. His fellow citizens often came to view the gaping cellar excavation and meditate on the uncertainty of human affairs. High man on the sucker list was undoubtedly the wealthy farmer of Greene County, Illinois, who "took" nineteen copies of the atlas when first canvassed and subsequently bought everything offered by the biography men, the view artist, and the portraitist, including a crisply rendered drawing of his monument in the local cemetery. The boys took him for $642 all told, and left him forever confused by their rapid-fire talk of brevier type, mezzotints, and steel engravings.

What did a county history contain? After the "corps of experienced historians" from Chicago had shuffled through local courthouse records, made transcripts of the minutes of early court sessions and other docu-

Twain's publishing firm sent Grant's widow this royalty check for the General's Memoirs. *In all, she got over $420,000.*

ments, and taken down the biographies of old settlers and their anecdotes of early times, the material was forwarded to the home office to be worked up. Often the manuscript was puffed out with a brief history of the United States and the Northwest Territory, short biographies of the Presidents and state governors, the text of the Constitution, a digest of state laws, general material on Indians and pioneer customs. The title pages, prefaces, and introductions saw hard service, with only the names of the counties changed where it was necessary.

The real meat of the volume was its chapters on the county's geography, geology, flora and fauna, early settlement, its record in various wars, annals of the church, press, "bench and bar," and long lists of local officials. Often dry reading, the county histories were illuminated, nevertheless, with occasional vivid episodes—the story of a robbery, the winter of the Big Snow, the frontier law of bees, bits of folklore, details of dress and manners. There are homely and charming touches to be found in these fat quartos: "Mr. Francis Jackson related to us that he saw at one time nine coons in one tree." The *History of Pike County, Illinois* (Charles C. Chapman and Company, Chicago: 1880) contains a reference to John Hay which is delightful in its emphasis: Hay was described as "son of Dr. Hay, of Warsaw, and nephew of Milton Hay, and for some time a resident of Pittsfield," and he "was a companion of Mr. Nicolay in the study of law in Mr. Lincoln's office at Springfield and in being private secretary to the President. While in Pittsfield he published 'Pike County Ballads,' a collection of capital pieces of poetry. . . ." Usually the biographies appeared helter-skelter at the end of the general history of the county, or if the biographical material was to predominate, the book was published as a "portrait and biographical record."

The books were, to some extent, works of autobiography, since the biographee supplied the account of his struggles on a printed form entitled "The Story of My Life." One may be pretty sure of the source when it is recorded as a high point how a man from Ulster County, New York, stood on the roof of the Tremont House in Chicago and assisted in firing the first salute when Lincoln was nominated for the presidency. The flattering sketches made a statesman out of every county politician, a merchant prince out of every storekeeper, a hero of every militiaman. The "historians" spread it on thick, but the paying customers loved it. If there was sometimes snickering among their peers, there was by that time nothing to be done except face it out and live it down.

We might try on, just for size, an excerpt from the tribute paid by Chapman Brothers of Chicago to Gerhard Sander, a respectable member of the large Ger-

One publisher used this cartoon to attract agents in 1892.

man community of the pretty Mississippi River town of Quincy, Illinois:

GERHARD SANDER. If a pleasant manner and accommodating disposition bear any relation to success in life, then the comfortable circumstances in which the subject of this sketch now finds himself can easily be explained. The gentleman is an old settler, and has been engaged in the manufacture of brick since 1875.

A man's political views and church affiliations were staples, as were his acres, his children, and his record in the temperance movement. "The political views of Mr. Walton," the anonymous historian would write in his orotund style, "are embodied in the principles of the Republican party, and since casting his ballot for Frémont, he has always voted with the party of his choice." One would gladly know more about Dr. James Asbury Mitchell, of whom it is recorded, "He was a strong Union man, though when war came on he went the bond of some Southern sympathizers who were captured by General McNeil, and taken to Palmyra." The writing was by turns annalistic and high-flown. A man who kept a store was "engaged in merchandising." A grain dealer with a taste for politics "has held several local offices of trust in the gift of the people."

After the development of the halftone process for reproducing photographs, the cameraman replaced the lightning artist. When a photograph was lacking, the front fighters for local history got a black box out of their buggy, slipped an ingenious contrivance, widely known in mortuary circles, over the subject's sweat-stained shirt. It was made secure behind with a safety pin, and they had him to the life in "a natty cutaway coat with collar and tie attached." Sometimes they backed the farmer up against a painted canvas drop curtain, decorated with magnificent barns, flags flying from the ridge. In the background was an elegant residence, complete with wife, windmill, and an iron deer grazing on the lawn.

The county histories have come in for a good deal of condemnation from scholars because of their weakness in interpretation, their euphuistic and infelicitous writing, their haphazard sources, and their commercial origin. Certainly few of the western volumes compare favorably with the best of the New England town histories, such as Sylvester Judd's *History of Hadley* or Frances Manwaring Caulkins' *History of Norwich, Connecticut: From its Possession by the Indians, to the Year 1866*. But there was often a spirit of devotion and enthusiasm which redeemed, in part at least, the clumsiness and naïveté.

Chicago was the undisputed capital of this business. In eight years, from about 1869 to 1877, the subscription publishers made $3,000,000 out of Illinois on the atlas bonanza alone. Several county history houses grossed over $1,000,000 a year between 1870 and 1890, with forty books in preparation at a time, and twenty crews in the field.

No practitioner of this school of biography was more accomplished than the historian Bancroft—not George, but Hubert Howe—who mass-produced West Coast history on the fifth floor of a San Francisco building. A solicitor named Fowler, working southern California, landed a big fish, former Governor John G. Downey, who had escaped to America from a mud house and a life of turf-cutting in Ireland. Fowler invented a fancy tale about Downey's castle in Munster and his noble descent from King Brian Boru. The proof sheets of this biography are still extant, in the Bancroft Library of the University of California, docketed in Bancroft's hand: "Hold till 5M is paid."

When a friend remonstrated with Downey, the old gentleman replied, in substance:

"Well, I'm rich now. I would rather pay five thousand dollars to be lied about in this way than to leave the five thousand dollars for a lot of hungry Munsterians to fight over when I die."

The work in which Downey's touched-up life story appeared was *Chronicles of the Builders of the Commonwealth: Historical Character Study*, in seven volumes and index (San Francisco: 1891-92). It was one of the great "mug books" of all time. The total subvention amounted to $219,225. Bancroft went to California to participate in the Gold Rush. He did. One can almost hear in imagination the smooth chatter of the Bancroft canvasser making his rounds, well drilled in *Information for Agents to Assist in Selling the Works of Hubert H. Bancroft:*

"It may sound to you, Mr. ——, something like exaggeration, or at least superabundance of enthusiasm, what I have said about Mr. Bancroft and his work. But I can assure you, sir, the half of the truth has not been told."

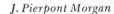

J. Pierpont Morgan

When the

Charles M. Schwab

The Monte Carlo capers of U.S. Steel's

new president outraged Andy Carnegie

but never ruffled J. P. Morgan

On the thirteenth of January, 1902, William E. Dodge, a large stockholder in the United States Steel Corporation, was reading his copy of the New York *Sun* in his comfortable Madison Avenue residence. No event of unusual importance dominated the staid *Sun's* front page, but Mr. Dodge found a small item in the right-hand column that stirred him deeply. Beneath the headline, SCHWAB BREAKS THE BANK, the story ran as follows:

Monte Carlo, Jan. 12.—Charles M. Schwab, President of the United States Steel Corporation, who has been playing roulette very high here during the past few days, broke the bank this afternoon. He had backed 26 plain and in various ways in maximums had won 50,000 francs. He left the table

amid great excitement and a large crowd followed him.

He resumed playing later on another table and lost 15,000 francs on five successive coups. He then resumed his practice of backing a certain number and the contiguous numbers on the cloth to the extent of 1,000, 2,000 or 3,000 francs. He lost every time and his winnings nearly vanished.

Although Mr. Schwab had occasional runs of luck late in the afternoon in addition to his recent winning of 75,000 francs on two successive coups, he has already dropped several thousand dollars.

To Dodge, this brief narrative threatened disaster. The giant United States Steel Corporation, capitalized at $1,400,000,000, was less than one year old. Its creation by the mighty banker J. Pierpont Morgan, who

...eadlines said:

CHARLIE SCHWAB BREAKS THE BANK

By JOHN A. GARRATY

brought together the tremendous holdings in ore, blast furnaces, mills, and transportation of Andrew Carnegie, John W. "Bet a Million" Gates, John D. Rockefeller and other tycoons, had been accompanied by serious misgivings and much criticism. Its promise of expansion, order, and efficiency in the vitally important steel industry had yet to be made good. Meanwhile, the monopolistic nature of the company was apparent to every observer; its policies and its very existence were being challenged in the courts. The new corporation was plainly on its good behavior before the public. Should the public form the impression that the president of the corporation was a reckless gambler, the future of what Dodge called "the

largest Experiment of Co-operation and Consolidation ever attempted" might be imperiled. That very day Dodge wrote an indignant letter to the chairman of the corporation's finance committee, George W. Perkins, who represented the interests of the House of Morgan. "I have no right to criticize [Schwab's] habits or pleasures," Dodge wrote, "but as the President of the U.S. Steel Corporation the fact that he plays 'roulette very high' and sees no harm in it absolutely changes the view the public has had of his caution, care & business methods. A loss of twenty millions of dollars would have been nothing to this."

At this time President Schwab was blissfully unaware of the excitement he was causing in his native land. He was not to remain so for very long. The next day the *Sun* carried another account of his exploits.

Monte Carlo, Jan. 13.—C. M. Schwab, President of the United States Steel Corporation, who has been playing roulette here for high stakes for several days and who broke the bank yesterday afternoon, repeated this performance ten minutes before the rooms closed last night. He won 54,000 francs on No. 20, which he backed in various ways on maximums.

The Casino was thronged at the time and Mr. Schwab's feat was greeted with cheers.

Previous to this Mr. Schwab had lost many thousands of francs on the same number. Mr. Schwab won three maximums today in fifteen minutes.

Other papers also carried the story. The *World* had him winning heavily on No. 36 while onlookers stood on chairs and cheered, but reported that in the end he lost $20,000 on his evening's play. The more restrained New York *Times* reprinted the *Sun*'s earlier dispatch, and ran in addition an ominous editorial. "A man who is at the head of a corporation with more than a billion dollars of capital stock, which controls a great part of one of the chief industries of a great Nation, and of which the securities are offered to the public as a safe and profitable investment, is under obligation to take some thought of his responsibilities," the editorial ran. "We should suppose that the friends of Mr. Schwab would call these strange stories to his attention in order that he may deny them *if he is in a position to say that they are untrue.*"

The "friends of Mr. Schwab" were quick to take the *Times*' suggestion. An Associated Press reporter named Martin Egan recognized the gravity of the situation when the first reports came over the wires. After failing to reach Schwab's brother, he telephoned his New York office, and urged the steel man's secretary to cable a warning at once. This was done. Independently, James Gayley, first vice president of United States Steel, also cabled an account of what was going on. On the fourteenth alone, Schwab re-

269

ceived forty cablegrams dealing with his alleged gambling. But the most drastic action was taken by Schwab's former boss, Andrew Carnegie.

Carnegie was not directly engaged in the management of United States Steel. When the great trust had been created, Carnegie had pocketed over $225,000,000 and prepared to devote the rest of his life to philanthropic pursuits. But he was naturally interested in the welfare of his former property. Moreover, he was deeply attached to Schwab. He had picked up Schwab, a "round-faced country boy" of nineteen fresh from Spiegelmire's general store in Braddock, Pennsylvania, in 1881, and raised him within five years to be superintendent of the vast Carnegie Homestead Works. Schwab had become his trusted lieutenant and his close personal friend. When Carnegie had decided to sell out, it was Schwab who had conducted the delicate negotiations with Morgan. The news that Schwab was gambling at Monte Carlo was a bitter blow to the strait-laced Scot, who was fond of pointing out to the youth of America that the gravest dangers besetting the road to business success were liquor, gambling, and lending money to one's friends. After reading the *Times* editorial, Carnegie cabled to the culprit at once, signing with his code name, "Wakeful":

Andrew Carnegie was outraged at protégé Schwab's gambols.

PUBLIC SENTIMENT SHOCKED. TIMES DEMANDS STATEMENT GAMBLING CHARGES FALSE. PROBABLY HAVE [TO] RESIGN. SERVES YOU RIGHT.   WAKEFUL

This done, he clipped the *Times* editorial and sent it to J. P. Morgan, with the following letter:

Confidential   5 West Fifty-First Street, New York.
                          Jany 14th, 1902

My Dear Mr Morgan

I feel in regard to the enclosed as if a son had disgraced the family.

What the Times says is true. He is unfit to be the head of the United States Steel Co.—brilliant as his talents are. Of course he would never have so fallen when with us. His resignation would have been called for instanter had he done so.

I recommended him unreservedly to you. Never did he show any tendency to gambling when under me, or I should not have recommended him you may be sure. He shows

a sad lack of *solid* qualities, of good sense, & his influence upon the many thousands of young men who naturally look to him will prove pernicious in the extreme.

I have had nothing wound me so deeply for many a long day, if ever.

                          Sincerely Yours
                          Andrew Carnegie

Schwab, the unsuspecting cause of this righteous indignation, received the cables of Carnegie and his other "friends" at Nice. He had arrived in France for what was later described as a combined business and pleasure trip with his wife and a small party of friends, including his personal physician, Dr. C. O. Goulding, and Charles T. Schoen, recently retired president of the Pressed Steel Car Company. He had been working hard for months, first at arranging the sale of the Carnegie holdings to Morgan and then at the complicated task of helping to create the world's first billion-dollar corporation. A charming, witty, happy-go-lucky sort, he knew how to enjoy himself when opportunity offered. In Paris he had purchased "a big fast automobile," which he proceeded to drive to Nice in the then sensational time of eighteen hours. In Nice he had joined other friends, including Baron Henri Rothschild and Dr. Griez Wittgenstein, head of the largest steel works in Austria, who was known to the press as "the $100,000,000 steel man from Vienna." They made, as Schwab later confessed, "a jolly party . . . racing all over the Riviera" in the new automobile. On four separate occasions they dropped in at the casino in Monaco to play roulette.

Their play, Schwab insisted, was completely casual "and simply for amusement." True, they were betting what were called "maximums" (nine louis d'or), which were worth about $36, and occasionally when a member of the party won he left his chips on the cloth for a second play. But at no time did any of them win or lose any considerable sum. Indeed—and for some reason this seemed vital in Schwab's eyes—they had never actually sat down at the table. They had created no disturbances, attracted no special attention, and had certainly not broken the bank. When indignant cables began to descend upon him, Schwab was dumfounded. "To say that I was astonished and chagrined," he wrote a friend, "is putting it mildly."

He was also badly frightened, especially by the thought of what might be going on in the New York office of J. Pierpont Morgan. No cable had reached him from that source, but President Schwab knew who really ran the United States Steel Corporation. He therefore cabled George Perkins, who was known to readers of the newspapers as "Morgan's right hand man":

This cable reached the Morgan offices at the corner
of Broad and Wall streets at about the same time as
Carnegie's letter to Morgan. The great financier and
his "right hand man" compared notes. As a result,
Perkins cabled Schwab:

VERY SENSATIONAL REPORTS IN NEWSPAPERS. . . . THINK
IT ADVISABLE AND IMPORTANT YOU CABLE SUCH A MES-
SAGE AS GAYLEY CAN GIVE NEWSPAPERS AND STOP BAD
EFFECT.

When this order reached Nice, Schwab prepared a
brief statement, which was published in the New
York papers on the fifteenth. "I have been on an automobile trip through the south of France with a party
of friends," he announced. "I did visit the Casino at
Monte Carlo, but the statements of sensational gambling are false." But he realized that this was a pretty
lame explanation, although it did have the virtue of
being true. Mr. Morgan deserved a fuller account.
However, one does not approach an emperor directly;
Schwab addressed his letter to Perkins.

"I am sorry that my visit to the Riviera and especially to Monte Carlo should have provoked so much
publicity," he wrote. He described what had actually
taken place, stressing his erect position while following the little spinning ball and the respectable company he had been with ("Lord Rothschild was with
me"). He also admitted the error of his ways. "I can
see now that it was a mistake. Of course. If the mistake was of such a character as to injure our company . . . by all means you should permit me to
quietly resign. . . . Frankly cable me what Mr. Morgan and yourself think." But he could not resist adding that fate had treated him very badly. "I have been
coming here for 15 years," he complained. "I always
visit the Casino on acct of its orchestra." And he signed
himself "Sorrowfully Yours." He also dispatched another long cable to Perkins, summarizing the situation:

MY ONLY REGRET IS THAT MR MORGAN SHOULD BE AN-
NOYED AND I WILL DO ANYTHING HE DESIRES. . . . HAVE
GAYLEY DO ANYTHING IN THE MATTER YOU SEE FIT.

Back in New York the excitement and indignation
were not stilled by Schwab's weak public statement.
The yellow press pushed the story for all it was worth.
Wall Street was full of rumors that Morgan had given

Schwab a terrible dressing-down via cable, and even
before Schwab's announcement was released the *Journal* had carried the headline: MORGAN TO SCHWAB: STOP
GAMBLING. The *Times*, which had questioned the au-
thenticity of the original reports, now condemned his
actions. How, asked the *Times*, could a man of
Schwab's responsibilities "join the intellectual and social dregs of Europe around the gaming tables of
Monte Carlo, and there make a more or less prolonged
effort to 'beat' a game which to a mathematical certainty cannot be beaten?"

Fortunately for Schwab, the House of Morgan was
unmoved by the clamor. Perhaps Morgan, whose own
pleasure seeking was a con-
stant source of interest to
the newspapers, shared
Schwab's fondness for the
casino orchestra. In any
case, Perkins had begun to
"straighten out" the press
as early as the evening of
the fourteenth, and after
receiving Schwab's elabo-
rate cable of the fifteenth,
he hastened to reassure the
beleaguered gambler that
he would not have to re-
sign. "Any friends that
cable you as you say are
pretty poor sort of friends
and under no circum-
stances should you take any
such step," he ordered. Af-
ter another day of "straightening" the situation was
well in hand, and Perkins cabled again to Schwab, who
was by then in Vienna:

*George W. Perkins: Morgan's
"right hand" and spokesman.*

EVERYTHING ALL RIGHT. ANDREW CARNEGIE AND SEVERAL
OTHERS WERE VERY MUCH EXCITED BUT THEY DID NOT
MAKE THE SLIGHTEST IMPRESSION ON MR MORGAN. DO
NOT GIVE THE MATTER ANY FURTHER THOUGHT OR CON-
SIDERATION. GO AHEAD AND HAVE BULLY GOOD TIME.

The worst of Mr. Schwab's ordeal was over. "Many
thanks," he cabled Perkins. "Appreciate Mr Morgan's
attitude more than possible to express. Am his to
command always."

For the remaining three weeks of his tour the president of the United States Steel Corporation attended
strictly to business. "If I have injured our great company in America," he wrote from Berlin on January
26, "I have done it very much good in Europe." In
Vienna he was received by Emperor Francis Joseph;
in Berlin he made a speech on the expansion of American trade. But he was still worried about his adven-

tures at Monte Carlo, and inquisitive reporters plagued him continually for further statements about his future in the great trust. Finally he wrote Perkins again for reassurance, and he asked how he should handle the American reporters when he arrived in New York. "Steel Co. first—me second," he said. "Do what you think best. . . . I'll do anything Mr. Morgan wants. He's my idea of a great man. Carnegie has condemned me without a hearing. Mr. Morgan, a new friend, is broader gauged by far. I'm his to command."

But Schwab had no reason to fear for his job. By the last week of January his letter explaining the affair had reached Perkins, and Perkins, of course, had read it to Morgan. "That's a good letter," Morgan had commented. "He's all right." Since J. Pierpont Morgan did not make such statements lightly, the incident could be considered closed.

The only remaining problem was the reporters. Schwab's arrival would have been newsworthy in any case, for the corporation's first annual report had just been published, and a stockholders' meeting was scheduled for the day after his ship docked. Because of the Monte Carlo incident, it was sure to be a major event. Perkins, however, went to the editors of the "decent" papers ("it is impossible," he said, "to do anything with the *World* or the *Journal* in such matters"), and "arranged" for them to avoid the subject of gambling. Then he wrote a final letter of instruction which was delivered to Schwab by special messenger just before he came ashore. If Monte Carlo was mentioned, Schwab should treat the affair as "one of those wild rumors." Then he should "shoot right off into what really took you to Europe"—the study of commercial conditions. He should stress the great interest of European businessmen in the United States Steel Corporation, and his own deepened sense of responsibility as the head of that great exemplar of America's methods and aims. "This will have the effect of reassuring the weak brethren over here who thought you had ceased to be a serious-minded business man and had turned into a gay butterfly," Perkins told him. And he added: "I want to see you as soon as you arrive."

On February 16 Schwab reached New York on the *St. Paul.* A terrible blizzard was raging, but he talked at length with the reporters. Naturally, they tried to get him to discuss his visit to Monaco, but he would not do so. A *World* reporter overheard Dr. Goulding whisper to him as the reporters approached: "Don't say a word; not a word." The best the man from the *World* could obtain was a statement by Charles T. Schoen, who said that Schwab was "an all-round good fellow and a dead game sport every time." (In Vienna he had lent Schoen 600 kronen and when Schoen had tried to pay him back he had pulled out a coin, asked him to call it, and, when Schoen had done so correctly, refused to accept the money.)

"Mr. Schwab declined to discuss the personal details of his trip," the *Times* man reported respectfully. "He said he preferred to speak as the President of the United States Steel Corporation."

"While I had a delightful trip," Schwab told the newsmen, "I also did a great deal of work. I found a feeling of the utmost friendship for our country existing everywhere in Europe. I found also intense interest in the question of industrial combinations. . . . I come back with my ideas broadened and my enthusiasm unbounded." The European political situation seemed calm, and the future of American trade limitless, he added. And he left the reporters with this thought: "My visit abroad this year was notable in the change I found when I, who had been there so often before as an individual, presented myself as the President of the United States Steel Corporation." This "greatest of American consolidations," Schwab said, "was the centre of curiosity among enquiring men of all nations."

That evening, according to the *Times,* Mr. Schwab was the guest of George W. Perkins for dinner at Sherry's.

THE
Delusion Mouse Trap.

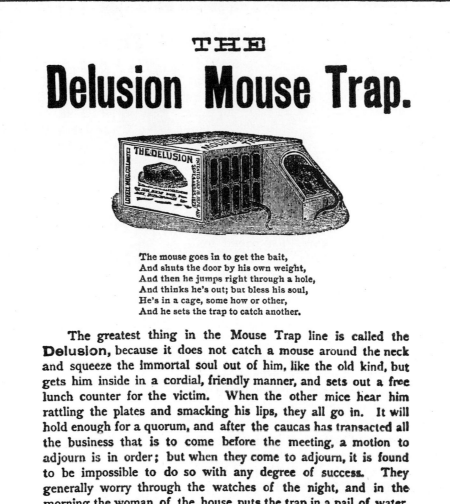

The mouse goes in to get the bait,
And shuts the door by his own weight,
And then he jumps right through a hole,
And thinks he's out; but bless his soul,
He's in a cage, some how or other,
And he sets the trap to catch another.

The greatest thing in the Mouse Trap line is called the **Delusion**, because it does not catch a mouse around the neck and squeeze the immortal soul out of him, like the old kind, but gets him inside in a cordial, friendly manner, and sets out a free lunch counter for the victim. When the other mice hear him rattling the plates and smacking his lips, they all go in. It will hold enough for a quorum, and after the caucas has transacted all the business that is to come before the meeting, a motion to adjourn is in order; but when they come to adjourn, it is found to be impossible to do so with any degree of success. They generally worry through the watches of the night, and in the morning the woman of the house puts the trap in a pail of water, and the work is done. Thousands of mice are now climbing the golden stair in this manner. This trap is more fatal than the yellow fever, and about as prompt and efficient as a Leadville vigilance committee. The way this trap is going on, it won't be long before the women of this glorious republic will have nothing to jump up in a chair and squeal at whatever. The **Delusion** is filling up the little mouse cemeteries throughout the land at an appalling rate.

Manufactured exclusively by the

Lovell Manufacturing Company
(LIMITED),
ERIE, PENNSYLVANIA, U. S. A.

CULVER PICTURES

While the world did not quite beat a path to the door of the Lovell Manufacturing Company when it introduced "the Delusion," near the turn of the century, the trap did sell in the millions. One reason must have been the enchanting style of the copywriter, who seems to have learned a lot from Mark Twain. The company, although it no longer makes mousetraps, still exists, producing such things as TV cabinets—which may, of course, work on more or less the same principle.

PURVEYOR TO THE WEST

A not inconsiderable number of agencies have been credited with bringing what passed for civilization to the Old West. First and foremost is the United States Cavalry, with the assistance of Sam Colt's single-action frontier model pacifier and the Winchester magazine rifle. The peace officers and city marshals of the Kansas cow towns, again with an assist from Colt and Winchester, also rank high in popular esteem as agents of sweetness and light. So does the princely banking and express firm of Wells, Fargo & Company, aboard whose Abbot & Downing Concord coaches, routed and administered from Montgomery Street, San Francisco, the amenities of urban life—strolling players, clergymen, prostitutes, forty-rod whiskey, and frontier newspaper editors—reached mining outposts like the Comstock, the Coeur d'Alêne country, and the diggings at Treasure Hill.

Still another claimant as a vehicle of *lux et veritas* was the iron horse. In its trailing palace cars rode the frock coats and gold-headed walking canes of lordly finance; it brought to the frontier grand opera troupes, and English commentators whose patrician snarls in print and condescending approval were received with local raptures in Cherry Creek and the adobes of Santa Fe. Finally, it brought the refining influence of civilized dining to an area where burnt cow and rifle whiskey had hitherto constituted the height of gastronomic ambition. Its agent in this last endeavor was a young Englishman named Fred Harvey.

There was little about Harvey to suggest a Roman proconsul bringing the enlightened authority of the Empire to the farthest reaches of Gaul or Asia Minor. Nor, except for a common English ancestry and background, was there much about the mild-mannered man of pots and sauces to suggest the shapers of the British reign who for three abundant centuries gave Britannia dominion over palm and pine. And yet on a scale and to a degree of perfection that has become

To a culinary wilderness

civilized cooking—and

By LUCIUS

part of the folklore of the trans-Mississippi West, Harvey imposed a rule of culinary benevolence over a region larger than any Roman province and richer than any single British dominion save India.

Where the grunt and growl of frontier barbarism had held sway, Fred Harvey endorsed a law of "please" and "thank you." Where the inhabitants had rooted about in a beans-and-bacon wilderness, he made the desert bloom with vintage claret and quail in aspic. It was quite an achievement.

In 1876 the Atchison, Topeka & Santa Fe was fairly small punkins as railroads went in the West. Starting at the Topeka of its corporate title, it had barely reached Pueblo, Colorado. It had yet to engage in its epic struggle with the narrow-gauge Denver & Rio

Fred Harvey brought pretty girls to serve it

Grande Western for possession of Raton Pass, which was to give it access to the high plains of New Mexico and, eventually, to all the great Southwest. It was nowhere near the Santa Fe of its title, and, in fact never did include that city in the main line, though the line was to run all the way from the shores of Lake Michigan to Los Angeles.

The Santa Fe was, like all railroads of the time, full of optimism. When its founder, side-whiskered Cyrus K. Holliday, turned the first spadeful of earth at Topeka in 1868 and, in his inaugural speech, mentioned going to the Pacific coast, the townsfolk smiled tolerantly. Any railroad with pretensions to respectability in those days included the word *Pacific* in its title, but, as everybody knew, the Union Pacific, when it was com-

pleted the following year, would be all the railroad connection needed by California for the next couple of years.

In 1876, Frederick Henry Harvey, the future César Ritz of the false fronts, was just forty-one years old. Born within sound of Bow bells in London in 1835, he had emigrated at the age of fifteen and gained his first experience as a restaurateur in New York. He was a pot-walloper at Smith & McNell's chophouse and ordinary at 229 Washington Street for $2 a week and found. A few years later, fulfilling the universal ambition of all restaurant workers, he opened his own business in St. Louis. But the coming of war in 1861 made chaos of most private enterprise in that turbulent, half-southern river town; in the early sixties Harvey got a job as a mail clerk on the Hannibal & St. Joseph Railroad, whose western terminus was the jumping-off place for the Far West. The Hannibal & St. Joe, known to its early passengers as the Horrible & Slow Jolting, was the first carrier of a railway post office in which mail was sorted en route, and Harvey was the first mobile mail clerk. Some of the letters he sorted may well have gone overland by the immortal Pony Express.

Subsequently he worked for other railroads and for a time sold advertising space in the Leavenworth *Times & Conservative,* making, according to James Marshall, annalist of the Santa Fe, as much as $3,000 a year. This, in the minted gold of the time, was real money, the equivalent of perhaps five times as much today.

We next encounter Fred Harvey in the capacity of western freight agent for the Chicago, Burlington & Quincy Railroad; it was one up on the Santa Fe because it actually served all three elements of its corporate title. The Burlington was a granger railroad; it was going places in a hurry, and Harvey was known as a hustler. But then he came down with a stomach complaint that today would probably be diagnosed as ulcers. It may have been the result of too much railroad food.

At this juncture, it may be well to insert a footnote on the gastronomy of travel in the years before clever George Mortimer Pullman placed in service the first dining car on the Chicago & Alton. Depot restaurants were spotted along the right of way at appropriate intervals, and three times a day the cars were hand-braked to a smoking halt; their occupants then engaged in a pitched battle with the management to get fed in the conventional twenty minutes allowed at each stop. No favorable commentary on the depot fare of the Southwest has survived, although contemporary reports indicate that things weren't nearly so bad on the Union Pacific a few hundred miles to the north. Without exception the depot-lunch proprietors of Kansas, Missouri, and Colorado were descendants of the Borgia family. To their talents as poisoners, some of them added those of brigands. They would bribe the train crew to sound the "all aboard" whistle before the prescribed twenty minutes had elapsed. The passengers had paid in advance; nevertheless, what they left on their plates was sold again to the next trainload of arrivals. The food was simply terrible.

There were, to be sure, two alternatives to risking one's health in such establishments. One was to go without food at all and subsist solely on bottled nourishment. The other was the shoe-box lunch.

"Many years ago when you went for a trip on the cars," said the Kansas City *Star* in 1915, "somebody at home kindly put up a fried chicken in a shoe-box for you. It was accompanied by a healthy piece of cheese and a varied assortment of hard-boiled eggs and some cake. When everybody in the car got out their lunch baskets with the paper cover and the red-bordered napkins, it was an interesting sight. . . . The bouquet from those lunches hung around the car all day, and the flies wired ahead for their friends to meet them at each station."

In this extremity it occurred to Fred Harvey that perhaps a railroad restaurant which offered reasonably edible fare and honest treatment of the customers might attract favorable attention and even make money for its altruistic proprietor. Its very novelty would occasion comment.

The Burlington management had other things on its mind when he brought the idea to its attention. But the management of the Santa Fe—in the person of Charles F. Morse, a general superintendent with a taste for unsalted butter and underdone steak—saw eyetooth

to eyetooth with Harvey, and in 1876 the first Harvey restaurant came into being in the railroad's Topeka depot and office building.

The impact was sensational. Word that "an eating house with a conscience" was in operation, serving tastefully prepared food in clean and well-ordered surroundings, spread far and wide, nowhere more swiftly than among the drummers or commercial travellers who formed a ponderable part of the railroad patronage in those days and who began planning their itineraries so as to be in Topeka at mealtimes, just as a later generation of continental travellers took pains to stay only in cities where they knew there was a Ritz Hotel.

"For a few months it looked as though civilization were going to stop short in her onward march at the capital of Kansas," wrote a contemporary, "and that the westward course of empire . . . would end at the same spot. Travellers positively declined to go further once they had eaten with Fred Harvey. Traffic backed up, and it became necessary for the Santa Fe to open similar houses at other points along its right of way in order that the West might not be settled in just one spot."

The next stop in the westward progress of gastronomy was at Florence, Kansas, where Harvey, using the profits from his venture at Topeka, purchased an entire hotel. Here was the first Harvey House that offered sleeping accommodations. At Topeka Harvey had merely operated a depot restaurant, but at Florence he maintained not only a formal dining room but bedrooms for his guests as well.

It was an overnight success, and the Santa Fe at once made a gentleman's agreement with Harvey providing that in future the railroad should furnish the premises and equipment, and Harvey the food and service. A handshake between Fred Harvey and Superintendent Morse was all that bound the two companies for some time, until their operations reached a degree of complexity that indicated written contracts.

At Dodge City, when Fred Harvey arrived in the eighties, the gunsmoke of frontier times had not yet blown from the scene, and it was still a rough, tough cow town. In the absence of more formal accommodations, two primeval boxcars were taken off their trucks and set on the ground, one to serve as kitchen and the other as dining room. The waddies were amazed at the amenities of dining that prevailed in this impromptu setting. Across the range the word spread: "They make you take off your hat and put on a coat there in an old boxcar, but the grub is strictly A-No. 1."

BEFORE *the advent of Fred Harvey, mealstops (left) were chaotic affairs, with passengers fighting for service, then gulping the far-from-appetizing food, which they were often forced to finish on the run.* AFTER *(right): The Harvey Houses—like this one at Cleburne, Texas—brought order and graciousness to trackside dining. As this photograph shows, the Harvey Girls were not always raving beauties, but they were neat and polite, and they knew their jobs. Harvey advertised in eastern newspapers for "Young women of good character, attractive and intelligent, 18 to 30." He paid them $17.50 a month, plus room and board, and required them to be in every night by 10 P.M. Curfew didn't stay the course of true love: many made good marriages, thus not only helping to improve the eating habits of the West, but also bringing it some social stability.*

As the Harvey system expanded its operations to include Newton and Hutchinson in Kansas, La Junta in Colorado, Las Vegas, Lamy, and Albuquerque in New Mexico, Winslow and Williams in Arizona, and Needles and Barstow in California, it was only natural that Harvey and all the details of his benevolent autocracy should enter into the folklore of the region. It may reasonably be supposed that Harvey himself encouraged a certain amount of embellishment, for he was well versed in the uses of publicity, but the ascertainable facts were fairly sensational.

It was a source of great pride to the owner, for example, that some of the Harvey Houses lost money for a time on their initial operations. Harvey made no secret of the fact that he was giving more in food and service than he was taking in in currency. At one depot hotel there had been a steady loss of $1,000 a month until an ambitious manager came along and, with an eye to gaining the good graces of his employer, cut portions and corners until the loss had been pared to a mere $500. Outraged, Harvey fired him at once, and started looking around for a manager who would promise to lose the original sum.

The railroad co-operated handsomely to supply Harvey with the best of everything. His menus began to teem with luxuries unheard-of on the Great Plains in a day innocent of deepfreezing and with nothing but the most primitive refrigeration. Fresh whitefish from the Great Lakes began appearing in the high deserts of New Mexico. It was an age when game was still plentiful everywhere in America, and Harvey specialized in sage-fed Mexican quail and antelope fillets. The antelope originated "on line" and made its way east and west as the steamcars moved between points on the Harvey map. The Harvey chef at Florence had been lured away from Potter Palmer's ineffable hotel in Chicago and made $5,000 a year, more than the president of the Florence bank. He paid local lads $1.50 a dozen for prairie chicken, seventy-five cents a dozen for quail, ten cents a pound for creamery butter, and was generally regarded as an easy mark.

Next to the food itself and the impeccable conduct of the Harvey Houses, the aspect of their operation which aroused the widest admiration was what came to be known as the Harvey Girls. The personal appearance and moral character of every applicant for work as a waitress was inspected by Mrs. Harvey. No Gold-Tooth Tessies or Fat Maggies were hired, and the character, intelligence, and good sense of Harvey personnel became legendary. Quite literally thousands of them made good marriages to ranchers, railroad men, prospectors, and businessmen of the Old West on the basis of acquaintances struck up over the service of apple pie and coffee; Elbert Hubbard claimed that 4,000 babies were christened Fred or Harvey, or both, by parents with sentimental recollections of a lunch-counter courtship. Fred Harvey himself was in great demand to give away his waitresses as brides; he probably appeared at more weddings than any member of Ward McAllister's celebrated Four Hundred back in New York and Newport. Humorist Will Rogers said of him: "He kept the West in food and wives."

In contrast to the shabby devisings of his predecessors on the ptomaine circuit, Fred Harvey's railroad restaurants bestowed upon the business of refreshing the inner man not only the best steaks and chops available, but a method and organization that functioned with fine precision where only chaos had existed before. The routine began at the last telegraph stop the train made before arriving at a Harvey depot. The conductor filed a wire specifying the number of customers who would be arriving and indicating any special requests for food or service that might seem reasonable. At the yard limits the engineer blew his whistle to warn the chef and, when the cars were braked to a stop at the station platform, they were greeted by a white-coated porter smiting loudly on a big brass gong and directing the customers toward the dining room.

The pretty Harvey girls taking orders from customers, who were usually seated eight to a table, arranged the cups and glasses according to a code and were followed by the "drink girl," who poured tea, coffee, or milk. Soup or fish having been served, the stage was set for the big moment when the manager of the premises made a grand entrance from the kitchen bearing an enormous platter, piled high with steaks or a partly carved roast that was expeditiously portioned out to the waitresses and arrived at its destination still smoking hot. The business of what the French call *présentation* was much admired and widely reported by the awed customers. It was also a direct link with an older tradition of innkeeping that was still observed in the United States until the early nineteenth century; under its terms meals in all public dining rooms of consequence were served by the proprietor in person. Fred Harvey insisted that his managers fill the ancient function; they were never allowed to delegate it to an underling.

To counteract the legacy of suspicion derived from an earlier time, the patrons were reassured at intervals during the meal that the train would on no account leave without them and that there was plenty of time for leisurely enjoyment of the Harvey bounty. Nobody had to run for the cars with a wedge of pie in his hand.

A loyal partisan of Fred Harvey was William Allen White, "the Sage of Emporia," who categorically stated in the editorial columns of the Emporia *Gazette* that Harvey food was head and shoulders above all the competition. "It is the best in America," White testified. "Deponent has in the past six months eaten meals on ten of the great railway systems of the country. Harvey meals are so much better than the meals of other railroads, east, west, north and south, that the comparison seems trite."

In the opening years of the last decade of the nineteenth century, it was becoming apparent that the universal meal-stop along main-line railroads was becoming a thing of the past. Faster schedules and limited trains caused operating departments to take a dim view of three half-hour stops a day in addition to the operational and switching stops dictated by abso-

The cover of this Harvey menu suggested comfortable dining. But the inside (opposite) was even better.

lute necessity. The introduction of dining cars on the faster and more luxurious trains was the solution of the problem. In the beginning, because of the limited tractive force of locomotives, diners were more frequently cut into trains at division points and carried only long enough for the service of a single meal, or perhaps breakfast and lunch, before being switched to a siding and then cut into a following train, or one bound in the opposite direction, for dinner. It was an intricate and vexatious process, but even the pauses required to pick up and set out diners once or twice a day didn't add up to the delay involved in three full meal-stops.

In 1892, the Santa Fe placed in service the first of the great trains that were to make its operations the transportational glory of the West. The California Limited, a name radiant in the lexicon of the Old Southwest and one that ornamented the Santa Fe timecards until well after the Second World War, carried a luxurious innovation in the form of a through diner that rode with the Pullmans all the way from Chicago to Los Angeles. Thus a new pattern of de luxe travel made its appearance, and from that day until comparatively recently much of the best food served in the United States was served on flanged wheels.

For Fred Harvey to take over the operation of the Santa Fe's dining cars was little more than an extension of an already well-established and elaborately routined service operation. The same organization that purchased Texas steers on the hoof at Kansas City, supplied California citrus to Chicago terminal restaurants, and distributed game, seafood, and dairy products at strategic points over half a continent, lent itself with a minimum of strain to the operation of mobile eating establishments that rolled night and day over the same huge territory.

To the dining cars Harvey brought the same decorum and the elevated amenities of food and service that had been the hallmark of his wayside operation. Irish table linen from Belfast and Sheffield silver as heavy as that in the best private clubs were the rule. There was a variety and quality of food in keeping with the opulent Harvey tradition of frontier generosity. The diners of the California Limited set the standard; those of the Colorado Express, the Missionary, the San Francisco Limited, the Grand Canyon, the Navajo, and eventually the Chief and Super Chief, followed in its footsteps. The best of everything was none too good for the Santa Fe's patrons, and until his death Fred Harvey saw that that rule was enforced on thirty-odd Santa Fe dining cars.

Although other western carriers like the Great Northern might advertise the luxury of eating aboard their crack name-trains, it was the Santa Fe which travellers always used as the standard of culinary excellence. "Real railroading begins west of Chicago" has long been an American aphorism, and by "real railroading" most passengers mean the quantity and quality of the food available to them. Other railroads have had dining-car stewards of national celebrity, such as Wild Bill Kurthy aboard the Union Pacific-Southern Pacific's Forty-Niner and Dan Healey on the Milwaukee's Pioneer Limited. But the Harvey organization has eschewed spectacular personalities in favor of an urbane worldliness and *savoir-faire* that would have pleased the legendary and monocled Olivier of the Paris Ritz.

The high-water mark in Santa Fe sumptuousness was to be found aboard a once-a-week, all-Pullman, extra-fare limited between Chicago and Los Angeles inaugurated in 1911 under the name De-Luxe. Aboard it a strictly limited sixty passengers were carried in upholstered surroundings never before experienced in public travel. They slept in private staterooms in individual brass beds instead of berths. Valets and ladies' maids and barbers crouched in the shadow of potted palms ready to spring at any unwary passenger who

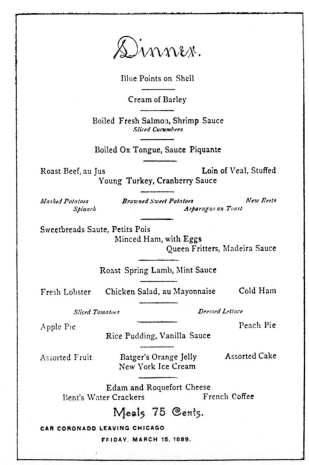

Ox tongue, roast beef, turkey, lamb—you could take your choice; and the price was the kindest cut of all.

tried to do anything for himself. Gentlemen passengers received pigskin billfolds as souvenirs of their trip, and at the California border uniformed messengers came aboard with corsages for each lady traveller. For such service a surcharge of twenty-five dollars was exacted —the equivalent in the hard-gold currency of the time of, say, one hundred dollars today. And, of course, the food in the diner was Fred Harvey's.

Nothing like it has ever been seen before or since, not even the yard-long menu on the first Super Chief when that pleasure barge was inaugurated in 1936 with fresh beluga caviar at $1.50 and larded tenderloin of beef for 95 cents. Passengers on the De-Luxe didn't dress for dinner, as they are reported to have done aboard the Blue Train to Monte Carlo at the turn of the century, or on the Simplon–Orient Express, but this was the only touch of grandeur that was lacking.

A footnote to the style in which Harvey operated in the mid-thirties, both on wheels and when grounded, can be discovered in the fact that for a decade or so the most socially and gastronomically acceptable restaurant in Kansas City was the Harvey Restaurant in Union Station. Here the most lavish dinner parties of the season were given by local magnificoes.

In those days the carding of the Chief westbound brought it to Kansas City shortly after nine in the evening for an operational stop that often lasted thirty minutes, and knowing regulars aboard the cars were met by friends and spent the interval profitably in the Harvey bar downstairs. Film celebrities occasionally were overserved and had to be helped aboard, while impatient locomotives panted to be on their way.

Until the spring of last year, when some of the stock was sold to the public, the ownership as well as the management and administration of the Harvey system was always a family affair. Upon Fred Harvey's death in 1901 at the age of sixty-six, the business provided service for fifteen hotels, forty-seven restaurants, thirty dining cars, and a ferryboat crossing San Francisco Bay. The company passed intact to Harvey's oldest son, Ford, who headed the organization until he died in 1928, when Fred's younger son, the late Byron Harvey, Sr., took over. The late Byron, Jr., succeeded *him,* and at the present time two more of the founder's grandsons, Daggett and Stewart Harvey, are still active in the company's management.

In general terms the operation has been kept fluid, to accommodate itself to the changes of national habit, taste, and travel patterns that have been the direct result of the motor-car age. Most of the earlier on-line hotel operations that were integrated into the Santa Fe's passenger traffic have been closed or modified. Mobile restaurants aboard dining cars and buffets have been geared to the class of patronage of the trains themselves—ranging from the epicureanism of the Super Chief to lunch-counter cars on the shorter runs in Texas and Kansas.

The original intention of Fred Harvey was to provide a Harvey facility approximately every 100 miles along the Santa Fe main line between the Great Lakes and California, but the trend in recent years has been away from on-line services and in the direction of operations entirely disassociated from the Santa Fe, such as inns, hotels, and restaurants, away from the railroad's tracks and terminals. And the company has recently undertaken the merchandising of a number of proprietary-brand food products, including the special blend of coffee that has been sold at Harvey Houses everywhere since the firm was founded.

The original Fred Harvey with his well-bred English notions of the proprieties, the Harvey who tamed the western frontier of gastronomy, might not recognize the many diversifications of his company in the second half of the twentieth century. He would, however, recognize its guiding principle—no compromise with mediocrity, and only the best of everything for Harvey patrons—which served so well in the cow towns of the Old West.

GUSHER

The story of the first great Texas oil well,

which ushered in a new century and a

new age, as remembered by participants

By WILLIAM A. OWENS

Texas, as everyone knows, is synonymous with oil. But how many know, at least in any detail, the story of the fabulous strike which ushered in the age of the Lone Star billionaire?

The history of Texas oil really begins on a dramatic morning in January, 1901, when the Lucas gusher, afterward world-famous as Spindletop, was brought in near Beaumont. (The name Spindletop is said to be derived from a tree in the vicinity shaped like an inverted cone.)

Beaumont in January of 1901 was an obscure and unpromising lumber and rice market. But then the Lucas gusher was brought in, four miles south of the town, and overnight Beaumont became a mecca. Adventurers flocked from far and near. Every Texan began to dream of a fortune under his ranch, farm, or town lot; and many of the dreams came true: within two years Texas' oil production increased twentyfold.

The remarkable narrative which appears here was obtained by Dr. William A. Owens, novelist and scholar in English literature, who took to Texas the methods of the Columbia University Oral History Project. It is an account of Spindletop derived direct from the lips of the three observers best qualified to tell it: Pattillo Higgins, since dead, who had faith that oil was to be found at Spindletop, but whose money ran out before he could prove it; and the Hamill brothers, Curt and Al (also now dead), who were at work on the drill the day a 160-foot geyser of oil suddenly leaped into the Texas sky.

AT SPINDLETOP

Tuesday, January 1, 1901. First day of the first year of a new century.

Early in the morning three men in a buckboard were driving slowly across the Texas coastal plain south of Beaumont. Their destination was a prairie mound called Spindletop, where a rough wood derrick rose above the marsh grass. They were intent on the job ahead of them only as a job. Not one of them imagined the impact it would have on the new century.

The men were Allen W. Hamill, his brother Curt, and Will "Peck" Byrd. They were the entire crew of an outfit engaged to drill an oil well at Spindletop, the well that turned out to be the first gusher in American oil history.

Al Hamill, 24, tall and slender, was a partner with his brother Jim in the Hamill Brothers Contracting Company. Jim Hamill, after getting a start drilling artesian wells at Waco, had moved on to the Corsicana oil field near Dallas, where a small boom had begun after the discovery of oil by two enterprising Pennsylvanians in 1897. There Al joined him; they formed a partnership and offered Curt a job as tool dresser. Curt, four years older than Al, was heavier of build, with the strength of an ox and the tenacity of a bulldog. For the well at Spindletop they hired Peck Byrd as fireman and man of all work. They had begun drilling in October, but so far they had failed to strike oil.

Now, on New Year's Day, the three of them bounced along the muddy track toward a well that seemed unlikely to pay the cost of drilling. They had shut down on December 24 so Al and Curt could spend Christmas in Corsicana. On their return, Curt had brought his wife and family and settled them in a shack not far from the well. Al and Peck boarded with them.

They came to the fence that marked Perry McFaddin's tract, opened a gate, and drove through. McFaddin, having little faith in the prospect for oil, was planning to turn the tract into a large rice farm; beyond the derrick, within hollering distance, he had six carpenters at work building a rice barn.

The men came to the derrick, which jutted up from a wide expanse of gray prairie toward a wider expanse of gray sky. Al stopped the horses and ran his eyes over the derrick, bull wheel, and boiler. Everything seemed to be in order, ready for them to get on with the job. Al, who was in charge, had contracted to drill down to 1,200 feet, when he would receive payment in full, $2,400. For Curt and Peck, the job represented a living—$80 a month and lodging.

Al was eager to get started.

"Peck, fire her up. Curt, check the derrick."

Peck filled the boiler from a water well and fired it with pine slabs. Curt climbed to the double board, forty feet up, and checked the pulleys and ropes of the draw works. From the floor of the derrick to the crown block—the pulley and rope which moved the bit up and down—the rig was ready to go.

With a heavy wrench Al tightened the ring clamps that fastened the rotary drill to the drill pipe and inspected the fishtail bit. With luck it would hold out for another day or two of drilling. Then, standing at the driller's place on the derrick floor, he got a signal from Peck, who had built up a head of steam. Al looked up at Curt, above him on the derrick.

"Ready?"

"Ready."

Al kicked in the clutch that set the rotary to its auger-like grinding and they settled down to the task.

Theirs was not the first attempt to find oil at Spindletop. For ten years Pattillo Higgins, a local man, had tried to harness the natural gas that bubbled in the five sour mineral wells at Spindletop. Managing, after some difficulty, to obtain backing, Higgins proceeded to lay out a part of the prairie in a real-estate development, which he called Gladys City, and to bring a succession of drillers to Spindletop. As well after well failed, people almost laughed him out of town.

At this point Higgins brought in Captain A. F. Lucas, an Austrian mining engineer who had been prospecting for sulphur in Louisiana. Lucas drilled another well. It was a failure, but he did manage to extract some crude oil—enough to fill a small vial—and took it east in search of more financial backing. (His capital exhausted, Higgins had been forced to drop out, though he still owned land at Spindletop.)

Curt Hamill, seen here in an early photograph, is the only survivor of the crew that brought in the gusher, starting the boom which built Texaco, Gulf, and other large companies.

In Pittsburgh Lucas interested J. M. Guffey and John H. Galey, both experienced in the oil fields of Pennsylvania. In September, 1900, Lucas was back in Texas, at Corsicana; it was he who had contracted with the Hamill brothers to drill the test well at Spindletop.

The Hamills had arrived in Beaumont with their drilling equipment about October 1. Lucas had met them and taken them to the location, where they saw a six-inch pipe extending above ground—all that remained of the earlier attempts to find oil. Lucas lighted a match and dropped it into the pipe. There was a puff. A flame shot up and died away.

Convinced of the presence of natural gas, the Hamills hauled their rotary drill and boiler to Spindletop. With their own hands they unloaded a carload of pipe, hauled it to the location, and stacked it on a crude pipe rack.

In Corsicana there had been derrick builders, but here in Beaumont they could not find one. There was not even a carpenter who would undertake the job. There was nothing to do but build it themselves.

They trampled down marsh grass that grew high as fences, stirring up swarms of mosquitoes that made life almost unbearable. The timber was green, wet, unsized, and would not fit the derrick pattern they had brought with them. In a kind of desperation they laid the timber out on the ground and made a new pattern, much as a woman cuts out a pattern for an apron.

After ten days they had a derrick 84 feet high, rough in appearance but strong and sturdy. In it they installed their Chapman rotary drill. Then they dug a slush pit sixteen by thirty by three feet and lined it with red Beaumont clay. Finally they began digging a water well to supply the boiler; twenty feet down they struck a good flow of water that bubbled with gas.

On an October morning they started drilling, using a twelve-inch bit. As the bit dug down, they forced water into the hole, and the fishtails worked up a sludge that was pumped out into the slush pit. As they bore downward, they hit, successively, formations of water sand, hard sand, and gumbo; having no geologist to advise them, they had to experiment to get through each one. The work was time-consuming; more than six weeks had passed and they were far behind schedule.

But finally they got through them all. Then, at something over 600 feet, gas suddenly blew water out of the hole and damaged the drill. Sharp sand shot out as if from a blast furnace, damaging the machinery. The men waited while the gas blew itself out; then they repaired the rig and began drilling again.

Worried that another blowout might destroy their equipment, they decided to keep the rotary and pump going day and night. That meant going on eighteen-hour "towers" (as oil men called tours of duty).

One night about midnight Al came on to find that Peck had made hardly any headway at all. He took over and thumped along until about three in the morning, when the rotary began to turn with ease. Daylight showed oil in bubbles in iridescent slicks on the slush pit.

When Curt came, Al showed him the oil and sent him for Captain Lucas. Lucas smelled and tasted the oil and then wired for John Galey. He was convinced the well was ready to be brought in and wanted Galey to share the excitement.

When Galey finally arrived he examined the oil on the slush pit.

"You might bail it," he told Al.

They put on a bailer made of perforated pipe wrapped in a bed sheet, a device that strained out sand and mud. The sample they brought up showed a little flow of oil.

"Try it again," Galey ordered.

When they went in again, the pipe stopped 300

feet from the bottom. They tried several times but could get no deeper.

Galey soon saw there was no use trying to bring the well in at that depth. He had them rig up a string of two-inch pipe and wash the bottom of the well out with clean water.

It was near Christmas time. Anyone could see that the men were near exhaustion.

"I'll tell you what to do," Galey told them. "You try to pull that pipe. Can't do anything with it the way it is. Set the six-inch through that and go down and see if there's anything below. When you get that done, shut down for Christmas."

They followed Galey's orders and on December 24 set the six-inch to a depth of 920 feet.

That is how the drilling operation stood when they returned on the morning of January 1, 1901.

All of New Year's Day Al held the lever of the rotary and watched the slowly turning drill pipe sink into the earth. Again they were on eighteen-hour towers, constantly facing the danger of a gas blowout. At 1,020 feet Al hit a crevice, or what he took to be a crevice, in the rock. If he turned the bit in one direction, it would go down five or six inches farther than if he turned it in the other. If he turned it a quarter revolution more, it would start to back up. Baffled, he called Curt and Peck.

When they were unable to make headway, they decided to pull pipe. It was discouraging work, pulling up twenty-foot lengths at a time when they should be going steadily toward their 1,200-foot depth. They found the fishtail bit dull from battering rock. They sharpened it and went in again.

Another night of keeping the boiler going and the rotary turning. Still the rock would not give way. Another day of drilling with no progress. All their bits were worn down to nubbins. Finally, on the morning of January 10, Al brought a new bit from Beaumont and they put it on.

Suddenly, at about 700 feet, mud commenced boiling up through the rotary. It got higher and higher. Then the drill pipe began rising—something they had never seen before. It moved up and started going through the top of the derrick.

Al and Peck yelled to Curt and ran. Curt scrambled down from the derrick, covered with slimy mud. From a safe distance they watched as the pipe kept on rising. It took the elevators and traveling block off and then knocked off the crown block. Fascinated, they watched pipe break in sections of three or four lengths and fall like crumbled macaroni. It knocked down the smokestack of the boiler and curled on the ground around the derrick. The last length of pipe was followed by rocks, and then by a deafening roar of gas.

McFaddin's carpenters scrambled like monkeys from the nearby barn and raced on horseback toward Beaumont.

The roar died down gradually and within a few minutes all was quiet. Peck and the Hamill brothers crept back to find a discouraging mess: engine and boiler seemed ruined; mud stood six inches deep on the derrick floor. They could see no signs of oil.

Al picked up a shovel.

"Let's get some of this off the floor," he said.

Of a sudden, a chunk of mud shot out of the six-inch hole with an explosion like a cannon. Then a stream of mud blew up, with a little blue gas following it. Again the men ran.

Then it quieted down and ceased altogether. The crew looked at each other wonderingly. Again they inched forward till they stood on the derrick floor in the mud. Al walked over and peered down the hole. They could hear a kind of bubbling deep in the earth. Then they could see frothy oil starting up. The well seemed to be breathing: oil was coming up and settling back with the gas pressure; with each breath it came a little higher.

When it poured out over the derrick floor they moved back. With each pulsation the flow went a little higher and a little higher and a little higher. Finally the momentum was so great that oil shot through the top of the derrick. With it came rocks and sand and shale from the conglomerate formation they had drilled into. It spurted skyward in a stream over 160 feet high —at least twice the height of the derrick. Once the oil was in full flow, there seemed to be no lessening.

After a few minutes, when their excitement had subsided somewhat, they crept closer, getting soaked with a spray of black oil. Their excitement changed to disgust. The machinery was damaged. Mud flowed all over the derrick floor. Strings of drill pipe lay on the ground, twisted and useless. They saw no way to control the power they had unleashed.

Al shouted for Peck to go for Captain Lucas. Peck drove at a gallop across the prairie to Captain Lucas' house, more than a mile away, only to find that Captain Lucas had gone to Beaumont.

Mrs. Lucas located him at Louis Meyer's Dry Goods Store, where he had set up his headquarters while waiting for something to happen. She had seen the gusher from her door. Quickly she told him what she saw.

Peck got back to the well as fast as he could. Some of McFaddin's carpenters had returned, but they stood far off, watching.

In a short time they saw Captain Lucas come over the hill in his buckboard, his horse at a dead run. At the gate, the horse stopped short, pitching Lucas to the ground. He landed on his feet and came running—panting, out of breath.

"Al, Al," he called, his Austrian accent more pronounced in his excitement. "What is it? What is it?"

"Why, it's oil, Captain. Oil!"

Captain Lucas grabbed Al and hugged him.

"Thank God, thank God," he cried. Then he hugged Curt and Peck.

Within an hour people began to arrive from Beaumont—in buggies, on horseback, on foot—attracted by the rumors spreading from Louis Meyer's store and by the roar of the gusher, which could be heard as far as Beaumont and beyond. They came as near as the fence, about 150 feet from the well, and watched in fear and astonishment. Every time the wind shifted, a spray of oil drove them back.

Lucas, when he had regained his composure, hurried to Beaumont and wired John Galey to come at once.

The effect of oil was already beginning to be felt in Beaumont. Oil spray drifted in on the Gulf breeze. Sulphur gas filled the air. People held their noses against it. They watched it tarnish their white houses with black and orange stains. They told of Negroes holding prayer meetings, thinking the end of the world had come.

Back at Spindletop Captain Lucas, seeing the danger of fire, had Curt sworn in as a deputy sheriff to keep everyone away from the well. Together they drove the curious onlookers back beyond the fence. Lucas hired extra guards, armed them with shotguns, and stationed them in lines on the east and west. To the south, marsh grass stretched unbroken.

"Keep the people back and don't let them smoke," Captain Lucas told Curt. "Don't let anybody smoke."

At sunup the curious again lined the fence. Pattillo Higgins rode his horse close and sat watching the fulfillment of his dream. Though he no longer held stock in the Gladys City Oil, Gas and Manufacturing Company, he had valuable land near the well, more than enough to establish him in the oil business.

About ten that morning the well blew wild again, with a mighty roar of gas that heaved rocks high into the air. Those who had come to watch were rewarded. After the well had cleaned itself of rocks and shale, it settled down to a steady flow that spouted above the top of the derrick.

There being no tankage in the Beaumont area, they had to let the oil bubble out on the ground. Captain Lucas had some levees thrown up to contain it until he could get cypress tanks built. The railroad men protected their tracks with an embankment. Oil flowed over fields intended for rice farms and collected in a draw near the railroad.

During the day Jim Hamill arrived from Corsicana,

and, for the first time since the well blew in, Curt and Peck went home to clean up. They took off their oil-soaked clothes and rubbed their bodies dry with gunny sacks. Then they scrubbed off the remaining oil with lye soap and water as hot as they could stand it.

Sunday morning broke clear and cold. A heavy frost coated the grass. Curt and Peck were on duty, Al having gone home to sleep. By midmorning some five or six hundred people were milling about in the pasture. Curt and Peck, in their slicker suits, took turns working around the well and keeping people away.

Then they saw a man come riding on horseback across the pasture, with a Negro boy mounted behind him. Just when they reached the oily area the boy lighted a pipe and dropped the match into the grass. Flames burst up and black smoke began to rise. A stampede toward Beaumont began, in a wild rush of horses and buggies and running men.

Curt went running toward the fire, with Peck close behind. They took off their slicker coats and beat at the flames. When their coats were burned up, they took off their denim jumpers, and then their shirts. Still the fire spread, nearer and nearer the well. Some of the stampeded men returned.

"Bring me some boards," Curt shouted.

The men brought boards from McFaddin's barn, fifty or more of them. Curt and Peck threw them on the line of flame nearest the well. Gradually they brought the fire under control, but not until more than an acre of grass had burned over.

By the time Al arrived, alerted by the smoke, the fire was out. He looked at Curt and Peck. They were out of breath and their faces were black with oil smoke. Al looked at the blackened patch.

"If it had ever got to the well," he said, "I don't know what we'd have done with it."

This fire put fear into them: the well had to be shut off. But how? Great pressure was needed to cap the well; it had to be supplied by human muscle, and the work was perilous because a single spark might trigger a tremendous explosion.

Stories of the wild well had appeared in newspapers across the country. Telegrams began to arrive from as far away as San Francisco, with offers to shut off the well. Estimates for the job ranged up to $10,000. A man who claimed to be a hydraulic engineer appeared at Spindletop with a telegram from John Galey, authorizing him to shut off the well. He studied the gushing oil and then turned to Al and said, "You can certainly have the job if you want it. I wouldn't shut it off if they gave me the well, lease, and everything belonging to it. It's too dangerous."

Galey himself arrived soon afterward, and Al took

him to the well. Elated, Galey estimated the flow to be between 80,000 and 100,000 barrels a day. Ruefully they looked at the wasted oil which had run over the flat land and been washed down the bayou by heavy rains. They talked immediately about capping the well.

Galey turned to Jim and said, "Well, you boys drilled the well. What do you think about shutting it in?"

"Well, Mr. Galey, I think we can do it."

"All right, go to it."

All that night the Hamill brothers and Captain Lucas worked on plans for capping the well. Early next morning Jim arranged for heavy timbers and clamps to be delivered. Al swiped two steel rails from the Southern Pacific Railroad.

During the drilling they had put a collar on the ten-inch pipe to protect the threads when they set the eight-inch pipe inside. While driving the pipe through the first sand the collar had become welded to the pipe. It had to be cut off and the threads re-dressed before the shutoff could be started.

Al, the only one of the three Hamills who was unmarried, volunteered to cut the protector off. He went to Beaumont and got a pair of goggles, the kind he had used on the farm when threshing grain. These he taped to his face to keep oil and gas out of his eyes.

Then he went in with a hacksaw and diamond points. He straddled the pipe all afternoon, working away carefully and patiently, with oil raining down on him and running off his slicker suit and hat.

J. S. Cullinan, later a founder of the Texas Company and considered the father of the Texas oil industry, had arrived a few days before, and now he and Jim Hamill stood watching.

"Now, Jim," Cullinan warned, "you watch that kid. He's in great danger. If he hits a spark there, why, he just—it'd be impossible to get him out."

The men stood close, ready to pull Al out in case of fire or in case he should be overcome by gas. As fatigue set in, he had to come out for air, some work intervals lasting only two or three minutes; but finally he succeeded in cutting the collar in two and springing it enough to get it off. Then, in spite of the rain of oil, he dressed the threads perfectly.

When the pipe was ready, they took the floor boards off. Then they buried two four-by-twelve timbers and bolted them to the legs of the derrick. They bolted the steel rails to the timbers. Then they built a carriage arrangement and bolted it to the rails. With the fittings, the valves and the "T," and the connections, it looked like a crate. It was actually the beginning of

Fires like this one were common in Spindletop's early days because the wild gusher had spewed 2,520,-000 gallons of oil onto the ground. Sparks from a locomotive finally touched off this entire "lake."

what was later called the "Christmas tree," a set of pipes and valves for reducing internal pressure in a well. All parts were solidly bolted to the derrick; if the carriage were dislodged by the pressure, the whole derrick would go.

Their equipment was ready, but the well was still throwing rocks—rocks that went up as high as a man could see and then came down in a spray of oil and sand.

"We'd better not shut that in today," Jim said. "One of those rocks might damage our valve—might knock it off."

Again they settled down to fearful watching and waiting. A spark might set it off, the well would be lost, and there would be little hope of escape for three oil-soaked men.

On January 20 they watched as they had watched every day. In the middle of the morning Jim came out.

"Well, boys," he asked, "how's it been acting?"

"No rocks this morning," they assured him.

He watched with them until after eleven.

"Well, let's shut her in," he said.

The brothers looked at each other. The most dangerous moment had arrived. Al was the first to speak.

"Curt, I'll work the carriage. You turn the valve there, will you?"

With chain tongs Al pulled the unwieldy carriage until the valve was directly over the pipe. Then Curt rushed in, lowered the valve over the pipe, and screwed it tight. One moment there was a hissing roar—the next, silence. The well was shut off. But Curt had fallen to the ground, overcome by gas. They dragged him to fresh air and revived him.

The flow finally stopped. They pounded rope between the six-inch and eight-inch pipes, poured cement in over the rope, and finally covered the valve with a mound of dirt, to protect the well from fire.

It was fortunate they did. A few days later a spark from a locomotive set fire to the lake of oil that stretched between the well and the railroad tracks, three-fourths of a mile away. This time there was no chance to fight the fire. The flames leapt fast; the smoke was overpowering. Men worked feverishly to drag their equipment out of the path.

The fire started about noon. By middle of the afternoon it was burning along the entire side of the lake bounded by the tracks. If the wind changed, flames would sweep across the whole of Spindletop.

A man on horseback (some said it was McFaddin trying to save his pasture) set fire to the other side of the lake. Smoke boiled up and shut out the sun. The two walls of flame rushed toward each other. When they were close, with only a deep alley between, explosions began to shake the earth. The walls would meet, throw sheets of oil into the air, and then recede under the impact of explosions that shook Beaumont, four miles away.

Smoke rolled over the city and turned day into night. Then a rain storm came and washed soot down upon the town. Houses stained orange before were now turned black. Again people, frightened by this great unknown force, held prayer meetings and prepared themselves for the end of time.

But the fire passed, and the well was safe. Its stored-up power became both the symbol and the incentive of a new century.

THE COAL KINGS COME TO JUDGMENT

When the anthracite miners downed tools in 1902,

economic feudalism went on trial

By ROBERT L. REYNOLDS

The highways leading south and west out of Scranton, Pennsylvania, wind through the graveyard of a dying industry. Its monuments are decaying company houses, boarded-up collieries, and mountainous piles of culm—the black, gravelly residue from the mining of anthracite coal.

Most of the area's younger men have moved away now, unwilling to endure the bone-wearying labor and irregular pay checks their fathers knew, or unable to get jobs at all in the dwindling number of underground shafts still open or in the strip-mining operations that gouge great scars across the face of the land. The obituary pages of the local newspapers tell the story plainly: when old miners die, their funerals bring their surviving sons and daughters—and there are many of them, for this was a prolific immigrant stock—from New York, New Jersey, and other nearby states where they have gone in search of a better life.

Anthracite is finished now, replaced by oil and gas. Yet only fifty years ago northeastern Pennsylvania was a prosperous region. For here, in a 500-square-mile triangle of low mountains, deep valleys, and sharp outcroppings of rock, lies nearly all of the country's hard coal, and at the turn of the century anthracite heated most of the homes, factories, and offices of the Atlantic seaboard. Along with food and shelter, it was a major necessity of life, and when in 1902 the supply was cut off by a bitter, five-month strike, the entire East was thrown into turmoil. The governor of Pennsylvania sent the state's entire National Guard into the coal fields to keep order. In Wall Street J. P. Morgan, who seldom worried, was very worried indeed. So, as winter neared, was New York's reform

mayor, Seth Low, who feared bloody coal riots in the streets. Before it was over, the strike had helped spark a national revolution in the relationships among employers, employees, and the federal government. It had also thrust into national prominence a young union leader named John Mitchell, launching him on one of the most brilliant yet heartbreaking careers in the history of American labor.

In Scranton and Wilkes-Barre, in Shamokin, Mount Carmel, and Shenandoah, there are still men and women who remember John Mitchell. An elderly Hazleton librarian, then a little girl, recalls being taken by her father to Mitchell's headquarters in a local hotel so that the child could shake the hand of a man who was making history. And many an immigrant miner's son remembers when the family parlor proudly displayed two pictures side by side: a chromo-

United Mine Workers' President John Mitchell (right), by organizing the anthracite strike of 1902, made the plight of the miners a national issue.

THE MINER'S CASTLE

"His wife is his queen and his home is his palace," says an old ballad of the anthracite miner. But as these photographs show, the lot of the miner's wife was something less than queenly, her home not quite a palace. Above, mine-field mothers, with children too young for the breaker, scavenge coal for drafty houses like those at right on the "Street of Rocks" in Shenandoah, Pennsylvania. "Their homes are not really what we call homes," a priest remarked, "they are simply . . . resting places, if they can obtain rest in the company buildings that are given out to them."

lithograph of Jesus Christ and a photograph of "Johnny d'Mitch."

These old likenesses of Mitchell reveal a handsome man with dark hair combed straight back and luminous brown eyes set in a swarthy face. His slight, wiry figure is dressed in a plain black suit with a frock coat and a high, plain collar, giving him the appearance of a priest. The son of a soft-coal miner from Braidwood, Illinois, he had gone into the mines himself at twelve as a "trapper boy," standing in the underground darkness and opening the heavy wooden doors to let the mule-drawn coal trucks go by. A shy, introspective man, he would as his world widened feel his lack of education keenly: dutifully, as he finished a book, he would write "Read" on its flyleaf and replace it on the shelf. Nevertheless, by sticking to the United Mine Workers in their earliest, most difficult days, by hard work, a talent for conciliation, and a quiet maturity that inspired confidence, he rose through the union's ranks to become national president in 1898, when he was only twenty-eight years old.

Nearly all of the organization's 40,000 members were then in the bituminous fields of western Pennsylvania, Ohio, Indiana, and Illinois. A year after Mitchell's inauguration the union decided to organize the anthracite, and in the fall of 1899 Mitchell himself, with two lieutenants, Miles Dougherty and John Fahy, headed east to take on the job.

The industry was in the grip of a handful of coal-carrying railroads, all controlled by the giant among them, the Philadelphia and Reading Coal and Iron Company, commonly called "the Reading." The grip was tight and it squeezed the miner hard. An old epitaph in a coal-country cemetery reads:

> *Forty years I worked with pick and drill*
> *Down in the mines against my will*
> *The Coal King's slave but now it's passed*
> *Thanks be to God I am free at last.*

The slavery began, for most miners' sons, at the age of ten or eleven, when they went to the breaker, separating slate from coal for as little as thirty-five

cents a day. "I have seen boys going to the breaker that did not seem really able to carry their dinner pail," said the Reverend James Moore, a Methodist minister from Avoca. "I am not very tall myself, but I have seen some little fellows with the bucket nearly touching the ground." The breaker was at once the miner's grammar school and old-age home—for after thirty or forty years underground he would return to it, crippled by accident or racked by miner's asthma, and sit on the dusty floor with the little boys, doing the same work for the same pittance as they.

In between, if all went well, he might work his way up through a variety of jobs inside the mine to become a laborer and, finally, a contract miner. This was the top of the profession. Most of the anthracite was produced, in those days, by small teams working under an experienced older miner who entered into a contract with an operator to produce coal at so much a carload. Out of this gross income, which in a very good year might amount to as much as nine hundred dollars, he was expected to hire as many laborers as

he needed, to furnish his own tools, and to buy—usually from the company, at highly inflated prices—the fuses and powder with which he blasted the coal out of the ground. George R. Leighton, in his *Five Cities*, has graphically described the miner's daily routine:

It was up to the miner to fire the shots, to use the most delicately exact skill in placing the timber. The work required an alert mind and great physical strength. . . . The pitching coal veins made the work never the same; sometimes erect, sometimes on his knees, sometimes on his side or back, the miner worked in an endless night, a soft black velvet darkness, with only the light of his miner's lamp to see by.

Death—from a sudden fall of rock, from gas, from a premature explosion caused by a faulty fuse—was everywhere about him. In the year 1901 alone, 441 miners were killed, to say nothing of scores of others deprived of sight or limbs, or condemned to an early death by the irritating coal dust. According to a mine-field doctor who had performed many an autopsy, a

LABOR IN THE EARTH

lifetime of breathing the dust made a miner's lungs resemble nothing so much as lumps of anthracite coal.

Safety devices were pitifully primitive, and the effectiveness of the state-appointed mine inspectors was often nullified by the fact that the foremen accompanied them on their rounds. One miner, asked why he didn't voice his complaints to the inspector, answered that "if the boss was along with him I would sooner be still."

Fluctuations in the market price of coal made work irregular—in an average year a miner might work only two hundred days—and unemployment compensation was a generation away. Miners complained that they were forced to put up to eighteen inches of "topping" on the cars before they left the mines, for coal was naturally shaken down, and some of it was jarred off, as the cars rumbled over the uneven rails to the weighing point. At the scale there was no representative of the miners to check the weight jotted down by the company weighmaster, so a man had no way of knowing whether he was receiving honest pay for an hon-

est day's work. To compensate for the unmarketable impurities always present in anthracite as it comes out of the mine, the operators arbitrarily fixed the "miner's ton"—the basis on which he was paid—at 3,360 pounds, and even higher.

There was no such thing as a standard scale of wages; often men working side by side in the same mine, doing the same work, received different amounts in their pay envelopes. This had the effect of depressing all wages to the lowest level—"mining the miners," the men called it. Under circumstances like these, not even the mine operators knew what the average miner's salary amounted to. John Mitchell, after investigation, placed it at about three hundred dollars a year, and the chances are he was not far wrong. What that meant in human terms can be gleaned from the description by a miner's wife of what happened when her husband brought home his pay envelope. "People comes in and wants money so quick we haven't time to have it in our hands, hardly," Mrs. Sophia Bolland said. "I can't count it up; sure not . . . I throw it to

Teams of men (far left) went down the shaft in rickety cages early in the morning. The contract miner placed the powder and fuses and blasted out enough coal to keep his laborers shoveling and loading for the day. The "chamber" at left was relatively easy to work; often the vein pitched sharply, making digging a contortionist's nightmare. Once loaded and hoisted above ground, the coal went to the breaker (above), where the boys removed the slate. The remainder was sorted into various sizes, depending on the use intended.

his feet sometimes, when there is nothing in it. . . . Eight dollars was not so bad, or ten or twelve, but when he brings home only three or four, or two dollars, I had to cry." She was speaking of two weeks' pay.

As he toured the mine fields John Mitchell heard story after story of the heartlessness of the operators. For example, the husband of Mrs. Kate Burns had operated a pump at the G. B. Markle mine at Jeddo until he was killed by a locomotive. She began scrubbing floors and taking in washing seven days a week to support her children, of whom the oldest, a boy, was eight. When the boy was fourteen he too went to work in the breaker, but after a month brought home only a due bill; the family owed the company $396— the rent that had accumulated on the miserable, two-room company house they had occupied since Burns's death. It took Mrs. Burns, her son, and one of his younger brothers twelve years to work off the debt. In Pennsylvania's steel towns you will find an occasional library, clinic, or park donated by the Mellons or the Carnegies. In the anthracite towns you will

look hard and long before finding anything of the kind. What happened to Mrs. Sophia Bolland and the Widow Burns happened to the people and the region as a whole. "They never give me anything," Kate Burns said, "but all they took off me."

Against conditions like these the miners had made several attempts to organize. Each in its turn had been defeated—by the hated coal and iron police ("coalies," the miners called them) hired and armed by the operators; by the lack of unity among the twenty or more nationality groups among the men themselves; or simply by gnawing hunger, which drove strikers back to work one by one.

John Mitchell, then, had to reverse a tradition of failure as he sought to build a new union. He had also to cope with the divisive antagonisms among the nationality groups in the area. The original anthracite miners had been largely Welsh and Irish, but in the 1870's and 1880's successive waves of foreign-speaking immigrants arrived. Rivalries—between old-timers and newcomers and among the newcomers themselves—

MEN ON THE MARCH

The strike began in May, and as summer ended, coal in metropolitan areas like New York (above) was scarce and prohibitively expensive. New Yorkers were buying coconut shells for fuel, Chicagoans were reported tearing up the wooden paving blocks, and in many places the opening of schools had to be delayed. Meanwhile, in the coal region itself, official union demonstrations like the parade at right were remarkably peaceful, though hunger sometimes drove unofficial groups of strikers to violence, particularly against the non-striking "scabs" and members of their families.

were unbelievably strong, extending even to the altar. Most of the immigrants were Catholics and all of them were poor; yet so closely did they cling to their native language and customs that each group willingly made the sacrifices necessary to support its own Catholic parish. Today it is not rare to see even in a small anthracite town as many as three or four churches—monuments to an earlier disunity now happily blurred by time.

Leaving his assistants, Fahy and Dougherty, to organize the English-speaking miners, John Mitchell concentrated on these foreigners, going from town to town and from mine patch to mine patch, speaking in turn to Poles, Italians, Ukrainians, Hungarians, and Lithuanians. He spoke everywhere he could gather an audience—in miners' kitchens, in taverns, in parish halls—securing the backing of their priests and convincing the men themselves that in unity lay their only hope. And gradually he won them over. "To a great many of the newly arrived miners, John Mitchell is the one great man in the United States," wrote Walter

Wellman of the Chicago *Record-Herald;* ". . . ask the first Hun or Polander on the streets who is president of the United States and the odds are about even that he will reply, 'Johnny d'Mitch.'"

And Mitchell seems to have been ahead of his time in understanding the necessity for all the workers in an industry to act together. The contract miners, for example, sought to keep the breaker boys away from union meetings; Mitchell insisted on their right to attend: they worked as hard as the men and were even more shamelessly exploited. Of the young slate-pickers Mitchell, a man not often capable of eloquence, said: "They have the bodies and faces of boys but they came to meetings where I spoke and stood as still as the men and listened for every word. I was shocked and amazed . . . as I saw those eager eyes peering at me from eager little faces; the fight had a new meaning for me; I felt that I was fighting for the boys, fighting a battle for innocent childhood . . ." The boys repaid him with the unalloyed devotion that only the young can give.

Philadelphia & Reading Railway Company.
President's Office.
Reading Terminal. Philadelphia.   17th July 1902.

My dear Mr. Clark:-

    I have your letter of the 16th instant.

    I do not know who you are. I see that you are a relig-
ious man; but you are evidently biased in favor of the right of
the working man to control a business in which he has no other interest than to secure fair wages for the work he does.

    I beg of you not to be discouraged. The rights and in-
terests of the laboring man will be protected and cared for - not
by the labor agitators, but by the Christian men to whom God in His
infinite wisdom has given the control of the property interests of
the country, and upon the successful Management of which so much depends.

    Do not be discouraged . Pray earnestly that right may
triumph, always remembering that the Lord God Omnipotent still
reigns, and that His reign is one of law and order, and not of violence and crime.

    Yours truly,

    Geo. F. Baer
    President.

Mr. W. F. Clark,

    Wilkes-Barre,

        Pennsylvania.

A key break for the strikers came in August with the publication of the famous "divine right" letter (left) from operator George F. Baer (above) to a Wilkes-Barre photographer. Public opinion rallied to the miners, the New York Tribune, *for example, calling Baer "God's viceregent at the mines."*

Little by little, Mitchell began to lay the foundations of an enduring union which has engendered a loyalty probably unsurpassed in any other labor organization in America. Touring the anthracite area four decades later, Leighton could write:

It would be inaccurate to say that the miner's attitude toward the union resembles that of the Roman toward the citizenship, but the feeling invoked is as powerful and as subtle. To utter the word is to touch a vital nerve. The union may be hoary with age, may be racked with faction, officials may be corrupt, a miner's card may have lapsed years ago . . . he may be a judge on the bench after a slate picker's childhood, he may have quit the mines and the region—it makes no difference. Under all these ashes the idea of the union is still a live coal.

Still, organizing was slow, slogging work, and by the beginning of 1900 the United Mine Workers could count just 8,993 members—only about six per cent of the anthracite working force of more than 140,000. But the accumulated weight of their grievances began to engender among all the men a determination to strike. Mitchell held them off as long as he could, doubting that the union was strong enough to win and knowing its national treasury could not sustain many families should the stoppage be prolonged. But despite all he could do, the vote to strike was taken.

To his unlooked-for delight, between 80,000 and 100,000 men walked out of the mines on September 17. Their number grew to 125,000, but the mine operators, believing that once they recognized the union their control over their men would be lost forever, refused even to meet with Mitchell to negotiate the issues.

At this point politics entered the scene. Mark Hanna, running McKinley's "Full Dinner Pail" campaign, impressed upon the operators that if the strike were not settled, it might spread into the midwestern bituminous states—which also happened to be the core of McKinley's support—and seriously hurt Republican chances. Reluctantly, the mine owners yielded. They still would not deign to meet with Mitchell. But at their collieries they posted notices of a ten per cent wage increase, and on October 29 the miners, mollified by this partial victory, returned to work. Ever since then, October 29, known as "Mitchell Day," has been a holiday throughout the anthracite.

Both sides seemed to realize that it was a phony peace. After the settlement the operators complained that wildcat strikes were multiplying. They regretted having yielded to Hanna's coaxing. For their part, the miners complained that management was doing everything it could to stamp out the union. The operators began building stockades around their collieries, hiring "coalies" to guard them, and stockpiling coal against another strike. Meanwhile, Mitchell and his corps of organizers sought to extend their membership gains. All through the mine fields, the stage was being set for another test; on both sides the feeling grew that this one would be fought to a finish.

Again Mitchell, an innately conservative man who preferred to settle differences by arbitration, sought to stave it off. Throughout 1901 "the cold coal war," as Robert J. Cornell has called it in his excellent recent study, went on. Several times Mitchell sought a conference with the railroad presidents. His courteously phrased requests were refused—or ignored. Once when he and the union presidents of the three major anthracite districts went to New York to see President E. B. Thomas of the Erie, they were informed he had gone to Europe, and when Thomas returned he would not even answer Mitchell's letters.

Finally, in March of 1902, after a year of trying, a full-dress conference was arranged. Mitchell outlined the union's demands:

Recognition of the United Mine Workers

A minimum wage scale

An eight-hour day

A twenty per cent wage increase

The weighing of coal using as the legal ton 2,240 pounds, for which the minimum rate would be sixty cents.

The operators replied that granting these demands would drive some of them into bankruptcy, and negotiations dragged on without practical result, except to postpone a strike that now seemed inevitable.

And yet, looking back, one has the distinct impression that it was not.

One of the operators remarked after the conference that he "did not know but what it was the best thing to do—to make a contract with Mr. Mitchell's organization"; Mitchell, he said, had impressed him "with being a very fair and conservative man." Another said: "I am not prepared to go that far, but I will say this: that I have changed my mind on several points. This man Mitchell is quite a man. I am beginning to like him."

Nevertheless, because those on each side of the table were what they were, a strike became a certainty. Behind the intransigence of the rank-and-file miner was not his immediate condition (though by modern standards that was bad enough) but the long, hard past, with its crippled and dead, its endless grubbing to make ends meet, the years of dreary living in dreary company houses with the debts piling up at the "pluck-me" company store. The miners held the firm opinion, based upon hard experience, that whatever concessions the operators had ever granted had had to be wrung out of them. The only wringer the miners knew was the strike. Behind the obstinacy of the operators, on the other hand, lay a longing for the free-wheeling past, when they could run their businesses as they pleased.

And so, on May 12, 1902, 147,000 miners walked off the job. The great anthracite strike was on.

As the days of idleness mounted into weeks and the weeks into months, the strike laid a heavy burden on the miners and their families. What savings they had were soon used up. And yet children had to be fed, and household expenses, pared to the minimum, could be pared no further. Nerves frayed, tempers flared easily, and crowds of idle men turned suddenly ugly.

Some miners, uncommitted to the union or simply driven by need, returned to work, and these soon became prime targets for the strikers. Wherever they went they—and their wives and children—were taunted by cries of "Scab!" Some were even set upon by mobs, and a few were killed. One man awoke in the middle of the night to find his house on fire; outside was an angry mob calling for him to be shot. He barely escaped with his life.

When the Reverend Carl Hauser, a Lutheran minister, went to Lansford to conduct burial services for one of his foreign-born parishioners, he was met by a committee and told he should not bury the man, because he was a scab. "He is a Lutheran," Mr. Hauser answered, "he is a Christian and belongs to my church, and I am called by the Lutheran people . . . to bury that man and I will bury that man." But nobody would even go into the house to carry the corpse to the hearse. When finally the minister managed to corral four reluctant pallbearers, they emerged from the house to find an angry crowd—"they were not so-called foreigners but were American people," Mr. Hauser noted—lining both sides of the street and yelling: "Let that dog lie. Bury somebody else," and, "It's a shame to bury a scab." When the lonely little funeral cortege reached the cemetery, more strikers lined the fence. "Nobody went to the grave," Mr. Hauser recalled later, "only the undertaker and a few women, I guess. I went back and before the big crowd

I told the sexton, 'You are responsible for that body.'" He was afraid they might desecrate the grave.

Pent-up emotions finally came to a head on July 30 in the town of Shenandoah. Deputy Sheriff Thomas Beddall, escorting two nonunion men, was surrounded by a crowd of five thousand strikers and forced to take refuge in the Reading Railroad depot. When Beddall's brother Joseph attempted to get arms and ammunition to the beleaguered men, he was mobbed and beaten to death. The sheriff managed somehow to escape and to wire Pennsylvania's Governor William A. Stone to send troops into the region to restore order. Next morning two regiments of National Guard infantry and a troop of cavalry under the command of Brigadier General John P. S. Gobin marched into Shenandoah.

Through August the strike dragged on, with no end in sight. The presence of so many soldiers patrolling the streets, as well as the large number of

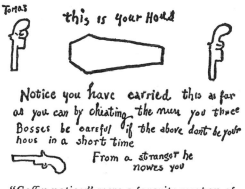

"Coffin-notices" were a favorite weapon of the Molly Maguires, a lawless element that terrorized the coal fields after the Civil War and helped discredit legitimate unions.

armed coal and iron police, grated on the nerves of men and women whose morale was already sagging from long weeks of want. The scattered violence increased, and on August 29 General Gobin felt compelled to issue an order to his unit commanders which concluded:

In moving troops, place reliable, competent and skilled marksmen on the flanks of the command and arm your file closers with loaded guns, and instruct them that in case of attack upon the columns by stones or missiles, where the attacking party cannot be reached, the men thus selected shall carefully note the man attacking the columns, and being certain of his man, fire upon him without any further orders.

To union sympathizers it was soon known as the "shoot-to-kill" order—though in fact the soldiers killed no one—and it made the mood of the strikers even uglier. With the strike going into its fourth month,

their morale was at its lowest ebb. Early in August Mitchell himself had doubts; long afterward he recalled: "I am fully convinced that the strike would have collapsed had the operators at this time opened their mines and invited the strikers to return."

But they did not. Instead, just at this juncture their principal spokesman made the greatest tactical blunder of the strike. Back in July a Wilkes-Barre photographer named William F. Clark had written to George F. Baer, president of the Reading, asking him to settle the strike. Clark hoped, he wrote, that God would "send the Holy Spirit to reason in your heart." Baer's answer, which for some reason did not become generally known until August, has become a classic example of capitalistic arrogance at its apogee:

My dear Mr. Clark:
I have your letter of the 16th inst. I do not know who you are. I see that you are a religious man; but you are evidently biased in favor of the right of the workingman to control a business in which he has no other interest than to secure fair wages for the work he does.
I beg of you not to be discouraged. The rights and interests of the laboring man will be protected and cared for—not by the labor agitators, but by the Christian men of property to whom God has given control of the property rights of the country, and upon the successful management of which so much depends. Do not be discouraged. Pray earnestly that right may triumph, always remembering that the Lord God Omnipotent still reigns, and that His reign is one of law and order, and not of violence and crime.

The newspapers of the country, which already favored the strikers, had a field day. "A good many people think they superintend the earth," said *The New York Times* dryly, "but not many have the egregious vanity to describe themselves as its managing directors." From then on public opinion was almost unanimously on the side of the miners.

Meanwhile autumn was at hand, and in great cities coal supplies were dwindling dangerously. Even President Theodore Roosevelt was worried. He had been worried, in fact, for some time. As early as June 27, he had asked Attorney General Philander Chase Knox if there was any way in which the federal government could intervene. Did the coal and railroad companies constitute a combination in restraint of trade liable to prosecution under the Sherman Act? The statute was too vague, Knox had answered. As Mayor Low of New York City and other local officials communicated to Washington their fears of the consequences of a continued fuel shortage, Roosevelt wrote to Robert Bacon of J. P. Morgan and Company: "The situation is bad, especially because it is possible it may grow infinitely worse. If when the severe weather comes on there is a coal famine I dread to think of the suffering, in parts of our great cities especially, and I fear there will be fuel riots of as bad a type as any bread riots we have ever seen."

He was not oblivious to the political effect of the strike, either. Anthracite, which normally retailed for five or six dollars a ton, was up to twenty dollars in New York, and from Massachusetts Senator Henry Cabot Lodge was warning the President that factors like this could defeat the Republican party in the forthcoming congressional elections. At least, Roosevelt decided, he would do what he could. He dispatched telegrams to Mitchell and to the principal representatives of the operators, asking them to confer with him in Washington on the morning of October 3.

The meeting was held at No. 22 Lafayette Square, for the White House was undergoing repairs. At one end of the room were Baer and the other coal operators; Attorney General Knox; Roosevelt's secretary, George B. Cortelyou; and Carroll D. Wright, Commissioner of Labor. At the other end were Mitchell and the presidents of the three United Mine Workers anthracite districts. A few seconds after 11 A.M. the President entered the room in a wheelchair—he had been injured in a traffic accident the month before—and launched at once into an earnest appeal for peace. Disclaiming any legal right to intervene, he asked both parties whether they had considered the interests of a third—the public. He went on to detail the horrors of a winter coal famine and concluded: "With all the earnestness there is in me I ask that there be an immediate resumption of operations in the coal mines in some such way as will, without a day's unnecessary delay, meet the crying needs of the people. I appeal to your patriotism, to the spirit that sinks personal consideration and makes individual sacrifices for the general good."

Mitchell was on his feet immediately. "I am much pleased, Mr. President, with what you say. We are willing that you shall name a tribunal which shall determine the issues that have resulted in the strike; and if the gentlemen representing the operators will accept the award or decision of such a tribunal, the miners will willingly accept it, even if it be against our claims."

Baer quickly demonstrated an attitude that showed that his famous "divine right" letter had not been a temporary lapse of common sense. To the President of the United States, his tone was almost as condescending as to the obscure Wilkes-Barre photographer: "Thousands of other workmen are deterred from working by the intimidation, violence, and crime inaugurated by the United Mine Workers, over whom John Mitchell, whom you have invited to meet you, is chief." John Markle, representing the independent

operators, asked Roosevelt bluntly: "Are you asking us to deal with a set of outlaws?" And he proceeded to instruct the President in his responsibilities: ". . . I now ask you to perform the duties invested in you as President of the United States, to at once squelch the anarchistic conditions of affairs existing in the anthracite coal regions by the strong arm of the military at your command."

Baer and Markle had threatened the wrong man. Roosevelt kept his temper, but just barely. Inwardly he was seething. Afterward he said, speaking of Baer: "If it wasn't for the high office I hold, I would have taken him by the seat of the breeches and the nape of the neck and chucked him out of that window." And again: "There was only one man in that conference who acted like a gentleman, and that man was not I." The reference was to Mitchell. Indeed, the President wrote to his friend Joseph Bucklin Bishop: "Mitchell shone so in comparison with [the operators] as to make me have a very uncomfortable feeling that they might be far more to blame relatively to the miners

NURSERY RHYMES FOR INFANT INDUSTRIES.

Little Boy Blue, come blow your horn;
There are trusts in the meadow and trusts in the corn!
To curb the fat trusts not an effort he'll make,
As a champion sleeper he captures the cake!

These two cartoons, which appeared in the
New York Journal *during the strike, are the*

298

than I had supposed. I never knew six men to show to less advantage." That was, in fact, the only effect the meeting had: to convince the President that maybe the miners were right.

Once the conference had failed, however, there seemed little he could do. He had no power to send federal troops, as Markle had demanded, unless the governor of Pennsylvania asked for them. But that did not for a moment discourage the President. "The one condition Roosevelt's spirit could not endure," his friend Mark Sullivan wrote, "was any situation in which individuals or groups seemed able to defy or ignore the people as a whole and their representative in the White House. . . . He could not endure to be dared." If a request from the governor was necessary, Roosevelt would make sure one came. Through Senator Matthew Quay of Pennsylvania he sought to persuade Stone to ask for federal assistance; then he would send in the Army to operate the mines. He had even chosen a troop commander—Major General J. M.

NURSERY RHYMES FOR INFANT INDUSTRIES.

Old King Coal was a jolly old soul,
And a jolly old soul was he:
When he felt in the humor
He'd rob the consumer
And chuckle with fiendish glee.

work of Frederick B. Opper, famous political cartoonist and creator of Happy Hooligan.

Schofield. But the Quay-Stone gambit failed: no request for troops ever came.

Nevertheless, sentiment for a settlement of some kind continued to build up. The operators were under particularly heavy pressure. Roosevelt was too shrewd a politician not to let some word of his take-over plan get through to them. In addition, their conduct at the Washington conference, coming on top of Baer's infamous letter, placed the coal-hungry public even more squarely behind the miners. The strike had now been in progress for almost five months. Violence was increasing; the entire Pennsylvania National Guard—8,750 strong—was now on duty in the coal region.

To Secretary of War Root, who on his own initiative had carefully reviewed the proceedings of the October 3 meeting, it seemed clear that the strike had now reached the point where pride, more than the issues, prevented either side from backing down. He felt the only hope of settlement lay in an agreement similar to the one Mitchell had suggested: the miners to return to work pending appointment of an impartial board of arbitration whose award both they and the operators would consent in advance to accept.

Still on his own hook, but with Roosevelt's acquiescence, Root on October 11 met with J. P. Morgan in New York. Together they worked out a memorandum —which Morgan next day persuaded Baer and his colleagues to sign—asking Roosevelt to set up an arbitration commission. The operators did not, however, entirely abandon their pride. Though they refrained from naming the members for him, they told the President exactly what kinds of men to select: an engineer from one of the military services, a professional mining engineer, a federal judge from the eastern district of Pennsylvania, a businessman familiar with the anthracite industry, and, finally, "a man of prominence, eminent as a sociologist."

Roosevelt was chagrined—and so was Mitchell, when he learned of the memorandum—to note that not one man with a labor background had been suggested. Both felt there should be at least one such individual, and that in addition, because so many of the miners were Catholics, a high-ranking Catholic prelate ought to be named. The operators could not very well oppose the latter suggestion, but they could and did fight very vigorously the naming of any pro-labor representative. A crisis was reached late in the evening of October 15. Roosevelt and two of Morgan's junior partners, Bacon and George W. Perkins, were in the White House with telephone lines open to the offices of Morgan and Baer. All at once there ensued a scene of high comedy, which only Roosevelt could appreciate fully; for suddenly it dawned on him "that the mighty brains of these captains of industry would

299

rather have anarchy than tweedledum, but that if I would use the word tweedledee they would hail it as meaning peace." The President explained:

... it never occurred to me that the operators were willing to run all this risk on a mere point of foolish pride; but Bacon finally happened to mention that they would not object to any latitude I chose under the headings that they had given. I instantly said that I should appoint my labor man as the "eminent sociologist." To my intense relief, this utter absurdity was received with delight by Bacon and Perkins who said they were sure the operators would agree to it! Morgan and Baer gave their consent by telephone and the thing was done.

To Finley Peter Dunne, creator of Mr. Dooley, Roosevelt wrote: "I feel like throwing up my hands and going to the circus, but as that is not possible I think I shall try a turkey shoot or bear hunt . . ." For the benefit of the country, however, he played it straight: in naming as the "eminent sociologist" E. E. Clark, Grand Chief of the Order of Railway Conductors, the White House spokesman added, with tongue in cheek, ". . . the President assuming that for the purpose of such a commission the term sociologist means a man who has thought and studied deeply on social questions and has practically applied his knowledge."

John Lancaster Spalding, Bishop of Peoria, Illinois, was the Catholic prelate selected, and the other members of the commission were Judge George Gray of the United States Circuit Court, who was elected chairman; Edward W. Parker, editor of the *Engineering and Mining Record;* Thomas H. Watkins, a businessman who for twenty years had operated a mine in Scranton; and Brigadier General John M. Wilson, formerly the Army's Chief of Engineers. "Clark and Spalding," wrote Walter Wellman, "would be set down as leaning toward the miners; Parker and Watkins to the owners; with Gray and Wilson as wholly neutral." The President also appointed Labor Commissioner Wright as recorder, and the others promptly elected him a full member of the commission. Roosevelt had chosen an extremely well-qualified group, and in the process had managed to please both parties to the strike. The miners returned to work and the commission members, after a personal inspection tour of the mines, began their formal hearings in Scranton on November 14. There, in a high-ceilinged Victorian courtroom, economic feudalism went on trial.

No one, apparently, expected that the hearings would be brief, and Judge Gray allowed lawyers for all three factions—the nonunion mine workers were presenting their case separately—as much time as they wished. As a result, the hearings continued, in Scranton and later in Philadelphia, for over three months,

with a recess at Christmas. A total of 558 witnesses were heard—240 for the United Mine Workers, 153 for the nonunion men, 154 for the operators, and eleven called by the commission itself. The fifty-six volumes of testimony—by turns bitter and shocking, funny and sad—constitutes a remarkable historical document.

As chief of its legal staff the union had hired Clarence Darrow, who in the next quarter century would make his name as the ablest defense attorney in modern courtroom history. Darrow, playing his cards skillfully, led with his ace: he called John Mitchell to the stand.

If any members of the commission had expected a wild-eyed, fire-eating agitator, they were soon disappointed. Mitchell, dressed as usual in his near-clerical black, the strain of the long strike written clearly in his still-youthful face, stated the union's case calmly and fairly. After Darrow had completed his friendly questioning, Wayne MacVeagh, a former United States attorney general, took over for the operators. His long and grueling cross-examination lasted more than four days, but not once—despite ample provocation—did Mitchell lose his temper. On the contrary, he managed occasionally to enliven the proceedings with rare darts of dry wit. MacVeagh had been badgering him about how, when profits were low, he expected the operators to give the men a raise without passing it on to the consumers, many of whom were poor families:

MACVEAGH: . . . If you demand an increase and they have no profits, where are they going to place it except on the bowed backs of the poor?
MITCHELL: They might put it on the bowed backs of the rich.

With one eye on the commission, the other on public opinion, Darrow followed Mitchell with 239 witnesses, for the most part ordinary miners and their families. Day after day, week after week, there moved across the stand a pitiable parade of the blinded and maimed, the widowed and orphaned, the oppressed and exploited. Darrow was also careful to include a generous leavening of priests and ministers—and in truth such men were in the majority among the minefield clergy—who favored the union's cause. Compared with their powerful stories, the testimony of the nonunion miners and that of the operators' witnesses fails to move one nearly so deeply, at least when read at a remove of nearly sixty years.

But the hearings did more than lengthen the short and simple annals of the poor. The last two men the commission heard before adjourning to consider its decision were Baer, summing up for the operators, and Darrow, for the miners. American history rarely presents such an opportunity to study within a narrow compass the contrast between two utterly opposed philosophies of the social order. Baer—spade-bearded, almond-eyed, self-assured, quoting Seneca, Cervantes, and the Roman law—spoke for the glories of the half century just passed, when capitalism was unrestricted and capitalists answered only to their stockholders. Darrow—given to the florid phrase and the dramatic gesture—spoke for the century just beginning, which would assert the rights of the individual workingman and his union, and would bring an end to the world George Baer had known. A few statements from their long summations, selected at random and juxtaposed, will point up the contrast:

BAER: . . . we do not admit the right of an organization . . . to coerce us . . . or [interfere] with our management. The employer ought, I think, to meet his employees personally . . .

DARROW: . . . these gentlemen who all these long and weary months have refused to know us, to recognize us, have demanded as a condition that these men must give up their union . . . and must come to them with their hat in their hand, each one in a position to be discharged the next moment if they dare to raise their voice.

BAER: [The strike furnished] a record of lawlessness and crimes unparalleled in any community save where contending armies met on fields of legal battle . . .

DARROW: So far as the demands of the Mine Workers are concerned, it makes no difference whether crimes have been committed or not. If John Smith earned $500 a year, it is no answer to say that Tom Jones murdered somebody in cold blood. . . . The question is, what has [Smith] earned?

BAER: If a man comes to me and offers to work for me and I am willing to pay him $2 a day and he is content to take it, that is a bargain as good and as sacred in the eyes of the law as any bargain could be . . .

DARROW: Mr. Baer and his friends imagine no doubt that they are fighting for a grand principle when they fight for what they say is the God-given right of every man to work for any wages he sees fit. . . . But that is not [the] God-given right these gentlemen are interested in. They are interested in the God-given right to hire the cheapest man they can get.

BAER: . . . the eight-hour system, it is proposed, shall bring about . . . the leisure to enable [the miners] to learn to read good novels and sound religious books. (Laughter)

DARROW: It is no answer to say, as some employers have said in this case, "If you give him shorter hours he will not use them wisely." . . . One man may stumble; ten men may stumble; but in the long sweep of time, and in the evolution of events, it must be that greater opportunities mean a more perfect man . . .

And Darrow had the last word:

The blunders are theirs, and the victories have been ours. The blunders are theirs because, [in] this old, old strife they are fighting for slavery, while we are fighting for freedom. They are fighting for the rule of man over man, for despotism, for darkness, for the past. We are striving to build up man. We are working for democracy, for humanity, for the future, for the days that will come too late for us to see it or know it or receive its benefits, but which still will come . . .

And so it has turned out.

When the commission finally announced its award on March 22, 1903, it granted the contract miners a ten per cent wage increase, and there were a few other gains important enough for the rank and file of the strikers to regard the settlement as a victory. Yet since the primary object of the strike—recognition of the United Mine Workers—was not achieved, there were those who said that the miners had lost the strike. But what mattered more was that they had won the battle of public opinion; formal recognition of their union would come. And quite as important—for organized labor and for the nation as a whole—the federal government, for the first time in its history, had intervened in a strike not to break it, but to bring about a peaceful settlement. The great anthracite strike of 1902 cast a long shadow.

Roosevelt went to Mississippi for his bear hunt, and Lodge and the Republicans got their majority at the polls. For Mitchell, however, the fruits of victory were bitter. He stayed on as the United Mine Workers president for five more years, but they were years full of factionalism and eventually, in 1907, he failed to win re-election. The opposition, it was true, came mostly from the bituminous delegates; in the anthracite John Mitchell was still a demigod. But the defeat was final, for all that.

Mitchell was still a young man, but there seemed nothing for him to do. There was some talk of his succeeding Samuel Gompers as president of the American Federation of Labor, and later of his becoming the first Secretary of Labor when Woodrow Wilson made that appointment in 1913. But neither job materialized. Away from the union and the mines Mitchell was lost, and he died, frustrated and worn out, in 1919. He was forty-nine.

THE LEGEND OF

Long before his death, more than forty years ago, Jim Hill had become a legend in the American West. Whether he was hero or villain matters little. He died something of a giant in the vast region where many contemporaries came often to think him less a man than an elemental force. Time has not diminished his stature; neither has it quite managed to condemn him nor to put him safely on the side of the angels.

First of all came the blizzards. Then the droughts. Then the grasshoppers, and hard on the leaping legs of the parasites came James Jerome Hill, Jim Hill, the Little Giant, the Empire Builder, the man who *made* the Northwest, or who wrecked it—Jim Hill, the barbed-

PHOTOGRAPHS FROM GREAT NORTHERN RAILWAY

This was the weathered face of James J. Hill not long before he died in 1916. The New York Times *obituary said: "Greatness became him, and was a condition of his errand here."*

wired, shaggy-headed, one-eyed old so-and-so of western railroading.

Lasting legends are seldom ready-made. They are built from inconsequential stories laid end to end, or piled one upon the other. Of two of the best remembered stories of Jim Hill, one shows him as hero, the other as villain. Once, when a crew was trying to clear track for a Great Northern passenger train stalled in a blinding snowstorm, President Hill came out to snatch a shovel from a man and send that working stiff into the president's business car for hot coffee, while Hill himself shoveled like a rotary plow. One after the other, the gandy-dancers were spelled off and drank fine Java in unaccustomed elegance while the Great Northern's creator faced the storm. *That* was Jim Hill for you. Again, because the mayor of a small Minnesota town objected, mildly, to all-night switching in his village, Hill swore that its people should walk. Then he had the depot torn down and set up two miles away. That, too, was Jim Hill.

The legend carries on: Hill began life with nothing. He died lord of an empire that reached from the Great Lakes to Puget Sound, from the Canadian border to Missouri and Colorado. He had staked out provinces in China and Japan. He died worth $53,-000,000, won in a region so sparsely settled that it was believed by most easterners to be an intact and worthless wilderness. There is more of substance to the Hill legend than shadow.

Born in 1838 in Ontario, Upper Canada, young Hill arrived at eighteen in the raw new settlement at the head of navigation on the Mississippi that was beginning to dislike its pioneer name of Pig's Eye, and was calling itself St. Paul. The time was mid-1856. St. Paul was in its first notable boom. The prosperity was to last a little more than twelve months longer before the Panic of '57 turned the city into what a local historian described as a place of "no business, . . . no banks, . . . no courage, no hope, . . . no foundation to build on."

Twelve months, however, was all young Hill needed. Neither then nor later did panics hurt him. Like his contemporaries, Rockefeller and Carnegie, he wel-

302

JIM HILL

By STEWART H. HOLBROOK

Minnesota, built a railroad empire from the Great Lakes to Puget Sound

This flat, empty country in eastern Montana typifies the terrain through which Hill built his railroad. The photograph was taken in 1887, when in seven and a half months 8,000 men laid 643 miles of track—from Gassman Coulee, North Dakota, to Helena, Montana. It was one of the great construction jobs: every timber, tie, and rail had to be hauled out from Minnesota.

comed them. Panics shook the stuffing out of insecure institutions, leaving useful fragments that able hands might pick up and make into something solid. One year in St. Paul before the debacle of 1857 was time enough. In that period young Hill's energy put down such firm roots in the city that it was to remain his base of operations for the next six decades.

His first job was on the St. Paul water front, where he clerked and made himself useful for an outfit running a line of packet steamers. He saw the first ship-ments of Minnesota grains go down-river. With his own hands he cut the first stencil for the first label of the first flour made in Minnesota. He noted the in-creasing number of immigrants, the steadily mounting tonnage of freight. By 1865 he had set up for himself as a forwarding agent. Within months a local daily paper observed that "J. J. Hill is now prepared to give shippers the lowest rates ever quoted from here to Eastern points. Mr. Hill has nearly all the important carriers of freight in his own hands." When winter

closed river navigation, his big warehouse was not idle; he converted it into a hay-pressing establishment, bringing the admiring editorial comment that "this remarkable young man evidently intends to keep abreast of the times." This was not quite exact; young Hill was keeping ahead of the times. He presently organized what became the Northwestern Fuel Company and virtually a monopoly to supply wood for St. Paul's stoves and furnaces then, having first leased several thousand acres of Iowa coal lands, he introduced that fuel to the city and region. He also contracted to supply fuel to the St. Paul & Pacific Railroad, Minnesota's chief source of revenue for corruptionists, lobbyists, and legislators.

Among the older businessmen who had been observing young Hill's career was Norman W. Kittson, Canadian-born in 1814, a fur trader from youth, who had arrived in Minnesota in the 1830's, served in the territorial and state legislatures, done well in real estate, and was acting as agent in St. Paul for the venerable Hudson's Bay Company. Before accepting this post, Kittson had acted for the independent trappers and traders. He continued to act for them. This odd arrangement satisfied nobody, and Kittson proposed to Hill that he might find it worthwhile if he could devise a way to transport the independents and their supplies from the United States to the fur and farming regions of the Canadian province soon to be called Manitoba.

The Hudson's Bay Company was operating what it considered a monopoly steamboat line on the Red River, which flowed north out of Dakota to the Bay Company's post at Fort Garry (Winnipeg). Hill put a boat of his own on the Red. He added another. He had taken care to bond his steamers, thus complying with a United States customs law which, until then, had been a dead letter. The Bay Company's vessels were suddenly barred from carrying freight; and until the Canadian firm could comply with the forgotten law, the Hill boats enjoyed a lucrative monopoly. When Donald A. Smith, governor of the Bay Company, learned of the coup, he remarked of Hill that "he must be a very able man."

Hill promptly began a rate war against the Bay Company boats so effective as to cause Donald Smith to visit St. Paul. The outcome was a coalition. What the public saw was that Norman Kittson, the Hudson's Bay agent at St. Paul, organized the Red River Transportation Company, in which Hill was a secret partner. Shipping rates on the Red went high and

In 1904 the Great Northern distributed this poster in the East to lure settlers westward. It also sold land along its right of way cheaply and sent immigration agents to Europe.

stayed high. It is of interest to know what "high" meant: during its first season the Kittson-Hill combine returned a net profit of 80 per cent.

Yet Hill was not content. While engaged in his now numerous activities he watched the steady decay of the St. Paul & Pacific Railroad. If they could lay hands on that streak of rust and corruption, he told Kittson, it could be made into a profitable enterprise. Soon came the Panic of 1873 to add the ripening touch. The railroad promptly went into receivership.

Hill and Kittson together could muster a few thousand dollars. To get a firm hold on the St. Paul & Pacific called for infinitely more money. Through Donald Smith and Smith's cousin, George Stephen, head of the Bank of Montreal, $6,000,000 was raised. Hill and Kittson then borrowed and mortgaged and added $780,000 to the syndicate. The four men took over the bankrupt company and reorganized it as the St. Paul, Minneapolis & Manitoba Railroad.

To get it so cheaply, Hill had guided a bondholders' committee over the road—or, as legend has it, over the most worthless stretches of it and in the most decrepit rolling stock Hill could find. While so engaged, he gently admonished them to behold their folly.

Even at $6,780,000, the bondholders' folly was something of a bargain. The new owners promptly sold the major part of the company's land grant for $13,068,-887. They still owned the railroad, such as it was. Of the four partners, Smith was soon to become Lord Strathcona, Stephen was to be made Lord Mount Stephen. The others were to remain Kittson and Hill. Hill took charge of building the Manitoba, as the line was commonly known, into a railroad that would pay its way wherever it went.

Hill was just forty when he set out to make something from the dismal remains of the bankrupt line. Directing the job in person, he drove his construction crews at a furious rate. Across Minnesota went the rails, then north to the border to meet the Canadian Pacific, which built a line south from Winnipeg, a "happy conjunction" made possible by the fact that Hill's Canadian partners were heavy stockholders and leading spirits in Canada's first transcontinental line.

Two thumping wheat harvests followed completion

Construction crews on the St. Paul, Minneapolis & Manitoba—the Great Northern's predecessor—took their own out-size dormitory cars with them as they pushed the road across North Dakota and Montana late in the 1880's. Farther west, the cars had to be sawed down to get through tunnels dug in the mountains. Soldiers went along to ward off hostile Indians.

of the first Hill railroad; the freight traffic grew immense. What had been a trickle of immigrants from Norway and Sweden turned to flood, and not without reason: Hill's agents had been in Scandinavia singing the glories of the Red River of the North. Homesteads could be had free, or Hill would sell them some of the land still in possession of the Manitoba railroad at $2.50 an acre.

Jim Hill's idea of a railroad was not a piece of track to connect the Twin Cities and Winnipeg. As early as 1879 he told his directors he meant to push the line across the continent to Puget Sound. Some of his colleagues were alarmed. No other concern had attempted to build a transcontinental railroad without a subsidy from the government in lands and often in loans. Hill could get no land grant other than the one the road already had in Minnesota, and that would be of no aid in building across Dakota, Montana, Idaho, and Washington. Even if by some quirk he did manage to lay rails to Puget Sound, how then could he hope to compete with the old subsidized lines, the Northern Pacific and the Union Pacific? When Hill's presumptuous plan became public, his railway inevitably was labeled "Hill's Folly."

Hill's Folly moved westward with speed, though not so fast as to preclude short feeder lines being built as the main rails went forward, heading for the northwest shore. Hill seemed to know just where a branch would become a profitable feeder almost as soon as it was laid. Soon the main line started the long haul across Montana, running well north of the Northern Pacific, which Hill pretended to ignore, except to set his freight and passenger rates very low in territory where he could compete with the older road.

Hill was ruthless. Near Great Falls, Montana, which Hill's Folly reached in 1887, he showed what he could do to a stubborn community. He laid his rails in a graceful arc clean around Fort Benton, whose shortsighted townsmen had rejected his demand for a right of way free of charge, and left the settlement a good mile from the tracks. Great Falls had been debating how much to charge Hill for a strip through the city, but observing what had occurred at Fort Benton, it decided to be openhanded, and presented him with a dandy right of way through the center of its city park.

Hill always protected his rear. Grain elevators went up as the main line continued west. More immigrants came to settle on what by now had become the Great Northern Railway. Hill was ready to haul a good healthy peasant from Europe halfway across the United States for $25 if he would promise to drive his stakes along Great Northern rails.

At last the Great Northern reached Puget Sound at Everett, Washington, early in 1893. It was a bad year for railroads. The Santa Fe and the Union Pacific went into receivership. And, to the great delight of Hill, so did his major competitor, the Northern Pacific. Of all the rails that reached the West Coast, only the Great Northern remained intact.

Jim Hill himself was still intact. At 55 he had long since reminded many of a grim old lion—a thickset man with massive head, gray beard and gray hair shaggy as a shorthorn's. He had immense shoulders and one good eye (he had lost the other in a childhood game of bow and arrow) which often seemed to glow in his dark, weathered countenance—said one who saw it—like a live coal at the bottom of a cinder pit.

Men often look the way they do because conditions and their own bent have forged their personality. Hill was one of these. He made people think of some craglike geologic outcropping, a neolithic fact, old Rock of Ages. Yet his was a volcanic base. His temper was such that once he tore a telephone from its moorings and heaved it the length of his office. Again, he fired an inoffensive Great Northern clerk who, when asked by Hill, replied that his name was Spittles. It *was* Spittles, too, and Hill fired him because of it.

Hill had studied the failing Northern Pacific closely; and now, with his old associate of the Bank of Montreal, Lord Mount Stephen, he made an offer to stockholders of the bankrupt line; he would take over and operate it. The deal was halted by an injunction in support of a Minnesota law prohibiting the merger of parallel and competing railroads. But there was nothing to stop Hill from buying Northern Pacific stock copiously. This Hill did. The road was reorganized with the help of J. Pierpont Morgan. Henceforth, for all practical purposes, the NP was a second track for the Great Northern. The two roads became known as the Hill lines, and for them Hill was planning further expansion; he wanted nothing less than the great midwestern property called the Chicago, Burlington & Quincy Railroad.

Hill wanted the Burlington for several reasons, among them the fact that it would give him entry to Chicago and St. Louis. That road touched the Great Northern at St. Paul, and the Northern Pacific at Billings, Montana. It operated large mileages in Iowa and adjacent states, which together comprised America's best domestic lumber market. (The far-western portions of Hill's GN and NP relied heavily on lumber for eastbound freight.) Then, too, the Burlington would give Hill connection with the cotton-hauling roads entering St. Louis and Kansas City, and with the smelters of Colorado and South Dakota, and the packing houses of Omaha. Hill and J. P. Morgan bought the Burlington from under the nose of Edward H. Harriman, who also wanted it.

Ten years younger than Hill, Harriman "looked like a bookkeeper." A rather frail man, he wore thick glasses, had a soft voice, and was both shy and silent. He was also one of the few men who did not fear Morgan. In fact, Harriman feared nobody. At 21 he had owned a seat on the New York Stock Exchange. He headed a syndicate to take over the foundering Union Pacific. (He was soon to get control of the Central Pacific and Southern Pacific as well.) Now he felt ready to begin what went into railroad history as the Hill-Harriman wars. Both men were ruthless enough. Both meant to dominate railroading in the northwestern United States from the Great Lakes to the Pacific.

The Hill-Morgan coup—getting the Burlington—occurred in March, 1901. At almost the same time Harriman, with the backing of Kuhn, Loeb & Company, New York bankers, started secretly to buy into the Northern Pacific. If he couldn't get the Burlington, then he meant to buy control of Hill's second road and be in a position to dictate to Hill. The stock buying was begun so astutely that neither Hill nor Morgan seemed to suspect what was going forward. In fact, everything looked so serene that in April Morgan sailed for Europe, where he planned to take the waters at Aix-les-Bains. That same month, Hill set out to roll westward across his own empire.

During the last week in April Hill, then in Seattle, was perturbed to note a sudden sharp rise in Northern Pacific shares. It troubled him because the Hill-Morgan crowd owned less than half of the NP stock. True, in most cases a strong minority interest was sufficient to hold control of a railroad. But not always. Hill acted promptly. In Seattle he had his car hitched to a locomotive, ordered the tracks cleared, and started a fast run to Chicago, and then on to New York. In New York he went immediately to the office of Jacob H. Schiff of Kuhn, Loeb and demanded to know if Schiff were buying NP shares for E. H. Harriman. Yes, said Schiff, he was. What was more, if the Hill-Morgan crowd would not let Harriman have the Burlington, then Harriman was going to buy the Northern Pacific from under their feet, which, said Schiff, were not planted firmly enough to hold it. Indeed,

Harriman already had control. (Schiff was bragging a little; Harriman needed approximately 40,000 more shares.)

Hill went to the House of Morgan with the bad news that they had been caught napping in the Old Man's absence. The Morgan partners cabled to Aix-les-Bains, asking Morgan for permission to buy 150,-000 shares of NP Common. This happened on a Friday. Next day, while the Morgan partners awaited a reply, Harriman thought to play safe by purchasing another 40,000 shares. He called Schiff's office and gave the order. It was never executed. The devout Schiff was at the synagogue.

By Monday it was too late. Trading on the Exchange had barely begun when the House of Morgan poured buying orders into the market. On Monday alone brokers bought some 127,500 shares of NP Common for the Morgan account. The price climbed from 114 to 127½. And the buying continued. On Tuesday the price hit 149. On Thursday it rose to 1,000.

A sudden if brief panic followed the boom, and many stocks went tumbling. But Hill-Morgan reached an understanding with Harriman. In what was really no more than a partial and temporary armistice, it was agreed Harriman should have representation on the Northern Pacific board. Control of the three railroads, however, remained with the Hill-Morgan people. Hill continued to run the Northern Pacific, the Great Northern, and the Burlington as he thought best.

A business commentator once observed that "Mr. Hill's judgment has never been seriously at fault in any of his undertakings." He had noted that Hill's plans for the three Hill lines became apparent at once. Hill's agents in the Orient prevailed on Japanese industrialists to try a shipment of American cotton to mix with the short-staple article from India they were using. It proved successful; from then on the Hill lines carried an increasing tonnage of American cotton for shipment at Seattle. Minnesota flour began crossing the Pacific in huge volume. Jim Hill liked to say that if each inhabitant of a single province in China could be induced to eat an ounce of flour daily, it would require some fifty million bushels of midwest wheat annually. Hill carried the flour dirt-cheap to Seattle. In fact, his over-all policy was not to charge rates as high as the traffic would stand, but as low as the Hill lines could stand.

Hill's campaign to populate the so-called wastelands between Minnesota and the Cascade Mountains of Oregon and Washington was only too successful. The end result was bad. In the twelve years after 1910, 42 per cent of Montana's great area was tentatively settled by

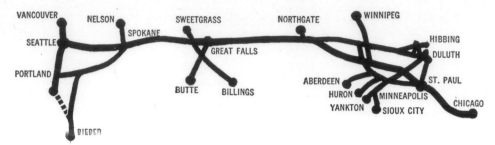

As this outline map shows, the Great Northern spans two thirds of the continent, connecting the principal centers and sending off profitable feeder lines to the smaller cities.

homesteaders, a majority of them induced thither by Hill's agents and his continuous publicity efforts. They plowed this short-grass country deep; erosion followed, and Montana's topsoil was blown away. As a result, the average yield of wheat fell, and abandoned homesteads became a characteristic scene in Montana. Hill's judgment, at least on this occasion, *was* seriously at fault.

Four years after the armistice of 1901, the Hill-Harriman wars broke out anew. Hill was nettled because Harriman, through his Union Pacific and his large interest in the Northern Pacific, considered Oregon to be his domain and may well have believed his position impregnable. Hill, however, thought differently. Before Harriman got wind of it, Hill had completed surveys down the north bank of the Columbia River to occupy a water-level route through the Cascade Mountains, which the Northern Pacific had originally planned to use but which for some reason or other it had deflected to the south bank.

No sooner had Hill's gangs started grading and laying track down the north bank than they were met with injunctions and other legal harassments conjured up by a couple of paper-railroads hastily incorporated by Harriman. Although most of this engagement was fought in the courts, violence broke out in the field. Some of Hill's equipment was dynamited in night raids by unknown parties. Harriman's surveyors were shot at and driven off.

Hill won the north bank fight; and his new line, the Portland & Seattle, went into joint operation by the Great Northern and the Northern Pacific, with headquarters in Portland. Yet he still was not content. He had a foothold in the extreme northwest corner of Oregon. He wanted more. The outcome went into history as the last of the classic railroad battles that had shaken and often entertained the United States periodically for half a century.

Under an assumed name and posing as a wealthy sportsman, John F. Stevens, Hill's incomparable chief engineer, went into central Oregon to buy options on ranches and other property along the Deschutes River.

He also purchased the charter for a nonexistent railroad, the Oregon Trunk, which had never laid a rail. Only then did Jim Hill announce he planned to "open up" central Oregon by building 165 miles of railroad up the river to a place named Bend.

The news of Hill's plan to "develop" a region given over largely to sagebrush, extinct volcanoes, and lava beds, yet hedged with a vast stand of virgin ponderosa pine, gave Harriman a start. Almost nobody lived in the region, even in Bend, its metropolis. Harriman rightly comprehended that Hill planned to build not only to Bend but right on through that town in a direct line to San Francisco, and California was a Harriman province.

To parallel Hill's Oregon Trunk, Harriman hastily moved surveyors and huge gangs of laborers into the neighborhood, and they went to work making grade and laying track up the east bank of the Deschutes River. All Oregon, and much of the Far West, watched with interest while the armies of the two railroad generals massed for an old-fashioned construction war.

In the narrow Deschutes Canyon, little more than a cleft in high, craggy cliffs of rock, the opposing crews used dynamite on each other. For close fighting the weapons were shovels, crowbars, and pick handles. In more open spaces, the factions harassed one another's right of way with fences, barricades of rock, and court orders. Armed guards occasionally lay flat on the rimrock to shoot at any mysterious movements below.

The campaign came to a head at the ranch of a man named Smith, who sold his property to Harriman. There was no other route to Bend except through this ranch. Hill decided to arbitrate. Harriman was willing. A truce was signed by which Hill agreed to build no farther south than Bend. But west of the Cascade Range the war continued, no longer with violence but with electric lines and coastwise steamships.

This struggle was still going on when Harriman died in 1909. It was not finished in 1916, when Hill died. Only by the mid-1920's, when the Great Northern at last gained entry to San Francisco, over the tracks of the Western Pacific, could the Hill-Harriman wars be said to be over. By then it was something of a hollow victory anyhow; in the very year Harriman died, Henry Ford had announced his Model T. One era was ending, a new one dawning.

308

What might be called Hill's private life presented no difficulties to his official biographer. There were no family skeletons to be concealed. No de-spicing was necessary. Seemingly his private affairs were as placid as his business career was stormy. His marriage, in 1867, to Mary Theresa Mehegan, daughter of Irish Catholic immigrants, was "one of those perfect unions of which the world hears little because of their completeness." Three sons and seven daughters were born to the Hills. Of her husband Mrs. Hill remarked that "he never brought his business home."

Though Hill seems never to have embraced the Catholic Church as a communicant, he first and last made it gifts of something more than one million dollars. His will also set aside a million dollars to establish the James Jerome Hill Reference Library in St. Paul, opened in 1917. His hobbies, such as raising fine cattle and swine and experimenting in the growing of grain, were closely related to his railroad interests. Yet he took no little satisfaction from his collection of paintings. He began it with a Corot, a good Millet, then added works by Daubigny, Dupré, Deschamps, T. Rousseau, and one of Delacroix's better pictures. All these artists were much admired at the time. Yet, early in the eighties, Hill was purchasing paintings by younger men like Monet and Renoir.

Thus there is little in James J. Hill at home on which to build a legend. It was Jim Hill in action who went into legendry. One of his appealing qualities was that he was not an absentee-emperor whose knowledge of his realm came solely from his agents and captains. In person he had walked on snowshoes across Minnesota in the days when the Sioux were on the warpath. He had camped on the banks of the Red River when Manitoba was still Prince Rupert's Land. By foot, horse, or rail he had been to all the limits reached by the Hill lines. When the Great Northern's Number One train, the *Empire Builder,* whistles for Sauk Centre or Fargo or Whitefish or Spokane on its way two thousand miles across the top of the United States, the echoes find scarcely a stark butte or valley that Jim Hill himself had not seen at first hand.

One who has been riding the Hill lines for many years is likely to fancy that in them he finds certain qualities of Jim Hill the man. By this I mean the land, the climate, and the very towns and flag stops of this now spectacular, now monotonous, but often handsome, harsh, desolate, wild, and bitter region. Take little Malta, Montana, an angry sun beating down, baking the false fronts, roasting the soil . . . or Havre, Montana, at night, snapping from cold, coyotes yelping within sound of the roundhouse . . . or the glittering hill that is Butte at twilight—Butte twinkling with astonishing brilliance in this thin air, seen from the Northern Pacific's limited as she comes suddenly out of the high pass of the Rockies, while away to the south stands the enormous stack marking Anaconda, spewing yellow fumes and death to vegetation. . . . The Kootenai, a tumult of white water boiling over rocks, sea green in the pools . . . then the immense lushness of the Wenatchee orchards . . . and at last the long thundering bore straight through the Cascade Range and emergence into the fog-ridden silence of the towering firs, the most somber and melancholy forest on earth; then the lights of Puget Sound and the hoarse calls of ships bound for the Orient.

Jim Hill hitched these places and things together, then went on to tie them to Chicago, to Omaha, St. Louis, Kansas City, and Denver. They comprised the Hill lines. The Hill lines comprised an empire. I can think of few other Americans who had quite so much direct influence on quite so large a region.

The patent medicines of the Nineteenth Century claimed much and cured little.

Who put the borax in Dr. Wiley's butter?

False cures and adulterated foodstuffs were flooding the market when a chemist and his "poison squad" pushed through the first Pure Food and Drugs Law

By GERALD CARSON

On a hot and humid July morning in 1902, a burly, 200-pound scientist and connoisseur of good food and drink sat hunched over his desk in a red brick building in Washington and planned deliberately to feed twelve healthy young men a diet containing borax. Dr. Harvey W. Wiley, chief chemist of the Department of Agriculture, had in mind a double objective: first, to determine the effects upon human beings of certain chemicals then commonly used to preserve processed foods; and, more broadly, to educate the public in the need for a federal "pure food" law. Food preparation was becoming industrialized and subject to more complicated processing; products were traveling longer distances, passing through many hands. Manufacturers, facing a novel situation, turned to dubious additives to make their products appear more appetizing or to preserve them. Borax compounds, the first object of Dr. Wiley's investigations, were used to make old butter seem like new.

Volunteers for the experiment were recruited from the Department of Agriculture. They pledged themselves to obey the rules. A small kitchen and dining room were fitted out in the basement of the Bureau of Chemistry offices with the assistant surgeon-general in attendance to see to it that the subjects of the experiment did not get too much borax, and Dr. Wiley to see that they got enough. A bright reporter, George Rothwell Brown, of the Washington *Post,* gave the volunteers an enduring handle, "the poison squad"; and before long the public began referring to Wiley, affectionately or otherwise according to the point of view, as "Old Borax."

Six of Dr. Wiley's co-operators at the hygienic table got a normal ration plus measured doses of tasteless, odorless, invisible boracic acid. The other six also enjoyed a wholesome diet, with equally tasteless, odorless, invisible borate of soda added to their menu. The resulting chemical and physiological data was quite technical. But the meaning was clear. The effects of borax included nausea and loss of appetite, symptoms resembling those of influenza and overburdened kidneys. The feeding experiments continued over a five-year period. After the borax initiation, which made a popular sensation, the squad subsequently breakfasted, lunched, and dined on dishes containing salicylates, sulfurous acid and sulfites, benzoates, formaldehyde, sulfate of copper, and saltpeter. Seldom has a scientific experiment stirred the public imagination as did Dr. Wiley's novel procedures in, as he said, "trying it on the dog."

"My poison squad laboratory," said Dr. Wiley, "became the most highly advertised boarding-house in the world."

A popular versifier wrote a poem about it, the "Song of the Pizen Squad." Lew Dockstader introduced a topical song into his minstrel show. The chorus closed with the prediction:

Next week he'll give them mothballs à la New-
*   burgh or else plain:*
O they may get over it but they'll never look the
*   same!*

The New York *Sun* sourly handed Wiley the title of "chief janitor and policeman of the people's insides," an expression of one line of attack which the opposition was to take—invasion of personal liberty.

The movement to protect the health and pocketbook of the consumer was directed no less at "the patent medicine evil" than it was at the chaotic situation in the food manufacturing field. The "cures" for cancer, tuberculosis, "female weakness," the dangerous fat reducers and "Indian" cough remedies were a bonanza for their proprietors, and many an advertising wizard who knew little enough of drugs or materia medica came to live in a jigsaw mansion and drive a spanking pair of bays because he was a skillful manipulator of hypochondria and mass psychology. Slashing exposés in the popular magazines told of babies' soothing syrups containing morphine and opium, of people who became narcotic addicts, of the use of tonics that depended upon alcohol to make the patient feel frisky.

"Gullible America," said Samuel Hopkins Adams in an angry but thoroughly documented series of articles, "will spend this year [1905] some seventy-five millions of dollars" in order to "swallow huge quantities of alcohol . . . narcotics . . . dangerous heart depressants . . . insidious liver stimulants."

The nostrum vendors at first looked upon the Food and Drugs Act as a joke. In time the manufacturers of Pink Pills for Pale People learned the hard way that they were living dangerously when they ignored the precept, "Thou shalt not lie on the label."

As public interest rose in "the food question," powerful groups took their places in the line of battle to contest the pure food and drug bills which appeared, and died, in Congress with monotonous regularity. On the one side were aligned consumer groups—the General Federation of Women's Clubs, the National Consumers' League, the Patrons of Husbandry, and the labor unions. With them stood food chemists who had had experience in state control work, the American Medical Association, important periodicals (*Collier's Weekly*, Bok's *Ladies' Home Journal*, *World's Work*, *The Independent*, *Cosmopolitan*), President Theodore Roosevelt, and Dr. Wiley.

In opposition were the food manufacturers and manufacturers of articles used in the adulteration of foods and drugs such as cottonseed oil, the proprietary medicine industry, the distillers, canners, *Leslie's Weekly* (to which Dr. Wiley was anathema), newspaper publishers opposed for business reasons, Chicago meat packers, and powerful lobbyists holed up at the Willard and the Raleigh Hotel; also an obdurate Senate, responsive to pressures from big business. Wiley, as the leading personality in the fight for a food bill, achieved the uncommon distinction of acquiring almost as many enemies as did President Roosevelt himself.

When the average member of Congress, newspaper publisher, or pickle manufacturer smelled socialism and deplored the effects of the proposed legislation upon business, he was only responding normally to two powerful stimuli: self-interest and the nostalgic memory of his lost youth. Most mature Americans of the 1880-1900 period were born on farms or in rural areas and knew the conditions of life of a scattered population. The close-knit farm family was the dominant economic unit. It raised, processed, cured, and stored what it ate, and there is abundant evidence that it ate more and better food than the common man of Europe had ever dreamed of tasting. There was no problem of inspection or of deceptive labels. No "Short-weight Jim" invaded the home kitchen or smokehouse. If the preparation was unsanitary, it was no one else's business. What wasn't raised locally was obtained by barter. There were adequate forces of control over that simple transaction—face-to-face bargaining, community of interest, fear of what the neighbors would say.

As to drugs and medicines, grandma could consult the "family doctor" book and compound her home remedies from roots, herbs, and barks gathered along the edge of forest, meadow, and stream: catnip for colic, mullein leaf for asthma, the dandelion for dyspepsia, and so on through the list of simples, essences, flowers, tinctures, and infusions, whose chief merit was that they did not interfere with the tendency of the living cell to recover.

When Americans were called to the cities by the factory whistle, a dramatic change took place in their food supply. No longer was there personal contact between the producer and consumer, nor could the buyer be wary even if he would. For how could a city man candle every egg, test the milk, inquire into the handling of his meat supply, analyze the canned foods which he consumed in increasing quantities?

Since foodstuffs had to stand up in their long transit from the plant to the home, it is not surprising that unhealthy practices developed. During the "embalmed beef" scandal, for example, there was a debate as to whether a little boric acid in fresh beef was after all only an excusable extension of the ancient and accepted use of saltpeter in corning beef. Analytical chemistry was called upon increasingly to make cheap foods into expensive ones, to disguise and simulate, to arrest the processes of nature. The food manufacturers raided the pharmacopœia. But the salicylic acid that was approved in the treatment of gout or rheumatism was received with mounting indignation on the dining room table where it proved to be a depressant of the processes of metabolism. It was objectionable on another ground too—that it led to carelessness in the selection, cleansing, and processing of foodstuffs.

It is difficult to picture today the vast extent of adulteration at the beginning of this century. More than half the food samples studied in the Indiana state laboratory were sophisticated. Whole grain flour was "cut" with bran and corn meal. The food commissioner of North Dakota declared that his state alone consumed ten times as much "Vermont maple syrup" as Vermont produced. The *Grocer's Companion and Merchant's Hand-Book* (Boston, 1883), warned the food retailer, in his own interest, of the various tricks used to alter coffee and tea, bread and flour, butter and lard, mustard, spices, pepper, pickles, preserved fruits, sauces, potted meats, cocoa, vinegar, and candies. A New York sugar firm was proud to make the point in its advertising of the 1880's that its sugar contained "neither glucose, muriate of tin, muriatic acid, nor any other foreign, deleterious or fraudulent substance whatever." The canned peas looked garden-fresh after treatment with $CuSO_4$ by methods known as "copper-greening." The pork and beans contained formaldehyde, the catsup benzoic acid. As a capstone of inspired fakery, one manufacturer of flavored glucose (sold as pure honey) carefully placed a dead bee in every bottle to give verisimilitude.

The little man of 1900 found himself in a big, big world, filled with butterine and mapleine.

This is not to suggest that the pioneer food manufacturer was as rascally as his contemporaries, the swamp doctor and the lightning rod peddler. What was occurring was less a collapse of human probity than an unexpected testing of human nature in a new context. Someone has said that all morality is based upon the assumption that somebody might be watching. In the milieu of late Nineteenth-Century business, nobody seemed to be watching. Thus the food crusade became necessary as a means of redressing the balance in the market which had turned so cruelly against the ordinary American and, indeed, against the honest manufacturer.

The ensuing controversy was symptomatic of the passing—painful, nostalgic to many, including no doubt many a big business senator—of the old, simple life of village and farm which was doomed by the expanding national life. It was, one feels, not solely in defense of the hake (sold as genuine codfish with boric acid as a preservative) that Senator George Frisbie Hoar of Massachusetts rose in the Senate to exalt "the exquisite flavor of the codfish, salted, made into balls, and eaten on a Sunday morning by a person whose theology is sound, and who believes in the five points of Calvinism."

The friends of food reform needed all the courage and public discussion they could muster. Since 1879, when the first federal bill was proposed, 190 measures to protect the consumer had been introduced in Con-

A FERTILE FIELD FOR THE MUCK-RAKE
THE SAUSAGE DEPARTMENT IN A CHICAGO PACKING-HOUSE

This interior view of a Chicago packing-house occupied a full page of a 1906 issue of Collier's. *Such vivid reportage greatly abetted the long fight for a pure food and drugs bill.*

gress, of which 49 had some kind of a subsequent history, and 141 were never heard of again. Meanwhile the states did what they could. About half of them had passed pure food laws by 1895. But there was no uniformity in their regulations. Foods legal in one state might be banned in another. Some of the laws were so loosely drawn that it was quite conceivable that Beechnut Bacon might be seized by the inspectors because no beechnuts were involved in its curing. Was Grape-Nuts misbranded because the great Battle Creek "brain food" had only a fanciful connection with either grapes or nuts? One bill actually proposed a numerical count of the contents of a package—the grains of salt, the cherries in a jar of preserves. What if Mr. Kellogg had to count every corn flake which went into his millions of packages?

Conflicts and foolish regulations could be ironed out over a period of time. The fatal flaw was that individual states had no power to get at the real problem:

interstate traffic in the "patented" bitters, cancer cures, and strawberry jellies made out of dyed glucose, citric acid, and timothy seed.

The act which Wiley drew up was first introduced in 1902. It was successfully sidetracked in one legislative branch or the other for four years. The provisions were simple. In essence, it was a labeling act.

"Tell the truth on the label," Dr. Wiley said, "and let the consumer judge for himself."

Some of the legislators who opposed the act were states' rights Democrats, concerned about constitutional interpretation, who in the end fortunately saw the wisdom of sacrificing principle for expediency. Others were Old Guard Republicans who were special custodians of the *status quo* and highly sensitive to the sentiments of the business community: men like Senators Aldrich of Rhode Island (wholesale groceries), Kean of New Jersey (preserving and canning), Platt of Connecticut (home of the great Kickapoo Indian remedies), Hale and Frye of Maine, along whose rock-bound coast the familiar Maine herring became "imported French sardines," packaged in boxes with French labels.

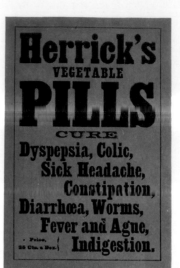

The tactic in the Senate was one of unobtrusive obstruction and lip service to the idea of regulation. Open opposition was never much of a factor. "The 'right' to use deceptive labels," observed *The Nation*, "is not one for which impassioned oratory can be readily invoked." When a serious try was made to pass a general pure food law in 1902-3, Senator Lodge was able to direct the attention of the Senate to legislation more urgently needed, such as a Philippine tariff bill. In the last session of the 59th Congress (1904-5) the food bill was considered less pressing than a proposal to award naval commissions to a couple of young men who had been expelled from the Academy for hazing but still wanted very much to become officers in the United States Navy.

President Roosevelt finally decided to push the issue. "Mr. Dooley" offered a version of how it happened. "Tiddy," he said, was reading Upton Sinclair's novel, *The Jungle,* a grisly sociological tract on "Packingtown." "Tiddy was toying with a light breakfast an' idly turnin' over th' pages iv th' new book with both hands. Suddenly he rose fr'm th' table, an' cryin': 'I'm pizened,' begun throwin' sausages out iv th' window. Th' ninth wan sthruck Sinitor Biv'ridge on th' head an' made him a blond. It bounced off, exploded, an' blew a leg off a secret-service agent, an' th' scatthred fragmints desthroyed a handsome row iv ol' oak-trees. Sinitor Biv'ridge rushed in, thinkin' that th' Prisidint was bein' assassynated be his devoted followers in th' Sinit, an' discovered Tiddy engaged in a hand-to-hand

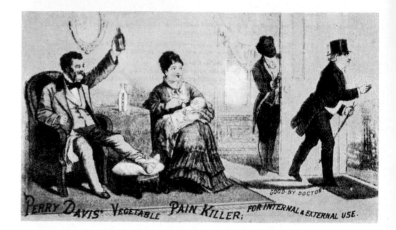

PERRY DAVIS' VEGETABLE PAIN KILLER; FOR INTERNAL & EXTERNAL USE.

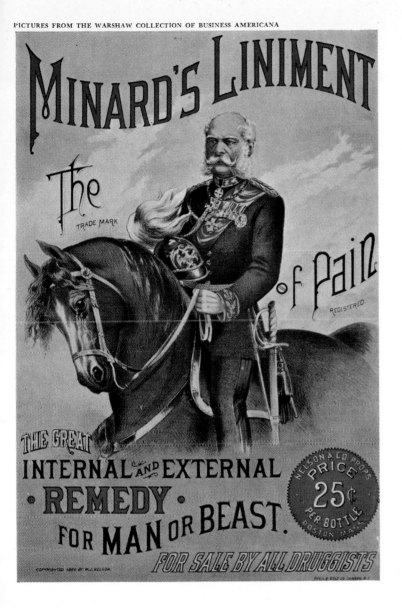

The men in the gray flannel suits had few verbal restrictions before the passage of the Pure Food and Drugs Act in 1906. Their products, displayed here on posters, trade cards, and pamphlets, were emphatically declared to be good for either man or beast, mother or child, one's inside or one's outside. Experiments on patent medicines showed that some of them had as high an alcoholic content as corn whisky, but of course ingredients were never listed on the label in those days.

conflict with a potted ham. Th' Sinitor fr'm Injyanny, with a few well-directed wurruds, put out th' fuse an' rendered th' missile harmless. Since thin th' Prisidint, like th' rest iv us, has become a viggytaryan. . . ." At any rate, in his annual message to Congress, December 5, 1905, Roosevelt recommended in the interest of the consumer and the legitimate manufacturer "that a law be enacted to regulate interstate commerce in misbranded and adulterated foods, drinks and drugs," and the bill was re-introduced in the Senate by Senator Weldon B. Heyburn of Idaho. Pressure from the American Medical Association, the graphic exposé of revolting conditions in the Chicago packing houses, and Roosevelt's skillful use of the report of an official commission which investigated the stockyards, finally forced a favorable vote in the Senate and then the House on the Pure Food and Drugs Bill. The meat inspection problem was, actually, a different matter. But an angry public was in no mood to make fine distinctions. Meat, processed foods, and fake medicines all tapped the family pocketbook, all went into the human stomach, and all smelled to high heaven in the spring of 1906. Roosevelt signed the bill into law on June 30, 1906.

The enforcement of the law was placed in the hands of Dr. Wiley. According to the Doctor, it was after the bill became law that the real fight began. Most food and drug manufacturers and dealers adjusted their operations to the new law, and found themselves in a better position because of it, with curtailment of the activities of fly-by-night competition and re-establishment of the consumers' confidence in goods of known quality. But there were die-hards like the sugar and molasses refiners, the fruit driers, whisky rectifiers, and purveyors of wahoo bitters, Peruna and Indian Doctor wonder drugs.

The administration of the Food and Drugs Act involved the Bureau of Chemistry in thousands of court proceedings, *United States* v. *Two Barrels of Desiccated Eggs, United States* v. *One Hundred Barrels of Vinegar;* and one merciful judge noted that Section 6 extended the protection of the act to our four-footed friends. Pure food inspectors had seized 620 cases of spoiled canned cat food. When the case of the smelly tuna fish turned up in the western district court of the state of Washington, the judge cited man's experience with cats throughout recorded time: "Who will not

feed cats must feed mice and rats." He confirmed the seizure and directed an order of condemnation.

The law was subsequently strengthened both by legal interpretations and by legislative action, as experience developed needs not met by the original act. Government technicians worked with private industry in the solution of specific problems such as refrigeration and the handling of food. When Dr. Wiley retired from public service in 1912, a revolution had occurred in food processing in only six years' time. Yet the food industry had hardly begun to grow.

"The conditions created by the passage of the act," said Clarence Francis, former president and chairman of the board of General Foods Corporation, "invited responsible business men to put real money into the food business."

The next 25 years saw the decline of the barrel as a food container and its replacement by the consumer unit package; the setting of official standards for the composition of basic food products; and the banning of quack therapeutic mechanical devices such as the electric belt, whose galvanic properties were once presented so vividly to the "Lost Manhood" market. We still have with us in some measure the "horse beef" butcher and the "butterlegger." Tap water remains a tempting means of "extending" many foods. But there is no question about the general integrity of our food supply, the contribution to the national well-being of the original food law, as amended, and the readiness of today's food industry leaders to accept what is now called the Food, Drug, and Cosmetic Act as a proper blueprint of their obligation to the nation's consumers.

By JOHN A. GARRATY

How J. P. Morgan,

like a "one-man Federal Reserve,"

calmed the bankers

and helped ease the Panic of 1907

A LION IN THE STREET

On August 8, 1911, a committee of the House of Representatives was interrogating George W. Perkins, a former partner of the House of Morgan, about the control of the Morgan firm over the steel industry. Tempers matched the heat of the Washington weather as the questioning ranged over every aspect of the firm's affairs. Time and again the witness and Chairman Augustus O. Stanley clashed—interrupting each other repeatedly, their voices rising. Stanley asked Perkins about his personal contributions to political campaigns, and when Perkins, upon advice of counsel, refused to answer, Stanley threatened to cite him for contempt. Thereupon the members of the committee wrangled endlessly in a partisan discussion of the propriety of the question. Finally, perhaps to clear the air, Congressman Charles Lafayette Bartlett of Georgia turned to the role of J. P. Morgan in the Panic of 1907. "Is it not a fact," he asked the witness, "that Mr. Morgan and his associates, not only in that panic but in all panics and at all times, so control and dominate the financial situation in New York that they can control it as they please?" Perkins leaped from his chair, pounding the committee table with clenched fists. "Absolutely not," he snapped. "There never was anything further from the facts. . . . Mr. Morgan was able to do what he did in that panic because of the man and his personality, and because people believed in him."

"You need not get excited about it," said Bartlett soothingly. "I am not getting excited," Perkins stated quietly. "But I am in earnest."

Perkins' vehemence was understandable. No one had been closer to Morgan during the spectacular days of October and November, 1907, when the whole structure of American finance tottered on the verge of the abyss. He remembered the white and shaken faces of the nation's leading bankers as they crowded into Morgan's offices literally begging for direction, while mobs ranged aimlessly through Wall Street and panicked depositors clamored for their savings before the doors of some of the largest trust companies in the city. Morgan had been indeed, in the words of Frederick Lewis Allen, a "one-man Federal Reserve Bank" in the crisis.

The troubles of the autumn of 1907 were unexpected only in their violence. As early as May, Wall Street was predicting "a pretty serious time next fall." The stock market was sluggish, new bond issues almost impossible to move; everyone seemed afraid to lend money. Through the summer things got no better. The great Union Pacific Railroad tried to float a $75,000,000 bond issue but could dispose of only $4,000,000. Industrial activity faltered; steel production was down about 20 per cent from the summer of 1906. In October conditions grew worse, for crops were late that year and farmers were straining the already precarious credit structure by seeking extensions of their loans to tide them over.

Suddenly the financial community was rocked by news of the failure of a big copper speculator named F. Augustus Heinze. Heinze controlled a chain of banks; it was rumored that these banks were involved in his personal collapse, and frightened depositors flocked to withdraw their funds. Their fear was contagious. Heinze's banks were basically sound, but other institutions could not withstand the infection. By October 21 the Knickerbocker Trust Company, with deposits of $60,000,000, was in serious difficulty. Its president had been associated with the unfortunate Heinze, and its affairs were in bad shape. Lacking liquid funds, it could not meet the sudden demands of its frightened depositors without outside help. That afternoon its officers descended upon J. P. Morgan in search of assistance.

John Pierpont Morgan, the Banker's Banker.

Morgan had spent the summer in Europe and the weeks immediately preceding the crisis at an Episcopal convention in Richmond, Virginia. Seventy years old and semiretired, he had not followed events closely. He was faced suddenly with the terrified clamor of hundreds of uncertain, befuddled financiers. Yet in a matter of hours he had a firm grasp of what was happening. Then, calmly but with iron determination, he took over.

Quietly he assembled a group of young banking experts who could examine the assets of doubtful institutions and find out whether or not they were worth helping. The Knickerbocker Trust, they said, was not sound; Morgan (although he owned stock in the company himself) coldly decided to let it go to the wall. By the afternoon of Tuesday, October 22, after doling out $8,000,000 to an unending line of creditors, the Knickerbocker closed its doors.

It was now clear that the financial world was "in for it." For a decade previous to 1907 there had been a remarkable growth of a new kind of bank—the trust company. Ordinary banks were required by law to maintain large cash reserves, but trust companies were not. With only 2 or 3 per cent of their assets lying idle in the form of cash, trust companies could afford to pay high interest rates to depositors. Between 1898 and 1906 their business more than quadrupled. But all at once, with the collapse of the Knickerbocker Trust, the public became frightened. And it was all too obvious to the financiers that the trust companies, with their low reserves, would be hard pressed by even a moderate panic among their depositors. Still worse, there was no organization among them comparable to the Clearing House, which operated as a bulwark for hard-pressed banks.

George W. Perkins, top Morgan lieutenant.

The Knickerbocker Trust gave up the ghost at two o'clock on the twenty-second. At once Morgan decided to ask Secretary of the Treasury George Cortelyou to come to New York. While Cortelyou was en route, Morgan instructed his partner Perkins to try to get the presidents of the city's trust companies to organize for their mutual defense, but Perkins discovered that none of them was willing to call a meeting, fearing that if he did his own institution would be suspected of weakness. Morgan and Perkins then conferred at length with George F. Baker of the First National Bank and James Stillman of the National City Bank, and when Cortelyou arrived at about nine in the evening, their group was closeted with him for hours in his rooms at the Manhattan Hotel. Cortelyou agreed to deposit government cash in the New York *banks,* but the danger to the trust companies remained.

The most likely scene of future trouble seemed to be the Trust Company of America. This company, one of the biggest in New York, held a large block of stock in the Knickerbocker Trust as collateral for loans, and rumors connected it with the Heinze copper speculations. That day the company had experienced heavy withdrawals, although not of panic proportions. As a result, Morgan's committee had begun to look over its records to see if it was worth helping. But in the meantime, nothing further could be done. The conference broke up at two o'clock, Cortelyou and Perkins issuing "reassuring" statements to the newspapers.

These statements, however, did not have a reassuring effect. Evidently, in emphasizing the intention of Morgan to help deserving trust companies, Perkins gave too much stress to the Trust Company of America. Although he later denied referring specifically to that company, some newspapers quoted him as saying that it was "the chief sore point" in the crisis. Perhaps because of this statement, on the morning of the twenty-third long lines of depositors were waiting when the company opened its doors. President Oakleigh Thorne put on extra tellers in an effort to reduce the lines, but they seemed without end. Soon the main lobby was jammed with people, while hundreds more milled about in the street. Attendants struggled desperately to organize the mob; finally the police had to be called in. The huge pile of $11,000,000 in gold and banknotes that Thorne had collected to meet the rush dwindled rapidly. This was panic.

Meanwhile, Morgan's team of investigators was rushing its evaluation of the company's assets, while Perkins, with Morgan's approval, shuttled through the financial district urging the presidents of other trust companies to attend a meeting that Morgan had called for twelve thirty in his office. So long as Morgan was willing to call the meeting, the presidents (now thoroughly frightened) were eager to attend.

By noon President Thorne was in desperate straits. He hurried up Wall Street to tell Morgan that he simply must have help. Morgan promised to do his best, but he was still depending on the other trust companies to save the Trust Company of America by raising a fund to tide it over the crisis. However, when the heads of the trust companies began to drift into his office, they were not in a co-operative mood. Their lack of organization was complete; many did not even know one another and had to be introduced. Morgan outlined the problem and suggested joint action, but when he finished his speech no one said a word. He tried again, but the heads of the largest and most secure companies said flatly that the Trust Com-

George B. Cortelyou,
Secretary of the Treasury.

George F. Baker,
First National Bank.

pany of America's problem was none of their business and that weak companies would only obtain their just deserts if the panic spread.

While these discussions were going on, Thorne was sending bulletin after bulletin to Morgan describing his dwindling cash reserves. One o'clock: $1,200,000. One twenty: $800,000. One forty-five: $500,000. Two fifteen: $180,000. Still the other companies would not help. Leaving them fruitlessly debating, Morgan went to another office and called for a report from his special crew of experts. These experts had not finished their complicated task, but when Morgan asked one of them whether the company was solvent he was told that it probably was. "This, then," said Morgan decisively, "is the place to stop this trouble." Baker and Stillman, who were at hand, agreed; together with Morgan they would supply the cash to keep the trust company going until closing time at three o'clock. Morgan ordered Perkins to the phone. If the company would send over half a million of its best securities as collateral, cash would be provided. This was done, and as Perkins said later, "we kept them open until three o'clock, with cash sent down every few minutes."

Morgan had saved the Trust Company of America for the day; he still felt that the other trust companies must take up the burden on the morrow. But it was not until late in the evening that, under continued pressure from Morgan, they agreed to contribute to the support of the Trust Company of America. Even so, the key factor in their decisions was the willingness of Secretary Cortelyou to make federal funds available to the trust companies indirectly. At a time when the trust company presidents were deadlocked, Perkins had slipped away from

Oakleigh Thorne,
Trust Company of America.

319

the meeting and had gone to Cortelyou's room at the Manhattan Hotel. Cortelyou had agreed to allow the *banks* (where he could legally deposit the government's cash) to lend the money to the trust companies if they in turn would make it available to the beleaguered Trust Company of America. Thus a $10,000,000 fund was raised, seemingly enough to bolster the company against any trouble.

But the next day, October 24, brought only further crises. Morgan arrived at his office at about ten to find the building jammed with frightened bankers and brokers. The fact that the Trust Company of America was able to pay off its demand deposits had not ended the run; indeed, the panic now had struck at another institution, the Lincoln Trust Company. Still worse, the Stock Exchange itself was in serious trouble. In a matter of hours blue chip securities lost 8 to 10 per cent of their value. Money for loans had practically disappeared, and hundreds of brokers faced ruin. Speculators ready and willing to meet their obligations and take their losses, men possessed of ample (and solid) securities, simply could not borrow money at any price. Morgan was besieged by men with tears in their eyes, others feeble and benumbed with terror, all faced by the dread specter of bankruptcy. Early in the afternoon the president of the Exchange, R. H. Thomas, squeezed his way into the House of Morgan with the dreadful news that the Exchange must close down if countless failures were to be avoided.

Morgan would not hear of this. The crucial moment for the Exchange would come at about twenty after two when it was customary to compare the day's sales and adjust accounts. Morgan summoned the city's leading bankers to a two o'clock meeting. When they arrived he told them that $25,000,000 must be raised in ten or twelve minutes. James Stillman promptly offered $5,000,000 of National City Bank cash, and others fell in line. By sixteen minutes past two the subscription had been filled. The word was announced to the waiting brokers, who cheered wildly and then rushed out to save themselves. When the market closed at three (after absorbing $18,000,000 of the $25,000,000 in half an hour) a mighty roar went up from the floor that Morgan heard in his office up the Street; upon inquiry he learned that the members of the Exchange had been cheering him as the savior of the situation.

Morgan, however, did not share in this feeling of relief. As he and his inner circle of advisers headed uptown to the Morgan Library for further conferences they were despondent. The runs on the trust com-

The 1907 panic jammed Wall Street to overflowing with clamorous, worried depositors. This photograph shows the run on the Trust Company of America (white façade, right).

panies had not slackened. The $10,000,000 trust company fund had almost evaporated. Millions of dollars of actual cash had been poured into the troubled situation by Cortelyou without producing any improvement whatsoever. During the evening Clark Williams, the state superintendent of banks, informed the group that Governor Charles Evans Hughes was considering a two-day bank holiday and wished to know what the bankers thought of the idea. Everyone but Morgan approved; he said that closing the banks would be disgraceful. But shortly after midnight word came that Hughes had decided that he lacked the authority to declare a bank holiday. At one o'clock the weary group broke up, feeling, as one of them remarked, "that we had about reached the end of our rope and no one having any idea what would happen the next morning." To cap their troubles, the twenty-fifth was a Friday. The psychological effect that this fact might have on superstitious and already frightened investors added to the general gloom.

Dawn did nothing to revive their spirits. In the morning the Morgan offices were once more haunted by desperate men facing utter ruin. By noon the Stock Exchange was in trouble. Money was simply not to be had at any price, for the trust companies were calling their loans right and left in a desperate effort to retrench. Morgan had served notice on "the big bear operators" that "if they attempted to break prices and throw the market into a panic he would crush them." Through Perkins he asked President Thomas to stop executing orders on margin and the brokers had responded "most splendidly," but even so, by early afternoon the demands for money became critical.

Again Morgan called the bank presidents to a meeting, this time at the Clearing House. He asked them to raise another $15,000,000 but could get promises for only $13,000,000. Many felt that their reserves had already been depleted beyond the danger point. (Morgan was contemptuous of this attitude. When, earlier in the panic, one banker had protested that his reserve was already down to 26 per cent, Morgan had said with scorn: "You ought to be ashamed of yourself. . . . What is a reserve for if not to be used in times like these?") But time was short; Morgan took what he could get.

Herbert L. Satterlee, Morgan's son-in-law, has left us a graphic picture of Morgan, derby hat set solidly on his head, a cigar clamped between his teeth, his coat unbuttoned, sailing along Nassau Street from the Clearing House to his office. He walked fast, eyes straight ahead, mind engrossed in his problems. Those who recognized him stepped deferentially from his path; those who did not, according to Satterlee, "he brushed aside." He neither dodged nor wove in and out through traffic nor slackened his stride. "He simply barged along . . . the embodiment of power and purpose."

Once again the money was enough to save the Exchange, though by the barest of margins. The situation looked a little better that evening, but Morgan was in conference with financial leaders until after midnight and then with Stillman, Cortelyou, and Perkins at the Manhattan Hotel until the small hours of Saturday morning. It was decided (over Morgan's strenuous objections) to issue Clearing House certificates in lieu of cash, for the huge sums that Cortelyou had been pouring into the banks were evaporating rapidly. Depositors were simply withdrawing their money and salting it away. Perkins checked with the leading banks of the city and discovered that nearly 2,000 new safe deposit boxes had been rented during the past week.

Psychological warfare was also employed. Cortelyou issued a strong and confident statement to the newspapers, and the bankers set up an information committee and undertook to reach religious leaders with an appeal for optimistic sermons. Saturday showed some improvement, and Cortelyou ostentatiously returned to Washington in order to create the impression that the crisis was over. Morgan also left the city for the weekend.

Sunday was calm and Monday also. There was another shortage of money on the Stock Exchange, but this time the desperate brokers were able to make individual arrangements with their banks and no heroic action was necessary. But the runs on the trust companies went on. No longer did the beleaguered companies try to stop the runs by paying rapidly; now they doled out cash as slowly as possible to conserve their dwindling supplies. Slow payment, however it might conserve funds, did nothing to calm the fears of depositors. Each morning found the grim-faced crowds waiting, many clutching lunch boxes along with their passbooks, determined to remain as long as necessary to collect their money. By Tuesday, despite their appearance of serenity, the men in the inner circle that had gathered around Morgan were desperately worried. "Three o'clock never seemed so long in coming nor so welcome when it did come as on this day," Perkins reported. On Wednesday the timid officers of the Lincoln Trust Company almost failed to open their doors. Only a tongue-lashing from the House of Morgan kept this company and the Trust Company of America going. On Thursday the State Superintendent of Banks, exasperated by the dilatory tactics of tellers at these institutions, informed them that they must begin to pay off depositors at a reasonable rate or

A cartoon of Morgan grasping the globe warned: "Like Alexander his plans of conquest embrace the . . . world, but where the Grecian . . . drew his sword, the American draws his check.

he would close them both. All Thursday afternoon and well into the night the Morgan group discussed the problem. Disgust with the management of the two companies was patent. "The officers seemed hopelessly at sea; we couldn't get them to get down to business and try to collect their loans or realize on their assets," Perkins complained later. Yet they must be saved in spite of themselves. "It was not because we were particularly in love with these two trust companies," he said. "Indeed, we hadn't any use for their management and knew that they ought to be closed, but we fought to keep them open in order not to have runs on other concerns."

The entire second week of the panic was made up of muted but deadly serious crises. Suddenly the city government found itself pressed for funds. At a time when money was almost impossible to borrow Morgan underwrote a $30,000,000 bond issue (his price was 6 per cent interest and the promise of fiscal reform by city officials) and saved New York from bankruptcy. The top-heavy credit structure of the nation's banking system was increasingly complicating the New York situation, for banks all over the country were drawing upon assets deposited in New York institutions. By the end of that week the strain was beginning to tell on everyone. Morgan was an old man; he was plagued by a heavy cold; yet he was up late every night, making vital decisions and assuming immense responsibilities. His partner Perkins had not been to bed before two o'clock for fourteen consecutive nights. Twice within the week he had made secret night trips to Washington to see Secretary Cortelyou. On one of these he left New York in the evening, conferred with Cortelyou from midnight until three, then returned at once to New York, arriving at eight o'clock for a working "day" that extended until three in the morning.

Upon men so fatigued there fell, during the second weekend of the panic, a blow that threatened to wipe out all their past efforts. The brokerage firm of Moore & Schley, it suddenly developed, was in desperate straits. Grant B. Schley, head of this company, belonged to a syndicate that controlled a small independent steel plant called the Tennessee Coal & Iron Company. Schley's firm had put up the money for the purchase, receiving T. C. & I. stock as collateral. It had then deposited this stock in banks as collateral for time loans. Now these time loans were falling due, but Moore & Schley lacked the cash to meet them. Under normal circumstances there would have been no great tragedy in this for anyone but Moore & Schley; the banks would have simply sold the T. C. & I. stock. However, this stock, being owned by a small group, had not been actively traded on the Stock Exchange for some time. Its price had been held steady around 130, yet the market as a whole had declined precipitously in recent months. Should the banks attempt to dispose of the stock, it would probably have to fall at least fifty or sixty points before buyers could be found for it, wiping out Moore & Schley, of course, but also gravely embarrassing the banks and perhaps triggering a general collapse of the whole stock market.

When this situation was called to Morgan's attention on Friday, November 1, he concluded at once that Moore & Schley must be saved; the problem was how to save them. The simplest way was to lend them money, but they needed about $25,000,000, and after two weeks of panic such a sum seemed impossible to raise. So another of the innumerable conferences of those desperate days was convened at the Morgan Library on Saturday morning. Lewis Cass Ledyard, lawyer for the T. C. & I. syndicate, presented this conference with a "brilliant" plan. Why not have the United States Steel Corporation purchase the Tennessee Coal & Iron Company? No money need be raised, for the steel company could simply exchange some of its own bonds (in which the public had confidence) for the T. C. & I. stock.

Morgan, who dominated U.S. Steel, quickly grasped the possibilities of this transaction. Here was a chance to add a valuable property to the steel trust and at the same time avert trouble on the stock market. Perhaps, if the deal could be combined with a final settlement of the trust company problem, the whole panic would be ended. He ordered a meeting of the finance committee of U.S. Steel for that very afternoon. At that meeting, however, he ran into unexpected opposition. Some of the members were afraid that the merger would provoke an antitrust suit. Henry C. Frick, a powerful member of the committee, argued vehemently against the idea on the ground that the Tennessee Company had extremely high costs of production and would not be a valuable addition to U.S. Steel. Morgan retaliated by saying that its coal and ore deposits alone were worth the cost. Finally, after much debate, the committee voted to make two offers to Moore & Schley. They would buy the stock at ninety dollars a share or they would lend Moore & Schley $5,000,000. But both propositions were turned down by the brokers because neither would yield enough cash to save them, and the conference broke up.

On Library notepaper Morgan scribbled his initials, handing over $30,000,000 that saved New York's credit in return for interest at 6 per cent and a promise of fiscal reform.

In desperation Perkins sent a Morgan accountant to go over the books of the Tennessee Coal & Iron Company in hopes that he could make a more favorable report as to its condition. Perkins also persuaded Schley to send for the president of the company, who might be able to make a better case in argument with Frick. On Sunday afternoon the U.S. Steel finance committee met again in the Morgan Library. After much argument the T. C. & I. men were able to convince Frick that a new rail mill, just being completed, would enable them to produce more efficiently than in the past. Finally the finance committee voted to offer par for the T. C. & I. stock (paid for in U.S. Steel bonds valued at 84) *provided* that President Theodore Roosevelt would approve the merger, that the transaction would definitely save Moore & Schley, and that some other arrangement could be worked out to save the two struggling trust companies.

Frick and Judge E. H. Gary, chairman of the board of U.S. Steel, left at once for Washington to see Roosevelt. While they were en route attention reverted to the two trust companies. Expert investigators had by now prepared detailed reports on the value of their assets which showed that the Trust Company of America was completely sound and the Lincoln Trust no more than a million dollars short of being able to pay off all its depositors, but under panic conditions these assets could not be liquidated. All Sunday night the Library was buzzing with conferees; at three in the morning there were about 125 financiers in the building, while outside knots of reporters waited for word on the debates. But there was no statement forthcoming. Finally at five in the morning the conference broke up, the directors of the Lincoln Trust Company having decided not to open their doors that day.

Monday morning, November 4, was in many ways the most disheartening time of the whole crisis. Cables from London indicated that American securities were falling there in morning trading. Should Wall Street follow this trend, many brokers would be caught without funds to meet their margin requirements. The Lincoln Trust Company's failure to open might produce a wave of further runs.

But when things looked blackest there was a turn for the better. Gary phoned from Washington that Roosevelt had approved the T. C. & I. merger; this news was allowed to leak and the market rallied. Representatives of Morgan and the leading bankers persuaded the State Superintendent of Banks to permit the Lincoln Trust to continue its slow payment policy, and the directors voted to open up after all. However, final consummation of the steel merger depended upon a permanent solution of the trust company problem, and this had not yet been worked out.

In desperation Morgan appealed to John D. Rockefeller, the titan of the oil industry. George Perkins had come to Morgan with a bold plan. Suppose a fund of $40,000,000 could be pledged to support the two companies. This sum represented all their remaining deposits. Surely the runs would end when depositors learned that they could definitely get their money. If Rockefeller would pledge half of this sum, Morgan and the bankers would somehow find the rest.

The negotiations were conducted by Perkins. He called on John D. Rockefeller, Jr., and explained to him the straits of the trust companies, how they had assets which in time could be liquidated and how, therefore, there would be little risk in the loan. "I told him that I believed his father had a very great opportunity to be of immense service to the business of the country and to win fame for himself in a most worthy cause," Perkins recalled in describing the interview. "I explained . . . that . . . his father would be in the attitude of having protected over fifteen thousand depositors, which step, I felt sure, would bring him the commendation and good will of hundreds of thousands of people all over the United States. I pointed out to him how the President at Washington had commended Mr. Morgan . . . and others for what they had done, and how I believed such action on Mr. Rockefeller's part would unquestionably make a favorable impression on the President and other governmental officials at Washington." Perkins's last point was, no doubt, particularly weighty with the Rockefellers because an antitrust suit against Standard Oil was then in the courts, on appeal from Judge Landis' astronomical $29,000,000 fine, levied in August, 1907. The younger Rockefeller promised to take the matter up with his father, but after much debate their decision was negative. This effort, too, thus ended in nothing.

Tuesday, fortunately, was election day and a bank holiday, which gave the bankers a respite. During the day, Morgan, Stillman, and Perkins worked out a new scheme. With the help of the committee of trust company presidents they would undertake to raise $20,000,000 for the Trust Company of America and the Lincoln Trust. In turn, these companies would place 66 per cent of their stock in a voting trust consisting of the heads of some of the other companies to be named by Morgan. The leverage that would force *all* the trust companies to agree to these terms would be the T. C. & I. deal. Unless they agreed, the finance committee of U.S. Steel would not approve the merger and in the resulting chaos no trust company would be safe.

The grand climax came on Tuesday night in the

Morgan Library. In one room were the executives of the Trust Company of America, in another the executives of the Lincoln Trust Company. A third held the presidents of all the major trust companies, and a fourth the finance committee of U.S. Steel. Morgan men circulated from room to room, pressing for agreement. On into the night the negotiators debated, while outside the reporters waited impatiently for an announcement. At one point there was a great stir—a mysterious woman in black entered the Library and a rumor circulated that she was Hetty Green, the famous miser. It turned out, however, that she was only a lady who held an important mortgage on the chief office of the Trust Company of America. Finally, at three o'clock on Wednesday morning, the news broke. U.S. Steel had absorbed the Tennessee Coal & Iron Company; the trust companies would be supplied with ample cash and would be taken over by a committee under the universally respected Edward King, president of the Union Trust Company.

When trading began on Wednesday there were sharp advances on the stock market. The bonds of U.S. Steel fell slightly in active trading as they were sold to meet Moore & Schley's obligations. (Business stimulating cash came out of safe deposit boxes to pay for these securities, of course.) At the trust companies, the lines of waiting depositors moved briskly for the first time in two weeks. Observing reporters estimated that customers were being serviced at the rate of one every three minutes, whereas previously as few as three a day had actually received their money. Seven million dollars in gold had just arrived from Europe, and the *Lusitania* was expected momentarily with ten million more. BANKERS SAVE BIG TRUST COS. BY FLOOD OF CASH, the headlines proclaimed. MORGAN CLEARS UP THE WHOLE TRUST SITUATION. A tremendous change for the better had taken place; all talk of failure and collapse ceased as if by magic. The panic was over.

The Panic of 1907, although it was followed by a brief industrial depression, had many salutary results. More than anything else it was responsible for the creation of the Federal Reserve System and for the stiffening of regulations controlling trust companies. Centralized control of finance, long overdue in rapidly industrializing America, could be achieved only after the weaknesses of the old system had been so effectively demonstrated. In the crisis, Morgan, as Congressman Bartlett suggested in 1911, had indeed "controlled and dominated the situation." But as Perkins said at that time, he did so not through his financial power, great as it admittedly was, but through the force of his personality, through his courage, determination, and skill. J. P. Morgan was no saint. He took his 6 per cent along the way. But while others cringed before the force of the storm, he braved its wildest winds and piloted the financial community to safe harbor.

THE STANLEYS AND

Teetotaling twin brothers

built the most wonderful car of

their era, and its day of glory

may not be over yet

At the turn of the twentieth century, the American automobile industry was in a stage of youthful indecision. Two courses lay open to it: to follow the already well-defined path of steam propulsion, or to explore the lesser-known byway of gasoline power. Steam seemed to have the brighter future and, at this point, was heavily favored by the early auto makers. In the year 1900 more than 1,600 steam cars were produced, compared to only 900 driven by gas.

The course of an industry, however—like that of an individual or an entire nation—is sometimes influenced by isolated incidents. Such an incident occurred in 1907 at Ormond Beach, Florida, where a crowd had gathered to watch the annual automobile speed trials. After a number of gasoline cars had made their runs, none reaching the 100 m.p.h. mark, the Stanley Steamer entry appeared. It was a frail vehicle that looked like a canoe turned upside down and mounted on spindly wheels. The press of the day had dubbed it "The Flying Teapot."

As the Steamer started its run, it was silent except for a low, soft whistle. This rose to a faint whine, and a jetlike white stream flowed from the tail of the car. Soon the head of the driver could hardly be seen in the blur of speed. The car passed the 100 m.p.h. mark

THEIR STEAMER

By JOHN CARLOVA

F. E. and F. O. Stanley in a handmade 1897 Steamer. Two years later they began producing the car commercially.

story, would be rewarded by the company with a prize of $1,000. Rumors went the rounds about men who had been blown to bits trying to win this prize.

These stories persist to this day, although all are false. The truth is that the Stanley Steamer was constructed in such a way that it was impossible for it to blow up. Early models, however, did have a tendency to let off steam in a noisy manner. One time in Boston, for example, a man drove up to a tavern, parked his Stanley Steamer at the curb, and went inside, forgetting to turn off a valve. The Stanley Steamer, in protest, gave off a thunderous blast of steam. The tavern windows rattled, glasses danced on shelves, and several startled patrons fell to the floor. The Stanley Steamer owner glanced at the prostrate patrons, remarked to the bartender, "Mighty powerful stuff you're serving here these days," and calmly walked out to his car.

This *savoir-faire* was typical of adventurous Stanley Steamer owners, who, according to a company announcement of 1916, had "the courage to buy the house they want, or the overcoat they want, or the automobile they want, even though their neighbors advise them not to." They had to have courage of another kind, too. The fuel burners of the early Stanleys used to "flood," shooting out sheets of smoke and flame. This looked a lot more dangerous than it actually was, since the front part of the car was virtually a fireproof compartment and the flames would go out of their own accord. Some drivers simply ignored the blaze and continued on their way, much to the consternation of all human and animal life in the vicinity. They did not always escape unscathed, however. One of them was driving a flaming Steamer through the streets one day, when a hastily summoned horse-drawn fire engine clattered around a corner, pulled alongside, and doused both vehicle and driver.

Incidents such as this—and the tales that grew out of them—eventually contributed to the death of the Stanley Steamer in 1925. This was a sad passing, for the Stanley Steamer was more than an automobile. It was the symbol of an era, an era of individuality and independence—an era that has been replaced, for better or worse, by standardization and conformity.

and surged up to 197 m.p.h. As it was about to touch 200 m.p.h., however, the racer hit a slight bump on the beach. The light car took off like a wingless glider, soared for about 100 feet at a height of 10 feet, then crashed to the cement-hard sand in an explosion of steam and flames. The driver was flung clear, badly injured but not dead.

Out of the flaming wreckage was born another of the legends surrounding the Stanley Steamer, the best car of its era but also the most misunderstood and maligned. No man, it was said, could open the throttle and stay with the Steamer. Anyone who could even hold the throttle open for three minutes, went another

EVELYN CURRO

Like other early cars, the 1903 Stanley Runabout (above), manufactured at Newton, Massachusetts, had the seats, and appurtenances of a horse-drawn carriage; some owners even added a fringed umbrella top. But by 1908 the Steamer (below), along with its gas-driven competitors, looked like a conventional automobile.

CLARENCE P. HORNUNG

Appropriately, the highly individualistic Steamer was the brain child of two of the most rugged individuals in American industrial history—the Stanley twins, Francis E. and Freeland O., better known as "F. E." and "F. O." They were born in 1849 into a particularly large family in Kingfield, Maine—where, according to a local historian, "you couldn't throw an apple without hitting a Stanley."

F. E. and F. O. were identical twins. One was seldom seen without the other, and both were always whittling. This led them into their first enterprise, the carving and making of fine violins. Such an artistic beginning for a pair of auto makers is not as incongruous as it may seem. The Stanley Steamer, when it was produced, was as much a work of art as it was of mechanics. For instance, instead of employing patternmakers, the Stanleys themselves whittled the precise wooden forms required for casting machinery.

From violins the twins moved on to photography. They pioneered the dry photographic plate and perfected early X-ray equipment. The sale of these inventions set them up financially for the next stage of their career—the production of the Stanley Steamer. This important stage opened almost casually. In 1896 the Stanley twins went to a fair to see a widely advertised "horseless carriage." The car, imported from France, was billed as "The Marvel of the Age." Actually it was not very impressive, continually snorting, jerking, and stalling.

The Stanley twins decided they could do better. Within a year, without any previous knowledge of steam engineering, they turned out the first Stanley Steamer. This was simply a small engine and boiler slung beneath a carriage, but it was an immediate success. Spectators were particularly impressed by the vehicle's brisk pace and strange silence. "It was like watching a pair of pants run down the street with nobody in them," one old-timer graphically recalls.

The Stanley twins had the New England characteristics of taciturnity and dry humor. They enjoyed a practical joke and were not above taking advantage of their car's silence. Noiselessly pulling up to a toll bridge one time, they found the keeper sound asleep. When awakened, the keeper stared at the two men in the carriage and demanded, "How did you get up here without me hearing you? Where's your horse?"

"He got away from us," said F. E. "Have you seen him?"

The keeper shook his head. "No—but you're blocking the bridge. You'll have to get that carriage out of the way."

"Of course," said F. E., and covertly touched the throttle. The carriage silently glided across the bridge, leaving the keeper staring after it with open mouth.

Horses also suffered from the silent Steamer. They apparently couldn't figure out what kind of invisible beast was drawing the carriage, and some horses wouldn't even go near a trough that had been used by a Steamer taking on water. Dogs were another story. As soon as a Stanley Steamer appeared, the entire canine population would come running, barking, and howling. It used to be a mystery how a dog, sometimes more than a mile away, would know an unobtrusive Stanley was in the neighborhood. With today's scientific knowledge, it is not hard to guess that the sharp-eared dogs were attracted by the supersonic pitch of the Steamer's burner.

To discourage dogs, some Stanley owners installed steamboat whistles on their cars. One blast and the dogs would scamper for home. More than a few humans were sent scampering, too—astonished by the sudden sound of a steamboat in the heart of, say, Syracuse, New York.

Train whistles were used on Stanleys, too. These were fine for "whistling down" the barriers at a train crossing—*after* the Stanley was safely across the tracks and on its way. The crossing keeper would then come out and stand scratching his head, wondering what had happened to the train he had heard.

Despite such wry humor, the Stanleys were austere in their private lives. Neither of the twins drank or smoked, and both were shrewd, hardheaded businessmen. They took pleasure, however, in mystifying people with their similarity in appearance. They dressed alike and wore the same full-blown type of beard. For such a conservative pair, they also developed a strange passion for speed. This led to confusion among police all over New England.

For instance, in taking trips, the Stanleys would start out in two Steamers, F. O. a few minutes in advance of F. E. Sooner or later, F. O. would be stopped by a constable. While the lawman was lecturing F. O. on the evils of speeding, his twin would solemnly whiz past, identical in all respects. This numbed more than one rural arm of the law.

In 1899, after several years of making and selling individual Steamers, the twins bought a factory at Newton, Massachusetts, and formally launched what soon became known as the Stanley Motor Carriage Company. Two hundred cars were made that year, and the firm went down in history as the first American company to produce steam automobiles on a commercial scale.

This by no means meant that the Steamers were turned out on anything resembling a mass-production basis. On the contrary, the mechanics—all hand-picked by the Stanleys and all highly skilled if somewhat temperamental craftsmen—were encouraged to assem-

This photograph of cars and spectators at the Ormond Beach races of 1907 shows the wildly individualistic character of early auto design. This was the meet at which a Steamer became air-borne and crashed; the Stanley twins never raced again.

ble the cars as they thought best. Consequently, each craftsman put into his cars something of himself as an individual, and, unlike the twins, no two Stanley Steamers were ever exactly alike. One mechanic even insisted on putting in the engine upside down, a principle he claimed was better than the Stanleys'. This was too much for F. E., who, after fruitless argument, went to F. O. and complained about the stubborn mechanic. "Better let him have his way," F. O. advised. "He's just as cussed as we are."

And the Stanleys were "cussed" indeed. A customer simply couldn't walk in and buy a Stanley Steamer. He had to be "screened," like a candidate for an exclusive club. If the Stanleys decided he didn't have the right personality for their car, they wouldn't even take his order. Even when a customer's order was accepted, this didn't necessarily mean he would get a Steamer. If he did or said anything to displease the Stanleys between the time of placing the order and the actual production of the car, he would be refused delivery. This happened to a customer who asked for a written guarantee. The Stanleys, who figured their word was guarantee enough, showed the gentleman to the door.

This was hardly the way to build a business, let alone sell cars, and a modern automobile salesman would blanch at such treatment of a customer. It is a measure of the Stanley Steamer's worth that it continued to sell as well and as long as it did, especially since one never left the factory until it had been paid for in hard cash. The Stanleys just didn't believe in credit or installment buying, which they regarded as somewhat immoral.

The price of a Steamer was high for its day—in 1917, about $2,500—and there weren't many people around who had that kind of cash. Sales were steady but never spectacular. The Stanley was a prestige car, and al-

though many people would have liked one, they simply couldn't afford it. If the car had been sold on credit, and more people had gotten to own one and know its wonderful qualities, it is possible the Steamer would never have been allowed to pass away.

However, there were other matters that contributed to its death. The Stanleys didn't believe in advertising. They figured that it was a waste of money that should go into the improvement of their product. In later years, when the Stanley Steamer was suffering from all sorts of rumors, some judicious advertising might have saved the firm. Instead, the Stanleys stubbornly stuck by their policy of letting the Steamer "advertise itself."

Nor would they give in to the demands of style and mass production, which would have increased the popularity of the car and brought its price down. Except for a few streamlined racers and an early rakish model known as the Gentlemen's Speedy Roadster, the lofty, solid, individually-created Stanleys bore a resemblance to a prairie schooner. Almost always painted black, they had long, rounded hoods, which added to their funereal aspect. They looked like coffins.

Beneath that dark, gaunt exterior, however, beat a heart of mechanical ingenuity. The Stanley Steamer was—and still is—a model of engineering skill, combining comfort and economy with almost unbelievable speed and power. Yet with all this, it was surprisingly simple. The 1916 model, for example, had only 32 moving parts, including the wheels and the steering wheel.

George Woodbury, a New Hampshire sawmill owner who reconstructed a 1917 Steamer, wrote a book about his experiences. The source of the car's power, Woodbury wrote in *The Story of a Stanley Steamer*, was a twenty-gallon water tank set under the floor boards. The water was pumped into a small, drumlike boiler—23 inches in diameter and 18 inches high—located under the hood. This boiler, bound with three layers of fine, high-grade steel wire, could easily take the 600 pounds of pressure considered necessary for ordinary driving. Actually it was virtually impossible to burst the boiler, as the Stanleys once proved. They dug a hole in a field, placed a boiler in it, and pumped steam pressure up to 1,500 pounds. At that point, instead of exploding, the tubes within the boiler began to leak, allowing the steam to escape.

Inside the boiler were 751 small, seamless steel tubes, looking somewhat like metallic spaghetti in a big pot. In effect, they were tiny chimneys, conveying heat through the boiler from the pressure burner beneath and turning the water to steam. The cheaply operated kerosene burner—its jets fed from a twenty-gallon tank safely situated at the extreme rear of the car—worked on the blowtorch principle. Although small, the burner could generate intense heat.

The steam drove a two-cylinder horizontal engine, geared directly to the rear axle, which almost literally had the power of a locomotive, although its horsepower rating was low. Its tremendous performance sprang mainly from the peculiar nature of steam. This is best described by John Bentley, who states in *Old-time Steam Cars:* "At best, the thermal efficiency of the internal-combustion engine may reach 35 per cent, whereas that of the steam engine tops 90 per cent."

The Stanley Steamer also benefited from its single gear. In other words, when the engine turned over once, the rear wheels also turned once. This means that in a mile the simple Stanley engine turned only 980 times, compared to the 4,000 or 5,000 times of a complicated internal-combustion engine. No wonder the Stanleys asserted that their engine could "last forever."

When the live steam had accomplished its job at the rear of the Stanley, it was piped back to a condenser in the nose. Here it was cooled to water and returned to the water tank, where it could be used again on an endless circuit. In this way, a Steamer could go for more than 200 miles before taking on a fresh supply of water. This was not so with the early Stanleys, which had no condenser and could manage only one mile on a gallon of water, requiring so many stops at horse troughs that an outraged legislator in Vermont once demanded that "these vile, smelly, snorting steam demons be barred by law from facilities set out for the comfort and well-being of man's noble friend and helper, the horse."

The actual driving of a Stanley Steamer was simplicity itself. In fact, the Stanley anticipated modern automatic transmission by nearly half a century. A touch of the throttle—a sliding lever conveniently located just beneath the steering wheel—set the Steamer into silent motion. There was no clutch, and no gears to shift, which meant that a speed as low as 1 m.p.h. could be maintained all day without shaking, shuddering, rattling, overheating, or stalling. Another touch of the throttle would accelerate the car instantly.

There were two foot-pedals on the floor. The right one was for the brake, the left for reverse. The Stanley, incidentally, could go as fast backward as forward—and Stanley pranksters sometimes *passed* gasoline-driven cars in that manner.

The Steamer could also be thrown into reverse even while it was going ahead at speed. Since the old-time rear-wheel brakes were none too efficient anyway, this quick reverse action was helpful in times of emergency. During one race in New York State, a Stanley whirled around a corner just as a group of spectators was straggling across the road. The driver threw the Steamer into reverse, even though it was doing better than 60 m.p.h. With a shriek the tires tore loose, and then the body, which slid along the road and came to rest a few inches from the spectators, the driver draped over the windshield. The chassis, meanwhile, was obediently going backward. It slanted off the road, bumped across a field, and disappeared into a forest; finally it encountered a solid line of trees, and only then did it grind to a halt.

On another occasion, a brick wall failed to stop a Stanley. It happened in a garage in Chicago, where a mechanic was tinkering with a Steamer. He "fired up" all right and opened the throttle, but still the car wouldn't go—for the simple reason that the emergency brake was on. After steam pressure had been building up for some time, the mechanic finally remembered the emergency brake. As soon as he released it, the Stanley rammed through the wall of the garage and emerged into the street, leaving a trail of bricks behind it.

This trick of building up steam with the emergency brake on was used by racing drivers to get greater acceleration out of a Stanley. The Steamer, in its heyday, was limited in acceleration only by the amount of strain its old-type wheels and structure could stand. As early as 1914, however, a Stanley went from 0 to 60 m.p.h. in 11 seconds. This compares with the 11.7 seconds it takes a 1958, 310-horsepower Cadillac to go from 0 to 60 m.p.h. At a recent sports-car meet in California, this writer did 0 to 60 m.p.h. in 9 seconds in a reconstructed and improved Stanley, which put the old Steamer right up there with such modern speedsters as a British-made Triumph and a Studebaker Golden Hawk.

The accelerating action of a Steamer is different from that of a gasoline car. Instead of a grabbing, jerking, neck-snapping forward lunge, the motion is smooth and gliding, strangely rubbery, like being flung out of a slingshot. Out on the highway, at speed, it is the ground, rather than the Steamer, that seems to be moving. With the silence, one has the feeling of forever coasting down a hill—even when the car is going *up* a hill.

It was at hill climbing, in fact, that the Stanley Steamer first attracted nationwide notice. In 1899 F. O. Stanley, with his wife as a passenger, drove a Steamer to the top of 6,288-foot Mount Washington, the highest peak in New England. The rugged dirt wagon-track wound for ten miles at a twelve per cent grade, but the Stanley made it in two hours and ten minutes —a remarkable feat for its day and the first time a motor vehicle had accomplished anything like it. It was not until three years later that the first gasoline-powered car managed to struggle up Mount Washington in a little less than two hours. F. E. promptly took a new model Stanley up the mountain in only 27 *minutes*.

This showed how much the Steamer had been improved—and, incidentally, stopped any argument as to which was the best car on the road in those days. One proud Stanley owner even boasted that his Steamer could "climb a tree if it could catch ahold." There was more than a little truth in the boast, for a Stanley once literally climbed a tree—in fact, two trees. The car had been left standing at the foot of a bank of earth, which was topped by a grove of young birch trees. A boy, playing around the car, opened the throttle wide. The Steamer threw the boy aside, plunged up the bank, and slammed into two trees growing close together. The pliant trees bent back nearly to the ground, and the Steamer stopped only when it became entangled in the branches. A few minutes later the birch trees, noted for their elasticity, rose into the air again, carrying the car with them. There it was eventually found, suspended about ten feet from the ground.

This was the sort of incident that wove an almost mystic aura around the Stanley Steamer. Owners of the car were not above thickening the mystery. One of their favorite tricks was to walk down the road about a dozen yards ahead of a parked Steamer, then turn and whistle. The car, responding like an alert and well-trained dog, would roll down the road to its master.

The explanation for the trick was simple enough. The Steamer, after standing for half an hour or more, would "cool off." If the throttle was open very, very slightly, there would be a space of some seconds before the engine took hold. This would give the owner time to walk down the road and "whistle" his car to him. The effect on a group of spectators can easily be imagined.

Fred Marriott at the wheel of the Stanley Rocket, virtually identical with the racer which took off and crashed in 1907.

Another trick was more nerve-racking. F. O., who once accompanied a Stanley Steamer shipped to New Orleans, assembled the car in a field near the Mississippi River. Every day a crowd gathered to watch the vehicle taking shape. When the Steamer was ready to roll, F. O. began "firing up." The crowd stared in tense apprehension. Up and up went the steam pressure—100 pounds, 200 pounds, 400 pounds, 600 pounds. Suddenly there was a terrific explosion.

F. O., not too concerned, turned to reassure the crowd. There was nobody to reassure. Everyone had scuttled out of sight. F. O. turned back to the car and examined it. There didn't seem to be anything wrong. Perplexed, F. O. finally heard a snicker in some bushes behind him. Turning, he saw a couple of kids trying to hold back their mirth. One pointed beneath the Steamer, where F. O. spotted the remains of a big firecracker.

Some Stanley owners enjoyed this joke so much they took to carrying firecrackers around with them. When a crowd gathered to watch them "fire up," they would wait till a particularly suspenseful moment, then drop a firecracker beneath the car.

These pranks—which, of course, added to the wild tales about the Stanley Steamer—also obscured many practical (although unusual) uses of the car. For instance, it made a fine peanut roaster. Before starting on a trip, a bag of peanuts could be placed on top of the boiler. By the end of the journey, the peanuts would be done to a turn.

A Stanley's steam pressure was also excellent for blowing out clogged drains. In addition, several cities used Steamers to thaw out frozen fire hydrants in winter.

On the other hand, there were a number of drawbacks to the old Stanley. It sometimes took up to half an hour to get up steam in a cold boiler. Although driving the car was easy enough, the "firing up" process was complicated and cumbersome, calling more for a plumber than a mechanic. The driver's seat, faced with a bewildering array of gauges, valves, and pump controls, looked something like a boiler room. In fact, one of the most persistent canards about the Stanley was that a driver needed a steam engineer's license, as well as a regular driver's license, to operate it competently.

There was also the matter of smell. Kerosene, although cheap, has a pungent, penetrating odor. An old saying went, "You can see a Stanley Steamer before you hear it—and you can smell its owner before you see him."

The Stanley twins and the head of their maintenance department, Fred Marriott, raced Steamers all over the country, particularly at fairs. Nothing on wheels could stand up to the Stanley, which usually beat its nearest opponent by as much as five minutes in a twenty-mile race.

In 1906, at Ormond Beach, driving a streamlined but otherwise stock-model Steamer, Fred Marriott set a world speed record of 127.66 m.p.h. and became the first human to travel two miles a minute. This record was set by a car weighing only 1,600 pounds. Actually, it was lack of weight that hurled the little "Flying Teapot" to its doom in 1907 on the same track. In that year, so fateful to the Steamer, Fred Marriott brought the racer back to Ormond Beach. Piling the pressure up to 1,300 pounds, Fred opened the throttle and sent the car speeding down the beach. Nearly fifty years later, Marriott was still around to describe what happened next:

I quickly got up to 197 miles an hour and the speed was rising fast when the car hit a slight bump. I felt it lift and then rise clear off the ground and twist a little in the air. It took off like an airplane, rose about 10 feet off the beach and traveled 100 feet before it struck. I was thrown clear and pretty badly

smashed up. The machine broke in two and was bashed to kindling wood. The boiler rolled, blowing steam like a meteor, for a mile down the beach.

The cause of the crash was a simple one, although few could understand it at the time. In designing the streamlined body of the car, the Stanleys had left the underside flat. When the wind got under this at high speed, it lifted the light car and made it air-borne, creating the myth that a Steamer was just too fast to stay on the ground. It is interesting to note that the 200 m.p.h. mark touched by the 1,600-pound Stanley was not bettered by a gasoline car until 1927, and then only by a four-ton monster powered by two twelve-cylinder airplane engines.

The Stanley twins were badly shaken by the near disaster at Ormond Beach. They never built another racer and, in fact, tried to play down the speed potential of the Steamer. This, then, brings up the natural question: What about that well-known and widely believed story that the Stanleys would pay $1,000 to anyone who could hold the throttle open for three minutes? Fred Marriott had a definite answer:

I'll tell you what's in that yarn—*nothing.* We did our best to kill it, but it always kept coming back. It used to make the Stanleys sore—and kind of sad, too. I guess they could see the way things were going.

In 1918, F. E. Stanley started out on a trip in his Steamer. Coming up over the crest of a hill, he found the road blocked by two farm wagons. Rather than hit them and possibly kill the drivers and horses, he turned off the road and crashed into a ditch. He was killed instantly.

F. O., heartbroken over the tragedy, retired. (He eventually died of a heart attack in 1940.)

Early English steamer, built by James and Anderson in 1829, had two boilers and engines and traveled fifteen m.p.h. carrying fifteen passengers, including a tootling footman.

First successful U.S. steamer was Oliver Evans' "Orukter Amphibolos" (Amphibious Digger), a combined boat-carriage which was "launched" in 1805 to dredge Philadelphia docks.

The Stanley Motor Company passed into other hands. It lingered on for a few years, out of tune with the fast-changing times, lost without those "cussed" dreamers and craftsmen, the Stanley twins. In 1925, the firm went out of business. In its last full year of production it turned out only 65 cars. Ford alone was producing more than that in a single day. Mass production and the internal-combustion engine had won out over steam and individuality.

Today there are many automobile experts who cannot understand why the Steamer was allowed to pass away. They argue that with modern improvements—such as a boiler capable of a quick start—the Steamer would be a far better car than the present gasoline auto. And who can deny that our cities would be finer, pleasanter places if we all had silent Steamers, rather than the noisy, fumes-belching gasoline cars that now pollute the air?

There is also the matter of economy. During World War II, with gas rationing, many old Stanley Steamers were brought out of barns or rescued from junk yards. Aside from the low cost of operation, the gallant Stanleys brought back to many motoring enthusiasts the thrill of driving a truly outstanding and individual car. This set off a revival of interest in steam autos that is still growing. The era of the Stanley Steamer is gone, but the spirit of the time and the car has not perished.

Not long ago a petroleum engineer, who improved an old Stanley, drove from Los Angeles to New York on $4.50 worth of furnace oil. Another engineer designed and built a steam car capable of taking off from a cold start in one minute and maintaining a steady seventy or eighty m.p.h. on the open road. Some steam fans, like Charles Keen, a Wisconsin businessman, hide their silent secret under the modern exterior of a reconverted gas car. Others, like Hollywood writer Nick Belden, take their improved Stanleys to sports-car meets and beat some of the latest models from the Detroit assembly lines.

Some observers contend that it is performances such as these that keep the steam car from coming back. They claim that powerful automobile and gasoline interests, having long ago won the battle against steam, are certainly not going to allow their old rival to be revived commercially. In at least one instance, this is not true. Not long ago, the Chrysler Corporation brought Calvin and Charles Williams to Detroit from Philadelphia to demonstrate their highly improved steam motor, which works equally well in cars, trucks, buses, or boats. It can be built for one third the price of a gasoline engine and can perform with greater efficiency and economy, operating on fuel oil costing sixteen cents a gallon.

The Chrysler Corporation is reported to be interested in producing the Williams' steam motor. It is perhaps significant that the Williams brothers are twins. Automobile history may yet repeat itself. In fact, one auto expert, Ken Purdy, writes in *Kings of the Road*: "The steam-lovers may have to wait just a bit longer—until the atomic-powered automobile is ready. Chances are that it will be a steam car, for it seems doubtful that we will find a way to use atomic energy for transport except by converting it to steam."

The greatest glory of steam cars, therefore, may lie just ahead.

Deliveries by steam were made in this buglike wagon produced by the White Sewing Machine Company, which made steamers until 1910, then switched to gasoline automobiles.

DRAWINGS BY EVELYN CURRO

Stanley's last stand was the 1922 phaeton, continued until 1924, when the company was sold. The purchasers made Stanley cars for another year or so, but steam was about dead.

THE MACHINE THAT KEPT THEM HONEST

J. H. Patterson, the first supersalesman,
put his cash register in every emporium
and banished itchy fingers from the till

By GERALD CARSON

he machine was the cash register. The clangor of its bell fell pleasantly upon the ear, whether activated by dollars and cents, pounds and pence, francs, marks, florins, lire, pesetas, or pesos.

The man behind the bell was an Ohio farm boy who promoted a novel counting device of wheels and springs grandly encased in an ornate bronze or nickel sheath. When a clerk pressed a key the machine gave out with its joyous tintinnabulation. In the beginning no one had heard of the cash register. But John Henry Patterson changed all that. To do it he had to invent American Salesmanship.

John H. Patterson was a not-so-young hustler lightly endowed with this world's goods when in 1884 he offered $6,500 for the controlling interest in an obscure little factory in Slidertown—a slum area of Dayton, Ohio—which manufactured the new machine that was to make the open cash drawer obsolete. Dayton laughed so hard that Patterson panicked and tried, unsuccessfully, to back out of the deal. It was too late. The seller confided that he wouldn't take the stock as a gift. But Patterson's fortune was as good as made,

and the story of selling had to be rewritten. What the small, sandy-haired, intense promoter did with the cash register made entrepreneurial history; and the tales told of the man himself will be repeated, with no embellishment needed, as long as men wearing name tags convene to learn how to sell widgets, or management types gather at country clubs to relax at the nineteenth hole. Patterson's solid achievements, his impressive list of business "firsts," are enough to secure him a high and enduring place in mercantile history.

The Autocrat of the Cash Register was born in 1844 of pioneer stock on the family farm near Dayton. He attended the local schools, spent a year at Miami University in Oxford, Ohio, and was graduated from Dartmouth College. There he acquired, Patterson often remarked, much useless knowledge. His prejudice against higher education lasted through the rest of his idiosyncratic life. After college, Patterson worked on his father's farm, later became a toll collector on the Miami and Erie Canal, and still later, with his two brothers, ran a coal yard, developed coal and iron mines in Jackson County, Ohio, and was for several

335

years the general manager for the Southern Coal and Iron Company at Coalton, Ohio.

The Southern operated a company store. Instead of turning in a profit of $12,000, which the books said it should, the store was actually losing $6,000 a year because, Patterson discovered, his clerks were dishonest. At this point he read that James S. Ritty, a Dayton saloonkeeper with similar problems, and his mechanically minded brother, John, had invented a contraption that tabulated sales as they were made and registered them publicly. In order to open the

NATIONAL CASH REGISTER COMPANY

The door to Patterson's office was always open, but the sign outside discouraged idle chatter. In our still life opposite, observe the great man himself—and his brain child that struck down the thieving clerk. We strive also to suggest the sloganeering, the paternalism (health, gardens, schools), and even the "magic number."

cash drawer and make change, the clerk was compelled to ring up the sale. The bell on the device—at the time Patterson heard about the register, it gave out a loud *bong*—forced him to deposit the money received. In sum, the magic money box provided publicity, protection, and compulsory morality.

The cash register was expensive, costing all of fifty dollars. But Patterson, even though he had probably never seen one, promptly telegraphed for two. At the time there were only about a dozen in use, under the name "Ritty's Incorruptible Cashier." With the introduction of the new machines the profit picture at Ritty's oasis in Dayton brightened, and John H. Pat-

terson's store also moved into the black. The Patterson brothers immediately purchased a block of cash register stock—this was in 1882—and two years later, with John H. in the lead, acquired control of the business and soon changed the name to National Cash Register Company.

Thus, at the age of forty, with no manufacturing experience and little capital, Patterson started in to build a business upon an article almost no one wanted or knew how to use. Known as a "thief catcher," the device aroused such fury among bartenders and café cashiers that a travelling man who was handling another item, say sewing machines, found it prudent when entering a drinking parlor to say loudly and distinctly that he was not associated with the N.C.R.

The man in absolute control of that company—"the Cash" it came to be called in Dayton—was small, wiry, a natty dresser; he had penetrating gray eyes, a florid complexion, luxuriant white handlebar mustaches, and a quick mind untrammelled by convention. Patterson quickly improved the cash register, took out several patents in his own name, introduced a system of quality control, and turned his attention to the problems of advertising and selling.

The important businessmen of the time were converters of raw materials, railroad presidents, and hardshelled merchants who had survived the panic of '73. Advertising by and large consisted of drab announcements. Selling was glad-handing, a matter of exploiting a genial personality that attracted a following in "the trade." Look the part. Sell yourself and you sell your product. Manufacturing was getting men to work for as little as possible. Card indices, filing systems, and duplicating machines had not been heard of.

Into this traditional business environment Patterson introduced several startling new concepts. He began by building (with borrowed money) a model plant on the old family farm. It was a revolutionary concept in industrial architecture, a "daylight" building with eighty per cent of its walls made of glass and with ampelopsis climbing up the brickwork; the grounds were landscaped and dotted with flower beds. Inside, the revolution was just as complete. There were lockers and showers, swimming pools and other recreational facilities, hot lunches, medical care, and inspirational lectures to give wings to the mind.

These pioneering efforts in industrial welfare—and the high rate of pay at "the Cash"—attracted so much attention locally, nationally, and even internationally that Patterson, who explained gruffly, "It pays," hung a sign by his office door: "Be Brief—Omit All Compliments About Welfare Work."

In exchange for his unusual attentions to the N.C.R. employees, Patterson exacted absolute obedience and

336

a high rate of productivity. In a day when good management meant cost-cutting, Patterson took the opposite tack—the way to make money, he believed, was to spend it. Secrecy, too, was highly regarded as a competitive weapon. But Patterson welcomed visitors to his plant and even wined and dined—no, just dined—competitors and would-be competitors. He inevitably showed them "the Gloom Room," where they were urged to gaze upon piles and piles of rusty registers, the products of bankrupt companies that couldn't stand the pace set by National. It was unforgettable evidence of the folly of bucking John H. Patterson.

Patterson soon demonstrated his native flair for showmanship. One day when he was escorting some friends through the factory, he stopped before a shiny new register that had been checked out for shipment. He started to point out the model's special features. One key stuck. Another wouldn't depress. Patterson reached for a hammer and reduced the register to a mass of junk.

"That is how we take care of faulty machines," he said casually.

But the glory of N.C.R. was what Patterson called "the American Selling Force." With nothing in hand but the legal right to make a mechanism for which there was no demand, but with an almost apocalyptic vision of a universal market of prospective purchasers who needed a cash register and didn't know it, Patterson put together the most aggressive corps of salesmen the world had ever seen. He argued with his men, coaxed and criticized, often lashed them with biting sarcasm, preached and exhorted. He supported the Force with aggressive advertising, and tried to generate in each man an incentive equal to religion's fear of damnation and hope of salvation. It was the missionary spirit of spreading the gospel to the heathen, hooked up with American boosterism.

A man who looked like a comer was often taken by Patterson to New York at company expense to stay at a luxury hotel, get measured for a good suit, visit the finest hatters and custom shirt shops, see a couple of shows, and generally, in Patterson's words, "get the hayseed off him." A taste of the fleshpots, Patterson figured, was a sure-fire way to spark the imagination of a good man who would like to have a new davenport and join the local country-club set. Patterson introduced the idea of the guaranteed territory and paid straight commissions on which a man could really make money. Refusing to follow the common practice of the times, he did not cut back the commissions when business was good. "If you can sell a million dollars in a week," he declared expansively, "we'll hire a brass band to take your commission to you."

The idea of the sacrosanct commission took hold

These early twentieth-century pamphlets issued by the National Cash Register Company show some of founder Patterson's interests: employee welfare, education, gardening, salesmanship.

slowly. Years afterward Thomas J. Watson, brilliant leader of the International Business Machines Corporation and a member of the distinguished body of Patterson alumni, remembered how back home in Painted Post, New York, when a local man boasted that he had made thirty dollars selling a cash register, he was deemed to be the biggest liar in the Cohocton River valley.

One of Patterson's early formulations now regarded as an invaluable business tool was the establishing of sales quotas, based upon an objective analysis of potential opportunity in a territory. The quota system ironed out the inequities, applied the same measure to all salesmen, meant the same thing in Portland, Oregon, as in Utica, New York, in Indianapolis as in Bangkok.

Among the new concepts Patterson introduced was the standardized sales talk, codified into a revolutionary document known as the *N.C.R. Primer*. At first the use of the new method of selling was merely recommended. Later it became compulsory. Patterson never justified it from any theoretical standpoint. He didn't need to: the men who followed the *Primer* sold more registers and earned fatter commissions than those who stuck to personality selling. From this pioneering effort emerged the first sales manual. It brought together all the objections and excuses which had ever been advanced for not buying a cash register. A training school soon followed, later elaborated into conferences and conventions with intracompany competitions that provided rewards and distinctions for the fortunate winners. There were company songs, bunting, and banners. A Patterson sales convention was a Rotarian gala, the atmosphere one of emotion touched with grandeur. Part circus, part chautauqua, it resembled a church revival except that there was never any letdown. Early in each year, flags were flung to the breeze over the home office when the first salesman made his quota. The annual Sales Derby was on!

The men who survived Patterson's schooling came out casehardened and wily. They never simply sold a piece of machinery; rather, they promoted a business function. It was the principle later expressed by Elmer Wheeler, inspirational lecturer sometimes called "America's Number 1 Salesman," in the memorable slogan: *Don't sell the steak, sell the sizzle.* Patterson's men were forbidden to carry screw drivers, lest they become diverted into service work. Nor were they encouraged to become more than casually conversant with the innards of the machine they sold, although in the cash register field it was useful to have a working knowledge of a competitive register so as to be able, on occasion, to put it out of commission.

"I have called to interest you in a way to increase your profits," the polite N.C.R. man would say. He was itching for an argument, never happier than when the prospect, known in Patterson's lexicon as the "P.P." (Probable Purchaser), raised such childish and moth-eaten objections as:

I don't need one.

Times are hard.

I can't spare the money.

My present system is satisfactory.

You make too great a profit.

The next step was to entangle the P.P. in a net of admissions about his losses on *cash sales, credit sales, cash received on account, cash paid out,* and *charging money as an accommodation.* Healthy, shaved, with clean linen and no cigar, his blue serge suit well brushed, the N.C.R. agent staged his demonstration outside the store—usually in a sample room at the best hotel in town—with such theatrical trappings as curtains painted to represent a store interior. There were large business charts and diagrams. Real merchandise and real money were used to heighten the dramatic impact. The P.P. was comfortably seated, and there were no distractions in the room such as a clock, which might suggest that he had better be getting back to the store, or a calendar, a possible reminder that he had a note coming due at the bank.

The closing of a sale was as stylized as a Japanese kabuki play. When the salesman had the prospect sagging on the ropes he was too much the artist to ask crudely for the order; instead, he moved on smoothly to, "Now, Mr. Brown, what color shall I make it?" Or, "How soon do you want delivery?" If the store owner drew back, the N.C.R. man prepared him once more for signature, gently urging him up to the mark again, pen at the ready—"Just sign here." With the ceremonial signing went a twenty-five-cent cigar and the ego-boosting assurance that the customer had proved he was a real live wire as a businessman. Nor was that the end of the relationship between the purchaser and the company. The N.C.R. man was already making a note of the date when the register would be obsolescent and should be traded in on a new, improved model, for it was one of the most attractive discoveries made in the early days of specialty selling that the

We cannot forbear to share with our readers this little masterpiece of sentiment, a booklet put out by *"the Cash" in 1909. It illustrates with a tale of unalloyed bathos the point that purchase of a cash register is good not only for one's business but also for the moral well-being of one's employees.*

THE STOREKEEPER'S DREAM

"Oh, why don't you speak to us, grandpa ?
   What makes you so sad tonight ?"
Said a little girl with face aglow
   And eyes both pretty and bright

The gentleman looked at them sadly,
   And a tear stole down his cheek,
As he patted Robby's curly head,
   Who waited to hear him speak.

But he gently motioned them away,
   And sat at his desk to write,
While the pen drooped in his hand so tired,
   No work could he do that night.

Then as he mused, and his grandchild sang
   Her beautiful childish hymn,
With his daughter playing soft and low,
   To him came a vision dim,

Of his sweet and gentle wife again,
   Showing her pride and her joy;
While they built their castles in the air,
   With hopes for their darling boy.

Proud day when his boy left school to work
 Along with him in his store,
And watching his progress day by day
 His fatherly pride grew more

Again he recalled that fateful time
 When his son began to change;
Loving so well that beautiful girl,
 Who was visiting at "The Grange."

Together they would wander away,
 Ne'er thinking they soon would part;
When her father took her away to town.
 She left a sorrowful heart.

This answer from her he loved so well
 Seemed somehow his hopes to dim,
And as he grew more dejected still
 The Tempter reasoned with him.

"One side, a life of toil and hard work,
 The other, easy will be;

Too sad, at last, without her to stay,
　His boy bade them all good-bye,
To go to New York, to business there,
　Yet leaving with tearful eye

After months of toil he saw her once more
　Renewing his love again,
"My father," she said, "will not consent,
　Unless you money obtain."

Take that money, it will not be missed,
　You'll marry her then," said he.

And though his training began to tell,
　'Twas not enough for that life.
Blunt grew his conscience and he forgot,
　In that fight to gain a wife.

He fell, alas! how simple it was,
　Again and again he fell;
Sad that the path to Heaven's so hard,
　So easy the one to Hell.

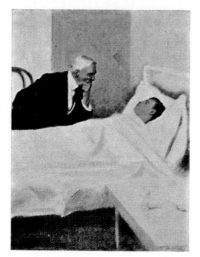

Entangled deep confessed he that night,
　While she begged her father there
To give him one more chance to do right,
　And save from utter despair.

But alas, too late! there came the crash,
　He could not conceal his works;

The door of his guilt wide open there,
　To many suspected clerks.

The horror and shame of that dread trial
　Sent his mother to the grave;
The loss of his love and parent, too,
　From prison his freedom gave.

"Father, good-bye," the dying man said,
　"But first to you I must tell
How your open cash drawer drew me on
　To the road that leads to Hall."

It broke him down, but his daughter's love
　Kept him, again to share
The battles and strife of this, our life,
　Upheld and aided by prayer.

And assisting others day by day,
　His business prospered the more,
Providing work for women and men,
　With the aid of his great store.

And when his grandchildren came to see
　The beautiful things so bright,
He showed them that, which enabled him
　To help his people do right.

customer who had been knocked over once could be upgraded later.

Patterson scoffed at the going idea that salesmen were born. Not N.C.R. salesmen, he vowed. They were made—by the head man, who often played store-keeper with them in this wise: "Good morning," the president of N.C.R. would say mildly to a sweating member of the Selling Force, "I have a drugstore down the street. Will you kindly explain the cash register to me?" If the salesman was quick, verbalized well, or was just lucky that morning, Patterson might give an occasional grunt, his most demonstrative expression of appreciation. More often he jumped up in the middle of the pitch, grabbed a piece of red chalk, and scrawled on the easel pad which always stood handy, "ROT-TEN!" Before the merciless examination was over, some men faltered, some blacked out. And some just plain quit.

But by about 1910, the Cash was doing ninety per cent of the cash register business. The U.S. Department of Justice thought this was a very high penetration of the market. But the pebble in Patterson's shoe was that other ten per cent. He could not honestly see a legitimate reason for *any* cash register to be sold except the National.

John H. Patterson loved to instruct. And he was a convinced eye-minded man. "Visualize! Analyze! Dramatize!" he urged, and installed in his offices hundreds of blackboards and pedestals bearing pads of coarse paper three feet long by two feet wide for jotting down problems or plans. Sometimes he drew pictographs, and he liked others to do the same. It wasn't enough to say "cow." At the Cash, one had to draw the cow.

"The optic nerve is twenty-two times stronger than the auditory nerve," the boss of N.C.R. declared as he made a quick chalk talk or scribbled THINK on the sheet. This cabalistic word was, incidentally, the inspiration of the kinetic Thomas J. Watson, who started out in the world selling pianos, organs, and sewing machines from a bright yellow democrat wagon. Watson got his postgraduate training in Patterson's University of Hard Knocks and went on to transform a faltering combination called the Computing-Tabulating-Recording Company into the fabulous International Business Machines Corporation.

To Patterson the number five was what seven was to the ancients, a digit endowed with occult power. Significantly, he thought, man has five senses, five fingers, five toes. There were five steps to making a sales pitch. Every problem, Patterson saw, had five parts. The figure was woven into the very fabric of the National Cash Register Company. In 1920, at the end of his life, filled with eagerness to see the League of Nations succeed, Patterson went to Geneva, studied the structure of the world organization, got out the old N.C.R. textbook, and charted the purposes of the League—under, of course, five headings.

The center of Patterson's training of his male employees was the N.C.R. Hall of Industrial Education, or the Schoolhouse, where salesmen and agents sometimes acted out little allegorical dramas resembling the old miracle plays with which the Church taught its children in the Middle Ages. An example: men on crutches, others with bandaged arms or legs or eyes, attempted to climb steps toward a bag with a dollar sign on it hanging over the stage. But they could not reach it. Other men emerged from a replica of the Schoolhouse carrying additional steps marked "Uses Advertising Matter," or "Cuts out Cigarettes." With these aids they successfully reached the bag and gave it a mighty wallop; out showered salary checks and special cash prizes.

The female counterpart of the Hall of Education was the Vacation House, where women employees gathered to learn about the menace of the housefly and were taught how to manage their homes. And frequently little N.C.R. children were herded into one of the buildings to learn how to save their money, how to masticate their food, and how coughing and sneezing scattered germs. All this they endured patiently, knowing that later there would be cookies and a movie about Indians. To an extraordinary degree, Patterson regarded the company's assets, human as well as material, as a simple extension of his own personality. Indeed, Patterson took the whole city as a part of his demesne, even at one time exhorting the clergy to drop the Scriptures in favor of his own pet causes—landscape gardening, the city-manager form of municipal government, and the proper care of the teeth.

Some of Patterson's utterances sound trite today, such as his call for "Head-Power, Hand-Power, Heart-Power"; or this one: "By Hammer and Hand All Arts Do Stand." Maybe they sounded that way when he said them. But those who entertained such a heretical attitude were quickly rinsed out of N.C.R.'s hair. Patterson was a great man for signs that expressed the little truisms in which he placed great faith. "It Pays" appeared on walls all through the N.C.R. buildings. He painted "We Progress Through Change" on a tall factory chimney, put cards on every office desk saying "Do it Now" and "Verbal Orders Don't Go."

Patterson was always open-minded, and sometimes credulous, when he encountered a theory that was apparently based upon scientific or quasi-scientific premises. He became interested, for example, in the study of business cycles long before most businessmen had ever heard of the concept, and believed that the price of pig iron was a clue to a certain periodicity in business trends. Scientific or not, it is a fact that Patterson was getting ready for a storm long before the depression of 1893 arrived. When it came he "had his fighting clothes on"; he made the panic year one of the brightest the company had experienced, successfully selling, in those shaky days, a $350 model.

The vegetarian dietary ideas that were disseminated from the Battle Creek Sanitarium in Michigan by another skillful publicist, Dr. John Harvey Kellogg, attracted Patterson's favorable attention. He often journeyed to Battle Creek when he felt the onset of managerial fatigue. As the Dayton *Daily News* said, he was "more than strong for all that Battle Creek stuff." During a trip abroad to expand the N.C.R. business in Europe, Patterson met Horace Fletcher, a health faddist who also had Battle Creek associations. Fletcher was a eupeptic millionaire who had passed through New Thought and Yoga, had once lived for fifty-eight days on potatoes, and was then propagandizing for a physiological regimen known as "Fletcherism." Fletcher believed that people ought to eat less and that the more one chews the less he needs to eat. He dramatized his ideas by prescribing that his followers chew every bite thirty-two times—one chew for each tooth in man's normal complement.

Patterson was fascinated. He plunged into a thirty-seven-day fast which left him so weak that he turned to Sandow in London, then known as "The Strongest Man in the World," to build him up again. When Patterson returned to Dayton, he brought with him a cockney trainer, or rubber, from Sandow's entourage, a wizened little man named Charles Palmer who claimed to have an extraordinary ability to read human character. This odd-ball gym attendant established an almost hypnotic ascendancy over the cash register millionaire and interfered in company affairs, causing many resignations and dismissals.

Charles Palmer hated Dayton. While under Palmer's influence and at a time when he was displeased with the city government, Patterson put together a bitter indictment of the city and announced that the N.C.R. was pulling out. Meanwhile, under Palmer's direction, butter, eggs, salt, and pepper disappeared from the officers' dining room. Even the sacred American Selling Force was not immune to the new regimen. The men were ordered to cut out coffee, tea, and cigars when they were assembled at the home office. Executives obediently drank bottled water, did their calisthenics, and turned out at dawn for horseback riding. Many of them had never been on a horse before. Naturally, the N.C.R. official family became known as "The N.C.R. Rough Riders." The Horse Period was regarded as one of Patterson's more hilarious antics. But for one family it spelled tragedy when the breadwinner, a company official, was thrown and killed.

Patterson brought a series of libel suits against the Dayton *Daily News* when it raised its voice in protest against his eccentric mania for the diminutive English chap. Patterson huffed and puffed but backed down when the *News* began to take depositions. Palmer wore out his welcome and failed to return after a European sojourn. Patterson soon relented in his attitude toward Dayton, later instituted many generous and far-sighted projects for community betterment, including in particular his dream that aviation research might be centralized at Dayton, where the Wrights were born. And Dayton remembers. There is a Patterson Boulevard, the great Wright-Patterson Air Force Base, linking the names of three famous Daytonians, and on parkland he gave to the city there is a heroic statue of Patterson. He is, of course, on a horse.

Over the years, the exodus of able men trained in the N.C.R. methods became legendary. Among the names of prominent alumni appear those of men who later became notable in other fields, such as the already mentioned Thomas J. Watson of I.B.M. and Hugh Chalmers, Edward S. Jordan, Alvan Macauley, Richard H. Grant, and C. F. ("Boss") Kettering of the automotive industry. At one time Patterson developed the habit of cleaning out his executives' desks and burning all the personal contents, even to the family portraits, on the theory that an executive should start fresh every so often. When a man began to look indispensable, he was as good as dead. In his deceptively meek manner Patterson would stutter, if disagreement developed, "Well, well, well, you ought to know best." But old hands knew it was the beginning of the end.

Once the president asked a foreman if he was satisfied with the work in his department. He said he was.

"All right," snapped Patterson, "you're fired."

In his last decade the founder was plagued with some of the penalties of leadership. The N.C.R. was charged with unfair competition in a Michigan state court by the American Cash Register Company, an old rival, which produced damaging testimony from a defecting N.C.R. agent. There were claims and counterclaims of harassment, industrial espionage, pirating, and bribery. Some of the battles became actual fist fights in the P.P.'s store. The verdict in this case was adverse to Patterson. At approximately the same time —in the U.S. District Court of Southern Ohio—the federal government brought suit against the president and twenty-nine other officials of the company for criminal and civil violations of the Sherman Antitrust Act. During the proceedings the court heard some of the uninhibited words Patterson had used in the old days, such as:

"The best way to kill a dog is to cut off his head."
"We do not buy out. We knock out."

Charges were aired of sabotage, industrial spying, payoffs, and harassment through patent litigation.

In 1913 the defendants were adjudged guilty and received jail sentences and fines of varying amounts. Patterson drew a fine of $5,000 and a year in the county jail at Troy. The verdict was appealed, of course. But before the Court of Appeals had handed down its decision, John H. Patterson had the chance to become a national hero.

On Tuesday, March 25, 1913, came the Dayton Flood. The city stood under six to eighteen feet of water. One hundred million dollars' worth of property was destroyed, and 90,000 people were made homeless. With his unconquerable spirit and the material resources he provided, Patterson saved the city. Crayon in hand, he quickly outlined a relief plan on his handy easel pad. Food, tents, medicines, and hospital equipment were moved to the N.C.R. property, which fortunately stood on high ground and had its own power plant. Company bakers started baking bread around the clock, and the assembly line at N.C.R. soon was turning out rowboats—one every seven minutes. Thousands of Daytonians were fed at the N.C.R. cafeteria, slept on hay in the offices (the hay was changed every night), drank bottled water out of mandatory paper cups that Patterson provided, and wore the heavy woolen stockings he prescribed for them. Five babies were born in the factory in one day alone. This explains why "Cash" can really be a man's name. Newspaper reporters, never neglected by Patterson, enjoyed free room and board on the top floor of the administration building, with such amenities available as pinochle cards and ewers of whiskey which were described for Patterson's benefit as "pop." One legend placed Patterson himself, at the age of sixty-five and then under a jail sentence, at the end of a tow line at Main and Apple streets, waist-deep in the swirling waters. Dayton needed a hero and Patterson had a legitimate claim to the role.

Miss Evangeline Cary Booth, commander in chief of the Salvation Army, announced that John H. Patterson was the instrument of the Lord and would be rewarded. And so he was. The United States Court of Appeals reversed the decision of the lower court, largely on the ground that the National Cash Register Company had been denied the right to show that its actions in the old, bad days were the consequence of patent infringements and other destructive practices by the rascally "opposition." One competitor had ridiculed N.C.R. improvements as "ornamental jim-cracks which cumber the machine and add little to its value but serve as an excuse for exorbitant prices." Another had unkindly distributed a circular entitled *Fourteen Ways of Beating the National Cash Register,* which listed ways to manipulate the Cash's machines so as to prove them inaccurate. The Supreme Court refused to consider the case, which meant that the decision of the Court of Appeals stood. To celebrate the triumph of justice twenty thousand Daytonians formed a victory parade with flags and brass bands.

The last sales conference conducted under Patterson's eye was held in January, 1922, to honor the men who had "helped to keep the smokestacks smoking" during the recession of 1921. The agents and salesmen who had bettered their quotas got three days of inspiration and elevation in Dayton, then boarded a

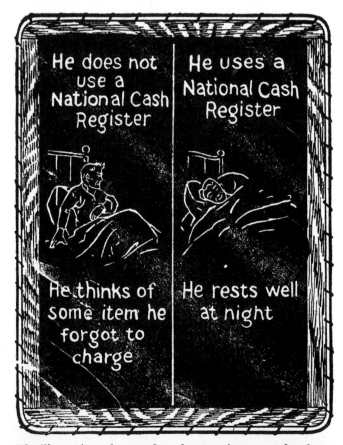

The illustrations above and on the opposite page, taken from a booklet called Chalk Talks, *are typical of the simple, forceful arguments Patterson used to sell his cash register.*

fourteen-car all-Pullman train for three exhilarating days in New York. The picked men thrilled to the N.C.R. chorus that welcomed them at Dayton with the Soldiers' Chorus from *Faust*. In response, they rose to their feet in roaring tribute to the bouncy Founder.

"With depression you went to the mat," said H. G. Sisson of the Publicity Department, as he recited a poem of his own composition:

You were there on the spot where the fighting was hot,
  And you won where the weaker men failed.
Though you may have been jarred when the sledding
    grew hard
  And your arguments seemed to be spent;
Why, you simply began on the old selling plan
  And you finished one hundred per cent.

Then the chevaliers of the N.C.R. Legion of Honor got the message for the next year. There was a door leading into 1922. Turn the knob and find Opportunity; remember such Patterson aphorisms as "Analyze —don't antagonize," "Every time you sell a merchant a National Cash Register you are doing him a big favor," and "Stay five minutes longer." There was the mass photograph on the steps of the Schoolhouse and the comradely fraternizing with the factory workers.

When the time came for the Hundred Per Cent Club to entrain for New York, Dayton put aside its ordinary preoccupations. On signal from the factory whistle, the men and women of N.C.R. formed eight abreast in a column a mile long, and then with flags flying, bands blaring, and symbolical floats, they paraded to the Union Station singing special lyrics arranged to the tune of "Marching Through Georgia." Patterson revelled in the convention, but for him time was running out. He died suddenly on his way to Atlantic City in May, at seventy-seven years of age. Just two days before, he had gone over plans with General William ("Billy") Mitchell, Assistant Chief of Air Service, for the development of Dayton as a great center for aviation research.

The company that Patterson created literally out of nothing has grown enormously; its last reported gross annual sales figure was a whopping $736,849,000, against $29,000,000 in the last year of Patterson's life. It has also become highly diversified, producing, in addition to cash registers, accounting machines, posting machines, and electronic data-processing systems.

The policies of the Cash are now far different from those of the unpredictable autocrat of its pioneering decades. But the heritage of a unique tradition remains. It is a tradition that links the gaslight era of Prince Albert coats and high collars, of wooden Indians and handwritten letters, with the business world of today, the world of the typewriter and the fountain

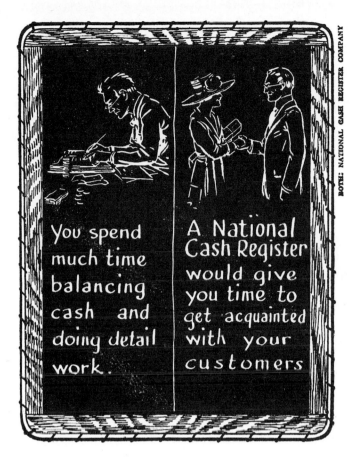

You spend much time balancing cash and doing detail work.

A National Cash Register would give you time to get acquainted with your customers

pen, the duplicating machine and the calculating machine, and, of course, the world of the cash register. This tradition places N.C.R. in the main stream of American business development.

Patterson showed the way to introduce not only "big ticket" merchandise like washing machines and refrigerators, but all products that require sampling and demonstration. To every doorbell ringer of the 2,700 companies whose salesmen make five million calls on every working day, to every bright, cheery, happy, polite, top-notch producer who ever made the Fine and Dandy Club of the Fuller Brush Company, or the Hoover vacuum cleaner Hall of Fame, some of Patterson's shrewd, practical psychology has been passed down. And every executive who has ever made a presentation, talked with the assistance of a slide projector, or handled a flip chart is an heir of the crotchety old man at N.C.R. with his blazing eyes, his scratch pads, his slogans, his food fads—and his touch of genius.

HENRY FORD

—a complex man

By ALLAN NEVINS

One of the most remarkable facts about Henry Ford is that his fame and the Ford legend were born almost simultaneously, and born full-grown. Both came late in life, when he was fifty. The industrialist, we may say without exaggeration, was little known until he suddenly became a world celebrity. He was tossed into international eminence on January 5, 1914, when the Ford Motor Company startled the globe with its "Five Dollar Day."

Until then, Henry Ford had touched the national consciousness but occasionally and glancingly. He had founded the Ford Motor Company in 1903, when already forty; after some years of uncertain struggle, he had produced a model, distinguished from previous Models B, N, and S by the letter T, which precisely filled a ravenous national want; he had erected at Highland Park, just outside Detroit, one of the best-planned and most efficient factories in the world. He and a group of tireless, gifted associates were bringing to birth that magic implement of global change termed mass production; still little understood (for most people ignorantly equate it with quantity production, which is merely one of its half-dozen chief components), and then not understood at all. Ford was, of course, known in the Detroit area as an astonishingly successful manufacturer, and in the automotive world as the dauntless leader of the battle against the Selden patent monopoly. But elsewhere until 1914 the name Ford connoted a brand, not a man.

Henry Ford's sudden fame did not burst and fade; it remained fixed in the skies as a brightening star.

Seekers for facts on the mind and character of the man before 1914 find that the materials are scanty, that most of them pertain to his activities as a racer and in the shop, and that when pieced together they furnish no real portrait. But after 1914, what a change! The spate of articles, books, interviews, and reminiscences becomes ever more torrential. "The Ford and Charlie Chaplin," remarked Will Rogers, "are the best known objects in the world." As the renown grew, unfortunately, so did the confusing legend. As one parodist of the Ford Motor Company slogan put it, "Watch the Ford myths go by!"

Lord Northcliffe extolled Henry Ford to the British public as symbol and exemplar of American energy, confidence and resourcefulness. In Paris Charles M. Schwab, invited to a dinner by Baron Rothschild, electrified the table by describing Ford's achievements. For a time in 1923-24 Ford's quasi-autobiography, translated as *Mein Leben und Werke,* was one of the two best-selling books in Germany. From Sweden to Turkey a new word, *Fordismus,* epitomized the new mass production engineering, the new low-price economy of abundance, and the new efficiency speed-up. Throughout Latin America Ford's personality was regarded as summing up the quintessential American traits and gifts. As for Russia, painfully aware of her industrial backwardness, Henry Ford was a figure about whom *moujiks* and mechanics wove wistful dreams. *Fordizatsia* or Fordization was one of the terms of power in the new era. A visit from Ford, wrote Maurice Hindus, would have called out Russian admirers in hordes.

In the United States, too, the Ford of fact and the Ford of myth were for a time indistinguishably blended. "While I do not accept all of Mr. Ford's industrial philosophy," wrote John A. Ryan, Director of the National Catholic Welfare Council, after reading *My Life and Work,* "I realize more strongly than ever that he has made the greatest contribution toward a solution of more than one of our industrial problems that has yet been made by any captain of industry." The public devoured books about him by Allan Benson, William L. Stidger, Rose Franklin Lane, Charles Merz, Ralph Graves, Dean Marquis and others. Technologists and manufacturers studied the classic work on Ford machines and Ford methods by Arnold and Faurote, an able primer of mass production requirements.

The fifteen years 1914-29 saw Henry Ford at apogee. The American masses took him to their hearts; every clerk and farmer had his own image of the man. But which lines in that image were false, and which true? The task of gaining a true portrait was not simplified by writers who tried to establish an artificial pattern, for of all human beings the complicated, disorganized Ford least responds to that effort. Nor was it simplified by the fact that Henry Ford discovered himself about the time the world did, and announced his discovery by pronunciamentos from on high and essays in self portraiture which wove oriental embroideries about the real man.

At once the most impressive and most disturbing fact about Henry Ford is the extent to which he held up a mirror to the modern American character. In his technological talents, his feats as organizer, his individualistic economics, his social blindness, his frequent brilliant insights, his broad veins of ignorance, prejudice and suspicion, he at first glance seems unique; a man fascinating in his intricacy even to those who most detest some of his traits. Assuredly, we say, nobody else ever existed like Henry Ford. Nothing in industrial history is more inspiring than the triumphs of his early days at the Piquette and Highland Park plants. Nothing in the same history is more depressing than some of the pages he wrote later; pages that would approach high tragedy but for their stupidity and harshness. We seek for threads to explain his labyrinthine complications, and we suddenly realize that in strength and weakness, pioneering thrust and reactionary conservatism, generosity and selfishness, he came near typifying the America of his time.

What made him a tremendous American force was his clear perception of four or five fundamental facts: that the American people not only wanted but needed cars in millions; that a single durable inexpensive model could meet that demand; that new technological elements (precise standardization of parts, the multiplication and perfection of machine tools, separation of the job into minutely specialized functions, quantity manufacture, continuous motion, Taylor time studies), when woven together to create mass production, could furnish the millions of cheap vehicles; that steady price reduction meant steady market expansion ("Every time I lower the price a dollar we gain a thousand new buyers"); and that high wages meant high buying power.

Ford had an imaginative feeling for machinery that could hold a group of children enthralled by his explanation of a watch.

All this was as obvious, when demonstrated, as Columbus' art of standing the egg on end. Until demonstrated it was so far from patent that the ablest manufacturers scoffed, and Ford had to battle his principal partner and the current trend to prove it. A special kind of genius lies in seeing what everybody says is obvious—once somebody thinks of it; and Ford, in relation to his time, had that genius. It changed the world.

Next to this insight, Henry Ford's most striking gift was unquestionably his peculiar engineering talent. In mechanics, he combined much of da Vinci's creative quality with much of James Watt's practical acumen. As a few rare men are born with the power of instantaneously performing intricate mathematical computations, Ford had the power of divining almost any mechanism at a glance. He *read* engines. Indeed, his associate, W. J. Cameron, says that the great engine collections he made in his museum and at Greenfield Village were his historical library. "They were living things to him, those machines. He could almost diagnose the arrangement by touching it. There was a peculiar sympathy between him and a machine." That gift had been with him when as a boy he took apart and reassembled every watch he could reach, and spent a Sunday afternoon, his father away, in disassembling and restoring much of a steam engine.

This flair generated a passion which explains another of his traits, his remarkable power of hard, sustained work. The relaxed air which the mature Henry Ford wore in public, together with his well-advertised recreations in square dancing, collecting Americana, and making excursions with Edison, Firestone and Burroughs, concealed from some observers the fact that from boyhood to old age (he was seventy in 1933) he led a singularly laborious, concentrated life. In his prime his frequent periods of intense industry would have exhausted a less resilient man. At Highland Park and River Rouge his responsibilities were always enormous. But his engineering passion made one important part of them—the responsibility for steady mechanical experiment—almost a refreshment.

Day-to-day study of his activities gives us the picture of a man in whose quick brain exploded a steady succession of technological ideas. A helical type of spring band to use in planetary transmission for holding the drum; a new element in the carburetor; a bolder mode of casting the engine block—always some novel ingenuity had to be tried. That side of his mind never rested. "He was up at Harbor Beach one time," writes E. G. Liebold, "where he had a summer cottage, and he was coming home with Edsel. Suddenly he said: 'I've got the idea. We're going to put a worm drive on the tractor.'" That idea solved the theretofore vexatious problem of power transmission to the rear axle—or so he hoped; and he drove his tractor factory ahead with enhanced zest.

In experimentation, pioneering, the quest for fruitful mechanical innovations, Henry Ford at his apogee was happiest. Anything was worth trying. In 1914-15 he became interested in making a better electric car than any on the market, and reports spread that he and Edison were collaborating. If the idea proved good (which it did not) he thought of forming a separate company. A later scheme called for the use of plastics in building cars; in fact, a plastic-body car *was* built. This experiment was connected with Ford's intense interest in promoting soy bean culture, for he realized that American agriculture needed new crops and that American industry suffered from a growing shortage of vegetable oils.

Now and then some incident suggested how far back in Ford's career his experimental passion reached. He once turned his attention to a slide-valve engine on which Knight, of Willys-Knight, held some patents. Reflecting that he might wish some time to build such an engine, Ford decided to protect himself by recovering an old slide-valve that, as a humble mechanic, he put in a Westinghouse steam engine. He actually recalled that the engine had been No. 345 and had been shipped to McKean County, Pa. A searcher found the battered engine; found an old bill of sale which proved that it *was* No. 345; and found the name-plate, which was being used on a stove-grate. Brought to Dearborn, the engine was triumphantly restored to the condition in which Ford had known it.

His technological genius was one aspect of a mind peculiar for its intuitive nature. Ford hit upon truths (and errors) by divination, not ratiocination. His aides credited him with what Dean Marquis called a "supernormal perceptive faculty" and W. J. Cameron "some gadgets in his head that the rest of us didn't have." Marquis termed him "a dreamer," adding that he had a different view from other men of what was possible and impossible. "I suppose the reason is that men who dream walk by faith, and faith laughs at mountains." As Ford himself told Fred L. Black, he worked partly by hunches. Even his understanding of his lieutenants was largely intuitive.

Obviously, if intuition moved some mountains, it collided disastrously with certain more massive ranges. Reliance on intuition was one reason why Ford was so amazingly unpredictable; men never knew which of a half-dozen Fords they were going to meet. It was also one reason for the crippling isolation of his mind, for a brain that cannot be reasoned with is a brain that cannot be penetrated. Down to 1914 Ford was open to the counsel of men who had a right to insist on being heard: his partners Alex Malcomson and John S. Gray, his indispensable business manager James Couzens, the brilliant designer Harold Wills, and others. Later, with the amazing expansion of the business, the rise of employees to six figures, his achievement of autocratic power by the ousting of all his partners, and increasing age, Henry Ford placed himself beyond advice. His mental isolation "is about as perfect as he can make it," wrote Marquis as early as 1923. Charles E. Sorensen, who ought to know, believes that Ford had only two lifelong friends: Sorensen himself, and the strong head of his British company, Percival L. D. Perry.

His complex, inconsistent, intuitive mind has naturally lent itself to a Jekyll and Hyde concept of two (or more) Fords dwelling in the same body; but we may repeat that these efforts at pattern-making are delusive. One clue, however, does explain much in the Dearborn wizard. The dreamer, the man of intuitive mind, is usually an artist; and many puzzling vagaries, many contradictions, even many repugnant acts in Ford become comprehensible if we view him as essentially a man of artistic temperament. His detachment, his arch, wry humor, his constant self-projection into the spotlight (though all his intimates call him essentially modest), his ability to lift himself above those business minutiae which absorbed most industrialists, his readiness to do some terrible things with as little seeming consciousness of their quality as Byron or Swift showed in *their* misdeeds, all suggest an artistic bent. The Model T was homely awkwardness itself—but it had artistic elements. Highland Park was the most artistic factory, in architecture, shining cleanliness, and harmonic arrangement, built in America in its day. The painter Charles Sheeler caught the beauty of the River Rouge plant. And what of the aesthetic element in the old dances, old folksongs, old buildings, and old machines Ford loved so well?

Above all, he had the artist's desire to remake the world after his own pattern. His gospel of abundant work, high wages, and low prices; his plans for decentralizing industry to combine it with rural life and rural virtues; his enthusiastic forays into "better" agriculture, "better" education, "better" recreation; his warm promotion from 1914-20 of the welfare work of his "sociological department"—what else were these but the artist's effort to impose his own vision on life? He would remold American society and the American economy to fit his vision, himself the potter at the whirling wheel.

If there was a Jekyll and Hyde element in the man, it lay in the complex enmity between Ford the artist and Ford the untutored countryman whose parents had been Michigan pioneers, and whose own formal educa-

tion was limited to a few years in a very common school. This conflict twisted the whole skein of his character. An artist needs a cultivated background: Henry Ford's background was that of Anglo-Irish tenant farmers, and of Springwells Township lately wrested from the forest. Though from his homely early environment he drew many advantages, its limitations always fettered him.

He always remained a countryman in his plain way of living, for despite Keith Sward's statements, it *was* plain. When his fortune first grew, he said plaintively that the chief difference in his way of life was that "Mrs. Ford no longer does the cooking"—and he preferred her cookery. He refused a butler, for he wanted no man behind his chair at dinner "while I am taking the potatoes' jackets off." His puritanic condemnation of smoking, drinking and marital irregularities con-

Ford drives his first farming vehicle, an "automobile plow."

formed to the principles described in Thorstein Veblen's essay *The Country Town*. He rejected the eminent Delancey Nicoll as attorney in the Sapiro case because, when the New York lawyer came to Dearborn, Ford saw him chain-smoking cigarettes. "I'm for Mr. Coolidge if he will enforce the Prohibition laws," he said in 1923. He was a countryman also in his devotion to work as a virtue in itself. His cure for nearly all ills was more work.

True to the frontiersman's instinct, he consistently preferred trial and error to precise planning. Contemptuous of elaborate record-keeping, he once shocked Perry by making a bonfire of forms used to keep track of spare parts. Hostile to meticulous organization, he ran even the huge Highland Park plant without formal titles or administrative grades. He long derided careful cost accounting. In this, thinks one surviving executive, H. L. Moekle, he was right. Success in the automotive industry at first depended not on computation of costs to the third decimal point in Rockefeller's fashion, but on courageous innovations in design and engineering and on the acceptability of models and prices to the public. Ford stayed in the field of bold experiment—cost accounting might have hampered him. He of course stuck to Model T too long; but meanwhile he was experimenting with tractors, a tri-motored airplane, a weekly journal, a railroad, and a dozen other matters.

He had also the frontiersman's intense hatred of monopoly and special privilege. To be sure, he long enjoyed a practical monopoly of the low-priced car, but he could say that he achieved it without favor and without warring on any competitor. His dislike of patents, his earnest counsel to George Holley to take out no patent on his carburetor, his course in throwing open to public view and general use Ford machines and methods, his determined battle against George Selden, all harmonized with the frontier attitude. He extended the principle beyond automotive patents. His early broadcasting station WWI carried on research, worked out (so associates say) the first directional airplane controls, and gained a patent—which he shared with all. Once his purchaser, Fred Diehl, was offered spark plugs free for River Rouge production if the supplier were allowed to sell all replacements to dealers. "Mr. Ford himself turned that down," reports a lieutenant. "He said he didn't want anything from anybody for nothing." A true countryman's speech; for a scheme that would have meant monopoly supply was abhorrent to Henry Ford.

Much more might be said on the pleasanter inheritances from the rural environment—on his rather appealing inarticulateness which kept him from making public speeches (the longest ever recorded was 28 words); on his dislike of class lines, which was one of several reasons for his aversion from Grosse Pointe society; on the rugged comradeship with fellow workers which he showed in his early career, but unhappily lost; on his warm love of nature, and the feeling for wild life which made him build shelters for rabbits, grow corn for crows, and keep warm water available all winter in the hope of retaining migratory songbirds in the North. One of the most important parts of his countryman's heritage was his stubborn originality of thought—when he did think. Neither from books nor men did he take ideas secondhand; he hammered them out for himself, usually on walks in field and wood. Often they were immature. But sometimes, between intuition and lonely thinking, he seized a concept which startled men with its novel glint of truth.

Meanwhile, what penalties his early environment, and his invincible ignorance in many areas, laid upon him! Like other untutored men, he had a deep sus-

picion of the uncomprehended, a strong inclination to prejudice, and a susceptibility to bad counsel. Some thought his antagonism to Wall Street traceable to a memory of Populist speeches, others to his anxieties in the depression of 1921; but surely three-fourths of it was simple distrust of what he did not understand. It is significant that his suspiciousness, hardly visible in his first years of success, grew marked when he came under fire. "Ford has the idea that he is persecuted," a writer in the Forum accurately stated in 1919. He thought that some journals had begun to "hound" him when he announced the $5 day, and others when he battled for peace and the League.

"A good part of the American press, not all, is not free," he told reporters. It lay, he thought, under various controls; it was warped by sensationalism. "They misquoted me, distorted what I said, made up lies." The gibing, malicious attitude of part of the press toward the Peace Ship, the aspersions on his motives in lifting wages from $2.25 to $5, the mean attacks on Edsel as an alleged draft-dodger, and the storm of ridicule accompanying the Chicago Tribune trial and the senatorial campaign, were indeed outrageous. Since Ford was a sensitive man, they had a perceptible effect in hardening his temper and converting his early idealism into cynicism. Had he possessed more education, poise, and perspective, he would not only have avoided some of the occasions for ridicule; he would have met ridicule with a heavier armor.

Out of his sense of needing an agency for defense and for stating his ideas came the Dearborn Independent. Out of his ignorance, sensitiveness, and suspiciousness came the lamentable anti-Semitic campaign of that weekly, for which he apologized only after vast harm had been done. In this unhappy crusade he had collaborators. The shrewd E. G. Pipp, who resigned as editor rather than share in it, made a brutally frank statement to Cameron: "You are furnishing the brains, Ford the money, and [E. G.] Liebold the prejudices." Cameron and Liebold furnished some of the methods, too, but as Liebold says, "As long as Mr. Ford wanted it done, it was done." His was the responsibility. That he had no deep-seated race prejudices, but really believed in a fictitious bogy called the International Jew, does not palliate his offense. We can only say that this, like the shortsighted harshness which he showed toward labor organizations, was the abortion of an uninformed mind and uncultivated spirit.

Some aspects of the man, defying any efforts to fix a pattern, remain—as in such other contradictory personages as Edwin M. Stanton or Woodrow Wilson—quite inexplicable. Highly diffident in some ways, he had an irrepressible desire to be oracular about topics of which he knew nothing. Kindly in most personal relations, he nevertheless countenanced such cruel treatment of subordinates as the smashing of their desks in token of discharge. At times he indulged a good humored liking for horseplay—"he was a proper Puck," as Lord Perry expressed it; at other times he was sternly unapproachable. Sharply practical, he yet cherished some curious superstitions. A churchgoing Episcopalian, he leaned strongly to an unorthodox belief in metempsychosis. There was always something in him of an urchin, a wry, cross-grained, brilliant adolescent; and like an energetic urchin, he was so kinetic that only a motion picture could have caught his multifarious activities and swiftly changing moods.

"A proper Puck," Ford had a mischievous sense of humor. Here he plays the Western badman on a summer outing.

Yet in this fascinating personality, with its bright lights, dark shadows, and intermediate *chiaroscuro* traits, we come back always to the image of the artist. John Reed, interviewing him in 1916, thought he looked like an artist, with "thin, long, sure hands, incessantly moving"; "the mouth and nose of a simple-minded saint"; "a lofty forehead"; "the lower part of his face extraordinarily serene and naïve, the upper part immensely alive and keen." His swiftness, his agility, his intense interest in everything he observed, contributed to the impression of an artistic temperament. Much that is otherwise puzzling becomes comprehensible if we think of him as an artist, struggling, despite many limitations and handicaps, to remake his world a little nearer to the heart's desire. He wanted to abolish war ("a habit, and a filthy habit," he said) from his world, and hence the great gesture of the Peace Ship. He wanted to exclude drink, class divisions, idleness and disorder. He wanted to get rid of money as anything but a part of the mechanism of production: "part of the assembly line," or "the connecting rod."

Perhaps his poignant failure lay in his relationship to his son, to whom he gave both intense devotion and total incomprehension. Edsel was a man of the finest qualities of character and mind, upright, idealistic, public-spirited, and hard-working. He was highly philanthropic. In the factory he got on well with other executives, many of whom felt a warm affection for him. In the world at large, as old associates testify, he had a broader vision than his father. Some of Henry Ford's acts, such as the anti-Jewish campaign, grieved Edsel greatly, though he was too loyal to speak out publicly. Yet the father, while justly proud of him, committed a fundamental error in their relationship. "He tried to make Edsel in his own image," says Mr. Sorensen. In the process he did incidental injustice to some men like Clarence W. Avery who, coming close to Edsel, aroused his jealousy. Of course he failed in his effort, with anguish to both himself and the son. But the attempt was again, in part, an expression of the artist's desire to make the world over to suit his own vision.

As the years pass and as we gain perspective, the absurd blunders and shabby misdeeds in Henry Ford's record will arouse less interest. His social primitivism will seem more a part of the general ignorance and gullibility of our adolescent American civilization. His great achievement, in the direct line of Watt and Stephenson, Eli Whitney and Cyrus McCormick, yet in some ways transcending theirs, will loom up as the really significant fact of his career. By his labors in bringing mass production to birth, by his gospel of high production, low prices, and large consumption, he became the key figure in a far-reaching revolution. This fumbling artist actually did remold the world according to his vision. Talking with Edsel one day, he said of his great company: "Well, we'll build this as well as we know how, and if we don't use it, somebody will use it. Anything that is good enough will be used." Of few of the industrial path-hewers of his time can it be said that they produced so much that is permanently and profitably usable.

At the Venetian Pool in Coral Gables, an aging W. J. Bryan daily

THE BUBBLE

Under the Florida palms William Jennings Bryan orated and Gilda Gray shimmied while real-estate promoters hawked lots. It was the greatest land boom in our history

The impulse which carried Theyre Hamilton Weigall into the Miami madness of 1925 was about as logical as that which carried anybody else into it. An unemployed English newspaperman wandering the streets of New York in the summer of that year, he was suddenly stopped by a sign in a window announcing that there were fortunes to be made in Florida real estate. "One Good Investment Beats a Lifetime of Toil. Say! YOU can do what George Cusack, Jr., did!" Cusack, Weigall judged from the accompanying photo, was a little half-witted anyway. If he could make $500,000 in four weeks in Florida real estate, anybody could.

When, a couple of days later, Weigall stepped off

sang Florida's praises. He carried his cross of gold—reputedly more than $50,000 a year—lightly. At left are some printed enticements.

IN THE SUN

By GEORGE B. TINDALL

a train into the blazing August sunlight of a Miami afternoon, he felt as though he had stepped into a tropical bedlam. Amid the din of automobile horns, drills, hammers, and winches, he later wrote, "Hatless, coatless men rushed about the blazing streets, their arms full of papers, perspiration pouring from their foreheads. Every shop seemed to be combined with a real-estate office; at every doorway crowds of young men were shouting and speech-making, thrusting forward papers and proclaiming to heaven the unsurpassed chances which they were offering to make a fortune. One had been prepared for real-estate madness; and here it was, *in excelsis*." Miami, Weigall was in-

formed, was "one hell of a place" . . . "The finest city, sir, in the U.S.A., and I don't mean mebbe."

The mob scene that Weigall was swept into was without question one of the supreme spectacles of the palmy years of the Twenties, a full dress rehearsal for the great bull market of 1929. The ebullience of Weigall's account merely reflects the excitement it inspired in almost every witness. The journalists and publicists who wrote of it nearly exhausted their stock of superlatives. The *New York Times* reported that more "pioneers de luxe" had settled in Florida within two years than in California in the ten years after the forty-niners. "All of America's gold rushes," Mark Sullivan wrote, looking back at the spectacle from the vantage point of the thirties, "all her oil booms, and all her free-land stampedes dwindled by comparison . . . with the torrent of migration pouring into Florida."

Amid that torrent of ambitious humanity, young Weigall soon realized that success was not automatic. He answered a newspaper advertisement and became a glorified salesman representing the "membership committee of an exclusive but nonexistent "International Yacht Club," and eventually found his role turning out promotion copy for the Miami subdivision of Coral Gables. He was here at last in the vortex of the boom.

Coral Gables, unlike many of the fraudulent and jerry-built promotions that imitated it, was the embodiment of an aesthetic vision. It had gestated for years in the mind of George E. Merrick, one of the towering geniuses of the Miami boom. He had come to Miami in the late nineties with his father, the Reverend Solomon Merrick, a New England Congregational minister who hoped the Florida climate would improve his wife's health. On a 160-acre tract south of town, the elder Merrick built a home which he called Coral Gables after the local coral limestone and after Grey Gables, Grover Cleveland's house on Cape Cod. He established a business selling fruit and vegetables in the village of Miami, and young George, on his daily trips to town with produce, trusted directions to his horse and spent the time reading, composing poetry, and building castles in Spain, castles that would eventually become the city of Coral Gables.

The family orchards prospered enough to begin shipping carloads to the North, and George went away to college and, later, to law school. When his father died in 1911, he was forced to return home and manage the family estate. Merrick built up one of the most prosperous fruit and vegetable plantations in the area and in 1914 moved into the real-estate business, developing some of the earliest subdivisions around Miami. His ultimate dream, though, was of a new model city, "wherein nothing would be unlovely," an American Venice planned not only for comfort and convenience but for aesthetic quality. "For ten years," he later told a reporter, "I worked night and day to build up a nucleus for the Coral Gables which consistently grew in my dreams. I never told anyone my plans, but as my profits in real estate grew, I bought adjoining land. The 160 acres the family originally owned increased to 300, then to 500, a thousand, and finally to 1,600."

Meanwhile, the situation slowly ripened for the realization of young Merrick's dream. For despite the impression it gave, the Florida boom did not spring to life full blown, like Aphrodite from the waves. It stemmed from a long line of promoters like Henry M. Flagler. The Florida historians A. J. and Kathryn Hanna have suggested that the Gold Coast from Hobe Sound, north of Palm Beach, to Miami could look back to Flagler "much as the human race recollects Noah." Before Flagler, Miami was but a lonely outpost on one of the last American frontiers. It had begun during the Seminole War of 1835-42 with the establishment of Fort Dallas at the point where the Miami River empties into Biscayne Bay. Until the nineties the little settlements that grew around the fort were populated by fishermen, traders, small farmers, and a few refugees from northern winters.

Flagler, an early partner of John D. Rockefeller in Standard Oil, had first seen Florida on a vacation trip in 1878. He returned to St. Augustine for his honeymoon in 1883 and soon embarked upon a career of developing a string of resorts along Florida's east coast. Starting with two hotels at St. Augustine, the Ponce de Leon and the Alcazar, and with the improvement of railroad connections from Jacksonville, he pushed his Florida East Coast Railway on south to Ormond and Daytona, and eventually, in 1894, into Palm Beach. That year, Flagler added to his hotel chain by building the Royal Poinciana in Palm Beach, and, two years later, the Breakers. These hotels, supplemented by a railroad parking lot for private palace cars, were for decades among the favorite resorts of the rich and the famous. When in April, 1896, the railroad reached Miami, Flagler launched the city by constructing still another Flagler hotel, the Royal Palm; an electric light plant; and a water and sewage system. By 1900, Miami could claim a grand total of 1,681 persons.

On June 13, 1913, a few weeks after Flagler's death, a landmark was dedicated in Miami. It was the first bridge to Miami Beach, the narrow strip of land that separates Biscayne Bay from the Atlantic. The bridge was the brain child of another great Florida pioneer, John S. Collins, a successful New Jersey horticulturist who, in the eighties, had invested $5,000 in a scheme to grow coconut palms in the area. Disappointed in that venture, Collins came to Miami himself in 1896, acquired land on Miami Beach with an eye to its future resort possibilities, and, for the time being, began raising avocados, potatoes, and bananas.

But in order to assure the development of the area, Collins realized that there had to be a bridge from Miami to the Beach. In 1912, with the backing of his three sons and his son-in-law, Thomas J. Pancoast, he began his bridge across Biscayne Bay. Halfway across, the contracting company failed, and with his Jordan nearly crossed, Collins' money ran out. The plight of the venture was brought to the attention of Carl

Graham Fisher, an Indianian who had founded the Indianapolis Speedway and the Prestolite Company and who, by good luck, was just then vacationing in Miami. Fisher met Collins, was impressed with his plan, and took $50,000 worth of bonds in the bridge, enough to complete it.

Fisher also inaugurated some of the more bizarre phases of Florida promotion. He dredged up the bottom of Biscayne Bay in order to fill a mangrove swamp, then dredged up more mud to make artificial islands in the bay. He incorporated the town of Miami Beach in 1915, and after World War I opened a campaign of hotel building and high-pressure advertising unlike anything seen before in the country. Among his gimmicks were Carl and Rosie, two elephants who hauled cartloads of children around the island. One even served as a caddy for President Harding. Finally, Fisher conceived the idea of the Miami Beach bathing beauty. According to Will Rogers, he was the "midwife" of Florida, who "rehearsed the mosquitoes till they wouldn't bite you until after you'd bought."

Thanks to the spadework of men like Flagler, Collins, and Fisher, Miami on the eve of the boom was already a playground for the rich. South Bay Shore Drive on Biscayne Bay, south of the city, had emerged as a millionaire's row in 1916 with the completion of the palatial Villa Vizcaya, home of the harvester magnate James Deering. In 1923 William H. Luden, the coughdrop king, arrived for the season at his home on the Drive, and William K. Vanderbilt came in his $3,000,000 yacht, *Alva*. Senator T. Coleman Du Pont of Delaware was staying at Flagler's Royal Palm Hotel, and Harvey S. Firestone came to visit and then to buy a great Georgian-style showplace. Other visitors of note that year included Labor Secretary James J. Davis, chain-store genius J. C. Penney, auto mogul William C. Durant, and the 1920 Democratic presidential candidate, James M. Cox, who purchased control of a Miami newspaper and transformed it into the Miami *Daily News*. A new resident was sometime-politician, sometime-evangelist William Jennings Bryan, who taught a Bible class for tourists every Sunday morning in the Royal Palm Park. But, naturally, the climax of the 1923 season was the arrival at the Flamingo Hotel of President and Mrs. Warren Harding.

Thus all was in readiness for the boom when, in 1924, the combination of Coolidge prosperity and the proliferation of Henry Ford's tin lizzies gave Americans extra money to spend and made Florida an accessible place in which to spend it. A number of factors contributed to the Florida boom. First of all, there was money to be made in land speculation. The value of

Florida real estate had been climbing since the turn of the century, and the state was particularly attractive to investors after 1924, when it outlawed both income and inheritance taxes.

But there was another more subtle and complex factor—a paradoxical revolt against the very urbanization and industrialization which were producing the new prosperity. The businessman made his money in the heart of the city, Frederick Lewis Allen suggested in *Only Yesterday*, but he wanted to spend it in exotic surroundings, in "a Venice equipped with bathtubs and electric ice-boxes, a Seville provided with three eighteen-hole golf courses." Florida promoters lost no opportunity to make it abundantly clear that Florida was *the* exotic place. "Florida is bathed in passionate caresses of the southern sun," one advertisement read. "It is laved by the limpid waves of the embracing seas, wooed by the glorious Gulf Stream, whose waters, warmed by the tropical sun, speed northeast to temper the climate of Europe. Florida is an emerald kingdom by southern seas, fanned by zephyrs laden with ozone from stately pines, watered by Lethe's copious libation, decked with palm and pine, flower and fern, clothed in perpetual verdure and lapt in the gorgeous folds of the semi-tropical zone." How could a small-town banker looking out his window at the frozen wastes of North Dakota resist *that?*

Every winter after the Armistice more and more "snowbirds" appeared. They were very different from the Vanderbilts and Du Ponts who had frequented Flagler's elegant hostelries. The arrivals of the Twenties were a part of what might be termed a "subdivision civilization," one which allowed the middle class to enjoy a comparatively inexpensive season in the sun and, if they were lucky, to turn a pretty penny in land speculation besides.

The prototype of the Florida subdivision was Coral Gables. By 1921, George Merrick had 1,600 acres just southwest of Miami, $500,000, and a sound experience in real-estate development. Now, with a highly organized sales force and a stable of architects, he took the first tentative steps toward making his dream city a reality, cautiously building a road or two, putting in lighting and water connections. The first sales of lots were made in November, 1921. Within two years the sudden inflation of land values was under way, and Coral Gables was one of the first areas to be caught up in the rapid expansion. Almost overnight Merrick found himself dealing in millions. He expanded his holdings to 10,000 acres, formed the Coral Gables Corporation under his sole control, and amid the speculative frenzy saw his dream begin to materialize.

Throughout the boom Merrick remained an enigma

to the host of extroverts that swarmed into Miami. A large, squarely built, pensive man in his late thirties, he avoided personal publicity and consistently refused to attend public functions. Even his dress—ill-fitting tweed trousers, Norfolk jacket, and old brogues—seemed strangely un-Miami. T. H. Weigall still regarded him worshipfully years later as "a very great man," "passionately in love with Florida," not for the sake of its exploitation but as "the last outpost of the United States, a fresh and unspoiled territory which it would be criminal to let develop along haphazard, ugly, or unscientific lines."

As the boom advanced, development of Coral Gables accelerated: the area was landscaped; lakes and waterways connected to Biscayne Bay were blasted out; and winding avenues and plazas were built through the pine woods. The quarry from which the coral rock had been dug for construction was converted into the colorful Venetian Pool. Carefully planned residential and business sections began to emerge, as well as the University of Miami, which was expected to rival the great academic centers of the East. There were golf courses, a country club, and a twenty-six-story hotel, the Miami-Biltmore. Everything was to be in a blend of Spanish-Italian architecture that Merrick called "Mediterranean."

As Weigall described Coral Gables later, "Its main boulevards were all 100 feet wide, and at their intersections there were fountains surrounded by tropical trees and wide plazas paved with coral rock. Everywhere there was brilliantly-colored foliage and running water. Its houses stood well back in their gardens, and even the offices, with their brightly-colored sunblinds, gave an impression of being almost countrified. Everywhere there were dazzling colors—white walls, striped awnings, red roofs, brilliant greenery, and the intense blue of the Florida sky." By the spring of 1925 it included five hundred homes.

Northward from Coral Gables the boom spirit spread up the coast and across the Florida peninsula into a hundred subdivisions of a hundred towns, each elaborating its own variations on Merrick's theme of a perfect city. There was Hollywood, "The Golden Gate of the South"; Fort Lauderdale, "The Tropical Wonderland"; Orlando, "The City Beautiful"; Winter Park, "The City of Homes"; Haines City, "The Gateway to the Scenic Highlands"; Sebring, "The Orange Blossom City"; Fort Myers, "The City of Palms"; and St. Petersburg, "The Sunshine City," where the *Independent* gave away its edition on any day the sun failed to shine.

Even staid old Palm Beach, at first inclined to look down its aristocratic nose upon the scrambling *nouveaux riches,* was caught up in the hurricane of expansion. Palm Beach was to be wooed and won into the heart of the boom by one of the great charlatangeniuses of the Twenties, Addison Mizner—painter, woodcarver, miner, interior decorator, prize fighter, writer, architect. Born in California in 1872, Mizner had gone to Guatemala with his father in his teens, and there had fallen in love with Spanish art and architecture. This love had later grown during a brief stay at the University of Salamanca in Spain. Over the years he had pursued his off-beat career as an exotic and romantic dilettante on four continents.

Mizner's first brush with fame had been as co-author of *The Cynic's Calendar.* "Where there's a will, there's a lawsuit"; "Many are called but few get up"; "The wages of gin is breath"; "Be held truthful that your lies may count." He was working in New York as a society architect and designer of Japanese landscapes when ill health carried him to Palm Beach in 1918.

There he fell in with a kindred spirit, Paris Singer, whose inheritance from his father's sewing machines gave him the time and the money to pursue both the arts and Isadora Duncan. Soon the combination of the Florida sun and Singer's generosity had helped Mizner recover to the point where he was busily designing a hospital—financed by Singer—for convalescent World War I soldiers. But the war was completed before the hospital was, and it was transformed into the Everglades Club, displacing Flagler's Breakers as the *ne plus ultra* of Palm Beach. The Everglades was the first of many architectural triumphs that established Mizner as the supreme master of the Florida Spanish motif. It led to a commission to build a villa for banker Edward T. Stotesbury, the first of dozens of rich patrons—including G. Rodman Wanamaker II, Drexel Biddle, Jr., and a pride of Vanderbilts—who were eager to pay for the privilege of being insulted by a great architect and of living in the gigantic pleasure domes he created for them.

The architecture of these latter-day Xanadus has been summarized by Alva Johnston in his book, *The Legendary Mizners,* as the Bastard-Spanish-Moorish-Romanesque-Gothic-Renaissance-Bull-Market-Damn-the-Expense Style. Their central theme was inevitably Spanish, but Mizner, a versatile antiquarian, sometimes threw ten centuries into one structure. "Most modern architects," he said, "have spent their lives in carrying out a period to the last letter and producing a characterless copybook effect. My ambition has been to take the reverse stand—to make a building look traditional and as though it had fought its way from a small unimportant structure to a great rambling house that took centuries of different needs and ups and downs of wealth to accomplish. I sometimes start a house with a Romanesque corner, pretend that it has fallen into disrepair and been added to in the Gothic spirit, when suddenly the great wealth of the New World has poured in and the owner has added a very rich Renaissance addition."

To get the all-important appearance of antiquity Mizner inflicted the wildest vandalism on his masterpieces. He deliberately smudged up new rooms with burning pots of tarpaper, took penknife and sledgehammer to woodwork and statuary, used ice picks and air rifles on furniture, hired inexperienced help to lay roof tiles awry, and once had men in hobnailed boots walk up and down a stairway before the cement set to get the effect of centuries of wear. One of his original contributions to architecture was the discovery that worm-eaten cypress gave the desired effect of age; thus pecky cypress, formerly considered almost worthless, suddenly became the mahogany of Palm Beach.

The one talent Mizner lacked was that of making conventional plans and specifications. Everything was done off-the-cuff. Plans for one house were drawn in the sand on the beach, a window in another was copied from a photograph of a house on Minorca. When one client asked for a blueprint, Mizner replied in amazement, "Why, the house isn't built yet." Occasionally, this resulted in oversights, such as the failure to include a staircase in one mansion; a staircase was eventually added—but outside, so that it would not spoil the perfection of the interior.

His landscaping experience gave him a distinct feeling for the setting of a house. To an admirer, the

Anything could help make a sale.

A charabanc for the prospects

Glimpses

of

Florida

in

Boom Time

Old windjammers pressed into delivering building materials

Golf all year around!

Building Miami for the multitude

Palm Beach was fancier.

journalist Ida Tarbell, he seemed "to have a veritable passion for utilizing all the natural beauties of the place," an ability "to make a typical Florida thing." Vistas of the ocean, the blue skies, the tall palms, all figured in his craft. Large windows and cross drafts let the balmy air into his rooms. He noticed that the prevailing winds were from the southwest, so his kitchens were invariably in the northeast corner of the house. As an artist he understood the dramatic effects of color—he preferred pastels. He looted Spain and Central America of tile roofs and furnishings and set up his own Mizner Industries, Inc., to make the latest thing in "antiques," wrought iron, artificial stone, stained glass, terra cotta, tiles, urns, pots, and fountains.

Not far from the Everglades Club were the Via Mizner, the Via Parigi, and the Worth Avenue Arcade, where Mizner created Old World alleys of little shops and sidewalk cafés with gay pink, blue, and cream-colored fronts. Up and down Palm Beach his talent ran riot, spawning a city of palaces with great watch towers and thick walls, cloistered arcades, high galleries, vaulted ceilings, and tiled pools. These edifices have been called by some the work of a quack, by others, including Frank Lloyd Wright, that of a genius.

Addison Mizner soon had a million dollars, he claimed, salted away in government bonds, but it was inevitable that he would be drawn into the subdivision madness that swept up from Miami. He was joined in that adventure by his scapegrace brother, Wilson, a latter-day Sir John Falstaff who had come down from New York in 1921 to manage the Mizner Industries. He was a master of the pulverizing phrase and was credited by some with the quip, "Never give a sucker an even break."

As the boom roared into fantastic excesses, Wilson found himself more and more at home in the Florida wonderland. The Mizners got a late start, but they made up for it by projecting the most ostentatious sub-

The promise: *The exotic atmosphere that all Florida subdivisions tried to create for themselves in the Twenties is typified by this ad for Coral Gables. Most of the "waterfront" was on man-made canals.*

division of all at Boca Raton (Rat's Mouth), a little stop on the Florida East Coast Railway south of Palm Beach. The plans featured El Camino Real, a highway 219 feet wide and only about twelve times as long, with twenty traffic lanes and a "Venetian canal" with powered gondolas running down its center. There was to be a hotel, an airport, a polo field, two golf courses, a yacht basin, and a church that was to be a memorial to Mama Mizner and a source of satisfaction to the Mizners' other brother, an Episcopal priest—the white sheep, as it were, of the family. Unfortunately, little of it got off Addison's mental drawing boards. "Beaucoup Rotten," the rival realtors labelled it, and so it turned out to be, for it got under way as the boom roared to a collapse. The only structure completed was the hotel, the Cloister, one of Addison's masterpieces.

At mid-decade the boom spirit soared to its peak. The Gold Coast, of which Miami was the heart, was geared to a winter-resort economy; from April to November it subsided into lassitude. But in 1925 the season never ended. The swarms of "tin can" tourists continued to arrive in their flivvers throughout that summer. Kenneth L. Roberts, covering the scene for the *Saturday Evening Post,* estimated that 4,000 people a day entered the state by automobile, supplemented by another 3,000 on trains and 200 on ships, making perhaps more than 2,500,000 in the boom year.

The new arrivals included a liberal sprinkling of real and pseudo celebrities. Indeed, the number of celebrities a town or subdivision had was considered a good barometer of its prestige. Thus Miami Beach boasted that it was the resort of "America's wealthiest sportsmen, devotees of yachting and other expensive sports." The subdivision of Floranda had the Earl and Countess Lauderdale, Lord Thirlestane, and the ex-King of Greece; Gene Tunney regularly appeared at another subdivision; Bobby Jones was at Davis Islands in Tampa Bay; while Helen Morgan and Elsie Janis could be seen at Hollywood-by-the-Sea. And Florida's famous visitors did not have to go around thirsty in the sun just because of the Eighteenth Amendment. Liquor was as readily available as it was in Al Capone's Chicago. The primary source for this cheer was the Bahamas. In 1922 a friend just back from Nassau reported to a horrified William Jennings Bryan, "The Bahamians are very proud of the fact that Prohibition in the United States has made their country independent. They boast of the fact that theirs is the only government known to be out of debt, with millions in the Treasury and a monthly income of more than $500,000 in revenue from the sales of whiskey alone."

Amidst this combination of boom times, dazzling celebrities, and free-flowing booze, the most ludicrous scenes became commonplace. At the Miami Western Union office those unable to reach the desk wrapped their messages in rocks and tossed them over the heads of the crowd. Every evening on the streets of Miami, charabancs of "realtors" passed slowly through the crowds shouting out their bargains to the accompaniment of trombones and saxophones. One of the most conspicuous features in promotion was the boom orator. There were all kinds among these spellbinders: side-show barkers, auctioneers, and free-lance orators willing to talk on any subject for a minimum of ten dollars an hour. Bible-Belt gospel shouters, many of them carried away with a semireligious enthusiasm for Florida, earned the premium wages. "It was a common sight," Weigall reported, "at any wayside barbecue on the Dixie Highway, to see some purple-faced orator mounted on the back seat of his car under the blazing sun bellowing of the land of hope to an awestruck audience standing round him in the white dust."

It was scarcely an exaggeration to say that everybody in Miami was "in real estate" in one way or another. The city was finally forced to pass an ordinance against making sales in the street or on the side-

The aftermath: The hurricane that swept across the state on September 18, 1926, dealt the final death-blow to the Florida land boom. Thousands of homes, like this one in Miami, were damaged by the storm.

walks. Since all ordinary office and salesroom space was taken up, the realtors had to operate from partitioned sections of hotel lobbies and warehouses, in cleared basements, enclosed porches, and boxed-in spaces between buildings.

In the better-organized operations, lots were sold from blueprints or models. D. P. Davis promoted development at St. Augustine with a forty-foot mock-up that featured tiny powered boats running around a minuscule island. Actually to see the lots was not possible, since they were offered "predevelopment," before the streets had been laid, the yacht basin opened, or even the mud dredged up to raise the land above water level. Underwater lots were among the standard frauds, but customers stood in line—some of them reportedly for forty hours—to buy lots on Davis Islands in Tampa Bay and Venetian Islands in Biscayne Bay while they were still under water. (Surprisingly, these particular speculations returned a tidy profit to the investors when the operations proved successful.)

To attend the opening of a subdivision sale, one frequently needed a reservation. Many a customer, having made a down payment of ten per cent, would step up when his turn came, select a lot from the blueprint, see it stamped "Sold," accept his receipt, and then rush out in search of a buyer. In the speculative fairyland of fast turnover and quick fortunes, the careless plunger was more likely to profit than the prudent investor. No matter how outrageous the price, there always seemed to be somebody else to whom one could "pass the baby" for more money.

Even well-planned Coral Gables became more and more involved in the boom-time hoopla. Merrick soon had three thousand salesmen hawking building lots and a fleet of seventy-six buses "to take you to Coral Gables at any time you desire"—as a guest of the corporation. The Coral Gables fleet made regular runs to and from the larger southern cities and occasional runs to and from New York, Chicago, and even San Francisco. And to guarantee that prospective buyers would be in a receptive mood once they reached his heaven on the Atlantic, Merrick had band leaders Paul Whiteman and Jan Garber making sweet music at the Venetian Pool, with "When the Moon Shines on Coral Gables" one of their most popular numbers. In addition, from a platform in the pool itself, the champion of silver, William Jennings Bryan, earned a little gold by orating on the miracle of Miami; it was, Bryan declared, "the only city in the world where you can tell a lie at breakfast that will come true by evening." For trumpeting this cheering news, Bryan received an annual salary of more than fifty thousand dollars. And just in case Bryan didn't do the trick, he was sometimes followed by the original "shimmy girl," Gilda Gray, who shook her chemise with such gusto that it took the viewers' minds off the prices quoted for lots by salesmen circulating through the audience.

But the Mizners' Boca Raton was not about to play second string to Merrick's Coral Gables or any other subdivision in the Florida promotion game. Wilson Mizner imported an old friend, the publicist Harry T. Reichenbach, to make Boca Raton into what Wilson called a "platinum sucker trap." The bait—overpowering snob appeal. It was announced that only the "best" people could get into the place, which meant, quite simply, only those with lots of ready cash. (Palm Beach, Wilson said, would be converted into servants' quarters for Boca Raton.) In Reichenbach's unmeasured terms, it was the habitat of "the world of international wealth that dominates finance and industry . . . that sets fashion . . . the world of large affairs, smart society and leisured ease." The Mizners collected, among other celebrities, two Du Ponts, one Vanderbilt, Elizabeth Arden, Irving Berlin, Herbert Bayard Swope, James M. Cox, George Whitney, and Marie Dressler, "the Duchess of Boca Raton." At one point sales of lots, on paper, averaged two million dollars a week.

The legends of money to be made in Florida real estate began to rival those of the California Gold Rush. Kenneth Roberts told of a strip of land in Palm Beach which was sold in 1915 for $84,000, in 1922 for $240,000, in 1923 for $800,000, in 1924 for $1,500,000; in 1925 it was estimated to be worth nearly $5,000,000. Weigall knew a New York bank clerk who went to Florida with a thousand dollars and returned three weeks later with $375,000, which he had the good sense to invest in gilt-edged securities. A New York cab driver took a passenger, who could not get train accommodations, all the way to Miami, stayed, and made a fortune speculating with the money he earned driving his cab. Land on West Flagler Street in Miami, which had been worth $30 an acre in 1910, was bring-

The Americans who hurried down to Florida in the Twenties were the spiritual heirs of the forty-niners.

ing $75,000 an acre by 1925.

But it was the "binder boys" who perfected into a fine art a method of making profits on little or no investment. The principle was to pay a nominal "binder" fee on the promise of a down payment to be made perhaps a month later and additional payments "as of one, two, and three years." The profit then would be reaped by the simple process of trading binders which might pass through a dozen or more hands before the initial down payment was made. The practice was finally broken up by Miami realtors who caught a group of smart operators from New York on binders and quickly produced abstracts with an agreement that cash payment was due immediately.

Even the clearest vision seemed to become dazzled by all this glitter. Both Weigall and Reichenbach actually began to believe that there was genuine twenty-four karat gold to be had in speculation, and plunged in with their own savings. Roger Babson, who was to make his reputation by warning of the 1929 stock market crash predicted an endless rosy future for Florida real estate.

It was all too good to last. Here and there skeptics began to raise their voices. Walter J. Greenbaum, a Chicago investment banker, warned against "wildcat land speculation" in Florida, and the Massachusetts Savings Bank League cautioned depositors against withdrawing money to invest there. Walter C. Hill of the Atlanta Retail Credit Company predicted that it would all end in the winter of 1925–26. The alarm seemed especially severe in Ohio. State Commerce Director Cyrus Locher went to Florida to investigate. "When the boom has subsided, there will be headaches all over America," he reported. "The rise in Florida will continue as long as northern money is sent to Florida, and the end will be that of every boom, where few prosper and many hold the bag at the end." Ohio passed "blue sky" laws in 1925 forbidding certain firms to sell Florida property.

These doubts suddenly began to take their toll of confidence. It was calculated that within ten miles of Miami there were enough building lots on the market to provide sites for houses for two million people. The first hard sign that the boom was going sour came when a lot on Miami Beach, which had been sold for $50,000, brought only $25,000. Other clouds, too, began to appear in the sunny Florida skies. In the summer of 1925, a fire started by an electric hair curler burned down both the Breakers and the Palm Beach Hotel. Then, Flagler's East Coast Line and the Seaboard found that their tracks had taken so much punishment from increased traffic due to the boom that urgent repairs were necessary at once. To make this possible, an embargo was declared in August, 1925, on all carload lots except fuel, petroleum, livestock, and perishable material. In September, a "less than carload lot" embargo went into effect.

The embargo had disastrous effects on the boom, leaving thousands of desperate builders with unfinished construction on their hands. (One frantic contractor smuggled in a carload of bricks buried in ice and labelled "lettuce.") The only alternative was to bring in material by water, and scores of abandoned hulks were resurrected for the purpose. But in January, 1926, an old Danish training ship, the *Prinz Valdemar,* which was being renovated to serve as a floating cabaret in the Miami harbor, capsized in the middle of the channel, completely halting all inbound and outbound shipping for several weeks.

As though these problems were not enough, other developments cast further gloom. For one thing, federal income-tax troubles began to dog the speculators. The rumors of a tax reduction in 1926, and the report that a number of special revenue agents had been sent into Florida, led many speculators to hold up sales in order to postpone profits until January, 1926. In December, 1925, the Internal Revenue Service announced that all notes on real-estate transactions would be considered as cash received and that full tax payment was due on them. The National Better Business Bureau

commenced an investigation of frauds in Florida real estate, and a stock market break in February and March of 1926 forced back to New York many businessmen who had gone to Florida to plunge.

Through Christmas week, 1925, Miami was able to disguise its nagging doubts behind a cheerful holiday mask. On Christmas Eve the *New York Times* reported that rents were coming down, but the planned festivities went on. In a joint statement the mayors of Miami, Miami Beach, Hialeah, and Coral Gables proclaimed the last day of 1925 and the first two days of 1926 "The Fiesta of the American Tropics," a season "when Love, Good Fellowship, Merrymaking, and Wholesome Sport shall prevail throughout Our Domains." They declared that "through our Streets and Avenues shall wind a glorious Pageantry of Sublime Beauty Depicting in Floral Loveliness the Blessing Bestowed upon us by Friendly Sun, Gracious Rain, and Soothing Tropic Wind." But the market would no longer respond to this kind of ballyhoo. The new season saw real-estate prices breaking sharply as optimists whistled in the dark about "stabilization," "levelling-off," and "salutary readjustment." On February 14, 1926, the *New York Times* reported a decided lull. By July, Stella Crossley wrote bluntly in *The Nation:* "The Florida boom has collapsed. The world's greatest poker game, played with building lots instead of chips, is over. And the players are now cashing in or paying up." The roads north, she said, were black with "a strangely quiet exodus."

The *coup de grâce* to the boom was administered by a formidable tropical hurricane, with winds in excess of 128 miles an hour, which roared over the Gold Coast and the Everglades on September 18, 1926. The storm killed 115 people in the Miami area and another 300 in the village of Moore Haven when it was flooded by the waters of Lake Okeechobee. Miami Beach was entirely inundated, and at one point during the storm the ocean extended deep into Miami itself. Four thousand homes were destroyed and nine thousand more damaged in the area from Fort Lauderdale to Miami, with property losses in the Greater Miami area alone put at $76,000,000.

Yet the wreckage left by the hurricane was as nothing compared to the wreckage left by the collapse of the boom. On Singer's Island, just north of Palm Beach, an unfinished hotel begun by Paris Singer became a luxurious resort for sea birds. In Miami, a hotel near the airport was transformed into a haven, not for snowbirds but for chickens. With property holders defaulting to creditors and to the tax collector, the only land-office business in Florida was being done in the courts.

The Mizners' Boca Raton was never finished, and the brothers, when they died in 1933, were both financially ruined. But Addison left behind more than a score of houses that are among the supreme artistic artifacts of the Twenties. George Merrick's Coral Gables, which had never relaxed its rigid zoning or its architectural standards, remained one of the most beautiful towns in America. And though Merrick himself lost heavily when the bubble burst, he made something of a comeback. In 1934 he re-entered the real-estate business and soon had branch offices throughout Greater Miami. When he died in 1942 he was Miami's postmaster.

Not all of the new arrivals of the Twenties departed when the bubble burst. Miami's population had grown from 9,471 in 1910 to 29,571 in 1920; it had risen to 110,637 by 1930. In the Twenties the metropolitan area led all others in the nation in its rate of growth, and the twin cities of Tampa and St. Peters-burg ranked sixth. And in the thirties, Florida as a whole continued to grow at a more rapid rate than any other state in the Union. But, when compared to the boom time of the Twenties and the boom time which was to come in the fifties, the peninsula was as in a great sleep.

In 1928, Henry S. Villard described a trip to Miami for *The Nation:* "Dead subdivisions line the highway, their pompous names half-obliterated on crumbling stucco gates. Lonely, white-way lights stand guard over miles of cement sidewalks, where grass and palmetto take the place of homes that were to be. . . . Whole sections of outlying subdivisions are composed of unoccupied houses, through which one speeds on broad thoroughfares as if traversing a city in the grip of death."

CLUB LIFE IN AMERICA
The Stock Brokers

The Days of BOOM and BUST

By JOHN KENNETH GALBRAITH

As the twenties roared on, a market crash became

inevitable. Why? And who should have stopped it?

The decade of the twenties, or more precisely the eight years between the postwar depression of 1920-21 and the stock market crash in October of 1929, were prosperous ones in the United States. The total output of the economy increased by more than 50 per cent. The preceding decades had brought the automobile; now came many more and also roads on which they could be driven with reasonable reliability and comfort. There was much building. The downtown section of the mid-continent city—Des Moines, Omaha, Minneapolis—dates from these years. It was then, more likely than not, that what is still the leading hotel, the tallest office building, and the biggest department store went up. Radio arrived, as of course did gin and jazz.

These years were also remarkable in another respect, for as time passed it became increasingly evident that the prosperity could not last. Contained within it were the seeds of its own destruction. The country was heading into the gravest kind of trouble. Herein lies the peculiar fascination of the period for a study

in the problem of leadership. For almost no steps were taken during these years to arrest the tendencies which were obviously leading, and did lead, to disaster.

At least four things were seriously wrong, and they worsened as the decade passed. And knowledge of them does not depend on the always brilliant assistance of hindsight. At least three of these flaws were highly visible and widely discussed. In ascending order, not of importance but of visibility, they were as follows:

First, income in these prosperous years was being distributed with marked inequality. Although output per worker rose steadily during the period, wages were fairly stable, as also were prices. As a result, business profits increased rapidly and so did incomes of the wealthy and the well-to-do. This tendency was nurtured by assiduous and successful efforts of Secretary of the Treasury Andrew W. Mellon to reduce income taxes with special attention to the higher brackets. In 1929 the 5 per cent of the people with the highest incomes received perhaps a third of all personal income. Between 1919 and 1929 the share of the one per cent who received the highest incomes increased by approximately one-seventh. This meant that the economy was heavily and increasingly dependent on the luxury consumption of the well-to-do and on their willingness to reinvest what they did not or could not spend on themselves. Anything that shocked the confidence of the rich either in their personal or in their business future would have a bad effect on total spending and hence on the behavior of the economy.

This was the least visible flaw. To be sure, farmers, who were not participating in the general advance, were making themselves heard; and twice during the period the Congress passed far-reaching relief legislation which was vetoed by Coolidge. But other groups were much less vocal. Income distribution in the United States had long been unequal. The inequality of these years did not seem exceptional. The trade-union movement was also far from strong. In the early twenties the steel industry was still working a twelve-hour day and, in some jobs, a seven-day week. (Every two weeks when the shift changed a man worked twice around the clock.) Workers lacked the organization or the power to deal with conditions like this; the twelve-hour day was, in fact, ended as the result of personal pressure by President Harding on the steel companies, particularly on Judge Elbert H. Gary, head of the United States Steel Corporation. Judge Gary's personal acquaintance with these working conditions was thought to be slight, and this gave rise to Benjamin Stolberg's now classic observation that the Judge "never saw a blast furnace until his death." In all these circumstances the increasingly lopsided income distribution did not excite much comment or alarm. Perhaps it would have been surprising if it had.

But the other three flaws in the economy were far less subtle. During World War I the United States ceased to be the world's greatest debtor country and became its greatest creditor. The consequences of this change have so often been described that they have the standing of a cliché. A debtor country could export a greater value of goods than it imported and use the difference for interest and debt repayment. This was what we did before the war. But a creditor must import a greater value than it exports if those who owe it money are to have the wherewithal to pay interest and principal. Otherwise the creditor must either forgive the debts or make new loans to pay off the old.

During the twenties the balance was maintained by making new foreign loans. Their promotion was profitable to domestic investment houses. And when the supply of honest and competent foreign borrowers ran out, dishonest, incompetent, or fanciful borrowers were invited to borrow and, on occasion, bribed to do so. In 1927 Juan Leguia, the son of the then dictator of Peru, was paid $450,000 by the National City Company and J. & W. Seligman for his services in promoting a $50,000,000 loan to Peru which these houses marketed. Americans lost and the Peruvians didn't gain appreciably. Other Latin American republics got equally dubious loans by equally dubious devices. And, for reasons that now tax the imagination, so did a large number of German cities and municipalities. Obviously, once investors awoke to the character of these loans or there was any other shock to confidence, they would no longer be made. There would be nothing with which to pay the old loans. Given this arithmetic, there would be either a sharp reduction in exports or a wholesale default on the outstanding loans, or more likely both. Wheat and cotton farmers and others who depended on exports would suffer. So would those who owned the bonds. The buying power of both would be reduced. These consequences were freely predicted at the time.

The second weakness of the economy was the large-scale corporate thimblerigging that was going on. This took a variety of forms, of which by far the most common was the organization of corporations to hold stock in yet other corporations, which in turn held stock in yet other corporations. In the case of the railroads and the utilities, the purpose of this pyramid of holding companies was to obtain control of a very large number of operating companies with a very small investment in the ultimate holding company. A $100,000,000 electric utility, of which the capitalization was represented half by bonds and half by common stock, could be controlled with an investment of a little over $25,000,000—the value of just over half the common stock. Were a company then formed with the same capital structure to hold *this* $25,000,000 worth of common stock, it could be controlled with an investment of $6,250,000. On the next round the amount required would be less than $2,000,000. That $2,000,000 would still control the entire $100,000,000 edifice. By the end of the twenties, holding-company structures six or eight tiers high were a commonplace. Some of

PRESIDENT HARDING: *"America's present need is not nostrums but normalcy, not surgery but serenity."*

them—the utility pyramids of Insull and Associated Gas & Electric, and the railroad pyramid of the Van Sweringens—were marvelously complex. It is unlikely that anyone fully understood them or could.

In other cases companies were organized to hold securities in other companies in order to manufacture more securities to sell to the public. This was true of the great investment trusts. During 1929 one investment house, Goldman, Sachs & Company, organized and sold nearly a billion dollars' worth of securities in three interconnected investment trusts—Goldman Sachs Trading Corporation; Shenandoah Corporation; and Blue Ridge Corporation. All eventually depreciated virtually to nothing.

This corporate insanity was also highly visible. So was the damage. The pyramids would last only so long as earnings of the company at the bottom were secure. If anything happened to the dividends of the underlying company, there would be trouble, for upstream companies had issued bonds (or in practice sometimes preferred stock) against the dividends on the stock of the downstream companies. Once the earnings stopped, the bonds would go into default or the preferred stock would take over and the pyramid would collapse. Such

a collapse would have a bad effect not only on the orderly prosecution of business and investment by the operating companies but also on confidence, investment, and spending by the community at large. The likelihood was increased because in any number of cities—Cleveland, Detroit, and Chicago were notable examples—the banks were deeply committed to these pyramids or had fallen under the control of the pyramidors.

Finally, and most evident of all, there was the stock market boom. Month after month and year after year the great bull market of the twenties roared on. Sometimes there were setbacks, but more often there were fantastic forward surges. In May of 1924 the New York *Times* industrials stood at 106; by the end of the year they were 134; by the end of 1925 they were up to 181. In 1927 the advance began in earnest—to 245 by the end of that year and on to 331 by the end of 1928. There were some setbacks in early 1929, but then came the fantastic summer explosion when in a matter of three months the averages went up another 110 points. This was the most frantic summer in our financial history. By its end, stock prices had nearly quadrupled as compared with four years earlier. Transactions on the New York Stock Exchange regularly ran to 5,000,000 or more shares a day. Radio Corporation of America went to 573¾ (adjusted) without ever having paid a dividend. Only the hopelessly eccentric, so it seemed, held securities for their income. What counted was the increase in capital values.

And since capital gains were what counted, one could vastly increase his opportunities by extending his holdings with borrowed funds—by buying on margin. Margin accounts expanded enormously, and from all over the country—indeed from all over the world—money poured into New York to finance these transactions. During the summer, brokers' loans increased at the rate of $400,000,000 a month. By September they totaled more than $7,000,000,000. The rate of interest on these loans varied from 7 to 12 per cent and went as high as 15.

This boom was also inherently self-liquidating. It could last only so long as new people, or at least new money, were swarming into the market in pursuit of the capital gains. This new demand bid up the stocks and made the capital gains. Once the supply of new customers began to falter, the market would cease to rise. Once the market stopped rising, some, and perhaps a good many, would start to cash in. If you are concerned with capital gains, you must get them while the getting is good. But the getting may start the market down, and this will one day be the signal for much more selling—both by those who are trying to get out and those who are being forced to sell securities that are no longer safely margined. Thus it was certain that the market would one day go down, and far more rapidly than it went up. Down it went with a thunderous crash in October of 1929. In a series of terrible days, of which Thursday, October 24, and Tuesday, October 29, were the most terrifying, billions in values were lost, and thousands of speculators—they had been called investors—were utterly and totally ruined.

This too had far-reaching effects. Economists have always deprecated the tendency to attribute too much to the great stock market collapse of 1929: this was the drama; the causes of the subsequent depression really lay deeper. In fact, the stock market crash was very important. It exposed the other weakness of the economy. The overseas loans on which the payments balance depended came to an end. The jerry-built holding-company structures came tumbling down. The investment-trust stocks collapsed. The crash put a marked crimp on borrowing for investment and therewith on business spending. It also removed from the economy some billions of consumer spending that was either based on, sanctioned by, or encouraged by the fact that the spenders had stock market gains. The crash was an intensely damaging thing.

And this damage, too, was not only foreseeable but foreseen. For months the speculative frenzy had all but dominated American life. Many times before in history—the South Sea Bubble, John Law's speculations, the recurrent real-estate booms of the last century, the great Florida land boom earlier in the same decade—there had been similar frenzy. And the end had always come, not with a whimper but a bang. Many men, including in 1929 the President of the United States, knew it would again be so.

The increasingly perilous trade balance, the corporate buccaneering, and the Wall Street boom—along with the less visible tendencies in income distribution—were all allowed to proceed to the ultimate disaster without effective hindrance. How much blame attaches to the men who occupied the presidency?

Warren G. Harding died on August 2, 1923. This, as only death can do, exonerates him. The disorders that led eventually to such trouble had only started when the fatal blood clot destroyed this now sad and deeply disillusioned man. Some would argue that his legacy was bad. Harding had but a vague perception of the economic processes over which he presided. He died owing his broker $180,000 in a blind account—he had been speculating disastrously while he was President, and no one so inclined would have been a good bet to curb the coming boom. Two of Harding's Cabinet officers, his secretary of the interior and his attorney general, were to plead the Fifth Amendment when faced

PRESIDENT COOLIDGE: *"When more and more people are thrown out of work, unemployment results."*

with questions concerning their official acts, and the first of these went to jail. Harding brought his fellow townsman Daniel R. Crissinger to be his comptroller of the currency, although he was qualified for this task, as Samuel Hopkins Adams has suggested, only by the fact that he and the young Harding had stolen watermelons together. When Crissinger had had an ample opportunity to demonstrate his incompetence in his first post, he was made head of the Federal Reserve System. Here he had the central responsibility for action on the ensuing boom. Jack Dempsey, Paul Whiteman, or F. Scott Fitzgerald would have been at least equally qualified.

Yet it remains that Harding was dead before the real trouble started. And while he left in office some very poor men, he also left some very competent ones. Charles Evans Hughes, his secretary of state; Herbert Hoover, his secretary of commerce; and Henry C. Wallace, his secretary of agriculture, were public servants of vigor and judgment.

The problem of Herbert Hoover's responsibility is more complicated. He became President on March 4, 1929. At first glance this seems far too late for effective action. By then the damage had been done, and while

President Hoover Issues a Statement of Reassurance On Continued Prosperity of Fundamental Business

Special to The New York Times.

WASHINGTON, Oct. 25.—A reassuring statement that the fundamental business of the country was on a sound and prosperous basis was made by President Hoover at the White House this afternoon. It was made in reply to questions by newspaper men asking his opinion on the possible effect on the nation's prosperity of yesterday's collapse in the stock market.

Prior to his announcement, the President is understood to have received detailed reports of the break in securities values, and of the current activities of the country's industries, from Secretary Mellon and other officials at the Cabinet meeting this morning.

The text of his statement headed, "In reply to press question as to the business situation, the President said," was as follows:

The fundamental business of the country, that is production and distribution of commodities, is on a sound and prosperous basis. The best evidence is that although production and consumption are at high levels, the average prices of commodities as a whole have not increased and there have been no appreciable increases in the stocks of manufactured goods. Moreover, there has been a tendency of wages to increase and the output per worker in many industries again shows an increase, all of which indicates a healthy condition.

The construction and building material industries have been to some extent affected by the high interest rates induced by stock speculation and there has been some seasonal decrease in one or two other industries, but these movements are of secondary character when considered in the whole situation.

A temporary drop in grain prices sympathetically with Stock Exchange prices usually happens, but as the Department of Agriculture points out, the overriding fact in grain is that this year's world wheat harvest is estimated to be 500,000,000 bushels less than that of last year, which will result in a very low carryover at the end of the harvest year.

This box reporting President Hoover's confidence in the economy appeared on page one of the New York Times of October 26, 1929, three days after leading bankers had pooled $240,000,000 to prop up the market. But, contrary to general belief, Hoover apparently never made another famous statement credited to him: "Prosperity is just around the corner."

the crash might come a little sooner or a little later, it was now inevitable. Yet Hoover's involvement was deeper than this—and certainly much deeper than Harding's. This he tacitly concedes in his memoirs, for he is at great pains to explain and, in some degree, to excuse himself.

For one thing, Hoover was no newcomer to Washington. He had been secretary of commerce under Harding and Coolidge. He had also been the strongest figure (not entirely excluding the President) in both Administration and party for almost eight years. He had a clear view of what was going on. As early as 1922, in a letter to Hughes, he expressed grave concern over the quality of the foreign loans that were being floated in New York. He returned several times to the subject. He knew about the corporate excesses. In the latter twenties he wrote to his colleagues and fellow officials (including Crissinger) expressing his grave concern over the Wall Street orgy. Yet he was content to express himself—to write letters and memoranda, or at most, as in the case of the foreign loans, to make an occasional speech. He could with propriety have presented his views of the stock market more strongly to the Congress and the public. He could also have maintained a more vigorous and persistent agitation within the Administration. He did neither. His views of the market were so little known that it celebrated his election and inauguration with a great upsurge. Hoover was in the boat and, as he himself tells, he knew where it was headed. But, having warned the man at the tiller, he rode along into the reef.

And even though trouble was inevitable, by March, 1929, a truly committed leader would still have wanted to do something. Nothing else was so important. The resources of the Executive, one might expect, would have been mobilized in a search for some formula to mitigate the current frenzy and to temper the coming crash. The assistance of the bankers, congressional leaders, and the Exchange authorities would have been sought. Nothing of the sort was done. As secretary of commerce, as he subsequently explained, he had thought himself frustrated by Mellon. But he continued Mellon in office. Henry M. Robinson, a sympathetic Los Angeles banker, was commissioned to go to New York to see his colleagues there and report. He returned to say that the New York bankers regarded things as sound. Richard Whitney, the vice-president of the Stock Exchange, was summoned to the White House for a conference on how to curb speculation. Nothing came of this either. Whitney also thought things were sound.

Both Mr. Hoover and his official biographers carefully explained that the primary responsibility for the goings on in New York City rested not with Washington but with the governor of New York State. That was Franklin D. Roosevelt. It was he who failed to rise to his responsibilities. The explanation is far too formal. The future of the whole country was involved. Mr. Hoover was the President of the whole country. If he lacked authority commensurate with this responsibility, he could have requested it. This, at a later

Whitney

M. J. Van Sweringen

Insull

O. P. Van Sweringen

Mellon

date, President Roosevelt did not hesitate to do.

Finally, while by March of 1929 the stock market collapse was inevitable, something could still be done about the other accumulating disorders. The balance of payments is an obvious case. In 1931 Mr. Hoover did request a one-year moratorium on the inter-Allied (war) debts. This was a courageous and constructive step which came directly to grips with the problem. But the year before, Mr. Hoover, though not without reluctance, had signed the Hawley-Smoot tariff. "I shall approve the Tariff Bill. . . . It was undertaken as the result of pledges given by the Republican Party at Kansas City. . . . Platform promises must not be empty gestures." Hundreds of people—from Albert H. Wiggin, the head of the Chase National Bank, to Oswald Garrison Villard, the editor of the *Nation*—felt that no step could have been more directly designed to make things worse. Countries would have even more trouble earning the dollars of which they were so desperately short. But Mr. Hoover signed the bill.

Anyone familiar with this particular race of men knows that a dour, flinty, inscrutable visage such as that of Calvin Coolidge can be the mask for a calm and acutely perceptive intellect. And he knows equally that it can conceal a mind of singular aridity. The difficulty, given the inscrutability, is in knowing which. However, in the case of Coolidge the evidence is in favor of the second. In some sense, he certainly knew what was going on. He would not have been unaware of what was called the Coolidge market. But he connected developments neither with the well-being of the country nor with his own responsibilities. In his memoirs Hoover goes to great lengths to show how closely he was in touch with events and how clearly he foresaw their consequences. In his *Autobiography*, a notably barren document, Coolidge did not refer to the accumulating troubles. He confines himself to such unequivocal truths as "Every day of Presidential life is crowded with activities" (which in his case, indeed, was not true); and "The Congress makes the laws, but it is the President who causes them to be executed."

At various times during his years in office, men called on Coolidge to warn him of the impending trouble. And in 1927, at the instigation of a former White House aide, he sent for William Z. Ripley of Harvard, the most articulate critic of the corporate machinations of the period. The President became so interested that he invited him to stay for lunch, and listened carefully while his guest outlined (as Ripley later related) the "prestidigitation, double-shuffling, honey-fugling, hornswoggling, and skulduggery" that characterized the current Wall Street scene. But Ripley made the mistake of telling Coolidge that regulation was the responsibility of the states (as was then the case). At this intelligence Coolidge's face lit

Sixteen Leading Issues Down $2,893,520,108;
Tel. & Tel. and Steel Among Heaviest Losers

A shrinkage of $2,893,520,108 in the open market value of the shares of sixteen representative companies resulted from yesterday's sweeping decline on the New York Stock Exchange.

American Telephone and Telegraph was the heaviest loser, $448,905,162 having been lopped off of its total value. United States Steel common, traditional bellwether of the stock market, made its greatest nose-dive in recent years by falling from a high of 202½ to a low of 185. In a feeble last-minute rally it snapped back to 186, at which it closed, showing a net loss of 17½ points. This represented for the 8,131,055 shares of common stock outstanding a total loss in value of $142,293,446.

In the following table are shown the day's net depreciation in the outstanding shares of the sixteen companies referred to:

Issues.	Shares Listed.	Losses in Points.	Depreciation.
American Radiator	10,096,289	10⅜	$104,748,997
American Tel. & Tel.	13,203,093	34	448,905,162
Commonwealth & Southern	30,764,468	3⅛	96,138,962
Columbia Gas & Electric	8,477,307	22	186,500,754
Consolidated Gas	11,451,188	20	229,023,760
DuPont E. I.	10,322,481	16⅜	169,030,625
Eastman Kodak	2,229,703	41⅞	93,368,813
General Electric	7,211,484	47½	342,545,490
General Motors	43,500,000	6¾	293,625,000
International Nickel	13,777,408	7⅞	108,497,088
New York Central	4,637,086	22⅝	104,914,071
Standard Oil of New Jersey	24,843,643	8	198,749,144
Union Carbide & Carbon	8,730,173	20	174,615,460
United States Steel	8,131,055	17½	142,293,446
United Gas Improvement	18,646,835	6	111,881,010
Westinghouse Elec. & Mfg.	2,589,265	34¼	88,682,326
			$2,893,520,108

The stocks included in the foregoing table are typical, but include only a few of the "blue chips" that fell widely. Some of the medium-priced stocks were swept down almost as sharply as the "big stocks." The loss in open market value by General Motors, for instance, was greater than that of some of the higher priced issues such as Steel, Consolidated Gas and New York Central.

For some of the market's trading favorites yesterday was the most disastrous day since they were admitted to trading.

This is the Times's *summary of losses on Monday, October 28, 1929. The next day, Black Tuesday, 16,000,000 shares were dumped on the New York Exchange, with even greater losses, and the newspaper attempted no summary. Brokers "roared like a lot of lions and tigers," an Exchange guard recalled later. "They hollered and screamed, they clawed at one another's collars. It was like a bunch of crazy men."*

Raskob
Warburg
Wiggin
Mitchell
Robinson

up and he dismissed the entire matter from his mind. Others who warned of the impending disaster got even less far.

And on some occasions Coolidge added fuel to the fire. If the market seemed to be faltering, a timely statement from the White House—or possibly from Secretary Mellon—would often brace it up. William Allen White, by no means an unfriendly observer, noted that after one such comment the market staged a 26-point rise. He went on to say that a careful search "during these halcyon years . . . discloses this fact: Whenever the stock market showed signs of weakness, the President or the Secretary of the Treasury or some important dignitary of the administration . . . issued a statement. The statement invariably declared that business was 'fundamentally sound,' that continued prosperity had arrived, and that the slump of the moment was 'seasonal.'"

Such was the Coolidge role. Coolidge was fond of observing that "if you see ten troubles coming down the road, you can be sure that nine will run into the ditch before they reach you and you have to battle with only one of them." A critic noted that "the trouble with this philosophy was that when the tenth trouble reached him he was wholly unprepared. . . . The outstanding instance was the rising boom and orgy of mad speculation which began in 1927." The critic was Herbert Hoover.

Plainly, in these years, leadership failed. Events whose tragic culmination could be foreseen—and was foreseen—were allowed to work themselves out to the final disaster. The country and the world paid. For a time, indeed, the very reputation of capitalism itself was in the balance. It survived in the years following perhaps less because of its own power or the esteem in which it was held, than because of the absence of an organized and plausible alternative. Yet one important question remains. Would it have been possible even for a strong President to arrest the plunge? Were not the opposing forces too strong? Isn't one asking the impossible?

No one can say for sure. But the answer depends at least partly on the political context in which the Presidency was cast. That of Coolidge and Hoover may well have made decisive leadership impossible. These were conservative Administrations in which, in addition, the influence of the businessman was strong. At the core of the business faith was an intuitive belief in *laissez faire*—the benign tendency of things that are left alone. The man who wanted to intervene was a meddler. Perhaps, indeed, he was a planner. In any case, he was to be regarded with mistrust. And, on the businessman's side, it must be borne in mind that high government office often nurtures a spurious sense of urgency. There is no more important public function than the suppression of proposals for unneeded action. But these should have been distinguished from action necessary to economic survival.

A bitterly criticized figure of the Harding-Coolidge-Hoover era was Secretary of the Treasury Andrew W. Mellon. He opposed all action to curb the boom, although once in 1929 he was persuaded to say that bonds (as distinct from stocks) were a good buy. And when the depression came, he was against doing anything about that. Even Mr. Hoover was shocked by his insistence that the only remedy was (as Mr. Hoover characterized it) to "liquidate labor, liquidate stocks, liquidate the farmers, liquidate real estate." Yet Mellon reflected only in extreme form the conviction that things would work out, that the real enemies were those who interfered.

Outside of Washington in the twenties, the business and banking community, or at least the articulate part of it, was overwhelmingly opposed to any public intervention. The tentative and ineffective steps which the Federal Reserve did take were strongly criticized. In the spring of 1929 when the Reserve system seemed to be on the verge of taking more decisive action, there was an anticipatory tightening of money rates and a sharp drop in the market. On his own initiative Charles E. Mitchell, the head of the National City Bank, poured in new funds. He had an obligation, he said, that was "paramount to any Federal Reserve warning, or anything else" to avert a crisis in the money market. In brief, he was determined, whatever the government thought, to keep the boom going. In that same spring Paul M. Warburg, a distinguished and respected Wall Street leader, warned of the dangers of the boom and called for action to restrain it. He was deluged with criticism and even abuse and later said that the subsequent days were the most difficult of his life. There were some businessmen and bankers—like Mitchell and Albert Wiggin of the Chase National Bank—who may have vaguely sensed that the end of the boom would mean their own business demise. Many more had persuaded themselves that the dream would last. But we should not complicate things. Many others were making money and took a short-run view—or no view—either of their own survival or of the system of which they were a part. They merely wanted to be left alone to get a few more dollars.

And the opposition to government intervention would have been nonpartisan. In 1929 one of the very largest of the Wall Street operators was John J. Raskob. Raskob was also chairman of the Democratic National Committee. So far from calling for preventive measures, Raskob in 1929 was explaining how, through stock market speculation, literally anyone could be a millionaire. Nor would the press have been enthusiastic about, say, legislation to control holding companies and investment trusts or to give authority to regulate margin trading. The financial pages of many of the papers were riding the boom. And even from the speculating public, which was dreaming dreams of riches and had yet to learn that it had been fleeced, there would have been no thanks. Perhaps a President of phenomenal power and determination might have overcome the Coolidge-Hoover environment. But it is easier to argue that this context made inaction inevitable for almost any President. There were too many people who, given a choice between disaster and the measures that would have prevented it, opted for disaster without either a second or even a first thought.

On the other hand, in a different context a strong President might have taken effective preventive action. Congress in these years was becoming increasingly critical of the Wall Street speculation and corporate piggery-pokery. The liberal Republicans—the men whom Senator George H. Moses called the Sons of the Wild Jackass—were especially vehement. But conservatives like Carter Glass were also critical. These men correctly sensed that things were going wrong. A President such as Wilson or either of the Roosevelts (the case of Theodore is perhaps less certain than that of

Franklin) who was surrounded in his Cabinet by such men would have been sensitive to this criticism. As a leader he could both have reinforced and drawn strength from the contemporary criticism. Thus he might have been able to arrest the destructive madness as it became recognizable. The American government works far better—perhaps it only works—when the Executive, the business power, and the press are in some degree at odds. Only then can we be sure that abuse or neglect, either private or public, will be given the notoriety that is needed.

Perhaps it is too much to hope that by effective and timely criticism and action the Great Depression might have been avoided. A lot was required in those days to make the United States in any degree depression-proof. But perhaps by preventive action the ensuing depression might have been made less severe. And certainly in the ensuing years the travail of bankers and businessmen before congressional committees, in the courts, and before the bar of public opinion would have been less severe. Here is the paradox. In the full perspective of history, American businessmen never had enemies as damaging as the men who grouped themselves around Calvin Coolidge and supported and applauded him in what William Allen White called "that masterly inactivity for which he was so splendidly equipped."

The
MILLION
& the
MIDGET

By JOHN BROOKS

Almost everyone remembers the picture of a midget sitting on J. P. Morgan's knee, but few recall, or ever knew, the end of that story. It is nearly unbearably sad. The thing happened in the Senate Caucus Room on the morning of June 1, 1933, while Morgan, surrounded by a cortege of partners and lawyers and assistants, was sitting in a leather-upholstered chair waiting to testify before the Senate Banking and Currency Committee. Reporters, photographers, and spectators were milling around. Suddenly, in the confusion, too quickly for official intervention, a press agent for the Ringling Brothers Barnum & Bailey Circus, apparently with the connivance of a Scripps-Howard reporter named Ray Tucker, popped the midget, a member of the circus troupe, into Morgan's lap. Instantly the photographers were climbing onto chairs and pushing people aside to get into position for pictures.

AIRE

Morgan at the time was a dignified, avuncular-looking man in his middle sixties. The circus lady, whose name was Lya Graf and who was twenty-seven inches tall, was a plump, well-proportioned brunette with sparkling dark eyes and a fresh peasant prettiness, and she was decked out in a flounced blue satin dress and a red straw hat of fishnet weave. Morgan's cortege stiffened as if frozen; but Morgan himself did not. His face, previously set into hard lines by a week of hostile questioning by the committee, relaxed, became disturbed, then turned kindly, and a small, warm smile crossed it under the bushy black eyebrows and the neat white mustache.

"I have a grandson bigger than you," he said.

"But I'm older," Miss Graf replied.

"How old are you?"

The press agent said she was thirty-two, but Miss Graf corrected him:

"I am not—only twenty."

"Well, you certainly don't look it," Morgan said.

The photographers clamored for one more shot, and the press agent told Miss Graf to take off her hat. "Don't take it off, it's pretty," Morgan said; then he lifted her from his lap and set her carefully on the floor. The partners, who had been looking on in rigid dismay, exhaled and collapsed in their chairs; one of them brusquely shooed the press agent and Miss Graf away; and Morgan went on smiling, more feebly now. Next day the picture was famous everywhere in the world where newspapers are published.

Morgan, and even Wall Street as a whole, profited adventitiously from the encounter. From that day forward until his death a decade later, he was in the public mind no longer a grasping devil whose greed and ruthlessness had helped bring the nation to near ruin, but rather a benign old dodderer. The change in attitude was instantaneous, and Morgan took advantage of it, seizing, whether by calculation or instinct, on further chances to "humanize" himself. The following day, asked to comment on the incident by reporters possessed of a new interest in his personality, he replied unaffectedly that it had been "very unusual and somewhat unpleasant," but that he didn't blame the photographers, who had merely been doing their job. Asked about a bloodstone set in a gold crescent that he was wearing as a watch charm, he became positively garrulous: "Oh, that. Well, now, I'll tell you about it. My father's mother was J. Pierpont's daughter. She had that made. It has the Pierpont coat of arms on one side. She gave it to her father. He wore it day in and day out. I don't think I would have known him without it. My father gave it to me. Does that tell the story?"

"Your father's father gave it to your mother's brother . . ." a reporter began in a puzzled tone.

"No, no." Morgan said with a chuckle, and launched into another round of ancestral rigamarole. "I still don't ——" the reporter began again, but Morgan had waved and swept grandly out. Could anyone hate such a man?

But Lya Graf did not benefit from the encounter. She was shy and sensitive, and where the role of ordinary circus freak, a kind of craft requiring skill, had been supportable to her, the role of celebrity freak was not. Two years later, hounded by fame, she left the United States and returned to her native Germany. She was half Jewish. In 1937 she was arrested as a "useless person" and in 1941 was shipped to Auschwitz, never to be heard of again. There had been no place for her anywhere; the New World had exploited her, the Old had obliterated her. Her gift to a rich and famous old man had cost her first her peace of mind and then her life.

The story might be a cozy and manageable fable except for the picture, in which Miss Graf is smiling proudly and has a plump hand splayed out on Morgan's coat sleeve to steady herself. They both look happy and at ease; that is the unbearable part.

First among all nations the United States made "restraint of trade" a crime, and voted an economic ideal into law. One of its most energetic exponents looks back on that unique, vague, and unenforceable bit of legislation: the Sherman Antitrust Act

The LAW *to* MAKE FREE ENTERPRISE FREE

By THURMAN ARNOLD

The author became the Roosevelt Administration's chief "trust buster" in March of 1938.

Ever since the Civil War there has been a continuous conflict between two opposing ideals in American economic thinking. The first of them says that business management, if relieved from the rigors of cutthroat competition, will be fair and benevolent. The age of competition is over, the theory continues, and great corporations with the power to dominate prices benefit the economy. In the field of big business, this philosophy justifies giant mergers. In the field of small business, it leads to the passage of fair trade laws and similar forms of legalized price fixing.

J. P. Morgan is the traditional hero of this philosophy. He organized United States Steel, our first billion-dollar enterprise, to make investments secure, and to eliminate cutthroat competition in steel. Andrew Carnegie, who was doing pretty well as an aggressive competitor, was paid twice what he thought his business was worth to go along. Morgan made the steel business safer for the investor but tough on the consumer, and it has been so ever since.

The opposing economic ideal says that industrial progress can best be obtained in a free market, where prices are fixed by competition and where success depends on efficiency rather than market control. Under this theory it becomes the government's function not to control or regulate but only to maintain freedom in the market place by prosecuting combinations whenever they become large enough to fix prices. Henry Ford represents this ideal. By producing cars at cut prices on a nationwide scale, he helped wreck many of the existing automobile companies. But at the same time he revolutionized the industry.

This second ideal is also represented by a remarkable piece of legislation called the Sherman Antitrust Act, passed by Congress on July 2, 1890, which states that "Every contract, combination in the form of trust or otherwise, or conspiracy, in restraint of trade or commerce among the several States, or with foreign nations, is hereby declared to be illegal." The act goes on to authorize the federal government to proceed against trusts which violate the act, and empowers federal circuit courts with jurisdiction over such violations.

If I may be permitted to say so, as one who has had some experience with enforcing it, this law is historically unique. Prior to the Second World War, no other nation had any legislation like it. It is different from any other criminal statute because it makes it a crime to violate a vaguely stated economic policy—and a policy, what is more, on which public attitudes often change. The average American citizen—and, indeed, the average court which administers the Sherman act —would like to believe simultaneously in both of the conflicting economic ideals described above. For that reason, the Supreme Court swings back and forth in Sherman act cases, in more important ones splitting five to four. The history of the Sherman act is the history of the conflicts and compromises between these two economic ideals.

But the dominant ideal in our American economic thinking has been the ideal of the Sherman act. The business pressures against its actual enforcement are great, but support of the *principle* of the act is so unanimous that no one ever suggests its repeal. Big business, labor, farmers—each economic group wants the Sherman act strictly enforced, against everyone but itself.

In meeting these pressures the Sherman act has shown extraordinary elasticity. It may bend at times, but it always bounces back. Thus it is like a constitutional provision rather than an ordinary statute, and its history tells much about our national attempt to create an economy that will be at the same time both disciplined and free.

How was this ideal born in the first place? The most improbable feature of the Sherman act is that this apparently anti-big business measure was introduced by a senator who was a high-tariff advocate and an extreme conservative, and was passed with only one dissenting vote by a big-business Republican Congress.

The initial pressure for it came from agriculture, which since the Civil War had been reduced to a fairly steady depression. Railroad monopolies were charging farmers all the traffic would bear, and sometimes a little more. Rates were rigged to favor big railroad customers and ruin small ones. As farm income fell, prices that farmers had to pay rose steadily. Monopolies kept them high. If the pressure from the agricultural states was strong, so was the rebellion against other aspects of the dog-eat-dog business ethics of the times. The necessity of some restraint on such practices came at last to be recognized even by business itself.

Big business during the latter half of the nineteenth century had come to regard competition as an unmitigated evil which could be alleviated only by combination. At first the combinations took the form of "pools" or agreements—regional rather than national—to restrain trade, to control prices, to restrict output and divide markets. But businessmen soon learned that agreements between members of an industry were too weak. Only the surrender of business independence by the units could make domination of the market certain.

Pools gave way to trusts, the first of which, established by Standard Oil in 1879, became a model for subsequent business combinations. Each party to the trust surrendered his stock-voting power to trustees, receiving trust certificates in return. Thus the nine trustees of the Standard Oil Trust, without the investment of a dollar, obtained absolute power over the nation's oil industry. The pattern set by Standard Oil was so widely followed that the name "trust" became a byword for any large industrial combination even after the trust device had been abandoned.

Prior to the Sherman act the federal government had no power to prevent predatory business activities. Therefore, the states themselves began an ineffective attack on the trusts in state courts. In 1887 Louisiana prosecuted the Cotton Oil Trust. In 1889 California prosecuted the Sugar Trust; in 1890 Nebraska prosecuted the Whiskey Trust. The attorney general of Ohio sought to repeal the charter of the Standard Oil Company of Ohio.

In 1892 the supreme court of Ohio ordered the local oil company to sever its connections with the Standard Oil Trust. The order was never effectively enforced. But these state attacks on it made the device so risky that corporate organizations looked for some other form of combination that could not be prosecuted under state law. New Jersey provided the model, by amending its incorporation statute to permit one corporation to own the stock of another. From then on it was easy.

Corporations A, B, and C would give 51 per cent of their stock to holding company X. Holding company X would in turn give 51 per cent of its stock to holding company Y. Thus holding company Y, with only about 25 per cent interest in the operating companies, controlled them completely. Y would transfer enough stock to Z, at which point Z needed only 12½ per cent

Senator John Sherman, young brother of the General, gave the law his name and prestige.

to control the industry. And so on until fantastic pyramids were built up. No state could attack these pyramids because they were legal in the state of incorporation. Only Congress could interfere with this process.

In July, 1888, John Sherman, senator from Ohio, introduced the resolution that led to the passage of the Sherman act. He had been Secretary of the Treasury under President Hayes and was known as an expert in finance and taxation. He was big business-minded and an ardent advocate of high tariffs. In this important respect, he was opposed to the very interests that were demanding antimonopoly legislation. In the farm belt the tariff was called the mother of monopoly. Sherman could have no part in such radical doctrine. His resolution reconciled that contradiction very neatly. It asked the Finance Committee to report on a bill that would

tend to preserve freedom of trade and production, the natural competition of increasing production, the lowering of prices by such competition, and the full benefit designed by and hitherto conferred by the policy of the government to protect and encourage American industries by levying duties on imported goods.

In other words, Sherman contended that the increased production by local industry protected by tariffs would more than offset the increased prices due to the tariffs, if domestic competition was free and unrestrained.

The Sherman act as it reads today was passed in the Senate 52 yeas to 1 nay, and signed by President Harrison on July 2, 1890. No votes were cast against it in the House.

The act is unexampled in economic legislation. In effect it says: "We want competition in the United States and we will leave it to the federal judiciary to determine, case by case, just what action constitutes a restraint on competition." That this law could be passed by a conservative Republican Congress whose most influential leaders were closely associated with big business is remarkable in the extreme. Many writers have argued that the act was a hypocritical piece of legislation, designed as a political sop to the farm belt, and that no one expected it to be of any consequence. For example, Senator Nelson W. Aldrich, who was known as J. P. Morgan's floor broker in the Senate, voted for it.

Such facts are sometimes cited to support the view that the original passage of the bill was only an attempt to placate western senators in exchange for votes on higher tariffs. But this interpretation has been completely refuted by Hans B. Thorelli in his recent book, *The Federal Antitrust Policy*, the most complete and objective analysis of the history of American monopoly policy. Thorelli concludes that a majority of congressmen were sincere and that the Sherman act represented for men of both parties the symbol and the image of what they sincerely desired the American economy to become.

By that I do not mean that the Republican supporters of the act would have welcomed the breakup of great American combinations into smaller units. At the same time, they would have instinctively rejected the system of domestic and international cartels that had been growing up in Germany and spreading to France from 1870 on, which would surely have become the American pattern if the Sherman act had not been passed.

The Sherman act fitted in with the American economic and legal philosophy that was religiously held in 1890 and which is still our dominant philosophy today. In 1890 Americans distrusted any form of governmental regulation. It was the tradition of the American common law that the relation between business and government should be based on some broad

"Big Gun in Danger," one newspaper warned.

The act came alive in 1902 when Teddy Roosevelt used it, in the Northern Securities case, to attack the central fortress of financial power. Roosevelt directed Attorney General Knox to go after the railroad holding company, hoping that his new Supreme Court Justice, Holmes, would concur. When the Court split, Holmes disappointed him, but Justice Brewer's vote won the decision for Roosevelt and saved the law.

President Roosevelt

common-law principle which would acquire definite meaning only through a series of court decisions. The Sherman act followed that tradition. Our faith in the common law was such that Congress believed that the courts could give a better and more practical meaning to the principles of the act than Congress could possibly do by further definition or regulation.

The Sherman act was definitely on the shelf during the administrations of Presidents Harrison, Cleveland, and McKinley. Cleveland's attorney general not only instituted no proceedings but dropped the prosecution of the notorious Cash Register Trust, even though he had won a victory in the lower court. Under Cleveland the principal impact of the Sherman act was against labor in breaking the Pullman strike. McKinley was equally indifferent to the Sherman act. During his four and one-half years only three suits were brought.

The first Sherman act decision by the Supreme Court was in the case of United States v. E. C. Knight & Co. It amounted to a virtual repeal of the act. The Supreme Court held that the Sugar Trust, in acquiring a monopoly over sugar manufacturing, affected interstate commerce only indirectly and, therefore, did not violate the act. As Justice John Marshall Harlan pointed out in his dissent: "While the opinion of the Court in this case does not declare the Act of 1890 to be unconstitutional, it defeats the main object for which it was passed." The Knight case thus emasculated the Sherman act. As a result of that decision the government became powerless to prevent the formation of a monopoly through the device of a holding company.

Yet within the short space of eight years, through the daring and ingenuity of Theodore Roosevelt, the Sherman act was transformed again from a meaningless and ineffective formula into a sharp weapon.

Theodore Roosevelt was one of the few politicians of his time who had seriously studied the antitrust problem. He had his first experience with monopoly power as a New York State assemblyman during the investigation of Jay Gould. He campaigned for re-election on the antimonopoly issue in 1882. In 1899, as governor, he wrote: "I have been in a great quandary over trusts. I do not know what attitude to take. I do not intend to play a demagogue. On the other hand, I do intend, so far as in me lies, to see that the rich man is held to the same accountability as the poor man, and when the rich man is rich enough *to buy unscrupulous advice from very able lawyers, this is not always easy.*" (Italics added.)

It was the empire-building ambition of J. P. Morgan that gave Theodore Roosevelt his chance. During the last year of the McKinley Administration the Northern Securities Company had been formed as a compromise between E. H. Harriman and Morgan in their fight to control the Northern Pacific Railroad. The holding company device was used to combine under one management two of the nation's largest competing railroads, the Northern Pacific and the Great Northern. Had the scheme succeeded, it could have led to the domination of all American railroads by this group. It could have created a pattern for the cartelization of all American industry.

Roosevelt, as one of the first acts of his Administration, determined to attack this respected citadel of corporate power. This enterprise was very different from that of using the act to attack mere dishonesty in business, and Roosevelt must have realized that the legal odds were very much against him. A careful lawyer would have advised him that the Knight case exempted J. P. Morgan's ambitious plans. The decision in the Knight case stood for the principle that the acquisition of monopoly control was immune from at-

Attorney General Philander Knox

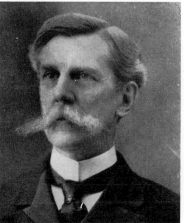

Justice O. W. Holmes

Justice David J. Brewer

tack because, though it affected prices "indirectly," it was not a conspiracy to fix them "directly."

The issue as Roosevelt saw it went far beyond the merger of the two railroads involved in Northern Securities. The issue was nothing less than effective national sovereignty. The federal government had been relegated to such minor roles as distributing the mail and collecting tariff duties. Big business was the real sovereign in infinitely more important areas. In the Northern Securities case, Theodore Roosevelt was to obtain for the federal government a magna carta limiting the power of the business princes.

Roosevelt gambled that the Supreme Court, with new faces in it since the Knight case, would repudiate or at least alter that decision. He directed Attorney General Philander C. Knox to draw up a case against the Northern Securities Company. It was to be a head-on attack on the philosophy of the Knight case decision. Fully aware of the tremendous pressures that would be exerted against him, he directed Knox to prepare the prosecution in complete secrecy. Not even his close friend and adviser, Elihu Root, the Secretary of War, was told.

When Knox finally released to the press his intention to prosecute Northern Securities, there was consternation and panic in the financial world. Root, a Wall Street lawyer, was dismayed and resentful. Morgan and his like-minded friend, Senator Chauncey Depew of New York, descended upon the White House like the emissaries of some independent sov-

ereignty whose rights were being invaded. But by that time the prosecution was a *fait accompli.*

On this case all of Roosevelt's antitrust program depended. It came before the Supreme Court in March, 1904. By that time, Roosevelt had appointed Oliver Wendell Holmes to the Court, believing that Holmes's reputation as a liberal was an indication that he would vote against the tremendous extension of monopoly power. In this hope he was to be bitterly disappointed. Had Holmes been able to win over to his side Justice David Brewer, as he thought he had, the legitimacy of monopoly would have been established, perhaps for all time, in this country as it was in Europe.

The Court was bitterly divided, five to four. The majority held that the Sherman act was intended to prevent giant combinations formed under any device and that such exercise of congressional power over industry was not unconstitutional.

Holmes, who wrote one of the two principal dissents, made the statement, believed by many at that time, that the Sherman act was not intended to prevent combinations in restraint of trade. He said: "It was the ferocious extreme of competition with others, not the cessation of competition among the partners, that was the evil feared."

Justice Holmes had faith in the benevolence and efficiency of the rich. He believed that the Constitution should protect them in their efforts to create industrial empires. But the ideal of a dynamic competitive economy and government-maintained freedom of industrial opportunity, I believe, was beyond him. He would have sincerely approved of the system of domestic and international cartels that dominated industry and caused it to stagnate in Europe before World War II.

Roosevelt, though a rich man himself, was one of the few men of his time to realize the destiny of America as a land of economic freedom. He had the ability to infuse the public with his point of view. Senator Sherman initiated the antitrust act, but it was Teddy Roosevelt who gave it vigor and meaning, made the policy of the Sherman act an economic religion and its violation an economic sin, and, finally, made it emotionally impossible for American business to co-operate in the European cartel system.

To appraise the effect of the Sherman act on American business institutions correctly we must view it apart from particular prosecutions, or particular periods of enforcement or nonenforcement. Theodore Roosevelt's achievement was to enshrine the ideal of the act as part of our national folklore. And its influence has continued in a far more potent way than perhaps any other statute on the books. The image of the Sherman act has not prevented tremendous concentrations of economic power, but it has prevented

Theodore Roosevelt was the first President to make vigorous use of the Sherman Antitrust Act. This 1904 cartoon showing the trust-buster at work was entitled "The Lion-Tamer."

such concentrations from obtaining legitimate status.

Only once since its passage has the principle of the act been repudiated. That was in production codes of the National Recovery Administration during Franklin D. Roosevelt's New Deal. They were designed to raise prices and restrict production, after the European model. The theory was that this would protect investments and rescue business from insolvency.

But the competitive tradition represented by the Sherman act was too strong for the NRA. The Sherman act over the years, even when it was unenforced, had built up an abiding faith that the elimination of competition in business was morally and economically wrong. Then the Supreme Court threw out the NRA, and Franklin Roosevelt turned back to the antitrust laws as a major instrument of economic policy, and placed me in charge of their enforcement.

When I took office, years of disuse of the Sherman act, culminating in its repudiation by NRA, had made violation of the antitrust laws common, almost respectable. I will never forget the amazement of the Wisconsin Alumni Research Foundation, an organization whose profits were used to support the University of Wisconsin, when the Justice Department charged it with using a vitamin patent to raise prices and restrict manufacture of important food products. It never occurred to the high-minded management of this foundation that it was doing anything wrong. The indictment was considered an attack on education itself.

I believed that my principal function was to convince American businessmen that the Sherman act represented something more than a pious platitude; second, that its enforcement was an important economic policy. But there was very little support among economists for the latter notion.

As indictments of respectable people began to pour out from the Justice Department in unprecedented numbers, cries of outrage could be heard from coast to coast. I will never forget the pain and astonishment caused when criminal charges were brought against the American Medical Association, which had established a pretty effective boycott on all forms of group health plans. I was pictured as a wild man whose sanity was in considerable doubt. One major newspaper referred to me as "an idiot in a powder mill." Letters of protest poured into the White House. Adverse publicity reached its peak when the Associated Press was charged with violation of the Sherman act for refusing to sell its news service to any new newspaper that would be competing with one of its member publications. Editorials appeared from coast to coast accusing the department of destroying freedom of the press.

Yet the enforcement program of the Antitrust Division on a nationwide scale between 1938 and the out-

Thirty-four years later, under the second Roosevelt, the author's revival and energetic application of the long-dormant statute made new grist for the cartoonist's mill.

break of World War II survived all such attacks. This was because American businessmen did not want to repudiate the principle of the Sherman act, however much they disliked particular prosecutions. It showed that the Henry Ford tradition was still dominant.

It is difficult now to appraise the economic effect of the revival of the Sherman act at that time. Opinions differ, and my own is, of course, biased. But this at least can be said: American business learned that the Sherman act was something more than a false front to our business structure. The public gained an idea of the purpose of the act, the act itself gained renewed vitality, and American business approved this revival.

There are two principal evils of concentrated economic power in a democracy. The first is the power of concentrated industry to charge administered prices rather than prices based on competitive demand. A second is the tendency of such empires to swallow up local businesses and drain away local capital. Prior to the Depression this condition had advanced so far that our concentrated industrial groups had helped destroy their own markets by siphoning off the dollars that could have been a source of local purchasing power.

It is idle to say that periodic enforcement of the

antitrust laws has solved these problems, but the laws themselves have given us an image of what our economy should be. In a cartel economy no one could question the legitimacy of the recent rises in steel—or any other—prices. In an antitrust-minded economy it seems a legitimate and natural thing for a congressional committee to call the companies to account.

Some indication of what American industry might have become without the curb of the Sherman act is to be found in the Senate hearings on labor so widely publicized this past year. It had been my belief when I took office that labor unions, like any other organizations in business, were subject to antitrust laws when the large ones tried to swallow up the smaller ones by using the predatory practices of the old-fashioned trust.

A liberal majority on the Supreme Court of the United States refused to accept my argument that labor coercion (*i.e.,* collective bargaining) should be limited to legitimate labor objectives. They gave the unions a broad and sweeping exemption from any application of the Sherman act, whatever they did, unless they combined with their employers. They permitted one union, by strike or boycott, to destroy another. Thus the Teamsters with their control over transportation became the fastest growing labor union in the world. The only way employers could survive was to buy them off. The brigandry of the 1880's was repeated, but now by unions in control of bottlenecks in transportation and building. The unhappy spectacle that is presented to the American public today is a direct result of the Court's decision.

No doubt the liberal majority that bestowed the exemption felt, as Holmes felt about business in the Northern Securities case, that labor leadership if not curbed by the Sherman act would nevertheless be benevolent. But what has actually happened in the labor movement is the picture of what would have happened in American industry had Teddy Roosevelt lost his fight in the Northern Securities case fifty-six years ago.